# English Medieval Industries

Noah building the ark. English *c.* 1420-30.
(Bodleian Library, MS Barlow 53 (R).) (*Detail*)

# English Medieval Industries

## CRAFTSMEN, TECHNIQUES, PRODUCTS

EDITED BY

## JOHN BLAIR

AND

## NIGEL RAMSAY

THE HAMBLEDON PRESS

LONDON AND RIO GRANDE

Published by The Hambledon Press, 1991

102 Gloucester Avenue, London NW1 8HX (U.K.)

P.O. Box 162, Rio Grande, Ohio 45672 (U.S.A.)

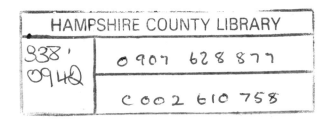

ISBN 0 907628 87 7

*British Library Cataloguing in Publication Data*

English medieval industries: craftsmen, techniques, products
   1.  England – Industries – History
   I.  Blair, John    II.  Ramsay, Nigel
338.0942          HC254

*Library of Congress Cataloging-in-Publication Data*

English medieval industries: craftsmen, techniques, products/
   edited by John Blair and Nigel Ramsay
   Includes bibliographical references and index
   1.  Great Britain – Industries – History
   I.  Blair, John (W. John)    II  Ramsay, Nigel
HC254.E54    1991          90-28993
398.0942′09′02 – dc20        CIP

Designed by Derek Brenner
Typeset by Vitaset, Paddock Wood, Kent
Printed on acid-free paper and bound in Great Britain
by Biddles Ltd., Guildford

# Contents

*Acknowledgements*

This book has been long in the making. The editors' foremost obligations are to the various contributors, and above all to the publisher Martin Sheppard, for their patience and good humour through the protracted stages of its production. The quick and accurate typing of Pat Lloyd has facilitated an arduous task. Anne Hudson compiled the index. Among many friends and colleagues who have helped in various ways, the editors would especially like to thank Justine Bayley, Sarah Brown, Claude Blair, John Cherry, T.W. French, David O'Connor, Karel Otavsky, Nigel Saul, Richard Sharpe and Timothy Wilson.

The editors and the publisher are grateful to the Abegg-Stiftung, Riggisberg, the Armourers and Brasiers' Company, the Carpenters' Company, the Pasold Research Fund and the Twenty-Seven Foundation for their generous grants towards the costs of publication.

John Blair
Nigel Ramsay

## Acknowledgements for Illustrations

The editors and publisher are extremely grateful to the following owners of copyright for permission to use illustrations:

Barber Institute of Fine Arts, Birmingham: Fig. 10; Musées Royaux des Beaux-Arts de Belgique: Fig. 141; Bedford Museum: Fig. iv; Guy Beresford: Fig. 183p; Birmingham Museum and Art Gallery: Fig. 25; Basil Blackwell Ltd: Fig. 4; Bodleian Library, Oxford: Figs. v, 45, 172, 192; P.J. Bowden: Fig. 180; Glenys Boyles: Figs. 163, 175a-c, 178a-c, 179; British Library: Figs. i, 60, 86, 109, 128, 140, 164, 165, 166, 189; British Museum: Figs. iii, 41, 59, 65, 87, 88, 89, 90, 91, 92, 93, 94, 95, 148, 149, 152, 153, 154, 155, 158, 160, 191; Brixworth Archaeological Research Committee: Fig. 5; Buckinghamshire Archaeological Unit: Fig. 194; Burrell Collection, Glasgow Museums and Art Galleries: Figs. 49, 131; Cambridge University Collection of Air Photographs: Fig. 1; Chapel Studio: Fig. 143; John Cherry: Fig. 183t; Chester City Council: Fig. 123; President and Fellows, Corpus Christi College, Oxford: Figs. 58, 69; Conway Library, Courtauld Institute of Art: Fig. 12; Rosemary Cramp: Fig. 6; D.W. Crossley: Fig. 79; Devon Record Office: Fig. 70; M. Duffy: Fig. 176; Dean and Chapter of Durham: Fig. 83; University of East Anglia: Fig. 62; Nick Griffiths: Figs. 183a, 185c, 187a; Goldsmiths' Company: Figs. 54, 56, 74; James Graham-Campbell: Fig. 183i; B. Harbottle: Fig. 177; T. Haysom: Fig. 14; D. Hill: Fig. 4; K. Hughes: Figs 147, 156; Humberside Archaeological Unit: Fig. 173; Jones Photography, Gloucester: Fig. 186; G.H. Kenyon: Figs. 113, 119; L.L. Ketteringham: Fig. 80; G. King & Sons, Norwich: Figs. 132, 138; Dean and Chapter of Lincoln: Fig. 37; Ministry of Defence (Crown Copyright): Fig. 9a; Museum of London: Figs. 17, 18, 21, 22, 26, 29, 30, 31, 32, 34, 36, 42, 44, 183j, 183u, 185a, 185c, 187a; Musée du Louvre: Fig. 63; Master and Fellows, Magdalene College, Cambridge: Fig. 126; R. Marks: Figs. 136, 145; S. Meyer: Figs. 157, 161, 162; Tom Middlemas: Fig. 6; R.K. Morris: Fig. 2; Moyses Hall Museum, Bury St Edmunds: Fig. 151; Norwich Survey: Fig. 174; David O'Connor: Pl. III; David Patrick: Figs. 167, 168; Pewterers' Company: Fig. 27; Derek Philips: Fig. 183k-l; Public Record Office: Figs. 71, 72; Canon M.H. Ridgway: Fig. 12; Royal Commission on the Historical Monuments of England: National Monuments Record (Crown Copyright): Figs. 46, 127, 130, 134, 135, 137, 142, 144, 146, 198; Mick Sharp: Fig. 150; Sussex Archaeological Society: Fig. 51; Master and Fellows, Trinity College, Cambridge: Figs. 169, 170; Trinity College, Dublin: Fig. ii; Ingrid Ulbricht: Fig. 182; Victoria and Albert Museum: Figs. 39, 47, 61, 67, 76, 77, 196, Pls. I, II, IV; J. Vila-Grau: Fig. 129; National Museum of Wales: Figs. 23, 64; Malcolm Watkins: Fig. 186; Peter Wenham: Fig. 188; Dean and Chapter of Westminster: Fig. 85; Winchester Excavations Committee: Fig. 114; Winchester Museums Service: Fig. 117; Dean and Chapter of Windsor: Fig. 84; Worcester Diocese: Fig. 190; York Archaeological Trust: Figs. 167, 168, 176, 177, 183e, 185b, 197; York Glaziers' Trust: Fig. 133; York Minster Archaeology Office: Fig. 183k-l; Yorkshire Museum: Fig. 159; G. Zarnecki: Fig. 19; R.J. Zeepvat: Fig. 194.

## List of Contributors

CLAUDE BLAIR. Formerly Keeper of Metalwork at the Victoria and Albert Museum; Liveryman of both the Goldsmiths' and the Armourers and Brasiers' Companies of London; a Vice-President of the Society of Antiquaries of London. Author of many publications on the history of metalwork, especially arms and armour.

JOHN BLAIR. Fellow of The Queen's College, Oxford, formerly Editor of *Oxoniensia*, and author of several publications on medieval history and archaeology, including monumental brasses.

MARIAN CAMPBELL. Deputy Curator in the Metalwork Collection of the Victoria and Albert Museum. Formerly Hon. Sec. of the British Archaeological Association. Author of publications on medieval goldsmiths' work, enamels and ironwork.

ROBERT J. CHARLESTON. Formerly Keeper of Ceramics at the Victoria and Albert Museum; a leading authority on glass, and author of numerous publications on early glass and ceramics.

JOHN CHERRY. Deputy Keeper in the Department of Medieval and Later Antiquities in the British Museum. Secretary of the Society of Antiquaries of London. Author of many publications on medieval art and archaeology.

JANE GEDDES. Formerly Inspector of Ancient Monuments; author of several papers on medieval decorative ironwork.

RONALD HOMER. Leading authority on pewter; Liveryman of the Pewterers' Company. Author of many publications on the subject, including *Five Centuries of Base Metal Spoons*.

ARTHUR MACGREGOR. Assistant Keeper in the Department of Antiquities,

Ashmolean Museum, and author of several works on bone artefacts including *Bone, Antler, Ivory and Horn: The Technology of Skeletal Materials since the Roman Period*.

RICHARD MARKS. Formerly Keeper of the Burrell Collection, Glasgow, and now Director of the Royal Pavilion, Art Gallery and Museums, Brighton. Author of several works on window glass and on medieval and renaissance art, including a forthcoming monograph on English medieval stained glass.

NICHOLAS MOORE. Independent architectural historian, formerly Investigator with the Royal Commission on Historical Monuments. Author of a thesis and various articles on brick building in medieval England.

JULIAN MUNBY. Leading authority on medieval structural carpentry; author of several papers on timber-framed buildings.

DAVID PARSONS. Archaeologist and architectural historian; formerly editor of *The Archaeological Journal*; editor of *Tenth-century Studies* and *Stone: Quarrying and Building in England, AD 43-1525*; author of several works on early medieval church buildings in England and Europe.

NIGEL RAMSAY. Curator in the Department of Manuscripts, British Library, and Research Editor of *A History of Canterbury Cathedral*. Author of many papers on medieval crafts, the medieval book trade and medieval legal history.

PENELOPE WALTON. Textile consultant; author of *Dyes in Medieval Textiles*.

# Abbreviations

| | |
|---|---|
| *Antiq. Jnl.* | *Antiquaries Journal* |
| *Arch. Jnl.* | *Archaeological Journal* |
| *Arch. Cant.* | *Archaeologia Cantiana* |
| B.L. | British Library |
| *Bull.* | *Bulletin* |
| *Cal.* | *Calendar* |
| *Cal. Hustings Wills* | *Calendar of Wills Enrolled and Proved in the Court of Husting, London*, ed. R.R. Sharpe (2 vols., 1889). |
| *Cal. Letter-Book A* (etc.) | *Calendar of Letter-Books . . . of the City of London . . . Letter-Book A* (etc.), ed. R.R. Sharpe (11 vols., 1899-1912). |
| *Cal. Plea & Mem. R. 1323-1364* (etc.) | *Calendar of Plea and Memoranda Rolls . . . of the City of London . . . 1323-1364* (etc.), ed. A.H. Thomas et al. (6 vols., Cambridge, 1926, etc.). |
| C.B.A. | Council for British Archaeology |
| *Chron.* | *Chronicle* |
| Drury | G.Dru Drury, 'The Uses of Purbeck Marble in Medieval Times', *Proc. Dorset Nat. Hist. & Arch. Soc.* lxx (1948). |
| *Econ. Hist. Rev.* | *Economic History Review* |
| *Eng. Hist. Docs.* | *English Historical Documents*: I: *c.500-1042*, ed. D. Whitelock (2nd edn., 1979); II: *1042-1189*, ed. D.C. Douglas and G.W. Greenaway (2nd edn., 1981); III: *1189-1327*, ed. H. Rothwell (1975); IV: *1327-1485*, ed. A.R. Myers (1969); V: *1485-1558*, ed. C.H. Williams (1967). |
| Harvey, *Mediaeval Craftsmen* | J.H. Harvey, *Mediaeval Craftsmen* (1975). |
| Inst. | Institute |

| | |
|---|---|
| *J.B.A.A.* | *Journal of the British Archaeological Association* |
| *J.B.S.M.G.P.* | *Journal of the British Society of Master Glass-Painters* |
| *Jnl.* | *Journal* |
| *King's Works* | *The History of the King's Works*, general editor H.M. Colvin, I and II etc. (1963 etc.). |
| Knoop and Jones, *Med. Mason* | D. Knoop and G.P. Jones, *The Mediaeval Mason* (3rd edn., Manchester, 1967). |
| Leach | R. Leach, *An Investigation into the Use of Purbeck Marble in Medieval England* (2nd edn., privately printed, 1978). |
| Lehmann-Brockhaus, *Schriftquellen* | O. Lehmann-Brockhaus, *Lateinische Schriftquellen zur Kunst in England, Wales und Schottland vom Jahre 901 bis zum Jahre 1307* (5 vols., Munich, 1955-60). |
| *M.E.D.* | *Middle English Dictionary* (Ann Arbor, Mich., etc., 1956 etc.). |
| P.R.O. | Public Record Office |
| *Proc.* | *Proceedings* |
| *R.* | *Roll(s)* |
| *Rep.* | *Report(s)* |
| Riley, *Memorials* | *Memorials of London and London Life, in the XIIIth, XIVth and XVth Centuries . . .*, ed. H.T. Riley (1868). |
| *Rot.Parl.* | *Rotuli Parliamentorum* (7 vols., *c.*1780-1832). |
| Salzman, *Building in England* | L.F. Salzman, *Building in England down to 1540* (reprinted with additions, Oxford, 1967). |
| Salzman, *Industries* | L.F. Salzman, *English Industries of the Middle Ages* (2nd edn., Oxford, 1923). |
| Salzman, *English Trade* | L.F. Salzman, *English Trade in the Middle Ages* (Oxford, 1931). |
| Singer, *Hist. of Technology* | *A History of Technology*, ed. Charles Singer and others (1955 etc.). |
| Soc. | Society |
| *S.R.* | *Statutes of the Realm. Printed by Command of his Majesty King George the Third* (11 vols., 1810-24). |
| *Test.Ebor.* | *Testamenta Eboracensia . . .*, ed. J. Raine and J.W. Clay (6 vols., Surtees Soc., iv, xxx, xlv, liv, lxxix and cvi, 1836-1902). |
| Theophilus, *De Div. Artibus* ed. Dodwell | *Theophilus, De Diversis Artibus*, ed. C.R. Dodwell (Oxford, 1961). |

| | |
|---|---|
| Theophilus, *On Divers Arts*, ed. Hawthorne & Smith | *Theophilus. On Divers Arts*, trans. and intro. John G. Hawthorne and Cyril S. Smith (Chicago, 1963; repr. with additions, New York, 1979). |
| *Trans.* | *Transactions* |
| *V.C.H.* | *Victoria County History* |
| *Wool Text. Ind.* | J.G. Jenkins, *The Wool Textile Industry of Great Britain* (1972). |

# Introduction

## NIGEL RAMSAY

How medieval craftsmen worked, what techniques they used and how specialised they were – these are questions that archaeological excavation can rarely answer by itself. Nor can the evolution of English crafts and industries easily be understood from the scattered documentary evidence that survives. Much of the craftsman's work, which of course took place above ground, has left no physical evidence, and few documents reveal anything about working methods, as opposed to administrative or financial details. Yet by juxtaposing documentary and archaeological evidence with surviving objects, a surprising amount of information can be gleaned about how craftsmen set about their work and what they made. The essays in this volume take this approach and apply it to the different materials that they used: wool and linen, the diverse stones and metals, wood, ceramics and glass, horn and bone, and leather.

Previous studies have tended to look at English crafts and industries obliquely, concentrating on the institutions that became prominent in their organisation and control. For instance, most of the surviving livery companies of London and other cities have sponsored the writing of their own histories.[1] Some of these companies have preserved a wealth of archival evidence of their medieval activities. Economic historians have written a few of these corporate histories, but they have otherwise concentrated their attention on the activities of the greatest economic importance in the medieval period, such as the textile and dependent industries. In so far as this book has a predecessor, its inspiration has been L.F. Salzman's *English Industries of the Middle Ages*, first published in 1913.[2] It remains of value, since Salzman based it on documentary evidence, and he had a wide knowledge of the royal works accounts

---

1 For bibliographies of the medieval London gilds see W.F. Kahl, *The Development of London Livery Companies: an Historical Essay and a Select Bibliography* (Boston, Mass., 1960), and John Greenwood, *The Industrial Archaeology and Industrial History of London: A Bibliography* (Cranfield, 1988), 32-53, as well as Appendix B to George Unwin, *The Gilds & Companies of London* (3rd and 4th edns., 1938 and 1963). A discursive account of gild historiography is given by W.F. Kahl, introduction to Unwin's *Gilds & Companies* (4th edn., 1963). All four 'editions' of Unwin's book have the same basic text.

2 In 1913 he spelled his surname Salzmann; he changed it to Salzman in *c*.1918.

and other materials in the Public Record Office. But the essays in this book are able in addition to draw on all the archaeological investigation that has taken place since Salzman's day, and they are also more technical and more sharply focused. While Salzman's scope included coalmining, fishing and brewing, the emphasis in this volume is on craftsmen, how they worked and what they produced.

Like Salzman's, this book follows a material- or else an artefact-based approach; each main category of material is treated separately, since craftsmen commonly worked in only one medium, and often only at one stage of its preparation. For instance, men who carved alabaster were usually called alabastermen, rather than coming under the generic term carver,[3] just as the men who worked gold and silver into jewellery were generally called goldsmiths rather than jewellers. A purely craftsman-based approach would be difficult, however, because a medieval craftsman might work in related materials or make objects that were drawing on more than just his principal skill: a goldsmith worked in the less precious metal, silver, for much of his time, while an agletmaker did not confine himself to making the metal tags of shoelaces but also made the laces themselves.[4] Many other goods were made by different craftsmen at their different stages of manufacture – shoes, for instance, were a product of the tanner's skills as much as of those of the cobbler. And there was an increasing tendency in the later medieval period for such occupational terms to be applied to men whose principal activity was to trade, and who were merchants rather than craftsmen. Woolmen, for example, were dealers in wool rather than being involved in any stage of its preparation.

Records of the 13th and even the 14th century abound in references to men whose occupation may seem remarkably specialised – forcermaker (maker of coffers or caskets), traventer (hirer-out of carts), quernpecker (indenter of the surface of a millstone), wimpler (maker of wimples or veils) or sheather (maker of leather sheaths). Some of these terms survived as surnames, for hereditary names began to become established from about the first half of the 13th century,[5] but otherwise they tend to occur less in the 15th century, and still less thereafter. Changes in fashion account for the wimpler's disappearance (just as they account for the rise of the hatter). However, a factor of greater importance was the shift in how goods were marketed and the way in which the men who finished and sold goods tended to achieve predominance in their field. The sheathers and bladesmiths, for instance, came to be dominated by the cutlers in a process of which one stage can be seen in a

3   But see below, 38, for the question of whether 'alabasterman' meant salesman as well as carver.

4   Elspeth M. Veale, 'Craftsmen and the Economy of London in the Fourteenth Century', in A.E.J. Hollaender and W. Kellaway (eds.), *Studies in London History* (1969), 131-51, at 143.

5   See generally Gustav Fransson, *Middle English Surnames of Occupation, 1100-1350* (Lund Studies in English, iii, 1938), and Bertil Thuresson, *Middle English Occupational Terms* (Lund Studies in English, xix, 1950); for London craftsmen see E. Ekwall (ed.), *Two Early London Subsidy Rolls* (Lund, 1951), and idem, *Studies on the Population of Medieval London* (Stockholm, 1956); for Norfolk and Suffolk and other counties, see the volumes by George Redmonds and Richard A. McKinley in the English Surnames series – *Yorkshire, West Riding* etc. (London and Chichester, 1973, etc.).

City of London ordinance in 1408 that followed a petition to the mayor and aldermen from the cutlers. The cutlers explained that they were accustomed 'to sell knives fully prepared and decorated, to all buyers whatsoever; but that every knife is prepared separately by three different crafts, first, the blade by smiths called "bladsmythes", the handle and other fitting work by the cutlers, and the sheath by the sheathers; and that if the articles are good, commendation is the result, but if bad, then blame and scandal falls and is charged upon the said trade of the cutlers. And . . . for any default in the sheaths, being not properly made, no little blame and scandal falls upon the said trade of the cutlers . . .' The mayor and aldermen thereupon conceded that in future two of the masters of the cutlers should be entitled to make scrutiny of the sheaths in London and elsewhere in England, with the power to present any defaults for punishment by the mayor and aldermen.[6] As mere suppliers to the cutlers, the sheathers were in an inherently weak position, while the cutlers controlled the market.

## *Techniques: Literary and Archaeological Evidence*

Surviving artefacts do not reveal who made them, and documentary evidence for how things were made is all too often limited to recording what was thought to be illegal. After seven years' apprenticeship, no craftsman was likely to need to be told how to do things, and a written exposition of techniques would in any case be useful only if he was literate.

Certain books with technical instructions do survive, mostly concerned with painting and the skills required for the arts of book decoration; none of these books, however, can be shown to have belonged to an English craftsman, and very few of them were copied or owned in England.[7] They are of immense value, nonetheless, both because the processes that they describe were practised throughout Europe and because some processes and products would not otherwise be explicable. Many medieval texts survive only in corrupt versions, for it was the common practice of medieval writers to excerpt and copy freely from their predecessors and to make 'silent' changes throughout their texts. Where the arts are concerned, they also tended to copy from classical texts, such as Pliny's *Natural History* or one of its derivatives.

The most valuable medieval instructional treatise is that 'Concerning Various Arts' (*De Diversis Artibus*) by Theophilus: he was a monk, and his aim was to explain

---

6  Riley, *Memorials*, 567-8.
7  A useful list of artists' and craftsmen's treatises is provided by S.M. Alexander, 'Towards a History of Art Materials – A Survey of Published Technical Literature in the Arts. Part I. From Antiquity to 1599', *Art and Archaeology*, *Technical Abstracts*, vii (1969), 123-61. For all aspects of book illustration see François Avril, *La Technique de l'Enluminure d'après les Textes Médiévaux. Essai de Bibliographie* (Paris: Bibliothèque Nationale: Cabinet des Manuscrits [1967]), listing monographs, articles and MSS.

Fig. i. Blacksmith's softening iron. Flemish-Burgundian, 2nd quarter of the 14th century (B.L., MS Sloane 2782, f. 5).

the craftsman's methods in terms of the production of works of Christian art.[8] His work is composed of three books, on painting, glass, and metalwork; the third is the longest, and the fact that its preface was written in answer to Bernard of Clairvaux's attack on the lavish decoration of Benedictine monastic churches suggests that Theophilus was writing in about 1122-3.[9] He was from north-west Germany, and some scholars have identified him with the metalworking craftsman Roger of Helmarshausen; his importance, in any case, lies in his being (or having been) a practising craftsman. Although some of his ideas and descriptions came from Pliny (via Isidore of Seville's excerpts), most of his writing was based on his own experience. He was also remarkably encyclopaedic in his approach, covering every stage of the process required, say, to found a bell or build an organ, from the making of tools and moulds to hanging the bell and tuning it or making a pulley-mounted cover to protect the organ. He was not commercially motivated, and shows no interest in mass-production except at the simple level of dye-making or the use of moulds; in this he reflects his age, for manual labour was thought positively to be virtuous and to exalt man.[10]

8.  There are two modern editions: Theophilus, *De Diversis Artibus*, ed. and transl. C.R. Dodwell (1961); and Theophilus, *On Divers Arts*, transl. J.G. Hawthorne and C.S. Smith (Chicago and London, 1963; reprinted with additions, New York, 1979); they were critically reviewed, from the point of view of interpreting the text's meaning, by D.V. Thompson, 'Theophilus Presbyter: Words and Meaning in Technical Translation', *Speculum*, xlii (1967), 313-39. A major recent study of book iii is Erhard Brepohl, *Theophilus Presbyter und die Mittelalterliche Goldschmiedekunst* (Vienna, etc., 1987).

9   Lynn White, 'Theophilus Redivivus', *Technology and Culture*, v (1964), 224-33.

10  Lynn White, 'What Accelerated Technological Progress in the Western Middle Ages?', in Alistair C. Crombie (ed.), *Scientific Change* (1963), 286-91. Technological progress was desirable, nonetheless, for it eased the burden of material life in a world that man was directed to subdue.

The techniques that Theophilus describes were virtually all practised throughout Europe, but his treatise did not have a wide circulation and it is very likely that no copy of it ever came to England. No knowledge of it is shown in the encyclopaedic but theoretical treatise *De Proprietatibus Rerum* (On the Properties of Things) by the English scholar Bartholomew Anglicus (*fl.* 1230-50).[11] Bartholomew's book was long a classic in English and continental universities, and in the 14th century was translated into English;[12] it would, however, have been of little practical use to any craftsman.[13]

In 1503 a York glazier, Robert Preston, left to his apprentice 'all my bookes that is fitte for one prentesse of his craffte to lerne by'.[14] What he was probably referring to was a book of designs, that is *vidimuses* or cartoons,[15] and his bequest is puzzling only in the use of the word 'bookes', for one might have expected him to keep his designs as loose sheets of parchment. Sheets of designs were as essential to stained-glass painters or freemasons as moulds were to bellfounders, bucklemakers and many other sorts of metalworker.[16] Sometimes these sheets may have been bound up at a slightly later date, like the Pepysian Sketchbook (made up of 14th- and 15th-century designs),[17] but it is probably only because bound volumes survive so much better than loose sheets that a fair number of medieval modelbooks survive, by contrast with a very few *caches* of designs.[18] That medieval masons carried around with them designs for buildings (generally as the profiles of mouldings rather than as elevations) can be inferred from close examination of medieval buildings and is also occasionally referred to in contemporary documentation.[19]

The question of the separation of design from execution is raised by documentary references that show designs crossing from one medium to another. Equally, the

11 See the *Dictionary of National Biography*, under Glanville, Bartholomew de.

12 [M.C. Seymour (ed.)], *On the Properties of Things. John Trevisa's Translation of Bartholomaeus Anglicus, De Proprietatibus Rerum . . .*, 3 vols. (Oxford, 1975-88).

13 One compilation that was aimed at the craftsman was the collection of nearly 300 recipes, mostly for painters' materials, known as the *Mappae Clavicula*; this was first compiled around A.D. 800, and is printed in translation, from a 12th-century copy, by C.S. Smith and J.G. Hawthorne, 'Mappae Clavicula. A Little Key to the World of Medieval Techniques', *Trans. American Philosphical Soc.* n.s. lxiv, pt. 4 (1974).

14 D.M. Palliser, *Tudor York* (Oxford, 1979), 172.

15 For which see below, 267, 269 and 283-5.

16 See N.L. Ramsay, 'Artists, Craftsmen and Design in England, 1200-1400', in J.J.G. Alexander and P. Binski (eds.), *Age of Chivalry. Art in Plantagenet England, 1200-1400* (Exhibition Cat., Royal Academy of Arts, 1987), 49-54.

17 The Pepysian Sketchbook (Cambridge, Magdalene College, Pepys MS 1916) is briefly discussed by J.J.G. Alexander, ibid., 402, no. 466, with references to further literature.

18 Surviving modelbooks are described by R.W. Scheller, *A Survey of Medieval Model Books* (Haarlem, 1963); a 2nd edn. is in preparation. The best known modelbook is that of the 13th-century French architect Villard de Honnecourt, most readily available in Theodore Bowie's edn. (Bloomington and London: Indiana U.P. 1959 and later printings); an invaluable companion to this is the bibliography by Carl F. Barnes, *Villard de Honnecourt: the Artist and his Drawings* (Boston, Mass., c.1982).

19 See Ramsay, art. cit. note 16, and the cautionary observations of R.K. Morris, 'Mouldings and the Analysis of Medieval Style', in Eric Fernie and Paul Crossley (eds.), *Medieval Architecture and its Intellectual Context: Studies in Honour of Peter Kidson* (London and Ronceverte, W. Va., 1990), 239-48.

similarity of surviving objects, say, of a set of 14th-century floortiles to a contemporary set of illuminations of the infancy of Christ in a book, or of the silver-gilt Swinburne Pyx to another book illustration, show how craftsmen might take a design from one context and re-apply it on a larger or smaller scale in their own work.[20] This does not however indicate a lack of artistic originality or freedom on the part of the craftsman: pictures in illuminated books might be used as sources of a work's iconographic scheme or elements of its design, but usually they were so altered and adapted that modern art-historians are left guessing as to their identity. Craftsmen and artists worked within established traditions, but they were not copyists. They would naturally wish to keep abreast of changing styles and follow the latest court-style, if they could learn what this was, just as the English court often looked to Paris or elsewhere on the continent for its fashions.

Mass-production of objects was technically possible only for a limited range of materials, principally those where moulds were employed. Moulds provided an easy way for designs to pass from one medium to another, enabling commonplace objects to be made in the most up-to-date style, although the use of moulds must also often have had the effect of perpetuating old designs. All sorts of materials were used for making moulds, from the potter's clay to the bucklemaker's fine-grained limestone, but the same mould might serve several or many craftsmen, either within the same craft (as is known to have been the case with the London pewterers)[21] or even transgressing craft boundaries. In cheaper materials, such as tin or pewter, craftsmen often sought to reproduce designs that were first popularised in more precious metals. The existence of men termed mouldmaker is suggestive of there being some craftsmen who specialised in making moulds; waxchandlers may have specialised as mouldmakers, since moulds were essential for the mass-production of wax votive effigies and the like.[22]

## Gild Organisation: Craftsmen and Merchants

The word gild is derived from the Old English word *geld* (itself of Old West Germanic origin), meaning payment or contribution. It was applied both to the associations of people who shared a particular religious devotion (as to a particular saint), and to the groupings of leading citizens of towns who came together for financial reasons, to help them in their dealings with the Crown as well as with the other inhabitants of their town. In the 12th century there is evidence for the first gilds of craftsmen of particular skills: fullers at Winchester (1129-30), and weavers at London, Lincoln, Oxford, Winchester, Nottingham and Huntingdon (also by 1129-30) and at York

20   Ramsay, art. cit. note 16.
21   See below, 71-2.
22   P. Norman in *London Topographical Record*, vi (1909), 76-9, printed details of a late 15th-century lawsuit which show a London gold-smith to have commissioned a waxchandler to 'make, mould, cast and cleanse in lead all such tabernacles, battlements and imagery' as a new Cheapside Cross should require, for £80.

Fig. ii. Building St. Alban's church; from Matthew Paris's Life of St. Alban, written at St. Alban's Abbey, *c.* 1240s (Trinity College, Dublin, MS 177, f. 60).

(1164-5).[23] Other citizens of these and other leading towns, perhaps at about the same time, organised themselves into more general gilds, of all the other merchants, traders and craftsmen, and these gilds, known as 'gilds merchant', ran their town's general affairs and represented it in its dealings with the Crown;[24] both sorts of gild owed their legitimation to grants or charters obtained (at a price) from the Crown.

From the late 12th century, the gilds merchant tended to be displaced in their control of the town by fresh charters of self-government issued by the Crown: citizenship of a town, with certain financial and legal obligations as well as the right of free trading within it, became the requisite of its craftsmen. A craftsman could only become a freeman of a town if he satisfied one or other of certain criteria –

23    E.M. Carus-Wilson, *Medieval Merchant Venturers. Collected Studies* (2nd edn., 1967), 225-6. 1129-30 is the date of the earliest surviving Pipe Roll, in which payments from these gilds are recorded; it is likely that most of the gilds that made payments in that fiscal year had already existed for some time. For gilds in 12th-century London see further Christopher N.L. Brooke and G. Keir, *London, 800-1216: The Shaping of a City* (1975), 278-82. Earlier gilds were not of a craft-related character;

they have most recently been discussed by G. Rosser, 'The Anglo-Saxon Gilds', in John Blair (ed.), *Minsters and Parish Churches. The Local Church in Transition, 950-1200* (Oxford, 1988), 31-4.

24    See discussion by Susan Reynolds, *An Introduction to the History of English Medieval Towns* (Oxford, 1977), 164-8; the authoritative survey remains Charles Gross, *The Gild Merchant*, 2 vols. (Oxford, 1890).

principally, birth in the town, or the completion of apprenticeship to a freeman of the town. The craftsmen of each particular skill or material were a clearly identifiable group, and it was not long before other crafts matched the example of the woollen industry's fullers and weavers in obtaining some form of recognition from the Crown of their identity and rights and needs. The goldsmiths of London, for instance, did not obtain a royal charter until 1327, but had existed as an organisation at least as early as 1179-80 when the 'gild of goldsmiths' was fined £30 for forming itself without leave from the Crown.[25]

In the 12th century, the Crown sought to control the formation of gilds, but as it ceded powers of self-government to towns, the town authorities (mayor and aldermen, mayor and bailiffs, etc.) gained the power of authorising the making of formal organisations of craftsmen. Royal charters then became an extra plank of authority and independence, a luxury even, that gilds of craftsmen rarely wished to buy, for what mattered was the validation of their rules by the town authority.[26]

Even though a town did not necessarily make a charge for validating the ordinances of a craft gild, the members of a particular craft might not bother to have what seemed to them their own private rules and customs set out in writing and copied into a town register. In this they differed from the religious gilds or fraternities, for it was of the essence of those gilds that their members should employ a priest to pray for them and they might well wish to have legal identity so as to be able to purchase land to support him, while they would certainly all wish to have their names written on a roll or in a book so as to be remembered. It was not found too difficult to distinguish the religious gilds from the craft gilds, either in 1389, when the religious gilds' foundations and properties were required to be stated, or in 1545 when they were suppressed by Henry VIII.[27] On the other hand, this distinction was rarely absolutely clear-cut, for most of the craft gilds also employed priests to pray for their dead members and might well have properties set aside to provide funds for these and other religious purposes.

In what may seem a strange reversal of the 12th-century picture, the government came to accept that the organisation of the different crafts into gilds had its uses. For instance, in 1363 parliament passed an ordinance restricting all traders to a single class of wares and all craftsmen to a single craft.[28] The aim was to stop traders from engrossing and holding up merchandise, and in July 1364 charters were accordingly granted to the fishmongers, vintners and other London gilds forbidding anyone to take part in their trade unless he was a member of their gild. The granting of

25 T.F. Reddaway and L.E.M Walker, *The Early History of the Goldsmiths' Company, 1327-1509* (1975), xix.

26 A number of towns purchased from the Crown charters that conceded certain rights to them: for instance, Richard I when in need of money for crusading granted to several towns charters with rights of fee-farm. See R.H.C. Davis, 'An Oxford Charter of 1191 and the Beginnings of Municipal Freedom', *Oxoniensia*, xxxiii (1968), 53-65.

27 H.F. Westlake, *The Parish Gilds of Mediaeval England* (1919), 137-238, provides a calendar of the gild certificates of 1389 which give some indications of craft links.

28 Statute 37 Edward III, cc. 5, 6; *S.R.*, i, 379.

monopolies in these victualling trades led to immediate price rises, allegedly of as much as a third, and to riots in the same month, forcing the repeal of the ordinance in the next session of parliament.[29]

Behind the events of 1363-4 lay a major change that was taking place in other parts of England as well as in London – a shift in importance away from the gilds that were almost solely composed of craftsmen to those that were or came to be primarily of merchants. In the 14th century the gilds of mercers, grocers, drapers, fishmongers, goldsmiths, skinners, tailors and vintners became, in effect, gilds of merchants, and in the next century they were joined by the ironmongers, salters and haberdashers.[30] These merchant gilds or 'companies' (a word that came to be applied to them instead of 'gild', and which fashion then led other gilds to use too) were increasingly predominant in the government of London, as can be seen from the fact that their members came to provide the majority of the mayors and aldermen.

It is a debatable question how far there were naked tensions between the two sorts of gild. The short-lived statute of 1363 that sought to limit each trader to a single class of wares and each craftsman to a single craft has been seen as an attempt by the merchants or 'mercantile class' to stop producers retailing their own goods and thereby keeping business out of the hands of the merchants.[31] Yet it was a long-established custom, in London and other towns, that every citizen could buy and sell wholesale whatever commodities he wished, and in practice the distinction between craftsman and merchant was often blurred. By the 15th century, the merchant companies themselves divided their membership into those who were entitled to wear the company's own coloured clothing or 'livery' and those who were not: the latter group was made up of those who might never succeed in joining the livery, such as modest artisans who worked by themselves or for the more successful merchants, as well as young men who were perhaps working for older members of the company and were building up experience so that at about the age of thirty they might be admitted to the livery.[32]

On the other hand, not all craftsmen wished to come together in anything so formal as a gild. In 1421-2 the clerk of the brewers' gild in London listed 111 crafts,[33] and it has plausibly been suggested that by craft he meant just that, and that he was not implying that each of those crafts was organised into a gild: the members of a craft (or of a 'mystery', from Latin *misterium* or French *métier*, as their activity was

29 J. Tait (ed.), *Chronica Johannis de Reading . . .* (Manchester, 1914), 39, 317.

30 Sylvia L. Thrupp, *The Merchant Class of Medieval London [1300-1500]* (Chicago, 1948), 6.

31 R.H. Hilton, 'Women Traders in Medieval England', reprinted in his *Class Conflict and the Crisis of Feudalism: Essays in Medieval Social History* (1985), 205-15, at 208. But see rather S.L. Thrupp, 'The Grocers of London: A Study of Distributive Trade', in E. Power and M.M. Postan (ed.), *Studies in English Trade in*

the Fifteenth Century (1933), 247-92, at 259-62, and P. Nightingale, 'Capitalists, Crafts and Constitutional Change in Later Fourteenth-Century London', *Past & Present*, no. 124 (Aug. 1989), 1-35, at 33.

32 Thrupp, op. cit. note 30, 12-13.

33 The Brewers' clerk's list of the names of various crafts in the City of London (*nominum diversarum arcium in civitate Londonie*) is printed by Unwin, op. cit. note 1, 370-1, and reproduced by him in facsimile (reduced) on p.167.

alternatively known) were readily enough identifiable in any case and might be so few in number as to make a formal organisation wholly superfluous.[34] For instance, in late 14th-century London there were just seven botellers, or makers of leather bottles.[35]

Yet gild formation offered its members great advantages, as did the validation of gild ordinances by the town authorities. The London cutlers in 1408 were strengthened in their case against the sheathers by the fact that the sheathers had never presented any rules to the chamberlain of the city.[36] The connections between gilds and town authorities came to be so close that by the 14th century it was the gilds who presented men (and occasionally women, as in the case of the London silkwomen's gild)[37] to the town for admission to its freedom.[38] But the *raison d'être* of the gilds was that they were associations formed for the mutual benefit of their members. They maintained professional standards within their craft, both by controlling admission of their members (as by regulating apprenticeship) and upholding certain standards in their behaviour towards each other, as well as by inspecting their members' products to ascertain that they were of reasonable quality. As early as the 12th century, the gilds were attempting to keep their members' differences from getting to the law courts, by insisting on such differences being settled within the gild's own jurisdiction.[39] The gain to members, apart from the maintenance of their own standards of life and work, was the exclusion of non-members from their activity. The gild monopolies were never entirely free from threat of breach, for even within each gild's town there might be liberties, or areas of ecclesiastical jurisdiction where the town's authority was null. In the later Middle Ages, moreover, there was an influx of 'aliens' from northern Europe who established themselves outside the City of London's jurisdiction in such places as Southwark; glaziers and goldsmiths were prominent among these.[40] The gilds sought to counter this threat by gaining or claiming control over the practice of their craft within a much greater area than their town, and perhaps even throughout the kingdom. As early as Henry II's reign the London weavers had been given the sole

34  Veale, art. cit. note 4, 140.
35  Ibid., 142.
36  Riley, *Memorials*, 567.
37  Widows might also present apprentices for admission to London's freedom: see M. Curtis, 'The London Lay Subsidy of 1332', in G. Unwin (ed.), *Finance and Trade under Edward III* (Manchester, 1918), 35-92, at 59. For women in the London craft gilds see generally K.E. Lacey, 'Women and Work in Fourteenth and Fifteenth Century London', in L. Charles and L. Duffin (eds.), *Women and Work in Pre-Industrial England* (1985), 24-82; M. Kowaleski and J.M. Bennett, 'Crafts, Gilds and Women in the Middle Ages: Fifty years after Marian K. Dale', *Signs*, xiv (1988-9), 475-501; and C.M. Barron, 'The Golden Age of Women in

Medieval London', *Reading Medieval Studies*, xv (1989), 35-58.
38  W. de G. Birch, *Historical Charters and Constitutional Documents of the City of London* (1887), 45-50, at 46-7 (London's charter of 1319); cf. *Cal. Plea & Mem. R., 1364-81*, pp.xviii-lvi.
39  This is implicit in the laws of the weavers of London, allowed to them by Henry II: Henry T. Riley (ed.), *Munimenta Gildhallae Londoniensis*, ii, *Liber Custumarum*, pt. i (Rolls Ser. 12, 1860), 33. See also Brooke and Keir, op. cit. note 23, 284-5.
40  See below, 273, 277 (glaziers) and 147-8 (goldsmiths), and see further Sylvia L. Thrupp, 'Aliens in and around London in the Fifteenth Century', in Hollaender and Kellaway (eds.), op. cit. note 4, 249-72.

right to engage in their craft within London, while the making of dyed or rayed cloth throughout Yorkshire was restricted to members of the weavers' gilds of York and the other boroughs in the county.[41] In the 14th and 15th centuries the London gilds were to the fore in getting authority to regulate their craft's products throughout England; this sort of national control was first given to the goldsmiths of London, when Edward I ordered the goldsmiths of other towns to observe the rules laid down for London.[42] Other gilds followed in gaining the right to vet goods for quality throughout England – principally, no doubt, at the fairs and markets at which their own members would expect to be present.[43] Both the embroiderers and the horners of London claimed rights specifically over certain country fairs.[44]

In addition to whatever extra rights their gild might obtain for them outside their town, gildsmen were already privileged in being citizens with the right of trading freely within it. There were often considerable tensions between gild members and the other inhabitants of each town, for the gildsmen were in a minority. In London, it has been estimated that only one-twentieth of the inhabitants were enfranchised citizens.[45] The others made persistent though ill-recorded attempts to organise themselves and obtain some sorts of rights and privileges: in London and other towns, a variety of journeymen's and other gilds can at times be detected, sometimes clinging legitimately to the coat-tails of the established gilds and sometimes in opposition to them, seeking like a trade union to better their members' pay.[46]

## Craftsmen's and Merchants' Marks

The marking or identification of goods as being those of a particular craftsman or merchant was one way of reassuring the buyer that the goods had indeed come from a reputable craftsman or merchant. Such marks were not intended to be readily identifiable by the buyers as the marks of particular people, and still less should they be seen as akin to artists' signatures or as craftsmen's substitutes for coats of arms. It is true that in the 15th and 16th centuries a few merchants became so proud of their marks as to treat them as though they were like coats of arms, fit to be represented on their rings or tombs, but craftsmen's marks originally were only intended to be recognisable to the officers of their gild, or to the town authorities who were

41  E. Miller, 'The Fortunes of the English Textile Industry during the Thirteenth Century', *Econ. Hist. Rev.* 2nd ser. xviii (1965), 64-82, at 69.

42  See below, 140-1.

43  The City of London's charter of 1327 allowed it to have its own wardens at all fairs in England, to determine all pleas about its citizens' contracts: Birch, op. cit. note 38, 52-8, at 55; cf. *Cal. Letter-Book E*, 230, for the exercise of this right.

44  *Rot. Parl.*, iv, 255. The embroiderers' petition was granted insofar as embroidery with gold or silver thread was concerned; the fairs were those of Stourbridge, Ely, Oxford and Salisbury. For the horners see below, 370.

45  *Cal. Plea & Mem. R., 1364-81*, lxi-ii.

46  Journeymen's gilds are touched on by R.H. Hilton, 'Popular Movements in England at the End of the Fourteenth Century', reprinted in his *Class Conflict and the Crisis of Feudalism: Essays in Medieval Social History* (1985), 152-64.

Fig. iii. Mould for making the backs of seal matrices. From Great Thornham (Suff.). 13th century? (1¾ x size) (British Museum, M. & L.A., OA 7484).

responsible for checking on standards of production.[47] For this reason the marks of the members of a particular craft may look extremely similar to one another:[48] they could only be matched to craftsmen's names by the official who had copies of them all. Only a master craftsman would have a mark: it would be applied to all the products of his shop, whether made by him, by his apprentices or by any journeymen whom he might have working for him.

The marking of English products is first documented in 1300 in the statutory requirement that gold and silver plate that had been assayed and had reached a certain standard of purity was to be marked with a leopard's head.[49] But the practice

47　Many late medieval English merchants' marks are illustrated by F.A. Girling, *English Merchants' Marks. A Field Survey of Marks made by Merchants and Tradesmen in England between 1400 and 1700* (1964). A useful discussion is provided by F.W. Kuhlicke, 'Merchant Marks: their Origin and Use', *Amateur Histor-*

*ian*, v (1961-2), 98-106.
48　E.g. the marks of the London coopers, 1420, reproduced by Salzman, *Industries*, 325.
49　*Articuli super Cartas*, 28 Edward I, c.20; *S.R.*, i, 140-1. The practice of marking gold and silver plate was followed in Paris from an earlier date: see below, 140 note 165.

of marking products was evidently followed earlier. For example, a 13th-century knife in the Museum of London bears a deeply-stamped crescent as its maker's mark,[50] while one or two memorial brasses of about the 1330s have been stamped with what are probably to be seen as casters' marks (i.e. made by the makers of the latten sheets), since they have been cut into subsequently by the engravers.[51] The London turners were required to mark their barrels from 1347,[52] and by the same date the London helmers had their helmetry assayed and marked by their wardens and also marked with their own sign or mark.[53] Likewise, each master blacksmith of London was ordered to put his own mark upon his larger pieces of work 'in case default shall be found in the same',[54] and brasiers' marks are mentioned in their ordinances of 1416.[55]

Next to goldsmiths' hall-marks, the best-known medieval marks are 'masons' marks', about which, as L.F. Salzman has stated, 'so much, including some fanciful nonsense, has been written'.[56] There are virtually no contemporary documentary references to these, there being nothing about them in the ordinances of the London masons' gild of 1356, 1481 or 1521, and it is not even certain whether they were chiselled onto stones by masons at the quarry or in the masons' lodge at the building. The marks rarely appear on tracery or carved stones, and it is possible that they differ from other craftsmen's marks in having been applied only by the men who were on piece-work or the casual labourers, and not by the masters.[57]

No system of control is foolproof, and the craftsmen's marking system was readily enough abused by the practice of forging other masters' marks. In 1408 the cutlers' and bladesmiths' companies of London came together before the mayor and aldermen with the complaint that people from other parts of England were selling defective knives and blades to the cutlers, bringing both trades into disrepute; the remedy that they sought, and were granted, was that henceforth the cutlers should only buy marked knives or blades from the bladesmiths of London.[58] That forgery within one craft was not unknown either is shown by the inclusion in the London blacksmiths' ordinances (1372) of the rule that no-one in that trade should counterfeit the mark of another.[59]

Other than hall-marks and masons' marks, the medieval marks likeliest to be found today are assembly marks – on wooden structures as well as on metalwork and tiles. It was the common practice to prefabricate the wooden frames of houses and stone vaults of roofs, and numbering systems can sometimes still be seen on the

50  Makers' marks on knives and shears are discussed and illustrated by J. Cowgill, M. de Neergard and N. Griffiths, *Knives and Scabbards*, Medieval Finds from Excavations in London, 1 (Museum of London, 1987), 17-24.
51  Malcolm Norris, *Monumental Brasses. The Craft* (London and Boston, 1978), 86.
52  *Cal. Letter-Book F*, 160-1, 307.
53  See below, 185.
54  Riley, *Memorials*, 361.
55  Ibid., 626.

56  Salzman, *Building in England*, 127; for another sane discussion see D. Knoop and G.P. Jones, 'The London Masons' Company', *Economic History*, iii, no. 14 (1939), 157-66, at 163-5.
57  Salzman, loc. cit. note 56.
58  Riley, *Memorials*, 568-9.
59  Ibid., 361. See also below, 185, for forged helmers' marks; for counterfeit leopard's head marks see Reddaway and Walker, op. cit. note 25, 141.

components of such work, as on the upper side of the stone vault of the chapel of King's College, Cambridge.[60] Roman rather than arabic numerals tended to be used, since they were made up of straight lines and were more clearly distinguishable from each other.[61]

### The Localisation of Industries; Markets and Fairs

Almost all industries were localised close to the source of their raw materials, at least for the initial stages of their transformation into finished products. Stone could only be quarried where it was found, and it was only practical to smelt metals close to where their ore occurred. Likewise, the best wool came from sheep that grazed in the Welsh marches and the richer agricultural areas, such as Lincolnshire, the Cotswolds and south-east England (wool from the north of England was always thought less good), and so the clothmaking industry tended to operate in the same regions.[62] Only carpentry and the other building trades, and metalworking and leatherworking, were practised throughout England.

Nonetheless, certain places came to specialise in the production of particular goods, even though their raw materials were not necessarily obtainable locally. A metrical list of English towns and their characteristic products or attributes, of the mid or late 13th century, well illustrates the range of specialities available.[63] Some are humorously intended, like the *puteynes* (whores) of Charing, by London, or perhaps York's *regraterie* (cornering the market, so as to be able to charge higher prices), but many of the specialities seem highly appropriate, and it is even fair to say that York, the second city in England, was perhaps a trading rather than a manufacturing centre. Corfe is rightly associated in the list with (Purbeck) marble,[64] Lincoln with scarlet cloth, and Stamford with hauberget cloth,[65] and although it may seem strange to find needles at Wilton, wimples at Lewes or cutlery at Thaxted, the poll tax records a century later show that in Thaxted cutlers still comprised 78 out of the total male population of 250.[66]

Such localisation of activities reflects both the small size of most towns and, more

60  Walter T. Leedy, *Fan Vaulting: A Study of Form, Technology and Meaning* (1980), plates 90 and 91, illustrates the Arabic and Roman numerals used in the assembly of the main vault of King's College Chapel, Cambridge.

61  Carpenters continued sometimes to use Roman numerals as assembly marks into the 19th century. Arabic numerals were used on floor tiles that have been found at Warden Abbey (Beds.): see below, 199.

62  J.H. Munro, 'Wool-Price Schedules and the Qualities of English Wools in the Later Middle Ages, c.1270-1499', *Textile History*, ix (1978), 118-69.

63  C. Bonnier, 'List of English Towns in the Fourteenth Century', *English Historical Review*, xvi (1901), 501-3; printed in translation in H. Rothwell (ed.), *English Historical Documents, 1189-1327* (1975), 881-4; discussed by Carus-Wilson, op. cit. note 23, 212-3.

64  See below, 41.

65  See below, 338-9, 348.

66  Norah Kenyon, 'Labour Conditions in Essex in the Reign of Richard II', *Econ. Hist. Rev.* 1st ser. iv (1932-4), 429-51, at 434. The difficulty of finding out more about these cutlers from documentary sources is noted by K.C. Newton, *Thaxted in the Fourteenth Century* (Essex Record Office Publications, xxxiii, 1960), preface, and cf. 20-1.

Fig. iv. Floor-tiles with designs cut from stencils. From Warden Abbey (Beds.). 14th century. (*Bedford Museum*).

importantly, the way in which goods were marketed. In the 13th century and, to a lesser extent, the 14th, it was usual for merchants to have to travel around England in search of goods, for the greatest markets for goods were not the large cities but the leading fairs.[67] It is true that the fairs were concentrated on the eastern side of England, between Lincoln and Bury St. Edmunds, with celebrated ones at Stourbridge (beside Cambridge) and St. Ives (Huntingdonshire), but there were other important ones throughout the country, notably those of St. Giles at Winchester and at Oxford. And even in the 15th century the fairs remained of regional importance, both as a means of communicating money and correspondence as well as for their basic role of providing goods for individual consumers as well as for merchants. The accounts of the household steward of Lady Alice de Bryene of Acton Hall (Suffolk) in 1418-19 show how much her household was still dependent

---

67  St. Ives and other fairs are discussed by Ellen Wedemeyer Moore, *The Fairs of Medieval England* (Toronto, 1985); St. Giles's fair, Winchester, by Derek Keene, *Survey of Medieval Winchester*, ii, Winchester Studies, 2 (Oxford, 1985), 1091-1132; fairs from the 8th to 13th centuries by P.H. Sawyer, 'Fairs and Markets in Early Medieval England', in *Danish Medieval History: New Currents*, ed. N. Skyum-Nielsen and N. Lund (Copenhagen, 1981), 153-68; A.R. Bridbury, 'Markets and Freedom in the Middle Ages', in B.L. Anderson and A.J.H. Latham (ed.), *The Market in History* (1986), 79-119. For a study of fairs and markets as used by particular consumers, see C. Dyer, 'The Consumer and the Market in the Later Middle Ages', *Econ. Hist. Rev.* 2nd ser. xlii (1989), 305-27.

on Stourbridge fair: she might herself buy wine in London, but stockfish (dried fish), salt, pepper, cloves and iron pans were all bought at Stourbridge, by herself or her servants.[68]

A major factor in the decline of the fairs' importance must have been the increasing importance of London as a mercantile centre. Even when due allowance is made for the distorting effect of the wealth of documentary material that survives for London, it is evident that in the 14th and 15th centuries the city became the leading place for many crafts and the base for the principal merchants.[69] It was by far the largest city in England, and it was so well able to attract people to work in it that its population was much less affected by the Black Death than were most other towns in mid 14th-century England. The 1377 poll tax figures gave London a total of 23,300 adults, far ahead of York's 7,250 and Bristol's 6,350; on this basis its actual population was perhaps 35,000, only 5,000 down from the 40,000 estimated to have lived in it thirty years earlier.[70] But both sets of figures should probably be revised upwards; recent research suggests that London's population in the early 14th century was more than double 40,000, and perhaps nearer to 100,000.[71]

Most of England's population lived in the country, however. For them, the likeliest alternative source of supply for goods that they could not buy locally or at a fair was the travelling merchant. By the 16th century such merchants were mere chapmen,[72] and 'tinker's ware' meant nothing better than pewter goods.[73] In the 13th century, by contrast, when distribution patterns were less clear-cut, a travelling salesman might bring all kinds of costly goods with him. For example, the stock-in-trade of a pedlar who died at Beaumaris in about 1328 was valued at £2 2s., and included ginger, pepper, wax, combs, gloves, purses, belts, needles, thread, kerchiefs, and 60 ells of fabric, as well as a myriad other items.[74]

### Overseas Trade: the Role of Wool and the Evidence of Customs Accounts

Wool formed the basis of England's trading activities in the Middle Ages.[75] The country's lead mines enabled it to export a sizeable amount of lead, tin and pewter,

---

68   *Household Book of Dame Alice de Bryene . . .*, transl. V.B. Redstone (Ipswich, 1931), Appx. iii, 119-23.

69   D. Keene, 'Medieval London and its Region', *London Journal*, xiv (1989), 99-111.

70   Ekwall, *Early London Subsidy Rolls*, op. cit. note 5, 71-81; Gwyn A. Williams, *Medieval London. From Commune to Capital* (corrected reprint, 1970), 315-17.

71   Derek Keene, 'A New Study of London before the Great Fire', *Urban History Yearbook*, 1984, 11-21, at 20, and the same author's booklet *Cheapside before the Great Fire* (Economic and Social Research Council, 1985), 19-20.

72   The chapman remained of importance as a distributor of cheap goods: Margaret Spufford, *The Great Reclothing of Rural England: Petty Chapmen and their Wares in the Seventeenth Century* (1984).

73   Below, 98.

74   Anthony D. Carr, *Medieval Anglesey* (Anglesey Antiquarian Soc. 1982), 187. 14th-century pedlars feature in J.J. Jusserand, *English Wayfaring Life in the Middle Ages*, transl. L.T. Smith (2nd edn., 1920), pt. ii, ch. 2.

75   Still the clearest introduction is Eileen Power, *The Wool Trade in English Medieval History* (1941).

and it was also a substantial exporter of leather hides, but wool was its most important commodity, whether as sacks of the raw material or as woven cloths. Wool was probably being sold to the continent in the 12th century, and very likely earlier,[76] but since all England's trade was free (save for local tolls) until 1275, it cannot be quantified from documentary evidence until that date. The custom on wool and hides that Edward I imposed in 1275, payable by both English and foreign merchants, both provided a great deal of revenue for the Crown (generally approaching £10,000 p.a.) and must have stimulated the development of the cloth industry, since the English weavers could now buy their wool cheaper than their continental rivals, and it could then be sold abroad free of custom charges. English merchants were encouraged by the limitation to foreign merchants of the 'New Custom' that was imposed from 1303 onwards, and cloth exports, subjected to only a modest duty in 1303, were deemed strong enough to cope with a 'Cloth Custom' from 1347.[77] From about this time, the combined customs revenues yielded the Crown between one-third and a half of its total revenue, thus making the country's overseas trade into a matter of permanent political importance.

The English customs records survive comparatively well, and are sufficiently detailed to enable the wool and cloth exports to be charted precisely in most years; they also give some clue as to the country's overall trading success. The story is essentially one of an increase in wool exports until about 1305, and of a fairly steady climb in cloth exports from a trickle in 1347 to about 40,000 cloths p.a. in *c*.1400 and a peak of about 60,000 in *c*.1447, then a decline until *c*.1470, followed by a resumption of fairly steady growth to *c*.130,000 cloths in the late 1540s. Within these overall figures, London's prosperity can be seen from its wool exports having continued climbing from under 6,000 sacks in *c*.1280 to a peak of four times that number in the 1350s, while its share of the nation's cloth exports grew from roughly half in the years 1400-30 to two-thirds in *c*.1490, three-quarters in *c*.1510 and five-sixths in *c*.1540.[78]

The medieval English government was constantly concerned that there was, or at least might be, an outflow of gold and silver bullion, but the inflow of money from the wool and cloth sales must have far exceeded even the costs of the Hundred Years' War. England enjoyed a major balance-of-payments surplus. Consequently it is likely that other English industrial activities were depressed, for the country must

---

76  For 12th-century and perhaps earlier exports to Scandinavia see P. Sawyer, 'Anglo-Scandinavian Trade in the Viking Age and After', in *Anglo-Saxon Monetary History. Essays in Memory of Michael Dolley*, ed. M.A.S. Blackburn (Leicester, 1896), 185-99, at 190-1; cf. J. Campbell, 'Was it Infancy in England? Some questions of Comparison', in M. Jones and M. Vale (ed.), *England and her Neighbours, 1066-1453. Essays in Honour of Pierre Chaplais* (London and Ronceverte, W.Va., 1989), 1-17, at 15, commenting on 11th- and 12th-century English silver bullion inflows.

77  E.M. Carus-Wilson and O. Coleman, *England's Export Trade, 1275-1547* (Oxford, 1963), 1-3.

78  Ibid. All this information is presented as a single graph in Carus-Wilson, op. cit. note 23, opp. p.xxii. Note, however, the cautionary words of Peter Ramsey, 'Overseas Trade in the Reign of Henry VII: the Evidence of Customs Accounts', *Econ. Hist. Rev.* 2nd ser. vi (1953-4), 173-82. N.S.B. Gras, *The Early English Customs System* (Cambridge, Mass., 1918), remains a useful introduction and contains transcripts of customs accounts.

have imported far more than would otherwise have been the case.[79]

The customs accounts do not allow any quantification of imports to be made, for imported goods and raw materials are jumbled in with exported goods since all were subject to the same poundage. However, the details of ships' cargoes (or 'particulars' of customs) do survive for some ports for some years, and these show an enormous quantity of finished goods coming into England. In 1390-1 ships brought into London cargoes of such things as ivory, mirrors, paxes, armour, paper (none was made in England for another century), painted cloths, spectacles, tin images, razors, calamine, treacle, sugar-candy, marking-irons, patens (or clogs; 7,000 in one cargo alone), ox-horns and quantities of wainscot (boards).[80] Most of these seem to have been imports from abroad, and not just shipments from other parts of England, although all save the calamine and wainscot could easily have been produced in England. Far too little research has yet been done to enable one to say how often it was men who were primarily craftsmen or merchants who were importing these goods, although it seems generally to have been the latter.[81] On the other hand, the craftsman's ability to trade freely must not be forgotten: there was nothing to stop a craftsman importing finished goods and then marking them and selling them just as if he had made them in his own workshop. The London brasiers' ordinances of 1347 recognise this in their provision that helms and other arms brought from overseas are to be assayed by the wardens of the craft and marked with their mark.[82] Equally, one may sometimes find imports of raw material, such as the 10,000 lb. of pure copper that the Crown imported at the start of the 15th century from two merchants of Dinant (in Namur), the great centre of finished copper products (commonly called dinanderie): the copper was being acquired, at a cost of £135, so that a big gun could be made from it in England.[83]

## Overseas Trade: the Ports

From the 14th century, Italian merchants came to the ports of London or Southampton almost every year, with fleets of ships and especially galleys: they took English cloths and other goods to the Mediterranean, where English ships rarely

79  The export of wool (and other commodities) was inevitably matched by the import of either foreign coin and bullion or foreign goods. The Crown preferred the former. See M. Prestwich, 'Currency and the Economy of Early Fourteenth Century England', and T.H. Lloyd, 'Overseas Trade and the English Money Supply in the Fourteenth Century', in N.J. Mayhew (ed.), *Edwardian Monetary Affairs (1279-1344). A Symposium held in Oxford, August 1976* (British Archaeological Reps., British Ser., xxxvi, 1977), 45-58 and 96-124.

80  P.R.O., E122/71/13.

81  Of course, the merchants might be members of the craftsmen's gild – craftsmen who had turned to full-time marketing, for instance. The mercantile dealings of some York craftsmen are discussed by Heather Swanson, *Medieval Artisans. An Urban Class in Late Medieval England* (Oxford and New York, 1989), 141-8.

82  Riley, *Memorials*, 238.

83  W.J.B. Kerr, *Associated Architectural Societies' Reports & Papers*, xxxiii (1915-16), 372, from a Duchy of Lancaster account roll of 1400-1. For dinanderie, see below, 93.

ventured, and they brought to England luxuries such as fruits and spices as well as goods that were thought to be superior to their English-made equivalents, such as silks and Spanish iron.[84] London's importance as a centre for the distribution of goods was thus enhanced: it was almost as though London and Southampton themselves became great fairs, for the fleets tended to come and go at fixed points in the year, and English merchants could prepare stock and come to the cities accordingly.

Yet although London's trade was all-embracing, many English and continental merchants who traded with the Low Countries and the Baltic also used the ports on the eastern coast of England – Newcastle, Hull, Boston, Lynn, Yarmouth and Ipswich, as well as the Cinque Ports in Kent and Sussex.[85] The Low Countries were quite as important a market for English wool as was Italy, while they exported linen and other finished goods to England. Hull and Winchelsea were re-established as ports by Edward I in the 1290s, and rapidly grew to prosperity in the early 14th century, the time of peak prosperity for the Cinque Ports.[86] Both Hanseatic and English merchants brought English cloth, tin, pewter and coal to the Baltic, returning with essential commodities such as corn and timber (the 'Estrich' or Prussian boards that, like Flanders chests, came to be generic terms rather than truly indicative of the wood's source),[87] fine osmund iron from Sweden,[88] copper from Hungary, and wax and furs.

A similar tale of diversified trading could be told of the ports on the south and west coasts of England and Wales – Southampton, Exeter, Bristol, Beaumaris and Chester, as well as the scores of lesser places.[89] Their trade was with France and the west Mediterranean, with Ireland and even with Iceland. Less of the trade at these places was in the hands of alien merchants, but they too came to be dominated by the export of cloth and overshadowed by the rise of London.

All ports also saw a great deal of coastal traffic, as it was easier to move goods by water than overland, whether on packhorses or in carts. The two systems of transport were mutually interdependent, however. For instance, alabaster carvings might be shipped from Hull if being sold to Scandinavia, from London, Southampton, Dartmouth or Poole if for France, Spain or Portugal, or from Bristol if

84  Alwyn A. Ruddock, *Italian Merchants and Shipping in Southampton, 1270-1600* (Southampton Records Series, i, 1951), chapter iii, 'The Commodities of Trade'.

85  R.A. Pelham, 'Medieval Foreign Trade: Eastern Ports', in H.C. Darby (ed.), *An Historical Geography of England before A.D. 1800* (Cambridge, 1936), 298-329, remains the best introduction, to be supplemented by E.M. Carus-Wilson, 'The Medieval Trade of the Ports of the Wash', *Medieval Archaeology*, vi-vii (1962-3), 182-201. The Continental context is provided by M.M. Postan, 'The Trade of Medieval Europe: the North', in M.M. Postan and E. Miller (ed.), *Trade and Industry in the Middle*

*Ages*, Cambridge Economic History of Europe, ii (2nd edn., Cambridge, 1987), ch. 4.

86  Pelham, art. cit. note 85.

87  See below, 380.

88  See below, 168, noting that osmund iron, too, became a generic term.

89  D.T. Williams, 'Medieval Foreign Trade: Western Ports', in Darby (ed.), op. cit. note 85, 266-97; E.M. Carus-Wilson (ed.), *The Overseas Trade of Bristol in the Later Middle Ages* (Bristol Record Soc. vii, 1937). A tendentious and anecdotal contemporary account of the commodities traded by England in *c*.1436 is given in *The Libelle of Englyshe Polycye*, ed. G.F. Warner (Oxford, 1926).

for Ireland, Iceland, France or Spain; but to get to any of these ports they had to be transported overland, from the midlands or the towns of the east.

Small quanties of goods needed to be transported for long distances as an inevitable result of industries being small-scale and, in many cases, highly localised. The merchant, as middleman, was all the more indispensable because he had to distribute the goods of what were commonly very small establishments of craftsmen. A craftsman's shop was a place of work and, if he had any apprentices, of instruction; only secondarily might it have been a sales outlet.[90] Most of the craftsmen with whom the studies in this book are concerned were exactly what craftsmen are today – people exercising a manual skill and making artefacts.

Fig. v. Blacksmiths at work. Detail from a Romance of Alexander. Flemish, *c.* 1340 (Oxford, Bodleian Library, MS Bodley 264, f. 84).

90   The size, location, numbers and rents of the shops of Winchester are discussed by Keene, *Survey of Medieval Winchester*, op. cit. note 67, i, 137-9, 162-5 and 237-41.

1

*Stone*

DAVID PARSONS

The construction of a masonry building is a complex operation involving the use of several quite different raw materials and demanding the services and skills of a wide variety of craftsmen and workers. Before work ever begins on site, the materials must be selected, ordered and assembled: stone has to be quarried and at least roughly shaped before being transported to the site, and limestone or chalk needs to be dug for burning to quicklime, the active ingredient of mortar; similarly, sand must be dug to supply aggregate for bulking out the mortar; timber has to be felled and cut, not only to make roofs or panelling or floorboards in the finished building, but also for use as scaffolding and as centring to support arches and vaults in the course of construction; roofing material is also required, and this may range from thatch through wooden shingles to earthenware tiles and lead. Each of these materials implies the activity of tradesmen both off and on the site: quarrymen and masons; woodsmen and carpenters; reed-cutters and thatchers; potters and tilers; miners, refiners and plumbers; to say nothing of the finishing trades and their requirements – plasterers, who need horsehair as well as lime and sand, and painters, who need pigments and quantities of linseed oil, egg-white or some other medium.

Once the initial materials have at least been ordered, work can begin on site. First the lines of the building must be surveyed, and then labourers can dig trenches for the foundations. Typically the foundations consist of rough rubble, broken brick and other hard material in a mortar matrix, but may be no more than pebbles bound with clay. When this stage is complete the masons (layers or setters) can begin building the walls with stone prepared by the banker masons, working at their benches or 'bankers'. By the time the wall has reached chest height they will need the assistance of the carpenters to build scaffolding, from which all subsequent building is done, and to rig hoists and cranes for lifting materials to the working platform. On a big medieval building project the carpenters would have been active at an earlier stage, if only in the construction of the 'lodge' in which the masons worked, ate, and on occasions slept. The whole of this complex operation was controlled by a senior master mason and an administrator. Smaller medieval stone buildings, mainly minor parish churches or chapels of ease, called for a less elaborate organisation, and no doubt the local general builder combined the functions of most of the trades, though the range, if not the quantities, of materials required would have been much the same as for a big project. The local builder's basic training is likely to have been in carpentry rather than masonry; despite the acceleration in demand for stone buildings (see below, p.17) it remained true throughout the Middle Ages that many substantial buildings and most minor ones were made of timber. In most villages the church would have been the only masonry structure, and in some cases even the church would have been a wooden building. In such circumstances it is not surprising to find ineptness in the construction of minor stone buildings and on occasions direct evidence for carpentry techniques carried out in stone (e.g. the the western turret staircase at Hough on the Hill (Lincs.)).

Of all the trades represented on a building site, the masons were the most specialised and tended to be the best paid. Most medieval towns could support quite a number of carpenters, plasterers, plumbers, and the like, but very few masons.[1] Many of the large building projects were outside the towns, for example monasteries like Fountains or castles such as Norham. No wonder that masons moved about from site to site and seem not to have founded municipal craft gilds, as many other trades did. Not until the end of the Middle Ages do they seem to have developed any coherent craft organisation, though as early as the 13th century there was apparently some machinery for regulating wages and by the 14th there was some codification of masons' customs. It is nevertheless clear from a much earlier date that the craft was organised on highly hierarchical lines. The distinctions between the various categories of craftsmen are apparent not only from the nomenclature but also – and most strikingly – from the wage differentials. Best paid were the master freemasons, so called because they were qualified to work the finest and most expensive stone, the 'freestone', that is fine-grained stone capable of being cut freely in any direction. Such stone may be used not only for architectural detail (mouldings, inscriptions, and so on) but also for decorative carving from low relief to sculpture in the round. Freemasons and carvers were probably identical, or at least of equal status. The range of medieval terms for these craftsmen included *cementarius libre petre, mestre mason de franche pere, sculptor lapidum liberorum*. There seem in addition to have been some specialist sculptors, called variously *imaginator, imaginarius, factor imaginum*, while a more general term for carver was *entayller*. Finished stone from the benches of these men was incorporated into the walling by another class of mason, the layers, setters or wallers: *ligiers* (and variant spellings, such as 'leggers'), *cubitores, positores*.

Much of the less skilled work, including we may imagine the construction of random rubble walling, was in the hands of 'roughlayers' and 'hardhewers'. Below this, and probably not accounted as belonging to the craft, were the unskilled labourers, who were employed in relatively large numbers to carry hods, to work hoists and to push barrows. Labourers (*operarii*) and roughmasons were also

---

1  For example, York: see H. Swanson, *Building Craftsmen in Late Medieval York* (Borthwick Paper lxiii, 1983), which gives much valuable background information relevant to this sec- tion, as do Knoop and Jones, *Med. Mason*, 109-84, and Salzman, *Building in England*, 30-67.

*Fig. 1* Barnack (Soke of Peterborough): abandoned quarries at TL 07 04 from the air.

*Fig. 2* Stonegrave (Yorks., N.R.): evidence for superficial quarrying, possibly of Anglo-Saxon date.

required to do the heavy work in the quarries, but the actual extraction of the stone was a specialist occupation, carried out by *quareatores* or *quarerarii* and perhaps even by the masons themselves. The main reason for employing masons in the quarry, however, must have been to cut the blocks of stone to shape and to carve them when necessary, for it is clear that in some cases stone was fully finished before being transported to the building site, for example the bosses for Exeter Cathedral mentioned below (p.24).

Few of the men just described could expect permanent employment at their trade. Most building projects were too small to guarantee continuous work for any length of time, and in any case many building operations were suspended during the winter because the weather was unsuitable. Most men were hired by the day, and the few privileged masons who were continuously employed for forty or more weeks in the year could count themselves fortunate. This opportunity was most likely to arise at a major religious site in a town, for example the Minster or St. Mary's Abbey in York, where running repairs might provide enough work for a small resident staff even during the winter. The greatest employer of labour, however, was the king, who would have a number of projects in hand simultaneously, some of which might be very large indeed, such as the palace and monastery at Westminster, or Edward I's series of massive Welsh castles. These gave work to a large number of craftsmen drawn from all over the country, and provided security of employment for senior masons who supervised individual projects or the king's works as a whole. The office of king's mason offered a comfortable pension, status and privilege, as well as the opportunity to act as architect-designer and controller of important and demanding building projects and thus ultimately to affect the course of architectural history.

In view of the complexity of a major building project, it is not possible in a survey such as this to describe in detail either the organisation of the work or the methods of building construction. These have in any case been dealt with more than adequately in the literature.[2] In what follows the emphasis will be on the supply of common building stone and related materials, such as lime mortar, but excluding marble and alabaster and brick-making, all of which are discussed in separate chapters. The sources of medieval building stone are often difficult to identify on the ground, either because the quarries have been exhausted and filled in (though extensive ones like Barnack, shown in Fig. 1, are still visible, especially from the air) or because it is still possible to work them and modern quarrying has obliterated all signs of medieval activity. Undoubtedly the easiest method of quarrying stone in the Middle Ages, when explosives and power tools were not available, was to dig back into a hillside (as at Stonegrave, Fig. 2) or the bank of a river. First the overburden of topsoil would have to be removed, to reveal what in the case of sedimentary rocks would generally be stone of poor quality, friable and full of fissures (Fig. 3). This could be

2  Knoop and Jones, *Med. Mason*, 1-79 for the organisation of the work; Salzman, *Building in England*, chapter 5 onward, and W. Rodwell, 'Anglo-Saxon Building: Aspects of Design and Construction', *The Anglo-Saxon Church: Studies . . . in Honour of Dr H.M. Taylor*, ed. L.A.S. Butler and R.K. Morris (CBA Research Rep. lx, 1986), 156-75, for building methods.

*Fig. 3* Tadcaster (Yorks., N.R.): Smaws quarry at SE 463 430, showing heavily-fissured upper deposits; some small- to medium-sized blocks could nevertheless be obtained from this horizon.

extracted relatively easily with the aid of crowbars, or even pickaxes, but in fairly small pieces. Unlike the topsoil, this was not regarded as waste, since there were plenty of uses for small rubble – in foundations, in the core of ashlar-faced walls and (in the case of limestone deposits) for burning to make mortar. Indeed, many medieval walls were built largely of small rubble or of other apparently unsuitable material, such as the flint nodules which occur in the chalk of south-eastern England. Masonry of this type was made waterproof and aesthetically more pleasing by the liberal use of rendering on the outer surface and of plaster on the inside; it was made structurally efficient by the use of dressed stone blocks for the facings of windows, doors and other features, and in particular for the construction of the quoins or corners. A good example of this combination of materials is the church at Bishopstone (Sussex) where builders of at least three different periods have used the local flints set in a matrix of mortar (doubtless made from the equally local chalk) for the general walling, but have taken the trouble to bring in sandstone blocks from the Hastings Beds to form the quoins.

Blocks such as these would normally have to be obtained from strata below those producing the small rubble. Detaching them from the parent rock required considerably more skill than did the digging of the rubble. The method used is likely to have been the traditional plug-and-feather technique or a version of it.[3] Iron wedges are certainly referred to in medieval accounts.[4] Once quarried, the stone

3 A. Clifton-Taylor and A.S. Ireson, *English Stone Building* (1983), 65-6.

4 Salzman, *Building in England*, 331-2.

blocks were scappled, or roughly shaped;[5] in certain cases the opportunity was taken to work them up to their final shape while the stone was still full of 'quarry sap' and relatively soft. This implies the presence of masons at the quarry, and there is evidence that the masons themselves were sometimes responsible for the initial quarrying, and even owned the quarries. The partially or fully shaped stones were then transported to the building site, in the first place by cart (though sledges are occasionally mentioned), but wherever possible only as far as the nearest navigable water. From then on the stone was taken as close as possible to the site by boat.

   This brief summary of the supply of building stone has taken no account of the medieval practice of obtaining materials at second hand from redundant buildings. This topic, which is rarely discussed in the literature, is dealt with below in some detail.

### *The Early Medieval Building Industry: Historical Evidence*

Most of the general works on the history of the building industry concentrate heavily on the later medieval period (13th to 16th centuries). This is hardly surprising in view of the paucity of the evidence for the Anglo-Saxon period and, to a lesser extent, for the period from the Norman Conquest to *c*.1200. In part this is because there actually was less stone building in England before the Conquest. The developed quarrying and construction industries of Roman Britain came to an end, in England at least, with the collapse of the Roman administration. The succeeding Anglo-Saxon civilisation had no stone building tradition, and there is ample archaeological evidence that the Anglo-Saxon builders erected their timber structures within the remains of Roman masonry buildings. Many of these Roman buildings would have been capable of repair, had their new occupants had the skill and the motivation to carry it out. This is clear from Bede's accounts of the progress of the mission to the English around 600 and of the establishment of monasteries later in the 7th century. The early missionaries came from Rome and almost certainly expected that churches should be built of stone. In some cases the buildings already existed, whether or not they had previously had a Christian use; King Æthelbert's Frankish wife, Bertha, had already been using one as a chapel,[6] and St. Augustine recovered another to serve as his cathedral.[7] He went on to build from new the monastery of SS. Peter and Paul (how, we are not told) and to build *and repair* churches in other places.[8] We can only assume that the masons who carried out this work were brought in from abroad, as Bede specifically states was done in the case of the building of the monastery at Monkwearmouth about 675.[9] From this time on, churches were increasingly built of stone, though many were still made of wood, and there is very little evidence before the Norman Conquest of secular masonry buildings.

5  E. Gee, *Glossary of Building Terms* (1984), 74.
6  *HE*, i, 26: *Bede's Ecclesiastical History*, ed. B. Colgrave and R.A.B. Mynors (1969), 76-7.
7  *HE*, i, 33: ed. Colgrave and Mynors, 114-15.
8  *HE*, i, 26: ed. Colgrave and Mynors, 76-7.
9  *Historia Abbatum*, §5, in *Ven. Baedae Opera*, ed. C. Plummer (1896), i, 368.

Even with such a limited number of buildings being put up in the Anglo-Saxon period, it is valid to ask where the stone was coming from. Here again the evidence is scanty. A few place names suggest where quarrying may have taken place. The earliest and best attested of these is Stonegrave (Yorks. N.R.), which occurs in a charter of 757/8.[10] Ekwall postulates an early form, Old English *Stāngraef*, but his treatment of the name has now been superseded by Morris's discussion.[11] Despite the apparent meaning of the name ('quarry of the stone people') and the presence in Stonegrave church of Anglo-Saxon cross fragments 'carved from a stone very closely comparable' with the outcrop north of the church, it remains uncertain whether building stone as such was quarried there in the early medieval period. There is no doubt, however, that quarrying was carried out in Stonegrave at some date (Fig. 2). Shallow excavations into the hillside can be seen to the north of the church and this kind of superficial exploitation is consistent with other evidence for quarrying in the Anglo-Saxon period (see below). Nevertheless, these may be workings of Roman date which were still recognisable – though not necessarily in use – at the time when the place-name came into being. Other suggestive names seem to be open to a degree of doubt. Reservations have been expressed, for example, about the interpretation of Chalgrave (Beds.) and Chalgrove (Oxon.) as 'chalk quarry'.[12] Standhill or Standel in Oxfordshire, however, seems to be a more dependable example. It first occurs in 1002 as Old English *Stangedelf*, and the place is known to have been quarried later in the Middle Ages.[13] A more recently recognised example is Stanion (Northants.), in which the second element, Old English *ærn*, may have a specialised meaning connected in this case with the stone trade.[14] Other place names with this element suggest that it indicates a semi-industrial use, if only that of storage. Examples include Brewerne (brewhouse), Colerne (charcoal store) and Seasalter (salthouse).[15] By analogy Stanion may mean 'stone store' or 'stonemasons' workshop'. Even if this interpretation is correct, it does not necessarily imply contemporary quarrying, as will become clear from what follows, but since Stanion lies in the stone-producing area of north-east Northamptonshire (Weldon is a near neighbour), and since there were quarries in the parish both before and after this date, it seems reasonable to assume quarrying in the Anglo-Saxon period. Nevertheless, it is fair to point out that at the comparable Potterne (Wilts.) the reference may not be to pottery manufacture by the Anglo-Saxons, who coined the

10 *Eng. Hist. Docs. (c. 500-1042)* p.830, No. 184.
11 E. Ekwall, *Concise Oxford Dictionary of English Place-Names* (4th edn., 1960), 446; G.E. Morris, 'The Significance of the Place-Name, Stonegrave', *Jnl. Engl. Place-Name Soc.* xvii (1985), 14-19. The conclusions of the latter (kindly drawn to my attention by Dr. Margaret Gelling since the present chapter was first written), in particular the suggestion that quarrying may have been carried out at Stonegrave as early as the 6th century, deserve detailed consideration.

12 Ekwall, op.cit. note 11, 94; M. Gelling, *Place-Names in the Landscape* (1984), 194.
13 E.M. Jope, 'The Saxon Building Stone Industry in Southern and Midland England', *Med. Arch.* viii (1964), 91-118, especially 97.
14 Also drawn to my attention by Dr. Margaret Gelling; the discussion of the place-names owes much to the observations of Dr. Gelling and Professor Jope, but neither should be held responsible for the present conclusions.
15 Ekwall, op. cit. note 11, 64, 116, 410.

place-name, but to finds of Iron-Age pottery; huge quantities of high-quality ware are attested archaeologically, and the presence of this may have led the Anglo-Saxons to think that previous inhabitants had been large-scale potters. Similarly, Stanion may mean 'place where there is evidence of ancient stoneworking'.

Further documentary evidence seems to be provided by a charter in favour of Glastonbury Abbey, which refers to a *stangedelfe* in defining the bounds of the estate. The charter claims to have been granted by a Mercian king in 681 but in its surviving form it is a forgery of 10th- or even 12th-century date.[16] Another piece of charter evidence occurs in 940, when *Tigel leah* is mentioned. This can be identified with quarries for stone tiles at Wotton-under-Edge (Glos.) which were still being worked in the post-Conquest period.[17] A more substantial piece of evidence survives from just before the Norman Conquest. It exists in a number of different versions: a writ of Edward the Confessor in Old English and in Latin,[18] in the Ramsey Cartulary, and in two chapters of the Ramsey Chronicle.[19] The king confirmed an arrangement between the respective abbots whereby the monastery at Peterborough, in return for an estate at Marholm(e) and an annual rent of 4,000 eels, gave to Ramsey Abbey a quarry at Lutton and the right to obtain *wercstan* (*de lapidibus quadratilibus*) from Barnack and *walstan* (*de petris muralibus*) from Peterborough itself. The distinction is apparently between freestone suitable for ashlar work or for cutting mouldings or sculpture, and plain walling stone which may have been no better than rubble. It may also have been small rubble that was used by Æthelric (Egelric), who on his return to Peterborough after resigning the bishopric of Durham in 1056 'built roads of wood *and stone*' in the Fens, though it may have been paving slabs that were used.[20] Here, then, are the first indications of an organised stone industry with quarries and quarrying rights which could be rented or exchanged and with distinctions being made between the quality of products from different quarries. At about the same time (1061) Earl Waltheof, who likewise owned property at Barnack, gave it together with its 'well-known quarry' to Crowland Abbey, where a new church was being built.[21] The same chronicler claimed that Crowland had previously been granted quarrying rights in its own vicinity c.950.[22]

Despite these pieces of evidence, there are surprisingly few references to quarries in Domesday Book. Over the whole country only seven places had quarries, and two of those were producing millstones.[23] Not even the famous Barnack quarries are

16  Jope, art. cit. note 13.
17  P.J. Drury, 'The Production of Brick and Tile in Medieval England', in D.W. Crossley (ed.), *Medieval Industry* (CBA Research Rep. xl, 1981), 126-42, esp. 126.
18  F.E. Harmer, *Anglo-Saxon Writs* (1952), 262-5.
19  Lehmann-Brockhaus, *Schriftquellen*, No.3588; *Chron. Abbatiae Ramseiensis*, ed. W.D. Macray (Rolls Ser. lxxxiii, 1886), 165-6, §101, and 167-8, §102.
20  Lehmann-Brockhaus, *Schriftquellen*, No.1018; *Historia Ecclesiae Dunelmensis*, iii, ch.9, in *Symeonis Monachi Opera Omnia*, ed. T. Arnold, 2 vols.

(Rolls Ser. lxxv, 1882-5), i, 92.
21  Lehmann-Brockhaus, *Schriftquellen*, No.1168; *Chronicle of Croyland Abbey*, ed. W. de Gray Birch (1883), 115-16. This gift is also recorded by Orderic, but since Bondi, a dependent of Waltheof, held the property in 1066, it is likely that only temporary quarrying rights or consignments of stone were granted, rather than the land itself: *Eccl. Hist. of Orderic Vitalis*, ed. M. Chibnall, ii (1969), pp. xxviii & 344 n.2.
22  Lehmann-Brockhaus, *Schriftquellen*, No.1149; *Chron. Croyland*, 55-6.
23  H.C. Darby, *Domesday England* (1977), 287.

mentioned, though it is clear that they were supplying stone before the Norman Conquest. There are several possible explanations of this dearth of Domesday references, any one or any combination of which may prove upon closer investigation to account for it. First, there may actually have been so few quarries working that the enumerators failed to recognise them as a category worth taking systematic note of. Second, the existing quarries may have been largely in the hands of those actually using the stone (in practice the major monasteries) and independent private ownership and commercial exploitation may not have developed to a sufficient extent to produce any revenue worth recording. It was not until 1239 that a Council held at London decided that tithe should be paid on quarries,[24] which could imply that they had not previously been regarded as revenue-producing enterprises. Third, it seems possible that quarries may originally have been a royal prerogative, like forests, which are similarly under-recorded in Domesday Book. It is interesting to see how often early medieval monasteries acquired their quarries, or their right to work them, direct from the king; and it may be significant that even later in the Middle Ages quarries were often described as being 'in the forest'. It was King Eadred who was supposed to have granted quarrying rights to Crowland in the 10th century[25] and the bounds of the property which Ramsey acquired from Peterborough were defined by reference to the *Kingesdelf* (*Cnutes delfe* in the Old English version: does this indicate when the quarry was first opened?).[26] The king likewise provided the stone for Battle Abbey[27] and for Abingdon,[28] and in the 13th century gave the Totternhoe quarry to St. Albans;[29] the equally famous Quarr quarries had been in the king's hands since the Conquest.[30] The references to forests occur mainly in the first half of the 13th century. The prior of Lenton was granted quarrying rights in Nottingham Forest,[31] the monastery at Stanley had a concession in Chippenham Forest,[32] while the canons of Lichfield were permitted to quarry at Hopwas on condition that they did nothing detrimental to the king's forest.[33] An assart at Foresthill was identified by reference to a quarry,[34] and in 1307 Tintern Abbey was granted stone for building and other purposes from the forest of Weyeswode.[35]

In view of the limited amount of documentary evidence for the early Middle Ages,

24  *Councils and Synods*, ii: *A.D. 1205-1313*, ed. F.M. Powicke and C.R. Cheney (1964), 281 (pt.II, §5); repeated in §76 of the Statutes of Wells in ?1258 (ibid., 623), in §53 of the Statutes of Exeter in 1287 (ibid., 1053) and by the Bishop of Lincoln (*Roberti Grosseteste . . . Epistolae*, ed. H.R. Luard (Rolls Ser. xxv, 1861), 221). Quarries are not included in the list of tithable commodities in the *acta* of the Council of Westminster in 1175.

25  Lehmann-Brockhaus, *Schriftquellen*, No. 1149; *Chron. Croyland*, as in n.21, 55-6.

26  Harmer, *Anglo-Saxon Writs*, 263, 264.

27  Lehmann-Brockhaus, *Schriftquellen*, No. 249; *Chronicle of Battle Abbey*, ed. E. Searle (1980),

42-5.

28  Lehmann-Brockhaus, *Schriftquellen*, No. 45; *Chronicon Monasterii de Abingdon*, ed. J. Stevenson (2 vols., Rolls Ser. ii, 1858), ii, 51.

29  *Cal. Charter R.*, i, 10.

30  T. Tatton-Brown, 'The Use of Quarr Stone in London and East Kent', *Med. Arch.* xxiv (1980), 213-15, especially 213.

31  *Cal. Close R.*, *Henry III*, i, 196; iv, 474.

32  Ibid. ii, 100.

33  Ibid. iv, 46.

34  *Cartulary of Oseney Abbey*, ed. H.E. Salter, iv (Oxford Historical Soc., xcvii, 1934), p. 340, No. 295.

35  *Cal. Charter R.*, iii, 103.

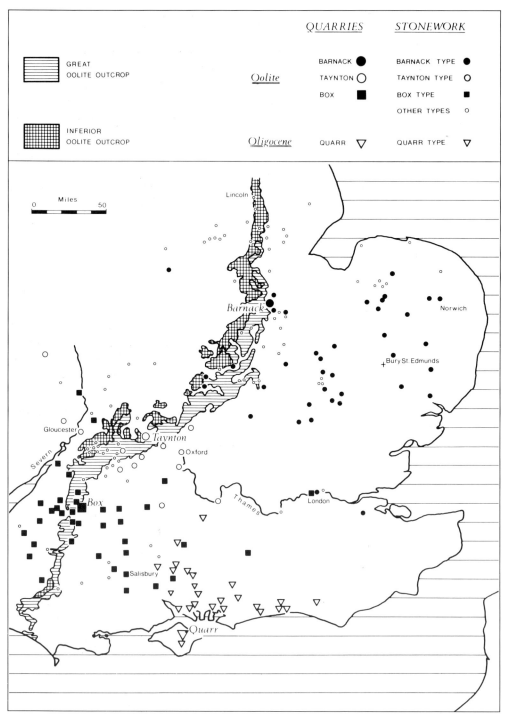

*Fig. 4* Distribution of building stone in the later Anglo-Saxon period, after Jope. (Drawing by D. Hill.)

it is particularly important to recover as much information as possible from the buildings themselves. E.M. Jope's distribution maps of building stones over southern and Midland England in the late Anglo-Saxon period (Fig. 4) show what can be achieved,[36] but his article as a whole takes a rather optimistic view of the extent to which original quarrying had developed before the Norman Conquest. There are very real difficulties in the way of this kind of study, not the least of which is the problem of identifying building stones correctly *in situ*, particularly inside standing buildings. Few Anglo-Saxon churches can be dated with any accuracy, and many may be later than the subjective date claimed for them. Jope's conclusions, based on a study of their fabric, may thus be valid only for the 11th century, but not for the 10th. Bradford-on-Avon church, with its rare ashlar masonry, is clearly an important example; it is claimed as 'early' by Jope,[37] but the extent of the disagreement between architectural historians about the date of this church is far more than 'of the order of half a century'.[38] If on the basis of the double-splayed windows one assumes a date in the late 10th century or later, then the implications for the development of deep quarrying are quite different. It must be said that many of Jope's dated examples are pieces of stone sculpture, rather than the buildings themselves. The stylistic dating of sculpture is somewhat more secure than that of the churches, but to use stone carvings, especially free-standing crosses, in an analysis of *building* stones begs several questions. It is possible that the supply of stone for carving was quite separate from the provision of routine building stone. Indeed, Jope's survey was concerned with special building components – quoins, pilaster strips, mouldings – which form only a small proportion of the total stone requirement of a complete building. Jope's article must be seen for what it quite clearly claimed to be: a study of the 'fine' end of the stone-supply range. It deals with *wercstan*, and its conclusions do not necessarily apply to *walstan*.

### The Early Medieval Building Industry: Archaeological Evidence

Archaeological investigations that have concentrated on general walling give a rather different picture of the supply of building stone, not only in the Anglo-Saxon period but also in the later Middle Ages. At Brixworth in Northamptonshire there has been a stone-by-stone survey of all the exposed elevations, including a detailed petrological examination of the building materials by an expert geologist, together with a study of the possible geological source for each stone type.[39] The church is devoid of any normal dressed stone features until the insertion of the south doorway in the latter part of the 12th century: imposts and string-courses are carried out in brick, while the remnants of pilaster strips on the north side of the apse are distinguished from the surrounding walling only by the alternating blocks of tufa.

36 Jope, art. cit. note 13, especially Fig. 25.
37 Ibid. 99.
38 Ibid. 94.
39 D.S. Sutherland and D. Parsons, 'The Petro-logical Contribution to the Survey of All Saints' Church, Brixworth, Northampton-shire: an Interim Study', *J.B.A.A.* cxxxvii (1984), 45-64.

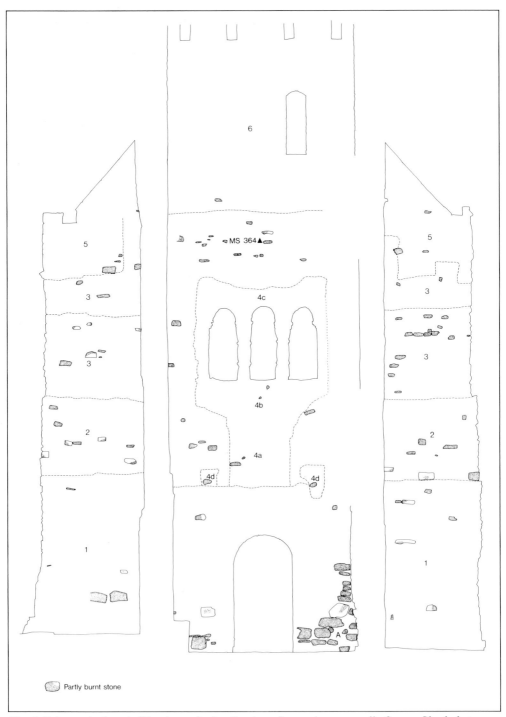

*Fig. 5* Brixworth church (Northants.): distribution of stone in west wall of nave. Shaded stones are burnt; numbers indicate various stone assemblages identified.

For much of the early life of the church, sources of *wercstan* do not seem to have been available. A detailed examination of the plain walling shows that much, if not all, of it was not the product of original quarrying, but came from earlier buildings, which may have been deliberately demolished to supply the Brixworth builders with material. One of the tell-tale pieces of evidence is the random distribution of burnt stone. Fig. 5 shows how in the west wall of the nave most blocks of burnt stone have unburnt neighbours, indicating that they cannot have been burnt *in situ*; they must have been salvaged from another building in which there had been a fire and mixed with unburnt stones before being built into this wall. This and other evidence for the reuse of materials is to be found in all phases of the early medieval fabric. It occurs in the primary building represented by assemblages 1, 2 and possibly 3 as shown in outline in Fig. 5, now dated by excavation to the 8th century. More important, it is apparent in the major reconstruction of the church, represented by assemblage 4. This includes the middle section of the tower and the whole of the attached western stair turret. The outside wall of the turret provides a classic example of the random pattern of burnt stones. This phase of the building can be assigned to the period 1040-1260 on the basis of radiocarbon dating of the construction mortar. The triple arch, which is such a prominent feature of assemblage 4, includes two baluster shafts, the only exceptions to the statement above about worked stones – but are they reused? The arch heads are constructed partly in tufa, alternating with other materials as in the apse pilaster strips. This stone, at least, may have been freshly quarried for the purpose.

The immediate sources of stone for the builders of the earliest surviving church at Brixworth were redundant Roman buildings. The stone-types identified in the fabric suggest that these buildings were as far away as Towcester in one direction (15 miles/ 25 km.) and Leicester in the other (27 miles/44 km.). What structures the later builders were robbing is less clear; by 1040 several generations of Anglo-Saxon buildings may have been available, but in this case the Brixworth builders are likely to have been recycling already reused material. If Brixworth is at all typical of pre-Conquest practice, it would appear that for much of the Anglo-Saxon period the building trade was reliant on salvaged materials; although by the mid to late 11th century some quarrying may have been undertaken, reused material was still a prominent component of Saxo-Norman walling.

This is borne out by other detailed studies which have been undertaken. At Kirk Hammerton (Yorks. N.R.), Richard Morris has identified many of the blocks of Millstone Grit, a stone foreign to the Vale of York, as reused Roman material.[40] Although it is possible that the salvaged stone was supplemented by fresh quarrying, Morris points out that the Bunter Sandstone, which outcrops locally, was not systematically exploited by the builders of the church. The tower is thought to date from the 11th century, though it is possible that the nave is earlier. Morris usefully

40 R. Morris, 'Kirk Hammerton Church: the Tower and the Fabric', *Arch. Jnl.* cxxxiii (1976), 95-103, esp. 100-3.

refs to other pre-Conquest and early Norman churches in the area in which Roman gritstone was reused.[41] In York itself, the Royal Commission's *Inventory* says of the Bishophill churches: 'in general the Saxon walls are built of re-used Roman material, large pieces of gritstone, *saxa quadrata* of magnesian limestone, and pieces of brick', and the same materials are noted in the fabric of the Norman churches.[42] Much the same picture emerged from the excavation of St. Helen's church in Aldwark.[43] None of this is surprising in York, or any other major Roman town. The survival of Roman buildings until quite late into the Middle Ages, and descriptions of them by medieval writers, have been discussed by J.C. Higgitt.[44] There were perfectly good precedents on the Continent for making practical use of the legacy of antiquity. The Emperor Charlemagne himself had obtained papal permission to carry away mosaics and marbles from Ravenna; his biographer, Einhard, speaks more specifically of 'marble columns', and claims that Charlemagne also obtained similar materials from Rome;[45] they were to reappear north of the Alps in buildings such as the Palatine chapel in Aachen.[46] Some of them perhaps reached England: this is a possible interpretation of the famous reference to 'black stones' in a letter from Charlemagne to Offa of Mercia.[47] A century later, Alfred the Great was clearly upholding this well-established tradition. Asser, his biographer, writes: 'And what [shall I say] of the royal residences of masonry, moved from their old position and splendidly reconstructed at more appropriate places by his royal command?'[48] One strongly suspects that the *villae regales* which were being 'moved' were the fora and other public buildings of the Roman towns that the Anglo-Saxon kings had inherited. Certainly the reuse of salvaged materials, whatever their source, for the building of a royal residence has been demonstrated archaeologically in a remarkable fashion by the excavation of a 9th-century masonry hall in Northampton. The building had been heavily robbed in its turn, possibly to provide stone for the town defences, but the surviving masonry of the foundations is thought to consist of recycled material.[49]

### Anglo-Saxon Carved Stonework

If the spoils of antiquity could reach such relatively isolated places (in Roman terms) as Brixworth, the motivation to develop a quarrying industry must have been small. Nevertheless stone, and stone in sizeable pieces, was required for carving – both for architectural sculpture and for free-standing monuments like the Hedda stone at

41  Ibid. 102.
42  R.C.H.M. (England), *City of York*, iii, pp. xlv-xlvi. See now L.P. Wenham et al., *St. Mary Bishophill Junior and St. Mary Castlegate, Archaeology of York*, 8.2.
43  J.R. Magilton, *The Church of St. Helen-on-the-Walls, Aldwark, Archaeology of York*, 0.1, 27.
44  J.C. Higgitt, 'The Roman Background to Medieval England', *J.B.A.A.* 3rd ser., xxxvi (1973), 1-15, especially 1-4.
45  B. Ward-Perkins, *From Classical Antiquity to the*

*Middle Ages* (1984), 218.
46  C. Heitz, *L'Architecture Religieuse Carolingienne* (Paris, 1980), 71.
47  *EHD* (as in n.10), p.782, No.197.
48  Asser, §91; *Alfred the Great*, ed. S. Keynes and M. Lapidge (1983), 101, from which this English version is taken; for the original Latin text see *Asser's Life of King Alfred*, ed. W.H. Stevenson (1904), 77.
49  J.H. Williams et al., *Middle Saxon Palaces at Northampton* (1985), 31.

Peterborough or the many grave covers, markers and crosses. There is evidence that some of the smaller pieces were fashioned from Roman worked stones. A cross-slab at Jarrow, which must originally have been about six feet tall, was made up from three Roman stones; of the two surviving pieces one retains traces of a Roman inscription and both bear original cable moulding.[50] At Warden (Northumb.), an 11th-century grave-slab appears to have been split from a large Roman altar, some of whose mouldings survive, and what was probably a Roman column has been reused as a grave marker.[51] In other cases the carving of the stone in Anglo-Saxon times was more complete and covered all the visible faces, so that it is impossible to tell whether the piece is reused or the product of contemporary quarrying. It is not entirely out of the question that many Anglo-Saxon carvings could represent recutting of Roman stones: lintels and pieces of architrave would have been of very suitable shape for conversion into cross-shafts. A few of the crosses are very large, however, and it is doubtful whether sufficient lengths of Roman material would have been available for reworking. The Bewcastle cross in Cumberland, for example, is a monolith more than 14 feet (4.4m.) tall, and even so is incomplete. Perhaps pieces of stone such as this had to be newly quarried, though there must have been serious technical and logistic problems in doing so. At least one example survives, however, of the sort of stone which might have been used for making such a cross-shaft. This is a sandstone block 16 feet (4.7m.) long, detached from its parent rock at the Long Bar outcrop some 4 miles (7km.) north-east of Bewcastle itself (Fig. 6).[52] It has long been regarded as a 'rough-out' for a similar cross-shaft, but geological opinion is now firmly in favour of its being a natural phenomenon.[53] Naturally occurring detached blocks of this sort would have offered a tempting prospect to would-be stone carvers, who were perhaps able to convert a block similar to that at Long Bar into the surviving cross at Bewcastle. Superficial exploitation of this sort was possibly sufficient to supply the stone carvers and ultimately to produce the mouldings, quoins and other features studied by Jope. The aerial view of the Barnack quarries (Fig. 1), which were worked both in Roman and in Saxon and medieval times, suggests that even here the quarrying was not very deep, for otherwise the heaps of spoil that seem to form the peaks in the 'hills and holes' conformation would hardly have filled the quarried area to this extent. Further quarry sites have been revealed by large-scale archaeological excavation. Foremost among these is Stamford, where several pits have been discovered dating from the Saxo-Norman period (11th century).[54] Another quarry found in an urban context was at Peterborough; it predated the construction of the castle in 1070 and may have been out of use for some time before that, but pottery found in it suggests a date no earlier than the 10th

50  R. Cramp, *Corpus of Anglo-Saxon Stone Sculpture*, i(1), 112-13: Jarrow 16.
51  Ibid. 229-30: Warden 1 & 2.
52  G.B. Brown, *The Arts in Early England*, v (1925), 104 ('Langbar').
53  R. Cramp and R. Bailey, *Corpus of Anglo-Saxon Stone Sculpture*, ii, 162 and illustr. 621. I am grateful to my colleague Dr. S. Becker for her comments on the photographs of the stone.
54  *Med. Arch.* xi (1967), 293; xiii (1969), 234; xv (1971), 127; xvii (1973), 162; xviii (1974), 201.

*Fig. 6* Long Bar (Cumb.): sandstone block detached from parent rock at NY 594 806.

*Fig. 7* Ravenstone (Leics.): remains of small quarry at Alton Grange, SK 389 147, used to provide facing stones for Kirby Muxloe Castle, 1480-4.

century.[55] The Peterborough quarry seems to have been quite extensive, but even in the later Middle Ages small superficial quarries were still quite common. The stone pits at Alton Grange in Ravenstone parish (Leics.), which appear to have been used once only, to supply Kirby Muxloe Castle in the 1480s, may give a better idea than a great complex like Barnack of the average medieval quarry (Fig. 7).

### After the Norman Conquest

It is very difficult to make an accurate assessment of the building stone industry in the pre-Conquest period. The evidence is sparse and somewhat contradictory but on balance it seems that while there may have been some quarrying for special uses from as early as *c.*700, it was carried out *ad hoc*, and most of the systematic acquisition of stone consisted of robbing the substantial remains of Roman buildings. Evidence for more extensive quarrying begins only in the 10th century and does not become even reasonably frequent until the 11th. Whether one can speak of an 'industry' before the end of that century is doubtful.

One of the effects of the Norman Conquest was to stimulate new building. The immediate founding of Battle Abbey may be taken as a microcosm of the building boom under the Norman kings. The Conqueror, faced apparently with an underdeveloped stone supply system in England, arranged to have stone imported from Caen. In the event this proved to be unnecessary, because a source of stone in the vicinity of the proposed abbey was miraculously revealed.[56] This episode serves to emphasise the *ad hoc* nature of English stone production. The opening of new quarries such as this and the importation of French stone clearly made a difference, but they by no means put a stop to the practice of cannibalisation. It continued apace, at least in the old Roman towns. When the abbot of St. Albans came to build a new church in 1077 he not only found building materials ready to hand in Verulamium but that his Anglo-Saxon predecessors had actually selected them and put them aside already.[57] In York the story of despoiling the Roman remains continued with the building of a new cathedral by Archbishop Thomas. Work began at much the same time as at St. Albans. All the major stone types of Roman York are represented in the massive Norman building; there is also a little freshly quarried stone, but it is not certain whether this belongs to the primary structure.[58] By this time, of course, there were Anglo-Saxon as well as Roman buildings available to rob, and the builders of the cathedral begun in Winchester 'obviously' used the Anglo-Saxon Old Minster as a quarry for their work.[59] The same is true of St. Peter's church, Northampton, which was built in the 12th century. In the course of the

55 D. Mackreth, 'Tout Hill Close, Peterborough', *Durobrivae*, ii (1974), 24-6, especially 26.

56 Lehmann-Brockhaus, *Schriftquellen*, No.249; *Battle Abbey Chronicle*, as in n.27, 42-5.

57 Lehmann-Brockhaus, *Schriftquellen*, Nos. 3791, 3807; *Chron. Monasterii S. Albani*, ed.

H.T. Riley (7 vols., Rolls Ser. xxviii, 1863-76), iv(1), 24-5, 52.

58 D. Phillips, *Excavations at York Minster*, ii, 182-4.

59 M. Biddle, 'Excavations at Winchester, 1964', *Antiq. Jnl.* xlv (1965), 230-64, especially 251.

Victorian restoration two original respond bases were discarded and are still lying loose in the south aisle of the church. The under-surfaces of these stones are carved with Anglo-Saxon interlace, perhaps of 9th-century date (Fig. 8). They must have come from a pre-Conquest church on the site or even from the middle Saxon stone palace that has recently been excavated to the east of the church.[60] The 12th-century masons recut them for use in the Romanesque building. It is important to note that St. Peter's was a large sophisticated building of high quality masonry with elaborately carved decoration,[61] and there is no justification for assuming that the reuse of salvaged material was confined to underfinanced or second-rate building projects.

The recycling tradition continued throughout the Middle Ages, with some curious twists as time went on. In the reign of King John, Falk, count of Bréauté, was granted the castle at Bedford, which he proceeded to extend and improve. He obtained the stone for this work by demolishing the ancient church of St. Paul near the castle as well as a further church dedicated to St. Cuthbert.[62] Poetic justice was done, however. Henry III subsequently slighted the castle and gave the demolition material to the canons of three churches: Newnham, Caldwell and St. Paul's, Bedford.[63] At some time before 1304 the chapel at Whitgift (Yorks. W. R.), was destroyed by the rector to provide material for his private house.[64] Around 1400 a remarkable chain of events linked a number of royal sites. First, in 1399, Richard II gave the manor of Northolt to Westminster Abbey. The sacrist of the abbey promptly sold materials from the manor house to the Clerk of the King's Works for use in the building of the king's new house at Sutton (Middlesex). No sooner had this been completed than the king decided to build another house at Sheen (Surrey), so Sutton (and a further house at Byfleet) were demolished and the materials were reused yet again.[65] These included not only stone, but timber, tiles, lead and even plaster. On occasion, indeed, old mortar was recycled, but it is not entirely clear whether it was reburnt or simply used as aggregate.[66]

### *Quarrying and Building from the 12th Century*

The pursuit of salvaged materials has carried us a long way past the Norman Conquest, and it is worth restating the changes which affected the industry from the end of the 11th century on. There was a huge acceleration in demand for masonry buildings which continued unabated for the rest of the Middle Ages. The actual

60 Williams et al., *Middle Saxon Palaces*, as in n.49, 31-5.

61 R.C.H.M. (England), *Archaeological Sites and Churches in Northampton* (Northamptonshire Inventory, v), 371, for the reused stones; the remainder of the St. Peter's entry and the accompanying plates illustrate the high quality of the building.

62 Lehmann-Brockhaus, *Schriftquellen*, No.291; *Radulphi de Coggeshall Chron. Anglicanum*, ed. J.

Stevenson (Rolls Ser. lxvi, 1875), 205.

63 Lehmann-Brockhaus, *Schriftquellen*, No.293; *Annales Monastici*, ed. H.R. Luard (5 vols., Rolls Ser. xxxvi, 1864-9), iii, 89.

64 Lehmann-Brockhaus, *Schriftquellen*, No.4589; *Fabric Rolls of York Minster*, ed. J. Raine (Surtees Soc. xxxv, 1859), 236.

65 *King's Works*, ii, 1004, 999.

66 Salzman, *Building in England*, 151-2.

*Fig. 8a* Northampton, St. Peter's church: 12th-century respond base.

*Fig. 8b* Northampton, St. Peter's church: Anglo-Saxon interlace on underside of base.

number of masonry buildings increased dramatically in comparison with the Anglo-Saxon period. The Normans undertook a wholesale replacement of cathedrals, some examples of which have been mentioned above. Left to themselves, the Anglo-Saxons probably would not have rebuilt them so completely or have tackled so many of them simultaneously. In addition to the cathedral monasteries there was a rapid growth of religious houses, particularly in the 12th century. The remains of famous monasteries like Rievaulx and Fountains, denuded as they are of stone, still give a strong impression of the huge demands made on the sources of stone by the monastic builders; not only the great churches but many of the conventual buildings were of masonry. Another characteristic of the Norman period is the building of castles. Despite two decades of research, it is still not entirely clear what form Anglo-Saxon 'castles' took, but those ringworks which are possibly of pre-Conquest date and town defences seem to have relied mainly on earth ramparts. Certainly they would not have demanded the huge quantities of dressed stone which were required by Norman tower keeps like Rochester or Norham or by the enormous circuits of the curtain walls which became common later. Finally, domestic buildings of all kinds, from royal palaces to private houses, were now increasingly built in stone. There are few parallels in the pre-Conquest period for, say, the Norman town houses surviving in Lincoln or the manor house at Boothby Pagnell.[67] In many cases these masonry buildings replaced houses that already existed in timber, and the shift from wood to stone also occurred in the field of church building. This process had already begun before the Conquest, for example at Chester-le-Street (Co. Durham), where Æthelric (Egelric, bishop of Durham 1042-56) demolished the wooden church in which St. Cuthbert's remains had rested in the 10th century, and built a new one of stone.[68] In 1187 the archbishop's church at Hackington (Kent) was similarly rebuilt in stone[69] and when the Dean of Salisbury visited the chapel at Earley (Berks.) in 1224 he found a collection of stones 'as though for building a stone chapel', the existing building being a wooden one.[70]

Not only were there more individual stone buildings and more kinds of stone buildings after the Norman Conquest, but many of them were considerably larger than their Anglo-Saxon predecessors. The first Norman abbot of St. Augustine's, Canterbury, built a new church which completely surrounded the Anglo-Saxon one.[71] Its walls were also thicker than the main run of Anglo-Saxon walling. Without knowing the heights of the two buildings or anything about their architectural detail, it is impossible to quantify the relative amounts of stone required to build them, but it is clear that the Norman church would have needed more than its predecessor. What is more, the pre-Conquest church, extensive though it was by contemporary

67  M. Wood, *Norman Domestic Architecture* (Royal Archaeological Inst., 1974).

68  Lehmann-Brockhaus, *Schriftquellen*, No.1018; *Symeonis Monachi Opera*, as in n.20, iii, p.92, §9.

69  Lehmann-Brockhaus, *Schriftquellen*, No.836; *Chronicles and Memorials . . . Richard I*, ed. W.

Stubbs (Rolls Series xxxviii, 1864-5), ii, 80.

70  Lehmann-Brockhaus, *Schriftquellen*, No.1495; *Registrum S. Osmund . . .* ed. W.H.R. Jones (2 vols. Rolls Ser. lxxviii), i, 309.

71  H.M. and J. Taylor, *Anglo-Saxon Architecture*, i (1965), 136, Fig.61.

standards, had grown stage by stage throughout the period. At no point would it have required an amount of stone comparable with the demands of the total Norman rebuilding. Only Wulfric's octagon, had it been completed, would have needed resources on the same scale, and that was a structure of the mid 11th century. Another similarly extensive composite building was the Old Minster at Winchester. By the end of the Anglo-Saxon period it had achieved a total length of some 240 ft. (73m.). The cathedral which replaced it measured about 536 ft. (163m.). The demolition material from the Old Minster can have made only a small contribution to the total stone requirement of the Norman cathedral.

### Sources of Stone

The huge growth in the amount of stone which had to be produced is matched by a sharp increase in the number of surviving documents referring to quarrying, transport of stone, building operations, masons' working conditions, and so on. This is particularly true from the 13th century onward. Salzman remarked in 1913 that 'it would be easy to fill pages with a list of casual references to the working of quarries in all parts of England, and after struggling through the list the reader would know that stone was dug in quite a lot of places at different times, which he might have assumed without the documentary evidence'.[72] Salzman nevertheless worked through it, and by the time he had completed *Building in England* he had 'examined some fifteen hundred manuscripts'.[73] Given this prodigious feat, and the parallel researches of Knoop and Jones, it is unlikely that new information will come to light which will materially alter the two classic accounts of the 1930s.

By extracting the information from these secondary sources and adding the results of archaeological excavations it would be possible to draw a map of known medieval quarry sites of the kind which Gee has published for south Yorkshire.[74] At best such a map would be uninformative, at worst misleading. The more spots were plotted, the more the map would tend to show the geology of England. Far more revealing would be a map of quarry sites in relation to building projects, but because of the quantity of information available this would have to be done site by site or quarry by quarry. What is noticeable about the later medieval period is the distances which stone might travel from quarry to building site and the multiplicity of sources on which a single project might draw. An outstanding example of this is Eton College, begun in 1442. The nearest sources of stone were Taynton (Oxon.) and Merstham (Surrey), but three Kentish quarries also supplied stone: Maidstone, Farleigh and Boughton. Further supplies of Kentish rag were obtained from the ruins of the Savoy Palace in London. In addition, Caen stone was brought from Normandy, continuing the tradition begun by William I, but by the winter of 1448-9 this had become

72 Salzman, *Industries*, 76.
73 Salzman, *Building in England*, v.
74 E. Gee, 'Stone from the Medieval Limestone Quarries of South Yorkshire', in A. Detsicas (ed.), *Collectanea Historica* (Kent Arch. Soc., 1981), 247-55, Fig.56 on 249.

unobtainable for political reasons, and magnesian limestone from Huddleston and Stapleton in Yorkshire was used instead.[75] Water transport was of course essential for bringing stone from abroad but it was also a desirable method of moving native stone from place to place, even between inland sites. In 1192, after a great deal of unpleasantness, the monks of Ramsey prevented their brethren of Sawtrey from using channels which they had made in the Fens, with the sole exception of the channel from Whittlesey to Sawtrey, which was specifically stated to be for the transport of building materials.[76] A hundred years later the archbishop of York was guaranteed free passage of stone for the building of the cathedral; it was brought by boat from Tadcaster.[77] The suggestion has recently been made that stone from Huddleston, 6 miles (10km.) south of Tadcaster, was carried to the Ouse by means of the still surviving artificial channel, known as Bishop Dyke, which runs from Sherburn-in-Elmet to Cawood (Fig. 9).[78]

Despite the use of waterways in some cases, the transport of large quantities of stone was both laborious and expensive. Salzman has calculated that for journeys longer than 12 miles the cost of transport was greater than the price of the stone.[79] The incentive to find stone near at hand must have been great, and the literary evidence for quarry sites and payments for carriage or the implications of stone distribution maps such as Fig. 4 tend to obscure the fact that many building projects obtained stone from the immediate vicinity of the site.[80] This had been the case at Crowland in the 10th century[81] and the immediate post-Conquest example of Battle has already been mentioned. In the 1090s stone for Lindisfarne Priory was obtained from Holy Island itself, though that from neighbouring villages was preferred because the stone from the island did not weather well.[82] In the second half of the 12th century the site of Finchale Priory, just downstream from Durham on the

75 *King's Works*, i, 281.
76 Lehmann-Brockhaus, *Schriftquellen*, No.4166; *Cartularium Monasterii de Rameseia*, ed. W.H. Hart and P.A. Lyons (3 vols., Rolls Ser. lxxix, 1884-93), i, 166.
77 Lehmann-Brockhaus, *Schriftquellen*, No.5057; *Fabric Rolls of York*, as in note 64, 153.
78 J.S. Miller and E.A. Gee, 'Bishop Dyke and Huddleston Quarry', *Yorks. Archaeol. Jnl.* lv (1983), 167-8. However, a scrutiny of the payments for this journey (*Fabric Rolls*, as note 64) shows that the cost of the first leg from Huddleston to Cawood remained stable at 10*d.* per cartload from 1419, when transport by cart is explicitly stated, until 1519, and rose slightly in 1526. This is well beyond the date at which Miller and Gee suggest that Bishop Dyke was in use for the carriage of stone, and one would have expected the cost to fall if water transport had replaced carts. The sledding of stone within Cawood before it was loaded on to boats is mentioned several times in the accounts; in 1458 the same entry includes a payment for

repairing the road from the quarry to Cawood. Similar information is recorded for 1432, when Thomas Bocher was paid for sledding stone 'from the bank of the Ouse to the boat'. This can hardly be taken as evidence for a canal basin. The entry for 1519 is the only one in which the same quantity of stone is accounted for on both legs of the journey. The shorter distance from Huddleston to Cawood cost more (at 10*d.* a cartload) than the longer distance by river from Cawood to York (at 6*d.*). The implication must be that the first leg of the journey was *not* made by water.
79 Salzman, *Building in England*, 119.
80 D. Knoop and G.P. Jones, 'The English Medieval Quarry', *Econ. Hist. Rev.* ix (1938-9), 17-37, especially 17-18 with 18 n. 1.
81 Lehmann-Brockhaus, *Schriftquellen*, No.1149; *Chron. Croyland*, as in note 21, 55-6.
82 Lehmann-Brockhaus, *Schriftquellen*, No.2446; *Reginaldi Monachi Dunelmensis Libellus de admirandis beati Cuthberti Virtutibus*, ed. J. Raine (Surtees Soc., i, 1835), 45.

*Fig. 9a*  Bishop Dyke, watercourse from Sherburn-in-Elmet, SE 49 33, to Cawood, SE 57 37 (Yorks., W.R.): aerial view of Cawood end from the west. In the left foreground the channel runs alongside the road leading to the bridge over the Ouse.

*Fig. 9b*  Bishop Dyke: detail of channel with Bishop Wood in distance.

River Wear, was flooded; the swollen river attacked the banks and miraculously dislodged the stone blocks from which the priory buildings were subsequently constructed.[83] In the 13th and 14th centuries Exeter Cathedral got its stone from a variety of sources: Barley, Colmanshay, Whipton and even Silverton were close to Exeter itself, but the main quarries were farther away at Beer, Branscombe and Salcombe. Since these are near the coast, however, transport would have presented no great problem and they may be regarded as almost local sites. The Dean and Chapter went farther afield than this only for special items. From Portland in Dorset they obtained great bosses, bases and capitals in 1304; two years previously they had paid 14s. for the carving of four bosses at Ham Hill (Somerset) and 8s. 8d. for their transport to Exeter, and they bought a further 300 stones from the same quarry to make the steps before the high altar.[84]

At the consecration of the new chancel of the church at Adderbury (Oxon.) in 1418 the sum of 6s. 8d. was paid for backfilling a quarry 'below the rectory garden' notwithstanding the earlier purchase of stone from Taynton.[85] It may be that the local stone was dug for lime-burning rather than for walling. Lime mortar was an essential component of masonry construction, and there are numerous references to the purchase of limestone or chalk for burning and of sand for aggregate and to the construction and firing of lime-kilns.[86] These include the mention in 1334 of a 'William the Mortar-maker' in the Denbigh area,[87] which implies that the preparation of mortar was becoming a specialist occupation. But there are no references to the mundane question of mixing the burnt lime and the aggregate, which for a big project must have been an enormous logistic problem. There is archaeological evidence from the Anglo-Saxon period, however, in the form of a series of circular mixers, varying in size from 2m. (6ft. 8in.) to 3m. (10 ft.) in diameter, discovered by excavation in Northampton; they were surrounded by wickerwork walls and the mixing was effected by paddles attached to a horizontal beam which rotated on a centrally-placed post.[88] The five mixers discovered probably supplied the mortar for the construction of the possible 9th-century minster church under the present St. Peter's, and of the (so far unique) stone-built royal palace.

83  Lehmann-Brockhaus, *Schriftquellen*, No.1717; *Libellus de Vita et Miraculis S. Godrici*, ed. J. Stevenson (Surtees Soc., xx, 1847), 112, §105.

84  *Accounts of the Fabric of Exeter Cathedral, 1279-1353*, ed. A.M. Erskine (Devon and Cornwall Rec. Soc., xxiv & xxvi, 1981-3), ii, pp.xiii-xv; i, 33, 35, 22, 24.

85  *Adderbury 'Rectoria'*, ed. T.F. Hobson (Oxford-shire Rec. Soc., viii, 1926), 23, 19, and *passim*. Since this chapter was written it has become clear that the quarry at Adderbury cannot have been a lime-pit. Elsewhere in the accounts are several references to the purchase of quick-lime, and the rectory garden was situated on marlstone, not on limestone or chalk.

86  Salzman, *Building in England*, 149-53.

87  E. Neaverson, 'Mediaeval Quarrying in North-Eastern Wales', *Flintshire Hist. Soc.* xiv (1953-4), 1-21, especially 9.

88  Williams et al., op. cit. note 49, 36-7, 72-3.

## Commercial Developments

In the later Middle Ages documents reveal a rapidly developing industry in which quarries could be privately owned, were commercially exploited and thus became assets that were worth buying and selling, or donating to good causes. In 1301 the Dean and Chapter of Exeter bought a plot of land at Barley (on the outskirts of the city) from a private individual, Robert le Hayward, with the implication that they would henceforth quarry it themselves. They had previously bought stone at Barley.[89] The Hazlewood quarries in the West Riding of Yorkshire belonged to the Vavasour family, and rights in them or parts of them were granted successively to Yorkshire churches in the 13th and 14th centuries.[90] Eventually the king obtained the use of the quarry at Thevesdale in 1447 to supply King's College in Cambridge. The Huddleston quarry was owned by the Langton family. In 1385 the Dean and Chapter of York took out an 80-year lease, and in 1415-16 bought a further 5 roods. In the 15th century the Langtons were selling stone by the load: stone had long since become a marketable commodity.[91] It was also resold by purchasers to third parties. Overproduction for particular building projects meant that stone could be sold off from store to other potential users. York Minster is a case in point. In the first half of the 15th century various quantities of stone were sold to Kirkham Priory, Beverley Minster, and other customers.[92] It is not surprising, therefore, to find master masons also acting as stone merchants. Most famous of these was Henry Yevele, best known as the king's mason and clerk of works. While employed on royal sites in London, he supplied all kinds of building materials over a wide area of Kent and Surrey, including 13 tons of stone to Rochester Castle in 1368.[93] Other suppliers of stone were mainly quarrymasters, though in some cases they also worked as masons. Roger of Reigate provided stone for Westminster Abbey in 1253, and Thomas of Weldon for Rockingham Castle later in the century. Roger, John and Thomas Howes supplied stone for Windsor Castle in the 1360s and for Merton College in 1448. They are one of the many families of quarrymasters which can be identified in the 14th and 15th centuries.[94] One of the best-known families were the Canons of Corfe, who supplied both Exeter Cathedral and Westminster.[95] But they specialised in marble work, the subject of Chapter 3, and will not be pursued further here.

## Acknowledgements

I am grateful to Dr. David Howlett, editor of the *Dictionary of Medieval Latin*, for kindly making available references to the documentary material; to Joan Stephenson, Fred Hartley, Stephen Moorhouse and Richard Morris (York) for their help in identifying

89  Erskine, op. cit. note 84, 18, 9 & *passim*.
90  Gee, art. cit. note 74, 247-8.
91  Ibid. 250, 253.
92  Knoop and Jones, *Med. Mason*, 54-5.
93  *King's Works*, i, 210.
94  Knoop and Jones, art. cit. note 80, 27-8.
95  Ibid. 24; Erskine, op. cit. note 84, ii, pp.xv and 250.

medieval quarry sites; to Richard Morris and Professor Rosemary Cramp for generously lending me original photographs from which Figs 2 and 6 have been made; and to Dr. Margaret Gelling for her advice on the place-names.

## Further Reading

The most influential general book on building materials is Alec Clifton-Taylor's *Pattern of English Building*. At least half of the book is devoted to stone and related materials. *English Stone Building*, by Clifton-Taylor and A.S. Ireson (1983), deals not only with the raw materials but also with traditional quarrying and masonry techniques and the tools used to carry them out.

The chapter in Salzman's *Industries* was the first concise account specifically of the medieval building stone industry, and included references to the cost of stone, masons' wages and the tools of the trade. *The Mediaeval Mason* by Douglas Knoop and G.P. Jones, an important book twice reissued, but now out of print, analyses a wealth of documentary information to present a comprehensive picture of the administration of the industry, of masons' wages, conditions of work and craft organisation, and of the cost of stone and its transport. The same authors also explored in detail the operation of the medieval stone quarry, including quarrymen's wages.[96] Salzman's *Building in England down to 1540* was completed in 1934 but not published until 1952. The expanded 1967 edition remains the most comprehensive single work on the medieval building industry. Part of its importance and interest lies in the large number of building contracts published as Appendix B.

J.H. Harvey's *English Mediaeval Architects: a Biographical Dictionary down to 1550* (revised edn., 1984) includes 'medieval masons, carvers, carpenters, building contractors and others responsible for design'. His *Mediaeval Architect* (1972) and *Mediaeval Craftsmen* (1975) present the information about the men working in the industry in narrative form.

The first two volumes of the monumental *History of the King's Works*, under the general editorship of H.M. Colvin, cover the medieval period, giving an authoritative site-by-site account of the palaces, castles, abbeys and churches erected by royal command. They include a great deal of information on the sources of building stone and its carriage to the site, on costs and on the organisation of the royal enterprises. The understanding of the original documents is now made easier by Eric Gee's *Glossary of Building Terms* (Frome, 1984), which defines the specialist vocabulary used in England from the Norman Conquest to the end of the Middle Ages.

Outstanding among the more detailed studies is the seminal paper by Professor E.M. Jope on the building stones of the Anglo-Saxon period.[97] Other researchers have concentrated on specific areas of the country or even particular stone types. In

---

96 Knoop and Jones, art. cit. note 80.          97 Jope, art. cit. note 13.

a series of publications beginning forty years ago E. Neaverson explored the medieval building stones of north Wales.[98] More recently, Eric Gee has collected together the evidence for the limestone quarries in south Yorkshire,[99] while Eileen Roberts has studied in some depth the Totternhoe quarries in Bedfordshire and the use of the chalk from them in Hertfordshire churches.[100] A short note by T.W.T. Tatton-Brown has extended the known distribution of stone from Quarr in the Isle of Wight to London and east Kent. [101] In addition there are numerous monographs, articles and reports devoted to the study of individual buildings or to the archaeological excavation of particular sites; all of these increase our knowledge of where the medieval masons obtained their stone and how they used it.

98  Neaverson, art. cit. note 87, and the references cited there on p.21.
99  Gee, art. cit. note 74.
100  E. Roberts, 'Totternhoe Stone and Flint in Hertfordshire Churches', *Med. Arch.* xviii (1974), 66-89.
101  Tatton-Brown, art. cit. note 30.

# 2

## *Alabaster*

### NIGEL RAMSAY

The carving of figures and panels of alabaster, for both religious images and tombs, was a major activity in the Midlands of England in the late medieval period. Like the pewterers or the carvers of Purbeck marble, the alabaster carvers owed much of their success to the rarity of their principal raw material outside England. In the course of roughly 50 years, from *c.* 1330 to *c.* 1380, the carving of alabaster developed from a single royal tomb commission to a small-scale industry producing religious imagery and tomb effigies. The Reformation had the effect of halting the production of all overtly religious sculpture but the stone continued to serve for tomb effigies into the later 17th century.

The stone had a twofold attraction which caused it to be widely adopted for sculpture once suitable quarries had been opened up. It could be found as white as marble, and though more brittle it was far softer and easier to work, especially when freshly sawn by the quarries: it thus lent itself to the mass-production of carved figures and reliefs. But alabaster appealed to the consumer no less than to the producer: by association with the practice of the Ancient World of storing costly ointments in *alabastra*,[1] the stone alabaster in the form found in western Europe was itself deemed precious in the medieval period. In the so-called Wyclif Bible, of the late 14th century, Matthew xxvi, 6 was translated as referring to 'a womman havynge a boxe of alabastre of preciouse oynement'.[2] At least two English cathedral churches – Canterbury and Exeter – were claiming in the 14th century to have the *alabastrum* used by St. Mary Magdalene.[3] In the 13th and 14th centuries,[4] as indeed

---

1   Cf. Pliny, *Natural History*, Book xiii, 3 (Loeb edn., 108); Mark, xiv. 3.

2   *The Holy Bible . . . in the Earliest English Versions made by John Wycliffe and his Followers*. ed. J. Forshall and F. Madden, 4 vols. (1850), iv, 73.

3   *Inventories of Christchurch, Canterbury*, ed. J. Wickham Legg and W.H.St.J. Hope (1902), 82 inventory of 1316); G. Oliver, *Lives of the Bishops of Exeter* (1861), 311 (inventory of 1327). The claim was also made by the abbey of Cluny: G.F. Duckett, *Charters and Records of the Ancient*

*Abbey of Cluni*, 2 vols. (priv. printed, 1888), ii, 224 (inventory of 1382).

In an antiphon for Lauds on the Feast of Becket's Martyrdom, 29 December, the breaking of the alabaster box was made to signify the Crucifixion: F.E. Gilliat Smith, *Dublin Review*, cxiv (Jan.-April 1894), 34.

4   E.g. at Canterbury Cathedral, 1331: *Arch. Jnl.* liii (1896), 266; at Norwich, 1368: *Archdeaconry of Norwich. Inventory of Church Goods temp. Edward III*, ed. A. Watkin (Norfolk Rec. Soc. xix (1), 1947), 21.

much earlier,[5] alabaster was often used for portable altars or superaltars, as well as for such secular items as cups and vases.[6] Since it is a soft stone (unlike the alabaster of the Ancient World),[7] it was not well suited to these functions, and in the 15th century, when its qualities were better understood, it can only very rarely have been applied to them.

*Quarries*

Alabaster is a fine-grained form of gypsum (which is chemically a hydrated sulphate of calcium); it is appreciably soluble in water, its solubility at 15°C (59°F) being about 1 part in 495 parts of water. At temperatures of between 128°C and 163°C (262°F and 325°F), gypsum is principally converted into plaster of Paris.[8] A quarry that did not yield economic quantities of alabaster might thus be viable because of the quantities of plaster of Paris that could be gained from it.[9] The alabaster was undoubtedly most prized when pure white, like the marble that it could easily be polished to resemble, but it was accepted that it was generally found 'with strakes of divers colours'.[10]

Small deposits have at different times been worked in Yorkshire, Lincolnshire, Nottinghamshire, Leicestershire and Somerset, but the principal quarries in medieval times and later were in Staffordshire and Derbyshire.[11] It has been quarried at Fauld, by Hanbury (Staffs.), or nearby ever since the 14th century,[12] the stone from this locality tending to have a mottled appearance due to red or brown colouring.[13] Stone from the other principal medieval quarry, at Chellaston (Derbs.), about ten miles east, tends rather to have a green mottling, but is also found with red colouring.[14] It is not possible by petrological analysis or any other scientific means to

5  E.g. at Conques (Aveyron), end of 11th century: *Les Trésors des Églises de France*, cat. of exhibition, Musée des Arts Décoratifs, Paris, 1965 (2nd edn.; Caisse Nationale des Monuments Historiques), No. 544.

6  E.g. a *ciphus* (cup), as a church ornament at Heytesbury (Wilts.), 1220: *Registrum S. Osmundi Episcopi*, ed. W.H. Rich Jones (Rolls Ser. 78, 1883-4), i, 295; vase repaired for the king, 1243: *Cal. Liberate Rolls, 1240-5*, 206; *cuppa*, 1363, belonging to Cambridge University Archives, Proctors' Indentures, C.U.R. 1.2(1a).

7  W. Smith et al., *Dictionary of Greek and Roman Antiquities*, 3rd edn. (1890), i, 95-6; Pauly-Wissowa, *Real Encyclopädie . . .*, i (1894), col. 1271-2 (*s.v.* alabastron).

8  R.L. Sherlock, *Gypsum and Anhydrite*, 3rd edn., ed. R.L. Sherlock and S.E. Hollingworth (Memoirs of the Geological Survey, Special Reports on the Mineral Resources of Great Britain, iii, 1938), 1.

9  In a lawsuit of 1363, land was said to have been dug for marl, clay, alabaster and plaster

of Paris, which were extracted to the value of £100: G. Wrottesley, *Extracts from the Plea Rolls of the Reign of Edward III and Richard II (Collections for a History of Staffordshire* (William Salt Arch. Soc.), xiii, 1892), 31. Various references to the making or importing of plaster of Paris are assembled by Salzman, *Building in England*, 155-7.

10  *On the Properties of Things. John Trevisa's translation of Bartholomaeus Anglicus, De Proprietatibus Rerum. A Critical Text*, ed. [M.C. Seymour], 3 vols. (1975-88), ii, 827.

11  R.J. Firman, 'A Geological Approach to the History of English Alabaster', *Mercian Geologist*, ix. 3 (March 1984), 161-78.

12  The two litigants in the 1363 suit, mentioned above in note 9, were both described as of Fauld although the case was about land at Marchington, which is about three miles north-west of Fauld.

13  Sherlock, *Gypsum and Anhydrite*, op. cit. in note 8, 3 and 51.

14  Ibid., 3 and 12.

determine the locality from which a piece of alabaster has been extracted.

The earliest remaining alabaster carving in England *in situ* is a 12th-century doorway surround at Tutbury (Staffs.): the local alabaster beds were no doubt the source for this, as for an early 14th-century effigy at Hanbury, only a couple of miles away.[15] The door surround was an unwise use of the stone, since it exposed it to the weather, and can be regarded as an experiment that was unlikely to be repeated over any significant period of time. The effigy at Hanbury may represent a more significant step in the development of alabaster working, for it was from around 1330 that alabaster began to be used for tomb effigies in other parts of England. The very high quality (and whiteness) of the blocks carved for Edward II's tomb argues for a well-established quarrying capability by *c.* 1330.

The documentary evidence for the different quarries and centres of alabaster working dates from more than a generation later. In 1362 Queen Philippa, wife of Edward III, had six carts laden with alabaster at Tutbury and brought to London,[16] and it was to Tutbury that John of Gaunt turned in the first instance, in 1374, for the alabaster for the tomb effigies of himself and his wife;[17] Tutbury (with Fauld) was part of his demesne property, and so he had an interest in meeting his requirements from it, and even developing its commercial potential.[18] Chellaston in Derbyshire had an equally well-documented quarry: it is about ten miles east of Tutbury, and across the border in Derbyshire, but it too was within Gaunt's honour of Tutbury. Alabaster was being dug at Chellaston at least as early as 1374,[19] and it was here, in 1414, that the abbey of Fécamp (Seine-Maritime dépt., Normandy) had some of the stone purchased for its needs,[20] while it was with two carvers of Chellaston that one of the few surviving medieval English tomb-contracts was made, in 1419, for a tomb to be erected at Lowick (Northants.).[21]

Alabaster occurs in workable masses or 'pillars', each of which is separated by 'coarsestone' and 'foulstone': the 'foulstone' is sufficiently soft, when weathered, to

15   The Hanbury effigy is noted by H. Tummers, *Early Secular Effigies in England. The Thirteenth Century* (Leiden, 1980), 15, 50, 116; Tummers also notes an early 14th-century alabaster effigy at Bedale (Yorks.).

16   *Cal. Patent Rolls, 1361-4*, 232.

17   *John of Gaunt's Register*, ed. S. Armitage-Smith, ii, Camden 3rd ser. xxi (1911), 212-3, No. 1394.

18   It cannot be mere coincidence that both an alabaster panel and alabaster tomb were commissioned to commemorate (respectively) the marriage and death of Sir Godfrey Foljambe (d. 1376) who was steward of the Duchy estates. The panel is discussed in J.J.G. Alexander and P. Binski (eds.), *Age of Chivalry: Art in Plantagenet England*, exhibition cat. (London: Royal Academy of Arts, 1987), 210-11, No. 26; the tomb, at Bakewell (Derbs.), is illustrated by Arthur Gardner, *Alabaster Tombs of the Pre-Reformation Period in England* (1940), pl. 3.

Details of the Duchy's exploitation in the 15th century of its alabaster at Castlehay Park in Needwood forest (Staffs.) are given by J.R. Birrell, 'The Honour of Tutbury in the Fourteenth and Fifteenth Centuries', M.A. thesis, University of Birmingham, 1962, 136.

19   I.S.W. Blanchard, 'Economic Change in Derbyshire in the late Middle Ages, 1272-1540', Ph.D. thesis, University of London, 1967, 374.

20   J. Bilson, 'A French Purchase of English Alabaster in 1414', *Arch. Jnl.* lxiv (1907), 32-7.

21   The contract is now in the Northamptonshire Record Office, Stopford Sackville Collection, 4239; it is translated by W.H.St.J. Hope, 'On the Early Working of Alabaster in England', *Arch. Jnl.* lxi (1904), 221-40, at 230-1. See also C. Ryde, 'An Alabaster Standing Angel with Shield at Lowick – a Chellaston Shop Pattern', *Derbs. Arch. Jnl.* xcvii (1977), 36-49.

be dug by hand. At Chellaston, and perhaps elsewhere in the east Midlands region, the whitest alabaster is found only in the top two or three feet of each pillar.[22] There would consequently have been a tendency for the quarriers to cut just the top layer of the stone, over a wide area: quarries must therefore have proliferated in the second half of the 14th century, as the industry developed.

## Workshops

The Lowick tomb contract of 1419 raises the question of whether alabaster was commonly carved at, or at least very near, the quarries at that date. The 14th- and early 15th-century evidence tends to suggest otherwise, particularly for the finest-quality work. Both Queen Philippa and John of Gaunt had their alabaster transported in carts – overland – to London, where John of Gaunt had his made into a tomb by the leading architect Henry Yevele and the mason-contractor Thomas Wrek, *c.* 1374-8.[23] Queen Isabella's alabaster tomb in the London Greyfriars had been made by 1358-9 in the London-based workshop of William Ramsey III.[24] It was from London that Lord Nevill had an alabaster and Caen stone reredos shipped (to Newcastle, for Durham) in 1372,[25] and in 1421 a London carver contracted to carve a tomb of alabaster and other stone, to be placed in Bisham Priory (Berks.).[26] It is clear, then, that a number of London-based sculptors were working in alabaster from the mid 14th to early 15th centuries. But it was also being carved closer to the quarries.

An alabaster *tabula* or reredos was ordered in 1367 for the high altar of St. George's Chapel, Windsor, from Peter the Mason of Nottingham,[27] and the Fécamp contract of 1414 (for stone from Chellaston) was drawn up in Nottingham, so it might seem tempting to regard this town, so easily accessible from both the Tutbury area and Chellaston by the River Trent, as being already a place where alabaster carvers thrived. On the other hand, there is no evidence for a century after Peter the Mason's time to link Nottingham with the carving of alabaster, either for tombs or for religious panels; it may well be that at this period much of the run-of-the-mill carving actually took place in the vicinity of the quarries, as is suggested by the 1419 tomb-contract with two Chellaston carvers. Quarries may have been owned or leased by carvers: it was from Thomas Prentys, one of the two carvers from Chellaston, that Fécamp had obtained its unworked alabaster five years earlier.

22  Firman, art. cit. in note 11, 171.
23  See J.H. Harvey, *English Mediaeval Architects.*
    *A Biographical Dictionary down to 1550* (2nd edn.,
    1984), 360; L. Stone, *Sculpture in Britain: the*
    *Middle Ages* (2nd edn., 1972), 262 n. 20.
24  F.D. Blackley, 'The Tomb of Isabella of
    France, Wife of Edward II of England', *Bull.,*
    *International Society for the Study of Church Monu-*
    *ments*, 8 (1983), 161-4.
25  C. Wilson, 'The Neville Screen', *Medieval Art*

    *and Architecture at Durham Cathedral*, British
    Archaeological   Association   Conference
    Trans., iii, for 1977 (1980), 90-104.
25  G.M. Bark, 'A London Alabasterer in 1421',
    *Antiq. Jnl.* xxix (1949), 89-91.
27  Hope, *Arch. Jnl.* lxi, 224-5; A.K.B. Roberts,
    *St. George's Chapel, Windsor Castle, 1348-1416:*
    *A Study in Early Collegiate Administration* (1948),
    93.

*Fig. 10* Coronation of the Virgin. Like other alabaster panels of this early date (*c.* 1400), it is relatively large (40½in., or 103 cm., high). (*Barber Inst. of Fine Arts, Birmingham*)

It was perhaps as a result of expansion in the activities of the alabaster carvers that they became based in certain towns, in the mid 15th century and later. The town in which carvers specifically called 'alabastermen' are first found is York, where seven were admitted to the freedom of the city at various dates between 1457-8 and 1487-9.[28] W.H.St.J. Hope suggested, in 1890, that representations of St. John the Baptist's head (of which many examples survive) might be associated with York, on the grounds that such representations were seen as standing for Christ and that there was a prominent gild of the Corpus Christi in York.[29] This theory is not tenable,[30] but Hope's suggestions have nonetheless been used to found the consequent possible political significance of certain of the St. John carvings.[31] Stylistic arguments have been advanced for other alabasters – certain of the panels with battlementing at the top – being carved in York.[32] There is no hard evidence, however, for either of these theories, and, as will be seen, even the fact that some alabasters have been found in the city gives no firm ground for assuming them to have been carved there.[33]

The next town with which there is reason to associate the carving of alabaster panels or figures is Burton-on-Trent, on the Nottinghamshire border of Staffordshire and only a few miles from Tutbury and Chellaston. In 1462 an alabaster image is mentioned as being bought from a painter of Burton,[34] and a lawsuit of 1481 shows two Burton alabastermen claiming payment, presumably for works in alabaster, from St. Albans Abbey (Herts.), Holy Trinity Priory, Wallingford (Berks.), and St. Batholomew's Hospital, Newbury (Berks.).[35] Relatively little medieval documentary material concerning Burton has survived, but there are references to two painters of Burton, in 1396-1403 and 1403-29, and to image-makers in 1459 and 1460.[36] It is likely that at these dates the words carver, imagemaker and even painter could all mean alabaster carver.

28  F.M. Collins, *Freemen of York*, vol. i (Surtees Soc. xcvi, 1896), 177 ff.; the dates are corrected by R.B. Dobson, *Econ. Hist. Rev.*, 2nd ser. xxvi (1973), 4.

29  W.H.St.J. Hope, 'On the Sculptured Alabaster Tablets called St. John's Heads', *Archaeologia*, lii, pt. ii (1890), 669-708.

30  The general identification of St. John the Baptist's death with that of Christ is doubtful, and there were Corpus Christi gilds in many towns: see M. James, 'Ritual, Drama and the Social Body in the Late Medieval English Town', *Past & Present*, xcviii (1983), 3-29.

31  P. Tudor-Craig, *Richard III*, cat. of exhibition, National Portrait Gallery, London, 1973 (2nd edn., 1977), nos. 21 and 27.

32  E.S. Prior and A. Gardner, *An Account of Medieval Figure-Sculpture in England* (1912), 479, 481ff, 492ff. P. Nelson, 'English Alabasters of the Embattled Type', *Arch. Jnl.* lxxv (1918), 310, 311, 317; W.L. Hildburgh, *J.B.A.A.* 3rd ser., xi (1948), 11-12.

33  Alabasters which were found in York in 1957 are now in the Yorkshire Museum at York;

they were described and illustrated by G.F. Willmot, 'A Discovery at York', *Museums Jnl.* lvii (1957-8), 35-6, and by G.B. Wood, 'A Saint's Life in Alabaster', *Country Life*, cxxiv (July-Dec. 1958), 1056-7 (6 Nov.).

34  Thomas Sharp, *Illustrative Papers of the History and Antiquities of the City of Coventry*, ed. W.G. Fretton ([Birmingham], 1871), 143.

35  Hope, *Arch. Jnl.* lxi, 239. A Wallingford Priory account roll of 1481-2 makes clear that its dispute was over an alabaster *tabula*: Oxford, Corpus Christi College muniments, Z/2/1/1, § *Debita soluta*.

36  I.H. Jeayes, 'Calendar of the Burton abbey and other documents of the Marquess of Anglesey' (unpublished typescript), Nos. 597, 1410 (John Redyng, painter, fl. 1396-1403); 1410, 1455 (Robert Bowde, painter, fl. 1403-29); 1511 (John Lende, image-maker, fl. 1459); 1512 (Robert Wade, image-maker, fl. 1460). For William Howeton, carver and painter, 1439, see I.H. Jeayes, *Descriptive Catalogue of Derbyshire Charters . . .* (1906), 330, No. 2618.

*Fig. 11* West end of tomb of William Rudhall, serjeant-at-law (d. 1530), Ross-on-Wye (Herefs.).
The carving combines sacred and secular subjects – The Incarnation of Christ and the Rudhall
family.

The contract (drawn up in 1508) survives for the tomb of Henry Foljambe which
is still extant in All Hallows church, Chesterfield (Derbys.), showing that it was
made for £10 by Henry Harpur and William Moorecock of Burton.[37] It is a brass
effigy, set on top of a partly alabaster table-tomb (though the contract calls for
'marble' alone), and stylistic similarities with other surviving alabaster tombs have
enabled one or more early 16th-century Burton workshops' tomb output to be
identified. An active alabaster industry in the town in this period is also confirmed by
John Leland's observation, made in the course of his travels around England in the
1530s and 1540s, that here were 'many marbelers working in alabaster'.[38] Marblers,
too, could be synonymous with alabastermen.

As a result of a rather one-sided interpretation of an article by W.H.St.J. Hope
published in 1904, Nottingham has become famous as the town where alabasters
were carved; Hope himself was perhaps unduly influenced by the wealth of
documentary material about medieval Nottingham which had just been published
when he was preparing his paper.[39] Alabastermen (other than Peter the Mason, in *c.*
1370) are not found in the city before 1478-9, and although it is undoubtedly the case
that between then and the 1530s the Nottingham records show that city to have been

37  Summary in *Collectanea Topographica et Genea-
logica*, i (1834), 354; discussed by Gardner,
*Alabaster Tombs*, op. cit. in note 18, 9-10, and
by S.A. Jeavons, 'The Church Monuments of
Derbyshire. The Sixteenth and Seventeenth
Centuries', pt. 1, *Derbs. Arch. Jnl.* lxxxiv, for

1964 (1965), 52-80, at 57.

38  *The Itinerary of John Leland . . .*, ed. L.T. Smith,
5 vols. (1906-10), v, 19.

39  *Records of the Borough of Nottingham*, ed. W.H.
Stevenson, 4 vols. (1882-9).

one of the main centres of the alabastermen, the records also suggest that some of the men (and women) were traders rather than sculptors and that the city's role in the alabaster industry was largely as a distributive centre. Furthermore, if a comparable quantity of medieval documentation survived for, say, Lincoln (where a gild is known to have been founded in 1525-6 for painters, gilders, stainers and alabastermen),[40] perhaps such towns would also be revealed as centres of the industry.

### Products

It is astonishing that alabaster's first major sculptural appearances in England were for the tomb effigies of no less important a trio than King Edward II (Gloucester Cathedral, *c.* 1330; its architectural surrounds recently attributed to Thomas of Canterbury, architect of the remodelling of the cathedral's south transept),[41] Edward II's son John of Eltham (d. 1336; Westminster Abbey) and Edward III's son William of Hatfield (d. *c.* 1340; York Minster). The first two of these tombs are of an outstanding quality, and both have been described as 'court' or London products:[42] it is remarkable that a novel material should have been used, and not, say, white marble (as for so many French royal tomb effigies).

The fashion for alabaster spread rapidly, other early instances being the tomb effigies of John de Hotham, bishop of Ely (d. 1337; Ely Cathedral)[43] and John Stratford, archbishop of Canterbury (d. 1348; Canterbury Cathedral), and a wider range of sculptors must have become used to working in the material. From about the 1360s onwards, references to alabaster sculpture in England became more frequent: there was the commission from St. George's Chapel, Windsor, to Peter the Mason of Nottingham in 1367 (paid by Edward III), and by 1374 Durham Cathedral had been given alabaster images of the Trinity and the Virgin Mary by its prior, John Fossour,[44] while Mary of St. Pol, the widowed Countess of Pembroke (d. 1377) gave to Westminster Abbey what was to become a celebrated image of the Virgin, also of alabaster.[45] From the 1370s or 1380s, the carving of alabaster statues, figures in high relief, and rectangular panels evidently developed at a quick pace into a fairly large-scale activity. Quite a number of figures and panels from this time or later in the 14th century still survive in England and France,[46] and from the 1380s documentary allusions to them multiply.[47]

Production must have been on a very large scale by early in the 15th century; a

40   H. Bradshaw, *Statutes of Lincoln Cathedral*, ed. C. Wordsworth, pt. ii (1897), p. cclv; cf. Hope, *Arch. Jnl.* lxi, 240.

41   C. Wilson, in *Age of Chivalry*, op. cit. in note 18, 416-7, No. 497.

42   Stone, *Sculpture in Britain*, op. cit. in note 23, 160-2.

43   See T.D. Atkinson, 'Queen Philippa's Pews in Ely Cathedral', *Proc., Cambridge Antiquarian Society*, xli, for 1943-7 (1948), 60-6, at 60, 64-6.

44   *Historiae Dunelmensis Scriptores Tres*, ed. James Raine (Surtees Soc. ix, 1839), 131; Fossour was prior from 1341 to 1374.

45   A.P. Stanley, *Historical Memorials of Westminster Abbey*, 3rd edn. (1869), 640; H.F. Westlake, *Westminster Abbey*, 2 vols. (1923), ii, 351-2.

46   See, for instance, W.L. Hildburgh, 'English Alabaster Tables of about the Third Quarter of the Fourteenth Century', *Art Bulletin*, xxxii (1950), 1-23.

47   E.g. in the testament of Roger de Freton, Dean of Chichester, 1382: Lambeth Palace Library, Register of Archbishop Courtenay, f. 203.

mid-century survey of 23 churches belonging to St. Paul's Cathedral shows that 16 of them possessed one or more alabaster images.[48] Six of these churches had alabasters of Christ's Passion, and nine had alabasters of the Five Joys of the Virgin Mary: by each of these subjects must be understood a reredos or retable that probably was composed of five or seven rectangular panels, surmounted by alabaster canopies and mounted on a wooden frame. Several dozen such retables still survive intact; they mostly date from the mid 15th century or later.

The carvings produced in the hundred years before the Reformation exhibit what today seems a decline from the simple elegance of the late 14th-century panels, being more deeply cut and showing crowded narrative scenes.[49] But although the details of costume or armour sometimes became so stereotyped that they failed to reflect changes in fashion, the industry's readiness to change its iconography is demonstrated by the survival of panels showing such saints as Erasmus, Armel and Roch (only popular in England from the later 15th century ownards). To judge from monastic dissolution inventories and other evidence, it is likely that every parish church and chapel in England, as well as every monastic church and many private individuals, had one or more alabaster or set of alabasters – and there were 10,000 or so churches and chapels.

## Sale and Distribution

Both parish records (churchwardens' accounts) and other documentary materials show that where churches paid for their alabaster carvings, it was with alabastermen that they most commonly made their contracts. For instances, the accounts of the churchwardens of Tintinhull (Somt.) record the payment in 1451-2 of 1*d.* to an alabasterman in earnest upon a contract, and in the following year the payment of 37*s.* 3*d.* for the alabaster table itself;[50] a church in Coventry in 1462 spent 40*s.* on an image of the Virgin Mary from one Couper, of Burton-on-Trent.[51] Wallingford Priory's dispute in 1481 was with two Burton alabasterman,[52] while in 1512 Ashton-under-Lyne church (Lancs.) litigated over a contract with a Nottingham alabasterman, Edward Hilton.[53]

As these examples suggest, alabastermen can generally be assumed to have been the men who carved the stone, and it is likely that they travelled around the country only for their more important contracts, such as these would have been; the churches in question would no doubt have wanted an iconographic scheme of a particular sort. Less demanding patrons, including the laity, who perhaps wanted a single panel or figure, were probably catered for by salesmen. In 1491 a Nottingham alabasterman,

48  *Visitations of Churches belonging to St. Paul's Cathedral in 1297 and in 1458*, ed. W. Sparrow Simpson, Camden Society, 2nd ser., lv (1895), p. lxiii.

49  See, however, the defence by L. Rollason, *Art History*, ix (1986), 86-94.

50  *Church-Wardens' Accounts of Croscombe . . .*, ed. W. Hobhouse (Somerset Record Soc. iv, 1890),

185, 186.

51  Sharp, *Coventry*, op. cit. in note 34, 143.

52  See above, 34 and note 35.

53  W.M. Bowman, *England in Ashton-under-Lyne* (1960), 134, 149 and photograph facing 134. The Hilton family is mentioned several times, from the 1480s onwards, in *Records of the Borough of Nottingham*, op. cit. in note 39.

Nicholas Hill, sued William Bott, his salesman, for payment for 58 heads of St. John the Baptist;[54] Hill had other means of selling his carvings, too, for he is also found paying for the carriage of St. John's heads to London.[55] In the middle of the 16th century, a Burton woman died leaving debts owing to her of over £22 for alabaster tables, and it would appear that she (or her deceased husband) had previously been trading in the tables;[56] her husband, however, may well have been an alabaster carver, and it is certain that her son-in-law was a tomb-sculptor who worked in alabaster, Richard Parker.[57]

One of the strengths of the alabaster industry was its sales overseas, and it is thanks to the fact that so many hundred carvings survive in Continental Europe, from Poland to Portugal and from Iceland to Yugoslavia, that they can today be assessed stylistically and iconographically. A large set of panels showing scenes from the life of St. Seurin, still in the church of St. Seurin, Bordeaux, is one instance of a special commission from England; there are also several cases of French churches in neighbouring parishes having alabasters that are stylistically so similar to each other as to make it likely that they are from the same workshop, and therefore likely to have come to France at the same time and presumably from the same salesman. The sales of alabasters by English parish churches at the Reformation, substantial though these were,[58] cannot account for the presence of more than a small proportion of the many panels and figures in France today.

Documentary evidence, especially that of the English customs accounts, shows finished alabaster work being exported from a relatively early date in the history of the industry. In 1382 a special licence was granted to Cosmato Gentilis, a papal collector in England, to export from Southampton three large figures, of the Virgin Mary, St. Peter and St. Paul;[59] this was hardly a commercial transaction, but it indicates the attractiveness of the carvings to one continental purchaser. A few years later, in *c.* 1390, a Dartmouth merchant is recorded as having *ymagez d'alabastre* on a ship bound for Spain.[60] Customs accounts of the 15th and early 16th centuries, patchily though they survive, reveal that alabasters were exported from the leading ports, such as London and Bristol, by ordinary merchants who dealt mainly in other commodities and for whom religious imagery can only have been a sideline.[61] The carvings cannot have been particularly well marketed, and indeed they tend to be

54  *Records of the Borough of Nottingham*, iii, 18.
55  Ibid., 28.
56  P.B. Chatwin, 'Three Alabaster 'Tables'', *Birmingham Archaeological Society, Trans. and Proc.* for 1922, xlviii (1925), 178-80.
57  For Parker see Harvey, *English Mediaeval Architects*, op. cit. in note 23, 228.
58  See, for instance, *Calendar of State Papers, Foreign, 1547-1553*, 55.
59  Thomas Rymer, *Foedera . . .*, orig. edn., vii (1709), p. 357; Record Commission edn., iv (1869), 146. The circumstances of the granting of this licence are discussed by W. Ullmann, *The Origins of the Great Schism . . .* (1948), 139-

41. W.L. Hildburgh, *Antiq. Jnl.* xxxv (1955), 186, has suggested that the statues of St. Peter and St. Paul are those now in the church of Sta. Croce in Gerusalemme, Rome.
60  *Select Cases in Chancery, 1364-1471*, ed. W.P. Baildon (Selden Soc. x, 1896), 45-6.
61  See e.g. Particulars of Accounts for London for 1438-9 (P.R.O., E. 122/73/12), 1442-3 (E. 122/77/4, mm. 26ᵛ, 27), 1450 (E. 122/73/25, fo. 40; noted by C.L. Kingsford, *Antiq. Jnl.*, iv (1924), 162), 1463 (E. 122/194/14, m. 2), and for Bristol for 1478-9 (E. 122/19/13, mm. 2,4), 1485-6 (E. 122/20/5, fos. 21ᵛ, 28ᵛ), and 1492-3 (E. 122/20/9, fos. 23ᵛ, 57).

*Fig. 12* Part of side panel of tomb said to be of William or John Lovell, Minster Lovell (Oxon.), *c.* 1460. The figure of St. Christopher is very similar to figures that were produced for individual sale.

found, even today, in the areas close to sea ports or beside the major rivers, and yet they appealed to the market sufficiently to exceed by far the sales of the German limewood carvings or, in the 16th century, the smaller alabaster panels of Malines (Mechelen).[62]

### The End of the Image-Making Industry

In the late 1530s the production of alabaster images in England must have come to

62  Alabasters' distribution in Normandy is touched on by A. Rostand, 'Les Albâtres Anglais du XVᵉ siècle en Basse-Normandie', *Bull. Monumental*, lxxxvii (1928), 257-309, at 268. Malines carvings have been treated by G. Derveaux-Van Ussel, *Exposition de Sculp-* *tures anglaises et malinoises d'Albâtre* (Brussels: Musées Royaux d'Art et d'Histoire, 1967), and by Michael K. Wustrack, *Die Mechelner Alabaster-Manufaktur des 16. und frühen 17. Jahrhunderts* (Frankfurt am Main and Berne, 1982).

an abrupt halt, as a direct result of the Reformation. There is no evidence to suggest that it recovered during Mary's reign.

The making of alabaster tombs can have offered no viable alternative employment for the alabastermen. In the first place, it was only from the 1580s that increased numbers of alabaster or partly alabaster tombs were commissioned, perhaps as there were fewer objections to the use of the mottled and veined stones that the quarries now principally yielded. And, secondly, the Midlands tomb-makers came increasingly to yield their share in the market to the carvers of the 'Southwark school' that thrived just outside the control of the City of London.[63]


## Further Reading

The largest collection of English alabaster carvings is in the Victoria and Albert Museum, London, and a fair proportion of it is on permanent display there. It has been catalogued by Francis Cheetham, *English Medieval Alabasters: With a Catalogue of the Collection in the Victoria and Albert Museum* (1984); his book also contains a general introduction to the subject, and a considerable bibliography.

The literature on alabaster is mostly concerned with the surviving examples, and especially with their iconography. W.H. St. John Hope's paper 'On the Early Working of Alabaster in England', *Arch. Jnl.* lxi (1904), 221-40, accordingly retains much of its value, even though it has been taken to show that Nottingham was the principal centre for the production of alabaster panels of all sorts; Hope argued only that Nottingham was the centre for the carving of representations of the Head of St John the Baptist. For the quarrying of alabaster, Hope must be supplemented by R.J. Firman, 'A Geological Approach to the History of English Alabaster', *Mercian Geologist* ix.3 (March 1984), 161-78.

The relations of alabaster panels and figures intended for reredoses or private devotional purposes with the panels carved for the sides of tombs need to be investigated further. A start has been made by C. Ryde, 'An Alabaster Standing Angel with Shield at Lowick – a Chellaston Shop Pattern', *Derbs. Arch. Jnl.* xcvii (1977), 36-49; the fullest collection of photographs of alabaster tombs is that of Arthur Gardner, *Alabaster Tombs of the Pre-Reformation Period in England* (Cambridge, 1940), but see also Pauline E. Routh, *Medieval Effigial Alabaster Tombs in Yorkshire* (Ipswich, 1976).

The best overall views of alabaster carving, from an art historical perspective, are Joan Evans, *English Art, 1307-1461*, Oxford History of English Art, v (Oxford, 1949), and Lawrence Stone, *Sculpture in Britain: The Middle Ages*, Pelican History of Art (2nd edn., Harmondsworth, 1972).

---

63   A table showing the numbers of alabaster tombs commissioned or erected in each decade from 1300 to 1700 is provided by Firman, art. cit. in note 11, 172, Text-fig. 5; cf. also 168, Text-fig. 4. An outline of some post-Reformation uses of alabaster is provided by K.A. Esdaile, 'Sculpture', in A.S. Turberville (ed.), *Johnson's England*, 2 vols. (1933), ii, 73.

# 3

# Purbeck Marble

## JOHN BLAIR

A distinctive and highly-prized material, Purbeck marble could be obtained from only one place: the neighbourhood of Corfe, on the Isle of Purbeck in south-eastern Dorset.[1] The thousands of architectural, ornamental and monumental works for which it was used passed through the hands of two small groups of men, the marblers of Corfe and London. These facts, and the widespread use during the 13th and 14th centuries of Purbeck marble components to embellish larger works, encouraged a standardisation of workshop practice and a uniformity of design unusual among non-portable medieval objects. Most products of the marblers' workshops can fairly be described as mass-produced; indeed, their high proficiency is largely a consequence of this fact. While there was a significant demand for Purbeck marble throughout the period c.1170-1550, the great age of the marblers was the century between 1250 and 1350: their wares answered perfectly the fashion for contrasting materials, rich, intricate detail, polished surfaces and hard, clean lines.

The 'marble' of Corfe is not a marble in the geological sense, but one of the polishable limestones which were so termed during the Middle Ages on account of their exotic character: they acquired, that is, the high-status connotations of true marble in the classical world. Other 'marbles' had similarities to Purbeck and were used in similar ways: the fine, dark stone of Tournai, for which it was essentially the English substitute, and English stones such as Frosterley, Alwalton, Black Bird's-Eye, Lias, Forest marble and Petworth which were in turn substitutes for Purbeck.[2] But after c.1200 Purbeck marble largely forced out the Tournai imports (apart from graveslabs shipped to the east coast during the 14th century), and none of the other native 'marbles' attained anything approaching its popularity.

---

1   I am extremely grateful to Sally Badham, Paul Binski, Claude Blair, Paul Foote, Treleven Haysom and Philip Lankester for their comments on an earlier draft.

2   See S. Badham, 'An Interim Study of the Stones used for the Slabs of English Monumental Brasses', *Trans.Monumental Brass Soc.* xiii(1985), 475-83.

## The Craft at Corfe

Purbeck marble is a polishable fresh-water limestone, characterised by close-packed fossil shells of the water-snail *Viviparus carinifer*. It occurs in various shades ranging from blue-grey to reddish-brown and green, and some beds have a scattering of shells of the fresh-water mussel *Unio valdensis*. 'Unio' and 'non-Unio' beds occur in the same horizon, and suggestions that different workshops deliberately selected one or the other should probably be discounted.[3] The marble lies in a bed, some 18 to 24 inches thick, which needs to be worked from the surface over an extensive area. It outcrops only on the southern range of the Purbeck hills on a line between Peveril Point and Worbarrow Tout, with the most extensive evidence for quarrying in the neighbourhood of Wilkeswood and Dowshay.[4]

The marble is dense and intractable, and carving it requires considerable skill: it was not normally worked, at least to complex forms, by anyone except specialist marblers. In art-historical terms it is important to establish which architectural and decorative components were produced near the quarries. Although specifications and templates for special commissions might be sent to Corfe (cf. below, p.49), the stylistic affinities of mass-produced items may be more with other marblers' work than with the buildings of which they became part.

This question cannot be answered until the evidence of quarry wasters has been seriously examined. Still the most informative comment is one published in 1861:

> The extent to which the stone was wrought in the town itself [i.e. Corfe] may be gathered from the fact, that in many parts, particularly near the extremity of West Street, on penetrating the soil the rubbish from the masons' banks is frequently found to be ten or twelve feet in thickness. In digging a drain a short time since a thick bed was pierced, which consisted entirely of the *debris* of this marble, largely interspersed with fragments of mouldings, foliations and other ornamental details.[5]

G. Dru Drury, who had a long-standing if amateur interest in the local history of Purbeck, believed that the marble was largely worked in Corfe itself. He envisaged laden sledges dragged along 'marblers' tracks' to West Street, which 'for the greater part of its length, was occupied on one side by the marblers' "bankers"'.[6] This seems to be no more than an inference from the layer of chippings, which, in the absence of controlled excavation, is ambiguous: Drury ignores the obvious alternative possibility that the chippings were carted from quarry sites to make up the road. The

3   Badham, art.cit. note 2, 476. Sections recorded at Peveril and Woodyhyde show both 'Unio' and 'non-Unio' beds (T. Haysom personal communication).

4   G. Dru Drury, 'The Use of Purbeck Marble in Mediaeval Times', *Proc. Dorset Nat. Hist. and Arch. Soc.* lxx (1948) [hereafter 'Drury'], 74-5; T. Haysom pers. comm. For marble taken out

of the cliff at Peveril in the 17th century, see B.L., MS Add. 29976, f.1.
T. Haysom pers. comm. For marble taken out of the cliff at Peveril in the 17th century, see Brit.Lib. MS Add. 29976 f.1.

5   J. Hutchins, *The History and Antiquities of the County of Dorset*, 3rd edn., i (1861), 466 note.

6   Drury, 75.

recent find of three shaft fragments in the back garden of 67 West Street may be more significant,[7] but the existence of 'marblers' bankers' in the town remains unproven.

Drury also wrote that 'there is no evidence at the site of the abandoned quarries of any carving having been worked on the spot, nor does it seem likely that anything should have been required there beyond splitting the blocks into sizes convenient for carting, and perhaps some rough squaring up of the sides'.[8] This is certainly wrong, as is proved by Treleven Haysom's important observation at Haycrafts Farm two miles south-east of Corfe.[9] The farm lies on the manor of Downshay (probably the source of marble given by Alice de Briwerre for building Salisbury Cathedral),[10] near a large dump of quarry waste. Here have been found not only moulded and foliate fragments, since lost,[11] but also a complete course from a large composite pier-base which still lies in the farmyard. These fragments are conclusive evidence that architectural components, including very large ones, were worked to a finished state in quarry workshops. Indeed, commonsense should suggest as much: there would have been little point in bringing this noisy industrial process into a small but thriving town when it could operate equally well beside the quarries only two miles away.

An important reason for the success of the Purbeck marble industry must have been its coastal location. The products were mostly taken off by ship, probably from quays at Ower, Swanage and Wareham around Poole Harbour. From a North-Eastern perspective the Purbeck columns used *c.*1175 at Durham Cathedral came from 'overseas parts',[12] and the shipment of shafts, capitals and bases to Norwich, Westminster, Vale Royal and other great churches is well-attested (below, p.49). In 1253 Robert de Bromley, the king's representative at Purbeck, wrote to one of the works staff at Westminster: 'I am sending you a shipload of marble by William Justise, who should be paid £4 3*s.* 4*d.* for the freight; and, God willing, I may send you one shipload before Whitsun and a third if I can find a ship to carry the said stone'.[13] In 1375-6 the *Margarite* of Wareham is twice mentioned as carrying cargoes of Purbeck marble bound for London: once with two high tombs for the Earl of Arundel and a big slab for the Bishop of Winchester, and again with two columns bought and loaded at Wareham.[14] In 1386 the same ship, then lying in Poole harbour, was bound for London laden with marble for Edward III's tomb.[15] The bringing of marble slabs to King's Lynn, presumably by water, is mentioned in 1318

7 Philip Lankester's observation. Mr. T. Haysom writes (pers. comm., 1988): 'Mr. H. Stockley, a Corfe builder, tells me he has found marble waste in diggings in West Street and in the common called Halves or Haws.'
8 Drury, 76.
9 Publication by Philip Lankester and John Blair forthcoming.
10 *Leland's Itinerary*, ed. L. Toulmin Smith, i (1907), 266, for the gift. Downshay lay on Alice's manor of Worth: see Hutchins, op.cit. note 5, 721.
11 Information from Mr. G.O. Bower.
12 *Historiae Dunelmensis Scriptores Tres* (Surtees Soc. ix, 1839), 11: 'a transmarinis partibus deferebantur columpnae et bases marmoreae'.
13 H.M. Colvin, *Building Accounts of King Henry III* (1971), 436. See ibid., passim, for regular shipments of marble from Corfe to Westminster, and Hutchins, op.cit. note 5, 466, for 13th-century Pipe Roll references to the shipment of marble to Westminster and London.
14 *Cal.Close R. 1374-7*, 59, 297.
15 *Cal.Pat.R. 1385-9*, 127.

and again in 1372.[16] Stylistic research has shown that Purbeck slabs were used by 14th-century makers of monumental brasses in York, Lincoln and other provincial centres.

The biggest shipments, however, must have come to London: for the great churches of the City and Westminster, for the London marblers' warehouses, and for carriage further inland up the Thames. In 1410/11 New College, Oxford, paid £25 6s. 8d. to a quarryman of Purbeck for 1,500 feet of marble paving, £2 to have it brought from London to Henley, and further sums for its carriage from Henley wharf to Oxford.[17] Most of this material seems to have been ready-worked: only to the very biggest projects, and then only sporadically, was raw marble taken for cutting and polishing on site. Just as Westminster attracted marblers to London, so other major projects may have generated permanent teams of craftsmen. One such may be Salisbury Cathedral: marble columns, capitals and bases were transported from Salisbury to Southampton in 1231-2, and in 1238 Master Elias of Dereham made a marble tomb at Salisbury.[18]

There is a small amount of evidence for the export of Purbeck marble to Normandy.[19] A fine effigy of an abbot in Lisieux Cathedral, probably of c.1170-80, is apparently of Purbeck,[20] as are the remaining original columns in the cloister at Mont St. Michel (under construction c.1228),[21] a tapered coffin-lid in Bayeux Cathedral,[22] a slab reused as a step in Coutances Cathedral,[23] and an altar-slab at Pontorson.[24] In 1397 two marble slabs for the tombs of John de Stratton and his wife Isabel,[25] marked with his arms, were exported from London to Gascony.

The existence of Purbeck marblers from early in the 12th century is demonstrated by their products (below, pp.47-8, 50-1 ). The first records of their names, however, are in accounts and contracts for metropolitan works of the 1280s and 1290s, when Robert le Blund, William Canon, Ralph of Chichester, Robert of Corfe and John Doget figure prominently as suppliers of both plain and worked marble.[26] By now marblers were starting to establish themselves in London, but despite their frequent Corfe origins and continuing Corfe contacts these seem to have operated independently from the 1330s onwards (below, pp.45-6). The leading Corfe-based marbling families of the 14th and 15th centuries were the Canons, the Bonevilles and the Bourdes.[27] Virtually nothing is known of their craft organisation, the earliest

16   D.M. Owen (ed.), *The Making of Kings Lynn* (1984), 316; *Cal.Close R. 1369-74*, 413.
17   New Coll. Archive 7372. I am grateful to Nigel Ramsay for this reference.
18   As argued by S. Whittingham, *A Thirteenth-Century Portrait Gallery at Salisbury Cathedral* (1972), 7-8.
19   I am extremely grateful to Philip Lankester for contributing this paragraph.
20   A. Gardner, *English Medieval Sculpture* (rev. edn., 1951), 152 n.1, and P. Lankester's observation, 1977.
21   T. Haysom's observation.
22   Ibid.
23   Ibid.
24   Philip Lankester's observation, 1977.
25   *Cal.Close R. 1396-9*, 99.
26   J.H. Harvey, *English Mediaeval Architects: a Biographical Dictionary down to 1550* (2nd edn., 1984), 53, 85; R. Leach, *An Investigation into the Use of Purbeck Marble in Medieval England* (2nd edn., privately printed, 1978) [hereafter 'Leach'], 84-5; B. Botfield (ed. T.H. Turner), *Manners and Household Expenses* (Roxburghe Club, 1841), passim.
27   Harvey, op.cit. note 26, 44, 29-30; Drury, 97; Leach, 84-5.

evidence for the 'Company of Marblers and Stonecutters of Purbeck' being the confirmation of their ancient customs in 1651.[28] Despite the virtual cessation of quarrying, there are wills and inventories of Corfe 'marblers' through the 17th to early 19th centuries, and from 1836 minute-books again record meetings of the Company.[29]

### The Craft in London

Probably the biggest single stimulus for Purbeck marblers to settle in London was service in the royal works, especially at Henry III's Westminster Abbey begun in 1245.[30] The larger the project, the more necessary and cost-effective it was to employ marblers on site: in 1253 there were 49 of them at Westminster, cutting and polishing marble blocks and shafts.[31] But too exclusive an emphasis on Westminster may be misleading. Other major buildings (mostly now destroyed) were in progress, notably the choir of St. Paul's Cathedral; and the great works may have been of less long-term significance than the far bigger volume of modest ones. In an age of growing prosperity the taste for Purbeck marble spread to the gentry and burgess classes, and it was to these that marblers with permanent London workshops and showrooms had the most to offer. Massive column-drums and bases could best be shipped direct from Corfe, but semi-portable items such as fonts, altars, tombs and shafts (as at Orsett (Essex), p.53 below) could be made or finished in workshops accessible to ordinary customers whenever they visited London on business.

The marketing zone of the early 14th-century London workshops is defined by the distribution of their monumental brasses, which concentrate in Hertfordshire, Buckinghamshire, Bedfordshire, Cambridgeshire, Northamptonshire, Essex, East Anglia, Kent and the Thames valley.[32] Although documentary evidence is lacking,[33] small-scale items had probably been disseminated by means of a London 'retail trade' from a considerably earlier date. Especially revealing are the distributions of fonts (*c*.1170-1230) and minor architectural features in parish churches (*c*.1210-1330),[34] which suggest two marketing zones: one around Dorset, the other almost identical to the area served by the London brasses and presumably also emanating from London.

A critical change, however, must have occurred around 1280, when the occupational name suddenly became familiar in London with the advent of John the Marbler, Godfrey the Marbler and Walter the Marbler.[35] Henceforth the London marblers were not occasional visitors from Dorset, but established citizens. Walter

28   *V.C.H. Dorset*, ii, 336-7; Drury, 77. The correct date is 1651, not 1551 as usually stated (ex inf. T. Haysom).
29   T. Haysom, personal communication.
30   Cf. Leach, 8.
31   Colvin, op.cit. note 13, 236, 252, 262, 266, 274.
32   J. Blair, 'English Monumental Brasses before 1350: Types, Patterns and Workshops', in J. Coales (ed.), *The Earliest English Brasses:*

*Patronage, Style and Workshops 1270-1350* (1987), map p.135.
33   Except for the bafflingly early reference to *Girardus Marbrarius* in a deed of 1106 concerning land by St. Paul's churchyard: *Early Charters of St. Paul's*, ed. M. Gibbs (Camden 3rd ser. lviii, 1939), No. 198.
34   Maps in Leach, 81, 14.
35   Blair, art.cit. note 32, 173 n.9.

was active between the 1280s and 1320s, though it cannot be demonstrated that he sold marble works; his association in 1287 with the Corfe marbler John Doget suggests that he came from Purbeck.[36] A Corfe background is certain for the man who dominated the London trade between *c*.1305 and his death in 1331: Adam of Corfe, otherwise Adam Laurenz or Adam the Marbler.[37] He was related to the marbling family of Boneville, and the bequest in his will of two tenements in Corfe shows that he maintained local interests throughout his working life. From his shops on the north side of St. Paul's churchyard he supplied bulk orders of marble paving and components to wealthy clients, and it is a fair inference that large quantities of lesser monumental and decorative works are from the same source. In the absence of known competitors, it seems that Adam enjoyed a virtual monopoly of the main commercial outlet for marble artefacts.

After 1331 Adam's Corfe and London properties were divided between his heirs, and his business was probably sold or disbanded; thereafter the London trade seems to have functioned independently. Normally there were only one or two active businesses at any one time: John Ramsey III, sometimes called marbler, was operating from the 1340s until his death in 1371; Richard and Henry Lakenham occur from the mid 1350s until Henry's death in 1387; Stephen Lote was associated with marble works in the 1390s; and John Mapilton appears as a working marbler between the mid 1390s and 1407.[38] The probable descent of one of the main brass-making workshops from Henry Lakenham to William West (d. 1453) and John Essex (d. 1465) is described below (p.54). These leading marblers had their workshops within one small area, and may have maintained them through several generations. Like Adam of Corfe before them, Henry Lakenham, William West and John Essex all operated from St. Paul's churchyard, while a testator of 1495 asked for his 'epitaph' to be made by James Remus 'marbeler in Poule's churche yerde'.[39] As well as the advantages of a base in the heart of London between the two great cemeteries of St. Paul's and the Greyfriars, it may be that the marblers' heavy materials and equipment encouraged a continuity of premises.

In London as in Corfe, there is surprisingly little evidence for craft organisation during the Middle Ages. Ordinances are not recorded until 1486, when the 'good men of the Craft of Marblers' were allowed to elect two wardens with jurisdiction over 'any stone-werk of marbyll, laton werke or coper werk belongyng or perteynyng to the same crafte'.[40]

36 Harvey, op.cit. note 26, 47; Leach, 86; Blair, art.cit. note 32, 168 and n.52.

37 For what follows see Blair, art.cit. note 32, 168-9.

38 J. Blair, 'Henry Lakenham, Marbler of London, and a Tomb Contract of 1376', *Antiq.Jnl.* lx (1980), 66-74; Blair, art.cit. note 32, 167-8.

39 Blair, art.cit. note 38, 67; R. Emmerson,

'Monumental Brasses: London Design c. 1420-85', *J.B.A.A.* cxxxi (1978), 67; *Test. Ebor.* iv, 104. For the later London marblers see also Leach, 85-6; Harvey, op.cit. note 26, passim; M. Norris, *Monumental Brasses: the Craft* (1978), 81-2.

40 *Cal Letter-Book L*, 233.

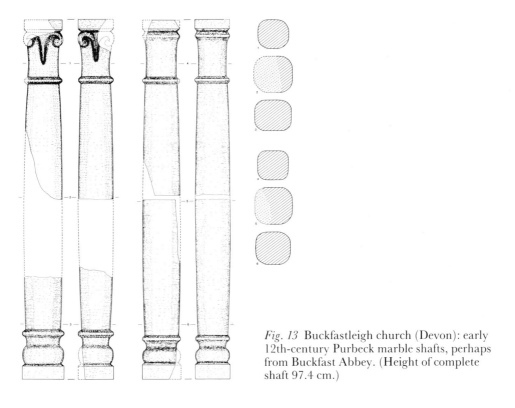

*Fig. 13* Buckfastleigh church (Devon): early 12th-century Purbeck marble shafts, perhaps from Buckfast Abbey. (Height of complete shaft 97.4 cm.)

## *Products: Architectural and Ornamental Components*

Purbeck marble was used by the Romans,[41] but at present there is no evidence for quarrying between the 4th century and *c*.1100. Systematic production of components may, however, have begun earlier in the 12th century than is usually thought. It is *prima facie* likely that the marblers' first run-of-the-mill works would have been rather crude, and would have had a restricted, south-western distribution. Evidence for such a category are the sets of dumpy, slightly bulbous monolithic Purbeck marble shafts, with volute capitals and undeveloped Romanesque bases, which support fonts at Buckfastleigh (Devon) (Fig. 13) and Kilpeck (Herefords.).[42] These can scarcely be later than *c*.1150 and may be some decades earlier; like a grave-slab at Oxford (below, pp.50-1), they suggest a first generation of products for which no systematic search has yet been made.

The industry rose to national importance between 1140 and 1170 thanks to the new fashion for dark marble shafting, which originated in the Tournai region but

41   See G.C. Dunning, 'The Purbeck Marble Industry in the Roman Period', *Archaeological News Letter*, March 1949; J.B. Calkin, 'Some Archaeological Discoveries in the Island of Purbeck: Part II', *Proc. Dorset Nat. Hist. & Arch. Soc.* lxxxi (1960), 121-2.

42   *R.C.H.M. Herefs.* i (1931), Pl. 38.

*Fig. 14* Canterbury Cathedral: Purbeck marble cloister shafts, *c.* 1150.

soon became distinctively English.[43] Like the fashion, the earliest shafts used in England were imported, and it took a generation for Purbeck marble to oust the fine black stone of Tournai. The key figure in this process was the great Henry of Blois (bishop of Winchester 1129-71), whose episcopal seat lay not far from the Purbeck quarries. Henry's first dark-marble works at Wolvesey Palace used Tournai, but alterations to the hall between 1141 and 1154 employed wall-shafts, capitals and bases of Purbeck marble; he may also have been responsible for elaborate marble colonnettes of the 1140s, now lost, at Hyde Abbey.[44] A splendid Purbeck capital of *c.* 1150 with naturalistic human heads amid foliage, from the abbey built at Faversham by Henry's brother King Stephen, belongs to the same artistic milieu.[45] The taste for complex small-scale Tournai shafting, in contexts such as font-bases

43   Tournai marble, already with a long tradition of architectural use, was employed at Tournai Cathedral in the 1130s to produce the characteristic contrast of dark shafts against white masonry, which was translated into a Gothic form at Valenciennes in 1171, four years before Canterbury. See J. Bony, 'French Influences on the Origins of English Gothic Architecture', *Jnl. of Warburg and Courtauld Insts.* xii (1949), 8-9; idem, *French Gothic Architecture of the*

*Twelfth and Thirteenth Centuries* (1983), 159.

44   M. Biddle in *Antiq.Jnl.* xlv (1965), 260; G. Zarnecki, 'Henry of Blois as a Patron of Sculpture', in S. Macready and F.H. Thompson (eds.), *Art and Patronage in the English Romanesque* (1986), 168.

45   *English Romanesque Art, 1066-1200* (Catalogue of Exhibition at Hayward Gallery, London, 1984), No. 146.

and cloister arcades, fostered an idiom well-suited to development on a larger scale and in Purbeck marble.[46]

Prior Wibert's cloister at Canterbury includes several Purbeck shafts (Fig. 14), but the earliest known major church piers in Purbeck marble are in the rotunda of the Temple Church, London (complete by 1161) and at Henry of Blois's hospital of St. Cross, Winchester (*c*.1160-70).[47] Henry's influence may also explain the use by his nephew Hugh du Puiset of monolithic Purbeck marble columns in the Galilee Chapel of Durham Cathedral, built *c*.1175.[48] Just as Purbeck had succeeded Tournai marble, so in the North-East the local Frosterley marble ousted Purbeck for work such as Puiset's slightly later hall at Bishop Auckland, or the Nine Altars chapel at Durham.[49] But at a national level the future lay with Purbeck: it was used for major piers in the Trinity Chapel of Canterbury Cathedral in 1182, and thenceforth until the Black Death almost every English church of importance included Purbeck marble shafts, bases or string-courses. The total output must have been enormous.

Between the late 13th and late 14th centuries payments to the marblers for pre-fabricated column-drums, shafts, capitals and bases are almost standard items in building accounts; such pre-fabrication is often betrayed by the awkwardness with which Purbeck components are fitted into their housings, a feature already apparent in the early 13th-century work at Chichester.[50] Thus in 1287 John Doget and Ralph of Chichester undertook to supply marble columns, capitals, bases and cornice mouldings for Vale Royal Abbey, worked to a pattern (*exemplar*) sent by the master-mason, which were to go by sea to Frodsham.[51] The Canons of Corfe sold columns, capitals and bases for Charing Cross in 1292 and for Exeter Cathedral in 1309-10 and 1332-3.[52] The carriage (from Yarmouth) and the setting and polishing of standard Purbeck shafts and accessories for the cloisters of Norwich Cathedral Priory is documented during the 1330s and 1340s.[53] After 1350 the new architectural styles gave much less scope for Purbeck piers and shafting; but the nave of Westminster Abbey (begun in 1375 in a continuation of of Henry III's style) provided a fresh impetus, and accounts between 1388 and 1413 contain the usual payments for prefabricated elements.[54]

46  As suggested by R. Halsey, 'The Galilee Chapel', in *Medieval Art and Architecture at Durham Cathedral* (B.A.A. Conference Trans. for 1977, 1980), 67; cf. Zarnecki, art.cit. note 44.

47  New dating of Temple Church, C. Wilson, personal communication. The piers and decorative details have now been renewed, but records of the 19th-century restorations in the Inner and Middle Temple libraries prove conclusively that they were originally of Purbeck marble (C.M. Gardam, personal communication). For St. Cross see Halsey, art.cit. note 46, 67.

48  Halsey, art.cit. note 46, 67-8.

49  Ibid. 68.

50  Leach, 7 (cf. Drury, 78).

51  Harvey, op.cit. note 26, 85.

52  Botfield, op.cit. note 26, passim; Drury, 97; A.M. Erskine, *The Accounts of the Fabric of Exeter Cathedral, 1279-1353* (Devon & Cornwall Rec. Soc. n.s. xxiv, xxvi, 1981, 1983), passim, esp. pt. 2, xv, xxxi-ii.

53  *The Early Communar and Pittancer Rolls of Norwich Cathedral Priory*, eds. E.C. Fernie and A.B. Whittingham (Norfolk Rec.Soc. xli, 1972), 38. See Leach, 7-8, for other documented cases of prefabricated components.

54  Drury, 97.

Smaller-scale works were equally standardised. Perhaps the commonest are the fonts produced between the late 12th and mid 13th centuries: square or octagonal, on shafted bases, and usually with shallow blind arcading around the bowls.[55] Adaptable, and therefore suited to the mass market, were small shafts with caps and bases which could be incorporated into tombs, sedilia, screens or even secular structures. Other once-common ecclesiastical items were piscinae, altars (one of which was made at Purbeck for the London Carmelites in 1273-4)[56] and lecterns.[57] Of domestic furnishings, probably common in great households, hardly anything is known. However, in 1308 Adam of Corfe supplied a marble slab for the king's high table at Westminster,[58] and a shafted marble leg, probably from this table, was found under the steps of Westminster Hall in 1960.[59] In the 15th and 16th centuries the trade in fireplaces preserved elements of what were, except in a funerary context, a dying fashion and a dying craft.

The marblers also produced huge numbers of mortars, fragments of which are found on domestic sites all over England; for example, four of the seven mortar fragments from Northolt manor-house (Middlesex) in contexts spanning c.1250-1350 are of Purbeck marble. Owing to the hardness of the material, and its tendency to crack along the bedding-plane, Purbeck mortars are more straight-sided and regular than ordinary limestone ones, and have solid rather than pierced handles. A few mortars have a sculptural quality which suggests production by marblers trained in decorative and monumental works.[60]

### Products: Tombs and Brasses

Effigies, tomb-chests, slabs and brasses were by far the largest and most successful class of Purbeck marble artefacts produced for the mass market. 'Enterd he was in a toumbe of stone/ And a marble-thrugh [i.e. slab] laid him opon' runs a late 14th-century verse from northern England:[61] whatever material was used for the rest of the tomb, to lie under a marble slab was prestigious from the 12th century to the 16th and even later. In 1307 a plain Purbeck tomb (a 'toumbe de marbre ben polye' as Peter Langtoft puts it)[62] was good enough for the king himself. This branch of the marblers' trade was undamaged by changes in fashion, and as their output of large-scale works declined the marblers concentrated more and more on tombs and, by extension, brasses.

Perhaps the earliest known monument in Purbeck marble is a rather crude slab from St. Frideswide's Priory, Oxford, showing a human head surmounting stylised crosses formed by groups of concentric arcs;[63] this kind of decoration is usually

55   Drury, 77; Leach, 4-5, 69-83.
56   Hutchins, op.cit. note 5, 466.
57   Drury, 81-2.
58   Blair, art.cit. note 32, 168.
59   John Steane, personal communication.
60   This paragraph is based on G.C. Dunning, 'Stone Mortars', *Med.Arch.* v (1961), 279-84.

61   *Northern Homilies: Altenglische Legenden*, ed. C. Horstmann (Heilbron, 1881).
62   *The Chronicle of Pierre de Langtoft*, ed. T. Wright, ii (Rolls Ser. 47b, 1868), 382.
63   J. Blair, 'An Early 12th-Century Purbeck Marble Graveslab from St. Frideswide's Priory', *Oxoniensia*, liii (1988), 266-8.

*Fig. 15* Rochester Cathedral: episcopal effigy (?Bishop de St.-Martin, d.1274) in Purbeck marble: detail of canopy.

assigned to the late 11th century,[64] and a date in the first half of the 12th century seems likely. Excepting this somewhat exotic and enigmatic item, the other early figural slabs were made after *c.*1160 and have a limited, south-western distribution. The ecclesiastical effigies at Exeter, Tolpuddle, Sherborne, Old Sarum and Abbotsbury[65] show the distinctive flatness, imposed by the limitations of the marble beds, which to a lesser extent characterises later Purbeck sculpture. A simple coped and coffin-shaped tomb in Winchester Cathedral, traditionally King William II's, is more convincingly (and appropriately) ascribed to that great patron of the infant Purbeck marble industry, Bishop Henry of Blois (d. 1171).[66]

More sophisticated are the gabled tombs with busts in quatrefoils for Hubert Walter (d. 1205) at Canterbury and Gilbert de Glanville (d. 1214) at Rochester, perhaps inspired by metalwork,[67] and the great series of full-scale Purbeck marble effigies of the 13th century. If episcopal (and presumably abbatial) patrons were the mainstay of the workshops during *c.*1210-50, orders from knightly clients of

64  Cf. L.A.S. Butler, 'Minor Medieval Monumental Sculpture in the East Midlands', *Arch.Jnl.* cxxi (1964), 119-21 and Fig. 2A.

65  Drury, 77-8, Pls. IX-XII; H. de S. Shortt, 'The Three Bishops' Tombs moved to Salisbury Cathedral from Old Sarum', *Wilts. Arch. Mag.* lvii (1958-60), 217-19.

66  Zarnecki, art.cit. note 44, 168-9 and n.58.

67  L. Stone, *Sculpture in Britain: the Middle Ages* (1955), 104-5, 116; P. Tudor-Craig in *Medieval Art and Architecture at Canterbury* B.A.A. Conference Transactions for 1979, 1982), 72-80.

increasing wealth and social pretensions rose sharply from the 1230s onwards.[68] As with the later brasses, high production levels resulted in an output of episcopal and knightly effigies which are sumptuous, proficient but rather monotonous. The dominant series are generally ascribed to London workshops, but their distribution[69] does not in fact show so clear a grouping around London as fonts and, later, brasses. In the absence of evidence for marblers' workshops in London before the 1280s, the origin of the Purbeck marble effigies must remain an open question: there is strong evidence that at least one (now lost), sent to Tarrant Monkton Priory in 1252-3, was carved in Dorset,[70] and the two military effigies at Wareham must surely have been made locally.[71]

The output of Purbeck marble effigies declined sharply after *c.*1280, their market being captured by cheaper works in freestone and wood which could be gessoed and painted. But the contemporary taste for rich, intricate detail and contrasting materials, seen in such top-quality works as Edward II's tomb, the Lady Chapel at Ely and the cloister of St. Paul's, made Purbeck components more popular than ever. The late 13th-century fashion for rehousing the relics of local saints brought commissions for sumptuous arcaded shrine-bases, such as those which survive at St. Albans, Stanton Harcourt (from Bicester Priory) and Oxford.[72] Simple, standardised tomb-slabs and coffin-lids, mostly carved with crosses in low relief, satisfied a mass market throughout the 13th and 14th centuries and are numerous in southern and eastern England.[73] If unpretentious, they show a proficiency and consistency seldom attained by freestone cross-slabs. The few incised slabs in Purbeck marble are inferior both to their French counterparts and to English brasses, though clearly related to the latter and competent by the standards of incised slabs in England.

Both the standardisation of the cross motif and the use of incised lines point the way to the marblers' most successful mass-produced product: the monumental brass. Introduced in the 1270s and 1280s as monuments for the higher clergy, brasses rapidly acquired an astonishing popularity: there is evidence for over 800 (doubtless only a fraction of the total made) from the period 1270-1350.[74] The figure-brasses of the episcopal and knightly classes were outnumbered by inexpensive busts, crosses and plain inscriptions (in separately-inlaid brass letters) bought by parish clergy, manorial gentry and prosperous freeholding families. Such was the degree of standardisation that prefabricated brass components could be arranged

68    For Purbeck marble effigies see E.S. Prior and A. Gardner, *An Account of Medieval Figure Sculpture in England* (1912), 568-602; Stone, op.cit. note 67, 116-17; Leach, 25-33. The standard work on military effigies is now H.A. Tummers, *Early Secular Effigies in England: the Thirteenth Century* (Leiden, 1980).

69    Map in Leach, 28.

70    P.J. Lankester, 'A Military Effigy in Dorchester Abbey, Oxon.', *Oxoniensia*, lii (1987),

164 and n.144.

71    Philip Lankester's observation.

72    Stone, op.cit. note 67, 134; Drury, 82-3; Leach, 46-8; N. Coldstream, 'English Decorated Shrine-Bases', *J.B.A.A.* cxxix (1976), 15-34.

73    Drury, 85-6; Leach, 34-40; Butler, art.cit. note 64, 142-6.

74    For statements in this paragraph see Blair, art.cit. note 32, esp.166-9.

on the surface of the slab in various permutations to suit various pockets. From the uniformity of nearly all the early 14th-century London brasses it is evident that they emanated from one large workshop. The production of London-made brasses by marblers is consistent and explicit during *c*.1350-1550, and is implied for the earlier period by the almost invariable use of Purbeck marble slabs, and by the incorporation of fragments of brass-indents into the plinth of Edward I's tomb and into early 14th-century sedilia at Orsett (Essex), both of which are made of Purbeck marble.[75] The most likely candidate for master of this workshop must therefore be the dominant London marbler Adam of Corfe (above, p.46).

This mass-production suited both the London marblers and their ordinary customers; but an important patron with special needs and contacts might obtain his brass in a different fashion. The option of buying a Purbeck slab direct from the quarry, and then having it embellished by a brass-maker in London or the provinces, was always open. The slabs for the brasses to Dean Andrew de Kilkenny (d. 1302) and Bishop William Bitton (d. 1307) in Exeter Cathedral were both bought separately, the former being carried to Exeter by cart at a cost of 10*s*.[76] Especially revealing is a letter written *c*.1400 by a monk of Westminster to an unnamed prelate, who seems to have obtained his slab cheaply by taking advantage of the regular shipments of marble for the new nave of Westminster Abbey:

As for the other business which you mentioned to me when we last spoke, reverend father, I have made the greatest possible efforts on this account, which indeed I owe you. For you will shortly be the owner of a marble slab according to the measurement which you gave me, nine feet long, unblemished, polished and finely squared up at the edges. But since I could not find a slab like this in the London area at what seemed to me a fair and moderate price, I have caused such a stone to be prepared in the place where the marble for our church is cut, that is in the marble-quarry next to Corfe Castle, at a better and fairer enough price estimated for it. This slab should be brought to Westminster, God willing, around the feast of the Purification of St. Mary, where the craftsman should receive 5 marks 40*d*. on that feast by the agreement made between us. If you would like the blank slab sent to your part of the country, I shall certainly do this to the best of my ability so long as you send me appropriate expenses. But if you would like your image placed (*exsculpi*) on the slab, and verse or prose written around the edge or in the middle, please send me written instructions and I shall immediately carry out everything you wish.[77]

Brasses made in London between the mid 14th and mid 16th centuries fall into rigidly formulaic pattern-series, which diversify with time but still betoken a remarkable continuity in workshop control.[78] The earlier products of the prolific

75 J. Blair, 'Orsett, Essex: a New Clue to the Early London Brass Workshops?', *Monumental Brass Soc. Bulletin*, 23 (Feb. 1980), 15.

76 Coales, op.cit. note 32, 52-3, 162.

77 J. Blair, 'A Bishop Orders his Brass: Buying a Slab from the Purbeck Quarries, *c*.1400', *Trans. Monumental Brass Soc.* xiv.3 (1988),

243-6.

78 J.P.C. Kent, 'Monumental Brasses – a New Classification of Military Effigies c.1360-c.1485', *J.B.A.A.* 3rd ser. xii (1949), 70-97; Emmerson, art.cit. note 39; M. Norris, *Monumental Brasses: the Memorials* (1977), 51-99.

'series B' can probably be associated with the marbler Henry Lakenham, who contracted in 1376 to supply a freestone effigy on a plain Purbeck tomb with brass inlays, resembling surviving tombs with 'series B' brasses.[79] Lakenham's apprentice was William West, a leading London marbler from the early 15th century until his death in 1453. At Sudborough (Northants.) is a 'series B' brass of *c.*1440 commemorating West's parents, with an unusual extra inscription for the children including *Willelmus West marbler*'; it is a reasonable inference that this was made in his own workshop.[80] Control of the 'B' workshop may have passed from West to the marbler John Essex, whose death in 1465 heralds the breakdown of the pattern-series into variant styles.[81] The purchase of a brass from an unnamed marbler in 1479, the jurisdiction over marble, latten and copper works given to the London Marblers' Gild in 1486 (above, p.46), the bequest of 'marbylle stonys and laten werke' by the marbler John Lorimer in 1499, and a reference to 'marbelors plate' in a customs book of 1507 are all testimony to the grip which London marblers continued to hold on the monumental brass trade.[82]

Monumental work without brass inlays, notably panelled tomb-chests, still came direct from the quarry workshops. Even when a tomb was made wholly of Purbeck marble, the brass-inlaid top might be bought in London but the carved sides at Corfe. The contracts of 1454 for Richard Beauchamp's tomb at Warwick show that John Bourde of Corfe made the elaborate canopied chest, whereas John Essex of St. Paul's churchyard made the top slab with its 'series B' brass inscription.[83] Standard Corfe products in the 15th and 16th centuries were tomb-chest panels bearing shields framed in cusped quatrefoils and lozenges, two of which, presumably wasters, remain built into cottages in West Street.[84] Accounts of 1519-22 for a tomb in Bisham Abbey (Berks.) include payments of £8 'to the marbelers of Corff for a tombe of marble' and £3 6s. 8d. 'to a marbler in Powls church yerd for the picturs writyng and armys gilt ... and to sett them in the marble'.[85]

Some Purbeck marble tombs of the normal late medieval types were, however, made in London, notably the canopied wall-tombs with mural brasses which became increasingly popular in the 16th century and which often served as Easter Sepulchres. Henry Tooley's at Ipswich was made in 1567-9 by 'Allen Gamon of London', almost certainly the 'Aleyne Gaulyn' who with Roger Sylvester bought 'seven score poundes of olde and broken lattyn' from St. Faith's London in 1552.[86] These conservative works with their Gothic detail continued to be made well into Elizabeth's reign (Fig. 16); they show that the idioms and modes of production which were so long established in Corfe and London survived the Reformation by a generation or so.

79  Blair, art.cit. note 38.
80  Emmerson, art.cit. note 39, 52-8, 66-7.
81  Ibid. 66-8.
82  Ibid., 65-6; Norris, op.cit. note 39, 89.
83  Emmerson, art.cit. note 39, 67. For the various sets of extracts from the Beauchamp tomb contracts, which are now lost, see Stone,

op.cit. note 67, 266, n.43.
84  Drury, Pl. VII.
85  N.L. Ramsay, 'Makers of Sixteenth-Century Church Monuments', *Monumental Brass Soc. Bull.* 27 (June 1981), 9-10.
86  Ibid.

*Purbeck Marble*                                           55

*Fig. 16* A 'Gothic survival' Purbeck monument: the tomb of Anthony Forster (*c.* 1572) at Cumnor (Berks.).

## *Further Reading*

Only three works are devoted mainly to Purbeck marble: C.H. Vellacott, 'Quarrying', *V.C.H. Dorset*, ii (1908), 331-44; G. Dru Drury, 'The Use of Purbeck Marble in Medieval Times', *Proc.Dorset Natural Hist. & Arch.Soc.* lxx (1948), 74-98; R. Leach, *An Investigation into the Use of Purbeck Marble in Medieval England* (2nd edn., privately printed, 1978). On petrology, see S. Badham, 'An Interim Study of the Stones used for the Slabs of English Monumental Brasses', *Trans.Monumental Brass Soc.* xiii (1985), 475-83; W.J. Arkell et al., *Country around Weymouth, Swanage, Corfe and Lulworth* (British Regional Geology Series, H.M.S.O., 1947); A. Clifton-Taylor, *The Pattern of English Building* (2nd edn., 1972), ch. vii. Purbeck marble architectural components are discussed in numerous works on Gothic architecture and on individual buildings, but there has so far been no comprehensive analysis of forms and mouldings. Many marblers are listed in J. Harvey, *English Mediaeval Architects: a Biographical Dictionary down to 1550* (2nd edn., 1984), and in the above works of Drury and Leach. For effigies and tombs, see E.S. Prior and A. Gardner, *An Account of Medieval Figure-Sculpture in England* (1912), 568-602; H.A. Tummers, *Early Secular Effigies in England: the Thirteenth Century* (Leiden, 1980). For the making of monumental brasses by marblers, see M. Norris, *Monumental Brasses: the Craft* and *Monumental Brasses: the Memorials* (1977 and 1978); essays by P. Binski, J. Blair and N. Rogers in J. Coales (ed.), *The Earliest English Brasses: Patronage, Style and Workshops 1270-1350* (1987); R. Emmerson, 'Monumental Brasses: London Design c.1420-85', *J.B.A.A.*, cxxxi (1978); J. Blair, 'Henry Lakenham, Marbler of London, and a Tomb Contract of 1376', *Antiq.Jnl.* lx (1980).

# 4

## *Tin, Lead and Pewter*

### RONALD F. HOMER

Only three non-ferrous metals were mined commercially in medieval Britain: tin, lead and silver. Tin was fundamental to the country's economy, since between *c*.300 and 1300 England was the only significant European producer of this metal. Even much later it was an important export, and an unknown poet wrote in 1436:

> For Spayne and Flaundres is as yche othere brothere,
> And nethere may well lyve wythowghten othere.
> They may not lyven to mayntene there degrees,
> Wythoughten oure Englysse commodytees,
> Wolle and tynne....[1]

By contrast much lead was mined for the purpose of recovering the silver which occurs in argentiferous lead ores, for desilvered 'sterile' lead was produced in abundance throughout Europe and the market appears frequently to have been surfeited. The Crown's interest in tin for its own sake, and in lead for its silver content, led to early grants of extensive rights and privileges to the miners of both metals. Both King John's charter to the tinners of Devon and Cornwall in 1201 and that of Henry III to the lead miners of Alston Moor (Cumb.) in 1235 confirmed longstanding rights.[2]

Alloyed with copper, tin formed bronze, the only readily worked and readily available metal which was both resistant to corrosion and of reasonable strength and durability. Tin was used for the tinning of culinary and decorative wares made from copper alloys and iron, and alloyed with small amounts of lead or copper (or both of these) it provided the raw material for England's growing pewter industry. Much lead was used in building construction and for large domestic and industrial vats.

1   *The Libelle of Englyshe Polycye ...*, ed. George F. Warner (1926), lines 86-90.
2   Charter of King John, *Cal. Charter Rolls, 1225-57*, 380 (the document is an *inspeximus* of the 1201 charter). Charter of Henry III, *Cal. Patent Rolls, 1232-47*, 65, 132, 174.

Alloyed with tin it formed solder, and with copper it formed a range of bronze-like alloys used for cheap domestic utensils. The unsatisfactory quality of some of these was complained of in 1316, 'for the moment they are put upon the fire and exposed to great heat, they come to nothing and melt'.[3] From the mid 14th century the working of tin (as pewter) and of lead was regulated by 'crafts' which laid down rules for their members and for the protection of the consumer from poor workmanship and excessive prices.

The archaeological remains of medieval mining and working of tin and lead are unimpressive, and surviving artefacts are unrepresentative of much that was made.[4] Considerable reliance has therefore to be placed on documentary evidence in reconstructing these industries.

## Tin Mining and Trade[5]

Tin mining in Devon and Cornwall dates from *c.* 500 BC and was important in Roman times, particularly after the Spanish mines failed in the 3rd century AD. Archaeological evidence (mainly coin finds) indicates working in the 9th and 10th centuries and English tin was an article of commerce in Europe at this time.[6] Curiously, tin mines are not mentioned in the Domesday survey. From the 12th century all the tin produced in Devon and Cornwall (Cornwall being the dominant producer after *c.* 1220[7]) was subject to a tax, the coinage, for the levying of which it had to be brought at specified times to one of the coinage towns. These were Chagford, Ashburton, Tavistock and (from 1328) Plympton in Devon, and Lostwithiel, Bodmin, Liskeard, Truro and Helston in Cornwall. Coinage and coinage farm returns enable tin production to be calculated for much of the period after 1156 (Table I). The retail price of tin in Cornwall in the early 14th century was 1*d.*-1½*d.* per pound; it doubled after the Black Death, but steadied at 1½*d.*-2*d.* between about 1400 and 1460.[8] Hence the tin produced in 1400 was worth *c.* £10,000 to the ultimate local vendors.

The miners of tin, and equally of lead, could prospect for ore anywhere except in gardens, orchards, churchyards and on the highway. They could cut wood, dig peat, divert watercourses and make roads; they were subject to the jurisdiction of their own courts and were exempt from certain taxes.[9] This was not without repercussions. In 1314 Devon miners were said to be laying waste over 300 acres a

---

3   Riley, *Memorials*, 118. cf. p.82 below.
4   T.A.P. Greeves, 'The Archaeological Potential of the Devon Tin Industry', and I.S.W. Blanchard, 'Lead Mining and Smelting', in D.W. Crossley (ed.), *Medieval Industry* (C.B.A. Research Rep. xl, 1981).
5   See particularly J. Hatcher, *English Tin Production and Trade* (1973), for a comprehensive study. Much of the data in this section is taken from this source. Hereafter cited as 'Hatcher,

*Tin.*'
6   Ibid. 16-17. For an important recent discussion of Anglo-Saxon tin production in the south-west see J.R. Maddicott, 'Trade, Industry and the Wealth of King Alfred', *Past and Present*, cxxiii (May 1989), 3-51.
7   H.P.R. Finberg, *Tavistock Abbey* (1955), 173.
8   Hatcher, *Tin*, 90-1.
9   Finberg, op. cit. note 7, 169-70; Salzman, *Industries*, 46-9.

*Fig. 17* A one-pound lead weight cast with the arms of England ancient, within a border of pellets. Height 70 mm. (*Museum of London*)

*Fig. 18* The lead coffin of Anne Mowbray, child widow of Richard, duke of York, who died in 1481 aged eight. (*Museum of London*)

year,[10] and in Cornwall in 1361 John de Treeures complained to the Black Prince that:

whereas for a long time tinners have dug and gathered tin in the waste moor of himself and his ancestors ... and he and his ancestors ... have received from them as toll a third of the tin so dug ... now of late fully sixty tinners have entered on his demesne and soil, which bears wheat, barley, oats, hay and peas, and is as good and fair as any soil in Cornwall, and have led streams of water ... over part of his said demesne and soil, so that by reason of the great current of water they have obtained and the steep slope of the land there, all the land where they come will go back to open moor, and nothing will remain of all that good land except great stones and gravel...[11]

The secondary alluvial deposits of oxide ore, *cassiterite*, worked in the medieval period, the so-called 'stream works', required only crushing and washing before

10   Finberg, op. cit. note 7, 176.

11   *Register of Edward the Black Prince*, pt.2, *Duchy of Cornwall, 1351-65* (1932), 178.

## TABLE I

*Annual tin production in typical years between 1156 and 1487*[1]

| Years (see notes) | Production | Years (see notes) | Production |
|---|---|---|---|
| 1156-60[2] | 100-130 | 1366 | 508 |
| 1163-8 | 140-170 | 1379 | 919 |
| 1170-89 | 480-580 | 1385 | 1084 |
| 1198 | 869 | 1395 | 1341 |
| 1209 | 612 | 1407 | 1418 |
| 1214 | 1199 | 1418 | 1117 |
| 1303[3] | 874 | 1425 | 1263 |
| 1309[4] | 817 | 1435 | 926 |
| 1316 | 740 | 1445 | 852 |
| 1324 | 991 | 1455 | 823 |
| 1332 | 1644 | 1465 | 864 |
| 1342 | 1159 | 1477 | 1034 |
| 1351 | 237 | 1487 | 1103 |

1 Figures from Hatcher, *English Tin Production*, Appendix A. Quantities are in thousandweights of 1000 lbs. In Devon the thousandweight was of 1200 lbs.; in Cornwall 1000 lbs.
2 Figures for 1156-89 are estimates from the value of the farm.
3 Figures for 1243-1300 are available for Devon only.
4 Figures for 1309-1366 are those giving Cornish production only which is probably between 80 and 90% of the combined Devon/Cornwall production.

being smelted with peat or charcoal; in early medieval times, smelting was in simple open fires.[12] Although exhaustion of these deposits eventually necessitated deep open-cast and shaft mining of the main lodes, this does not appear to have been significant before about 1500. Until the late 12th century a second, refining, smelting of the metal was customary, but it became unnecessary as primary smelting improved, probably as a result of the introduction of furnaces with a forced draught.[13] The metal was cast into blocks in stone moulds and, after coinage, was stamped to show that duty had been paid.[14] Only then could it be sold freely.

Many miners were employed by the owners of large mines, and Abraham the Tinner in 1337 claimed to employ the exceptional number of 300 men in seven separate works.[15] Others worked as individuals, but their fortunes were mixed. No doubt for many of them tin mining was only a secondary occupation, but nevertheless many found difficulty in subsisting from one coinage to the next and were forced to pledge their tin in advance to speculators and merchants, some of

12   Finberg, op. cit. note 7, 169; Forbes, 'Metal-lurgy', in Singer, *Hist. of Technology*, ii, 47.
13   Greeves, op. cit. note 4, 87.
14   Ibid. 90.
15   Hatcher, *Tin*, 62.

*Fig. 19* The cast-decorated lead font at Frampton-on-Severn (Glos.), *c.* 1130-40. One of 30 surviving English decorated medieval lead fonts, of which 16 date from before 1200.

whom captured significant shares of the market. Tin presented for coinage varied from quantities exceeding 100 thousandweights by the great landowners and merchants, to only a few hundred pounds from some individual miners. It has been calculated that there were perhaps 2,000 Cornish miners in 1300 and 5,000 by 1400,[16] and that a miner presenting a thousandweight a year earned 3*d.* a day in 1330.[17]

In the 12th century tin was exported in quantity directly from Devon and Cornwall to France and Flanders and thence to other destinations in Europe and beyond. In 1195, 254 thousandweights were shipped to the king in La Rochelle.[18] Two Bayonne merchants bought no less than 240 thousandweights in 1198 and merchants from Brabant regularly visited Devon and Cornwall in the 12th and 13th centuries. The Hanseatic merchants had installed an agent in Falmouth in 1265, but indigenous production in Saxony and Bohemia led to a waning of their interest by the early 14th century. From about 1330 exports were dominated by the Italians; a

16 Ibid. 67.
17 L.F. Salzman, 'Mines and Stannaries', in J.F. Willard et al. (ed.), *The English Government at Work 1327-36*, iii (1950), 93.
18 Finberg, *Tavistock Abbey*, 172.

Bardi merchant exported tin worth £520 in 1339 and £724 in 1340. Forty years later the focus of the export trade had shifted to Southampton and to a lesser extent to London; there was significant trade with the Low Countries and elsewhere, and some of this was in English hands. Transport of the metal from the coinage towns to London and other destinations in Britain was frequently by sea, Southampton being a staging point whence some was diverted for export and some continued overland to London.[19]

## Lead Mining

The main centres of lead mining, which waxed and waned in their relative importance, included Yorkshire, Durham, the Peak District of Derbyshire, Flintshire, the Mendips and South Devon.[20] In the 1170s the Scots' incursions disrupted production in the north of England, and this, at a time of increasing demand for architectural lead, necessitated the exploitation elsewhere in England of ores of low or negligible silver content. Despite the ready accessibility of such deposits on or near the surface, the economics of working them were highly uncertain. In many mines the isolation of at least some silver was essential for survival. The Birland mine in Devon had total expenses between 1325 and 1334 of £870 against an income of £591 for silver and only £147 for lead.[21] The operation of the mine was subsidised by loans from the king and elsewhere. What this meant at the individual mine is strikingly illustrated by the meagre inventories of the Beer Alston mine for 1325 and 1338. These include 2 worn-out anvils, a worn-out cart, worn-out bellows, 13 worn-out sacks for ore, a worn-out boat and oars, a broken saw, a broken balance and a pack horse 'of practically no value'.[22] In 1335 the Beer Alston staff comprised an overseer at 14*d.* a week, a boler at 15*d.* with two assistants at 8*d.*, a furnaceman at 12*d.* with blowers at 2*d.* a day, a keeper of the woods and an overseer of the woodcutters, a smith at 10*d.* a week with an assistant at 1½*d.* a day and a chandler at 8*d.* In addition there were two silver refiners at 18*d.* a week with assistants at 8*d.*[23] The presence of a chandler, and the record in the inventory of the use of half-a-ton of candles a year, indicates that shaft mining was undertaken – an enterprise justified only for the extraction of silver-rich ores. The rudimentary technology available for the draining of mines, limited to bailing until the late 13th century and thereafter by means of adits (drainage tunnels) where the lie of the land permitted, was a serious constraint on anything other than open-cast mining. Where the silver content did not justify its extraction, economic viability depended on the extent and accessibility of the ore so as to allow easy migration from site to site as

19　Hatcher, *Tin*. Chapters i, iv and vi and Appendix B discuss both the internal and external medieval tin trade in considerable detail.

20　I.S.W. Blanchard, 'Lead Mining and Smelting', in Crossley (ed.), *Medieval Industry*, gives a detailed survey of the various lead fields and techniques.

21　Salzman, art. cit. note 17, 80.

22　Ibid. 70-71, for a full transcript of the inventories.

23　Ibid. 71.

deposits became depleted, and on the local availability of adequate timber as fuel.

Miners might work on their own account, giving a proportion of the ore to the owner of the mineral rights, or as employees paid on a piece-work basis. At the Beer Alston mine in 1298, miners received 5s. for a 'load' of ore amounting to nine 'dishes' of some 60 lbs. per dish. Those engaged in 'dead work', i.e. those prospecting in as yet unproductive workings, received wages, which in 1320-30 amounted to only 1d.-1½d. a day.[24]

The modern commentator will be struck by the small scale of medieval mining operations. The total production of the Derbyshire lead field in 1300 amounted to some 391 'fothers', about 370 tonnes.[25] The total English and Welsh output, from the efforts of thousands of miners, was 385 tonnes in 1400, 400 tonnes in 1450 and 625 tonnes in 1500.[26] A single miner might win no more than 30-40 lbs. of crushed and washed ore a day. As lead sold at the mine for about ⅓d. per lb. in 1330 and ½d. in 1430-1500,[27] the economic value of this geographically scattered industry was small indeed.

Smelting of the prevalent 'black ore', *galena* (lead sulphide), does not require a reduction with charcoal, and the metal results from a two-stage roasting of the ore. Until the end of the 13th century, and in places until much later, this was done in a simple 'bole' comprising a hearth surrounded by a stone wall with a wind tunnel in the side facing the prevailing wind.[28] On a foundation of logs were piled layers of brushwood and crushed ore and the bole was fired when the wind was favourable. Imperfectly controlled roasting resulted in much lead remaining in the slag as oxide and sulphate. This mattered little while ore and fuel were plentiful, but by the 1280s shortages of fuel became a problem. A partial answer was the 'turnbole', in which the hearth was mounted on a massive wooden platform which could be rotated to take advantage of the wind from any direction, thus eliminating firings which had to be aborted due to an unexpected wind change and the stock-piling of ore while a favourable wind was awaited.[29] Its advantages were more apparent in the sometimes urgent smelting of argentiferous ores, than in the more leisurely production of lead for its own sake.

Shrinking fuel resources and depletion of readily accessible ores eventually led to the need to recover residual lead from bole slag, the so-called 'blackwork'. From the 14th century this was reprocessed by reduction with charcoal in a 'blackwork oven', which was essentially a circular, stone-built blast furnace fed with air from bellows operated by 'blowers' or by water power.[30] Such charcoal reduction of lead ores was not new; the less common 'white ore', lead carbonate, was necessarily smelted in this way. For the isolation of silver from 'fertile' (argentiferous) lead, a process

24  Salzman, *Industries*, 51-2.
25  I.S.W. Blanchard, 'Derbyshire Lead Production', *Derbs. Arch. Jnl.* xci (1971), 119-40, 125.
26  I.S.W. Blanchard, 'Labour Productivity...', *Econ. Hist. Rev.* 2nd ser. xxxi (1978), 1-24, 24.
27  Salzman, op. cit. note 17, 78-9, and Blanchard,

'Labour Productivity...', 19, respectively.
28  Blanchard, 'Lead Mining and Smelting', 72 and Fig. 73.
29  Ibid. 77.
30  Ibid. 78 and Fig. 75.

unchanged from ancient times, fertile lead was subjected to cupellation in a current of air which oxidised it to litharge, leaving a residue of silver metal. The litharge was reworked by charcoal reduction to yield sterile lead containing only some 0.01 per cent of residual silver.[31]

## Lead Working

The essential use of lead in permanent buildings resulted in the early recognition of lead working as a separate trade. A leadworker and lead vessels are mentioned in an early 11th-century treatise on estate management, and Godric Plumberre is recorded sometime between 1102 and 1107.[32] Walter Plumarius appears in the Pipe Roll for 1175-6 which contains details of lead purchased for work on Westminster Palace, the Tower of London and the 'house of God at Grantmonte'.[33] Osbert Plumberius (alias Osbert le Plumer, le Plumbere and le Plummer) and William Plummerius witnessed various London deeds between *c.* 1200 and 1220.[34] Plumbers were also found widely in the provinces in the 13th century. In Oxford, John and Randolf Plumbator appear in 1260[35] and in rural Wales Simon le Plumber and Henry le Plumber are recorded in Welshpool in 1293.[36] No doubt they were employed on Edward I's castles. In 1335 it was reported of Portchester castle that 'the great tower is unroofed ... and can be repaired with 20 fodders of lead worth 60*s.* and for the wages of the plumbers and other expenses ... 60*s.*'[37] Lead, as an essential building material, was transported for long distances overland: for example, five-and-a-half fothers (about five tonnes) arrived in Southampton in five 'waynes' from Derby in 1444.[38]

Roofing lead was cast on a bed of sand into sheets *c.* 4mm. thick which were joined at the sides by being rolled round the edge of the adjoining sheet and were secured at their lower edges by iron clips.[39] Lead pipes were made from sheet on wooden formers and the seams soldered.[40] Window glass was secured in 'H'-shaped lead 'calmes' which were cast in two-part hinged iron moulds.[41] As a domestic vessel,

31  Forbes, 'Metallurgy', op. cit. note 12, 43-5.
32  'The Gerefa', printed by W. Cunningham, *The Growth of English Industry and Commerce: Early and Middle Ages*, i (6th edn., 1915), 571-5; for Godric Plumberre see P.H. Reaney, *The Origin of English Surnames* (1984), 191 (citing the Cartulary of Ramsey Abbey).
33  *Pipe Roll 22 Henry II* (Pipe Roll Soc. xxv, 1904), 120, 13, 14, and 141, respectively.
34  *Cartulary of St. Bartholomew's Hospital*, ed. N.J.M. Kerling (1973), Nos. 531, 533, 535, 541, 542, 543, 554 and 560.
35  *Cartulary of the Hospital of St. John Baptist*, ed. H.E. Salter, ii (Oxford Hist. Soc. xviii, 1915), 290, 293 etc.
36  R. Morgan, 'A Powys Lay Subsidy Roll', *Montgomeryshire Collections*, lxxi (1983), 111-2.
37  *Cal. Inquisitions Misc. 1307-49*, No.1472. The sum of 60*s.* for 20 fodders of lead appears to be an error for £60.
38  *Brokage Book of Southampton, 1443-1444*, ed. Olive Coleman, ii (Southampton University, 1961), 280.
39  Briggs, 'Building Construction', in Singer, *Hist. of Technology*, ii, 445.
40  A detailed account of the making and laying of the lead pipe-work for an aqueduct to Waltham Abbey in 1220, from B.L. MS Harl. 391, is given by G.H. Busby, 'The Holy Springs of Waltham Abbey', *Trans. E. Herts. Arch. Soc.* viii (1928-33), 177-83. See also R.A. Skelton and P.D.A. Harvey (eds.), *Local Maps and Plans from Medieval England* (1986), 59-70.
41  Theophilus, *On Divers Arts*, ed. Hawthorne & Smith, 67-8.

the *plumbum* of large size was in common use. The London eyre justices in 1244 found two cases of women being scalded to death by falling into such vats, one containing boiling water, the other hot mash.[42] Five similar fatalities were recorded in the eyre for 1276.[43] In *c.* 1252 'a woman named Cecily and her maid Juliana were fighting indoors and near a leaden vessel full of hot water. During the fight both fell into the vessel and were scalded to death'.[44] Christine de Bennington of Lincolnshire, who died in 1283, bequeathed a leaden vessel to her niece, and her inventory lists four such vessels. In 1327 Avice de Crosseby of Lincoln left 'one very small leaden vessel to mend the eaves or gutter of the church of St. Cuthbert'.[45] The inventory of a London brewer in 1335 includes leaden brewing vessels[46] and inquisitions taken of the goods of Michael de la Pole in 1388 record leaden hand basins, leaden stills, a lead vat, a lead cistern 'near the door of the chamber' and a lead pan in the slaughterhouse.[47] Clearly lead vessels were in widespread use, even though the toxic properties of the metal were well recognised. Nor were utensils the only risk to the citizen. A number of residents of Candlewick Street complained in 1371 that certain plumbers

> do purport to melt their solder in a vacant place called Wodehaw ... to the great damage and peril of death to all who shall smell the smoke from such melting for whoever has smelt the smoke therefrom has never escaped without mischief.

The mayor and aldermen ruled that the work could continue,

> it having been testified before them that the place aforesaid had for many years past been let to men of the trade,

but that the height of the chimney on the furnace should be increased.[48]

The 1365 Ordinances regulating the plumbers' craft provide for apprenticeship for seven years, forbid casual dealing in secondhand lead, provide for orderly marketing and lay down a rate of $\frac{1}{2}d$. 'for working a clove of lead for gutters or for the roofs of houses' and 1*d*. 'for working a clove for furnaces, *tappetroughs*, belfreys and conduit pipes'.[49] Among the minor uses for lead may be mentioned weights (Fig. 17), which for common trade purposes were usually made of lead (unsatisfactory though it was) until the 16th century; coffins, shaped to fit the corpse and soldered round the edge (Fig. 18); small cannon-balls, badges, ink-pots and writing points. Surviving examples of high quality decorative leadwork are the ornate relief-cast fonts dating

42   *London Eyre of 1244*, ed. H.M. Chew and M. Weinbaum (London Rec. Soc., vi, 1970), Nos. 95, 137.

43   *London Eyre of 1276*, ed. M. Weinbaum (London Rec. Soc., xii, 1976), Nos. 13, 14, 21, 43 and 211.

44   Ibid. No. 13.

45   *Lincoln Wills*, v, ed. C.W. Foster, i (Lincoln Rec. Soc., v, 1914), 2-3 and 6.

46   Riley, *Memorials*, 193-4.

47   A composite list from *Cal. Inquisitions Misc., 1387-93*, Nos. 68, 76, 94, 102.

48   Riley, *Memorials*, 355-6.

49   Ibid. 321-3 for the full text. The meaning of 'tappetroughs' is obscure.

Fig. 20 A 15th-century pewterer at work casting the body of a flagon. From the *Housebook of the Mendel Brotherhood*. (*Stadtbibliothek, Nuremberg*)

Fig. 21 A fragment of a stone mould for casting a pewter spoon, *c*. 15th-century. (*Museum of London*)

from the 12th century (Fig. 19).[50] Significant quantities of the metal must also have gone irreversibly into lead glazes for pottery and into lead-based pigments.

### Pewter

The earliest mention of English pewter vessels is found in a letter written by Ælfric for archbishop Wulfstan in *c*. 1006. This lays down that chalices should be made of fusible material, gold or silver, glass or tin (*tinen*), not of horn or wood.[51] However, there is no record of where or by whom these vessels were made. Theophilus, writing in the early 12th century, gives directions for making pewterware and it is possible that some manufacture took place within the religious communities themselves.[52] The technology is simple. The low-melting alloy can be cast in clay moulds, if necessary by the lost wax technique, or even in moulds of wood. The rough casting is finished on a lathe, the parts soldered together and the whole smoothed with abrasives and polished (Fig. 20).

Fragments of multi-part stone moulds for casting small items such as tokens,

50  Zarnecki, *English Romanesque Lead Sculpture*; see also G. Zarnecki et al. (ed.), *English Romanesque Art*, Exhibition catalogue, Hayward Gallery, London, (1984), 247-8.

51  *Councils and Synods, with Other Documents Relating to the English Church, A.D. 871-1204*, eds. D.

Whitelock, M. Brett and C.N.L. Brooke (1981), i, pt. 1, 292. See also Albert Way, *Suss. Arch. Collns.* ix (1857), 310.

52  Theophilus, *On Divers Arts*, ed. Hawthorne & Smith, 179-82.

*Fig. 22* A fragment of a stone mould for casting pewter badges, 15th-century.
(*Museum of London*)

*Fig. 23* An originally circular lead ingot from Criccieth Castle. Diam. *c.* 523mm.
(*National Museum of Wales*)

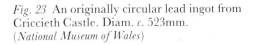

spoons and badges survive from the 14th century (Figs. 21, 22), but moulds of bronze were in general use by at least the later part of that century. No doubt these were expensive, and some elegant pewter flagons and cruets with hexagonal or octagonal bodies were made without the use of moulds by soldering together appropriately shaped strips cut from flat sheet (Figs. 24, 25). Probably these are the items described in contemporary documents as 'square pots'.

No mention of domestic pewterware has been found before the 1290s.[53] Pewter pitchers and a basin are recorded in the larder of Berwick-on-Tweed castle in 1292,[54] and the earliest London pewterer so-called appears to be John le Peutrer, recorded in 1305.[55] He, with Geoffrey, Thomas and William le Peutrer, appears later in the 1319 subsidy roll when they were assessed at rates typical of the modest craftsman and shopkeeper.[56] Thomas and William reappear in the 1332 roll paying 4s. (1319: 10d.) and 5s.4d. (1319: 13½d.) respectively,[57] indicating a rapidly expanding business. Significantly, another early London pewterer, Henry le Peautrer (dead in 1312), was known also as Henry le Calycer (chalice-maker); this not-uncommon name, which occurs as early as *c.* 1190, must conceal a number of 13th-century workers in pewter whose main business was the production of chalices.[58] Gilds of pewterers existed in

53   The 300 pieces of pewter attributed by M. Bell, *Old Pewter* (1905), 55 to Edward I in 1290 are now known to have been pottery vessels. See R. Weinstein in *Pewter, a Celebration of the Craft* (Museum of London, 1989), 33.

54   *Documents Illustrative of the History of Scotland, 1286-1306*, ed. Joseph Stevenson (1870), i, 342.

55   *Cal. of London Trailbaston Trials, 1305-6*, ed. R.B. Pugh (1975), No. 109.

56   *Two Early London Subsidy Rolls*, ed. Eilert Ekwall (Lund, 1951).

57   M. Curtis, 'The London Lay Subsidy of 1332', in G. Unwin (ed.), *Studies in Finance and Trade Under Edward III* (1913).

58   The identity is shown by Hustings Enrolled Deeds, Roll 53(85),(89) and Roll 57(119), (120) at the Corporation of London Records Office. See R.F. Homer, 'The Origin of the Craft in London', *Jnl. of the Pewter Soc.* v 1985-6 54-7.

*Fig. 24* The body of an octagonal pewter flagon made from segments of shaped sheet soldered together, mid 14th-century. Excavated in Gloucestershire. A similar flagon has recently been recovered from the Medway near Tonbridge and others have been excavated in Europe. Height 240 mm. Analysis (%): Sn, 97.7; Pb, 0.57; Cu, 1.55.

*Fig. 25* An elaborately cast-decorated pewter cruet body of almost pure tin, from Weoley Castle, Birmingham, first half of the 14th century. It is made from twelve separate panels and an inserted base, all soldered together. A similar cruet was excavated at Ludlow. Analysis (%): Sn, 99.9; Pb, 0.04; Cu, below 0.03. (*Birmingham Museum and Art Gallery*)

Europe well before 1300 (for example in Paris in 1268),[59] but ordinances were not granted to the London pewterers until 1348.[60]

Outside London, pewterers, as suppliers of consumer goods to the wealthier citizens, are to be found in many large towns before 1400 (Table II). In addition, for different reasons, there was a clandestine trade in Cornwall as early as 1327, where ware was being made from uncoined tin. Pewterers are recorded subsequently in Canterbury (1438), Hull (1464/5), Ipswich (1453), Northampton (1414), Reading (1468), Shrewsbury (1463), Southampton (1443), Wells (1435) and Wigan (1470). In 1474 the Pewterers' Company, exercising the countrywide right of search granted in its first charter, seized substandard wares from pewterers working in Abingdon, Bedford, Boston, Brainsford, Bridgwater, Bury St. Edmunds, Cambridge, Chelmsford, Chichester, Colchester, Leicester, Montacute, Taunton, Thetford, Winchester and Wookey, in addition to some of the earlier recorded towns.[61] Ware

59   E.S. Hedges, *Tin in History* (1964), 86.
60   Riley, *Memorials*, 241-2 for the full text.

61   Guildhall Library, London, MS 7086/1, Pewterers' Company Audit Book.

## TABLE II

*Provincial Pewtering Towns before 1400*

| Lostwithiel | 1327 | Richard peautrer[1] |
| Bristol | 1343 | John le peautrer[2] |
| York | 1348 | William de Ordesdale[3] |
| Kings Lynn | 1350 | Johannes Peutrer[4] |
| Coventry | *c.* 1370 | Hugo le peutorer[5] |
| Exeter | 1370 | Richard Osborne[6] |
| Norwich | 1371-2 | Nicholas atte Pirye[7] |
| Truro | 1379 | Richard Pyauterer[8] |
| Salisbury | 1397 | Geoffrey Peautrer[9] |
| Lincoln | 1398 | John Sparrow[10] |
| Walsall | ?1399 | John Filkes[11] |

1  H.L. Douch, *Jnl., Royal Inst. of Cornwall*, vi. 1 (1969), 65-80.
2  *Cal. Close Rolls, 1343-6*, 124.
3  J. Hatcher and T.C. Barker, *A History of British Pewter*, 40; Massé, *The Pewter Collector* (1921), 53, refers to William the wiredrawer who worked in pewter in 1320.
4  *The Red Register of Kings Lynn*, transcribed by R.F. Isaacson, ed. Holcombe Ingleby (n.d.), ii, 84, 170.
5  *Register of the Trinity Guild of Coventry* (Dugdale Soc., xiii, 1935), 11.
6  *Exeter Freemen*, ed. M.M. Rowe and A.M. Jackson (Devon and Cornwall Rec. Soc., extra ser. i, 1973).
7  J. L'Estrange, *Cal. of Freemen of Norwich*, ed. Walter Rye (1888). The record is incomplete between 1328 and 1364.
8  Douch, as in note 1.
9  *Cal. Patent Rolls, 1396-9*, 298. He owed £20 to a London pewterer.
10  *Cal. Close Rolls, 1396-9*, 348.
11  *Cal. Patent Rolls, 1396-9*, 496; *V.C.H. Staffs.* xvii, 196 and note.

seized at Abingdon included plates, dishes, saucers, small saucers, great saltcellars, middling saltcellars and tavern pots of quart, pint and half-pint capacity.[62]

The growth of the craft in London can be followed in considerable detail. From information collected from contemporary sources about some 200 London pewterers working before 1450[63] (believed to include the great majority) can be derived an indication of the numbers of pewterers working in the capital at the end of each decade (Table III). The depression following the Black Death and the upturn consequent on the growth of the economy and the increased number of monied people after 1400 is clearly apparent, and comparison with the relatively constant number of London goldsmiths shows the increasing importance of the pewterers. The output of these pewterers is conjectural, but present-day concerns, making pewterware by hand methods differing little from those used in the Middle Ages,

62  Ibid.
63  R.F. Homer, 'The Medieval Pewterers of London *c.* 1190-1457', *Trans. London & Middlesex Arch. Soc.* xxxvi (1985), 137-63. A list of London pewterers by R.F. Homer is also deposited at Guildhall Library, London.

## TABLE III

*Estimated number of Pewterers working in London 1310-1460*

| Date | Number of Pewterers | Number of Goldsmiths |
|------|--------------------|--------------------|
| 1310 | 5 | – |
| 1320 | 13 | – |
| 1330 | 17 | – |
| 1340 | 20 | – |
| 1348 | 30 | – |
| 1360 | 20 | – |
| 1368/9 | – | 135 |
| 1370 | 20 | – |
| 1380 | 13 | – |
| 1390 | 20 | – |
| 1400 | 33 | – |
| 1404 | – | 186 |
| 1410 | 60 | – |
| 1420 | 57 | – |
| 1430 | 57 | – |
| 1440 | 94 | – |
| 1444 | – | 140 |
| 1450 | 87 | – |
| 1457 (actual) | 100 | – |
| 1462 | – | 150 |

Figures for goldsmiths from T.F. Reddaway and L.E.M. Walker, *The Early History of the Goldsmiths' Company 1327-1509* (1975), 78-81, 90-91, 138-9.

The 1457 figure for pewterers is taken from C. Welch, *History of the Worshipful Company of Pewterers* (1902), i, 20-5, and comprises 56 masters, 34 journeymen and 10 individuals of uncertain status.

appear to average about one tonne of ware per skilled craftsman per annum. The London pewterers of the early 15th century were thus perhaps making some 60 tonnes of ware a year, say 200,000 individual items of domestic pewter. The sizes of individual pewterers' shops, based on information from the Pewterers' Company archives, are given in Table IV.[64] Journeymen's wages are indicated by an isolated figure of 40*s.* a year in a will of 1451,[65] and in 1538 they received between 2*d.* and 4*d.* a day, presumably in addition to board and lodgings.[66]

64  See C. Welch, *History of the Worshipful Company of Pewterers*, 2 vols (1902), i, 20-25.
65  S.L. Thrupp, *The Merchant Class of Medieval London* (1948), 114, citing the will of John

Paris.
66  'The Namys of all Clothing, Yeomandry and the Howseholders...', London, Guildhall Library, MS 22,179.

## TABLE IV

*Size of Pewterers' Shops in London in 1457*

| | | |
|---|---|---|
| Master alone | 18 | 32% |
| Master + one | 11 | 20% |
| Master + two | 15 | 27% |
| Master + three | 7 | 12% |
| Master + four | 1 | |
| Master + six | 1 | |
| Master + eight | 1 | |
| Master + eleven | 1 | |
| Master + eighteen | 1 | |

The largest shop, that of Thomas Dounton, who was also a mercer, comprised eleven apprentices and seven journeymen and is the largest enterprise so far discovered for any craft at that period.

The contents of a London pewterer's workshop of 1427, extracted from the inventory of Thomas Filkes,[67] include everything needed for casting, hammering, soldering, finishing and weighing the ware:

a small charger mould of brass, weight 80 lbs., value 26*s.* 8*d.* at 4*d.* per lb.
a middle platter mould of brass, 54 lbs., 18*s.*
a small platter mould of brass, 59 lbs., 19*s.* 8*d.*
a great dish mould, 50 lbs., 16*s.* 8*d.*
a counterfeit dish mould, 51 lbs., 17*s.*
a middle dish mould, 37 lbs., 12*s.* 4*d.*
a hollow dish mould, 20 lbs., 8*s.* 4*d.* (*sic*)
a greater saucer mould, 16 lbs., 7*s.* (*sic*)
a middle saucer mould, 16 lbs., 5*s.* 4*d.*
a small saucer mould, 16 lbs., 5*s.* 4*d.*
a dish mould and a saucer mould, 25 lbs., 8*s.* 4*d.*
a hollow platter mould, 57 lbs., 19*s.*
a great charger mould, 120 lbs., 44*s.* (*sic*)
a new charger mould, 93 lbs., 31*s.*
a middle charger mould, 106 lbs., 35*s.* 4*d.*
the greatest charger mould, 157 lbs., 52*s.* 4*d.*
14 'prynts', 155 lbs. at 2*d.* the lb., 27*s.* 4*d.*
7 pairs of 'clammes', 60lbs., 5*s.* 6*d.*
a wheel, an arbour and a 'tower' (i.e. a lathe and fittings), 3*s.* 4*d.*

67   Corporation of London Records Office, Letter
     Book K, f.49r.

*Fig. 26* A pewter plate, probably 15th century, from the Thames at London. Diam. 270 mm. (*Museum of London*)

*Fig. 27* A pewter saucer from Tong Castle with the mark of a pewterer's hammer on the rim, *c.* 1400. Diam. 137 mm. (*Pewterers' Company*)

a pair of clipping shears, 12*d.*
a burnisher, 2*d.*
8 turning hooks (i.e. lathe tools), 8*d.*
4 anvils and 2 swages, 3*s.* 4*d.*
7 'cleue' hammers, 2*s.* 4*d.*
2 scoring 'flotes', 12*d.*
2 chisels and a pair of lifting tongs, 8*d.*
2 bellows, 2 casting pans and a stirring staff, 8*d.*
4 soldering irons and 3 casting 'stocks', 8*d.*
4 'strake stones' and scales and weights, 21*s.* 3*d.*
20 marking irons, 6*d.*

The moulds listed would have cast saucers, plates and dishes between 4 inches and 20 inches in diameter[68] (Figs. 26, 27); they had a total value, at 4*d.* the lb., of over £16. Each was designated to be shared between from two to six pewterers, and other records also speak of the practice of sharing these expensive items. The will of John Childe (1441)[69] refers to 'my part of a dish mould which I and John Hulle, pewterer, share', and a further complex sharing arrangement was made by the Pewterers' Company in 1448.[70]

From apparently humble beginnings a few decades earlier, by the mid 14th century many London pewterers were acting as merchants, being involved in the shipping of tin from Cornwall and in the exporting of pewterware. In 1364 a ship

68   R.F. Michaelis, *Antique Pewter of the British Isles* (1955), 15-16, for a list of sizes dated 1438.
69   Guildhall Library, London, MS 9171/4, Com-missary Court Wills, f.92ᵛ.
70   Guildhall MS 7086/1, flyleaves.

owned by a consortium of London pewterers and carrying some 40 tonnes of tin was seized by the French[71] and in 1407 the pewterer John Megre is described as a merchant when he was sued for the delivery of 139½ cwt. of tin worth £150.[72] The prosperity of John de Hilton, pewterer, is indicated by the theft from him in about 1352-4 of gold, silver, amber, precious stones and cloth worth £30 14s.[73] In 1345 Nicholas le Peautrer of Ludgate bequeathed to his son his moulds and tools together with 2,000 lbs. of pewter (or tin, *stagnum*), an enamelled cup, silver spoons, mazers and ten marks of silver.[74] Evidence from over 40 London pewterers' wills provides a picture of a close-knit and generally prosperous community.[75] A number of them were summoned from time to time to assemblies of 'the wealthier and wiser commoners', and the craft paid 100s. in 1363 towards 'a present sent to the king'.[76] The trade was sufficiently buoyant in the late 14th century to attract craftsmen from the provinces. In 1397 James Quarrer (also Quarry) and John Seward had left the manor of Arlesey (Beds.) to work as pewterers in Candlewick Street, and Quarrer became affluent enough to purchase his own and his son's manumission.[77]

The Pewterers' Ordinances of 1348 stipulate two different pewter alloys, 'fine metal' and 'lay metal'. The former was an alloy of tin with copper and the latter of tin with lead. The lead alloy was in common use in Europe, but the London pewterers sought to conceal the exact nature of the fine metal, on which the high reputation of English pewter abroad rested. Thus the ordinances state only that 'the proportion of copper to the tin is as much as, of its own nature, it will take'. Lay metal is openly defined as 'an hundred' of tin to 26 lbs. of lead.[78] Modern analysis of fine metal reveals alloys of typically 1-3 per cent copper.[79] The harder fine metal was to be used for flatware such as plates and for wares classified as 'square', while lay was to be used for round wares. Quality control was enforced: 23 pottel pots and 20 saltcellars of leady metal were seized from John de Hilton in 1350 and a hand-basin from John Syward in 1373.[80]

Exports of English pewter are first recorded in 1307 with a shipment of about 50 lbs. weight of pitchers, plates and salts, but they rose rapidly to average 15-20 tonnes per annum by 1400, 45-50 tonnes by the 1430s and (exceptionally) 90 tonnes in 1466-7.[81] Indeed, at this time, pewter ranked second only to cloth among manufactured exports. In England, pewter is increasingly mentioned in wills and inventories during the 14th century. Twelve plates, 12 dishes, 18 saltcellars and 2 flagons valued

71  *Cal. of Letters ... of the City of London*, ed. R.R. Sharpe (1885), 96, No. 207.
72  *Cal. Plea & Mem. R., 1381-1412*, 285, 287.
73  *Cal. of Letters*, as note 71, 63, No. 138.
74  *Cal. Hustings Wills*, i, 502, supplemented from the original.
75  D.W. Hall, 'Some Early London Pewterers'; R.F. Homer, 'Medieval London Pewterers'; R.F. Homer, art. cit. note 63.
76  *Cal. Letter-Book G*, 172.
77  Beds. County Record Office, Arlesey Bury Manor Court Roll, IN58; see also Joyce God-ber, *History of Bedfordshire* (1969), 101.
78  A later transcript in the Pewterers' Company records gives 22 lbs. of lead.
79  R. Brownsword and E.E.H. Pitt, 'X-ray Fluore-scence Analysis of English 13th-16th Century Pewter Flatware', *Archaeometry*, xxvi (1984), 237-44.
80  Riley, *Memorials*, 259-60 and *Cal. Plea & Mem. R., 1323-64*, 264.
81  Hatcher and Barker, *A History of British Pewter*, 64-6.

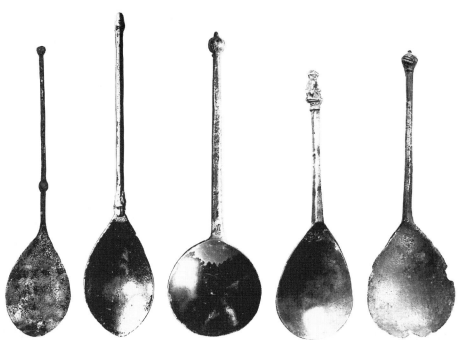

*Fig. 28* Five pewter spoons. *Left to right*: *c*. 1300; *c*.1300; 14th century; 15th/16th century; 15th/16th century. Not to uniform scale, *c*. 150-165 mm.

*Fig. 29* A pewter badge of an archer, early 15th century, 72 mm. (*Museum of London*)

*Fig. 30* A superbly detailed pilgrim souvenir in the form of a pewter ampulla cast with the figure of St. Thomas of Canterbury. From Trig Lane, London, mid 13th-century. Height 97 mm. (*Museum of London*)

*Fig. 32* A pewter seal-matrix with the legend 'S'. BEATRICIS FIL HUGONIS, late 13th century. Max. dimension 40 mm. (*Museum of London*)

*Fig. 33* A group of 13th-century tokens in eutectic tin-lead alloy. From the Thames at London. Diam. *c.* 16 mm. (*Private collection*)

*Fig. 31* A pewter pilgrim souvenir in the form of a scabbard containing a separate sword and symbolising the martyrdom by the sword of St. Thomas. From Trig Lane, London, before *c.* 1440 and probably late 14th century. Almost certainly a metal mould would have been needed for such a sophisticated product. Height 145 mm. (*Museum of London*)

*Fig. 35* Two pewter finger-rings of 13th- or 14th-century date from the Thames foreshore, London. (*Private collection*)

*Fig. 34* Jewellery of the 10th or 11th century from London. (*Museum of London*)

*Fig. 36* The lid of a lady's mirror-case, pewter, early 14th century. Diam. 53 mm. (*Museum of London*)

*Fig. 37* A 13th-century pewter sepulchral chalice from a grave at Lincoln Cathedral. (*Lincoln Cathedral*)

*Fig. 38* A hexagonal pewter cruet from Tong Castle, late 14th century. A very similar cruet was excavated at Ashby-de-la-Zouche. The body appears to have been cast in one piece and the base inserted. (*Tong church*)

*Fig. 39* A pewter receptacle, probably a chrismatory, with cast relief decoration on the lid including scenes of the Annunciation and Visitation and the arms of England and France; early 14th century. Height 90 mm. (*Victoria and Albert Museum*)

*Fig. 40* A pewter lidded baluster-shaped measure of two pints capacity. The base is inset with a medallion of a heart in a decorative surround. Second half of the 15th century; from the Thames at London. Height overall 211 mm. (*Private collection*)

*Fig. 41* A cast pewter crucifix figure, *c.* 1160-70, from Ludgvan church (Cornwall). The alloy is 68% tin, 32% lead, and the figure was originally painted over a gesso ground. Height 126 mm. (*British Museum*)

at 7*s.* appear in the 1317 will of Richard de Blountesham.[82] An inquisition at Wolverhampton in 1341 found that Thomas de Arleye and William de Marnham each had 24 pewter dishes and 12 saucers worth 4*s.*[83] In 1356 Stephen de Northerne, ironmonger of London, had 20 lbs. of pewter valued at 2*s.* 11*d.*;[84] 50 years later John Oliver, draper, owned 200 pieces weighing 400 lbs. and valued at 2½*d.* per lb.[85]

Both pewter and lead were of little intrinsic value and small items such as spoons, badges and tokens, when lost, were not worth retrieving. These have been excavated in large numbers. The earliest pewter spoons date from the end of the 13th century[86] and pilgrim badges in tin, lead and pewter survive from a century earlier (Figs. 28-31).[87] The production and sale of many millions of these badges was a profitable business and the church sought to monopolise it, though apparently with limited

82 Riley, *Memorials*, 123-5.
83 *Cal. Inquisitions Misc., 1307-49*, No. 1758.
84 Riley, *Memorials*, 283.
85 *Cal. Plea & Mem. R., 1413-37*, 4; other wills and inventories are given in Hatcher and Barker, op. cit. and in Homer, op. cit. note 63.
86 R.F. Homer, *Five Centuries of Base Metal Spoons* (The author, 1975); see also S. Muldoon and

Roger Brownsword, *Pewter Spoons and other Related Material* (City of Coventry Leisure Services, n.d. [?1985]).
87 Brian Spencer, 'Medieval Pilgrim Badges', in J.G.N. Renaud (ed.) *Rotterdam Papers: A Contribution to Medieval Archaeology* (1968), and 'Pilgrim Souvenirs from Trig Lane', *Trans. London & Middlesex Arch. Soc.* xxxiii (1982).

*Fig. 42* A pewter candlestick cast in one piece with a hollow stem, probably early to mid 15th-century. From the Thames at Queenhithe. Height 100 mm. Analysis (%): Sn, 78.5; Pb, 20; Cu, 1.29.
(*Museum of London*)

success.[88] The large-scale production of pilgrim badges may well have led to the first introduction of metal moulds, for their advantage in preserving the fine detail found on many badges is self-evident.[89] They were perhaps cut by seal engravers (Fig. 132). A token coinage bearing naive designs of animals, birds, human figures and heraldic and geometric designs was produced from *c.* 1200 onwards.[90] Before *c.* 1350 these tokens were cast in eutectic tin/lead alloy and later in lead alone. A few of the earliest are of pure tin (Fig. 33). A considerable quantity of pewter jewellery exists, some of late Anglo-Saxon and Viking date, as do finger rings and dress ornaments (Figs. 34-36). These last were the subject of a complaint by the Girdlers of London in 1327-9 who sought to ban girdles garnished with 'false work of lead, pewter and tin'.[91] In York, in 1427, John Lyllyng was convincted of supplying 'false tin' adulterated with lead to the city's girdlers for making into girdle decorations.[92]

Larger items, which wore rapidly due to the softness of the metal, were readily recast, and at least in the case of pewter records show that the recycling was well organised, old metal fetching about two-thirds the price of new. Thus the survival of significant items is rather rare. In pewter, sepulchral chalices and patens,

88    Idem, 'Medieval Pilgrim Badges', 141.
89    Ibid. 146, note 26; Thomas Hugo, 'Pilgrim Signs', *Archaeologia*, xxxviii (1860).
90    Michael Mitchiner and Anne Skinner, 'English Tokens', *British Numismatic Jnl.* liii (1984). This paper also contains analyses of the metal of tokens and pilgrim badges.
91    *Cal. Patent Rolls, 1327-30*, 40, 367, 379; see also

E. Smirke, 'On the Use of Tin in Girdles in the 14th Century', *Arch. Jnl.* ix (1852), 281-4.
92    J. Raine, 'An Account of the Proceedings in a Remarkable Case of Adulteration at York', *A Volume of English Miscellanies...* (Surtees Soc. lxxxv, 1888 (1890)), 1-10. He also traded in 'false iron' and 'false alum'.

deliberately interred with the priest from the 11th century onwards,[93] have been recovered in some numbers from graves (Fig. 37). Other ecclesiastical items include cruets, some elaborately decorated with relief-cast motifs (Figs. 25, 38), a chrismatory (Fig. 22) and a 12th-century cast pewter crucifix figure (Fig. 41). Of domestic items there survive a range of saucers and plates, a few flagons of uncertain provenance, even fewer baluster-shaped wine measures from the end of the medieval period (Fig. 40) and isolated examples of other utensils (Fig. 42). Of the vast and diverse output of the medieval pewterers of England, all that remains today is a random sample of just a few of their products.

## Acknowledgements

The author is indebted to Roger Brownsword and Ernest Pitt for permission to quote their analytical results on the objects shown in Figs, 24, 25 and 42.

## Further Reading

The most comprehensive work on the tin industry is John Hatcher's *English Tin Production and Trade before 1550* (1973). Earlier studies include G.R. Lewis's *The Stannaries* (1908) and 'The Stannary of Tavistock' which forms chapter 7 of H.P.R. Finberg's *Tavistock Abbey* (1955). L.F. Salzman's 'Mines and Stannaries' in J.F. Willard et al. (eds.), *The English Government at Work 1327-36*, iii (1950) provides much detailed information for the decade which it covers. T.A.P. Greeves, 'The Archaeological Potential of the Devon Tin Industry' in D.W. Crossley (ed.), *Medieval Industry* (C.B.A. Research Rep. xl, 1981) discusses surviving archaeological remains. The same publication contains I.S.W. Blanchard's 'Lead Mining and Smelting' which analyses a wealth of recently-discovered information. Salzman's earlier study in *English Industries of the Middle Ages* is nevertheless still very informative. Early mining and metalworking in general are well described in volume 2 of C. Singer (ed.), *A History of Technology* (1956).

John Hatcher and T.C. Barker, *A History of British Pewter* (1974) contains much of value on the medieval period. Welch's detailed *History of the Worshipful Company of Pewterers*, 2 vols. (1902), based on the Company's records, refers to little before 1451. Descriptions of medieval pewterware are, in general, scattered in the archaeological literature. Spoons are covered in the present author's *Five Centuries of Base Metal Spoons* (1975) and pilgrim badges in several papers by Brian Spencer (see

---

93  The earliest appears to date from 1087, see *Proc., Soc. of Antiquaries*, 2nd ser. xxii (1909), 394. Thirteenth-century chalices and patens at Lincoln cathedral are illustrated and described by R.F. Homer, 'Chalices and Patens at Lincoln Cathedral', *Jnl. of the Pewter Soc.* vi (1986).

bibliography). Works on pewter which contain some mention of medieval wares include R.F. Michaelis, *Antique Pewter of the British Isles* (1955) and (for continental pewter) H.H. Cotterell, *Pewter Down the Ages* (1932). *Pewter, a Celebration of the Craft, 1200-1700* (Museum of London, Exhibition catalogue, 1989) contains much of value. Decorative leadwork is dealt with in G. Zarnecki, *English Romanesque Lead Sculpture* (1957).

# 5

# Copper Alloys

## CLAUDE BLAIR and JOHN BLAIR

In modern usage, *bronze* is an alloy mainly of copper and tin, *brass* an alloy mainly of copper and zinc.[1] Both medieval terminology and medieval alloys were more variable than this, and modern scholars have increased confusion by their inaccurate usage. There has been a tendency to call red-coloured alloys 'bronze' and yellow-coloured ones 'brass'; and further, to apply 'bronze' to objects considered works of art and 'brass' to those thought merely utilitarian. In fact it is nearly impossible to distinguish between the two alloys and their variants by non-scientific means, and it is only now, with a growing body of analytical data, that it is becoming possible to generalise about medieval practice. For convenience, 'bronze' and 'brass' are used in this chapter in their modern senses except where otherwise stated.

In medieval Latin texts the classical words *aes* (with its derivatives *aeneus* and *aereus*) and *orichalcum* (or *aurichalcum*) occur in contexts which show that they were often, perhaps usually, applied to bronze and brass respectively. But Theophilus's treatise *On Divers Arts*, written in Germany in about 1125, uses *aes* for both brass and bronze, and *auricalcum* for brass made from copper that has been specially refined to remove the lead content so that it can be gilded.[2] In the 13th century, Albertus Magnus defines brass (*auricalcum*) as copper (*cuprum*) combined with calamine (*calamina*, in other words zinc ore) by the cementation process.[3]

Vernacular English included, in addition to *copper*, the words *brass*, *maslin*, *latten*, *auricalke* and *alkamine*.[4] The first two are of Anglo-Saxon origin, while the third

---

1 We are very grateful to Dr. Roger Brownsword, Miss Catherine Mortimer and Mme. Monique de Ruette for their comments on this chapter.

2 Theophilus, *On Divers Arts*, ed. Hawthorne and Smith, 143 note 1.

3 Albertus Magnus, *Opera Omnia*, ed. A. Borgnet, v (1890), 90; 'Hi autem qui in cupro multum operantur in nostris partibus, Parisiis videlicet et Coloniae et in aliis locis in quibus fui et vidi experiri, convertunt cuprum in aurichalchum per pulverem lapidis qui calamina vocatur; et cum evaporat lapis, adhuc remanet splendor obscurus declinans aliquantulum ad auri speciem.'

4 See *O.E.D.* and *Middle English Dictionary* under the relevant words. An early attempt to elucidate these terms, still of some value, is W. Papworth, 'Latten or Brass', *Notes and Queries*, 3rd ser. xii (1867), 301-3. See also A. Way (ed.), *Promptorium Parvulorum*, i (Camden Soc. xxv, 1843), 289 n; this, it should be mentioned, gives a medieval reference to the otherwise unrecorded word *goldfome* as an English translation of *auricalcum*.

(derived from Turkic *altun* through Arabic *latun* and Spanish *allaton*) first occurs in Middle English in the early 14th century. *Brass* seems to have been used loosely, with, if anything, a bias towards what we should call bronze (which is not a medieval word). The most favoured term for alloys containing zinc was *latten*; in contemporary sources *maslin* (i.e. 'mixture', cognate with modern German *Messing*) is likened to latten but differentiated from it. Trevisa, in his translation of Bartholomew the Englishman's *De Proprietatibus Rerum* (c.1398), writes: 'latone hat auricalcum and hath that name for, thogh it be brass of messelyng, it shineth as golde ... Also latyn is harde as brasse oither copour, for by medlyng of coper and of tynne and of auripigment [yellow arsenic] and with other metalles it is brought in to the fyre to colour of golde'.[5] A London text of 1440 lists basins, a colander, chafers and candlesticks of *laton*, but pots and pans of *brasse*.[6] A York founder of 1516 had quantities of both copper and 'messelyng', while an inventory of 1537 from Chesterfield (Derbs.) distinguishes between two 'brase potts', two 'laten basyns' and four 'maslen panes'.[7] The word *tyngbasse* (perhaps 'tin-brass') is used in one London text of 1417, apparently equated with *auricalcum*, as is *alkamine* in the 15th century.[8] In addition there was *pot-metal*, *pan-metal*, *bell-metal*, and, at the very end of the Middle Ages, *gun-metal*.

All these alloys could have been classified as brass, though their compositions must obviously have differed. Most early medieval copper-alloy objects from English sources are in the very mixed alloys produced by extensive reuse; but significant quantities of zinc normally occur, and latten in the later sense of the word was evidently commonplace in Anglo-Saxon England.[9] The contract for the mid 15th-century effigy of Richard Beauchamp in St. Mary's Church, Warwick, specifies 'the best latten', and analysis has shown this to be a copper-zinc-tin-lead alloy: 84.3 per cent copper, 9.4 per cent zinc, 3.3 per cent tin, 1.4 per cent lead, and the remaining *c.* 1.5 per cent nickel, iron, antimony, arsenic and silver.[10] In other words it is intermediate between bronze and brass, using the terms in the modern sense, but nearer the latter than the former. The majority of other medieval copper alloys are of a similar type but with varied proportions of the component metals, sometimes with a high lead content.[11] Exceptions are the alloys used for bells (below pp.89-90), and those used for utilitarian objects such as cooking vessels and weights. The latter are usually made from heavily leaded bronze, and it is significant that in 1316 some London makers of metal pots were accused of diluting their alloy with too much lead.[12] However, the finer medieval objects hitherto usually called 'bronzes' are, in

5　Quoted *Middle English Dictionary, s.v. latoun.*

6　Corporation of London R.O., A67 m.8ᵛ, calendared *Cal. Plea & Mem. R. 1437-57*, 31-2 (cf. ibid. 16, 35, 80).

7　*Test. Ebor.* V (Surtees Soc. lxxix, 1884), 79-80; J.M. Bestall and D.V. Fowkes (eds.), *Chester-field Wills and Inventories 1521-1603* (Derbyshire Rec. Soc. i, 1977), 16.

8　Riley, *Memorials*, 656; *Middle English Dictionary, s.v. alkamine.*

9　Information from Miss Catherine Mortimer.

10　See C. Blair, J. Blair and R. Brownsword, 'An Oxford Brasiers' Dispute of the 1390s', *Antiq. Jnl.*, lxvi (1986), 82-90, note 12.

11　On the addition of lead see M. de Ruette, 'Les Résultats d'Analyse de Teneurs des Laitons . . .', *Revue des Archéologues et Historiens d'Art de Louvain*, xvi (1983), 269-71, note 66.

12　Riley, *Memorials*, 118-19, cf. p.58 above.

*Fig. 43* Holy-water stoup,
mid 14th century, from
Wreay church (Cumb.). (See
p.102.)

fact, turning out on analysis to be made from complex copper-zinc-tin-lead alloys,[13]
closer to brass (again using the term in its modern sense) but for which it seems best
to use the medieval term *latten*.

Workshops contained both new metal and scrap for re-melting. In 1423 Nicholas
Broker, coppersmith of London and one of the makers of Richard II's tomb,
bequeathed 300 barrels *de auricalco cum eorum platis roughycasted*.[14] In 1421 the London
brasier John Brede left 1000 lb. of *marshhalbras*, perhaps some form of scrap-metal; the
half-hundredweight of *bawdeneys* left by John Burgess in 1405 were probably offcuts.[15] A *squachinghamer* left by Richard atte Weye (1374) and two *hakhamerys* left by
John Burgess (1405) must have been for breaking up the scrap.[16] But the main
problem concerns the newly-made latten or bronze: did English brasiers always buy
it as an alloy, or did they sometimes make it from the raw materials? The received
view is that all bronze and latten used in medieval England came from the Low
Countries and Germany, and customs accounts show that much latten was indeed
imported.[17] Nonetheless, the question of indigenous manufacture can perhaps be re-
opened.

13 Blair, Blair and Brownsword, art.cit. note 10,
   85 and n.14.
14 Guildhall Library, London, MS 9171/3, f.157.
15 Ibid. MSS 9171/3 ff.71ᵛ-72, 9171/2, f.75ᵛ
   (and cf. *Middle English Dictionary s.v. bauden*,
   'to trim').
16 Ibid. MSS 9171/1, f.5, 9171/2, f.75ᵛ. For the

wide range of hammers to be found in a
brasier's workshop see *Test.Ebor.*, loc. cit.
note 7.
17 N.S.B. Gras, *The Early English Customs System*
   (Harvard Economic Studies xviii, 1918),
   passim.

We suggest that the decisive characteristic of latten is likely to have been the intentional presence of zinc in its composition, irrespective of what other metals (apart from copper) it contained. Zinc was not known in metallic form in the medieval west.[18] Its boiling-point is only 907°C (nearly 180° less than the *melting-point* of copper), so it is driven off as a vapour if the zinc-bearing calamine ore is smelted in a shaft furnace. No method of separating metallic zinc from the ore seems to have been known in Europe before the 16th century, and it was not produced commercially until the 18th century. Previously it was used by means of the cementation process (described in detail by Theophilus), in which ground calamine ore, sealed in a crucible with charcoal and fragments of copper, is heated until the zinc is produced as a vapour which permeates the copper, so converting it to latten.

Thus the necessary ingredients for latten are copper and calamine ore. There are suggestions that copper was mined in Cornwall, Cumberland and Yorkshire from the 13th century, and clearer evidence that it was mined in the last two areas in the late 15th century.[19] Analysis has shown that some rather poor-quality copper-alloy objects contain high levels of antimony, which might suggest use of the antimonial sulphide ores mined in Devon and Cornwall and known as 'grey coppers'.[20] A proclamation of 1492, establishing a staple for metals mined in England, says that 'the continualle wirkyng of the saide mynes shalle dayly renew as welle golde and silver oute of the same as lede, tynne and copere';[21] but in fact the rest of the provisions deal solely with gold, silver and tin. A statute of 1529-30 states that 'there is no myne of metall of Coper within this realme of England founde or hadde where suficient coper may be gathered for the use of the Kyng oure Soveraigne Lorde and for the people of this his Realme', which implies that *some* copper was mined but not enough; and copper is actually listed among English exports to Venice in 1456.[22] So it seems fairly clear that late medieval England did sometimes produce copper, if only in small quantities. Calamine ores were apparently not discovered, and certainly not commercially exploited, in England until the 1560s, when German miners brought over specially for the purpose located them in Somerset.[23]

There is, however, evidence that both copper and calamine were imported raw. A

18  In 1967 two decorated fragments, apparently from an early 12th-century piece of plate, were found in a river-bank at Pipe Aston near Ludlow (SO 4585 7170). Analysis at Coventry revealed that they are of almost pure zinc. Metallic zinc was known in China and the Islamic world from an early date, so it may be legitimate to assume that this object was made from imported metal. The fragments are now in Ludlow Museum. (Correspondence in British Museum, Dept. of Medieval and Later Antiquities, kindly made available by John Cherry.) See also *Current Archaeology*, cxv (June 1989), 114-15.

19  *V.C.H. Cumberland*, ii (1905), 342-3; *V.C.H. Yorks.* ii (1912), 354; *V.C.H. Cornwall*, i (1906),

563. We are grateful to Dr. Jane Geddes for these references.

20  See H.H. Coghlan, *Notes on the Prehistoric Metallurgy of Copper and Bronze in the Old World* (Pitt Rivers Museum, Oxford, Occasional Paper in Technology 4, 2nd edn., 1975), 20; R.F. Tylecote, *A History of Metallurgy* (1976), 130; idem, *The Prehistory of Metallurgy in the British Isles* (1986), 13, 14.

21  *H.M.C. Middleton* (1911), 614-17.

22  *Statutes of the Realm*, iii (1817), 290: 21 Hen. VIII, cap.x; *Cal. State Papers Venetian*: i (1202-1509), 85-6, No.341. We are very grateful to Phillip Lindley for the last reference.

23  H. Hamilton, *The English Brass and Copper Industries to 1800* (2nd edn., 1967), Ch. I.

customs account of 1420-1 contains payments 'for 6½ barrels of grey copper' and 'for 27 barrels of red copper',[24] the former presumably the same as the *coper grey* (5 cwt. of of it) in John Brede's will of 1421 (above p.83). A customs account of 1384 lists not only a very large amount of copper beside a small amount of latten, but also six barrels each of *calamys* and *calamin*.[25] Since calamine also had medicinal uses, an alternative explanation for this last item is possible (if perhaps in the context unlikely). A contract of 1392 between two Oxford brasiers, with a list of grievances compiled in an ensuing dispute, takes us a little further.[26] The contract binds the master-brasier to find for his assistant 'certain metal, namely on one part *graycober* of the best [quality] and *stelebake*, and on the other part *old bras'*. If *graycober* is copper in some more-or-less pure-refined form, *stelebake* is presumably something to do with calamine ore (or, less likely, tin). We owe to Dr. Roger Brownsword the ingenious suggestion that *stelebake* is an anglicisation of the placename Stolberg, in the calamine-producing region to the east of Aachen. This is not conclusive, but the evidence now seems quite strong that late medieval English brasiers sometimes bought copper and calamine ore to turn into latten in their own workshops. It may be added that 14th-century crucible fragments and slag found in York have been interpreted as waste-products of the cementation process.[27]

*Methods of Working*

The two main methods of working copper alloys were those used for all metals, namely forging with the hammer and casting. For practical reasons related to their physical characteristics, copper has normally been worked by the hammer and bronze cast; brass has regularly been worked by both methods, though a high proportion of the brass objects surviving from medieval Europe were produced by casting.

The techniques for working brass and copper with the hammer are those still regularly employed by silversmiths. Sheet metal is invariably used and, after being cut into the basic pattern appropriate to the final object, is annealed to soften it, a process that has to be repeated as work progresses. It is then formed into the required shape – usually a hollow vessel of some kind – by hammering it cold over one or more of a series of anvils called *stakes*. Through the circumstances of survival, most extant medieval latten objects of any size are cast. One major product which, because of its size, seems likely to have been mainly hammer-worked was the lavatorium which John le Potter of London contracted to make for Ramsey Abbey in 1288: 'of good and durable metal, 33 feet long and 2½ feet or more high, with 16 copper taps (*claves*) of

24 Gras, op.cit. note 17, 502, 509; cf. also 456. This problem is discussed further by Blair, Blair and Brownsword, art.cit. note 10.
25 P.R.O., E122/71/8.
26 See Blair, Blair and Brownsword, art.cit. note 10.

27 *Archaeology of York*, 10.1, 25-6. For comparable Roman crucible fragments used for the cementation process, see J. Bayley, 'Roman Brass-Making in Britain', *Historical Metallurgy*, xviii (1) (1984), 42-3.

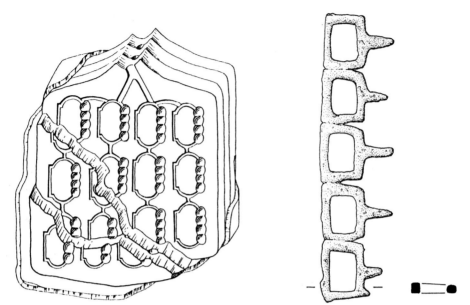

*Fig. 44a* Gang-mould for casting buckles. Scale 1:2. (*Museum of London*)   *b* Cast strap-loops in their rough state, before cleaning-up. Scale 1:1. (*Museum of London*)

subtle design and richly gilt, and fillets through the centre'.[28]

Casting, in essence, merely involves melting the metal or alloy until it is quite liquid, and then pouring it into a mould. The very simplest form of mould is open on top, like a modern jelly-mould (Fig. 44 A-B). It can only be used for producing simple shapes, with at least one face (corresponding to the open top of the mould) flat, especially if the mould is to be used more than once, since any undercutting or similar irregularity of shape prevents removal of the casting. The production of more complex patterns from permanent moulds was achieved in prehistoric times by the development of the two-piece mould, at first of stone and later of clay or metal. The two halves are bound together to form a mould that is completely closed, except for an aperture through which the molten metal can be poured and vents to emit the air displaced by the metal. The junctions of piece-moulds are often visible as thin lines on the finished objects. Still more complex shapes can be produced by making the mould in several pieces, while hollow castings can also be made in this way by incorporating a core.

The normal medieval method of casting objects in copper-alloy was the *waste-wax* or *lost-wax* process (in French *cire-perdue*), which has been used since prehistoric times. This involves modelling the object to be made in wax (over a clay core if a hollow casting is required) and covering this with clay, again leaving a pour-hole and vents. The whole is then heated so that the clay is hardened while the wax melts and

28  *Cal. Letter-Book A*, 172; G. Unwin (ed.), *Finance and Trade under Edward III* (1918), 33.

burns out through the vents, leaving a hollow mould ready to receive the molten metal. Since the mould has to be broken to release the casting, it can only be used once.

Many objects, especially large commercial ones, are now produced by sand-casting, in which the mould is formed of bonded sand of a special type closely compacted in one or more moulding-boxes around a full-sized pattern, usually of wood. Removal of the pattern leaves its impression in the sand, which can then be filled with molten metal. In its simplest form such a mould was an open one, used to make flat objects decorated on one side only, but it is possible to construct sand-moulds in many pieces for castings of great complexity. The earliest recorded description of this process is in Biringuccio's *Pirotechnica* (1540), but European cast-iron objects, mainly firebacks, from the second half of the 15th century which appear to have been made in sand moulds are evidence that the process was known at least a century earlier. We have been unable to establish when sand-casting became common in Europe (it was probably still unknown in *c.*1125 as Theophilus fails to mention it), but its occasional use for simple copper-alloy objects in the later Middle Ages is not impossible.

Fragments of simple crucibles for melting copper-alloys, sometimes associated with slag and metal drippings, are known from a number of pre-Conquest sites. More interesting is the evidence now coming to light for continued use of lost-wax casting throughout the Anglo-Saxon period.[29] Fragments of 10th-century clay bellmoulds, including ones with inscriptions, have been found at Winchester and at St. Oswald's, Gloucester.[30] The debris of bell- and pot-casting is sometimes found on post-Conquest urban sites; a tenement in Exeter, known to have been occupied by a brasier in the 15th century, has produced fragments of clay moulds for casting three-legged cauldrons.[31] Casting-clay seems to be mentioned in the 1392 Oxford text, where 'six cartfuls of earth' are valued at 2*s*. 3*d*., and in two early 16th-century York founders' inventories which include 'white earth'.[32]

London brasiers' wills provide further information. Richard atte Weye (1374) left a pair of bellows, two little pans called *meltyngpannys*, two pairs of tongs, two files, a *squachinghamer* and 100 *spyndelys ad plenam mold*'.[33] In 1421 John Brede left his brother 'all my instruments pertaining to my art of potter, with the moulds and spindles' (*cum*

29 D.M. Wilson (ed.), *The Archaeology of Anglo-Saxon England* (1976), 267-8. For other finds see J.H. Williams, *St. Peter's Street Northampton* (1979), 261-3.

30 J. Backhouse, D.H. Turner and L. Webster (eds.), *The Golden Age of Anglo-Saxon Art* (catalogue of exhibition at British Museum, 1984), 138. For later Gloucester bell-founding see H.B. Walters, 'The Gloucestershire Bell-Foundries', *Trans. Bristol & Glos. Arch. Soc.* xxxiv (1911), 110-19. This evidence for founding activity in Gloucester suggests a context for the Gloucester Candlestick (for which see p.162).

31 *Ex inf.* Christopher Henderson, Exeter

Archaeological Unit. For other finds of crucible fragments etc. see Alison R. Goodall, 'The Medieval Bronzesmith and his Products', in D.W. Crossley (ed.), *Medieval Industry* (C.B.A. Research Rep. xl, 1981), 63. The 'Medieval Britain' sections of *Medieval Archaeology* contain frequent notes of finds relating to copper-alloy working.

32 Swanson, op.cit. note 36 below, 493-7; *Test. Ebor.*, loc.cit note 7.

33 Guildhall Library, London, MSS 9171/1,f.5. A York founder of 1516 had 6 doz. 'spyndylles', which were distinguished from his 'yerne spyndylles' (*Test.Ebor.*, loc.cit. note 7).

*Fig. 45* Finishing a pot: line-filler in a 14th-century manuscript (Bodleian Library, MS Douce 6, f.136).

*les moldes et spyndell'*),[34] while in 1434 Walter Colt, brasier of Mile End, left a pair of *meltyngbelys* (i.e. 'melting-bellows') and *spyndeles de moldes*.[35] The spindles were presumably the iron rods around which were turned the clay cores for the moulds, also of clay, in which the pots were cast by the lost-wax method; Theophilus describes this process in detail.[36] The moulds bequeathed by Brede must have been reusable ones, and therefore piece-moulds or formers in stone, wood or metal. They were presumably the work of professional mouldmakers, four of whom appear in the York freemen's register between 1351/2 and 1409/10; 'patterns' occur regularly in late medieval York brasiers' wills, for instance six 'bell fete patoones' in 1492 and five 'greate fete patrones' in 1512.[37] These reusable moulds and patterns might have been for direct casting (copper-alloys as well as pewter can be cast successfully in brass moulds), but it seems more likely that they were used to make the wax or clay models.

Casting, of course, was only the first stage: saws, files, drills, lathes and soldering-irons all played their part afterwards. A marginal decoration in an early 14th-century Flemish manuscript (Fig. 45) appears to show a craftsman finishing off a latten pot with hammer and chisel. Candlesticks especially were often cast in more than one piece, lathe-turned and soldered or riveted together. In 1493 the York founder William Wynter left 'the lathe that he tornys in' together with his hooks, mandrells, hammers and burnishers.[38] The London Founders' Ordinances of 1389

34  Guildhall Library, London, MS 9171/3, ff.71ᵛ-72.
35  Guildhall Library, London, MS 9171/3, f.391.
36  *On Divers Arts*, trans. Hawthorne & Smith, 132-3.
37  For mouldmakers see *Register of Freemen of the City of York: I: 1272-1558* (Surtees Soc. xcvi, 1897), 56, 62, 113. For bequests of metal moulds and patterns in late medieval York see H.C. Swanson, 'Craftsmen and Industry in Late Medieval York' (unpub. Univ. of York D.Phil. thesis, 1980), 185, 496.
38  Ibid. 186.

are concerned both to stamp out poor-quality soldering and to control the more noisy activities:

> No one of the said trade shall make any manner of moulding, turning, filing, garnishing or any work in the way of hatching, in the said trade, by night, or on ... [the eves of certain feast-days] after noon rung out in his parish. But that anyone who has then begun to cast, shall finish what he has so begun; but he shall set no new mould to finish after noon rung ...; and he shall work only during the time of melting...'[39]

In 1603 John Stow proposed an informative (though false) etymology of Lothbury:

> This streete is possessed for the most part by Founders, that cast Candlestickes, Chafingdishes, Spice mortars, and such like Copper or Laton workes, and do afterwarde turne them with the foot & not with the wheele, to make them smooth and bright with turning and scrating (as some do tearme it) making a loathsome noice to the by-passers, that have not been used to the like, and therefore by them disdainedly called Lothberie.[40]

The process provided a conventional figure of speech for an especially horrible noise: in *Henry IV Part I* (III.1) Hotspur protests that he would 'rather hear a brazen canstick turn'd' than listen to poetry.

Fired enamel was used to decorate copper and latten as well as goldsmiths' work, but nothing is yet known for certain about the craftsmen who did this in Britain. Since the techniques involved are identical, whatever the metal used as a base, the reader is referred to the chapter on goldsmiths' work for further information. In fact, many sophisticated copper-alloy objects have every appearance of having been made by goldsmiths.

### Bell-Founding

Bell-founding was one of the most specialised of the copper-alloy crafts, not only because of the casting processes used, but also because, for all but the very earliest part of the period under discussion, the product was normally large and had to be tuned as well as made.[41] Considerations of sound required an alloy rich in tin, close to modern bronze. A proportion of four parts of copper to one of tin is prescribed by Theophilus and has remained normal ever since.[42] Thus when scrap was used, other than from old bells, extra tin had to be added. In 1318/19(?) a new bell at Bridgwater (Som.) was made from 180 lb. of pots, platters, basins, lavers, kettles, brass mortars and mill-pots, an old bell weighing 425 lb., 40 lb. of 'brass' (*aes*), 896 lb. of copper and 320 lb. of tin, giving a ratio of new tin to new copper of more than 1:3.[43] There was an

39  Riley, *Memorials*, 512-15. Cf. also the Company's first ordinances of 1365: W.N. Hibbert, *History of the Founders' Company* (1925), 285-91.

40  John Stow, *A Survey of London*, ed. C.L. Kingsford (2 vols., 1908), i, 277.

41  This section is based on Theophilus, and on the works by Walters, Elphick, Harvey, Feld-

haus and Salzman cited in the notes on p.105.

42  *On Divers Arts*, ed. Hawthorne & Smith, 167-79.

43  T.D. Dilks (ed.), *Bridgwater Borough Archives*, i, *1200-1377* (Somerset Record Soc. xlviii, 1933), 65-7.

*Fig. 46* Two stages in the making of a bell, shown on a window of *c.* 1300 at York minster.

ancient, and erroneous, belief that the addition of silver to the metal of a bell improved its tone.[44]

The earliest bells, which were small, or comparatively so, were either forged with the hammer (from iron and copper as well as bronze) or cast by the waste-wax process described above (p.86-7). After the advent of the church-bell, probably in the 6th century A.D., a variation of the wax process was evolved and used exclusively for the casting of bells and mortars, which are, of course, of similar form. The earliest record is Theophilus's account, but it was probably introduced long before his time, since what he describes is a fully-developed process that must already have had a long history. It was one that has persisted without essential change until the 20th century.

A bell has been aptly described as a layer of metal which has been run into a narrow space between two moulds: an inner mould forming the core, and an outer

44  See Feldhaus, op.cit. note 41, column 474, and
    Walters, op.cit. note 41, 34. For an apparent
    case of this practice revealed by analysis of

casting debris see P. Greene, *Norton Priory*
(1989), 120.

45  Walters, op.cit. note 41, 36.

one, called by bell-founders the *cope* or *mantle*.[45] The loops at the top (*canons* and *argent*), which secure the bell to the wooden headstock on which it swings, are added at the modelling stage but cast in one piece with the bell.

The bell-founding process as described by Theophilus is as follows: a square tapering oak spindle is made, slightly taller than the finished bell, and capable of being fitted horizontally into recesses in a wooden stand in which it can be rotated by means of a handle at one end. The spindle is covered with clay in successive layers, each layer being allowed to dry before the next one is applied, until it is thick enough to be made into the core of the bell. It is then placed in the stand and, while the handle is turned by someone else, the belyeter works it with appropriate tools until it is the right shape to form the core; finally he smooths it off with a damp cloth. Next it is covered with a layer of tallow of the thickness that the metal of the bell is to be, laid on in strips joined with a hot iron. The tallow is thickened in the appropriate place to form the rim and, when cold, turned to the exact size with sharp tools, and incised with any decoration that might be required.

The foundation of the cope is then formed by covering the whole with two layers of sifted and carefully mixed clay, of which the first is allowed to dry before the second is applied. Next, the mould is turned on its side, the spindle pulled out, and the upper part of the resulting hole filled with clay into which the iron crown-staple, for attaching the clapper, is embedded with its ends projecting upwards. When this clay has dried the projecting ends of the staple are thickly covered with tallow, and tallow models of the canons and argent and of a gate and a vent are applied to the top, of which the two last-named will form apertures in the completed mould through which molten bronze will be poured and hot air escape; when complete, these are all covered with clay. When the clay has dried all over, the whole mould is bound with close-set iron hoops and two further layers of clay are applied. When these are dry the mould is again turned on its side and, in order to reduce weight, its inside is scooped out until it is no more than a foot thick anywhere.

A pit is then dug wide and deep enough to contain the mould, which is placed on a low stone and clay base, containing a wide central channel, in the centre of the pit. A furnace is built all round the mould with an arched opening at each end of the central channel in the base. When the building of this has reached halfway up, a hole is pierced in each side of the rim of the mould through which melted tallow can escape into pots. A wood fire is then lit round the mould and, while the latter heats up and the tallow runs out, the building of the furnace is completed right to the top, where a small aperture, fitted with a clay or iron cover, is left. When all the tallow has been discharged the holes made for this purpose are made good with clay.

The fire round the mould is kept burning for a day and a night, and, at the same time, the pots in which the bronze for the bell is to be melted are heated in separate furnaces. The bell-mould is kept under observation through the opening left in the top of its furnace and, as soon as it is red-hot inside, the metal for the bronze is put into its pots to melt, while, very rapidly, the mould-furnace and its fire are removed and the pit is filled with lightly compacted earth. The purpose of this last is to support the mould and prevent it from breaking under the weight of the molten alloy that is now poured into it.

When the metal has solidified, but is still hot, the earth is again removed from the pit and the mould is taken out, laid on its side and the clay core extracted to prevent it from cracking the bell as it cools. The mould is returned to an upright position and, when it is completely cold, broken away from the bell, which is now ready for cleaning-up. This is done by fixing a piece of wood, supported by braces, centrally in the bell and placing the whole in a wooden stand, exactly as when the core was made, so that it can be rotated by means of a handle attached to one end while being smoothed and polished with appropriate tools and abrasives. The process is well illustrated in the famous bellfounders' window of *c*.1330 in York Minster (Fig. 46).[46] Finally, the bronze sprue from the gate through which the metal was poured is removed and the wooden headstock and the clapper are attached.

Theophilus, writing of small musical bells, decribes how to alter the tone of a bell by filing or honing metal away in the appropriate places. It is likely that some form of tuning larger bells was already being practised, though we have no definite evidence for it until the early 14th century. This is provided in a treatise by Walter of Oddington, a monk of Evesham, who describes a system of casting bells whole notes apart in a peal by making each ⁸⁄₉ths the weight of the next larger one.[47]

At some unknown date, possibly as early as the late 11th century, a variant method was introduced, in which clay (loam) was also used instead of tallow or wax in the mould.[48] This had become normal (at least in England) by the early 14th century, and survived in regular use until the mid 19th century. The centre of the core was of brick, made hollow so that a fire could be lighted inside it, and built round the vertical pivot of a template (*crook* or *sweep*) with two arms shaped respectively to the inner and outer contours of the proposed bell. The core proper was built up round this centre from layers of clay mixed with hair and straw, each of which was allowed to dry before the next was applied, and finally shaped with the appropriate arm of the crook to conform exactly to the interior of the bell. It was then greased liberally and what was, in effect, a false bell of fine clay was modelled on it with the aid of the other arm of the crook, its final surface being finished with a layer of wax or tallow.

From not later than the middle of the 13th century, decoration, including inscriptions, marks and signatures, was normally in relief, and not intaglio as decribed by Theophilus: during the Middle Ages this was produced by means of applied wax models produced from moulds. At this stage also the models of the canons and argent were added. They were at first of wax or tallow, as already mentioned, but, from probably no later than the late 12th century, were usually

---

46  Illustrated by Harvey, Pl.157, Salzman, 152, and Walters, frontispiece (opp.cit. note 41). It has been suggested that this picture – one of several in the window showing bell-making – illustrates the turning of the core of a bell, but as Salzman pointed out, the bell-shaped object shown being turned is decorated, whereas the surface of the core at this stage of manufacture would be quite plain.

47  See Harvey, op.cit. note 41, 90, and Elphick, op.cit. note 41, 3.

48  See Elphick, opt.cit. note 41, 8.

made of clay in wooden piece-moulds.[49] The surface was then greased again, a reinforced clay cope was built on to it, as described by Theophilus, and the whole was baked hard by means of a fire lit inside the core, which also served to melt out the wax or tallow. Finally, the cope was lifted off with a crane and, after the clay false bell had been broken away, replaced, so producing a mould with a gap between the cope and core, used in exactly the same way as Theophilus's mould.

### Nomenclature

The City of London records reveal a confusion of crafts directly involved in the working of copper and its alloys in the later Middle Ages: *potters, brasiers, copper-smiths, latteners, battours, founders* and *belyeters*.[50] There is also evidence that the *marblers* were indirectly involved in that they supplied monumental brasses, and in 1486 the ordinances of the Marblers' Company of London specifically mention latten and copper works;[51] in some cases at least, it is likely that makers of incised slabs also engraved brasses. Precise distinctions between these terms are today far from clear.

The four 'brass' crafts that are particularly confused are the potters, brasiers, founders and belyeters. The potters (about whom Pirenne and Unwin have written)[52] were not makers of earthenware, but founders of copper-alloy pots and other domestic utensils, as well as dealers in the small latten objects which were imported in such quantities from Dinant in the Low Countries.[53] In the record of an investigation into the sale of defective metal pots in London in 1316,[54] the potters chosen to undertake it are specifically described as four dealers and four founders of the trade.

The potters tend to disappear from London records in the middle years of the 14th century and, as was pointed out as long ago as 1884 by J.C.L. Stahlschmidt in his book on Surrey bells, were replaced by the brasiers.[55] These were making the same things as the potters, and were almost certainly the same craftsmen under a different name: for instance, as Stahlschmidt again pointed out, Robert Rider who appears in the records from 1351 is at first called a potter, but in his will, proved in 1386, is called 'citizen and brasier'.[56] Why the London potters changed their name is unclear: possible reasons are a growing confusion with the makers of earthenware, or a breakaway of the working craftsmen from the traders. In York, on the other hand, casters of copper-alloy vessels continued to be called potters until at least the beginning of the reign of Elizabeth I, the makers of earthenware being distinguished

49 For a brief discussion of the evidence provided by surviving bells for when this technique was introduced see Elphick, op.cit. note 41, 10-12.
50 See *Cal. Letter-Books*, passim; J.C.L. Stahlschmidt, *Surrey Bells and London Bell-Founders* (1884), 31; Harvey, *Mediaeval Crafts-men*, 91-3.
51 *Cal. Letter-Book L*, 233. See p.46 above.
52 H. Pirenne, 'Les Marchands-Batteurs de Dinant au XIV^e et au XV^e Siècle', *Vierteljahr-*

*schrift für Social- und Wirtschaftsgeschichte*, ii (1904), 442-9; Unwin, op.cit. note 28, 31-4. See also *Middle English Dictionary* and *O.E.D.* under the various terms.
53 Pirenne, art.cit. note 52.
54 See note 12.
55 Stahlschmidt, loc.cit. note 50.
56 Ibid. This will is Guildhall Library, MS 9171/1 f.153.

from them by the name 'erthpotter'. The craft name *tounder*, which appears to be synonymous with *founder*, occurs regularly in the freemen's register from 1364/5 to 1367/8 and is thereafter replaced by the latter term, apart from an isolated occurence in 1377/8. The first brasier is not found until 1472/3, and only in Henry VIII's reign does the term start to appear with any frequency in the register. The same confusion of usage with *potter* as in the London records also occurs in the York ones. In 1541/2, for example, John Mashroder 'brasyer', son of Richard Mashroder, 'potter', was made free, but when in 1548/9 his brother Roger, a pewterer, was also made free the father was described as 'brasyer'![57]

Unfortunately, the origins of the new term *brasier* are obscured by the fact that its contemporary forms are indistinguishable from those for 'brewer' (Latin *brasiator*) until at least the 15th century, so it is impossible to say which is which in documents where names are the only guide. Eilert Ekwall, in his study of the London Subsidy Rolls of 1292 and 1319,[58] calls all the many 'le Brasers' listed therein brewers, but it is by no means certain that he is right in every case. We have not, however, been able to find any 'brasier' who can be proved to have been a metalworker earlier than 1353-60, the period covered by a royal wardrobe account which mentions that William de Aldgate, 'brasier', supplied 4 'gunnis de cupro' to the King.[59] Gunmakers mentioned in similar accounts during the next few years seem all to have been brasiers, and many references to metalworking brasiers occur from the third quarter of the 14th century onwards. As already shown, the wills of late 14th- and 15th-century London brasiers make it abundantly clear that they were producing cast copper-alloy pots and other portable objects such as potters would have made a few generations earlier.

Latteners (or latoners) are never mentioned as frequently as the brasiers. They occur, both in London and in large provincial towns such as Oxford and Norwich, from *c*.1310 onwards; in York ten are mentioned in the register of freemen between 1309/10 and 1362/3, but only two thereafter, in 1443/4 and 1484/5.[60] The ordinances of the London Mistery of Latteners (which provide no technical details) were approved in 1417.[61] In 1403 a London lattener, John Domegode, was paid for

57  See *Register of Freemen of York*, op.cit. note 36, passim, but especially, for example, 4, 45, 47, 56, 62, 63, 64, 75, 113, 139, 156, 177, 178, 187, 193, 194, 195, 206, 244-50, 276; the references, to the Mashroders are on pp.262 and 269. Other terms found in the register are *potmaker* (194), *batour* (8, 27, 51, 58), *bellmaker* (51, 146, 211), *potter & bellmaker* (226, 229), *bellfounder & potter* (257), *mettelman* (254, 271). *Coppersmith* occurs only once, in 1411/12 (116). See also Swanson, op.cit. note 36, 188.

58  E. Ekwall, *Two Early London Subsidy Rolls* (Lund, 1951), *passim*.

59  T.F. Tout, 'Firearms in England in the Fourteenth Century', *Collected Papers of T.F. Tout*, ii (1934), 262 (reprinted with introduction by C. Blair (1968), 44. Cf. also payment in 1371

'Hugoni Brasier pro iij gunnes eneis ab eodem empto xxs' (P.R.O., E101/78/15).

60  For London, see *Cals. Letter-Book D*, 86, 174, 191; *Letter-Book E*, 1, 131, 177; *Letter-Book F*, 164; *Letter-Book G*, 112, 229, 293; *Letter-Book H*, 34. For Oxford, see H.E. Salter (ed.), *The Cartulary of the Hospital of St. John the Baptist* (Oxford Hist. Soc. lxvi, lxviii, lxix, 1914-16), passim. For Norwich, see W. Rye (ed.), *A Calendar of Norwich Deeds 1307-41* (Norfolk Arch. Soc., 1915), passim. For York, see *Register of Freemen of York*, op.cit. note 36, 12, 17, 21, 23, 33, 34, 36, 56, 161, 208, and Swanson, op.cit. note 36, 188-90.

61  For London, *Cals. Letter-Book I*, 186; cf. ibid. 173, and *Letter-Book K*, 29, 98, 149.

making a seal of *auricalcum*.[62] Three wills of 15th-century latteners were proved in the London commissary court (John Madur, 1445, John Alcock, 1459, and Thomas Murdag, 1453);[63] Alcock's has bequests of brass pots and dishes indistinguishable from those in brasiers' wills (below, p.98).[64] In 1552 Thomas Hawes of St. Margaret Lothbury, 'latten founder', left a lathe with mandrels and hooks (perhaps for turning candlesticks), a pair of small lamps, a 'myddell dysche', a small spice-mortar, and (perplexingly) 'a payre of small Synagogges'.[65] None of these sources gives any indication of why latteners should have been distinguished from brasiers or founders.

It is no easier to draw distinctions between the other terms. Obviously belyeters (first mentioned in 1247)[66] specialised in bells; but even they may also have made typical brasiers' wares (cf. Fig.48). William Burford of St. Botolph's Aldgate is called 'belyetere and citizen' in his will of 1391, but 'citizen and brasyer' in his widow's of 1397; while in 1312 a London potter covenanted to make a bell.[67] The term coppersmith (first recorded in 1305)[68] must originally have denoted the working of copper plate with the hammer, as distinct from casting. Yet Nicholas Broker, one of the makers of Richard II's cast effigy, is called coppersmith in his will of 1425, which includes bequests of cast latten.[69] In 1374 the London brasier Richard atte Weye bequeathed his best tin-mould (*tinmod*), presumably for casting pewter.[70] These examples merely emphasise what we might in any case expect: an absence of any rigid demarcation lines or exclusive specialisation.

## Organisation

In the list of London mysteries who lent money to Edward III in 1364 (which incidentally has a separate entry for brewers but not one for potters), the brasiers appear as an independent gild.[71] The earliest relevant ordinances, however, are those of the Founders' Company (1365).[72] These refer to making candlesticks, lavers, pots, stirrups, buckles and spurs, and the slightly later ordinances of the York founders forbid the use of poor or brittle latten for stirrups, spurs and candlesticks.[73] It is hard to see how their work differed from that of the brasiers. The London Brasiers' Ordinances, approved in 1416,[74] unfortunately contain little technical

62 C. Blair, 'An Early 15th-Century London Latoner', *Monumental Brass Soc. Bulletin* 38 (Feb. 1985), 129.

63 Guildhall Library, MSS 9171/4 f.160ᵛ, 9171/5 ff.289, 148ᵛ.

64 'Illam magnam patellam meam eream, . . . unam pelium counterfett de auricalco nov' fact', . . . unam pelium cum lavacro counterfett de auricalco.'

65 Guildhall Library, MS 9051/2 f.62ᵛ. Cf. the reference to Roger Taylor, citizen and 'lattyn founder', in a London will of 1538: I. Darlington (ed.), *London Consistory Court Wills 1492-1547*

(London Record Soc. iii, 1967), 66.

66 *Middle English Dictionary*, s.v. *belyeter*.

67 Guildhall Library, MS 9171/1, ff.230ᵛ, 411ᵛ; *Cal. Letter-Book D*, 287.

68 *Middle English Dictionary*, s.v. *coppersmith*.

69 See note 14.

70 Guildhall Library, MS 9171/1, f.5ᵛ.

71 *Cal. Letter-Book G*, 171-2.

72 Ibid. 194; another version (1389) in Riley, *Memorials*, 512-15.

73 *York Memorandum Book*, ed. M. Sellers, Part I (Surtees Soc., cxx, 1911), 93.

74 Riley, *Memorials*, 624-7.

information. There are references to 'divers works ... deceitfully made, as well in the mixing of metals as in other matters', and instructions about the use of 'good and sufficient metal, well and sufficiently mingled and tempered', and of weights of the proper standard. This last provision is explained in a statute of 1504 about pewterers and brasiers which mentions, among other things, people buying scrap metal with 'deceivable and untrewe Beames and Scales that ... wold stand even with xij lb. weight at one end ayenst a quarter of a lb. at the other end'.[75] Significantly, it is the Master and Wardens of the Pewterers' Company who are given the right of search 'of all such unlawefull peweter or brasse': it seems fairly clear from this that the Brasiers' Company, if not defunct, must have been moribund. Possibly it survived until early in the 16th century, since as late as 1527 one Simon Vaverser called himself 'Citizen and Braser' in his will.[76]

By this date the London brasiers may already have been involved with the Armourers' Company, in which they were prominent by the end of the century. The will (dated 1535) of William Vynyard, who had been Master of the Armourers' Company in 1503, 1513 and 1531, includes not only armour and armourers' tools but also 'a stake to torne candisstickes' and 'toles to make grates and lanterns'.[77] There is no reference to brasiers in the Armourers' Ordinances of 1571, but a brand-new charter of 1619 gave the Armourers rights of search of 'all manner of brasse and copper works' made by its members.[78] It is odd that the Brasiers should have joined the Armourers, rather than the much more obvious Founders' Company (which did indeed have brasiers among its members). Armourers' Hall is in Coleman Street, just round the corner from Lothbury where, according to John Stow, there were numerous workers in brass and copper. Possibly a group of these had some quarrel with the Founders and preferred to join the Armourers. A more interesting possibility is that there were long-standing links because of the brasiers' early involvement with making cannon (below, p.99).

As workers in moderately expensive materials, potters and brasiers were among the more prosperous London citizens. In 1312 the wealthy potter Richard de Wymbush cast the second of his two bells for Holy Trinity, Aldgate,[79] in an area on the eastern edge of the city which may already have become a centre for the copper-alloy trades. Bellfounders seem normally to have lived in Aldgate and Portsoken wards,[80] and the name of Billiter (i.e. Belyeter) Lane in Aldgate preserves a memory of the bell-founders.[81] Aldgate Ward had four potters in 1319,[82] and nearly all the late 14th- and 15th-century brasiers whose wills were proved in the London Commissary Court lived in St. Botolph's Aldgate. By contrast, the three 15th-century latteners with extant wills lived at the other end of the City, in the parish of St. Martin Ludgate.[83]

75  *Statutes of the Realm*, ii (1816), 651: 19 Hen. VIII, cap. vi.
76  Guildhall Library, MS 9171/10 f.102.
77  Ibid. f.261.
78  Ibid. MS 12,110, p.24.

79  Unwin, op.cit. note 28, 33-4.
80  Stahlschmidt, op.cit. note 50, 2.
81  Stow, *Survey of London*, i, 138.
82  Ekwall, *Two Subsidy Rolls*, 84.
83  See note 63.

The London Coppersmiths' Ordinances were approved in 1423.[84] In the accompanying petition they list such items as rings, beads, purse-rings, chalices and powder-boxes of copper and latten, and ask to be allowed to make search of all workers in gilt or silvered copper or latten. Whatever the problems of categorising the actual craftsmen, this makes it clear enough that the Coppersmiths' Company concerned itself with personal adornments and small-scale, semi-precious items, leaving the heavier cast goods to the Brasiers and Founders.

For the operation of workshops and the distribution of their products there is little evidence from London, still less from elsewhere, but the 1392 Oxford contract is again useful.[85] The master-brasier, William Cnurley, evidently ran his business by sub-contracting rather than by centralising production in one workshop. He provided his assistant, Richard Gyles, with a leasehold tenement, and undertook to find full-time work in *brasiercrafte* for him and for five other men. Cnurley was to provide all materials for Gyles, who was to make objects to his order at a flat rate of 8*s*. per cwt. The articles of complaint attached to the contract list some of Gyles's products: pots, bells, and no less than 202 *fawtys* (perhaps a contemporary misreading of *faucets*, i.e. taps or pierced spigots for barrels, cf. Fig.51). Gyles also claimed that Cnurley owed him 4*s*. 10*d*. 'for his work when he was with him at the fair', and accused him of trickery with false weights. This unique glimpse of one relatively humble business can probably stand for countless others: half-a-dozen men turning out small, portable objects in large quantities and touring the local fairs and markets.

## Products

Most brasiers would have worked within the standard range of portable copper-alloy goods.[86] Wills of 15th-century London brasiers usually mention items which were presumably their own products: two- and three-gallon brass pots or measures (*ollee*

---

84  Corporation of London Records Office, Letter-Book K, f.126 (noted but not calendared *Cal. Letter-Book K*, 18). The ordinances begin with a petition against dishonest vendors wishing to deceive the people who 'fount de jours en aultre fermail les anelx bedes signetz gipscyrynges chalices pouderboxes lyens & burcelx pur hangers & aultre choses de cupre & de laton & les sursorrent & sursargentent semblables a or & argent & les vendont & mettont a gage as plusours homes' as pure gold, pure silver or pure silver-gilt, causing the honest men of the mystery of coppersmiths great care and slander. They ask: (1) to be allowed to make search of all who exercise their mistery '& qi ferront ascuns oeueraigues de cupre ou de laton sursorez & sursargentez' in the City, and to search such wares and all other wares whatsoever they may make touch-

ing the mistery of the coppersmiths; (2) that nobody in the said Mistery, whether master or servant or any other condition, is to make or cause to be made 'les oeueraignes de cupre & de laton sursorrez ou sursargentez ou ascuns aultres oeueraigues qecongues de mesmes le Mistier en lours Chambres ne aultres lieux priueez & suspectz mais en shopes ou aultres lieux ment suspectz' and where the Wardens can enter etc.

85  See Blair, Blair and Brownsword, art.cit. note 10.

86  For good recent surveys, see: H. Drescher, 'Mittelalterliche Dreibeintöpfe aus Bronze', in J.G.N. Renaud (ed.), *Rotterdam Papers* (1968), 23-33; A.R. Goodall, art.cit. note 31, 63-71; H.P. Lochner, *Messing: Ein Handbuch über Messinggerät des 15-17 Jahrhunderts* (Munich, 1981).

*Fig. 47* Engraved, enamelled and gilt reliquary casket, *c.* 1400. (*Victoria and Albert Museum 634-1870*)

*enee*) (John Burgess, 1405); a brass three-gallon pot and a brass bowl (Alice, widow of John Langhorne, 1421); pots and pans of brass and candlesticks of latten (Nicholas Vavesour, 1479).[87] In 1577 the inventory of Ralph Heathcote, brasier of Chesterfield, provides a list of stock which, though late, may reflect a large producer's normal repertoire at the end of the Middle Ages.[88] Heathcote purveyed new pots, new mortars, 'myllne [Milan?] brasses', chafing-dishes, bell-feet candlesticks, smaller candlesticks, ladles, skimmers, and small bells. He also had a range of pewter goods, 'tynckers wares and suche lyke', and 160 lb. of 'flawnders ware pannes and kettles'. The last item shows that he was also a retailer of the imported Flemish goods ('dinanderie') which had dominated the late medieval market. That dinanderie was considered a threat to the home industry is suggested by an Act of 1464 which restricts the importation of 'harneys for gurdles of iron, of laton, of stele, of tyn or of alkamyn, ... chauffyngdisshes, candelstickes hangyng or stondyng, hangyng lavours, chauffyng-balles, sakeryngbelles, rynges for curtyns, ladles, scomours, counterfett basons, ewers ...'[89] 'Counterfeit' in such contexts evidently means 'decorated': in 1464 the Howard household accounts distinguish between 'a garnyshe of counterfet vessellys ... and half a garnyshe of playne vessellys'.[90]

87  Guildhall Library, MSS 9171/2, f.75ᵛ, 9171/3, f.75, and 9171/6, f.306.
88  Bestall and Fowkes, op.cit. note 7, 137-42. For similarly detailed York brasiers' inventories of 1512 and 1516 see Swanson, op.cit.

note 36, 493-7, and *Test.Ebor.* loc.cit. note 7.
89  *Rot.Parl.* v [n.d.], 507a.
90  B. Botfield, *Manners and Household Expenses* (Roxburghe Club, 1841), 279. See *O.E.D. s.v. counterfeit.*

Probably the most important products between the 13th and 16th centuries were baluster-shaped pots and pot-bellied cauldrons or kettles (Figs.48-50). The latter invariably, and the former often, had three legs designed to stand on the hearth:[91] an English calendar picture of *c.* 1375 shows a man cooking in what is clearly one of these cauldrons.[92] As mentioned above, some London potters were accused in 1317 of alloying their metal with so much lead that the pots melted when placed over the fire.[93] The skillet was simply a small version with a long handle and a lip or spout to facilitate pouring.[94]

Brasiers seem to have played an important role in the early development of firearms, probably because the techniques required for casting the pots that were their normal stock-in-trade were very similar to those required for casting the barrel of the earliest form of muzzle-loading gun in the same, or a similar, alloy. The earliest firm evidence for the existence of guns, anywhere in the world, is provided by a Florentine ordinance of 1326 and the well-known illustration of an arrow-firing cannon in the manuscript treatise of Walter de Milemete, dated 1327, in the library of Christ Church, Oxford. The English royal wardrobe accounts record payments for the ingredients for gunpowder from 1334, and for guns from 1344, many of the latter being supplied by London brasiers. It is interesting to note in this connection that some of the earliest continental references to cannon are as *pot* and *vasa*, while they are commonly described as being made to fire arrows (*quarreaux*). The form of the cannon shown in the Milemete manuscript is almost exactly that of a medieval baluster-shaped pot laid on its side, it fires an arrow, and its surface is coloured gold: it is extremely probable, therefore, that it represents one of the products of a potter (or brasier).[95]

Mortars, bells, skimmers, and other simple objects are known from surviving examples, as are more elaborate items such as flagons and two-spouted lavers. Some are highly decorated, with coats of arms, inscriptions and other motifs cast in relief.[96] The earlier domestic candlesticks generally have tripod legs; conical or bell-shaped bases (the 'bell-feet candlesticks' of Heathcote's inventory) developed in the later 15th century.[97] As already indicated (p.97), taps, spouts and spigots were

---

91  For a range of examples see K. Marshall, 'Cast-Bronze Cauldrons of Medieval Type in the Belfast City Museum', *Ulster Journal of Archaeology*, 3rd ser. xii (1950), 66-75. See also *Stadt im Wandel: Kunst und Kultur des Bürgertums in Norddeutschland 1150-1650* (cat. of exhibition, Brunswick, 1985), i, 197-8.

92  Bodleian Library, MS Rawl. D. 939. Cf. also 15th-century misericords at Ludlow (Salop.); a figure of Gluttony on a bench-end at Finningham (Suffolk) (Fig.50); and J. Seymour Lindsay, *Iron and Brass Implements* (1970), 26, 28. The lettering on an early 15th-century bell by Thomas Potter shows a tripod cauldron: Walters, *Church Bells of England*, 289.

93  Riley, *Memorials*, 118-19.

94  E.g. E. Jackson, 'On a Bronze Tripod Vessel', *Trans. Cumberland and Westmorland Arch.Soc.*, n.s. viii (1908), 72-4.

95  Cf. note 50. For *pot* and *vasa* see J.R. Partington, *A History of Greek Fire and Gunpowder* (1960), 102; for a discussion of the Milemete and Holkham Hall (now B.L.) MSS see ibid. 98-102, 132, 232, 276-7. See also C. Blair (ed.), *Pollard's History of Firearms* (1983), 27-8, and pl. 88 (coloured illustration of Milemete).

96  See for instance J. Cherry, 'A New Type of Dinanderie found in England', *British Museum Occasional Paper*, x (1980), 55-6.

97  See R. Brownsword, *English Latten Domestic Candlesticks 1400-1700*, Finds Research Group 700-1700, Datasheet 1 (n.d. [c.1984]).

Fig. 48 Seal of a brasier, 'Andrew of Gloucester', showing two products. After *Arch. Jnl.* xiii (1856), p. 73.

Fig. 49 Brass pot bearing the name of John de Walmer (*Burrell Collection, Glasgow*)

Fig. 50 Gluttony, holding a brass pot: 15th-century bench-end figure in the church of Finningham (Suffolk).

Fig. 51 Brass tap from Wallands, near Lewes, mid 13th century. (*Lewes Museum*)

produced in large quantities (Fig. 51).[98] At the bottom end of the scale were very small, simple objects such as buckles, badges, ornamental fastenings and girdle-mounts, which could be cast in open moulds (Fig.44). These did not require a fully-equipped brasier's workshop, and were made by by lorimers, girdle-makers and perhaps others concerned with the clothing trades.[99] Latten spoons are of much the same form as pewter ones, and some surviving examples were clearly cast in the same or similar moulds.[100] Spurs are exceptional metallurgically, being sometimes made of brass and often of virtually pure copper.[101]

It is rarely self-evident whether any of these cast copper-alloy objects are English or imported, and unjustified assumptions have often been made. Metallurgical analyses, notably Roger Brownsword's at Coventry, are now starting to provide more solid evidence. It may be, for example, that high levels of tin or lead point to the work of English brasiers, who bulked out imported latten with these less expensive metals.

A rather specialised copper-alloy product was the monumental brass.[102] The plates were cast as sheets, usually about 0.76 m. by 0.61 m. across and about 4 mm. thick; it is generally assumed (not necessarily rightly) that these were always imported. The designs were engraved by using hand-driven tracers and burins (gravers), both of which are sharply-pointed tools, the former for marking out the work and the latter for gouging out its lines; the section of the line depends on the shape of the burin's point. Until *c.* 1350, English brasses were laid in their indents with nothing but pitch to hold them down; rivets in lead (or occasionally wooden) plugs were generally used thereafter. Slabs were of the hard, polishable limestones known in medieval England as 'marbles', and except for a few provincial products, Purbeck marble was almost always used. This emphasises the fact (above, pp.52-4) that monumental brass manufacture was, at least in London, controlled by marblers rather than by brasiers.

A point worth emphasising in conclusion is that the use of durable moulds and patterns to form the wax models must have militated strongly in favour of conservative design. Moulds could have remained in a workshop for fifty years or more, whilst decorative panels, friezes, letters for inscriptions and other embellishments were certainly reused in different combinations on different kinds of object. A good illustration of this is a latten holy-water stoup now on loan to Carlisle

98 See G.C. Dunning, 'Medieval Bronze Tap-Handles from Lewes and Kirkstall Abbey', *Antiq. Jnl.* xlviii (1968), 310-11 and Pl. LXXX.

99 The London and York girdlers were making such objects. See Riley, *Memorials*, 154, 216, 399, 656, and for York, Swanson, op.cit. note 36, 114.

100 See examples illustrated by S. Muldoon and R. Brownsword, *Pewter Spoons and Other Related Material of the 14th to 17th Centuries* ([1985].)

101 Analysis of six spurs by Mrs. C. Girangrande indicates that five, mainly 14th- and early 15th-centuries, are of almost pure copper (between 98.55 and 99.52%), while the sixth, 15th-century, is of brass (Cu. 85.61%, Zn. 13.5%, Pb. 0.5%). We are very grateful to the Royal Armouries for permission to publish these results.

102 See M. Norris, *Monumental Brasses: the Craft* (1978), 32-43.

Cathedral treasury (Fig.43).[103] The object itself appears to be of the mid 14th century, and is inscribed, in raised Lombardic letters around its rim, PRIEZ PVR LALME G GLAVILE. On its sides are three decorative panels: the two figures of the Annunciation, and a very curious scene showing an emaciated enthroned man blowing a horn. All three scenes are rather too big for the stoup and have consequently been truncated, while Mary and Gabriel seem to have been divided out of a single panel. Stylistically, the figures look several decades earlier than the stoup. Whatever these panels were made for originally, it was not the object on which they now survive: they must derive from old models left in the workshop of the brasier who cast the stoup. This example should be a warning against applying too precise stylistic dating to a craft-form which, more than most, was suited to routine and prolonged mass-production of identical objects.

## *Technical Appendix*

## ROGER BROWNSWORD

Discussions of medieval alloys in archaeological and historical works have been prone to generalisation and error. Scientific approaches, including the analysis of several thousand copper-alloy objects (not all of English manufacture) at Coventry Polytechnic and elsewhere, are now providing a firmer basis.

Nowadays 'bronze' is often used loosely to mean any kind of copper alloy. Analytical evidence has, however, revealed almost nothing made in post-Conquest medieval England from copper-tin alloy without other significant constituents, except the very special type of high-tin bronze used for the casting of bells and known as 'bell-metal'. Since inscriptions on many 16th- and 17th-century skillets and mortars indicate that they were made by bell-founders,[104] who may well have produced such objects in earlier centuries, the assumption that 'bell-metal' was used is understandable, but the several hundred analyses of cauldrons, skillets and mortars do not support it. This is surprising, since tin was mined and smelted in England and could readily have been used to make true 'bronze'.

On the other hand, 'leaded-bronzes' were used for a wide variety of casting purposes in the Middle Ages and later; analysis has shown that the proportions of tin and lead varied widely, which in turn determined the properties and so the applications of the alloys. High-tin, low-lead alloys, close to a true 'bronze', were

---

103  From Wreay church, which acquired it in the 19th century: see J. Alexander and P. Binski (eds.), *Age of Chivalry: Art in Plantagenet England, 1200-1400* (Exhibition catalogue, Royal Academy of Arts, London, 1987), 242.

104  17th-century skillets by Clement Tosear (Salisbury) and Thomas Palmer (Canterbury) are known (the latter illustrated by Seymour Lindsay, op.cit. note 92, Fig. 119). See A.G. Hemming, 'Mortars by English Bellfounders', *Connoisseur*, xciii (1934), 393.

strong and not unduly brittle, and so were suited to the manufacture of objects subject to a degree of stress in use. A few cooking-pots and tripod ewers, probably of the 14th century, were made of this high-grade alloy. These and many more objects, such as skillets, large weights, measures and mortars, were later cast in 'leaded bronzes' with lower tin and higher lead levels, ranging to the very inferior 'lead-bronze', a copper-lead alloy. The nearer the 'leaded bronze' was to this extreme, the worse were its properties; such alloys were, however, cheap.

Heavily leaded 'bronzes' are weak and brittle: the lead particles do not dissolve in copper, and if too numerous they provide an easy facture path through the metal. This explains why broken fragments of cauldrons and skillets are often found in excavations. When cauldrons with a high lead content were placed over fires, their legs were especially vulnerable: the lead melted and ran out from surface sites, allowing internal oxidation to take place and leading to loss of the copper-rich parts of the alloy. Many late cauldrons and skillets, which generally have high lead contents, now lack the lower parts of their legs.

Comment is needed on the discussion of cauldron manufacture by K. Marshall,[105] which is in three respects misleading. First, his sketches show cauldrons cast on their sides, reflecting modern foundry practice which requires a horizontal parting plane between the two mould halves; to cast them mouth-downwards, with a vertical parting plane, would be more in keeping with the normal medieval method for bells and mortars. Secondly, his suggestion that cauldrons were made by sand moulding is contradicted by the recently excavated clay-digging pits and baked clay fragments from cauldron moulds; the clay contained some sand, but the mould was certainly not made with the reusable sand which founders know today. Thirdly, the use of separate sand cores let into the main mould for casting cauldron handles is a modern approach; wax models for handles and legs stuck to the clay body, involving a trivial cost in wax compared with the full wax model, are far more likely.

The brittleness of the leaded bronzes, and their dull colour, limited their use to relatively large and utilitarian objects. Where high resistance to stress was necessary, or the much-favoured golden colour was required, alloys were used which contained some zinc. Tin and lead were often still present, but were secondary to the zinc which coloured the metal. The complex copper-zinc-tin-lead casting alloys, best referred to as 'latten', are widespread in medieval metalwork.

These complex alloys vary from ones with a low zinc content, and so not very different from 'leaded bronze', through 'latten' alloys with all three additions at significant levels, to ones with high zinc content and so not very different from 'brass'. As this trend is followed the colour of the alloy changes towards the desirable golden, and the metal becomes more amenable to finishing or decoration by turning in a lathe or chasing. The best objects from the Meuse region, where calamine ore was readily available, were made in zinc-rich alloys.

English craftsmen knew such zinc-rich metal largely, if not exclusively, as an

105   Art.cit. note 91.

expensive import, and naturally tended to use it sparingly. A fair approximation to the golden colour of a high-zinc 'brass' is given by an alloy with several percent of tin substituted for an equivalent amount of zinc, and English craftsmen seem to have employed such dilution for all but the very finest objects. The resulting 'latten', its lead content depending on the type of object and the stress in service, has been identified in candlesticks, ewers, chafing-dishes, purse-frames, keys and no doubt others of the objects listed in the Act of 1464. The fact that the rival Flemish ware is frequently identified in documents suggests that the two types were readily separable, perhaps because of the more golden colour of the high-zinc Flemish alloys. Occasional English ewers cast in 'leaded bronze' tend to be cruder and less well-finished, and may be copies produced with limited means. Small domestic candlesticks show an evolution of alloy composition within the 'latten' range. 'Bunsen-burner' types, believed to be 15th-century, contain less zinc than their 16th-century derivatives. By the 17th century, English trumpet-based candlesticks have high zinc and low tin contents not very different from 'brass', perhaps reflecting the greater availability of zinc-rich metal in England from the late 16th century.

A notable exception is the case of late medieval spurs (14th to 15th centuries) which seem to be divisible on compositional grounds into two groups: one, mainly of fragments, is of 'brass' with low lead content, whereas the other is of almost pure copper. Both these materials are amenable to decorative chasing and finishing by gilding. No 'bronze' spur has yet been found.

The above comments all relate to casting. The alloys used in the shaping of objects by working with a hammer or similar implement, or such processes as wire-drawing, present a simpler picture, for the success of these operations places constraints on the material. Alloys must be largely free from lead particles, for these offer easy fracture paths which would lead to cracking during working. Extensive hammering of thin sheet, or drawing for wire, places heavy demands on the ductility of the metal, and for this copper itself or a true 'brass' are the most satisfactory materials. The high strength of the worked 'brass', together with its resistance to atmospheric corrosion, made it the ideal medium for finely executed repoussé work or, at the other end of the spectrum, wire for the making of wool-cards or pins. Some domestic or barber's bowls are of wrought 'brass', and it seems highly probable that at least the shaping of these was sometimes carried out in England. The raw material, in the form of 'brass' sheet or wire, was only produced in England from the end of the 16th century; and then only of inferior quality, it seems, compared with the Continental material which must have sustained such English trades as pin-making in the later Middle Ages.

## Further Reading

For technical processes, Theophilus is an original source of crucial importance. The best modern general works are R.F. Tylecote, *A History of Metallurgy* (2nd edn. 1976), and H. Hamilton, *The English Brass and Copper Industries to 1800* (2nd edn., 1967). In recent years a growing body of analyses have been carried out and published, in England mainly by the late Dr. H.K. Cameron and Dr. R. Brownsword; some of these are cited in the footnotes. For a good summary of current knowledge on the history of copper alloys, with a bibliography, see P.T. Craddock, 'Medieval Copper Alloy Production and West African Brass Analysis: Part I', *Archaeometry*, xxvii (1985), 17-41. See also O. Werner, 'Analysen Mittelalterlicher Bronzen und Messinge. I', *Archäologie und Naturwissenschaften*, i (1977), 145-200; M. de Ruette, 'Les Résultats d'Analyse de Teneurs des Laitons Coutes dans les Anciens Pay-Bas Méridionaux et la Principauté de Liège (Moyen Age et Temps Modernes)', *Revue des Archéologues et Historiens d'Art de Louvain*, xvi (1983), 252-79. For analyses of English copper-alloy jettons and coin forgeries of the 13th and 14th centuries, see M.B. Mitchiner and A. Skinner, 'Contemporary Forgeries of English Silver Coins: Henry III to William III', *Numismatic Chronicle*, cxlv (1985), 209-36.

Little of substance has been written on the organisation of the craft. London potters are discussed by G. Unwin in G. Unwin (ed.), *Finance and Trade under Edward III* (Manchester, 1918), 31-4, and Dinant merchants by H. Pirenne, 'Les Marchands-Batteurs de Dinant au XIV$^e$ et au XV$^e$ Siècle', *Vierteljahrschrift für Social- und Wirtschaftsgeschichte*, ii (1904), 442-9. The organisation of one small brasiers' workshop is discussed by C. Blair, J. Blair and R. Brownsword, 'An Oxford Brasiers' Dispute of the 1390s: Evidence for Brass-Making in Medieval England', *Antiq. Jnl.* lxvi (1986), 82-90.

On bells and bell-founding, see J.C.L. Stahlschmidt, *Surrey Bells and London Bell-Founders* (1884); H.B. Walters, *Church Bells of England* (1912), especially 36-47; G.P. Elphick, *Sussex Bells and Belfries* (1970), especially 1-22; John Harvey, *Mediaeval Craftsmen* (1975), 90-1; G. Elphick, *The Craft of the Bellfounder* (Chichester, 1988); F.M. Feldhaus, *Die Technik* (2nd edn., Munich, 1965), columns 462-74; L.F. Salzman, *English Industries of the Middle Ages* (2nd edn., 1923), 144-56.

Two important recent surveys of products, drawing much information from excavated finds, are: Alison R. Goodall, 'The Medieval Bronzesmith and his Products', in D.W. Crossley (ed.), *Medieval Industry* (C.B.A. Research Rep. xl, 1981), 63-71; H. Drescher, 'Mittelalterliche Dreibeintöpfe aus Bronze', in J.G.N. Renaud (ed.), *Rotterdam Papers* (1968), 23-33. See also J. Seymour Lindsay, *Iron and Brass Implements of the English House* (revised edn., 1970); G. Szabo, 'Medieval Bronzes: a Survey', in D. Mickenberg (ed.), *Songs of Glory: Medieval Art from 900-1500* (catalogue of exhibition at Oklahoma Museum of Art, Oklahoma City, 1985), 20-26; J.M. Lewis, R. Brownsword and E.E.H. Pitt, 'Medieval Bronze "Tripod" Ewers from Wales', *Med. Arch.* xxxi (1987), 80-93; O. von Falke and E. Meyer, *Romanische Leuchter und Gefässe. Giessgefässe der Gotik, Bronzegeräte des Mittelalters*, i (1935); Thomas Dexel,

*Gebrauchsgerät Typen* (Munich, 1981); U. Mende, *Die Türzieher des Mittelalters* (Munich, 1981); Hermann P. Lockner, *Messing. Ein Handbuch über Messinggerät des 15.-17. Jahrhunderts* (Munich, 1982); R.F. Homer, *Five Centuries of Base Metal Spoons* (Pewterers' Company, London, 1975). On monumental brasses, the standard work is now M. Norris, *Monumental Brasses: the Craft* and *Monumental Brasses: the Memorials* (1978); see also H.K. Cameron, 'Technical Aspects of Monumental Brasses', *Archaeological Journal*, cxxxi (1974), 215-37.

# 6

# Gold, Silver and Precious Stones

## MARIAN CAMPBELL

Throughout the Middle Ages silver formed the principal basis for the English coinage, as well as being used for the manufacture of plate and jewellery. The regulation of the purity of gold and silver, and of the activities of the goldsmiths who worked with the metals, were thus matters of critical importance to the Crown. The sterling standard (silver of 92.5 per cent purity) was enforced for silver plate and coin throughout the Middle Ages – the very expression 'sterling silver' originates in the term for the silver penny of the 11th century.[1]

Gold, only intermittently used for the coinage,[2] was consistently prized for use as plate and jewellery, and was indispensable for gilding, whether of silver, base-metals, wood, stone or manuscripts. Both gold and silver thread were used embroidered into textiles, the *opus anglicanum* for which England was renowned. Silver was used to produce the yellow silver stain prominent on stained glass from the 14th century onwards. Less significantly, both gold and silver played a part in medieval cookery and medicine: one of Edward I's more exotic remedies, provided to ward off leg-pains and dysentery, included crushed pearls, gems, gold and silver.[3]

Precious stones, valued as amulets as well as for their beauty and rarity, were used to adorn both plate and jewellery. The brilliant gem-like colours of enamel were similarly deployed, and enamel had the further and unique advantage of allowing a design on metal to be permanently coloured, thereby achieving an effect rivalling that of an illuminated manuscript. The craftsmen who made jewellery and plate in both gold and silver were called goldsmiths; those who made coins were called moneyers.[4]

1  P. Grierson,'Sterling', in R.H.M. Dolley (ed.), *Anglo-Saxon Coins* (1961), 266-84.
2  In 1257 Henry III introduced a gold penny (each weighing 2 silver pennies and worth 20) but the experiment failed: D. Carpenter, 'Gold and Gold Coins in England in the mid 13th Century', *Numismatic Chronicle*, cxlvii (1987), 110-13. Edward III reintroduced gold into the currency more successfully in 1344: C.H.V. Sutherland, *English Coinage, 600-1900* (1973), 72ff.; M. Mate, 'The Role of Gold Coinage in the English Economy, 1338-1400', *Numis-matic Chronicle*, 7th ser. xviii (1978), 126-41.
3  Provided in 1306 by the king's spicer Richard de Montpellier at the high cost of £129 16s. 4d.: L.G. Matthews, *The Royal Apothecaries* (1967), 18.
4  The role of moneyer, often an inherited office, was largely supervisory: Sutherland, *English Coinage*, 43, and see his index *s.v.* moneyer; P. Nightingale, 'Some London Moneyers and Reflections on the Organization of English Mints in the 11th and 12th Centuries', *Numis-matic Chronicle*, cxlii (1982), 34-50.

The passionate ostentation which led 15th-century magnates like Sir John Fastolf to amass plate and jewellery was not without reason; in an age without banks, such collections represented bullion, and were assets easily realised in times of financial difficulty. Partly as a result, and partly because of the Reformation and its after-effects, very few of these objects are left – the commonest being relatively small pieces such as rings, spoons and chalices. The largest, most spectacular and expensive masterpieces of the day – the shrines, altarpieces and crosses – have vanished.[5] Any study of the products made must therefore rely heavily upon documentary evidence. The other principal aspect of production, the method of working, can be examined from archaeological as well as documentary evidence.

## *Materials*

Much of the gold and silver used by goldsmiths was not new but consisted of old plate or coin. Native sources existed for both metals, but for gold these were negligible, although it had been mined by the Romans in Wales and was much prospected for in medieval England. That it was a rarity is illustrated by an incident in 1324, when the London goldsmith John de Wyrlingworth, after prospecting for a month, found gold in Devon weighing only 22 dwt. – and worth rather less than his expenses of 66s. 8d. Of the gold, 3 dwt. were refined in Exeter, and the remainder was refined in York; reduced to 17½ dwt. the little nugget was placed in a box, clearly a curiosity.[6] Most gold was imported, often in the convenient form of coins, in the 12th and 13th centuries, either as besants from the mint at Byzantium or as *obols de musc*, that is Almohade dinars from Moslem Spain or North Africa. In the late 15th century Germany was also a source of gold, according to a contemporary Italian account.[7]

Silver too was imported, perhaps as early as the 11th century, coming from the then freshly-discovered mines in the Harz mountains in Germany. In the 15th-century the *Libelle of Englyshe Polycye* also refers to imported silver ingots from Bohemia and Hungary.[8] England was however itself a silver producer, obtaining the

5  Surveys of surviving material are conveniently collected together in recent exhibition catalogues: J. Backhouse et al. (eds.), *The Golden Age of Anglo-Saxon Art, 966-1066* (British Museum, 1984); *English Romanesque Art, 1066-1200* (London: Arts Council, 1984); J.J.G. Alexander and P. Binski (eds.), *Age of Chivalry: Art in Plantagenet England, 1200-1400* (London: Royal Academy of Arts, 1987).

6  Welsh gold: R. Tylecote, *The Prehistory of Metallurgy in the British Isles* (1986), 2; John de Wyrlingworth: P.R.O. E 101/262/2, summarized by L.F. Salzman, 'Mines and Stannaries', in J.F. Willard et al. (eds.), *The English Government at Work, 1327-1336*, iii (Cambridge, Mass., 1950), 86.

7  Besants and obols: *The De Moneta of Nicholas of Oresme and English Mint Documents*, ed. and

trans. C. Johnson (1956), xxix-xxx; P. Nightingale, 'The London Pepperers' Guild . . . and Links with Spain', *Bull. Inst. Historical Research*, lviii (1985), 128; German gold: *Two Italian accounts of Tudor England*, transl. and ed. C.V. Malfatti (Barcelona, 1953), 37.

8  Harz silver: P. Sawyer, 'The Wealth of England in the 11th Century', *Trans. Royal Hist. Soc.* 5th ser. xv (1965), 160; Bohemian silver: *The Libelle of Englyshe Polycye . . .*, ed. G.F. Warner (1926), 17, lines 317-19. In 1235 Toulouse merchants were licensed to import to the royal mints at London and Canterbury sheet silver and ingots (*minis*): *Cal. Pat. R. 1232-47*, 90. For a discussion of the influx of foreign silver into early 14th-century England see M. Mate, 'High Prices . . . Causes and Consequences', *Econ. Hist. Rev.* 2nd ser. xxviii (1975), 2-3.

*Fig. 52* Stonyhurst chasuble; detail showing St. Dunstan, patron of goldsmiths, in his workshop; silk, gold and silver thread on velvet (*opus anglicanum*), *c.* 1470. In the cupboard are displayed rings, rosary beads and beakers and other types of drinking vessel, including a covered cup with 'writhen' decoration. (*Stonyhurst College*)

metal from mines of argentiferous lead or copper, the most significant being in Cumberland (Alston Moor), Derbyshire, Devon (Bere Alston), Durham, Flintshire, Glamorganshire and Somerset (the Mendips). All were active at different times during the period, those in Devon having the richest ores. In the five years 1292-7 the Devon mines produced £4,046 worth of silver, but their productivity was short-lived, from *c.* 1290 to 1340.[9] There is little evidence that all medieval lead was smelted for silver as a general practice; the mines so exploited may have been only those associated with a mint, such as those at Carlisle, Derby, Durham and Shrewsbury.[10]

Lead ores were of two kinds, the black ore galena (lead sulphide) being superior to the white (lead carbonate); the black ore could yield four times as much silver and twice as much lead as the white.[11] After the lead ore had been crushed and washed, it was smelted, and the silver extracted by cupellation. In this process the lead was melted on an open hearth at a temperature of 900°C and subjected to a strong blast of air. This caused the lead to oxidise and become litharge, which was absorbed by the porous materials (bone-ash, etc.) of which the hearth was made, leaving the silver in a reasonably pure form. The silver could be further refined by adding more lead and repeating the process. This process, carried out on a smaller scale, was used to test both gold and silver and is known as fire-assaying. Bone-ash was necessary both for lining hearths for refining and for making cupels, the shallow dishes in which assaying was carried out.[12]

Analysis of coins and plate shows that the small proportion of gold which silver normally contained was not generally recovered in the Middle Ages. By the 14th century, however, at least two methods were known for the separation of gold from silver. In the cementation technique, silver was extracted by heating together gold leaf with salt and brick dust, thus converting the silver to silver chloride. Both Theophilus and Agricola describe the process, and there is recent late Saxon and Viking archaeological evidence for it from Winchester and York. The sulphur method of refining (where the addition of sulphur converted the silver to silver sulphide) is first described by Theophilus, and is independently recorded in 14th-century England.[13]

9  Tylecote, op. cit. note 6, 71; Devon mines: Salzman, *Industries*, 63-40.

10  A. Raistrick and B. Jennings, *A History of Lead Mining in the Pennines* (1965), 86; for Carlisle, ibid., 47, 94, 97; for Durham, ibid., 52; for Derby, *V.C.H. Derbys.* i, 316, ii, 363; for Shrewsbury, W. Wells, 'The Shrewsbury Mint . . . and the Silver Mine at Carreghova', *Numismatic Chron.* 5th ser. xii (1932), 215-35.

11  Salzman, op. cit. note 6, 72, 79. The distinction was one known to the 13th-century writer Bartholomew the Englishman: *On the Properties of Things: John Trevisa's Translation of Bartholomeus Anglicus, De Proprietatibus Rerum*, ed. M.C. Seymour (1975), 865: 'De plumbo'.

12  Silver cupellation: Raistrick, op. cit. note 10, 15ff.; R.J. Forbes, *Studies in Ancient Technology*, 9 vols. (Leiden, 2nd rev. ed. 1964-72), viii,

234-46.

13  Gold refining methods (cupellation, salt and sulphur): Forbes, op. cit. note 12, 177-81; C.R. Dodwell, 'Gold Metallurgy in the Twelfth Century', *Gold Bulletin*, iv (1971), 52-3; W.A. Oddy, 'Assaying in Antiquity', *Gold Bull.* xvi (1983), 53-5. English 14th-century descriptions of the cementation process are in the *De Moneta*, op. cit. note 7, 84-5, and B.L. Sloane MS 1754, f.205, which also contains the first English mention of the sulphur method. Acid parting (in which the silver is dissolved out of the gold by nitric acid), though allegedly recorded in 14th-century France (Greenaway, op. cit. note 17, 821) is not a method evidenced in England unless by the exceptional purity of the 1477 trial-plate (see note 18).

After refining at or near the mine, the silver was cast into ingots; these were probably not of a standard size or purity, as indicated for example by five ingots weighing £26 10s. 9d. but worth only £25 2s. 5d. in 1333.[14] Had the ingots been up to standard the sums should have been identical. The specialist goldsmiths who refined the precious metal were known as finers. In London they were an autonomous group controlled by the Goldsmiths' Company, bound to sell only silver of the fixed standard, which they were to mark with a punch provided by the wardens of the company; no silver marked in this way is known to survive. The major part of their work was probably in refining old plate and foreign coin and plate; details of the different finenesses of silver they might encounter – those of Limoges (very pure) or of Ghent – are given in Turnemire's treatise of *c.* 1280.[15] Goldsmiths generally needed to buy little bullion for stock since their customers so often provided their own, in the form of plate to be reworked. For instance, Queen Margaret of Anjou in 1452-53 gave five silver *bolles de Roone* (Rouen?) to her goldsmith to be made into four silver parcel-gilt salts.[16]

When complete, all goldsmiths' work was by law subject to increasingly stringent scrutiny as to the purity of its metal by means of assaying. Both gold and silver were normally alloyed with some copper to add strength and hardness. One method used for assaying was fire-assay or cupellation, first clearly described in an English text of *c.* 1181 as a means of testing the coinage. Archaeological evidence in the form of cupels from numerous Anglo-Saxon sites suggests that knowledge of the process was widespread.[17] Specially prepared sheets of gold and silver of the fixed alloy, known as trial-plates, were used in the assay to provide a standard against which the coin and plate might be checked; pieces were sheared from them and used as controls. Four medieval trial plates survive, one gold, the rest silver: one of 1279 (Fig.54), two of 1477 (one gold) and one of 1530.[18]

A simpler although less accurate method of assaying was to use a touchstone –

14  Salzman, art. cit. note 6, 82-3.

15  London finers: T. Reddaway and L. Walker, *The Early History of the Goldsmiths' Company* (1975), 110-11, 246, give details of the 1435 regulations for finers which are repeated in the 1489 statute (4 Hen. VII c. 2) for finers of gold and silver: *Statutes of the Realm*, ii, 526-7. Limoges and Ghent silver: *De Moneta*, op. cit. note 7, 69-70, 96 (note).

16  A. Myers, 'The Jewels of Queen Margaret of Anjou', *Bull. John Rylands Library*, xlii (1959), 119.

17  Discussed by C. Challis, 'Assays and Assaying in the Reigns of Henry III and Edward I', in N. Mayhew and P. Spufford (eds.), *Later Medieval Mints: Organization, Administration and Techniques* (British Archaeological Reps. Internat. Ser. 389, 1988), 76-86, and R.L. Poole, *The Exchequer in the Twelfth Century* (1912), 76-7. Fire-assay of the coinage is again described in documents of *c.*1280 and 1350: *De*

*Moneta*, op. cit. note 7, 67, 78-82; *De Necessariis Observantiis Scaccarii Dialogus, commonly called Dialogus de Scaccario, by Richard, son of Nigel*, ed. C. Johnson et al., (2nd edn., Oxford, 1983), xl-xli, 10-11, 36-43; for a reference of *c.*1350 see *De Moneta*, op. cit. note 7, 78-82; another 14th-century description of silver refining is in B.L. Sloane MS 1754, f.205. There is useful material in F. Greenaway, 'The Historical Continuity of the Tradition of Assaying', *The History of Chemistry* (Ithaca, 1962), 820-3, and D.V. Thompson, 'Trial Index . . . for the History of Medieval Craftsmanship', *Speculum*, x (1935), 425.

18  J.H. Watson, *Ancient Trial Plates* (1962), 13-15, 43-7; J. Forbes and D. Dalladay, 'Metallic Impurities in the Silver Coinage Trial Plates', *Jnl. of the Institute of Metals*, lxxxvii (1958-9), 55-8; Tylecote, op. cit. note 6, 117-18, suggests that the 1477 gold trial plate was made from imported gold.

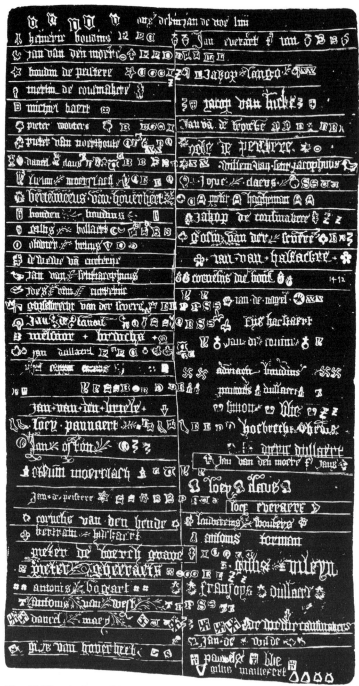

*Fig. 53* Touchplate of the goldsmiths of Ghent, showing the marks used by them (to the left of their names), and (on the right) the date letters used by the wardens; dated 1454. Height 26.2 cm. After J. Casier, *Les Orfèvres Flamandes et leurs Poinçons* (Ghent, 1923).

*Fig. 54* The earliest surviving silver trial-plate and two silver pennies of Edward I. The trial-plate, 1279, shows impressions used in the coinage of Henry III. The portion stamped with dies used in Edward's coinage has been used up in testing the purity of the coinage. (*Royal Mint*)

*Fig. 55* Detail of the Guy of Warwick mazer. Ancient repairs to the wood are patched in silver; the design of the central medallion has been achieved by hammering silver sheet on to an engraved die; *c.* 1325. Diameter of medallion *c.* 5.5 cm. (*Harbledown Hospital, on loan to Poor Priests' Museum, Canterbury*)

certainly more practical for the kinds of spot-checks which needed to be carried out on goldsmiths' premises by the wardens of the London Goldsmiths' Company before 1478. The gold or silver to be tested was rubbed onto the surface of the touchstone – a fine-grained black stone. The colour of the resulting mark on the touchstone was compared with marks produced on the same stone by alloys of known composition, in the form of touch-needles. Archaeological evidence shows the use of touchstones in England from before the Conquest right through the Middle Ages, although records make only passing mention of the method.[19]

Modern methods of metal analysis still have much to reveal about sources of metal supply and refining expertise. The presence and proportions of certain trace elements – bismuth, zinc and gold, for instance – have been identified as particularly significant diagnostic elements for determining the source of different metals.[20] It is

19  W.A. Oddy, 'Assaying in Antiquity', *Gold Bull.*, xvi (1983), 55-9 and plates, and cf. note 17; for records of touchstones see Reddaway and Walker, op. cit. note 15, 165, 319-20.

20  Considerable work has been published on the coinage, for instance J. Forbes and D. Dalladay, 'Composition of English Silver Coins (870-1300)', *British Numismatic Journal*, xxx (1960-1), 82-7; D. Metcalf and F. Schweizer, 'The Metal Contents of the Silver Pennies of William II and Henry I (1087-1135)', *Archaeometry*, xiii.2 (1971) 177-90; D. Metcalf, 'Metal Contents of Medieval Coins', in E. Hall and

D. Metcalf (eds.), *Methods of Chemical and Metallurgical Investigations of Ancient Coinage* (Royal Numismatic Soc. 1972), 407-21; D. Metcalf and W.A. Oddy (eds.), *Metallurgy in Numismatics* (Royal Numismatic Soc. 1980). There is almost nothing in print on plate and jewellery (although the Goldsmiths' Company of London maintains a confidential data-bank), but see David Jenkins, 'Trace Element Analysis in the Study of Ancient Metallurgy', in J.E. Jones (ed.) *Aspects of Ancient Mining and Metallurgy* (1988), 95-105.

*Fig. 56* Coconut-shell mounted in silver gilt, *c.* 1400-50. The lip and foot are pounced (a delicate form of engraving) with birds and flowers, the straps and lion feet are cast. Height 23.5 cm. (*Gonville and Caius College, Cambridge*)

not yet possible to see how the purity of, for example, silver chalices, dated on stylistic grounds to the 13th and 14th centuries, compares with that of contemporary coins, or whether the hall-marked silver Nettlecombe chalice of 1479 may match the 1477 trial plate. Although the medieval reuse of old plate is bound to distort such evidence, analysis may yet provide useful indications as to the source of metals, perhaps confirming the importance of Germany as a supplier.

Comparatively few surviving medieval gems set into objects ascribed to English workmanship have been investigated and identified mineralogically. Equally problematic are the vagueness or inconsistency of the terms in which gems are so often described in medieval sources. For instance, *camahieu* seems to mean a multi-coloured stone, but not always what we understand by cameo.[21] The term *amans*, *adamas* or *adamant*, although it sometimes means a diamond, often evidently does not.[22] It is nevertheless clear from both physical and documentary evidence that the gems most frequently used were pearls, rubies (both *balas* = spinel, and *orient* = corundum), sapphires, diamonds, turquoises and emeralds. Less precious materials employed included crystal, beryl, amber, coral, jet and garnets, as well as exotic shells – of ostrich and coconut – and horns, which were mounted in silver or gold and

21 Helmut Bethe, 'Edelsteine', in Otto Schmitt et al. (eds.), *Reallexikon zur Deutschen Kunstgeschichte*, iv (Stuttgart, 1958), cols. 714-42; Arthur H. Church, *Precious Stones* (Victoria and Albert Museum, 1924); R.J. Forbes, *Studies in Ancient Technology*, vii (2nd edn.) (Leiden, 1966), 237-41, 'Note on Precious and Semi-Precious Stones'; cameo: U.T. Holmes, 'Medieval Gem Stones', *Speculum*, ix (1934), 202-3.

22 See *Middle English Dictionary*, *s.v.* Adamas, Adamant; Otto Schmitt et al. (eds.), *Reallexikon zur Deutschen Kunstgeschichte*, iii (Stuttgart, 1954), cols. 1409-20: 'Diamant'.

used as cups, like the 15th-century coconut cup at Caius College, Cambridge[23] (Fig.56). Of all gems, the sapphire – 'most apt to fyngres of Kings' – was rated highest by the 13th-century encyclopedist Bartholomew the Englishman,[24] although in 16th-century Italy it took second place in price to the ruby, according to Cellini.[25] The diamond, so reliant on cutting for effect, only achieved its modern supremacy of price in the 19th century.[26] Most of these stones were credited with magical and often medicinal powers, whether to aid courage, victory or reconciliation, or to counter poison, envy or drunkenness. Such qualities were quite as important as value and appearance, and it was doubtless as a guide to them that the London goldsmith John Asshurst in 1442 bequeathed his 'lapidary book' to his fellow goldsmith William Rogersson.[27]

The sources for most of these materials were far distant, in Indian and Burma (corundum ruby, sapphire, diamond), the Mediterranean (coral, pearls) or the Baltic (amber).[28] They seem often to have been imported into England by foreign merchants, such as George Morsteyn of Cracow who in 1457-58 was licensed to import a huge ruby, weighing 214 carats.[29] Italian merchants probably played the major role as gem importers,[30] no doubt partly because of the convenient geographical coincidence which placed Italy mid-way between Alexandria (at the end of one route to India) and England. Direct purchases and gifts from abroad must also have been an important means of acquiring gems. They might be either set into an item later broken up for refashioning, or loose, such as the Black Prince's legendary ruby, given to him by King Pedro the Cruel of Spain in 1366-67 and traditionally identifiable with the spinel ruby now set into the State Crown, in the Tower of London.[31]

Pearls were to be found in fresh-water mussels in rivers in Wales, Cumberland and Scotland, and British pearls are mentioned by the Roman writers Tacitus and Pliny as well as by Bede. In *c.* 1070 the lapidary written by Marbodus refers to British pearls rivalling those of India and Persia, but by the 12th century, although there

23  C.J. Jackson, *An Illustrated History of English Plate* (1911), ii, 649-52; *Treasures of Cambridge*, exhibition cat. (London: Goldsmiths' Hall, 1959), No. 109.

24  *On the Properties of Things: John Trevisa's Translation of Bartholomeus Anglicus*, op. cit. note 11, 205 (book XV, ch. 86).

25  *The Treatises of Benvenuto Cellini on Goldsmithing and Sculpture*, transl. C.R. Ashbee (1888), 23.

26  Godehard Lenzen, *The History of Diamond Production and the Diamond Trade*, transl. F. Bradley (1970), 21.

27  Joan Evans, *Magical Jewels of the Middle Ages and the Renaissance* (1922); Ashurst's will is in Guildhall Library, MS 9171/4, f. 75v.

28  *Gemstones and Jewellery*, cat. of exhibition at Birmingham City Museum and Art Gallery (1960), 6-10; J. Ogden, *Jewellery of the Ancient World* (1983), 89-121.

29  *Appendix to the 48th Report of the Deputy Keeper of*

the *Public Records* (1887), 427. English merchants were undoubtedly active too: in 1484-5 Sir Edmund Shawe and Ralph Latham were licensed to import free of Customs 'perilles and precious stones sette or unsette polissched or unpolissched': *British Library Harleian Manuscript 433*, eds. R. Horrox and P. Hammond, i (1980), 207-8.

30  M.L. Campbell, 'L'Oreficeria Italiana nell' Inghilterra Medievale . . .', *Bollettino d'Arte*, Supplement (1987); A.A. Ruddock, *Italian Merchants and Shipping in Southampton, 1270-1600* (1951), 72, 74.

31  *Jewels and Plate of Queen Elizabeth I . . .*, ed. A.J. Collins (1955), 12-13 note 3. The ruby in the State Crown weighed 170 carats in 1838 (I am grateful to E.A. Jobbins for this information). Collins suggests that the ruby is the one set into one of Richard II's crowns which weighed 181 carats.

was a market for 'scotch pearls', they were cheaper than the oriental.[32] 'Scotch' pearls are specified in a 1324 inventory as adorning Edward II's crown, and were set also into a square brooch owned in 1370 by Queen Jeanne d'Evreux of France.[33]

Jet is found in England at Whitby, and Britain is lauded as its chief source by Bede as well as by the 13th-century writer Bartholomew the Englishman.[34] The earliest reference to an English jet worker, possibly of Whitby, is not until 1394, when Whitby Abbey paid Robert Car for making jet rings.[35] Not far away, at York, there is archaeological evidence for the working of jet, perhaps local material, from Roman times onwards.[36] Nearby Durham owned a jet super-altar in 1372.[37] Elsewhere in England there are jet objects of all sorts recorded, or surviving, such as a phylactery given to Salisbury Cathedral by Bishop Osmund (1078-99);[38] a crozier of *c.* 1175-1200 found at Chichester Cathedral;[39] a few 13th-century personal seals;[40] a paternoster owned by Humphrey de Bohun in 1322;[41] and, from the 15th century, beads, pectoral crosses and a corpus figure.[42] Jet was favoured throughout Europe, particularly because of its reputed powers over evil, and only technical analysis might indicate the geological sources for these objects,[43] for jet seems to have been imported to England, in 1438-39 at least, through London and Southampton.[44] Amber may have been retrieved from East Anglian beaches, where it is still sometimes washed up.

Artificial gems were also used. Crystals foiled with a colour to imitate a gem

32 G.F. Kunz and C.H. Stevenson, *The Book of the Pearl* (New York, 1908), 17, 159-61.

33 Crown: F. Palgrave, *Antient Kalendars and Inventories . . .* (1836), iii, 139. *Fermail*: C. Leber, *Collection des Meilleurs Dissertations, Notices et Traités relatifs à l'Histoire de France*, xix (Paris, 1838), 126.

34 H.P. Kendall, *The Story of Whitby Jet* (1936); *Bartholomeus Anglicus*, op. cit. note 11, book XV ch. 48, 851-2.

35 *V.C.H. Yorks.* ii (1912), 330.

36 D. Waterman, 'Late Saxon, Viking and Early Medieval Finds from York', *Archaeologia*, xcvii (1959), 68, 74, 94; A. MacGregor, 'Anglo-Scandinavian Finds from Lloyds Bank . . .' in *The Archaeology of York: Small Finds*: 17.3 (1982), 89-91; D. Tweddle, 'Finds from Parliament Street . . .', ibid. 17.4 (1986), 186-7.

37 D. Rock, *Church of our Fathers*, eds. G. Hart and W.H. Frere (1905), i, 201; in 1404 Walter Berghe bequeathed another jet super-altar to the Fraternity of St. George, York: *Testamenta Eboracensia*, i, ed. J. Raine (Surtees Soc. ii, 1836), 334.

38 O. Lehmann-Brockhaus, *Lateinische Schriftquellen zur Kunst in England . . . 901-1307*, 5 vols. (Munich, 1955-60), ii, 479-80, No. 4053.

39 *English Romanesque Art*, op. cit. note 5, cat. No. 272.

40 Five seals are in the British Museum: J. Cherry, 'Two Equestrian Seal Dies', in *Department of Medieval and Later Antiquities: New Acquisitions*, pt. 1 (British Museum Occasional Paper No. 10, 1980), 31-2 and note 2; another is in Maidstone Museum: W.J. Lightfoot, 'Note on an Ancient Seal . . .', *Arch. Cant.* iii (1860), 189-90.

41 T.H. Turner, 'The Will of Humphrey de Bohun . . . with Extracts from the Inventory of his Effects, 1319-22', *Arch. Jnl.* ii (1845), 348.

42 Beads (15th-16th cent.) from London: Baynards Castle site, unpublished, *ex inf.* Peter Marsden, Museum of London; from Toppings and Sun wharves, Southwark: *Proc. London and Middx. Arch. Soc.* xxv (1974), 103, Fig. 49 No. 22. Pectoral crosses found in Carlisle in 1987, and near Kirkleatham Hall, Yorks., illus. in *Proc. Soc. Antiq.* 2nd ser. i (1859-61), 399. Corpus found in London, 1987, unpublished, *ex inf.* Brian Spencer, Museum of London.

43 K.D. Sales et al., 'Identification of Jet and Related Black Materials with ESR Spectroscopy', *Archaeometry*, xxix, pt. 1 (1987), 103-9.

44 As 'gete bedes': 100 lbs. into London: P.R.O., E 122/73/10, f.12ᵛ; 1½ cwt., worth £8, into Southampton: P.R.O., E 122/141/23. The beads may have been rosary beads, or simply black glass.

adorned another of Edward II's crowns in 1324, and are found set into a 12th-century ring in the Lark Hill hoard, as well as being used to decorate William of Wykeham's girdle of *c.* 1400.[45]

Tiny white (glass?) beads, perhaps imitating pearls, were also used, as on the clothing in which Edward I was buried in 1307, and it may have been for producing just such beads that craftsmen used the early 14th-century English recipe *ad faciendum margaritas* (to make pearls); a recipe is also given for artificial amber.[46] Counterfeit gems – mostly of glass set into gold – account for many of the fines levied by the London Goldsmiths' Company from the 14th century onwards. The implication of legislation in 1300 and of the Company's ordinances in 1370 and 1478 that reiterate the prohibition against setting gold with glass seems to be that glass was permissible in silver and base metal, so that the makers of the objects listed above were perhaps not acting illegally.[47]

As with precious metal, it seems that customers accumulated their own stocks of gems for supply to the goldsmith. Edward I had various bags of stones stolen in 1302-3, one holding 26 pearls and another three turquoises and 110 small rubies and emeralds. Piers Gaveston, when arrested in 1313, had with him an unset ruby worth £1,000, while Humphrey de Bohun died in 1322 leaving branches of coral in his will.[48]

## *Methods of Working: Metals*

The basic techniques used by goldsmiths throughout the Middle Ages varied little from those employed today. The innovations of the period – gem-cutting, the use of *basse-taille* (translucent) enamelling – all reflected refinements in technique. There is no medieval English goldsmith's treatise, but that many of the methods described in *c.* 1125 by the German Theophilus were in use in England is confirmed by an examination of the objects themselves.[49]

The two principal methods of working gold and silver were forging with a hammer

45  Crown: Palgrave, *Antient Kalendars*, op. cit. note 33, iii, 140; Lark Hill ring: *English Romanesque Art*, cat. cit. note 5, cat. No. 320; girdle: *Age of Chivalry*, cat. cit. note 5, cat. No. 609.

46  Edward I: J. Ayloffe, 'An Account of the Body of King Edward I . . . in the Year 1774', *Archaeologia*, iii (1786), 382-3; recipe: B.L. Sloane MS 1754, f.205 (artificial pearls), f.208 (artificial amber). Glass beads representing eyes are set into the 12th-century Gloucester Candlestick (Fig.76) and occur – sometimes mingled with pearls – on *opus anglicanum*: [D. King], *Opus Anglicanum: English Medieval Embroidery*, exhibition cat. (Arts Council, 1963), cat. Nos. 77, 78. The term *perle* was translated as bead in English, so references

may be ambiguous.

47  Statute of 1300 in *Statutes of the Realm*, i, 141; the ordinance of 1370, cited in W. Prideaux, *Memorials of the Goldsmiths Company* (1896), i, 8-9, also forbade the setting of real stones in 'latten or copper unless for church ornaments'. For the 1370 and 1478 ordinances see Reddaway and Walker, op. cit. note 15, 212, 220-1, 227-8.

48  Edward I: Lehmann-Brockhaus, op. cit. note 38, 226, No. 2970; Gaveston: T. Rymer, *Foedera* . . ., ed. A. Clarke, ii, 204; Bohun: Turner, art. cit. note 41, 348.

49  Theophilus, *On Divers Arts*, ed. Hawthorne and Smith, Book III.

Fig. 57 Mould for ring-
brooches with inscriptions
'Ave Maria Gracia Plena',
c. 1300; found at Ashill,
Norfolk, c. 1798; present
whereabouts unknown. After
*Archaelologia*, xiv (1805).

(Fig.60), and casting.[50] Most vessels and dishes were probably forged; jewellery and
decorative finials were often cast. To forge metal, an ingot was hammered into sheet
metal of suitable thickness, cut to size, and raised – that is hammered into shape.
Frequent annealing (heating and then cooling the metal) was necessary to prevent
hardening. A smooth surface was given to the object first by planishing with special
hammers, then by polishing. Casting was achieved in two principal ways: by pouring
molten metal into open or piece moulds, and by using the *cire-perdue* (lost wax)
method. Piece moulds, sometimes even with inscriptions, might be used for simple
items of jewellery such as badges or brooches (Fig.57); the use of such a mould
avoided much subsequent labour of engraving.

The same type of motif – for example, small figures of the apostles or lions – may
recur on croziers or reliquaries, as spoon finials or cup-feet (Fig.56). Since
goldsmiths frequently bequeathed their moulds to their heirs it is not surprising
occasionally to find evidence that the same mould has been used, sometimes over
several generations, one instance being the apostle figures on the Astor spoons of
1536-37 (Fig.59) which match those on Bishop Fox's crozier of 1501 (Fig.58).[51]

Cast architectural elements – tracery and buttresses – are also found in differing
combinations on objects by different makers.[52] An inference may be that either the

50 Tylecote, op. cit. note 6, ch. 5; compare (for
methods used today) C. Schwahn, *Workshop
Methods for Gold and Silversmiths*, transl. W.
Jacobsohn (1980); W.A. Oddy (ed.), *Aspects of
Early Metallurgy* (British Museum Occasional
Paper 17, 1980), 142-6 (painter), useful on
tools.

51 T. Wilson, 'Bishop Fox's Crozier', *Pelican and
Annual Report of Corpus Christi College Oxford*
(1980-1), 14. A clay mould could be made
from an existing object.

52 M.L. Campbell, 'Bishop Fox's Salt', ibid.
(1983-4), 48-9 and notes 52-4.

*Fig. 58* Detail of Richard Fox's crozier, showing the cast figure of St. James the Greater under a cast canopy; silver gilt. Unmarked, commissioned *c.* 1501. Height of figure *c.* 4 cm. (*Corpus Christi College, Oxford*)

*Fig. 59* Finial of one of the Astor apostle spoons showing St. James the Greater; from the same model as Fig. 58, but worn. Silver-gilt, with London marks for 1536-7. Height *c.* 4 cm. (*British Museum, MLA 1981, 7-1, 1-13*)

moulds themselves or the ready-cast components were provided by specialists, although many goldsmiths may have made their own moulds, like the bucklemakers whose regulations refer to 'cuttyng of stones for muldes' and 'gravyng of muldes'.[53] Such stone moulds would have produced simple small-scale work – badges, brooches, buckles, and small seals. The term *opus fusile* (cast work) is occasionally found in medieval inventories, but can rarely definitely be identified with goldsmiths' work. Similar uncertainty hangs over interpretation of the trade designation *mould-maker*, found in 14th-century York but apparently not in London.[54] Mould-makers may have had nothing to do with goldsmiths' work: late medieval York had particular concentrations of pewterers and bell-makers, both of which were trades needing quantities of moulds (cf. above, pp.66-7, 88).

Seals, though generally engraved, were sometimes cast – a method lauded by

53  *Cal. Letter-Book L*, 186.
54  Gilbert, Richard, Nicholas, John, mould-makers of York: *Register of the Freemen of ... York*,

ed. F. Collins, I, *1275-1558* (Surtees Soc. xcvi, 1896), 30, 44, 56, 62.

Cellini for instance.[55] Simon de Keyles was paid in 1307 for *fundendo* a royal seal, and the payment to Hugh le Seler in 1333 for *fusing* a seal suggests casting.[56] It is impossible to tell from seal impressions what method was used, but at least two partly-completed matrices survive to suggest that they were ready-cast with designs (an eagle displayed, and a helmet with blank shield) but with the surrounding areas left blank, awaiting a specific inscription which would be engraved.[57]

The lost-wax casting technique entailed the modelling of a design in wax, or in wax over a clay core, and then the enclosure of this with more clay. The outer clay skin was then pierced in two places and the wax was melted out (and the mould fired at the same time), after which molten metal was poured in. Supreme examples of the technique are the Gloucester candlestick of 1107×13[58] (Fig.76), of low-alloy silver, and the effigies of Henry III and Eleanor of Castile, made of gilt copper-alloy, by the London goldsmith William Torel.[59]

The component parts of jewellery and of vessels were attached to each other either by rivets or by the use of solder. Solder might be soft – composed of lead and tin, with a melting point below 250°C – or hard. Hard (silver) solder, with a melting point of over 700°C, was made of copper alloyed with silver, and hard (gold) solder was of copper, or silver and copper, alloyed with gold.[60]

All goldsmiths would have needed a source of heat, probably provided by an open charcoal fire, and a pair of bellows in order to raise the temperature by making a forced draught. Clay crucibles or discs would be necessary for melting and refining the metal or to support delicate pieces of work over the fire. Essential tools would have been an anvil, different types of hammers, chisels, files, tongs, engraving tools, an assortment of punches and moulds, a burnishing stone, scales, a touchstone, and touch-needles (for assaying). In addition the goldsmith might have a draw-plate (for making wire) and enamelling equipment.[61]

Medieval documentary sources provide some evidence. The Englishman Alexander Neckam (1157-1217) gives and early description of a goldsmith's workshop, which, undoubtedly idealized, may derive from personal observations made in Paris, where he lived *c.* 1180-1200, or in St. Albans, where he grew up and whose abbey had a noted goldsmiths' workshop.

> The goldsmith should have a furnace, an anvil on which iron and gold may be softened, stretched and pulled with the tongs and the hammer, a hammer also for making gold leaf,

55 *Treatises of Cellini*, op. cit. note 25, 62-6.

56 Keyles: H.S. Kingsford, 'Some English Medieval Seal-Engravers', *Arch. Jnl.* xcvii (1940), 165-6, 172; Hugh le Seler: F. Devon, *Issues of the Exchequer* (1837), 143.

57 Eagle displayed seal: P. Nelson, 'Some British Medieval Seal Matrices', *Arch. Jnl.* xciii (1936), 33, No. 60; helmet and shield seal: 'An Unfinished Seal-Matrix', *Antiq. Jnl.* xi (1931), 171-2. Both matrices are bronze, of the 14th century, but there is no reason why precious metals should not have been cast too.

58 *Romanesque Art*, op. cit. note 5, No. 247.

59 *Age of Chivalry*, op. cit. note 5, No. 377.

60 M.J. Hughes, 'Solders from Classical to Medieval Times', in *Aspects of Ancient Mining*, op. cit. in note 20, 80-87.

61 Illustrations and descriptions of tools in M. Rosenberg, *Geschichte der Goldschmiedekunst* (Frankfurt, 1910), Figs. 33-41, 69-93 and 38-79; E. Steingräber, *Der Goldschmied vom alten Handwerk der Gold und Silverarbeiter* (Munich, 1966), 63-9.

as well as sheets of silver, tin (*stagneas*), latten (*oricalceas*), iron and copper. The goldsmith must have a very sharp chisel by which he can engrave and shape figures in amber, adamant, serpentine (*ophelta*), or marble, or jacinth, emerald or carbuncle or jasper, sapphire, or pearl. He should have a touchstone for testing metals, a hare's foot for smoothing, polishing and wiping clean the surface of gold and silver, and for collecting the small particles of metal in a leather apron, a toothed saw and a gold file, as well as gold and silver wire by which broken objects can be mended or properly constructed. The goldsmith should be as skilled in the work of the quill (*opus plumiale*: engraving or drawing) as in carving, and in casting as in *repoussé*-work. His apprentice should have a tablet either waxed or covered with whiting or clay, for portraying little flowers and drawing in various ways. He must know how to distinguish solid gold from latten and copper, lest he buy latten for gold.[62]

The account raises many points of interest: the fact that the goldsmith has base as well as precious metals in stock; the mention of gems (especially the diamond) and of gem-carving, and by implication the cutting of cameos and intaglios; the use of wax tablets for trial designs and of a touchstone for assaying; and the absence of any references to enamelling. Nearly two hundred years later, in 1380, the meagre contents of the workshop of a London goldsmith, William Bartilmeu, suggest no such versatility.[63] He owns no metal, and few tools: a pair of tongs, a mortar and pestle, a work bench, a *vernysh barell* and two *trebulettes* (treblets: taper mandrels on which rings are made). He is in other words an impoverished specialist jeweller. This bleak picture is perhaps more accurate than Neckam's idealised one.

On the other hand, about fifty years later (1426), the range of goods in the possession of a Winchester goldsmith, John Kynge, indicates a continuance of virtuosity. Three wire tools, 'five lead mould pieces', a pile of troy weights, precious stones and ivory handles for daggers, and borax are listed.[64] The borax would have been used as flux in hard-soldering gold or silver. The wire tools may suggest that he was engaged in wire-drawing, a comparatively specialised aspect of goldsmithing; the comprehensive list of tools in the possession of a London 'goldwiredrawer' in 1476 substantiates this.[65] The leaden moulds were more probably casting patterns for small items of jewellery, or for the decorative elements – feet, finials and handles

62 *De Nominibus Utensilium*, the Latin text of which is ed. by A. Scheler in *Lexicographie latine du XII<sup>e</sup> et du XIII<sup>e</sup> siècle* (Leipzig, 1867), 114-16. The Latin is obscure in places: for varying translations see R.W. Lightbown, *Secular Goldsmiths' Work in Medieval France* (1978), 4-5, and U.T. Holmes, *Daily Living in the 12th Century* (Madison, Wisconsin, 1952), 142 and notes 40-2. Neckam's picture is perhaps somewhat distorted as a result of his lexicographical interests, whereby he tried to embrace every noun possible connected with the theme under discussion. Compare Theophilus's account of setting up a workshop: Theophilus, *On Divers Arts*, ed. Hawthorne and Smith, 81-97, with useful technical comments, and also Dodwell's edition (which also gives the Latin).

63 *Cal. Plea and Mem. R., 1364-1381*, 267-8. The barrel of varnish is puzzling – is it connected with the technique of decoration known as 'vernis brun' – linseed oil – applied, usually to copper, for decorative effect? A Nuremberg ring-maker of 1425 is illustrated with his handiwork and tools in W. Treue, et al., *Das Hausbuch der Mendelschen Zwölfbrüderstiftung zu Nürnberg* (Munich, 1965), Pl. 54.

64 Derek Keene, *Survey of Medieval Winchester* (Winchester Studies II, 1985), I, pt. i, 281.

65 *Cal. Plea and Mem. R., 1458-82*, 112-13.

*Fig. 60* Goldsmith at work, hammering out a bar held
with tongs; bellows and files in foreground. From
Anselm's Treatise on the faculties of the mind, English,
*c.* 1220-30, from Abbey Dore
(B.L., MS Cotton Cleop. C.xi, f. 42).

– needed for plate, rather than for full-sized items like basins. When made of pewter
basins were certainly often cast, whereas all the half-dozen extant silver examples
have been hammered – slender evidence admittedly, in view of the enormous
numbers that might belong to individuals, such as the 272 plain silver dishes and 279
saucers owned by Edward II in 1326-27. It was probably more trouble to hand-raise
plain silver bowls than to clean up castings in silver. 'Silver' moulds are listed in the
1379 will of the London goldsmith John Broun, but without indication of their use.[66]

The very detailed inventory of a York goldsmith's workshop in 1490 adds a further
dimension to the range of a goldsmith's skills.[67] John Colan, probably a German
immigrant (to judge from his surname), owned a variety of hammers, anvils, and
tongs, equipment for enamelling, a small *tryblett*, several punches (*pounsones*) and
*stampes* including one of latten with *bossellys* (perhaps a die), and *pattrones*, possibly
wooden patterns from which clay moulds might have been made. Raw materials
included three pieces of tin worth 10*d.*, three leaves of *boke gold* (gold leaf) worth 3*d.*,
a mazer shell (the wooden part of a mazer) worth 12*d.*, a knife handle of green
serpentine worth 1*d.*, 20 pearls worth 2*s.*, two crystals worth 8*d.*, two ingots, and
broken silver weighing 12½ *oz.* that was valued at 41*s.* 8*d.* Finished items in the
workshop range from a gold bell, a tin chrismatory (2*d.*), two old books (2*d.*), a jet
rosary (2*d.*) and a silver spoon without knop (12*d.*). Like the Winchester goldsmith,
Colan obviously was making jewellery (including rings like Bartilmeu) as well as
plate, and he was mounting knife handles and mazer bowls. Was the *boke gold* an item
to be sold on to illuminators or for use in gilding?

His tools indicate activity in both forging and casting metal, as well as engraving

66  Edward II: P.R.O., E 372/172 m. 54/1 (1
    Edward III), printed in translation: William
    Rees, *Caerphilly Castle* (1974), 111; Broun, see

    Guildhall Library MS 9171/1, f. 65ᵛ
67  *Testamenta Eboracensia*, ed. J. Raine, iv (Surtees
    Soc. liii, 1868), 56-60.

and stamping or punching and enamelling it. It is interesting to note that Colan had tin, both in pieces and made up into a chrismatory, just as Neckam's goldsmith had pewter, latten and copper in stock. Goldsmiths were forbidden to use base metals, except in the making of church plate, so that Colan may have been acting quite legally. The mention of enamelling is of some note; it occurs in none of the other descriptions. Although enamelling is found on English goldsmiths' work (jewellery) well before the Conquest and is mentioned in inventories from the 13th century onwards as decorating plate, no post-Conquest enamel (on precious metal) survives from earlier than the 14th century.

Recent excavations, particularly on urban sites, have shed light on aspects of the technical side of goldsmithery about which the documents are silent. An important body of this evidence is non-metallic: clay crucibles, moulds and touchstones. Crucibles were used for refining or melting precious metals, moulds for casting them.[68] Crucibles had a short life ; used once, they were then usually thrown away. Their fragments are numerous but it is only possible to be sure of the material they contained when they retain the slag layers, which are fragile and vulnerable to washing. Recent study suggests that two basic shapes of crucible, of varying capacity, were in use – bag-shaped and dish-shaped, the latter probably used for refining and as heating-trays for small pieces of work. Crucible fragments have been found in 10th-century contexts at Northampton (with silver residues); in 10th- and 11th-century contexts at Cheddar (Somerset) (with gold and silver residues) and York (silver and gold); from the 9th to 12th centuries at Lincoln (silver) and Winchester (gold and silver);[69] and from the 10th to 14th centuries in various sites in the City of London, notably in Foster Lane (silver)[70] almost opposite the site occupied since 1339 by Goldsmiths' Hall,[71] the heart of the goldsmiths' quarter.

Moulds that have been found are of two sorts: open, for casting oblong or circular ingots, and composite (only one part usually surviving), for casting objects. A fine-grained limestone is commonly used for the latter. Medieval ingot moulds with associated traces of precious metal survive from Oxford, Lincoln, Chester, Exeter and York.[72] Object moulds have been found at Lincoln, Thetford and Netherton

68 Tylecote, op. cit. note 9, 81-102; J. Bayley, 'Non-Ferrous Metal and Glass-Working in Anglo-Scandinavian England: an Interim Statement', *PACT* 7 (1982; proceedings of the second Nordic conference on the application of scientific methods in archaeology, Elsinore, Denmark, 1981), 487-96; M. Tite et al., 'The Examination of Refractory Ceramics from Metal-Production and Metalworking Sites', in *The Archaeologist and the Laboratory*, ed. P. Phillips (C.B.A. Research Rep. lviii, 1985), 50-55; J. Bayley, 'Non-Metallic Evidence for Metalworking', in Y. Maniatis (ed.), *Proceedings of 25th international symposium on Archaeometry: Athens, 1986* (Amsterdam 1989), 291-303.

69 I am grateful to Justine Bayley for discussing this with me, and showing me her notes; full reports are filed in the Ancient Monuments Laboratory, English Heritage.

70 Found with fragments of a beaker in a cess-pit: J. Clark, 'Medieval Enamelled Glasses from London', *Med. Arch.* xxvii (1983), 152-5.

71 Reddaway and Walker, op. cit. note 15, 30.

72 Op. cit. in note 68, and see E.M. Jope and W.A. Pantin, 'The Clarendon Hotel, Oxford', *Oxoniensia*, xxiii (1958), 68, 72; J.P. Allan, *Medieval and Post-Medieval Finds from Exeter, 1971-80* (1981), 304, 347; for Netherton (Faccombe) see *Med. Arch.* xxiv (1980), 220-1. For comparable Viking material see J. Graham-Campbell, *Viking Artefacts* (1980), 123 ff.

(Hants.).[73] In addition finely-carved moulds, without context, survive: a 13th-century fragment of the Massacre of the Innocents scene (Norwich Castle Museum), a 14th-century fragment showing leashed hounds (Museum of London), deer-motif badges, and an elaborate belt-end of *c.* 1400.[74] It is of course impossible to judge what metals would have been used in these. The artistic argument that is sometimes advanced – that high-quality carving indicates a precious-metal use – is clearly false, judging by the high aesthetic quality of surviving pewter pilgrim badges. Since the metal constituted the prime cost, it is not impossible that moulds were used for both base and precious metals, depending on customer demand.

The discovery of two touchstones streaked with gold in 9th- and 10th-century contexts in Winchester, and of one in Exeter from a 13th-century pit close to a goldworking site, has led to a reappraisal of a body of material scattered in museums, and often previously described as whetstones.[75] Touchstones were used in conjunction with touchneedles for assaying. In 1430 a Warden of the Goldsmiths Company left to his successors 'a little touch and four needles', and the London goldsmith Robert Amadas had in 1532 a bundle of silver needles, fifteen needles of copper tipped with gold and a touchstone.[76] No pre-Renaissance touchneedles survive.

The survival of punches and dies, used for punching motifs onto finished objects (Fig.69) and for impressing designs onto thin sheet metal, implies metalworking and perhaps goldsmithing activity. Those few punches that are extant mostly show animals, and though they are often called 'bookbinders' punches', the evidence for this use is slender.[77] Dies are more certainly linked with fine metalworking. Survivals include the unprovenanced 14th-century multiple die-piece in the British Museum engraved with a variety of drolleries, the 13th-century die-piece with a winged gryphon found at Hartlepool, and the 15th-century die from Wimborne (Dorset) with a pelican in her piety, all these being within roundels; all are of copper-alloy.[78] The rapid production of repetitive motifs was made possible by successively placing on a die the sheets of metal that were to be decorated (overlaid with a piece of lead) and hitting each sheet sharply with a hammer. The resulting motifs could then be cut out and applied directly onto the silver, as on the Leigh cup, or set into wooden

73  Op. cit. notes 68-70, 72.
74  *Age of Chivalry*, op. cit. note 5, Nos. 447-449; hounds badge: J. Steane, *The Archaeology of Medieval England and Wales* (1985), 221.
75  D.T. Moore and W.A. Oddy, 'Touchstones: Some Aspects of their Nomenclature, Petrography and Provenance', *Jnl. of Archaeological Science*, xii (1985), 71, 77, Nos. 5, 6, 17.
76  Reddaway and Walker, op. cit. note 15, 319; Amadas: P.R.O., PROB 2/486, m. 10. For a set of touchneedles and stone of 1608 from Hamburg, see exhibition catalogue *Stadt im*

*Wandel*, ed. C. Meckseper (Brunswick: Landes-museum, 1985), II, No. 656.
77  *Age of Chivalry*, op. cit. note 5, Nos. 430-4; Theophilus, *On Divers Arts*, ed. Hawthorne and Smith, 149.
78  *Age of Chivalry*, Nos. 450, 452; Wimborne die: H.S. Kingsford, 'An Unfinished Seal-Matrix in the Dorset County Museum', *Proceedings of the Dorset Natural History and Archaeological Society*, lx (1938), 95-6; Theophilus, *On Divers Arts*, ed. Hawthorne and Smith, xxxii, 153-4, 156.

*Fig. 61* Studley bowl, silver, parcel gilt, engraved. *c.* 1400. Height 14.5 cm. (*Victoria and Albert Museum, M1-1914*)

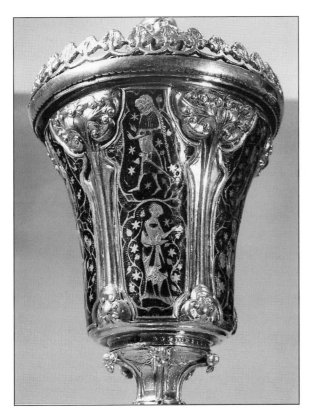

*Fig. 62* Detail of the bowl of the King's Lynn cup, silver-gilt, with translucent enamel, *c.* 1340. The heavy cresting on the list is cast, as is probably the body of the cup; the plaques of enamel, individually fired and attached to the cup, are held in place by a lip of metal. (*Corporation of King's Lynn, Norfolk*)

drinking bowls, such as the Warwick mazer (Fig.55),[79] or sewn onto textiles as spangles.

Scales for weighing metals would have been essential for any goldsmith; in 1490 Colan had five balances and weights, two being specifically for gold, while Amadas owned four sets of troy weights.[80] The arbiter of standards, the Goldsmiths' Company, installed in its treasury in 1417 a set of troy weights to serve as test weights for all others to use; only the set made in 1588 survives.[81] Excavation has so far produced a single weight from a 15th-century context in Exeter, and scales and weights from Roche Abbey (Yorks).[82]

## Decoration and Enamelling

The surface decoration of precious metals (other than gem-setting) included embossing or *repoussé* work, produced by working the metal with a hammer and punch from the back; chasing, where metal was worked from the front; and engraving, executed on the front of the metal with a fine tool which gouged out a thin sliver of metal. Stamped ornament (Figs.55, 69) was created where a steel punch with the design cut on it in relief (*cameo*) or concave (*intaglio*)[83] was hammered onto sheet metal, or where sheet metal was hammered directly into a die. Surface pattern could also be produced by the application (by soldering on) of wire filigree, or of *niello* (a sulphide of copper and/or silver fired onto the engraved metal surface) with a matt black appearance,[84] or of enamel (powdered glass fired onto the metal). Aside from gem-setting, enamelling was the most important means of surface embellishment available to the goldsmith, and therefore merits fuller discussion.

The word 'enamel' derives from the Old High German *smelzan*, 'to smelt' – the process crucial to the making of enamel. The constituents of enamel are the same as

79  Leigh cup with marks for London 1513 (re-attribution by Antique Plate Committee, Goldsmiths' Company): Jackson, op. cit. note 23, i, 144-5; Guy of Warwick mazer, 14th-century, *Age of Chivalry*, No. 155.

80  *Testamenta Eboracensia*, op. cit. note 67, iv, 59; Amadas: P.R.O., PROB 2/486, m.8.

81  Reddaway & Walker, op. cit. note 15, 112 and note 10, 245, Pl. 9.

82  Allan, op. cit. note 72; Roche scales (Ancient Monuments Laboratory 765351) illustrated as pl. 123 by J. Geddes, 'Cistercian Metalwork in England', in C. Norton and D. Park (eds.), *Cistercian Art and Architecture in the British Isles* (1986), 261. Compare the complete set of weights and scales dated 1497 for weighing gold and gems, owned by Hans Harsdorfer of Nuremberg, illustrated in *Gothic and Renaissance Art in Nuremberg, 1300-1550* (Metropolitan Museum of New York, 1986), No. 77. The question of what weights were used by goldsmiths, and when, is complex. The Tower

pound (5400 grains) was used for coin, both it and the Troy pound (5760 grains) for plate and jewellery: R.D. Connor, *Weights and measures of Medieval England* (1987), 117-129 and P. Nightingale, 'The Ora, the Mark and the Mancus: Weight Standards and the Coinage in 11th century England', pts. 1 and 2, *Numismatic Chronicle*, cxliii (1983), 248-57, ibid. cxliv (1984), 234-48.

83  Bishop Fox's basin, London 1493: the border consists of a repeated punched design, the edges of the punch being clearly visible: see P. Glanville, 'Bishop Fox's Ablution Basins', *Pelican and Annual Report of Corpus Christi College, Oxford* (1983-4), 74-86.

84  S. La Niece, 'Niello: an Historical and Technical Survey', *Antiq. Jnl.* lxiii (1983), 279-97; N. Stratford, 'Niello in England in the 12th Century', in S. Macready and F.H. Thompson (eds.), *Art and Patronage in the English Romanesque* (Society of Antiquaries Occasional Papers, n.s. viii, 1986), 28-49.

*PLATE I*

I.  The Gloucester Candlestick. Inscribed as being the gift of Abbot Peter (1107-13) to St. Peter's Abbey, Gloucester. Height 51.2 cm. (*Victoria and Albert Museum, No. 7649-1861*)

*PLATE II*

II. Diptych, silver gilt with translucent enamel, showing the Ascension and Resurrection of
Christ (left) and the Coronation of the Virgin, St. Christopher and St. George (right), *c.* 1340.
Height 4 cm. (*Victoria and Albert Museum, No. M544B-1910*)

those of glass. Flint or sand, sometimes red lead, and soda or potash were heated together to form clear flux, to which were added colouring agents in the form of metallic oxides – copper for green, cobalt for blue, and others. The enamel was then allowed to cool and solidify in slabs, each colour then being separately ground into a fine powder and washed to remove dirt. The powder was then placed on the prepared metal surface, allowed to dry, and fired in an enclosed kiln at a temperature of between 700°C and 800°C. Several firings were often necessary. When cool, the enamel surface was polished to remove imperfections and to add brilliance to the colours.[85]

The difference between the various enamelling techniques lies chiefly in the methods by which different metal surfaces were prepared for the enamel. In *cloisonné* (cell-work) thin strips of metal were bent to form the outline of a design and were soldered edge-on to the surface of the metal object. The resulting cells were filled with enamel, often restricted to one colour per cell. Because of the delicacy of such work, soft metals such as gold or silver were most suitable. This was probably the standard method of enamelling precious metals until the invention of *basse taille*.

*Champlevé* was in a sense the reverse of the *cloisonné* technique: the design was gouged from the surface of the metal (rather like a linocut), leaving thin ridges of metal standing above the resulting troughs and channels. Enamel was then placed in the depressions, often several colours in a single compartment. Since the process requires a substantial thickness of metal, it was usually used on copper or its alloys (Fig.65).

*Basse taille* (translucent enamel), a development of the *champlevé* technique, was invented in the late 13th century, substituting translucent for opaque enamel. A design in low relief was chased or engraved onto a base of gold or silver. Tonal richness and subtle modelling could be achieved by variations in the depth of the engraving, and hence in the thickness of the enamel, through which light was reflected back from the metal base (Fig.62).

*Email en ronde bosse* (encrusted enamel) was a technique of enamelling the irregular surface of figures or objects, in the round or in very high relief, and was developed in the 14th century. These small-scale sculptural compositions were invariably of gold or silver, whose surface was roughened to hold in place the enamel coating (Fig.63).

Recent work in analysing medieval enamels is beginning to make clear the degree of technological expertise of their makers. Whilst Theophilus in *c.* 1125 describes only the technique of *cloisonné* on precious metal[86] – the last two methods had yet to be developed – Cellini, writing in the 16th century, describes *basse taille*, and stresses the interaction of metal and enamel. Translucent red, the most difficult and beautiful of colours, could only be achieved on gold.[87] Silver for enamelling needed to be

85 M.M. Gauthier, *Emaux du Moyen Age Occidental* (2nd edn., Fribourg, 1972), 17-35.
86 Theophilus, *De Diversis Artibus*, ed. Dodwell, xxvi, 105-7.
87 *The Treatises of Benvenuto Cellini*, op. cit. note

25, ch. 3, 16; for early French examples see D. Gaborit-Chopin, in *Les Fastes du Gothique: le Siècle de Charles V*, cat. of exhibn. (Paris, 1981), 222.

particularly free of impurities, a fact evidently known also to the Norwich goldsmith who in 1426-27 charged 34*d.* per oz. of 'amelying' (enamelling) silver, as opposed to 32*d.* for silver (unspecified), presumably of sterling quality.[88]

Theophilus describes the re-use of glass tesserae from Roman mosaics in his day to make opaque enamels.[89] This practice appears to be confirmed by J. Henderson's unpublished analyses of 9th-century tesserae and other objects from Ribe (Denmark) and Århus (Sweden), and by the analysis of some continental 12th-century *champlevé* (opaque) enamels, in which the glass constituents are of a Roman type (soda-lime-silica), rather than of the potash glass prevalent in 12th-century vessel glass;[90] no work has yet been done on the few extant English 12th-century enamels. Tesserae or glass 'cakes' may also have been specially imported for enamelling, possibly from Venice or Byzantium, as they perhaps also were to produce *cloisonné* in 10th-century Germany.[91]

Tesserae have been found in a late 9th-century context in Lincoln (Flaxengate) where, however, they may be residual. X-ray fluorescence has shown them to be high in antimony and of quite different composition from the high-lead glass being made on the site at Lincoln, and in quantity at different sites in York from the 10th to 12th centuries.[92] Although this lead glass was made into beads and rings, it may have been used for enamelling too: the earliest known English recipe for enamel, *c.* 1300-50, is for high-lead translucent glasses:

> Enamel is thus made: take lead, and melt it, continually taking off the pellicle which floats on the surface, until the whole of the lead is wasted away; of which take one part, and of the powder hereafter mentioned, as much; and this is the said powder: take small white pebbles which are found in streams, and pound them into most subtle powder; and if you

88  G.A. Stephen, 'The Waits of the City of Norwich . . .', *Norfolk Archaeology*, xxv (1935), 53; on enamelling silver see E.A. Smith, *Working in Precious Metals* (reprinted 1978), 352-3.

89  Theophilus, *De Diversis Artibus*, ed. Dodwell, 43-4.

90  M. Bimson, 'A Preliminary Survey of Two Groups of Twelfth-Century Mosan Enamels', *Annales du 8ᵉ Congrès International d'Etude Historique du Verre, Londres-Liverpool 1979* (Liège, 1981), 161-4; D. Gaborit and C. Lahanier, 'Étude Scientifique de la Plaque Emaillé de Geoffroy Plantagenet', *Annales du laboratoire de recherche des Musées de France*, 1982, esp. 26. But Roman glass tesserae are uncommon finds in Britain: Neil Cookson, *Romano-British Mosaics* (B.A.R., Brit. Ser. cxxxv, 1984), 116-19. However, the chronology of soda/potash glass grows less certain with the discovery of 12th-century soda glass in York and 9th-century potash glass in Winchester: G. Cox and K. Gillies, 'The X-ray Fluorescence Analysis of . . . Glass from York Minster', *Archaeometry*, xxviii (1986), 57-68, and J. Hunter, 'Glass and Glass-Making', in *The Archaeologist and the Laboratory*, op. cit.

note 68, 65. Work in progress on 13th-century champlevé Limoges enamels by Julian Henderson (Oxford University Research Laboratory for Archaeology) may further modify the picture since his findings show a potash glass composition (high in potassium and magnesium oxides) but markedly different from medieval window glass.

91  German cloisonné: David Buckton, 'Necessity the Mother of Invention in Early Medieval Enamel', in *Transactions, Canadian Conference of Medieval Art Historians*, iii, 1982 (London, Ontario, 1985), 4, note 19; imported mosaic tesserae have been found on Viking glass-making sites: Graham-Campbell, op. cit. note 72, 462. For evidence that Venice was exporting glass 'cakes' (opaque and translucent) and beads for enamelling: R.J. Charleston, 'Glass "Cakes" as Raw Material and Articles of Commerce', *Jnl. of Glass Studies*, v (1963), 56-9, 65-6.

92  Bayley 1982, op. cit. note 68, 494, and J. Henderson and S. Warren in D. Tweddle, *The Archaeology of York: XVII, pt. 4: Small Finds from Parliament Street* (1986), 224-7.

wish to have yellow enamel, add oil of filberts and stir with a hazel rod; for green, add filings of copper, or verdigris; for red, add filings of latten with calamine; for blue, good azure or saffre, of which glaziers make blue glass[93]

Since no 14th-century English enamels have yet been analysed, it is not known if they follow this recipe. Lead allowed lower working temperatures and it improved fluidity, but it must also have had disadvantages, since lead glass was specifically forbidden to the *emailleurs d'orfevrerie* of Paris, in their statutes of *c.* 1307.[94] If not used on goldsmiths' work, was lead glass perhaps applied to base metals – pieces such as the Beauchamp and Valence effigies, or the Garter stall-plates in St. George's Chapel, Windsor?[95]

There is some evidence, from the 14th century, that 'amayl' (colours unspecified) was also imported into England, and individuals probably collected stocks of their own, as they did gems. Tesserae may once more have provided a source of material; the imported red and white glass mosaic inlaid into the 13th-century tombs of Henry III and the Valence children might otherwise have served for enamel.[96] The invention of *ronde bosse*, towards 1400, implies a technological progression of which we are largely ignorant. Paris – always a great centre for goldsmiths – was a major source of this new type of enamel. Of the surviving pieces only two can even tentatively be ascribed to English workmanship: the Dunstable swan jewel of *c.*1400, and the reliquary of the Order of the Sainte Esprit of *c.*1410 (Fig.63).[97] More certainly English is the section added to the stem of the Royal Gold Cup between 1486 and 1521: its red and white Tudor roses prove on analysis to be intriguing – the transparent red very close to the ruby glass used on the (French) 14th-century cup, while the opaque white is by contrast a high lead glass typical of 'post-medieval' enamel.[98] This sort of enamel must have been a particular boon to jewellers for delicate work, although both translucent and *champlevé* enamel continued in use into the 15th century and beyond. Bishop Fox's gold chalice of 1507 (Corpus Christi

93  B.L., Sloane MS 1754, f. 231, printed by A. Way, 'Decorative Processes . . . Enamel', *Arch. Jnl.* ii (1845), 171-2. Cf. R.J. Charleston, 'Lead in Glass', *Archaeometry*, iii (1960), 2.

94  René de Lespinasse, *Les Métiers et Corporations de la Ville de Paris*, ii (Paris, 1892), 97, 99-101.

95  Beauchamp effigy *c.* 1453: M.L. Campbell, 'English Goldsmiths in the Fifteenth Century', in D. Williams (ed.), *England in the Fifteenth Century* (1987), 51 and note 49; Valence effigy *c.* 1296: Gauthier, op. cit. note 85, 192; stall-plates, 15th century: W.H. St. John Hope, *Stall Plates of the Knights of the Order of the Garter* (1901).

96  For 'amayl' imported see P.R.O., E 122/71/13 mm.5, 10, 12 (for 1390: 13 Richard II) – the cost varied from 6s. 8d. for 4 lb. to 18s. for 1½ lb.; the 1326 will of Queen Mary of Hungary specifies 'saccum unum cum peciis vitrei Rubei pro faciendis smaltis decem et octo et

petiis vitri albi similiter pro faciendis *ysmaltis*': C. Minieri Riccio, *Saggio di Codice Diplomatico*, suppl. pt. 2 (Naples, 1883), 114; tombs of Valence children and Henry III: Joan Tanner, 'Tombs of Royal Babies in Westminster Abbey', *J.B.A.A.* 3rd ser. xvi-xvii (1953-4), 31-2.

97  Dunstable swan: *Age of Chivalry*, op. cit. note 5, No. 659; reliquary: *Fastes du Gothique*, op. cit. note 87, No. 221.

98  *Fastes du Gothique*, op. cit. note 87, No. 213; M. Bimson and I.C. Freestone, 'Rouge Clair and other late 14th Century Enamels on the Royal Gold Cup . . .', in *Annales du 9ᵉ Congrès International d'Étude Historique du Verre, Nancy 1983* (Liège, 1985), 221; P. Michaels, 'Technical Observations on Early Painted Enamels of Limoges', *Journal of the Walters Art Gallery*, xxvii-xxviii (1964-5), 21-9.

*Fig. 63* Detail of the reliquary of the Order of
Sainte Esprit, showing God the Father and
St. Bartholomew. Gold enamelled in *ronde bosse*,
set with pearls, balas rubies and sapphires. A
few gems are faceted, some are drilled with a
hole, most are simply polished. Made in London
(?) *c.* 1410 for Joan of Navarre (Henry IV's
second wife) who gave it to her son Jean, Duke of
Brittany, *c.* 1412. Height of whole 44.5 cms.
(*Musée du Louvre, Paris*)

College, Oxford) has a knop enamelled in translucent red and green, while the
iconographical rings characteristic of the 15th century, although of gold, were
covered with opaque enamel.[99]

The effects of some types of enamelling rely on the skill of the underlying
engraving. It therefore is logical enough that the 1370 ordinances of the Goldsmiths'
Company bracket enamellers with seal-engravers.[100] Early references to enamellers
in London include a John le Aumayller, goldsmith, mentioned in 1311-12, while
amongst the very large number of Englishmen (including five goldsmiths) who were
working in Paris in 1292 was a Richard *esmailleur de Londres*.[101] There is little evidence
to show whether English enamellers worked exclusively on precious metals or
whether they also worked on base metals, although in 1453 Bartholomew
Lambespring, goldsmith of London and York, was paid for the enamels (on copper)
on the monument of Richard, Earl of Warwick.[102] Enamel was useful as the only
permanent colorant for metals and was much used on the heraldic copper alloy

99  Fox's chalice: M.L. Campbell, 'Bishop Fox's
    Chalice and Paten', *Pelican and Annual Report
    of Corpus Christi College Oxford* (1981-2), 20-44;
    rings: C.C. Oman, *British Rings, 800-1914*
    (1974), 64-6, Pl. 65-9.
100 Reddaway and Walker, op. cit. note 15, 246.
101 John: *Cal. Letter-Book B*, 32; Richard: P.H.
    Géraud, *Paris sous Philippe le Bel, d'après . . . le*

*Rôle de la Taille imposée . . . 1292* (Paris, 1837),
23 (assessed at 3 sous).
A Bernard of Limoges, perhaps an enameller,
was in London in 1283: *Cal. Letter-Book A*, 109.
102 Campbell, art. cit. note 95, 51. Goldsmiths
    were forbidden to use paint instead of enamel
    as a colorant from at least 1366: Prideaux, op.
    cit. note 47, vol. I, 6.

horse-trappings which are the commonest surviving medieval form of enamel; invariably *champlevé*, they are unlikely to be the products of goldsmiths.

## Gold Leaf and Gilding

Gold and silver leaf are the thinnest forms of the metals, thinner than the finest modern tissue paper. They derive from foil (about the thickness of paper) which is itself thinner than sheet. Some metals cannot be made into leaf, because they are not malleable enough, but gold is almost infinitely malleable, although pure gold cannot be beaten quite as thin as alloyed gold. The standard gold leaf now is of 23¼ carat gold alloyed with ¾ carat silver and copper.[103] In the Middle Ages goldsmiths often obtained the gold for gold leaf and gilding by buying foreign gold coins.[104]

Goldbeating was a slow task; the coins were hammered into foil, which was further beaten with a variety of hammers between vellum (or parchment) leaves known as goldbeaters' skin. These served to protect the foil and maintain an even thickness. A square of gold was placed in the middle of a sheet of vellum with another piece of vellum on top, and further layers of metal foil and vellum above them. When hammering had caused the metal squares to spread to the edge of the parchment, the goldbeater cut up each piece of metal into further squares, and repeated the process.

Medieval gold leaf seems to have been rather heavier than modern leaf, although details are imprecise. It has been surmised that the 14th-century Italian painter Lorenzetti used gold leaves each about 3½ in. square, weighing about ½ troy grain, deriving 100 leaves from each florin.[105] English evidence is rare, but at Canterbury in 1324-25 four florins were beaten into 500 gold leaves (at a cost of 5s. for the workmanship), that is 125 leaves per florin, so they were presumably slightly lighter.[106] As to cost, 51 dozen (612) gold leaves were bought in 1253 for work at Westminster Abbey for 24s. 11d., that is about 4s. per 100,[107] while the prior of Canterbury in 1324-25 paid 8s. 6d. for 400 gold leaves (2s. 1½d. per 100). Silver leaf at Canterbury at the same time cost 2s. for 500 leaves, while at Ely only a dozen years later it was 8d. per 100 leaves.[108] Such variations in price may reflect the thickness of

---

103 G. Whilley, *Leaves of Gold* (1951), 56; a useful technical account is also D.V. Thompson, *Materials of Medieval Painting* (1936), 194-5. See also Theophilus, *De Diversis Artibus*, ed. Dodwell, book I, chap. 23.

104 For gilding Queen Eleanor of Castile's effigy, made 1291-3, 350 gold florins were bought from Lucca merchants, see *Age of Chivalry*, op. cit. note 5, No. 377; the York goldsmith Adam de Munketon in 1312-3 paid 12s. 10d. for 3 gold florins bought for gilding a cross: *Register of William Greenfield* . . ., ed. A.H. Thompson (Surtees Soc. cliii, 1938), p.21, No. 240.

105 Thompson, op. cit. note 103, 195-6.

106 Canterbury Cathedral Archives, Cathedral

Priory accounts, Collector Redditum (London) for 17-18 Edward II.

107 *Building Accounts of King Henry III*, ed. H.M. Colvin (1971), 228.

108 Canterbury Cathedral Archives, accounts of Collector Redditum, 17-18 Edward II; Ely: *Sacrist Rolls of Ely*, ed. F.R. Chapman (1907), ii, 83 for 1338-9; by 1345-6, 600 leaves of silver cost 6s., expensive when compared with 450 gold leaves for 4s. at the same date: ibid. 136. Nicholas Oresme (d. 1382) says that silver leaf was commonly called 'silver of Gutheron's Lane', i.e. Gutter Lane in the goldsmiths' quarter of London, parallel to Foster Lane, where the Company Hall stood.

the leaves as much as the cost of the metal, which in turn was conditioned by the purpose for which the leaf was intended: at Canterbury the gold was probably for gilding Becket's shrine, while at Westminster it was perhaps for gilding stonework.

The principal uses for gold and silver leaf were in the decoration of parchment, wood or stone surfaces, and in the gilding of metals. Painters found the lustrous reflective qualities of the metals attractive for embellishing books, panels and walls. The leaf was laid on a prepared surface, often gesso (gypsum rubbed smooth and covered with adhesive), and was then burnished bright. Painters, and later printers, also used powdered gold and silver. The metal was filed or sawn into a coarse powder and mixed with salt or honey, to prevent the particles sticking together, then finely ground with pestle and mortar. When washed clean, the powder was mixed with a binding medium and could be used as a pigment.[109]

The standard method of gilding silver and copper alloys in the Middle Ages was by mercury-gilding (also called fire-gilding).[110] There are two ways of carrying this out, but the end results are usually indistinguishable even by scientific analysis. In the first, the object is thoroughly cleaned and a gold amalgam (alloy of gold and mercury) spread on the parts to be gilded. The amalgam is made by dropping gold leaf or filings into boiling mercury, which is then allowed to cool. Eraclius, writing in the 10th or 11th century, cites the correct proportions as one part of gold to seven of mercury, and this may have been a working norm. Coated with amalgam, the object is then heated, causing the mercury to evaporate, and leaving behind a gold layer ready for burnishing. In the second method, the surface of the object is rubbed with clean mercury – a difficult process – and gold leaf is then laid on top. This dissolves immediately in the mercury, and further layers are added, each pressed on to the surface with a smooth leather, until no more will dissolve. The piece is then heated as before.

### Gold and Silver Thread and Wire

Gold and silver threads were used in textile production (and notably for the prestigious *opus anglicanum*), and wire served to decorate plate and jewellery.[111] Almost no post-Conquest filigree survives apart from the 15th-century collar of SS and the mid 13th-century drawing of a ring by Matthew Paris, so that it is impossible to determine which of the six available techniques, other than wire-drawing, was in

109 Use of metals in manuscripts: S. Alexander, 'Medieval Recipes Describing the Use of Metals in Manuscripts', *Marsyas*, xii (1964-5), 34-51, and T. Wright, 'Early English Receipts for Painting, Gilding', *Arch. Jnl.* i (1845), 64-5; V. Carter et al., 'Painting with Gold in the Fifteenth Century', *British Library Jnl.* viii (1983-4), 1-13; Thompson, op. cit. note 103, 192,

195-7.

110 W.A. Oddy, 'Gilding through the Ages', *Gold Bull.* xiv (1981), 75-9; Oddy, 'Gilding and Tinning in Anglo-Saxon England', in Oddy, op. cit. note 50.

111 J. Wolters, 'Filigran' in Otto Schmitt et al. (eds.), *Reallexikon zur Deutschen Kunstgeschichte*, viii (Munich, 1987), cols. 1062-1184.

use.[112] That much of the thread was imported is shown by the frequent English references to gold (thread) of Venice, Lucca, and Cyprus, and is implied by the ordinance of 1378 (2 Richard II) decreeing that alien merchants should be allowed to buy and sell freely in all cities *fil d'or et d'argent*.[113]

'Venice' and 'Lucca gold' thread consisted of finely beaten foil cut into strips and wound spirally round a silk core. 'Cyprus gold', cheaper because more sparing of metal, consisted of gilded animal membrane cut into strips and wound around a core of silk, linen or cotton.[114] By the 14th century, gold thread was a prized export from Cologne, where in 1397 a separate gild of gold spinners and beaters had been established.[115] Since this thread was being imported into the northern Italian silk towns in the 14th century, it may have been re-exported to England as Italian gold thread.[116]

It is not clear how pure the metals were. The 'gold' thread described by Theophilus was in fact a thin sheet of gold and silver, beaten together until bonded, appearing gold on one side and silver on the other.[117] If correctly wound onto the core thread it would seem to be gold. Analysis of thread has been so scanty that no conclusions can yet be drawn from the comparatively abundant evidence, especially that of *opus anglicanum*; we know only that the 10th-century gold thread used on St. Cuthbert's stole at Durham is almost pure gold on a silk core,[118] that some 14th-century silver threads proved fairly pure with traces of gold and copper, and that 14th-century 'gold' threads have so far proved in all cases to be gold plated onto

112  Collar: B. Spencer, 'Fifteenth-Century Collar of SS', *Antiq. Jnl.* lxv (1985), 449-51; ring: C.C. Oman, 'The Jewels of St. Alban's Abbey', *Burlington Mag.* lvii (1930), 82 and pl. Useful technical details on wire-production in W.A. Oddy, 'Gold Wire on Thetford Jewellery and the Technology of Wire-production in Roman Times', in C. Johns et al., *The Thetford Treasure* (1983), 62-4; N. Whitfield, 'Motifs and Techniques of Celtic Filigree', in M. Ryan (ed.), *Ireland and Insular Art A.D. 500-1200* (Dublin, 1987), 75-84.

113  1378 ordinance: *Rot. Parl.* iii, 47; details of imports in V. Harding, 'Some Documentary Sources for Imported Foreign Textiles in Late Medieval England', *Textile History*, xviii.2 (1987), 213-15; K. Lacey, '"Narrow Ware" by English Silkwomen', ibid., 187-191 and note 18.

114  M. Braun-Ronsdorf, 'Gold and Silver Fabrics from Medieval to Modern Times', *CIBA Review* (1961-3), 5-6.

115  M. Wensky, 'Women's Guilds in Cologne in the later Middle Ages', *Jnl. of European Economic History*, xi (1982), 636. There was nevertheless rivalry between the spinners who used the metal threads to wind around a silk core or spun the metal foil on its own and the beaters who produced fine thread by beating and stretching the foil.

116  See note 113; *Ribbon of gold of Venise* was bought by the Black Prince in 1359 and 1362: *The Register of Edward the Black Prince:* iv (*England*) (1933), 324-5, 463. Imports to England from Spain in 1474 included Venice gold and gold-wire: P.R.O., E 122/128/15, cited by W. Childs, *Anglo-Castilian Trade in the Middle Ages* (1978), 141. For qualities and prices of Florentine gold and silver thread: F.E. de Roover, 'Andrea Banchi . . . 15th-century Merchant . . .', *Studies in Medieval and Renaissance History*, iii (1966), 240-1.

117  Theophilus, *On Divers Arts*, ed. Hawthorne and Smith, book III, chap. 27.

118  A.G.I. Christie, *English Medieval Embroidery* (1938), 20 note 2; spectrographic analysis.

silver, as in Theophilus's account.[119]

The alternative way of making silver or gold thread was a development of wire-making: short rods of cast metal were drawn through successively diminishing holes in a draw-plate until a fine wire resulted.[120] Although it is often attributed to the 14th century, the technique of wire-drawing was known to the Vikings (several draw-plates have been excavated)[121] and it is described by Theophilus. It was very possibly practised by the craftsmen in London, York and Coventry who called themselves 'wire-drawers' from *c.* 1300 onwards.[122] By 1435 Coventry had a gild of 'wire-drawers';[123] 'goldwiredrawers' are recorded as members of the London Goldsmiths' Company from at least the 1460s,[124] while the list of a goldwiredrawer's tools in 1476 includes unequivocal mention of draw-plates.[125] Although none of the English pre-1500 thread or filigree examined has so far been identified as drawn, further investigation is likely to prove it so,[126] although it may be impossible to establish whether the production of drawn wire was continuous throughout the Middle Ages. Significant, too, may be the description in *c.* 1250 by Bartholomew the Englishman of making gold wire by cutting strips from foil, at about the same date that Parisian wire is described as being made in similar fashion.[127] In London, even in 1494, the same man could describe himself as goldbeater and goldwiredrawer, perhaps indicative of some technological overlapping.[128] Although there was no assay for gold or silver thread, quality was certainly of concern, as shown by a petition in 1495 by the craft of 'browderers' stating that all who embroidered 'velvet, satin and damask' should use 'fine gold and fine silver'.[129] 'Copper gold, lukes (Lucca) gold and counterfeit gold' were to be used only on inferior stuffs like 'satyn of bruges and sarcenet'.

119  Ibid.: examination of the Felbrigge Psalter cover (British Library) and the alb apparels (Victoria & Albert Museum, 8128-1863), the former on linen, the latter on velvet; see also P. Wallis, 'The Embroidered Binding of the Felbrigge Psalter', *British Library Jnl.* xiii (1987), 71-8; recent analytical work has been done by J. Darrah to whom I am grateful for discussing it with me: J. Darrah, 'Metal Threads and Filaments', in J. Black (ed.), *Recent Advances in the . . . Analysis of Artefacts* (1987), 213-4, Nos. 98-9: analysis by X-ray fluorescence spectroscopy of the 14th-century Jesse cope (V. & A., T. 175-1889) and magnification which showed the threads to be beaten and cut. See also N. Indictor et al., 'The Evaluation of Metal Wrappings from Medieval Textiles . . .', *Textile History*, xix (1988), 3-19.

120  W.A. Oddy, 'The Production of Gold Wire in Antiquity', *Gold Bull.* x (1977), 79-87.

121  Graham-Campbell, op. cit. note 72, Nos. 414-15 (found in Scandinavia).

122  The earliest is in London in 1292, a Henry Wirdrawere: *Two Early London Subsidy Rolls*, ed. E. Ekwall (Lund: Skrifter utgivna av Kungl. Humanistika Vetenskapssamfundet,

xlviii (1951)), 180; York wiredrawers are recorded in 1350 and 1358: *Freemen of York*, op. cit. note 54, 53.

123  P. Longmuir and J. Kenworthy, 'Early Wire-drawing Practice', *Engineering*, xcv (Apr. 18, 1913), 542.

124  An alien named Manntrot is recorded in 1468: Goldsmiths Company Archives, Minute book A, p.121.

125  *Cal. Plea & Mem. R., 1458-82*, 112-3.

126  Darrah, art. cit. note 119, 214, Nos. 8-9, found drawn round wire on a 16th-century nightcap. Could this be the 'round gold', costing 4s. 4d. per oz., bought in 1502 by Queen Elizabeth of York (N.H. Nicolas, *Elizabeth of York . . . Expenses* [1830], 55)?

127  Bartholomew: op. cit. note 11; Paris: *Le Livre des Métiers d'Étienne Boileau*, ed. R. de Lespinasse and F. Bonnardot (Paris, 1879), 63-4, Titre XXXI: *Des bateurs d'or et d'argent à filer*, who are distinguished from the *bateurs . . . en feuilles*, Titre XXXIII.

128  George Seneasco, alien: Goldsmiths' Company Archives, Minute book A, p.332.

129  *Cal. Letter-Book L*, 306-7; much of the *opus anglicanum* is on velvet.

*Coins*

These were produced by placing thin blanks of metal of the correct fineness (percentage of gold or silver) and weight between two iron dies – the trussel (upper die) and pile (lower die). When the moneyer struck the trussel with a hammer, the design on each die was simultaneously impressed onto the blank to produce a coin.[130] The commonest – and for a long time, the only – English coin in the Middle Ages was the silver penny (Fig.54), which bore on the obverse the sovereign's image and name and had a cross and the moneyer's name on the reverse.[131] The iron dies which produced these designs themselves consisted of an intaglio image, made by means of two types of tool: *burins* (engraving tools) and punches. The former were used to gouge metal from the die face; various shapes of punch were then hammered directly into the die face. The die design was built up from a small number of punches, effectively allowing the mass-production of dies. Letters were broken down into simple components so that the alphabet could be reproduced using only three or four punches; more complex shapes like crowns, crosses and faces could be built up using further punches. Later in the Middle Ages larger and more elaborate punches were used for complete elements in the design, a rose or individual letters, for instance; their use is particularly evident in the design of the gold coins. Since the dies were usually made in London, and distributed to the regional and ecclesiastical mints, the style for any given period is generally uniform, without regional or individual stylistic characteristics.[132]

*Methods of Working: Gems*

Colour, size and 'virtue' were the prime considerations for gems for much of the medieval period. Gems most commonly were not cut but simply polished.[133] The technique used for polishing may have been as described by Theophilus: the gem

130  D.G. Sellwood, 'Medieval Minting Techniques', *British Numismatic Jnl.* xxxi (1962), 57-65. A 14th-century moneyer's tools are listed in A. Beardwood, 'Royal Mints and Exchanges', in Willard et al., op. cit. in note 6, 43-4.

131  The moneyer's name did not appear after 1279: Barrie Cook, 'English Coinage in the 13th Century', *Age of Chivalry*, 314, and G.C. Brooke, 'Medieval Moneyers', *British Numismatic Jnl.* xxi (1931-3), 59-66; P. Spufford, 'Mint Organization in Late Medieval Europe', in *Later Medieval Mints*, op. cit. note 4, 9-17. For history of coining see B. Cook, 'English Coinage under Edward III', ibid. 490-1; M. Archibald, 'Coins', in *Romanesque Art*, 320-23 (with good bibliog.); Sutherland, op. cit. in note 2; P. Grierson and M. Blackburn, *Medieval European Coinage with a Catalogue of Coins in the Fitzwilliam Museum Cambridge: I: The Early Middle*

*Ages* (1986), chapters 8 and 10 on Anglo-Saxon and Viking coinage; VIII and IX, *British Isles 924-1279*, and *1279-1509* (to be published).

132  J. Craig, *The Mint: a History of the London Mint* (1953), 9-11, 17. Dies and trial pieces have recently been found in York in the context of a 10th-century goldsmith's workshop: *The Archaeology of York*, 18.1: *Post-Roman Coins . . .*, (1986), E. Pirie et al., 23-45, and 15th-century coin forger's dies at Exeter: Allan, op. cit. in note 72, 253-4. See also J. Field, 'Ancient Coyning Irons', *Numismatic Chronicle*, 1st ser. vii (1845), 18-22.

133  Discussed by R.W. Lightbown in *Medieval Jewellery* (forthcoming); see also J. Evans, *A History of Jewellery, 1100-1870*, 2nd edn. (1970), and F. Falk, 'The Cutting and Setting of Gems in the 15th and 16th Centuries', in *Princely Magnificence* (Victoria & Albert Museum exhibn. 1980), 20-26.

was temporarily stuck down to a piece of wood, which was then rubbed backwards and forwards against a fixed block of sandstone.[134] A final polish was given by rubbing the gem on a lead plate covered with tile-dust mixed with saliva. Many items would have needed piercing, although Theophilus mentions only the piercing of pearls by using a fine steel drill, and of crystal beads by hammering and filing.[135]

There is no known English evidence about the tools used, but some unfinished amber beads (15th century) from Baynards Castle, London, appear to have been drilled using a sharp conical bit, and their smooth regular polish suggests that they were mechanically turned, presumably on a lathe, and not hand-polished.[136] Horizontal lathe-drills (with the spindle operated by a fiddle-bow) were in use by at least the early 15th century in Germany.[137]

With the exception of cameos and intaglios, the cutting of stones probably began to develop in Europe *c.* 1200, although cut stones are rarely found or mentioned before *c.* 1300. The process of shaping gems could have been carried out by holding the gem, mounted on a slab, to the edge of a cutting wheel, mounted on the spindle of a lathe-drill. The process was one of abrasion, for the wheel would be made of a softer material (bronze or iron) than the stone to be cut, but would be coated with oil mixed with an abrasive such as carborundum (emery) sand; the friction of the rotating wheel against the stone would effect the cut.[138]

Early English representations of facetted gems are to be seen on a jewelled ring-brooch worn by the statue of a seated king of *c.* 1250-75 on the west front of Wells Cathedral.[139] Two of the stones on it are shown as table-cut (flat-topped with sloping sides) and are of trapezoidal shape. However, no actual object so sophisticated survives from an English context until much later. If a cut was used, the commonest was probably *en cabochon*: a simple rounding of the stone (Fig.65). The fact that 14th-century English lists of gems only rarely specify the cut, suggests that cuts were still a novelty. The 'jewels of St Thomas' at Christ Church, Canterbury, listed 1315-21, include rings set with a square sapphire, a triangular emerald and an oblong chalcedony;[140] in 1367 Edward III paid Benedict Zakarie £66 for a gold brooch

134  Theophilus, *On Divers Arts*, ed. Hawthorne and Smith, book III, ch. 95.

135  Ibid. book III, chs. 95-6; perhaps gems were imported already pierced? The re-use of pierced gems set into rings was not uncommon: *Age of Chivalry*, Nos. 634, 637, 639.

136  V. Mead, 'Evidence for the Manufacture of Amber Beads in London, 14th-15th Century', *Trans. London and Middlesex Arch. Soc.* xxviii (1977), 211-4.

137  See the Nuremberg paternosterer illustrated in *Hausbuch*, op. cit. note 63, Pl. 25.

138  A. Billing, *The Science of Gems, Jewels, Coins and Medals* (1875), 17-25 and pl. vi; M. Bimson, 'Dark-Age Garnet Cutting', in J. Campbell and S.C. Hawkes (eds.), *Anglo-Saxon Studies in Archaeology and History*, iv (1985), 127-8; H.R. Hahnloser, *Corpus der Hartsteinschliffe* (Berlin,

1985), 13-21; F. Falk, *Edelsteinschliffe und Fassungformen* (Ulm, 1975). The use of goat's blood to soften gems and glass prior to engraving is advocated both by Theophilus (III.95) and by the English 14th-century recipe in B.L., MS Sloane 1754: D. Thompson, 'Liber de Coloribus', *Speculum*, i (1926), 298-9. On gem-engraving see O. Dalton, *Catalogue of Engraved Gems of the Post-Classical Period . . . in the British Museum* (1915), xvii-xxxvii.

139  W.H. St.J. Hope and W. R. Lethaby, 'The Imagery . . . on the West Front of Wells Cathedral', *Archaeologia*, lix (1) (1904), Pl. 51 (N 10) and p.199.

140  Lehmann-Brockhaus, op. cit. note 48, No. 938; Osbert of Clare (d. *c.* 1170) refers to the sapphire and the beryl as too hard to be cut (*sculpi non potest*): ibid. Nos. 5500, 5504.

(*nouche*) set with a central squared (*quarrer*) balas ruby, surrounded by diamonds, sapphires and pearls.[141]

The diamond, hardest of all gems to cut, was at first left in its natural crystal shape, an octahedron, which was then split in half to form two pointed diamonds, often seen set in rings, or as in Princess Blanche's crown of *c.* 1400.[142] Success in cutting even the diamond was possibly achieved sometime before 1300 in one of the great European gem-cutting centres, perhaps in Paris or the Low Countries.[143] At the end of the 14th century, one of the jewels owned by Richard II was set with a large square diamond the size of a hazelnut,[144] presumably either a table-cut or a diamond crystal with the point sliced off. By the 15th century the variety of cuts for diamonds included the *hog-back* (an oblong with gable-shaped facets), the *rosette* (angular hog-backs fitted together into a rosette shape) and the *lozenge-cut* (a diaper of diamond-shaped facets). The first is seen set into the garter owned by Charles the Bold, who was created a Knight of the Garter by his English brother-in-law Edward IV in 1469;[145] an early example of the second cut is found on the bridal crown of Edward's sister Margaret, of 1461.[146] Neither is certainly of English workmanship. Lozenge-facetting, though not of diamonds, may be seen on a late 15th-century crystal set onto a salt, and on a sapphire set into a ring, both given by Richard Fox to his Oxford foundation, Corpus Christi College.[147]

Both cameos and intaglios were esteemed in Classical times, and many survived into the Middle Ages, to be reset into seals, rings and other metalwork.[148] Cameos were precious stones with two differently coloured layers, the upper of which was cut away leaving a design in relief, while the lower served as ground; intaglios were stones onto which a design was deeply engraved. Medieval gem-cutters produced both, but especially intaglios, which were easier to work and which lent themselves for use in seals (Fig.72). In addition the medieval lapidary attributed to engraved gems amuletic powers greater than those of unadorned stones.[149] Both were produced by using lathe-drills of varying sizes, put in place of the cutting wheel on a lathe. Examination of two 13th-century intaglio gem seal-impressions indicates that

141 P.R.O., E 403/431; Kay Lacey has drawn my attention to a document of *c.*1400 (P.R.O., E 163/9/21), apparently English, which lists six- and eight-sided rubies and sapphires, and lozenge and table-cut diamonds.

142 *Age of Chivalry*, No. 13; for diamond cutting see Falk, art. cit. note 133, which is a contracted version of his book, op. cit. in note 138.

143 See note 142, and H. Hahnloser and S. Brugger-Koch, *Corpus der Hartsteinschliffe des 12.-15. Jahrhunderts* (Berlin, 1985), 25-30.

144 Given by Richard to the Duke of Burgundy: R. Vaughan, *Philip the Good* (1970), 151.

145 Falk, op. cit. note 142, Pl. 11 and pp.35-6.

146 Ibid. Pl. 52 and pp.86-7.

147 Campbell, 'Bishop Fox's Salt', art. cit. note 52, Pl. 6; J. Cherry, 'Three Rings . . . Associa-

ted with Bishop Fox', ibid. 1981-2, Pl. 2c, p.50.

148 Amongst numerous examples, seals, set with intaglios, of Durham Cathedral Priory *c.* 1083 and Waltham Abbey in F. Wormald, 'The English Seal as a Measure of its Time', in *The Year 1200 Exhibition Symposium* (New York 1970), 591-9; gem-set rings in M. Henig, *Catalogue of Rings in the Fitzwilliam Museum* (forthcoming), and a Medusa head cameo set into a 12th-century cross: *Cat. Romanesque Art*, No. 241.

149 Evans, *Magical Jewels*, op. cit. note 27, 81-96; lapidaries of engraved gems were of Eastern origin and appeared in the West in the 12th century, the earliest English manuscript including such material being Bodleian Library, MS Digby 13: ibid., appendix C, 220-3.

both designs are made up of V-shaped cuts left by very coarse drills.[150] The need to add fine detail to a design may additionally have called for the use of a diamond-point – a diamond splinter fixed to the end of an iron handle – which is presumably what the encyclopedist Bartholomew the Englishman meant when talking of the 'adamante . . . gravers usen the peces therof to signe [mark] . . . and to thirle [pierce] precious stones'.[151] Surviving gems tend to be mounted in silver or gold, which coupled with the value of the gem itself must have made their cost considerable. Early English instances of seals which incorporated ancient intaglio gems are those of Henry of Blois, bishop of Winchester (d. 1171), and Thomas Becket, archbishop of Canterbury (d. 1170), whose privy seal appears to depict Minerva, promoter of wisdom and health according to one lapidarist.[152]

Cameos – more difficult to cut and fulfilling no secondary use – more rarely survive. Classical cameos are described by the chronicler of St. Alban's Abbey as having been collected (dug up?) since Saxon times for use in embellishing St. Alban's gold shrine.[153] The abbey's most illustrious cameo was kept separately: a huge Roman sardonyx depicting the Emperor Augustus, described and drawn by Matthew Paris in the 1250s.[154] The cameos for which Henry III paid handsomely in the 1230s are of unknown date and origin, but cameos were certainly being made in Paris by then. Only a handful of surviving examples of 13th- to 15th-century date have been credited, even tentatively, to English workmanship: pendants, unmounted gems, and those set into the Oxwich brooch of *c*. 1300 (Fig.64).[155]

Of the non-precious materials used, there is archaeological evidence for the working of jet, amber and coral in England, largely in the form of beads (finished and unfinished) that were presumably intended to make up rosaries. Jet rosaries gauded with coral, coral combined with precious metal, and amber alone are all recorded quite frequently from the 14th century onwards. In London, Baynard's Castle (not far from Paternoster Row where the sellers of rosaries had their shops) has yielded up a coral fragment, a few jet beads and a quantity of amber in different stages of working, all from 14th- to early 16th-century deposits. The amber consists of beads (some incomplete) and unworked pieces.[156] In York, amber-working was a well established industry in the Anglo-Scandinavian period; quantities of finished or

150  M. Henig and T.A. Heslop, 'Three 13th-Century Seal-Matrices with Intaglio Stones in the Castle Museum, Norwich', *Norfolk Arch.* xxxix (3) (1986), 305-9; medieval intaglios, perhaps English, are not uncommon: C. Hunter Blair, 'A Note upon Medieval Seals', *Archaeologia Aeliana*, 3rd ser. xvii (1920), 284-7; Dalton, op. cit. note 138, Nos. 895, 1119, 1121.

151  *On the Properties of Things*, op. cit. note 24, book XVI, chapter 8, 833.

152  Blois: *Romanesque Art*, 299; Becket: J. Burtt, 'Confirmation by Thomas, Archbishop of Canterbury . . .', *Arch. Jnl.* xxvi (1869), 84-7.

153  *Gesta Abbatum Monasterii S. Albani*, ed. H.T. Riley, I (Rolls Ser. xxviii.4, 1867), 29.

154  M. Henig and T.A. Heslop, 'The Great Cameo of St Albans', *J.B.A.A.* cxxxix (1986), 148-53.

155  Dalton, op. cit. note 138, Nos. 14, 16, 20; Oxwich brooch: *Age of Chivalry*, No. 653.

156  The coral had been cut into a bead but not drilled; for the amber see Mead, op. cit. note 136. In 1438, for example, both were being imported to London, the form unspecified: 2½ lb. of coral costing £6, 1 lb. of amber 12*s*. 5½*d*., see P.R.O., E 122/71/13, mm. 10, 14. By contrast, in 1290 Queen Eleanor bought 2,000 coral beads and 1,000 jet for 40*s*.: J.C. Parsons, *The Court and Household of Eleanor of Castile in 1290* . . . (Toronto, 1977), 106.

*Fig. 64* Oxwich brooch, gold set with cameos, which although almost contemporary fit their settings poorly and must replace the original stones; *c.* 1330 (cameos *c.* 1250). Excavated at Oxwich Castle. Diameter 4 cm. (*National Museum of Wales, Cardiff*)

*Fig. 65* Middleham jewel, gold, engraved and enamelled in champlevé on both sides with the Nativity, the Holy Trinity and saints, and set with a drilled sapphire; *c.* 1450. Found at Middleham (Yorks.), 1985. Height 6.5 cm. (*Private collection*)

partly finished beads have been found in 9th- to 12th-century contexts at Pavement, Clifford Street, and Coppergate, as well as rings and earrings at the latter.[157]

### *Gem-Setting*

Pearls were normally used pierced, either sewn onto clothing or mounted on goldsmiths' work. If mounted, they would be held in place by a short metal tang, usually as part of a cluster or *troche*, such as on the All Souls College mazer lid or on Blanche's crown of *c.* 1400.[158] Other gems were set in three principal ways. Collar settings, like those on the Oxwich brooch (Fig.64), were pinned to the main frame of the jewel, as seen on the back of the Founder's Jewel of *c.* 1450.[159] Simple four-pronged claw settings were also widely used (Fig.63). Lastly, in a development of the 14th century which continued in popularity throughout the 15th century, a petal-shaped setting is found, as on the Wytlesey ring, which may be the 'panse' (pansy)

157 A. MacGregor, *Archaeology of York: Small Finds:* *17.3, Anglo-Scandinavian Finds from Lloyds* *Bank, Pavement and Other Sites* (1982), 89-91, 152: the amber rings had been shaped on a lathe. The amber from Clifford Street had had the surface polished smooth on a wheel: D. Waterman, 'Late Saxon, Viking and Early

Medieval Finds from York', *Archaeologia*, lvii (1959), 68, 94-6.

158 Mazer: *Age of Chivalry*, No. 722; crown: ibid. No. 13.

159 Ibid. No. 640, which suggests that the jewel may be French, but the evidence is slender.

setting to which some documents refer.[160]

## *Organisation of the Industry*

The goldsmiths of London were among the first of the City gilds to receive a royal charter, in 1327; furthermore, it is clear that an organisation of goldsmiths had existed in the capital from at least the 12th century, and individual goldsmiths are recorded from the Conquest onwards.[161] The Crown's interest in controlling the activities of goldsmiths was inevitable, given their vital role not simply as makers and suppliers of plate and jewellery, but also as controllers of the exchange of old coin and plate for new, and as producers of the coinage.

The earliest recorded attempt to regulate the standard for gold and silver plate was in 1238, apparently as a result of the fraudulent activities of some goldsmiths.[162] The king ordered that the mayor and aldermen of London were to choose six goldsmiths to superintend the craft, stipulated standards for gold and silver, and forbade the plating of base metal with gold or silver. This latter regulation was in 1404 relaxed into an embargo on secular plate alone: it was permissible to make and gild church vessels in base metal.[163] It was forbidden to set base metal with real stones, as it was also forbidden to set gold with false ones.[164] The countless fines listed in the early minute books of the Goldsmiths' Company illustrate how frequently these rules were breached.

The Goldsmiths' Company of London based its authority on a statute of 1300 whose paramount intention was to protect the buying public from the use of inferior metals by dishonest goldsmiths.[165] Gold and silver plate were to be of fixed alloys: gold of the standard of Paris (19.2 carats), and silver, as supposedly from time immemorial, was to be of the same standard as the coinage, that is the sterling alloy of 92.5 per cent purity. Novelty lay in the introduction of a mark called *une teste de leopart* (leopard's head) to be punched on silver vessels by the wardens of the craft, before they left their maker's possession, as evidence that the metal had been assayed (tested) and found good. The leopard's head mark thus began as a sterling mark, a proof of quality.

160 Ring: ibid. No. 639; 'panse' setting: A.R. Myers, 'The Jewels of Queen Margaret of Anjou', *Bull. John Rylands Lib.* xlii (1959), 119.
161 Reddaway and Walker, op. cit. note 15, xix-xxx, 1-3, 222-4.
162 *Cal. Close Rolls, 1237-42*, 85: 'De auro fabricando in civitate London'. Silver was to be of no worse standard than money (i.e. sterling), gold to be worth at least 100*s*. per mark – as a unit of weight this was ⅔ lb. troy or 3,840 grains: Connor, op. cit. in note 82, 123.
163 Statute of 5 Henry IV c. 13: *Statutes of the Realm*, ii, 146-7.
164 Op. cit. note 162; this prohibition was repeated in 1300, see below.

165 Statute of 28 Edw. I c. 20: *Statutes of the Realm*, i, 140-1. England's marking system followed that of France, where town marks were already in use by at least 1275: R.W. Lightbown, *Secular Goldsmiths' Work in Medieval France* (1979), 6. See also S. Hare, *Touching Gold and Silver* (exhibn. cat., London, Goldsmiths' Hall 1978), 14. Interestingly, the earliest collection of Parisian goldsmiths' regulations, of 1260, stipulates that silver be of the sterling standard, 'Aussi bons qu'estellins . . . une monoye d'Angleterre ou d'Ecosse': P. Le Roy, *Statuts et privileges du Corps des Marchands Orfevres-Joailliers de la Ville de Paris* (Paris, 1759), 111.

Provincial goldsmiths were also controlled by the 1300 statute, which ordained that a representative goldsmith should be sent from each town where there were goldsmiths to London, there 'to seek their sure touch'. It is uncertain whether this meant that other towns were to use the leopard's head mark, or that the London company was to supervise the work of provincial goldsmiths. The company seems to have thought the latter, for its 1327 charter reiterated that the provinces were to follow the same ordinances as those of London and were to send representatives to London concerning the leopard's head punch.[166] The assertion of these powers appears to be confirmed by the appointment in 1330 of two York goldsmiths by the London Goldsmiths' Company, to ensure that the ordinances were being kept in York.[167] This authority may only rarely have been exercised, for an ordinance of 1378-79 further laid down that in towns with a mint, the master of the mint was to mark plate with the mark of the city or borough where the assay was.[168] A further safeguard of standards was an ordinance of 1363, which ruled that each master goldsmith was to have his own mark, to be known to the wardens of the company.[169] After an item of plate had been assayed it was to be marked twice, with the maker's mark and with 'the king's mark', that is, the leopard's head.

By a statute of 1423, seven towns other than London were ordered to be set up as assay towns, each with its own 'touch' or mark: York, Newcastle-upon-Tyne, Lincoln, Norwich, Bristol, Salisbury and Coventry.[170] The 'Keeper of the Touch' was liable to be fined if he marked with the leopard's head anything of less than sterling standard.

A further statute, of 1478, attempted to tighten control of malpractice, and made the Goldsmiths' Company itself liable to penalties for the misdeeds of the Keeper of the Touch.[171] The gold standard was lowered to 18 carats. In order to distinguish what plate had been made before the new statute, the old King's mark of the simple leopard's head was henceforth to be replaced by a crowned leopard's head. The Company appointed a salaried 'Common Assayer' who was to make regular assays at Goldsmiths' Hall, and wares found to be up to standard were to be given an additional mark, a letter of the alphabet, by him; the Touch Warden then added the crowned leopard's head. The letter used was changed each year after the election of

166 The 1327 charter speaks of provincial gold-smiths coming to London to 'fetch their certain touch': Reddaway and Walker, 223, which may be the correct interpretation of the 1300 statute 'de querre lour certeine tuche', often interpreted as meaning 'to ascertain'. Perhaps the provincial goldsmiths were issued with punches, just as the provincial mints were with dies?

167 *Cal. Patent Rolls, 1330-4*, 4: September 12th. Richard de Grymesby and Roger de Monketon were given responsibility well beyond York, for the counties of Lincoln, Lancaster, Westmorland, Cumberland, Northumberland and Durham as well.

168 *Rot. Parl.* iii, cols. 66b-67a; Hare, op. cit. note

165, 14-5; Reddaway and Walker, 45, 318. It seems most unlikely that this was ever put into practice, since minting in England was at this date confined to London, with the exceptions of the ecclesiastical mints at York and Durham: J. Craig, *The Mint* (1953), 81.

169 Statute of 37 Edw. III, c. 7: *Statutes of the Realm*, i, 380, see also Reddaway and Walker, 31, 317. The statute also forbade any maker of silver vessels to gild them, or gilders to make silver.

170 Statute of 2 Henry VI, c. 17: *Statutes of the Realm*, ii, 224, and Reddaway and Walker, 165-6, 318.

171 Statute of 17 Edw. IV, c. 1: *Statutes of the Realm*, ii, 454-60, and Reddaway and Walker, 165-7. The area of jurisdiction is stated as being the City of London and two miles beyond it.

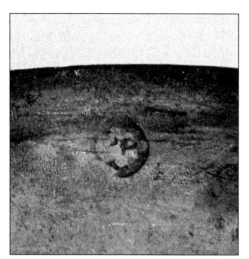

Fig. 66 Leopard's-head mark (for the sterling standard) on the silver Shrewsbury bowl; one of the earliest forms of the mark, c. 1350-1400. Diameter of mark c. 4 mm. (*Rowley's House Museum, Shrewsbury*)

Fig. 67 Leopard's-head mark on a silver diamond-point spoon of c. 1450. Diameter 5 mm. (*Victoria and Albert Museum, No. 1947-1900*)

Fig. 68 Leopard's head mark with an E on the tongue, on a silver spoon. May represent either an unidentified provincial town (York?) or a pre-1478 system of date letters. Mark c. 5.5 mm diameter. (*Private collection*)

Fig. 69 Rim of silver-gilt basin made for Richard Fox, showing a crowned leopard's head representing London, the date-letter Q for 1493-4, and an unidentified maker's mark of a horseshoe. The rim decoration is made up of the same motif stamped repeatedly; the edges of the punch are clearly visible to either side of the flower spray. Diameter of whole 48 cm. (*Corpus Christi College, Oxford*)

the new Touch Warden (on May 19th, St. Dunstan's day), and a 20-year letter cycle was adopted (omitting J,V,W,X,Y and Z). The earliest surviving fully marked pieces are the Nettlecombe chalice and paten, each with the date letter B for 1478-79, the crowned leopard's head, and a maker's mark of a tankard.[172]

Many of these regulations seem to have been evaded. Remarkably few pieces bear any marks at all, although the minute quantity of medieval goldsmiths' work which survives is in no way representative of what was made between 1300 and *c.* 1530. It is likely that old plate, which had been sent by its owner to be melted down and refashioned, would have escaped marking, as might jewellery because of its size or fragility. Items intended for retail sale, like spoons or dishes, were perhaps easier to control, although the frequency of goldsmiths' fines attests to the perpetual problem of inadequate workmanship and clandestine sale.

One of the commonest surviving marks is a leopard's head, which occurs in a number of varying styles (Figs.66-9). These different punches may represent differences in date, and a tentative chronological sequence has been proposed;[173] only one piece so marked comes from a secure archaeological context: the recently discovered Shrewsbury bowl, found in late 14th-century levels on the site of Shrewsbury Abbey.[174] Inventories of the 14th and 15th centuries sometimes record commonplace items, such as dishes and spoons, as being *signatus* (marked) with an initial, and yet others with a specified coat of arms, or a leopard or leopard's head. It seems probable that few, if any, of these are hallmarks, and that they instead represent ownership marks – very necessary in an age of constant travel. Surviving instances of these are found on the Coventry spoon[175] and the Bermondsey dish,[176] engraved respectively with an S and a leopard's head – the latter conceivably a mark of royal ownership. In at least one source – an account roll of 1323 – the leopard hallmark is clearly distinguished: silver dishes and saucers are described as 'without marks except for the impression of the leopard's head for tested metal'.[177] A related royal account itemizes saucers as both *signo de uno leopardo in uno circulo* and marked with a leopard lacking a circle;[178] these could well be hallmarks. More puzzlingly, the same account refers also to dishes and saucers 'of the touch of London' (*de tactu*

172  Hare, op. cit. note 165, No. 9; a spoon which may be a year earlier, ibid. No. 8, has an ambiguous mark.

173  G.E.P and J. How, *English and Scottish Silver Spoons . . . and Pre-Elizabethan Hallmarks on English Plate*, 3 vols. (1952-7), iii, 2, 11-13, which also ascribe all leopards' head marks to London. This surely cannot be the case (see below).

174  Of plain silver, punched on the rim, a typical piece of retail plate: M.L. Campbell, 'The Shrewsbury Bowl', *Antiq. Jnl.* lxviii (1988), 312-13.

175  *Age of Chivalry*, No. 209.

176  Ibid. No. 115; if the engraved leopard's head is derived from the royal arms it may be a

badge of royal ownership, and if so may be the prototype king's mark, forerunner of the sterling mark.

177  'Nullo signo signati nisi impressione caput leopardi pro metallo approbato': P.R.O., E 361/2, m. 22ᵛ: the King's chapel ornaments delivered to William de Langdale 14 December 1323.

178  Ibid. m. 29, for 1327-8. It is impossible to be sure exactly what is meant. Very often similar phrases are used which clearly do not describe hallmarks: *Discus . . . sign' extra in fundo de uno leopardo cum labell'* in C. Ord, 'Inventory of Crown Jewels, 3 Edward III', *Archaeologia*, x (1792), 246.

*London*'). These can only be hallmarks – and at this date only the leopard's head mark existed – but we do not know what feature made the mark distinctively a London one. Or is this merely an early instance of the assumption that the leopard mark must represent London because it originated there?[179]

Of the provincial marks, that used by Bristol – a bull's head, according to a 1462 document – is not known to survive.[180] Of the others, only that for York can be identified with certainty: half a leopard's head and fleur-de-lys conjoined within a circular punch, found on a few 15th- and 16th-century spoons. Although the mark is first described only in 1560, a York ordinance of 1410 alludes to a city mark and mentions too the presence of a local assay office,[181] some years before the 1423 statute naming the various provincial towns. It is possible that other towns were by then also using distinguishing marks, now unidentifiable; it has been conjectured that marks of a leopard's head distinguished by a prominent tongue incorporating a letter represent provincial versions of the King's Mark, the letter indicating the assay town (such as N for Norwich). Similar letters are found as town mint-marks on contemporary coins.[182]

The marks – other than the leopard's head – found on surviving objects are most commonly a symbol (Figs.69, 74) or letter mark, as used by the maker. All are obscure, although it may be suggested that a star mark described on Bristol spoons is that of some unknown local maker,[183] and that the fringed S mark found on some London spoons might be that of Simpson, a specialist spoonmaker.[184]

It is not clear why the seven towns specified in the 1423 act were chosen to be assay centres. For four of them – Salisbury, Lincoln, Norwich and Coventry – there is no evidence that they ever acted as assay centres in the Middle Ages,[185] although Coventry, for example, had documented metalworkers (including goldsmiths) by *c*. 1280, and was known as a centre for the metal trades by the 15th century.[186] By

179  P.R.O. E 361/2, m. 23, for 1324-5. Other instances of the 'touch of London' occur, as in 1416, cited by J. Wylie, *Henry V* (1912), i, 476 n. 4 – again a description is lacking. The reference might be thought to confirm the Hows' theory cited in note 173, except for the notorious inconsistency of medieval terminology. It seems likely that the leopard's head mark was associated with London by false analogy with the French system, whereby the fleur-de-lys represented Paris: Lightbown, op.cit. in note 62, 5-7.

180  Hare, op. cit. note 165, 24.

181  Ibid. 32, and T. Fallow, 'York Church Plate', *Yorks. Arch. Jnl.* viii (1889), 302-3.

182  G. How, 'Date-Letters on London Silver Prior to 1478 . . .', *Connoisseur*, cxxiii (1949), pp.106-7. But the N letter might have been confused between Norwich and Newcastle, and the letter I (on a spoon sold at Sotheby's, 13th Dec. 1973, lot 54) cannot be linked with an assay town. Alternative explanations are

that such marks represent either an early system of date letters or, most likely, the die-cutter's initial (as on coins).

183  How, op. cit. note 173, iii, 86-7 (who interprets the star as the Bristol town mark). Spoons marked with an arrowhead, probably also the maker's mark, occur in the 1451 will of Adelina Claydich of London: London, Guildhall Library, MS 9171/5, f.40.

184  T. Kent, *London Silver Spoonmakers . . .* (Silver Society, 1981), 9-10: William Simpson was active *c*. 1499-1546.

185  Hare, op. cit. note 165, 24-33, also C.J. Jackson, *English Goldsmiths and their Marks*, 2nd edn. (1921), chap. X (needs revising), and How, op. and loc. cit. note 183.

186  In the 13th century goldsmiths were centred on Broadgate: *Early Records of Medieval Coventry*, ed. P.R. Coss, 36-7, 40; for metalworkers in 1448 see B. Poole, *History and Antiquities of Coventry* (1870), 22, 48-9.

*Fig. 70a* Engraved silver matrix of the Common Seal of the city of Exeter (obverse), the earliest surviving civic seal in England; *c.* 1200-8. Diameter 6.5 cm. (*Devon Record Office*)

*Fig. 70b* Reverse side of the Exeter city seal, with the maker's inscription 'Lucas me fecit'.

contrast, many towns omitted from the 1423 act are known to have had active goldsmiths. *Opus Dunelm'* is recorded several times from the 13th century onwards, apparently referring to Durham goldsmiths' work. How was such work recognizably of Durham if it was not marked?[187] Exeter too is omitted from the 1423 statute, and yet goldsmiths are recorded there from the 12th century, there is 13th-century archaeological evidence of goldsmiths' activity, and the local mint was sporadically active until 1300.[188] The city's silver seal-matrix of *c.* 1200-8 (Fig.70), which is engraved *Lucas me fecit*, may be the earliest surviving example (excluding coins) of the work of an Exeter goldsmith.[189] Also omitted from the 1423 statute were Canterbury, Winchester and Chester. Goldsmiths are documented in Canterbury from *c.* 1150, and Canterbury was second only to London in the importance of its royal mint and exchange for much of the Middle Ages.[190] Equally, in Winchester in 1148 goldsmiths formed the most numerous group of craftsmen property-holders and, in 1302-3 at least, London goldsmiths were using a shop in Winchester's Goldsmiths' Row to sell their *iocalia* (jewels).[191]

London was undoubtedly always the predominant centre for goldsmiths in England; it had both the greatest pool of potential customers and ready access to such essential materials as precious metals and imported gems. The skilled engravers who produced the dies for the coinage, some of whom were goldsmiths, were concentrated in London from the end of Edward the Confessor's reign.[192] In 1130 a group of London goldsmiths (numbering perhaps eight) was kept permanently attached to the king's service by a grant for the purchase of charcoal.[193] Robert, abbot of St. Albans, bought *iocalia* (jewels) in London as presents for Pope Hadrian (1154-59);[194] in 1205 King John owned a sapphire brooch 'of London work' and a gold crown 'made at London'.[195] The writer Gerald of Wales, visiting London at about that time, marvelled at the abundance there of gold and gilt rings, gold belts adorned with ivory, earrings of gold and filigree, and signet rings.[196] In 1292, it was in London that Count Amadeus of Savoy ordered an engraved privy seal with a

---

187   Durham work: in 1295 a reliquary and in 1299 a silver mounted crozier: Lehmann-Brockhaus, op. cit. note 38, Nos. 2,902, 170, and 6,264, 304.

188   Hare, op. cit. note 165, 37; Allan, op. cit. note 72, 253-4, 353; N. Shiel, 'The Saxon and Norman Mint', in J. Andrews et al., *Exeter Coinage* (Exeter Industrial Arch. Group, 1980).

189   *Romanesque Art*, No. 378; Luke seems also to have made other Exeter seals, for Exe Bridge and the Hospitals of St. Alexius and St. John: Kingsford, art. cit. note 56, 156-7 and Pl. II b, c, d; also for the borough of Taunton nearby: ibid. Pl. II, all attributable on stylistic grounds.

190   W. Urry, *Canterbury under the Angevin Kings* (1967), 112-18; Craig, op. cit. note 168, *s. n.* Canterbury.

191   1148 survey: D. Keene, *Survey of Medieval Win-*

*chester* (Winchester Studies 2, 1985) i(1), 280-1; 1302-3 shop, ibid. Nos. 1,102-3, p.1,102. Chester was highly independent, being part of the Palatine County, and thus perhaps considered outside the scope of the 1423 act. There were goldsmiths and moneyers active there throughout the middle ages: M. Ridgway, *Chester Goldsmiths from Early Times to 1726* (1968), 3-9.

192   F.M. Stenton, 'Norman London', in his *Preparatory to Anglo-Saxon England*, ed. D.M. Stenton (1970), 44.

193   Ibid. 43.

194   Lehmann-Brockhaus, op. cit. note 38, No. 6,029.

195   Ibid. No. 6,138.

196   Ibid. No. 6,135: *vermiculatas* may mean inlaid rather than filigree.

chain made of gold.[197] It has plausibly been suggested that a number of 13th-century seals made for widely separated ecclesiastical foundations in Norwich, Faversham (Kent) and Milton Abbey (Dorset) are products of a single London-based workshop.[198]

The extent of London's pull as a centre can further be judged by the amount of business poached by London goldsmiths from their provincial peers. In 1288 John Peckham, archbishop of Canterbury, had a mitre made in London decorated with gold and gems at a cost of £173 4s. 1d.[199] In 1292 Beverley Minster commissioned a substantial gold and silver shrine (c. 5ft. by 1½ft.) from the London goldsmith Roger de Faringdon, who apparently completed it only in 1308.[200] The shrines of St. Hugh at Lincoln, of St. Thomas of Cantelupe at Hereford and of St. Cuthbert at Durham were repaired respectively in 1310, 1320 and 1400-1 by London goldsmiths, despite the great distances involved and the recorded existence of local craftsmen.[201] The pattern continues into the 15th century; in 1430 the abbot of Bury St. Edmunds commissioned a showy crozier in silver-gilt for £40 from John Orwell, goldsmith of London and the King's engraver, and it was Orwell who, in 1447, made a silver font for Canterbury Cathedral Priory, as well as carrying out minor repairs to its mazers.[202]

Although York could not equal London, it was a respectable rival. Archaeological evidence for goldsmithing and jewellery production exists from the Viking period onwards and York goldsmiths are recorded from the mid 11th century. Between 1272 and 1399 a total of 83 were admitted to the freedom of York, and another 105 between 1399 and 1509.[203] Figures for London seem dramatically larger, though they are not directly comparable; members of the London Goldsmiths' Company numbered 135 in 1369, 186 in 1404 and 210 by 1506.[204] These figures are a minimum and exclude some ancillary workers, as well as aliens and 'strangers' who worked in Westminster or Southwark, perhaps for the court and its circle, and were outside the effective jurisdiction of the Company.[205]

It is noticeable that the archbishops of York patronized their local goldsmiths.

197  Amadeus also ordered two silver seals: A. Dufour and F. Robert, 'Les Orfèvres . . . en Savoie', in *Mémoires et Documents, Soc. Savoisienne d'Histoire et Archaeologie*, xxiv (1886), 440.
198  Lehmann-Brockhaus, No. 6,538.
199  Kingsford, art. cit. note 56, 160-2.
200  *Cal. Letter-Book A*, 180-1; *Memorials of Beverley Minster: Chapter Act Book*, ed. A.F. Leach, ii (Surtees Soc. cviii 1903), 299-301.
201  St. Hugh's shrine, new lid: E. Venables, 'Shrine and Head of St. Hugh of Lincoln', *Arch. Jnl.* l (1893), 61; St. Thomas of Cantelupe: John de Werlyngworthe was paid £10 for ornaments for shrine, see P. Morgan, 'St. Thomas of Cantilupe's Shrine', in M. Jancey (ed.), *St. Thomas Cantilupe . . . Essays in his Honour* (1982), 150; St. Cuthbert: London goldsmith and

assistants paid 18s. travelling expenses to inspect the shrine, see J. Fowler, *Extracts from the Account Rolls of the Abbey of Durham*, ii (Surtees Soc. c, 1898), 499.
202  M.L. Campbell, 'English Goldsmiths . . .', in D. Williams (ed.), *England in the 15th Century* (1987), 51-2.
203  *V.C.H. City of York*, 115.
204  Reddaway and Walker, 79; by 1477 they numbered 180, ibid. 138. These figures also exclude apprentices.
205  The enormous 15th-century influx of aliens can be measured by the fact that between 1479 and 1510, 319 aliens swore to obey the rules of the London Goldsmiths' Company: ibid., 171.

Wickwane (1279-86) bought silver cups and cups 'de maser' from Walter the goldsmith of York;[206] Greenfield (1306-15) bought from Adam de Munkton; and Melton (1317-40) from his kinsman Henry Melton, who may have made the chalice and paten found in the archbishop's grave.[207] The shrine of St. William's head in York Minster was mended by local goldsmiths in the 1480s and 1490s.[208] York goldsmiths also worked elsewhere: Hugh 'le Seler' of York made a silver seal for the See of Durham in 1333,[209] and Richard de Grimsby, goldsmith of York, worked for Edward III, making at least one Great Seal (with another, for a total of £77 8s. 3d.), and altering the King's so-called 'chivalrot' privy seal of gold, inset with a rectangular engraved sapphire (Fig.72).[210] By the end of the 15th century, however, York's comparative economic decline was the counterpoise to London's prosperity, and the fortunes of their goldsmiths doubtless followed suit.

### Specialisations

Versatile craftsmen though goldsmiths were, there were various specialisms within their craft. These begin to define themselves in the 13th century, to judge from the evidence of wills and personal names, although some specialists, like moneyers, had certainly existed from before the Conquest. London and York were the major centres of goldsmiths, able to support such sub-groups as *finers* (refiners of precious metal), gold-beaters, gold-wiredrawers (see above), burnishers, gilders, spanglers (makers of the spangles sewn onto clothing),[211] *selers* (makers of seal-matrices), jewellers and mazerers. The three latter categories of craftsmen did not work exclusively with precious metals.

The use of seals grew dramatically between the 11th century and the 15th, when they were used by almost all sections of society. Although not exclusively of metal (jet, bone and ivory were also favoured), seals came to be commonly of copper alloy or precious metal. Goldsmiths undoubtedly found seal-making a profitable sideline – one that demanded principally a skill in engraving[212] – and they did not restrict themselves as to materials. In the 14th and 15th centuries goldsmiths like Thomas of

206  Lehmann-Brockhaus, op. cit. note 38, No. 6,231.
207  *Age of Chivalry*, No. 112; Melton's seal (impression only) also survives: W. Greenwell and C. Hunter Blair, 'Catalogue of Seals in Durham Treasury', *Archaeologia Aeliana*, 3rd ser. xiv (1917), 284, No. 3229.
208  John Gorrus of York worked on the shrine in 1478-9 and 1481-2: J. Raine, *Fabric Rolls of York Minster* (Surtees Soc. xxxv, 1858), 84, 86. Harmann (son of John Colan – see above) of York mended the shrine in 1497-8: ibid. 90.
209  See note 56.
210  Payment for seals in March and April 1340: *Wardrobe Book of William de Norwell, 1338-40* ed. M. and B. Lyon (Brussels, 1983), 428-9.

In 1351 Grimsby was given 'une piere quarre dun saphir ewage ove un chivalrot ove un toret dor pour . . . nostre secre seal': H.C. Maxwell-Lyte, *Historical Notes on the Use of the Great Seal* (1926), 105-6. This seems to correspond with the appearance of the fourth secret seal of Edward III, adopted in 1354, in which the central part is made up of a rectangular gem engraved with a horseman (Fig. 72): T.F. Tout, *Chapters in Administrative History*, v (1930), 175-6.
211  Though not a separate group in York, spanglers were by 1441 defined as such in London: Reddaway and Walker, 259.
212  Ibid. 57, note 58.

*Fig. 71* Impression of the second Great Seal of Henry III, designed and made in silver by the king's goldsmith, William of Gloucester, in 1259. The elaborately crocketed throne strongly resembles the shrine of Edward the Confessor at Westminster on which William is known to have worked. Diameter 8.2 cm. (*P.R.O. Ward 2/40/146L/34*)

*Fig. 72* Impression of Edward III's Secret Seal known as the 'chivalrot'; on a document dated September 1357. The original of gold, set with a contemporary sapphire intaglio of a horseman, was modified in 1354 by the king's goldsmith, Richard de Grimsby of York. The rectangular sides of the sapphire are clearly visible. Diameter 2.3 cm. (*P.R.O. E43/638*)

Chester, Adam de Thorp, Peter Hilltoft and John Orwell (all save Thomas being of London) each received payment for copper, brass or 'latoun' seals,[213] aside from their work in gold and silver. Although some *selers* were certainly goldsmiths, many were probably not.[214]

By a quirk of fortune, seals (in the form of wax impressions) are the commonest surviving witnesses to the art of the medieval engraver, goldsmith or not. The evidence for specialist goldsmith-engravers is slender and sometimes ambiguous (*graver* could also mean a sculptor or miner), but a York gold-engraver, Robert le Orgraver, is recorded in 1308,[215] and *ciselours* (chiseller or engraver) are known from the 13th century.[216] Any craftsman professionally involved with the production of dies for the coinage would have needed engraving skills, and these men tended to be goldsmiths, from Theoderic (*cuneator* to Edward the Confessor), Anketil of St. Albans, Theobald of Lyleston (dead by 1200; 'insculptor cuniorum monete tocius Anglie'), through to William of Gloucester, goldsmith to Henry III (see Fig.71), John Esmond, and John Orwell in the 14th and 15th centuries, all three of whom incidentally engraved seals.[217] It has been suggested on grounds of style that goldsmiths also engraved some monumental brasses, but there is no documentary evidence.[218] However, particularly earlier in the middle ages, it is known that engraving was also practised by painters or draughtsmen. It is recorded that the great 12th-century illuminator Hugh of Bury was a metalworker and engraver (*sculptor*) too, while the 14th-century Swinburne pyx is engraved with scenes (once enamelled) suggestively close to those in two contemporary manuscripts.[219]

213 Thomas made a copper seal in 1311-12: M. Ridgway, *Chester Goldsmiths to 1726* (1968), 30; Adam engraved a brass seal for Richard II in 1389-90: Devon, *Issues*, 242; Peter was paid in 1391 for engraving 17 brass seals, ibid., 246; Orwell was paid 40s. for making and engraving a *latoun* seal in 1461 for Edward IV: Kingsford, art. cit. note 56, 177, and M.L. Campbell, 'English Goldsmiths', in D. Williams (ed.), *England in the 15th Century* (1987), 51-2.

214 *Seler* could mean saddler too.

215 G. Fransson, *Middle English Surnames of Occupation, 1100-1350* (Lund, 1935), 135.

216 Ibid. 136.

217 Theoderic: M. Dolley and F. Jones, '. . . The Arms of St. Edward' in M. Dolley (ed.), *Anglo-Saxon Coins* (1960), 220-1; Anketil: Lehmann-Brockhaus, Nos. 3,836 (work on the coinage), Nos. 3,834,-6,-8 (work on the shrine and plate), No. 6,376 (seal), and C.C. Oman, 'Goldsmiths at St. Albans in the 12th and 13th Centuries', *St. Albans and Herts. Archit. and Archaeol. Soc. Trans.* 1932, 218-9; Theobald: Lehmann-Brockhaus, No. 2,639; William of Gloucester: R. Kent Lancaster, 'Artists, Suppliers and Clerks . . . to Henry III', *Jnl. of Warburg and Courtauld Inst.* xxxv (1972), 91-6, 99, 104; Esmond: Kingsford, art. cit. note 56, 172;

Orwell: Campbell, op. and loc. cit. note 213.

218 M. Norris, *Monumental Brasses: the Craft* (1978), 78; other examples in *Witness in Brass* (London: Victoria and Albert: exhibn. 1987), No. 206: a brass of *c.* 1420 with traces of gold, silver and enamel, and delicate pointillé engraving. The brass to Cristine, *d.* 1470, widow of Matthew Philip, London goldsmith has been thought to be goldsmith's work too: illustrated in *Arch. Cant.* xi (1877), 11; Philip is known only to have engraved seals: Kingsford, art. cit. note 56, 175.

219 Hugh cast the Abbey doors and a bell in bronze as well as illuminating in *c.*1135 the Bury Bible: C.M. Kauffmann, *English Romanesque Manuscripts, 1066-1190* (1975), No. 56, 14-5, 89. C. Dodwell most illuminatingly discusses the links between engravers and painters in the middle ages in 'The Meaning of Sculptor in the Romanesque Period' in *Essays for George Zarnecki* (1985), 97-8. It has been suggested that Anketil, goldsmith of St. Albans (see note 217), was the painter of the full-page miniatures in the St. Albans Psalter, that is the Alexis master: O. Pächt et al. *St. Albans Psalter* (1960), 172-7; pyx: C.C. Oman, 'The Swinburne Pyx', *Burlington Mag.* xcii (1950), 337-41.

The medieval understanding of the term *jeweller* is problematic, for it seems to mean variously a retailer of goldsmiths' work (including jewellery), a retailer of gem-stones, an appraiser of gem-stones, and only sometimes the craftsman who worked or set the stones. Jewellers are so described first in London in 1340 and in York in 1413, and the term becomes commonplace in the 15th century.[220] More investigation might reveal that although jewellers sometimes describe themselves also as goldsmiths, like John Wynne in 1446-47, they were as or more often drapers, like Richard Hercy of London (d. 1438) – a reminder of the intimate link between clothing and jewellery. That 'jewellers' were sometimes makers of rosaries – for which there must have been a steady market – is suggested by the description of Robert Nyke of London as jeweller and 'bedemaker'. The word bedemaker seems by the 15th century to have replaced 'paternosterer' (maker of paternoster or rosary beads), a term found as a personal name as early as 1199, and commonly from the mid 13th century.[221]

Amongst the material remains of the goldsmith's art, the predominance of rings might indicate specialist producers, but there is no evidence for this aside from one suggestive inventory and the mention in 1327 of a craftsman called John Goldehoper (maker of gold hoops or rings).[222] The term 'brochemaker,' found in London and York in the 1420s,[223] highlights the difficulty of dealing with personal names as evidence for the crafts, since it might mean either a maker of brooches, or of spits! Thomas the 'Perler' of London and John 'Peremaker' of York may respectively have sold pearls or their substitutes, and made *pierrerie* or artificial gems, but one cannot be certain.[224]

What of the evidence for the makers of the other common medieval survivals, mazers (maplewood drinking bowls mounted in silver or gold) and spoons? 'Mazerers' who were also goldsmiths are recorded in the 14th century: Thomas, imprisoned in 1336, and Simon and John, both members of the London Goldsmiths' Company.[225] The description of another John le Mazerer in 1309-10 as a *venditor*

220 London: Alice la Jueler listed in the 1319 subsidy roll: E. Ekwall, *Two Early London Subsidy Rolls* (Lund, 1951), 225 (jewellers Elena and Robert, see pp.239, 293). York: Hans Pollard in *Freemen*, op. cit. note 54, 119.

221 Wynne was a draper who transferred to the Goldsmiths Company: Reddaway and Walker, op. cit. in note 15, 117, note 82; Hercy's will describes him as draper and jeweller: *Index to Testamentary Records in the Commissary Court of London 1374-1488*, ed. M. Fitch (1969), i, *s.n.* Nyke appears in 1404 described as jeweller (*Cal. Close R., Hen. IV*, pt. 2, 381) and in 1410 as 'bedemaker' (ibid. pt. 4, 86). Robertus Paternosterer (1199): *Middle English Dictionary*: paternoster, pt. 3a.

222 Fransson, op. cit. note 215, 134.

223 B. Thurresson, *Middle English Occupational Terms* (Lund, 1950), 238: John Swan, London, 1421, Henry Bell, York, 1423.

224 Thomas the Perler: Ekwall, op. cit. note 220,

323; John Peremaker: Thurresson, op. cit. above, 238. Pierriers in 14th-century Paris made artificial gems: R. de Lespinasse, *Les Métiers et Corporations de la Ville de Paris*, 3 vols. (Paris, 1886-97), ii, 81-2.

225 'Thomas le Mazere Orfevre': *Cal. Pat. R., 1334-8*, 375-6; Simon le Mazerer, citizen and goldsmith, took apprentices from 1351 onwards, recorded in the Goldsmiths' Company Minute Book A[a], p.10, and left a will proved in 1381: Fitch, op. cit. note 221, i, *s.n.* John Maserer entered the Goldsmiths' Company in 1385: Goldsmiths' Company Minute Book A[a], p.63. The designation mazerer occurs at least by 1275: Thurresson, op. cit. above, 232. A 15th-century ordinance of the Goldsmiths' Company forbade any goldsmith from decorating or selling 'cups of plane-tree wood', the implication being that mazers were allowed: Reddaway and Walker, op. cit. note 15, 246, F. 55.

*ciphorum*[226] suggests that they were not always responsible for producing the mazers. The production of other tableware is reflected also in personal names – 'disshers', 'vesselers', 'hanapers' – but John Vesseler, fined by the Goldsmiths' Company in 1421 for defective work,[227] provides rare evidence that such craftsmen worked in precious metals, as well as in wood and base metals which must have been the predominant materials for these objects.

A rare reference to a *sponman* in 1327 probably indicates a maker of wood or horn spoons.[228] Yet surviving silver spoons themselves provide evidence, in the late 15th and early 16th centuries at least, of some specialisation, for a number of spoons are marked either with a heart or with a fringed S; the latter mark has recently been associated with the London spoonmaker Simpson.[229]

## Products and Design

Writing shortly after the Conquest, William of Poitiers mentions the renown of Anglo-Saxon goldsmiths and gold and silver embroidery. The reputation seems to have been one of longstanding, for Anglo-Saxon goldsmiths and their work had been prized in Germany and Italy for at least three centuries before. Although the records are considerable, few objects remain for us to judge, for in the way of all conquerors William carried much plate off to Normandy, and the heavy taxes he imposed on churches forced them to melt down their treasures, from life-sized gold and silver effigies, great crosses, reliquaries and altarpieces to the precious ornaments adorning vestments, altar cloths and bookbindings.[230]

Two outstanding survivals dating from just before the Conquest are the Cluny altar, of porphyry mounted in silver-gilt, and the silver Brussels reliquary cross;[231] both are engraved in a style close to that of contemporary manuscripts. The appearance of secular items in *c.* 1050 is suggested by an illustration (B.L., Cotton MS Tiberius C.VI, f. 10$^v$) of the treasures offered to Christ in temptation by the Devil: armbands and rings of twisted gold, a chalice-shaped cup and shallow bowl, a gold-mounted sword and a drinking-horn, the latter a distinctive token of northern taste that was to persist in England well into the 15th century.[232] The Bayeux Tapestry of *c.* 1066-82 shows Anglo-Saxons at a feast drinking from similar horns and bowls; the Normans, perhaps significantly, are shown drinking only from cups.[233]

226 *Cal. Letter-Book B*, 232.
227 John Vesseler fined by the Goldsmiths' Company for defective work in Goldsmiths' Company Minute Book A$^b$, p.76. Disshers etc are cited by Fransson, op. cit. note 215, *s.n.*; in no case is the material specified, and it must often have been wood.
228 Thurresson, op. cit. note 223, 233.
229 Heart maker: T. Kent, *London Silver Spoonmakers* (Silver Soc., 1981), 10-11; T. Wilson, '. . . Spoons', *Pelican and Annual Report of Corpus Christi College Oxford* (1983-4), 88; fringed S

mark: Kent, op. cit., 9-10.
230 C.R. Dodwell, *Anglo-Saxon Art: a New Perspective* (1982), 213-15.
231 *The Golden Age of Anglo-Saxon Art*, op. cit. note 5, Nos. 76, 75. See also the valuable summary on the period by J. Graham-Campbell, 'Viking Art Reviewed', in M. Ryan (ed.), *Ireland and Insular Art, A.D. 500-1200* (1987), 149-50.
232 Dodwell, op. cit. note 230, Pl. 5, 28.
233 D.M. Wilson, *The Bayeux Tapestry* (1981), Pls. 3, 48, and p.219.

The characteristic style of these objects is now hard to gauge, but it was one recognized as peculiarly English, for example, by the Italians, over a period of 350 years, from the 8th to the 11th centuries. It probably lay in a distinctive form of decoration, perhaps engraving, which is often mentioned in written sources, or filigree, which frequently adorns extant objects.[234]

Although evidence is sparse, the Conquest is less likely to have altered the goldsmith's repertoire than crucially to have affected his patronage, for the Normans seem to have concentrated their wealth into new building rather than goldsmiths' work. Material evidence for the half-century after the Conquest is negligible, one of the very few pieces from this time being the crozier of Bishop Flambard (d. 1128), made of silver and inlaid with *niello* decoration in a fashion akin to the Scandinavian Urnes style, an interesting illustration of the continuity of the Anglo-Scandinavian design tradition.[235]

The physical evidence increases from the start of the 12th century, the 15th century being the first period with more than a handful of survivals. Only in *c.* 1530 did English goldsmiths relinquish the Gothic style for that of the Renaissance. The sum is pitifully tiny – a random selection, preserved through institutional piety, accidental loss, or deliberate concealment. Only chalices and patens, spoons, rings, and mazers, and seals (mostly in the form of impressions) survive in any numbers. Almost all are silver-gilt, with the exception of rings, which are often of gold, and a few chalices of copper-gilt.[236] Few bear any hallmark, and, in the absence of diagnostic inscriptions or clear stylistic traits, attribution can usually only be tentative at best, even with pieces as celebrated as the King's Lynn cup of *c.* 1340 and Princess Blanche's crown of *c.* 1400.[237]

A 15th-century drawing of the arms of the London Goldsmiths' Company depicts what had probably long been staple products of the craft: buckles (ring-brooches) and covered cups. Many brooches survive (Fig.57) but only one similar cup, bearing the London mark for 1493-94, and now in the Goldsmiths' Company collection (Fig.74).[238] Part of an embroidery (Fig.52), the Stonyhurst chasuble of *c.* 1475, includes a scene depicting St. Dunstan, patron of English goldsmiths, seated in his shop with his wares before him: they consist of various forms of drinking cup (including one as in Fig.74), rosaries and rings. Although schematically depicted, these are the sort of standard items that a goldsmith would have needed to keep in stock, and they tally nicely with pieces listed in a London goldsmith's shop over a hundred years earlier.[239]

234 Dodwell, op. cit. note 230, 205-8.
235 *Anglo-Saxon Art*, op. cit. note 5, cat. No. 270, and Graham-Campbell, op. cit. note 231, 150.
236 For spoons see J. Ward-Perkins et al., *Medieval Catalogue of the London Museum* (1940), 127-132, and How, op. cit. note 173; otherwise see below. The base-metal products of goldsmiths are discussed in the legislation section above, and by C.C. Oman, 'English Medieval Base Metal Church Plate', *Arch. Jnl.* cxix (1962), 195-207.

237 *Age of Chivalry*, cat. Nos. 541, 13.
238 Drawing of *c.* 1480 in Peter le Neve's Book of Arms: B.L., Harleian MS 6163, illustrated in Reddaway and Walker, Pl. I(ii); 1493 cup: *Touching Gold and Silver* (exhibition, London: Goldsmiths' Hall, 1978), cat. No. 13.
239 Stonyhurst chasuble: N. Ramsay and M. Sparks, 'The Cult of St. Dunstan', in N. Ramsay et al. (eds.), *St. Dunstan and his Times* (forthcoming); Riley, *Memorials*, 470-1: inventory of 1382 of the shop of John Frensshe.

The increasing volume of records that survive from the 12th century onwards reveals how wide was the range of goldsmiths' work owned by ecclesiastical foundations and royal or noble households – objects that today are either obsolete or made in other materials. The Church must always have been a principal customer of goldsmiths: plate was needed for the Mass (chalices, cruets, pyxes, paxes, monstrances) and for other liturgical and sacred purposes (crosses, croziers, altarpieces, shrines, reliquaries, and embellishments for vestments). Aside from chalices, the losses have been almost absolute. The grandest commissions, the shrines, have utterly disappeared, melted down at the time of the Reformation.[240]

No processional or altar crosses survive to fill out such descriptions as that of the large gold cross set with over 200 precious stones and 22 relics which was given by Bishop Henry of Blois to Winchester Cathedral in *c.* 1162, or that evidently commissioned by Richard II, again made of gold and set with nearly 400 pearls, a few gems and images of the Virgin, St. John the Baptist and white harts, all enamelled (presumably *en ronde bosse*), and weighing 74 oz.[241] Only one extant piece, the reliquary of the Order of the Sainte Esprit (Fig.63), tentatively attributed to London *c.* 1410, approximates to these descriptions in either the lavishness of its materials (gold, gems and enamel) or the complexity of its decoration.[242] Images of gold or silver, whether votive or monumental, were numerous, a particularly detailed description being of that ordered by Henry III for his infant daughter Katharine from his goldsmith William of Gloucester in 1257: the wooden core was to be overlaid with sheets of silver, gilt and set with pearls and amethysts, for a total cost of 70 marks, of which the workmanship made up less than a third.[243] Nothing survives of these images or of the altar frontals, portable altars and altarpieces, except a handful of small devotional altarpieces of the 14th century, such as the Campion Hall triptych.[244] This is of gold and translucent enamel, and depicts the life of Christ and certain saints, prominent amongst whom is Edmund, king and martyr.

The two dozen chalices which survive are all of the cheaper sort, of silver or silver gilt, generally with little decoration. Even the most ambitiously ornamented, that of Archbishop Hubert Walter (d. 1205) (Fig.73), or the large Dolgelly chalice of *c.* 1250, are bare of gems, and bear little comparison with the more ornate and valuable

240  The subject has never been fully studied, although there is useful information in N. Coldstream, 'English Decorated Shrine Bases', *J.B.A.A.* 3rd ser. xxxix (1976), 15-34; J.C. Wall, *Shrines of British Saints* (1905), and C.C. Oman, *English Church Plate* (1957), 96-100.

241  Blois cross: E. Bishop, 'Gifts of Bishop Henry of Blois', in his *Liturgica Historica* (1918), 398, No. 1 (from B.L. Add. MS 29436, f.37ʳ.); Richard's cross, listed under 'crucifixes of gold recived of . . . Remayne', in Society of

Antiquaries MS 129, f.10, an inventory ascribed to *c.*1550 by Collins, op. cit. note 31, 238.

242  *Fastes du Gothique*, op. cit. note 85, cat. No. 221, and E. Kovacs, 'La Dot d'Anne de Bretagne: le Reliquaire . . .', *Revue du Louvre*, xxxi (1981), 246-51.

243  J. Tanner, 'Tombs of Royal Babies', *J.B.A.A.* 3rd ser. xvi (1953), 27.

244  *Age of Chivalry*, cat. No. 585; compare also Nos. 582-4, 586-7. Such altarpieces had their counterparts in ivory and wood.

*Fig. 73* Chalice found in the grave of Archbishop Hubert Walter (d. 1205). Silver, parcel-gilt, embossed and engraved (*c.* 1160). Height 14.2 cm. (*Canterbury Cathedral*)

chalices described in contemporary inventories.[245] A nice but rare example of how the written evidence can be matched with surviving pieces is provided by a contract of 1430 for a crozier for the abbot of Bury St. Edmunds, of which the crook was to enclose the abbey's patron saint, and the knop to be arcaded and adorned with apostle figures; decorated in just this way are the episcopal croziers of Wykeham of *c.* 1367, and of Fox of *c* .1501 (Fig.58).[246] It should be noted how little the overall design of these differs, although they were made well over a hundred years apart. Secular plate and to a lesser extent jewellery was owned in spectacular quantities, and it is likely that for much of the Middle Ages the production of such pieces constituted the major part of a goldsmith's work. The display of wealth in the form of plate was an important statement of status and power; some plate was made purely for show rather than use. Such perhaps was the elephant-and-castle shaped salt owned by Edward IV in 1468; it was made of gold set with nearly a hundred rubies, diamonds and sapphires and 249 pearls, and weighing over 16 lb. was valued at 1000 marks (£666 13*s.* 4*d.*). There is uncertainty over pieces like the Bermondsey dish of *c.* 1340 (Fig.78), which if not for display may have been used as a 'spice plate' in the postprandial dispensing of spiced cakes with sweet wine.[247]

Most secular plate was made for the service of wine or ale, whether for use at the table or for display; drinking vessels also make up the majority of surviving secular plate. In 1216 King John owned 157 cups and goblets and eight flagons (as opposed to only four shrines and two crosses).[248] Mazers are the most numerous form of surviving drinking vessel. Consisting of turned maple burrs mounted in gold or silver, mazers were fancy versions of the universal wooden bowl; their shape probably influenced that of the simple bowls of precious metal which no longer survive in England but are known from France and Scandinavia.[249] A number of types of drinking vessel are recorded: cups called 'bell' or in the shape of bells must have resembled the Anathema cup of 1481 (Pembroke College, Cambridge), and possibly the King's Lynn cup of *c.* 1340 (Fig.62). Chalice-shaped cups or 'bolepeces' seem clear enough, while 'flatpeces' were perhaps like the Campion cup of 1500 (Victoria and Albert Museum).[250] There is no extant parallel to the silver cup cast in

---

245  For a survey of extant chalices most detail is in T. Fallow and W. H. St.J. Hope, 'Medieval Chalices and Patens', *Arch. Jnl.* xliii (1886), 137-61, 364-402, on which Oman, op. cit. note 240, 299-309, is largely based; the most recent discussions of the Hubert Walter and Dolgelly chalices are in *Romanesque Art*, cat. Nos. 324 d and e, and *Age of Chivalry*, cat. No. 258. The St. Paul's Cathedral inventory of 1245 is especially rich and lists several gold chalices, gem-set and enamelled, or decorated with embossed (?)fleurs de lys or filigree: W.S. Simpson, 'Two Inventories of . . . St. Paul's . . .', *Archaeologia,* l (1887), 465-6.

246  For Fox's crozier and the 1430 indenture see Wilson, op. cit. note 51; for Wykeham's crozier see *Age of Chivalry*, cat. No. 608.

247  Salt: *Cal. Plea & Mem. R., 1458-82,* viii, 51-2; Bermondsey dish: *Age of Chivalry,* cat. No. 156.

248  A.V. Jenkinson, 'The Jewels Lost in the Wash', *History,* viii (1923-4), 164.

249  Mazers: *Age of Chivalry,* cat. Nos. 155, 542-3, 722 and W.St.J. Hope, 'On . . . Mazers', *Archaeologia* l (1887), 129-93; French 14th-century silver drinking bowls: *Fastes du Gothique,* cat. No. 198; Scandinavian: A. Andersson, *Medieval Drinking Bowls of Silver found in Sweden* (Stockholm, 1983).

250  M.L. Campbell, art. cit. note 93, 46-7; important 14th-century pieces are the Kings Lynn cup, *Age of Chivalry,* cat. No. 541, and the Studley bowl (possibly for drinking), ibid. cat. No. 728.

*Fig. 74* Wine cup, silver-gilt, with the crowned leopard's head (upside down) for London, the date-letter Q for 1493-4, and the maker's mark of a scallop. Embossed with 'writhen' work. Height 14 cm. From St. Andrew's church, Middleton on the Wolds (Lincs.). (*Goldsmiths' Company*)

*Fig. 75* Lacock cup, silver-gilt, *c.* 1400-50. Height 33.3 cm. (*Lacock Abbey (Wilts.), on loan to the British Museum*)

the shape of a man which was owned by Henry of Blois (d.1171); cups in the shape of animals were also made. Three cups owned by Londoners – two in 1442 called 'pere' and 'appull' and in 1470 another called 'pyneappyl' – have no extant English parallels, but strongly resemble surviving Nuremberg pieces, and may have been imports or products of alien 'Dutch' goldsmiths.[251] But all these are of silver and are comparatively plain, with the exception of the enamelled silver Kings Lynn cup. Even this must be contrasted with the enamelled gold vessels in royal ownership in the 14th century, often adorned with 'babewynes', or on occasion sirens with women on horses, as on a cup of Edward III.[252] Records alone attest to the great diversity of design or type of object: the silver basins decorated with David harping that

251 Blois cup: Bishop, op. cit. note 241, No. 31; fruit-shaped cups: Campbell, art. cit. note 95, 47 and note 26; for comparable Nuremberg pieces see H. Kohlhaussen, *Nürnberger Gold-schmiedekunst des Mittelalters ...,  1240-1540* (Berlin, 1968), cat. Nos. 354-5 (pineapple),

388, 392 (pear), 390-1 (apple).
252 For gold secular plate (far less common than silver) in the king's possession in 1338-40: *Wardrobe Book of William de Norwell, 1338-40*, ed. M. and B. Lyon (Brussels, 1983), 392, 397, 399; sirens cup: ibid., 397.

belonged to Edward III; the silver-gilt aquamaniles shaped as Samson with the lion and dragon, owned by Queen Margaret of Anjou in 1452-53; or the gridiron, spit, rake, skimmer and ladle, all of silver and weighing 13½ lb., owned by John Holland, duke of Exeter, in 1447.[253]

Jewellery was worn by both sexes, and included items essentially associated with dress such as buttons, brooches and girdles, which served a functional as well as decorative purpose.[254] Coronets, circlets, ornate chains, rings, seals and rosaries might also be worn, and men might also wear military gear – swords and spurs – mounted in precious metal. Surviving jewellery falls mostly into two categories, those of brooches and of rings. The commonest type of the former was the ring-brooch (Figs.57, 64), used from the 12th century onwards, made in all sizes, and sometimes set with gems. More ambitious brooches could be heart-shaped, or in the form of animals, like the white enamelled swan of *c.* 1400 found at Dunstable Priory, or the deer set with ruby owned by John of Gaunt in 1397. Letter-shaped brooches were also made, such as the gold M jewel (set with gems and enamel) given to New College by a Winchester family in 1440, its form very close to descriptions of M jewels owned by Edward III a hundred years earlier.[255]

Finger-rings required little metal to make, which must have been one reason for their popularity.[256] Another must have been the wide scope they offered: they might be plain, engraved (with inscriptions, arms, or motifs), set with gems as amulets, or used as seals. The range of different designs already in use in the late 12th century is illustrated by the Lark Hill hoard; enamel was increasingly employed from the 15th century. The inscription *en bon an* found on several rings suggests their use as New Year gifts.[257]

The long chains worn around the neck – collars – probably served both as decorative and portable forms of bullion and as gifts. A special type was the livery collar, that incorporating the device of SS being used for example by the 14th- and 15th-century Lancastrian leaders and their followers; it is found on the recently-

253  Pair of basins: bought by the king from the London goldsmith John Hiltoft in 1368: P.R.O., E 101/396/7; aquamaniles: Myers, art. cit. note 16, 122; gridiron etc: Westminster Abbey Muniment 6643.

254  J. Evans, *History of Jewellery* (2nd edn., 1970), chs. 1-3; Dodwell, op. cit. note 230, ch. 7; J. Cherry, 'Jewellery', in *Age of Chivalry*, 176-8. There will be much new material in R.W. Lightbown, *Medieval Jewellery* (forthcoming).

255  Ring-brooches: *Age of Chivalry*, cat. Nos. 641-4, 650-3; heart-shaped brooch from Fishpool: *Jewellery through 7,000 Years* (exhibn., British Museum, 1976), cat. 270b; Dunstable swan: *Age of Chivalry*, cat. No. 659; M-brooch, ibid., 640, and Edward's jewels, *Wardrobe Book*, op. cit. note 252, 407; Gaunt's jewel: J. Nichols, *A Collection of . . . the Wills . . . of the Kings and Queens of England* (1780), 155. Other early

forms of brooch are exemplified by the gold heraldic shield-shaped Folkingham jewel and a latten coin-brooch, both 12th-century: J. Cherry and J. Goodall, 'Brooch from Folkingham Castle . . .', *Antiq. Jnl.* lxv (1985), 471-2, *Romanesque Art*, cat. No. 468.

256  The subject is large, but see C.C. Oman, *British Rings, 800-1914* (1974); *Romanesque Art*, cat. Nos. 311-18; *Age of Chivalry*, cat. Nos. 634-9, 645-9, 654-8.

257  Lark Hill rings: *Romanesque Art*, cat. No. 320; 'en bon an' is inscribed on a gold ring found at Lewes Priory, W. Blaauw, 'On the . . . Priory of St. Pancras at Lewes', *Sussex Arch. Collns.* iii (1850), 210. The 15th-century gold and enamel Coventry ring decorated with the five wounds of Christ represents a type described in at least three medieval wills: *Jewellery . . . 7,000 Years*, op. cit. note 255, cat. No. 371.

PLATE III

III. Stained glass window, with figures of St. Thomas Becket and St. Alban, made by John Prudde of Westminster, *c.* 1447. Beauchamp Chapel, St. Mary's Church, Warwick. (*Photo: David O'Connor*)

*PLATE IV*

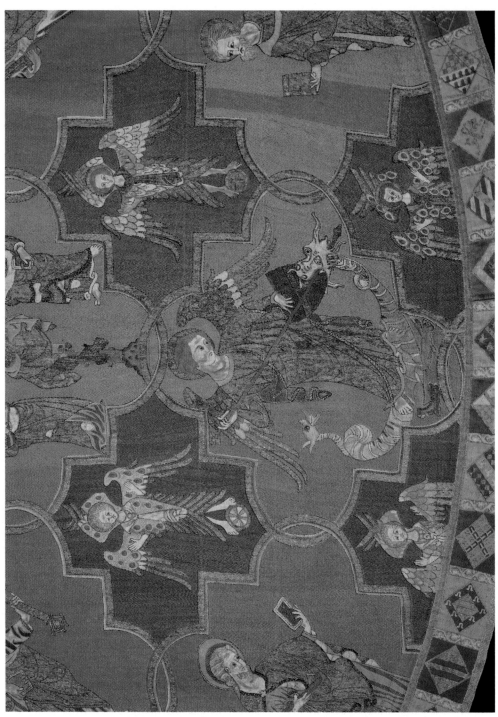

IV. The Syon Cope, *c.* 1300-20. At one time owned by nuns from the Bridgettine convent of Syon (Middlesex). (*Victoria and Albert Museum, No. 83-1864*)

discovered silver collar that is now in the Museum of London.[258]

Devotional jewels – often incorporating a relic – were worn around the neck. The few extant examples are mostly 15th-century, the most spectacular being the recently found Middleham jewel (Fig.65) of gold and enamel, set with a large sapphire. Similar in technique and style is the Langdale rosary, the only complete example to survive; this would have been worn suspended from the waist. Its rather clumsy style is in contrast to the sophistication of a rosary bequeathed to Richard Whittington in 1412: the gold beads enamelled in translucent red, the gauds shaped as John the Baptist heads enamelled in the round in white.[259] Only two girdles are known to survive, both male; the earliest was found in the tomb of Ferdinando de la Cerda (d. 1275). It is of silver-gilt set with heraldic motifs (of glass painted to imitate enamel), prominent amongst which are the English royal arms, and it may have been a gift from Henry III. The other girdle, also silver-gilt, is set with translucent enamels, pearls and pastes, and probably belonged to William of Wykeham (d. 1404).[260]

Seals might be worn suspended from the girdle; their use for authenticating documents grew enormously from the 12th century. Although thousands of seal impressions survive, it is impossible to determine the metal which made them. Seal matrices made of gold or silver (and sometimes set with intaglio gems) tended to be confined to ecclesiastical foundations, royalty, the nobility and bishops, and wealthy merchants and craftsmen.[261] Perhaps of gold was the seal of a 14th-century London goldbeater, John, which includes the head of Midas.[262] Jewellery of a special sort was made for the hawks and falcons which were so important for sport. Vervels of precious metal, sometimes enamelled, were the rings attached to one end of the jesse, or leather thong, which secured the bird's leg; a single poignant survivor is of gold, engraved *sum regis anglie* (I belong to the King of England).[263]

### Taste and Style

Little work has yet been done to analyse the taste of individual monarchs and their circle for goldsmiths' work, but it is clear that such men as King John, Henry III,

258 Of. *c.* 1422-6: B. Spencer, 'Exhibits at Ballots: . . . Collar of SS', *Antiq. Jnl.* lxv (1985), 449-51.

259 Middleham jewel: sold at Sotheby, 11 Dec. 1986, lot 196; Langdale rosary: Evans, *History* . . ., op. cit. note 254, 77; Whittington rosary: *Register of Henry Chichele, 1414-43*, ii, ed. E. Jacob and H. Johnstone (1937), 20.

260 Ferdinando's girdle (now at Las Huelgas monastery, Burgos) would have contravened regulations against counterfeit enamels: I. Fingerlin, *Die Gürtel des hohen und späten Mittelalters* (Munich, 1971), No. 61; Wykeham's girdle: *Age of Chivalry*, cat. No. 609.

261 The literature is large: see especially, *A Guide to Seals in the Public Record Office* (P.R.O. Hand-book 1, 1968) and A. Tonnochy, *Catalogue of British Seal-Dies in the British Museum* (1952), supplemented by A. Heslop in *Romanesque Art*: 'Seals', 298-300, and in *Age of Chivalry*: 'English Seals in the 13th and 14th Centuries', 114-17; cf. also notes 209-11.

262 R. Ellis, *Catalogue of . . . Seals in the P.R.O.: Personal Seals*, ii (1981), No. P 1450 and Pl. 15, on a document of 1348: E 213/123.

263 Since the other side is inscribed *comitis herfordie* it belonged presumably to Henry IV, one of whose titles this was. Vervels were made in pairs; for other examples A. Dillon, *Proc. Soc. Antiq.* 2nd ser., iv (1867-70), 355-8.

John of Gaunt, Richard II and Henry VII owned prodigious collections, the majority of pieces being secular plate and jewellery. While the wills or inventories which reveal this are useful as records of an individual's wealth and sometimes of his taste – the weight or value is usually specified, and the design occasionally – they are generally silent on the questions of maker and provenance. The terminology used for objects is often unclear. When foreign pieces are mentioned they are most commonly described as work of Paris, and far more rarely as marked, as in the case of spoons belonging to Edward I described in a 1299-1300 inventory as marked on the neck with the mark of Paris, that is a fleur-de-lis. Reference to other places occasionally occurs – Italy, Flanders and other parts of France, including what may be the earliest documentary reference to marked Tours silver, in a 1253 inventory of Henry III's wife Eleanor.[264] The amount of detail given in John of Gaunt's register of 1379-83 about design, cost of materials and workmanship and the names of goldsmiths is quite exceptional.[265]

Changes in fashion, the details of which are often unknown to us, must have affected production. Forks, for example, were scarcely used in the Middle Ages; none that is English survives and they are very rarely mentioned in inventories, being described there as for use with delicacies like green ginger or pears. The use of fingers as well as spoons and knives for eating necessitated a good deal of hand-washing before and during meals, and explains the production of basins for this purpose, with and without spouts.[266]

Legislation and taxation may also have exerted some influence. Throughout the 12th century the English bishops were urging the clergy to obtain silver chalices for use in their churches, culminating in 1195, when the Archbishop of Canterbury, Hubert Walter, ordered that every church was to obtain a silver chalice within the year.[267] The Crown's tax on personal property in 1290 exempted certain things. For example, each couple resident in a city, town or borough was allowed a ring, a buckle (brooch) of gold or silver, and a drinking cup of silver or mazer.[268] From 1363 onwards, the wearing of jewellery was legally restricted. Only knights were allowed to wear jewellery of gold or set with precious stones, and poor knights (with land worth less than 200 marks *p. a.*) were also forbidden silver brooches or girdles or cloth of silver. Only gentlemen and esquires of a certain income were allowed to wear silver brooches and girdles; only merchants of a certain income might wear silk or

264 Paris spoons: *Liber Quotidianus* (1787), 352; 'a cup of Tours work' given by Henry de Weng-ham, P.R.O. E 101/34/14; and see note 165.

265 *John of Gaunt's Register, 1379-83*, ed. E. Lodge and R. Somerville, Camden Soc. 3rd ser. lvi-lvii (1937), Nos. 327, 463, 524, 556-7, 803.

266 Piers Gaveston owned three silver forks for eating pears in 1313, an early reference: T. Rymer, *Foedera*, ed. A. Clarke and F. Hol-brooke (1818), ii, 204. Ablution basins were used in pairs, see the silver-gilt Chillenden

basins of the 14th century: *Age of Chivalry*, cat. No. 729; there was probably no design differ-ence between those used at table and those used during the Mass.

267 C.C. Oman, *English Church Plate* (1957), 24.

268 J.F. Willard, *Parliamentary Taxes on Personal Property* (Cambridge, Mass., 1934), 79. By contrast those residing in rural districts did better, for jewels and vessels of gold and silver belonging to knights, gentlemen and their wives were exempt, ibid. 77.

enamel girdles. Servants were forbidden gold, silver and enamel.[269]

The scale of losses is such as to make extraordinarily difficult any assessment of the relative popularity of gold or silver, and of the evolution of style and ornament. The earliest surviving gold vessel, for example, dates from the very end of the period: Bishop Fox's chalice, with paten, of 1507. Yet the records suggest that from the 13th century onwards plate and jewellery were increasingly made of gold (which was roughly ten times more costly than silver). It is perhaps significant that Henry III was a notable collector of gold treasure, as well as being the originator of the short-lived experiment of introducing a gold coinage in 1257.[270] The mid 14th century saw the permanent establishment of a gold coinage, when there seems to have been a shortage of silver.[271] Bullion supply is bound to have affected the plate and jewellery that goldsmiths produced. By the 15th century surviving pieces of jewellery – largely rings and brooches – are predominantly of gold.

The evolution of style is equally problematic. England probably conformed to the European pattern whereby the heavy forms of Romanesque architecture, and often the fussily-detailed intricacy of Gothic are found decorating goldsmiths' work. The column of foliage-entwined figures which makes up the Gloucester candlestick of 1107-13 (Fig.76) can be paralleled in contemporary architecture (though it is closer still to manuscripts); the Ramsey Abbey censer of *c.* 1325 (Fig.77a, b) takes the form of a miniature polygonal chapter-house, its style presumably being what is sometimes called *de masonerie*.[272] The style of the patterns and figures that were engraved, enamelled or nielloed on goldsmiths' work is often close to that found in manuscripts, the 12th-century Dune treasure bowl signed by Simon and the 14th-century Swinburne pyx, both mainly of silver, being two examples.[273] But difficulties in dating or even provenancing jewellery tend to arise from the fact that the styles and techniques employed are often unique to the genre.

269  For the 1363 statute: *Statutes of the Realm*, (1810-28), i, 380-1: 37 Edw. III, c. 8-14. By the time of the statute of array in 1463 (3 Edw. I c.5, in ibid. ii, 399-402), the emphasis is more on regulating the quality of the gold and silver worn, although servants and labourers are still forbidden silver.

270  D. Carpenter, 'The Gold Treasure of Henry III', in P.R. Coss and S.D. Lloyd (eds.), *Thirteenth-Century England. I: Proceedings of the Newcastle-on-Tyne Conference 1985* (Woodbridge, 1986), 61-88, and D. Carpenter, 'Gold and Gold Coins in England in the mid 13th Century', *Numismatic Chron.* cxlvii (1987), 106-13.

271  The question of the availability of gold and silver during the Middle Ages has been intensively debated over the last 15 years by economic historians and numismatists. There was a great diminution in the availability of silver in England between the 13th and 15th centuries, while gold predominated from the 1320s to the 1460s, after which new Alpine sources of silver were opened up: P. Spufford, 'Coinage and Currency', in *Cambridge Economic History of Europe: Trade and Industry in the Middle Ages*, eds. M. Postan and E. Miller, 2nd edn. (1987), 835, 851-60, with bibliography, 954-5. The difficulties of using surviving objects to gauge the availability of bullion are discussed by D. Hinton, 'Late Saxon Treasure and Bullion', in D. Hill (ed.), *Ethelred the Unready* (B.A.R. British ser. 59, 1978), 135-42.

272  Gloucester candlestick: *Romanesque Art*, cat. No. 247; Ramsey censer: *Age of Chivalry*, cat. No. 121; 'masoneria': Edward III inventory of 1338-40, op. cit. note 252, 401 (a cup with a 'pomell. . . de masoneria').

273  Dune bowl: *Romanesque Art*, cat. No. 305, and Andersson, op. cit. note 249, 25-9, 59-60; pyx: C.C. Oman, 'The Swinburne Pyx', *Burlington Mag.* xcii (1950), 337-41.

*Fig. 76* Detail of the lower stem of the Gloucester candlestick; the alloy includes silver (12.8%), copper, tin, zinc and antimony. The stem is made in one piece, a brilliant example of lost-wax casting. Probably by a Canterbury artist; inscribed as being the gift of Abbot Peter (1107-13) to St. Peter's, Gloucester. Total height 51.2 cm.
(*Victoria and Albert Museum, No. 7649-1861*)

The sketches or working drawings of goldsmiths are great rarities, even from the Renaissance; there is virtually no extant direct evidence from the Middle Ages – and certainly none that is English – to show how goldsmiths arrived at a design. Much plate and jewellery was probably made according to conventional types for which a pattern book of standard shapes would have sufficed. For important commissions, usual practice probably resembled both that described by the Italian 16th-century goldsmith Cellini and what we know of the procedures used to produce such base metal effigies as that of Richard Beauchamp, earl of Warwick, commissioned in 1439. First a design or series of designs would be drawn or painted, and submitted to the patron for approval, and then a three-dimensional model in wax, wood or terracotta would be made, followed finally by the finished piece.[274]

The evidence as to English goldsmiths is very slight, but suggestive. Writing in *c.* 1200, Alexander Neckam describes the use of wax or clay tablets by an apprentice for trying out patterns. In 1331 Queen Philippa paid the London goldsmith Simon de Berkyng 2*s.* for the drawing of a ship on parchment to serve as a model for a silver nef (for alms) which he was to make for her. In 1400 another London goldsmith, John Esmond, was paid to make a seal according to a pattern in his possession;[275] his

274 See J. Hayward, *Virtuoso Goldsmiths* (1976), 23-36, 54-7, for a perceptive discussion of workshop practice and technique; Beauchamp effigy: C. Stothard, *Monumental Effigies*, new edn. (1876), 165-8. See also R. Scheller, *A Survey of Medieval Model-books* (Haarlem, 1963).

275 Berkyng: the terms of the commission quoted from the original by N.L. Ramsay, 'Artists, Craftsmen and Design', in *Age of Chivalry*, 51-2, and note 27. Perhaps drawing was not so unusual: the contract of 1272 for the shrine of St. Gertrud of Nivelles (Belgium) specifies that it should be made following the drawing of a master goldsmith: Dodwell, op. cit. note 254, 66; in Paris in 1504 the commission for a gold nef was divided: a painter painted the design and made a terra-cotta model of it, to serve as the 'patron à l'orfèvre' for the goldsmith: Lightbown, op. cit. note 62, 108 and n. 44. For Esmond, see Kingsford, art. cit. note 56, 172.

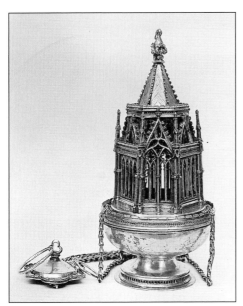

*Fig. 77a* Ramsey Abbey censer, silver-gilt, *c.* 1325. A combination of cast work (crestings, pinnacles) and hammered. Found in 1850 in Whittlesea Mere (Hunts.), with pieces bearing the badge of a ram's head, rebus for the name Ramsey. Height 26.5 cm. (*Victoria and Albert Museum, M268-1923*)

*Fig. 77b* Detail of inside of the Ramsey censer top, showing how the flat sheet has been cut out for the window tracery, and bent and soldered for attachment to the body of the censer.

method may perhaps be hypothesised from that followed much later by the royal goldsmith and miniaturist Nicholas Hilliard, whose 1584 commission to make the second Great Seal stated that he was first to draw the design on parchment, then to make a model, and finally to make the seal.[276] But a piece of evidence both cautionary and revealing is an instance recorded in 1545, when an English merchant sent a pattern abroad – to Antwerp – in order to have a gem for a ring cut following the pattern.[277]

The extent to which medieval (and Renaissance) goldsmiths themselves designed their products, and the moulds and stamps they used, must remain open to debate. Practice must have varied; even the slight evidence just cited indicates that a goldsmith might be responsible for all stages of a piece's making. That there was specialization is also evident. A particular skill, such as in drawing, might traverse the bounds of a medium, resulting in painters who were also engravers or vice versa.[278] Several such are known from the 12th and 13th centuries, notably Walter of Colchester and Matthew Paris, and Hilliard is of course from the same tradition.

276  E. Auerbach, *Nicholas Hilliard* (1961), 20.
277  The pattern 'of an arms' cut for John Johnson:
     *Letters and Papers, Foreign and Domestic, of the*
     *Reign of Henry VIII*, xx(2) (1907), appendix,
     No. 43, item 31 on p.566.
278  Dodwell, art. cit. note 219, 98.

*Fig. 78* Detail of the Bermondsey dish, silver gilt with traces of translucent enamel (on the medallion), *c.* 1325. The engraved medallion is a separate piece soldered into the centre of the dish, framed by embossed vine-leaves and lobes. Diameter of whole 26.4 cm.
(*Bermondsey parish church, London, on loan to Victoria and Albert Museum*)

Just such a craftsman may have decorated the Swinburne pyx.

In 15th-century Germany, specialist goldsmith-engravers developed the technique of making multiple impressions on paper from an engraved metal plate. Until then, there had been no method for reproducing a design, except by freehand drawing or pricked copying. The advent of this revolutionary technique – which was rapidly applied to the reproduction of all types of ornamental designs – meant that a design could be printed in quantity, and might travel anywhere. Work betraying Italian or German stylistic influence might now simply be the product of an English goldsmith with a foreign pattern-book, as is clearly the case with the silver pax of *c.* 1510 at New College, Oxford, its border decoration evidently inspired by an engraving in a Parisian Book of Hours of *c.* 1500 printed by Pigouchet.[279]

Throughout the Middle Ages gold and silver were relatively far more precious than they are today. England's wealth in precious metals had attracted the Vikings and before them the Romans. At the time of the Conquest she was still a country rich enough to be likened by the Conqueror's biographer, William of Poitiers, to the gold treasury of Arabia.[280] At the end of the Middle Ages, in *c.* 1500, it is interesting to find a similar reaction, this time that of an Italian, marvelling at the 52 goldsmiths' shops in London's Cheapside that were filled with salts, cups and basins: 'in all the shops in Milan, Rome, Venice and Florence put together, I do not think there would be found so many of the magnificence . . . to be seen in London'.[281]

## Acknowledgements

I naturally take full responsibility for errors and omissions; I am grateful for the critical comments of Justine Bayley, Claude Blair, Susan Hare, Julian Henderson and Nigel Ramsay.

## Further Reading

The literature of the subject is principally concerned with surviving artefacts; such studies are often subdivided into plate, jewellery, coins, seals, spoons and finger-rings. These artificial divisions – the creations of modern scholars – are not helpful when considering questions such as the range and quantity of a goldsmith's output, the importance of the output of provincial goldsmiths, or links in design or technique between different types of object. C.R. Dodwell's *Anglo-Saxon Art: a new Perspective* (1982) is exceptional in the use made of literary evidence to establish the social context as well as the physical appearance of lost pieces; there is also useful scattered material in J. Evans, *A History of Jewellery* (2nd edn., 1970).

Theophilus, writing in the 12th century (although not in England), provides detailed information of crucial importance on the techniques and practices of goldsmiths and, to a very limited extent, gem-cutters. The most useful modern writers, who provide metallurgical and archaeological information and details on metal extraction and refining, are R. Tylecote, *The Prehistory of Metallurgy in the British*

279  New College pax: Oman, *Church Plate*, op. cit. note 267, 77-8, Pl. 30b: the lower border closely parallels the upper border motif of daisies and backward-looking beasts in the Pigouchet Hours, reproduced by J. Harthan, *Books of Hours* (1977), 170.

280  Guillaume de Poitiers, *Histoire de Guillaume le Conquérant*, ed. R. Foreville (Paris, 1952), 254.

281  *A Relation of the Island of England about the year 1500*, trans. C. Sneyd (Camden Soc. xxxvii, 1847), 42-3.

*Isles* (1986) and R. Forbes, *Studies in Ancient Technology*, viii (2nd edn., Leiden 1971).

On gem-stones there is nothing dealing solely with the British Isles, but very good technical information in J. Ogden, *Jewellery in the Ancient World* (1982); the introduction to O.M. Dalton, *Catalogue of Engraved Gems of the Post-Classical Period . . . in the British Museum* (1915) is useful, as is A.H. Church, *Precious Stones* (1924).

For the organisation of the craft in London, T. Reddaway and L. Walker, *A History of the London Goldsmiths' Company 1327-1509* (1976) is indispensable, and gives a little information on provincial activity. No single work deals with the activities of medieval provincial goldsmiths. C.J. Jackson, *English Goldsmiths and their Marks* (1921 & reprints) is still the standard work on London and provincial goldsmiths and their marks, but is unreferenced and not always accurate. (The newly issued *Jackson's Silver and Gold Marks*, ed. Ian Pickford (1989), reproduces Jackson's text for the medieval period largely uncorrected and incorporates new inaccuracies). There is more up-to-date information on marks (although some interpretations are disputed) and on provincial and London goldsmiths in G.E.P. and J. How, *English and Scottish Silver Spoons and Pre-Elizabethan Hall-Marks* (3 vols. 1952-7), and in Susan Hare, *Touching Gold and Silver* (Exhibition catalogue, Goldsmiths' Hall, London, 1978).

Recent studies of provincial centres give a little more information, such as M. Gill, *A Directory of Newcastle Goldsmiths* (1976), and M. Ridgway, *Chester Goldsmiths from Early Times to 1725* (1968).

For goldsmiths' work the basic works are C.J. Jackson, *A History of English Plate* (1911) on plate generally; and on church plate: C.C. Oman, *English Church Plate* (1957); How, op. cit., on spoons; on jewellery: C.C. Oman, *British Rings 800-1914* (1974); Evans, op. cit., also Evans, *Magical Jewels* (1922), and David Hinton, *Medieval Jewellery* (1982); on coins: C.H.V. Sutherland, *English Coinage 600-1900* (1973) and J. Craig, *The Mint* (1953); on seals: A. Tonnochy, *Catalogue of British Seal-Dies in the British Museum* (1952) and *A Guide to Seals in the P.R.O.* (PRO Handbook No. 1, 1968).

In addition, for the most recent research and references the publications linked with recent exhibitions should be consulted: J. Backhouse et al. (eds.) *Anglo-Saxon Art* (British Museum, 1984); J. Graham-Campbell, *Viking Artifacts* (1980); *Jewellery through 7000 Years* (British Museum, 1976); G. Zarnecki (ed.), *English Romanesque Art 1066-1200* (Arts Council, 1984); J.J.G. Alexander and P. Binski (eds.) *Age of Chivalry: Art in Plantagenet England 1200-1400* (Royal Academy, 1987); *Money* (British Museum, 1986); P. Tudor-Craig, *Richard III* (National Portrait Gallery, 1973). For comparative material on developments in France see R.W. Lightbown, *Secular Goldsmiths' Work in Medieval France* (1978).

# 7

# *Iron*

## JANE GEDDES

The smith was an indispensable member of medieval society, for virtually all other crafts and occupations depended on his work. At the beginning of the 11th century Ælfric wrote an imaginary discussion between various craftsmen, each claiming to be the most important. The smith caps them all by saying that none of them could work without the tools he makes. The reply to this was typical of society's attitude to smiths: 'True, but all of us would rather visit the ploughman because he gives us bread and drink. And what do you give us in your smithy but iron sparks, the sound of your beating hammer and blowing bellows?'[1]

### *The Preparation of Metal: Sources and Bloom Smithing*

Iron is one of the most common ores found in England, occurring in almost every county. The main types of ore are carbonate, haematite and limonite. Carbonate ores are the most common and are found in the Weald, the Cleveland Hills and the counties of Oxford, Northampton and Lincoln. When ferrous carbonate ($FeCO_3$) is roasted, it is converted to ferric oxide ($Fe_2O_3$) which is chemically the same as haematite. Haematite is found in Cumbria and around Furness (Lancs.). Its great advantage is a low phosphorus content, which makes it suitable for the production of steel. Limonite, found in South Wales and the Forest of Dean, is a hydrated iron oxide ($Fe_2O_3.H_2O$ or $HFeO_2$). Bog ore is not a rock but a deposit formed in wet and cold locations, when iron-bearing surface waters meet organic materials and cause iron oxide to be precipitated. It is found on the moors of north England. In the Middle Ages the most important sources of ore were the Forest of Dean, the Midlands, South Yorkshire, Cumbria, Durham and Northumberland.[2] Although the Weald had copious supplies of ore, its heyday was in Roman times and the post-

I would like to thank David Crossley and Claude Blair for their comments on this chapter.

1   Michael Swanton (ed.), *Anglo-Saxon Prose* (1975), 107-15, at 113.

2  R.F. Tylecote, *The Prehistory of Metallurgy in the British Isles* (1986), 124-8; A.O. Fell, *The Early Iron Industry of Furness and District* (1908); I. Cohen, 'History of Ironworking in and near the Forest of Dean', *Trans. Woolhope Nat. Field Club*, xxxiv (1954), 161-77; H.R. Schubert, *History of the British Iron and Steel Industry* (1957), 77-108.

medieval centuries.[3]

Wrought iron, cast iron and steel are the main forms in which the metal is used. Chemically pure iron is of no commercial importance and is not generally prepared, except for laboratory use. Wrought iron of a commercial purity still retains a very small amount of other elements: carbon (up to 0.05 per cent), silicon, manganese, sulphur and phosphorus. Wrought iron is ductile and malleable, and, when heated to the correct temperature, can be fire-welded. Cast iron contains 3-4 per cent carbon, can be cast into complex shapes and has great strength in compression. It cannot be hammered or welded, and is very weak in tension. Steel can be made in several forms, each with its own characteristics. It contains more carbon than wrought iron but less than cast. Mild steel, containing *c.* 0.25 per cent carbon, rusts quickly and can only be fire welded within a narrow range of temperatures, but it is ductile and strong in tension. Medium-carbon steel (0-0.6 per cent carbon) is harder and stronger than mild steel. While it can be hardened, it cannot be tempered to hold a cutting edge. High-carbon steel (0.75-1.5 per cent carbon) can be both hardened and tempered to retain a cutting edge. Steel is hardened by heating it to a dull-red heat and then quenching it rapidly in cold water or oil. This process makes the steel very brittle, but it can subsequently be tempered or strengthened by heating and cooling it more gently.

In spite of England's abundance of ore, there was a considerable import trade in continental iron, especially from France, the Pyrenees, Sweden and Germany. Spanish traders from Bayonne and St. Sebastian are recorded as paying harbour dues in England in 1266, 1299 and 1308.[4] In 1338 a group of Spanish merchants were required to identify their ship's cargo. It included rods of long iron, pieces of pointed iron, pieces of iron plate, pieces of cut or tarred iron (*picati*) and welded iron.[5] Prior Henry of Eastry bought 15 cwt. of Spanish iron in 1308-9 for his improvements at Canterbury Cathedral.[6] The royal smith James of Lewisham used iron from Bayonne and Morlaix for his work on St. Stephen's Chapel, Westminster, in 1294.[7] 'Osmund' iron (strictly speaking, any iron derived from bog ore, but in the Middle Ages particularly applied to Swedish iron) was imported for hardening the edges of tools and weapons, and later on for wire-drawing. It had a low phosphorus content which allowed it to absorb carbon readily. It was brought to London by the Hansa, whose London office was called the Steelyard (*Stahlhof*). Royal building accounts highlight the different functions of English and imported iron.[8] The former was used for nails, horseshoes, wedges, spades and pickaxes, while iron from Normandy, Spain and Sweden was used for making siege engines and weapons. Long-distance transport of iron in England is frequently documented. A few examples will suffice to

3  E. Straker, *Wealden Iron* (1931); H.F. Cleere and D.W. Crossley, *Iron Industry of the Weald* (1985).
4  Salzman, *Building in England*, 409.
5  *Cal. Plea & Mem. R. 1323-64*, 149.
6  [R.C. Hussey], *Extracts from Ancient Documents*

*relating to the Cathedral . . . of Canterbury* (1881), 12.
7  *History of King's Works*, ed. H.M. Colvin (1963), ii, 512.
8  E.g. for 1278-9 see P.R.O., E 101/467/7 (6-7); Schubert, op. cit. note 2.

show that it was possible to overcome the practical difficulties of moving such a heavy commodity by road or water. In Domesday Book it is recorded that the city of Gloucester had to supply the king with 36 'dicres' (units of 10, probably in the form of horseshoes) and 100 rods of iron for making nails for the king's ships.[9] In the early 13th century, the ironworks in Weardale (Durham) sent 1,260 shovels, 160 picks and 100 hatchets to Wales, and 700 horseshoes, quarrels, nails and shovels to Chester, and the king's ship came up from Portsmouth to collect anchors and armaments in 1213.[10] In 1253 the sheriff of Sussex had to provide Henry III with 30,000 horseshoes and 60,000 nails for the army.[11] Even without this documentary evidence it is obvious that iron was moved freely around the country, because counties like Essex, Bedfordshire and Berkshire, low in local ores, have a large amount of surviving decorative ironwork.

In Roman times and the early Middle Ages, iron-mining skills were rudimentary and there was sufficient ore to work mainly the surface measures, but by the end of the 12th century quite extensive tunnels, trenches and bell-pits were being dug.[12] The improved skills of iron-miners were attested by their employment as sappers in 13th-century siege warfare, those from the Forest of Dean being recruited for campaigns in Scotland and Gascony.[13]

The ore was processed at a bloomery which could be either permanent or temporary. In 1298 the latter sort were described as small sheds 'without nail, bolt or wall'.[14] The middle-Saxon smelting site at Milbrook (Sussex) was protected by a screen, probably of hurdles.[15] The well-documented bloomery at Tudeley (Kent), which is known to have operated in 1329-34 and 1350-54, was protected by a daubed wooden shed built by a carpenter which needed rebuilding after seven years.[16] More substantial structures, 'great forges', had a proper forge house, workers' dwellings, stables and fuel sheds.[17] The excavated smithy at Alsted (Surrey) gradually developed between 1250 and 1405 from two small hearths used intermittently to a substantial working area and timber-framed house for the smith.[18] At Waltham Abbey (Essex) the 10th- to 12th-century forge was in a three-bay aisled building with stone walls.[19]

To produce workable iron from ore it is necessary to remove the 'gangue' or unwanted materials and reduce the iron oxide to purer iron. The methods for doing this changed remarkably little in England from Roman times to the late Middle Ages. Both the classical author Pliny and Theophilus, writing in the early 12th

9   *V.C.H., Gloucs.* ii (1907), 216.
10  *V.C.H., Durham,* ii (1907), 353-6.
11  Straker, op. cit. note 3, 33.
12  Schubert, op. cit. note 2, 123-24; Tylecote, op. cit. note 2, 178, 204; R.F. Tylecote, 'A Bloomery Site at West Runton, Norfolk', *Norfolk Archaeology*, xxxiv (1967), 187-214.
13  C.E. Hart, *The Free Miners of the Forest of Dean and the Hundred of St. Briavels* (1953), 21.
14  Schubert, op. cit. note 2, 125.
15  C.F. Tebbutt, 'A Middle-Saxon Iron Smelting Site at Milbrook, Ashdown Forest, Sussex', *Sussex Archaeological Collections*, cxx (1982), 20-35.
16  M.S. Giuseppi, 'Some Fourteenth-Century Accounts of Ironworks at Tudeley, Kent', *Archaeologia*, lxiv (1913), 145-64, at 148.
17  Schubert, op. cit. note 2, 125.
18  L.L. Ketteringham, *Alsted: the Excavation of a 13th- to 14th-Century Sub-Manor House in Netherne Wood, Merstham, Surrey* (Surrey Archaeological Society, Research Vol. 2 1976), 17-31.
19  P.J. and R.M. Huggins, 'Waltham Abbey', *Essex Archaeology and History*, v (1973), 131.

century, say that iron was smelted in the same way as copper, and this was basically true, except that iron required a much higher temperature.[20] Iron oxide can be reduced at 800°C, but 1150°C is required to liquefy the unwanted slag. The melting point of iron is 1540°C, but this temperature was not achieved in English furnaces, except by accident, until the end of the Middle Ages.[21] First the ore was washed and roasted to make it sufficiently friable to break into small pieces. In the detailed accounts from ironworks at Tudeley (Kent) (1329-54) and from Byrkeknott, Weardale (1408-9), this stage is described. At Byrkeknott a woman, John Gylle's wife, was paid 7*d*. a day for breaking up ironstone.[22] At Tudeley the smelters bought 'elyngwode', wood for burning, as opposed to charcoal, for the roasting process and, as only one furnace is mentioned, presumably the roasting and smelting took place on the same hearth.[23] At Withyham (Sussex) and Baysdale (N. Yorks.), roasting platforms were found, built of clay with low stone kerbs.[24]

Both shaft and bowl furnaces were used in England from Roman times until the end of the Middle Ages. The bowls gradually increased in size, but up to the 15th century they were barely more than 100cm. (3ft. 6in.) wide and 50cm. (1ft. 8in.) deep. The furnaces were lined with baked clay and were blown through by tuyères attached to bellows. The simplest type of bowl furnace was found at Alsted: 28cm. deep, 25cm. wide, with a bottom of flints lined with clay and no tapping facilities.[25] At West Runton the 11th-century developed bowl hearth was 50cm. (1ft. 8in.) in diameter, set in the natural clay. Slag was tapped from the hearth and two ceramic tuyères were used, set at right-angles to the slag hole. The superstructure probably formed a low dome, curving inwards to reduce the contact of oxygen with the ore and charcoal (Fig.79a).[26] A well-preserved shaft furnace has been excavated at Stamford (Fig.79b). It had a slag tap hole and tuyère slot at the bottom, and walls which could be reconstructed to the height of 1m. (3ft. 3ins.).[27] Three hearths from the 12th to 13th centuries were excavated at High Bishopley (Durham). Two were simple bowl hearths with slag tapping pits and the third was a kidney-shaped furnace 50cm. (1ft. 8ins.) in diameter, standing on a clay platform with a well insulated, slightly domed top.[28]

The furnaces were packed with layers of charcoal and crushed ore. A modern experiment using a 22cm. (8½ ins.) diameter bowl furnace showed that 16 lbs. of charcoal are needed to produce one pound of iron.[29] In the much larger late medieval

20  Pliny, *Natural History*, xxxiv; 213; Theophilus, 183; D.W. Crossley, 'Medieval Iron Smelting', in D.W. Crossley (ed.), *Medieval Industry* (C.B.A. Research Rep. xl 1981), 29-41.
21  Tylecote, op. cit. note 2, 144-5; Schubert, op. cit. note 2, 57-8.
22  G.T. Lapsley, 'The Account-Roll of a Fifteenth Century Ironmaster', *Eng. Hist. Rev.* xiv (1899), 511.
23  Giuseppi, op. cit. note 16, 153.
24  J.H. Money, 'Medieval Iron-workings in Minepit Wood, Rotherfield, Sussex', *Med. Arch.* xv (1971), 86-111; Crossley, op. cit. note 20, 31, fig. 26.

25  Ketteringham, op. cit. note 18. 17-31.
26  R.F. Tylecote, 'West Runton', op. cit. note 12, 187-214.
27  R.F. Tylecote, 'Recent Work on Early Iron-working Sites in the Stamford Area', *Bull. Hist. Metallurgy Group*. iv (1970), 24-7.
28  R.F. Tylecote, 'An Early Medieval Iron-Smelting Site in Weardale', *Jnl. Iron and Steel Inst.* cxcii (1959), 26-34.
29  E.W. Wynne and R.F. Tylecote, 'An Experimental Investigation into Primitive Iron Smelting Techniques'. *Jnl. Iron and Steel Inst.* cxc (1958), 339-48.

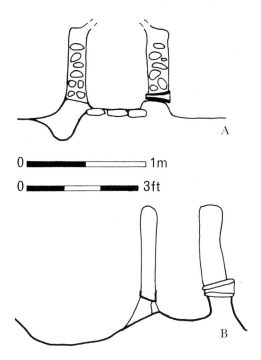

*Fig. 79a* Saxo-Norman smelting furnace: West Runton.  *b.* Saxo-Norman smelting furnace: Stamford. (From Crossley op. cit. note 20, 31.)

*Fig. 80* Ground-level hearth, *c.* 1340. Redrawn from the Romance of Alexander (Oxford, Bodleian Library, MS Bodl. 264 f. 82r).

furnace at Byrkeknott, 12 lbs. of charcoal were needed per pound of iron.[30] Thus the demand for charcoal was rapacious: at Tudeley, with an estimated output of 6,000 pounds of iron a year,[31] a minimum of 72,000 pounds of charcoal would have been required, if it was burnt at the same rate as at Byrkeknott. Even though the wood at Tudeley came from the forge owner's estate, the cost of making charcoal amounted to half of the forge's expenses. In the furnace, the slag, mainly silica, trickled to the bottom leaving the iron as a spongy mass combined with a few solid impurities in the centre of the hearth. The iron, now called a bloom, was extracted with tongs and hammered and heated to knock off the remaining impurities. At Byrkeknott, the fire used for this was called the 'stryng hearth'.[32] Although coal was not suitable for smelting, it could be used for forging when the iron was sufficiently consolidated to prevent it absorbing harmful sulphur from the coal.

The size of the bowl hearth and hence of the bloom was limited by the capacity of the bellows. At Tudeley these are described as being made of white leather, hareskins and oxhide, presumably attached between wooden boards.[33] Several bellows are illustrated in manuscripts (Figs. 80, 81, 86).[34] The drawings show that they were pumped by hand using a lever, and were operated alternately to produce a continuous draught. At Tudeley the heaviest item of the wage bill was not for smiths but for blowers, amounting to 20 per cent of the total forge expenses.[35]

30  Tylecote, op. cit. note 2, 206.
31  Ibid. 189.
32  Lapsley, op. cit. note 22, 520.
33  Giuseppi, op. cit. note 16, 150.

34  E.g. B.L., Sloane MS 3983, f. 5; B.L., Add. MS 47682, f. 31; Oxford, Bodleian Library, MS Bodley 264, f. 84, see Figs. 80 and 86.
35  Giuseppi, op. cit. note 16, 154

*Fig. 81* Bellows powered by a water-wheel located outside the forge. (From Agricola, *De Re Metallica*, trans. H.C. and L.H. Hoover (1950), 245.)

The adoption of water-power enabled smiths to increase their output. Bellows driven by a waterwheel could produce a continuous powerful draught from a free energy source, so it was at last possible to enlarge the size of the furnace and the bloom thus produced (Fig. 81). Water-powered hammers were also heavy enough to fashion the larger blooms. Waterwheels were used on the Continent to drive bellows and hammers at least as early as the 13th century.[36] In England, what appears to be the earliest known water-powered forge was set up at Chingley (Kent) in the early 14th century. Its timber wheel-race and the frame for the foundations of a hammer and possibly bellows have been excavated.[37] The accounts for Byrkeknott in 1408 show that a conduit was dug for a waterwheel. The site, now identified as Harthope Mill, would have had an intermittent water supply, which explains why only casual payments were made to the woman who operated the bellows.[38]

A technical improvement had obviously taken place there, for the Byrkeknott blooms, at up to 195 lbs., were much heavier than earlier products. The blooms at Tudeley in 1350 were about 30 lbs., whereas Roman blooms had ranged from 0.66 to

36 G. Magnusson, 'Lapphyttan – an Example of Medieval Iron Production', in N. Bjorkenstarn et al. (eds.), *Medieval Iron in Society* (Stockholm, 1985), 21-33; G. Heckenast, Le Développement de L'Entrainement par Roue Hydraulique dans la Sidérurgie Hongroise', *Revue d'Histoire de la Sidérurgie*, viii (1967), 73-94.

37 D.W. Crossley, *The Bewl Valley Ironworks* (1975), 2, 6-7.

38 R.F. Tylecote, 'The Location of Byrkeknott: a 15th-century Iron Smelting site in Weardale', *Jnl. Iron and Steel Inst.*, cxciv (1959), 451-8.

17 lbs.[39] References in Domesday Book to mills paying rents in blooms of iron and in the 13th century to a mill-race at Kirkstall forge are not sufficiently explicit to suggest the use of mechanical bellows.[40] Water was needed in the smelting process for washing the ore and quenching the final products. The existence of medieval bloomeries far from any water flow, as at High Bishopley (Co. Durham), Walney Island (Cumbria) and Peel Island (Cumbria), shows that even if mechanical bellows had been invented, they were not universally applied.[41]

Once the iron had been hammered into a fit state at the string hearth, it could either be worked up into objects for use or converted into steel. Medieval wrought iron contains up to 0.05 per cent carbon while steel has between 0.5 and 1.5 per cent carbon. Some ores, rich in manganese, produce a naturally steely iron when smelted with sufficient charcoal. The carbonates from Yorkshire, Shropshire and Staffordshire tend to do this. Wrought iron from haematite can be converted into steel by a process called case hardening or cementation. The surface of the iron would be hardened by prolonged contact with burning carbonaceous matter. The early 12th-century writer Theophilus describes the hardening of tools by sprinkling them with a mixture of burnt oxhorn and salt; they were heated red-hot and quenched in water. Another method was to smear them in pig fat and cover them with strips of goat leather and clay; they were then heated before being quenched in water or the urine of goats or, best of all, the urine of a small red-headed boy.[42] Both ways caused the iron to absorb a little carbon evenly, from the oxhorn and goat skin. Theophilus does not describe the process of tempering, which may be because his directions for making steel resulted in a carbon content too low for tempering.

Steel was needed primarily for the working edges of tools and weapons. Ensuring that a piece of high-quality iron absorbed carbon evenly was a long and skilled process, so it was easier to make a small piece of steely iron and then beat it onto the working edge of the tool. In order to obtain an even distribution of the carbonised iron it was necessary to beat it thin, fold it over and pile it together several times. Steel could be combined with the iron on an edge tool in several ways: using an iron core around which steel was wrapped; applying a steel tip; piling the iron and steel sufficiently to make a homogeneous metal; or sandwiching a strip of steel between strips of iron so the steel projected like the lead in a pencil.[43]

In the north of England, medieval methods of production lingered on till the 17th century: at Muncaster Head (Cumbria) a bloomery forge was built as late as 1636.[44] In the south, however, water-powered bloomeries were superseded by the blast-furnace during the early 16th century. The blast-furnace was introduced from

39  Tylecote, op. cit. note 2, 211.
40  Schubert, op. cit. note 2, 89, 143; Tylecote, op. cit. note 2, 64.
41  R.F. Tylecote, *Metallurgy in Archaeology* (1962), 290.
42  Theophilus, *On Divers Arts*, ed. Hawthorne & Smith, 93-5.
43  Schubert, op. cit. note 2, 119-121; R.F. Tyle-cote, 'The Medieval Smith and his Methods', in D.W. Crossley (ed.) *Medieval Industry* (C.B.A. Research Rep. xl, 1981), 44-7.
44  R.F. Tylecote and J. Cherry, 'The 17th-century Bloomery at Muncaster Head', *Trans. Cumberland & Westmorland Antiquarian and Archaeological Soc.* lxx (1970), 69-109.

abroad where shaft-furnaces, rather than the English type of bowl hearth, had been used to produce wrought iron blooms in the Middle Ages. Iron ore in a tall, narrow shaft furnace remained in contact with the charcoal and carbon monoxide for a much longer time than in the bowl hearth and was thus much more readily reduced to $Fe_3C$ (iron carbide). Iron carbide, having a lower melting-point than bloomery iron, would trickle to the bottom of the furnace where it could be cast into pigs or other artefacts. To convert brittle cast iron into malleable wrought iron, the metal had to be oxidised in a well-ventilated furnace called a finery, and then beaten into shape at a chafery. The adoption both of the blast-furnace for making cast iron and of the 'indirect process' for making wrought iron from cast was a slow evolution. Probably the earliest known European blast-furnace, in use from *c.* 1150 to 1350, has been excavated at Lapphyttan in Sweden; fully-developed examples were known in Italy in the mid 15th century; but the first known English blast-furnace was not built until 1496 at Newbridge (Sussex).[45] The introduction of cast iron and the indirect process of making wrought iron marked the end of the Middle Ages and the start of the modern era in the English iron industry.

### The Smith's Forge, Tools and Products

The blacksmith's forge has an impressive atmosphere of its own, vividly captured in the 14th-century 'Complaint against Blacksmiths':

> . . . The crooked codgers cry after: Coal! Coal!
> And blow their bellows till their brains are all bursting.
> Huff! Puff! says the one, Haff! Paff! says the other,
> They spit and they sprawl and they tell many tales,
> They gnaw and they gnash and they groan all together
> And hold themselves hot with their hard hammers.
> Of a bull's hide are built their bellies' aprons,
> Their shanks are sheathed against flickering flames
> Heavy hammers they have that are hard to handle
> Stark strokes they strike on a stock of steel...[46]

The noises and fumes of the forge could make blacksmiths unpopular, especially in towns. Night work was banned in London in 1298 because of the unhealthiness of the coal and the damage to their neighbours.[47] In 1257, when Queen Eleanor intended to make a long stay in Nottingham, she was forced to leave for Tutbury 'owing to the smoke of the sea coals'.[48] One hundred and forty years later the London smiths were

45  Magnusson, op. cit. note 36, 21-33; A.A. Filarète, Treatise on Architecture, *c.* 1464, *Rev. Hist. Sidérurgie*, i.4, (1960), 57-60; Schubert, op. cit. note 2, 162-3.

46  *English Historical Documents, 1327-1485*, ed. A.R. Myers (1969), 1055; E. Salter, 'A Complaint against the Blacksmiths', *Literature and History*, v (1979), 194-215.

47  *Calendar of Early Mayor's Court Rolls*, ed. A.H. Thomas (1924), 33-4.

48  *Annales Monastici*, iii, *Annales Prioratus de Dunstaplia*, ed. H.R. Luard (Rolls Ser. xxxvi, 1866), 203.

being indicted in ward-motes and asked to move house 'by reason of the great nuisance, noise and alarm experienced in divers ways by neighbours around their dwellings'.[49] The spurriers or spur-makers were even worse. They tended 'to wander about all day without working at their trade and when they are drunk and frantic, they take to their work to the annoyance of the sick and their neighbours. And then they blow up their fires so vigorously that their fires begin at once to blaze, to the great peril of themselves and the whole neighbourhood'. Neighbours also dreaded sparks 'which so vigorously issued forth from the chimneys in their forges'.[50] When necessary the smiths could turn the rigours of their work to their own advantage. In the 8th century when Ecgwin came to Alcester to preach to its 'wealthy and hard-hearted inhabitants..., the many smiths of the place drowned his words with the sound of their hammers and anvils'.[51] The neighbours of the London armourer Stephen atte Fryth complained in 1377 that:

> the blows of the sledge-hammers when the great pieces of iron called 'Osmond' are being wrought into 'brestplates', 'quysers', 'jambers' and other pieces of armour, shake the stone and earthen party-walls of the plaintiffs' house so that they are in danger of collapsing, and disturb the rest of the plaintiffs and their servants, day and night, and spoil the wine and ale in their cellar, and the stench of the smoke from the sea-coal used in the forge penetrates their hall and chambers.[52]

The smith's raw material was generally a bloom, of variable size and sometimes cleft in the middle to ascertain its quality. Some iron was sold in a half-finished state like that imported from Spain, and like the rods that Henry of Lewes, working in London, bought from a smith in the Weald.[53] The smith's hearth was sometimes on the ground, as excavated at Goltho, or on a raised fire bed, which seems to have been the case at Waltham Abbey.[54] At Alsted (Surrey) a waist-level hearth of stones replaced an earlier bowl hearth.[55] Both types are illustrated in manuscripts (Figs. 80, 86).[56] Apart from his hearth, the blacksmith's main tools were an anvil, hammers and tongs. The anvil was a block of iron set in a stout trunk of wood. Though he is mainly concerned with the working of bronze, Theophilus describes the different shapes of anvil: flat and square, or flat and horned; rounded like half an apple; or with two horns, one larger than the other and one slightly curved back like a thumb. He also explains how to make many tools such as flat, peened (rounded) and horned hammers, chisels and files.[57] Anglo-Saxon smiths' tools, including tongs, hammer

49  *Cal. Letter-Book H*, 415.
50  Riley, *Memorials*, 226.
51  *Chronicon Abbatiae de Evesham*, ed. W.D. Macray (Rolls Ser. xxix, 1863), 25-6.
52  *London Assize of Nuisance*, ed. H.M. Chew and W. Kellaway (London Record Soc. x, 1973, 160). I would like to thank R. Homer for this reference.
53  P.R.O., E 101/467/7(7), mm. 1-3.

54  G. Beresford, *The Medieval Clay-Land Village: Excavations at Goltho and Barton Blount* (Soc. Medieval Archaeol. Monograph Ser. 6, 1975), 46; Huggins and Huggins, op. cit. note 19.
55  Ketteringham, *Alsted*, op. cit. note 18, 17-31.
56  B.L., MS Sloane 3983, f. 5ʳ; Bodl. MS 264 f. 82ʳ.
57  Theophilus, *On Divers Arts*, ed. Hawthorne & Smith, 84-95.

*Fig. 82* Morville church (Salop): south door.

*Fig. 83* Durham Cathedral: south-west door of the nave. Partly restored.

and pritchel (a pointed tool used for punching holes), have been found, at Shakenoak, Thetford and Soham.[58] From the later Middle Ages, tongs, various hammers, chisels and punches have also been found, particularly productive sites being Deganwy Castle and Waltham Abbey.[59] However, nothing in England compares with the complete tool-chests from the Viking age found in Morgedal, Norway, and Mästermyr, Gotland.[60]

Surviving tools do not provide a complete inventory of the smith's equipment. Medieval anvils are very rare, though they are frequently illustrated in manuscripts.[61] It is clear from the surviving iron products that some specialised implements were needed for their manufacture. For instance, grilles with such regular scrollwork as those at Winchester and Lincoln Cathedrals must have been made with a beaked anvil, mandrel or, simplest of all, a scrolling iron. The latter is shaped like a corkscrew, curled to the required shape, and then slotted into the hardie hole of the anvil. It produces a more uniform result than a mandrel (an iron cone) for such repetitive work as a grille. A fuller, or round-nosed chisel, was clearly used on the cross on the door of Morville church (Salop) (*c.* 1175-1200) (Fig. 82).

58 D.M. Wilson, in D.M. Wilson (ed.), *The Archaeology of Anglo-Saxon England* (1976), 264-5.

59 I.H. Goodall, 'The Medieval Blacksmith and his Products', in Crossley (ed.), *Medieval Industry*, 51.

60 C. Blindheim, 'Smedgraven fra Bygland i Morgedal', *Viking*, xxvi (1962), 25-80; G. Arwidsson and G. Berg, *The Mästermyr Find* (Stockhom, 1983).

61 P. Oury, *L'Argus de l'Outil* (1978), illustrates a 14th-century example from Normandy; and various 16th-century examples are in the Metropolitan Museum of Art, New York: P. Walker, 'Collecting Craftsmen's Tools', *Connoisseur*, ccvi, No. 827 (Jan 1981), 52-7.

However, at Durham Cathedral (south-west doors of the nave)[62] a similar effect was produced with a swage, a percussive tool like a hammer with a profiled face (Fig. 83). On the latter example, the shoulder of the groove rises to a neat point (in section), an effect which could not have been achieved without a precise moulding tool. At Chichester Cathedral (Song School, outer door) some of the iron straps have a raised rib profile that was also achieved with a swage. Fullers and swages are not known from the Anglo-Saxon period and it is possible that these examples from late 12th-century door-hinges are the earliest evidence of their use in ironwork. In the early 13th century, probably influenced by coin makers and goldsmiths, the use of swages and dies for ironwork developed considerably. All sorts of floral and foliage motifs were stamped with swages onto the terminals of decorative iron scrolls, and used principally to embellish doors and chests. None of these swages is known to have survived: they took quite a battering, and on some door-hinges one can see the swage gradually disintegrating during the production of the hinge. The 14th-century coin dies from York, although only used to impress gold, show how the top hammered face became shattered and bent.[63]

Discussion of the products of a medieval iron-smith could cover almost every aspect of economic activity: as Ælfric's smith pointed out, no craftsman could work without his iron tools. The survival of craft tools is generally haphazard and does not necessarily reflect what was important at the time. The 11th-century tract on estate matters, *Gerefa*, provides advice for a 'sagacious reeve' on how to run an estate and lists in great detail all the tools which were necessary on an 11th-century farm. Many were of course made of wood: buckets, spinning equipment, brooms and rakes; but others such as axe, adze, awl, plane, saw, mattock, scythe and fire tongs were of iron.[64] From an urban context in 1356 comes the remarkable inventory of a London ironmonger, Stephen Northerne. Among his stock he had plenty of great hinges, garnets or decorative hinges, almarigarnettes or cupboard hinges, spadierns or the iron tips for wooden spades, goldsmiths' anvils, combs for wool-combers, battle-axes, masons' axes, a flesh-hook, a bow-shave, a baker's 'peel' of iron, and cartecloutes (the iron plates of an axle-tree). This collection would have supplied a wide variety of traders, and was worth £9 14s. 2d.[65]

The many surviving products of medieval blacksmiths fall into several specialised areas, of which clocks and decorative and cast ironwork will be discussed here. The clergy in particular needed accurate time-keeping devices to regulate their daily celebration of Divine Office, so it is not surprising that they pioneered technical improvements. Various time-keepers including the *clepsydra* or water clock had been used in the early Middle Ages but, between *c*.1280 and 1300, English monastic and collegiate records begin to refer to *horologia*, and by the early 14th century these are

62  J. Geddes, 'The Sanctuary Ring of Durham Cathedral', *Archaeologia*, cvii (1982), pl. xxviia.
63  P. Grierson, *Numismatics* (1975), 102, fig. 48.
64  P. Addyman, 'Archaeology and Anglo-Saxon Society' in G. de G. Sieveking et al., (eds.), *Problems in Economic and Social Archaeology* (1976), 318-19. Tools are discussed more fully by Goodall, op. cit. note 59, 51-62, and Wilson, op. cit. note 58, 253-81.
65  Riley, *Memorials*, 282-5.

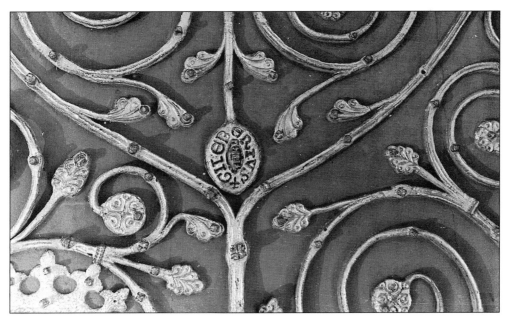

*Fig. 84* St. George's Chapel, Windsor: detail of the door.

clearly described as complex mechanical devices.[66] Their precisely made moving parts were of wrought iron. The earliest recorded *horologium* was made in 1283 by the canons of Dunstable Priory.[67] In 1322 the clock at Norwich Cathedral Priory had a large astronomical dial and automata including 59 images and a procession of monks.[68] Between 1327 and 1336 Richard of Wallingford designed for St. Albans Abbey a clock with hour-striking mechanisms to depict the movement of the sun, stars and planets.[69] The magnificent clock in Salisbury Cathedral, made in 1386, is the earliest existing clock in England and its delicate wrought iron construction testifies to the great skill of the early blacksmiths.[70]

Only two examples of decorative ironwork will be discussed here, selected because of the light they throw on the iron industry. In France, the first known use of stamped ironwork occurs on the hinges of the west doors of Notre Dame in Paris, originally made in the 1240s. The technique and even some of the designs seem to have been inspired by the innovative goldsmith Hugo of Oignies, who pioneered the use of naturalistic stamped leaves and flowers on book-covers and reliquaries.[71] A similar

66 C.F.C. Beeson, *English Church Clocks* (1971), 13-24.
67 Ibid. 13.
68 Ibid. 16.
69 J.D. North, *Richard of Wallingford* (1976), i, 461-527; ii, 1-5, 361-70.
70 C.F.C. Beeson, op. cit. note 66, 46. The clockmakers did not break away from the smiths to form their own gild until 1630: S.E. Atkins and

W.H. Overall, *Some Account of the Worshipful Company of Clockmakers ...* (privately pr., 1881), 2-7.
71 *Rhin-Meuse, Art et Civilisation*, catalogue of exhibition at Kunsthalle, Cologne, and Musées Royaux d'Art et d'Histoire, Brussels (1972), M5-8. S. Collon-Gevaert, *Histoire des Arts du Métal en Belgique* (1950), 247-51.

development seems to have taken place in England, illustrating how techniques could move from one craft to another, particularly when a craftsman was skilled in several fields. St. George's Chapel, Windsor, was built for Henry III between 1240 and 1249.[72] The delicate iron scrolls covering its original entrance doors are lavishly decorated with stamped terminals, the earliest known in England. Among the usual designs of leaves and flowers are two unique forms: a disc filled by a long-armed cross, with pellets between the arms; and a large stamp with the name Gilbertus (Fig. 81). If Gilbertus was the smith, he was exceptional in leaving his name in so prominent a position, as most medieval craftsmen left their work unsigned. Coins are the only category of medieval artistic or craft production which were consistently marked with the name of the moneyer or goldsmith. In 1247 Henry III had to change the design on the reverse of his coins, from a short to long-armed cross, in an attempt to reduce clipping.[73] The long-cross issue was made from 1247 to 1279 by 94 named moneyers. In 1248 Gilbert de Bonninton was sworn in as the king's moneyer at Canterbury, and he was the only Gilbert making long-cross coins.[74] The name and the use of the long-cross stamp at Windsor may well indicate that Gilbert de Bonninton, presumably a goldsmith, introduced the technique of stamping iron to England.

The iron grille over the tomb of Queen Eleanor at Westminster Abbey was made in 1292-3 by Master Thomas of Leighton, and brought by him from Leighton to Westminster[75] (Fig. 85). It is made with stamped terminals identical to those on the doors at Leighton Buzzard church (Beds.). This very scanty information has several possible implications: in 1292 it was preferable to commission a country smith rather than one from London for such a prestigious object; it was possible for a first-class artist in iron to run a viable business in a country parish; and the distribution trade in raw iron was efficient, because Bedfordshire had no supplies of its own. The skilled and successful royal blacksmith Henry of Lewes (who made Henry III's tomb railings, now lost) had died in 1291,[76] so Thomas of Leighton was possibly recommended for the job by Oliver Sutton, bishop of Lincoln, who conducted Eleanor's funeral service in 1290.[77] Sutton often stayed in his manors near Leighton Buzzard and is most likely to have consecrated the parish church there when it was completed shortly after 1288.[78] Thomas had earlier made the hinges for Turvey church using similar stamps to those at Leighton Buzzard. He may also have known through pattern-books about contemporary French ironwork design since a grille almost identical to the Eleanor grille was once at the abbey of Saint Denis.[79] How

72  *King's Works*, ii, 868-9.
73  G.C. Brooke, *English Coins from the Seventh Century to the Present Day* (1932), 107, 114-15.
74  L.A. Lawrence, 'The Long Cross Coinage of Henry III and Edward I', *British Numismatic Jnl.* ix (1912), 161.
75  *Manners and Household Expenses*, [ed.T.H. Turner] (Roxburghe Club, no. 57, 1841),

135-8.
76  *Cal. Husting Wills*, i, 102; H.M. Colvin (ed.), *The Building Accounts of Henry III* (1971), 226 and passim.
77  *Annales Monastici*, iv, *Annales de Oseneia*, ed. H.R. Luard (Rolls Ser. xxxvi, 1869), 326.
78  *Annales Monastici*, iii, op. cit. note 48, 34.
79  Viollet-le-Duc, *Dictionnaire*, vi, 61.

*Fig. 85* Westminster Abbey: detail of the Eleanor Grille, 1292-3.

Thomas acquired such knowledge and skills is not known, but he lived near Dunstable priory where, in 1283, the canons had made one of the very earliest mechanical clocks known in England.[80] This suggests that they had in their community an extremely skilled ironsmith who could have influenced Thomas's work.

The full exploitation of cast iron products lies beyond the medieval period. The initial impetus for the industry came from the Crown: Henry VII in 1496 commissioned Henry Finer to produce iron ordnance at the first known English blast furnace at Newbridge (Sussex).[81] Shortly after, in 1509, the first English cast iron cannon was produced at the same forge,[82] while by 1543-4 Ralph Hogge was casting cannons regularly at Buxted.[83] Other popular products were andirons, tomb-slabs and cast firebacks.[84] One of the earliest surviving firebacks, showing the initials, a fleur-de-lis, a four-leaved rose and a low crown, commemorates the crowning of Elizabeth of York as queen consort in 1487.[85]

80  *Annales Monastici*, iii, op. cit. note 48, 296.
81  Schubert, op. cit. note 2, 162-3.
82  Ibid. 164; the earliest certain reference to a European cast-iron artefact is in a Frankfurt document of 1391, B. Rathgen, *Das Geschütz im Mittelalter* (Berlin, 1928), 27-9. I would like to thank Claude Blair for this reference.
83  Straker, op. cit. note 3, 147-52.
84  At Burwash church (Sussex), is a cast-iron tomb slab inscribed 'Orate P annema Jhone Colins'. This inscription and accompanying cross appear to be in a 14th-century style, but for technical reasons it is unlikely that the slab could have been cast before the 16th century. Straker, op. cit. note 3, 306-7; Schubert, op. cit. note 2, 265-6.
85  J. Starkie Gardner, *Ironwork*, iii (1922), 158-64; Straker, op. cit. note 3, 142-76. The rest of this chapter is adapted from J. Geddes, 'The Blacksmith's Life, Wife and Work', *Tools and Trades*, i (1983), 15-37, and I should like to thank the Tools and Trades History Society for permission to reproduce it.

## *Organisation of the Industry*

'Smith' is a generic term covering the worker of any type of metal. Our word 'blacksmith', meaning a general worker of iron, was not used before 1376.[86] In Aelfric's discussion of Anglo-Saxon crafts, five types of smith are mentioned: smiths (*fabri* or *smithas*), iron-smiths (*ferrarii* or *isenesmithas*), and gold-, silver- and bronze-smiths.[87] In London it is possible to trace the growth of specialisation by the increasing numbers of smiths' gilds. They first appear on record in 1298, charged with an illegal attempt to form a fraternity. Sixteen men calling themselves 'masters of the trade of smiths', including three cutlers and one bell founder, were involved.[88] At roughly the same time a group of spurriers was arrested on similar conspiracy charges. They included two rowel-makers, one spurrier and one harness-maker.[89] Previously the lorimers had identified themselves, publishing their ordinances in 1260-1[90] Thus by 1300 in London there were at least six specialised branches of iron-smithing operating three organisations. By 1376 six ironworking gilds existed. They were the smiths (*feveres*), armourers, spurriers, lorimers, ironmongers and cutlers.[91] By 1422 this number had increased to fourteen: ironmongers, cutlers, armourers, clockmakers, lorimers, spurriers, wire-drawers, pinners, nail-makers, lockyers, furbours, smiths, ferrours and blacksmiths. (It is not possible to distinguish the functions of the last three.)[92]

## *Working Life*

The source material available for the study of the smiths' working life is greatly biased towards a few towns such as York, Beverley and Bristol, with London documents being overwhelmingly predominant. This means that very little is known at present about the majority of smiths who lived in the countryside.

There were three ways to become a master of a craft with licence or freedom to practise it in a particular city. These were by birth, if one's father was a master smith, by presentment by the gild or mystery before the mayor and aldermen, and by apprenticeship. An experienced craftsman who moved from one city to another would have to be judged by the masters of the mystery and then be presented to the mayor on payment of a considerable sum. Some of the pitfalls of moving to a strange town are illustrated by the tribulations of William Ward, a cutler from York, who came to London in 1382. William, not knowing the procedure, asked John Foxtone to help him. Foxtone first confused the bladesmiths (a branch of the cutlers) with the bladers (corn dealers) and signed William onto the latter, and then stole most of the money which William had given him pay the entrance fees.[93]

86  *Cal. Letter-Book H*, 245.
87  Swanton, op. cit. note 1.
88  *Cal. Early Mayor's Court Rolls*, op. cit. note 44, 33-4.
89  Ibid. 52.
90  *Munimenta Gildhallae Londoniensis, Liber Custum-* *arum*, ed. H.T. Riley (3 vols., Rolls Series xii, 1858-62), 78.
91  *Cal. Letter-Book H*, 35; *Cal. Letter-Book E*, 253.
92  Unwin, op. cit. note 70, 370.
93  Riley, *Memorials*, 474-5.

Apprenticeship was a slow and difficult way in. Detailed regulations for apprenticeship in the ironworking crafts only survive from the mid 13th century onwards. Clearly some effective system for training had operated earlier on, but perhaps on more of an ad hoc basis. The lorimers were among the first crafts to specify a term of not less then ten years and a fee of 30s. for apprentices, in 1269.[94] The first indentures for iron-workers appear somewhat later. In 1309-10 John, son of Saman the Knifesmith, apprenticed to Stephen atte Holt, a cutler, gained the freedom of the City of London after serving a term of ten years, and paying an entry of 2s. 6d.[95] Stephen then found as a replacement Ralph atte Holte, probably a relative, who came before the chamberlain and acknowledged himself an apprentice for a term of two years, and paid an entry fee of 2s. 6d.[96] Maybe Ralph had grown up in the trade and therefore needed less training.

The life of a journeyman was little easier than that of an apprentice. In theory a journeyman was a skilled craftsman who worked as a hired assistant to a master and was paid at a daily rate, *par jour*. In the 13th century it was normal for an apprentice, once qualified, to work for a few years as journeyman and then set up his own business.[97] A century later this was much harder and journeymen frequently remained as wage-earners all their lives, bound by long contracts. In some crafts they even set up journeymen's gilds to defend their interests. However, in some regulations it appears that the term journeyman was used simply for a paid labourer. Thus the London bladesmiths forbade masters to teach their journeymen the tricks of the trade as they would an apprentice.[98]

Before the gilds developed, a master-craftsman presumably was free to carry out his trade wherever he pleased. The movement of urban smiths is hard to trace at an individual level but can be demonstrated from gild regulations. Early on, the process was quite simple and the smiths were merely required to register at the gild hall and sometimes pay a small fee. Some qualified provincials came up to London and bought their freedom to start business. In 1310 Adam, a cutler from Thaxted, paid one mark to the commune of London and opened shop.[99] Gradually efforts were made to curb the free movement of labour. There were three reasons for this: shortage of manpower, surfeit of manpower and the need to control standards of production. Following the Black Death the King needed skilled metalworkers in London so in 1355 he forbade 'armourers of the city and suburbs to cross the sea to Gascony or elsewhere in the retinue of great men, on pain of imprisonment'.[100]

The travels of iron-merchants were also curtailed by the shortage of ore after the plague: in 1354 they were forbidden to export any iron from England even if it had originally been bought abroad.[101] The London cutlers were so badly hit by pestilence that they had to replace all their nine masters of the mystery in 1349 'in as

94  *Liber Custumarum*, op. cit. note 90, 78.
95  *Cal. Letter-Book D*, 109.
96  Ibid. 105.
97  Unwin, op. cit. note 70, 224-9.

98  Riley, *Memorials*, 569.
99  *Cal. Letter-Book D*, 46.
100  *Cal. Letter-Book G*, 44.
101  *Statutes of the Realm*, i (London, 1810), 345.

much as the wardens were all dead'.[102] When business was slack, gild members
wished to prevent competition from strangers and foreigners. (In gild parlance, a
stranger was a native who was not free of the city, and a foreigner or alien was anyone
coming from beyond the city or its suburbs.) While the blacksmiths were still an
illegal confederacy in 1298, the sixteen members tried to eliminate strangers'
production by saying 'no one was allowed to work with others than themselves'.[103]
Really restrictive measures were not introduced until the mid 15th century when
there was obviously a surplus of smiths in London. In 1434 the blacksmiths decided
that qualified strangers or foreigners coming to London and wishing to take up the
craft had to serve two weeks without pay and then make a three-year contract with a
London master, at a salary of 40s. per annum.[104] This was a mere pittance when a
master-smith was earning 16d. a day (roughly £18 a year).[105] It is possible that
restrictions like these persuaded many smiths to work in the country, or at least
outside towns like London, York and Bristol where the gilds had so much control.

### Gild Regulations

From the point of view of society as a whole, the maintenance of standards was
probably the most important function of the gilds. The ironworking gilds took
consumer protection very seriously and frequently took the initiative to improve or
uphold standards. For example, the blacksmiths in 1394 presented their articles to
the mayor and 'entreated that they might be granted', and in 1380 'in the
amendment of many defaults, the cutlers caused [their] articles to be written'.[106]
The gilds themselves had four ways of controlling quality: by authorising the sale of
goods in certain official places only; identifying and inspecting the wares of
strangers; specifying standards and confiscating falsework; and by limiting working
hours. In 1372 freemen wishing to sell their goods away from their shop, and
foreigners, were allowed to 'stand openly at Graschirche or else on the pavement by
St. Nicholas Flesshameles or near to the Tun upon Cornhill', in London.[107] The
cutlers forbade the sale of knives at hostelries 'except where some great lord or
reputable man shall send after cutlery for his own use, to be brought to his own place
to see whether it please him or not'.[108] The farriers and bladesmiths also forbade

102  *Cal. Letter-Book F*, 110.
103  *Cal. Early Mayor's Court Rolls*, op. cit. note 44, 34.
104  H.C. Coote and J.R.D. Tyssen, 'Ordinances of Some Secular Guilds in London', *Trans. London and Middlesex Archaeol. Soc.* iv (1871), 32-3.
105  W. St. John Hope, *Windsor Castle: An Architectural History*, 2 vols. (1913), ii, 403. It is impossible to be accurate in calculating an annual wage from a daily rate bacause of the variable number of feast days observed. They depended on the locality, occupation and contact between master and man. In the late 14th century a worker might have about 40 feast days without

work, but whether he was paid for them depended on individual circumstances. My estimate is based on 284 days pay in the year, according to Harvey's schedule for a carpenter in 1337: J.H. Harvey, *Mediaeval Craftsmen* (1975) 196-7. It also assumes that a man was employed for the whole year, which was not always the case: B.F. Harvey, 'Work and *Festa Ferianda* in Medieval England', *Jnl. of Ecclesiastical History*, xxiii (1972), 289-308.
106  Blacksmiths: *Cal. Letter-Book H*, 415; Cutlers: Riley, *Memorials*, 438.
107  Riley, *Memorials*, 361.
108  Ibid. 438.

hawking around inns.[109] To keep a check on quality, the application of individual marks for each smith was gradually introduced. These can often be found on armour, swords and knives. As the marks were frequently faked they are not a reliable means of identifying the smith. The King ordered all smiths of swords, knives and other armour to put marks on their work in 1365.[110] The helmet makers were already suffering from counterfeit marks in 1347. They showed a justified concern for quality, for 'persons coming in as strangers have intermeddled in the making of helmets whereas they do not know the trade . . . many great men have been slain by their default'.[111] Thereafter only heaumers, or helmet makers, who had been approved by the masters could set up forge in London, and no one was to employ a stranger.

Some details in the records of production and materials indicate the most common malpractices of the smithing trade. Sometimes, in spite of their rigorous training, the smiths were simply not 'sufficyantlith ylernyd', as the Bristol masters complained in 1403.[112] Sometimes they deliberately used defective materials or tried to sell secondhand goods as new. Furbours in 1350 were engaging in the dangerous practice of mending broken sword-blades instead of completely reworking them.[113] Both lorimers and spurriers were selling old wares as new, and spurriers were using 'iron that has been cracked for tin and putting gilt on false copper'.[114] The most detailed and urgent specifications came, not surprisingly, from the farriers. In 1356 in London 'many unskilled farriers were causing damage to the trade as they intermeddled with the works of farriery which they did not know how to bring to a good end, by reason whereof many horses had been lost'. To rectify this, farriers were not to use false metal for making shoes or nails. They had to give good and honest advice to those who asked for counsel, both in the purchase of horses and their cure.[115] There was also widespread concern about the dishonest manufacture of keys. The London blacksmiths were forbidden to make 'any manner of key from any kind of impress thereof unless they have the key itself present or the lock for which the same key was to be made, by reason of the mischiefs which have happened and which may happen in the time to come'.[116] Regulations for working at night varied from craft to craft, depending on the technical finesse required.[117] According to the London spurriers in 1345, 'no man can work so neatly by night as by day and many people engaging in deceitful work prefer to work by night'.[118] The London smiths banned night work in 1296 and the cutlers in 1344.[119]

A smith could have both his career regulated and his soul saved by his gild. The

109  L. Toulmin Smith, 'Ordinances of the Companies of Marshals and Smiths at York, A.D. 1409-1443', *The Antiquary*, xi (Jan.-June 1885), 105-9; *Cal. Letter-Book L*, 258.
110  *Cal. Letter-Book G*, 191.
111  Riley, *Memorials*, 237.
112  *The Little Red Book of Bristol*, ed. F.B. Bickley, 2 vols. (1900), ii, 181.
113  C. Welch, *History of the Cutlers' Company of*

*London* (1916), i, 239-40.
114  Riley, *Memorials*, 226.
115  Ibid. 292.
116  *Cal. Letter Book H*, 415. In 1394.
117  Salter, op. cit. note 46, 194-215.
118  Riley, *Memorials*, 217.
119  *Cal. Early Mayor's Court Rolls*, op. cit. note 44, 33-4; Riley, *Memorials*, 217.

differences between a fraternity founded for corporate religious purposes and a gild were blurred because the early gilds included religious along with professional activities. When the London smiths were still an illegal confederacy in 1298 they made a casket in which to collect a weekly subscription from each master to maintain a wax taper in honour of St. Mary and St. Laudus.[120] This appears to have been a spontaneous undertaking, but later, by the end of the 14th century, the religious dues became more onerous, and were backed up by penalties for neglect.[121] Fines were exacted for the failure to perform several gild duties: paying the quarterly subscription; buying the livery; and performing the mystery plays and supplying tapers for churches. The money from fines helped to pay for the poor-box. However, some economic security existed for gild members before fines became common. In 1269 the lorimers apportioned part of the strangers' entry fee to the poor-box;[122] the smiths arranged the same in 1298.[123] The cutlers were more definite than other branches of the trade about their insurance measures. They paid 10*d*. a week in compensation to members who suffered 'storm at sea, conflagration by fire or any other sudden mischance by the visitation of God'.[124]

## Women as Blacksmiths

In medieval literature the female blacksmith, 'a fell woman and full of strife', has a particularly evil reputation. She was supposed to have forged the nails for Christ's crucifixion after her husband had refused to do so, inventing a hand injury as an excuse.[125] The scene is vividly shown in the Holkham Bible (Fig. 86).[126] Even a craft as strenuous as smithing sometimes depended on women who were responsible partners in the family business and gild activities. Katherine the mother of Andrew of Bury, king's smith at the Tower, was paid a wage equal to his (8*d*. a day) so that she could 'keep up the king's forge in the Tower and carry on the work of the forge' while Andrew was away campaigning at Crecy, in 1346.[127] She had gained plenty of experience for this, having been married to Walter of Bury who had been the king's smith for nine years. On another occasion the king employed Katherine the smith-wife (*fabra*) for 'steeling and battering the masons' tools' at Westminster in 1348.[128] She may have been the same Katherine of Bury. Women could also be responsible for apprentices in the same way as male masters of craft. In 1364 Agnes the wife of John Cotiller promised to train Juseana as an apprentice, to feed, clothe and teach her, and not beat her with a stick or knife.[129] Women were not just given easy jobs

120 *Cal. Early Mayor's Court Rolls*, op. cit. note 44, 33-5.
121 E.g. Welch, op. cit. note 113, 249-54; A.F. Leach, *Beverley Town Documents* (Selden Soc. xiv, 1900), 36.
122 *Liber Custumarum*, op. cit. note 90, 78.
123 *Cal. Early Mayor's Court Rolls*, 33-4.
124 Welch, op. cit. note 113, 247-54.
125 *The Northern Passion* ed. F.A. Foster, E.E.T.S. orig. ser. cxlv (1913), 168-73, and cxlvii

(1916), 164-5.
126 B.L., Add. MS 47682, f. 31. Other examples in *Queen Mary's Psalter*, ed. G.F. Warner (1912), 28, 256; M.K. Ehrminger, *The Cathedral of Strasbourg* (1970), 24; T. Cox, *Jehan Foucquet* (1931), pl. xxxiv; G. Cohen, *Le Théâtre en France au Moyen Age* (1928), i, pl. 33.
127 Colvin (ed.) *King's Works*, i. 222-4.
128 Salzman, *Building in England*, 337.
129 *Cal. Plea & Mem. R., 1323-64*, i, 274.

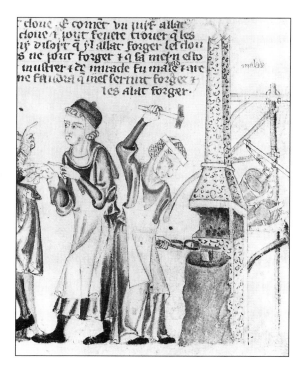

In the illustration, the manuscript text reads:

cloue . & comet vn iuif allac
cloue 7 pour fenere trouer q les
s ne pour forger l & il allar forger lef dou
tulfier & e miracle fu male tue
ne faudra q mef sernnt forger 7
les alat forger .

*Fig. 86* The Smith's Wife forging at
a waist-level hearth, *c.* 1325-30
(B.L., MS Add. 47682, f. 31).

like knife-grinding. The account roll of Byrkeknott, Weardale, isolates the women's tasks and their wages.[130] The tasks of the 'smytheman's' wife in 1408-9 are described as follows: helping to break up rock, blowing or working at the bellows, diverse labours, working at the bloom hearth and helping her husband.[131] She only earned a regular wage when she helped her husband: she was then paid a penny for every shilling he earned, in other words receiving a piece-rate of $\frac{1}{2}d$ per bloom.[132] She was generally better paid for breaking rock or working the bellows, but in a somewhat erratic way that related neither to the number of working days nor to the number of blooms. Women working at the smelters are illustrated in the paintings of Henri Bles (*fl. c.* 1490-1500) who lived in the region of Liège.[133]

Women were assumed to become members of a gild as soon as their husbands or fathers became masters. The ordinances of the girdlers of London and the rivet-makers of Paris forbade the employment of strange women, but allowed wives and daughters to work.[134] Women also came to the gild feasts, but presumably consumed

130  Lapsley, art. cit. note 22, 509-29.
131  Ibid. 511.
132  Ibid. 511-12. John Gylles the 'smytheman' smelted the ore and was regularly paid 6*d.* per bloom, in this case weighing 195 lbs. He earned from 1*s.*-5*s.* a week depending on output. Over the same period his wife earned between 2½*d.* and 1*s.* 6*d.* per week: Lapsley, art. cit. note 22, 516-29.

133  A. Dasnoy, 'Henri Bles', in *Etudes d'Histoire et d'Archéologie Namuroises, dédiées à Ferdinand Courtoy* (1952), ii, 619-26; Joseph Phillipe, *La Contribution Wallonne à la Peinture dite Flamande* (1956), 15.
134  Riley, *Memorials*, 216; Boileau, *Livre des Métiers*, ed. R. de Lespinasse and F. Bonnardot (Paris, 1879), 64.

less than the men: the cutlers in 1370 charged 2*s*. for a brother and 1*s*. for his wife.[135] In the lorimers' fraternity it was arranged for an equal number of masses to be sung at the death of any brother or sister, provided they had paid their subscriptions.[136]

By the end of the Middle Ages, iron-smiths had developed the potential of their metal to the limit of the technology available. Water-power had increased production from the bloomeries and was also used for mechanical hammers. The smiths could make heavy bars for wrought-iron cannon and architectural purposes or produce works of great precision and refinement for clocks, armour and decorative pieces. The major technical advances of making cast iron in a blast furnace and the indirect process for making wrought iron greatly increased the yield from ore and the range of products, marking the arrival of a new industrial era.

## Further Reading

H.R. Schubert's *History of the British Iron and Steel Industry* (1957) covers the historical and technical development of ironworking and makes ample use of documentary sources. More recent works tend to emphasise the metallurgical and archaeological aspects, in particular R.F. Tylecote's *Prehistory of Metallurgy in the British Isles* (1986), D.W. Crossley's 'Medieval Iron Smelting', in D.W. Crossley (ed.), *Medieval Industry* (C.B.A. Research Rep. xl, 1981) and H.F. Cleere and D.W. Crossley's *Iron Industry of the Weald* (1985).

There are regional studies of some iron-working areas, such as the Forest of Dean, covered by I. Cohen (*Trans. Woolhope Nat. Field Club*, xxxiv, 1954) and M.L. Bazeley (*Trans. Bristol & Gloucs. Arch. Soc.* xxxiii, 1910), and the Furness district by Fell (1908). The Weald has been explored by two major studies, E. Straker's *Wealden Iron* (1931), now somewhat out of date, and Cleere and Crossley's book (1985), incorporating all the latest archaeological and metallurgical discoveries.

There are a few original sources or tracts specifically concerned with the English iron industry but the accounts from Tudeley (ed. Giuseppi) and Byrkeknott (ed. Lapsley) are important records for the economics of medieval bloomeries. Theophilus, though not an English writer, gives a clear description of smithing practices in the early 12th century (ed. Hawthorne and Smith, 1979).

The products of the industry are covered in a few general works: tools by I.H. Goodall in D.W. Crossley (ed.), *Medieval Industry* (C.B.A. Research Rep. xl, 1981), and D.M. Wilson in D.M. Wilson (ed.), *The Archaeology of Anglo-Saxon England* (1976); clocks by C.F.C. Beeson, *English Church Clocks* (1971); and decorative iron by J. Starkie Gardner, *Ironwork* (3 parts 1922-30). The working life of urban iron-smiths is examined by E. Salter in *Literature and History*, v (1979).

---

135  Welch, op. cit. note 113, 249-59.                    136  *Cal. Letter-Book L*, 265-7. In 1489.

# 8

## *Pottery and Tile*

## JOHN CHERRY

The essential raw materials for the manufacture of pottery and tiles are a large supply of clay and sand, some water, and a source of fuel, generally wood. A well-drained working area is required with easy access by either road or water transport to a marketing area. Although the basic materials for the production of pottery and tiles do not differ from those used in Roman or post-medieval times, there was very little duplication of sites or continuity between the periods owing to the changing pattern of demand and marketing. Tileries and potteries are frequently sited on clay sub-soils which support managed woodland and tend to be in rural areas. The management of urban potteries probably differed from rural potteries even in the Middle Ages. For both types of pottery, material needed in small quantities – such as white clay for slips and inlays, or lead for glazing – could be brought from some distance away. White clay was brought to Thornton Abbey (Lincs.) from Leeds in 1313, and to Otterbourne (Hants.) from Farnham (Surrey) in 1395-6.[1]

Clay was normally dug quite close to the kiln, either on the peasant's croft or, by the 14th and 15th centuries, from the neighbouring common or from the open fields. The clay pits at Harlow (Essex) were either wells 14 ft. square or long narrow ditches 2 to 4 ft. wide. At Toynton (Lincs.) pits up to 20 ft. square are recorded, sometimes in the open fields. The potter had to pay for a licence to dig clay, whether from his own croft or elsewhere in the manor. The best clay on many peasant crofts was probably worked out at an early date. It was probably only when new supplies had to be taken from waste land or common land that payment became general. At West Cowick (Yorks.) it has been suggested that the sharp increase in payment in the second half of the 14th century is associated with the taking of clay and sand from the moor.[2]

Suitable clay for making medieval pottery and tile was available all over the country and the fabric of medieval pottery varies accordingly. An increasing amount

1   L. Keen and D. Thackray, 'A 14th-century Mosaic Tile Pavement with Line-impressed Decoration from Icklingham', *Proc., Suffolk Inst. Arch.* n.s. xxxiii (1973-5), 154, n. 12; E.C. Norton, 'Medieval Paving Tiles of Winchester College', *Proc. Hants Field Club & Arch. Soc.*, xxxi (1976), 23-42.

2   H.E.J. Le Patourel, 'Documentary Evidence and the Medieval Pottery Industry', *Med. Arch.* xii (1968), 114.

of work has been carried out in an attempt to relate the fabric of medieval pottery and tile to its clay sources by petrological analysis of the clay. For instance, Alan Vince's study of the medieval ceramic industry of the Malvern region showed that Malvernian products could be defined petrologically by the inclusion of igneous Malvernian rock fragments derived from the central spine of the Malvern Hills. This identification of source has enabled a pattern of development and distribution of both types of product to be traced from the 13th to the 16th century for that industry.[3]

### *Tiles: Manufacturing Process*

Our evidence for the making of tiles comes from the archaeological investigation of manufacturing sites, the tiles themselves, and from documentary material. From the latter, for example, an ideal picture of the time needed for the preparation of clay is given by the ordinance passed in 1477, which stated that clay should be dug by 1 November, turned before the beginning of February, and not made into tiles before March.[4] This ideal practice may not always have been followed.

The clay was stacked quite close to the workshop, as at Danbury (Essex) where it was placed in the northern part of the enclosures. The clay for roof tiles there would have received little preparation before the tiles were manufactured; evidence from Danbury would suggest this took place in a large timber-framed building.[5]

Although no contemporary documentation tells us how tiles were made in the medieval period, later practice suggests that they were shaped in a 'form' on a sanded board or table. The board was clearly sanded, since sand can still be found to be present fired into the undersides of tiles. The 'form' may well have been a wooden mould without top or bottom. The clay would be thrown into the 'form' and forced into the corners and then any clay left above the top of the mould would have been cut off with a knife or wire. For floor tiles, the sides of the tile were then trimmed to produce a bevelled edge and sometimes holes or 'keys' were scooped in the bottom of tiles. The tile would then be taken to the 'hack stead' to dry. At Danbury this was a large open-sided timber-framed building sited close to one of the kilns. After the tiles had dried they were decorated in a number of ways that will be discussed later. No equipment has yet been discovered at a tilery, and so for details of the type of equipment used one has to turn to Hull where the equipment of the brickyard was listed in 1425 as four wheelbarrows, three sand tubs, three forming stocks, one sty(?) which was 15 steles long, 14 old spars, three fletes, one trough, and five forms for the making of tile. At other times in Hull, shovels and water tubs are mentioned.[6]

3    A. Vince, 'The Medieval and Post Medieval Ceramic Industry of the Malvern Region: the Study of a Ware and its Distribution', in D.P.S. Peacock (ed.), *Pottery and Early Commerce* (1977), 257-302.

4    *Rot. Parl.* vi, 189 (17 Edw. IV).

5    P.J. Drury and G.D. Pratt, 'A Late 13th- and Early 14th-Century Tile Factory at Danbury, Essex', *Med. Arch.* xix (1975), 92-164.

6    F.W. Brooks, 'A Medieval Brickyard at Hull', *J.B.A.A.*, 3rd ser. iv (1939), 151-74.

Both floor and roof tiles were glazed. In England the glaze was applied to the unfired tiles. The basic glaze was lead, which could be prepared in several different ways. A 13th-century recipe is given in an addition to the 12th-century work of Theophilus:

> Take three earthenware jars and place them in the oven, and put in about two talents of lead.... When this has melted put in salt, and stir it diligently with a long iron rod with a round head, until it is well burnt. Then add nine parts of well-washed sand to the ashes and stir it with the rounded iron rod until it has liquefied completely. When it has melted take it out of the oven with tongs, and pour it on the ground. After it has solidified and hardened into glass, crush it with a pestle and sieve it. Lastly, mix these prepared ashes with sour wine or watered ale, paint this on the dry but unfired tiles with a brush and place the tiles in the kiln.[7]

Different colours were achieved by different additions. The lead glaze over a tile fired in an oxidising atmosphere looks brown. Addition of copper to the glaze gives a deep green, while the addition of more copper or iron gives a black colour.

Only a few pieces of archaeological evidence have been found for this process: one is the small earthenware mortar found at the site of the abbey tilery at North Grange, Meaux (Yorks.) where decorated floor tiles were made between 1249 and 1269, which could have been used for crushing the glass as referred to in the passage from Theophilus. Ash of lead oxide was found in a shallow flat-bottomed earthenware dish at the same site.[8]

Floor tiles were fired in wood-burning updraught rectangular kilns. The furnace was divided in two by a spine wall. This arrangement can be seen in the kiln excavated at Clarendon Palace (Wilts.) and now preserved in the British Museum (see Fig.87). The two chambers of the furnace were spanned by a series of arches from the spine to the side walls. The floor of the oven usually consisted of two or three layers of roof tile placed on top of the rows that bridged the gaps between the arches. The gap between the rear arch and the back wall was usually left open to act as a flue. The height of the oven is not known, but it is unlikely to have been built up more than 1.5 yards above the oven floor. The unfired tiles were stood on edge, placed so that the glazed face of one was toward the unglazed base of the next, with a space between so that they did not touch. The oven had no permanent roof but probably had a temporary cover of roof tiles or other pieces of fired tile. Kiln firing was usually carried out in the summer. It has been estimated that the temperature of the kiln would have been raised from a slow-drying firing (up to 200°C) to the higher temperature at which the glaze would be fired (*c*. 1000°C). The total firing of a kiln

7    J.S. Gardner and E.S. Eames, 'A Tile Kiln at Chertsey Abey', *J.B.A.A.* 3rd ser. xvii (1954), 27-8 and 42. Also quoted in E. Eames, *Catalogue of Medieval Lead-glazed Earthenware Tiles* (1980), 21. The manuscript reference is B.L.,

MS Harl. 3915, ff.146ᵛ-7ᵛ.
8    E.S. Eames, 'A 13th-Century Tile Kiln Site at North Grange Meaux, Beverley, Yorks', *Med. Arch.* v (1961), 137-68.

*Fig. 87* Tile-kiln excavated at Clarendon Palace (Wilts.) in 1937 and now reconstructed in the British Museum. This was used for firing the King's Chapel pavement in 1240-44.

probably took about a week. Kilns that were used regularly would not last for long even with regular repairs. Although most excavated kilns are similar to that found at Clarendon (with two parallel furnace chambers) other types such as the double-ended kiln at Chilvers Coton may have been quite widely used.[9]

Kilns for firing roof tiles were basically of the same nature as the floor tile kilns. They tended to be larger than the floor tile kilns and less carefully constructed, since the temperature required to fire unglazed roof tiles successfully is lower than that required for glazed wares. Roof tile kilns are known from North Grange, Meaux and Boston (Lincs.).[10]

The terms 'tiler' and 'paviour' can apply to either a worker with ceramic tile or a worker with stone or slate[11] (and see above pp.19-21). Throughout the medieval period the word 'tiler' (Latin *tegulator*) could mean either a maker or a fixer of tiles. Occasionally the same person may have done both. It may be assumed – though it is not certain – that Elias the Tiler who in 1352 laid 8,000 tiles in the floor of the chapter house of St. George's, Windsor (Berks.) also made them.[12] For a pictorial mosaic, such as that found at Old Warden (Beds.), the manufacture and laying clearly went together. The tilers who formed gilds in towns were presumably tile-fixers rather than tile-makers. The Lincoln gild founded in 1346 was of tilers commonly called

9   P. Mayes and K. Scott, *Pottery Kilns at Chilvers Coton, Nuneaton* (1984), 60, and Pl. V a.

10  P. Mayes, 'A Medieval Tile Kiln at Boston, Lincolnshire', *J.B.A.A.* 3rd ser. xxviii (1965), 86-107. For North Grange at Meaux see note 8.

11  E.M. Jope and G.C. Dunning, 'The Use of Blue Slate for Roofing in Medieval England', *Antiq. Jnl.* xxxiv (1954), 209-11. The term 'sclater' refers solely to workers in stone but the word 'paviour' can apply to either tile or stone. More work is needed on the geographical occurrences of tiler and slater names in relationship to the material employed in particular areas.

12  Eames, op. cit. note 7, 222.

'poyntours' (derived from the practice of sealing the gaps with mortar).[13]

The word 'tiler' can also mean someone who makes either floor or roof tiles. Unless the type of tile is specifically indicated in a document, the only way to distinguish between roof tile and floor tile is by price. Decorated floor tiles sold at between 6s. and 8s. a thousand in the late 14th century, while roof tiles were much cheaper.[14]

Most Tyler names are of men though occasionally women do appear, mainly as suppliers of tiles. Constance Tiler supplied tiles at 10s. a thousand in York in 1327 and Katherine Lightfoote supplied 2,000 tiles for the king's bathroom at Sheen in the period 1384-8.[15]

Crests, the elaborate roof tiles that protected the ridge of the roof, could be supplied by a potter. In 1373 John Pottere of Cheam (Surrey) was paid for two crests made in the fashion of mounted knights for the hall.[16] There is also a reference to a crest-maker at Lyveden (Northants.).[17]

### Roof Tiles

The use of different materials for roofing in the Middle Ages needs more study. Regional differences may reflect either the types of crop that were grown or the prevalence of local materials. Thatch was one of the most widespread of roofing materials, and straw or reed thatch was used according to the area. Thatch was not used for buildings of importance, and worries about its inflammability caused its use to be discouraged in towns. However, it served as the commonest type of roof well into the Tudor period. Shingles were commonly used where there was a good supply of oak. A 15th-century or older treatise on accounting comments that the cost of shingles is twice or thrice that of ceramic roof tiles.[18] Stone slates were frequently used in the limestone areas. Swithland slates were particularly used in Leicester in the medieval period.[19] There was also a considerable export trade in blue slates from Devon and Cornwall from the 12th to the 15th century. At Winchester such slates were used on royal buildings from the 12th century and large quantities were used in the city in the 14th and 15th centuries.[20]

Geographically the principal use of roof tile seems to have been in the south-east of England. Although by the 14th century the production of roof tiles occurred as far west as Somerset, as far north as York and even in North Wales at Denbigh,[21] it is

13  L. Toulmin Smith, *English Guilds* (Early English Text Soc. orig. ser. xl, 1870), 184-5.
14  J.E.T. Rogers, *A History of Agriculture and Prices in England:*, ii, *1259-1400*, 434-439 gives a range of prices for ordinary roof tiles.
15  Salzman, *Building in England*, 230; Eames, op. cit. note 7, 223.
16  Salzman, *Building in England*, 231.
17  J.M. Steane, 'Excavations at Lyveden, 1965-7', *Jnl. Northampton Museum*, ii (1967), 27-9.
18  Gloucester Cathedral Library, MS 33, quoted by D. Oschinsky, *Walter of Henley* (1971), 475.
19  C. Allin, The Roofing Slate, in J.E. Mellor and T. Pearce, *The Austin Friars Leicester* (1981), 67.
20  D. Keene, *Survey of Winchester*, Winchester Studies 2 (1985) i, 173; Jope and Dunning, art. cit. note 11, 209-11.
21  R. Newstead, 'A Medieval Potter's Kiln at Denbigh', *Archaeologia Cambrensis*, xciii (1938), 256-262.

clear that extensive tile manufacture beyond the limestone belt was uncommon at the end of the Middle Ages. It is noticeable that in Exeter there are no crests or other roof tile fragments among the 12th- and 13th-century deposits; although stratified crest fragments are present there in deposits dating from after 1250, the earliest sizeable groups belong to the 15th century.[22] London must always have needed a great number of tiles for its many buildings. There was a considerable production for the City in the Smithfield area. In the later 14th and 15th centuries Woolwich was a principal centre of supply for London and Westminster.[23]

In the 14th century Penn in Buckinghamshire became a major supplier of roof tiles in the Thames Valley. They were used at Windsor Castle, Westminster and the Tower of London. The Penn subsidy roll of 1332 gives some indication of the number of tilers and their relative prosperity. The tilers were the only villagers who were taxed on non-agricultural wealth. For instance, Henry the Tyler was assessed at 24s.; his property comprised one cow, one quarter of mixed grain, three quarters of oats, 7,000 tiles and five quarters of lime, indicating substantial dependence on agriculture. Production at Penn expanded considerably in the middle and latter part of the 14th century, possibly owing to the economic stimulus provided by the building works of Edward III at Windsor.[24]

All these were commercial tileries, operating on a small scale. There is some evidence that monasteries, particularly in the South-East, had their own tileries and invested considerable sums in establishing them. Both Boxley and Battle Abbeys had tileries and Battle Abbey also owned the great tileworks in the Kentish manor of Wye. It was Salzman who drew attention to the series of accounts relating to these tileworks from 1330 to 1380, and apart from his summary little further research has been carried out on these accounts. In 1355 the output of 10 kilns was 98,500 plain or flat tiles, 500 *festeux* (either ridge or gutter tiles) and 1,000 corners. The total expenses were £8 5s. 0d.[25]

Ceramic roof tiling was first used in England in the 12th century and the whole range of plain tile fittings that are available to the modern tiler had been developed by the late 13th century. This included ridge tiles, hip tiles, valley tiles and half tiles.

In London a large assemblage of late 12th-century tiles has been found behind the late 12th-century revetments of the Thames waterfront. These comprise three types: peg tiles, shouldered peg tiles and flanged and curved tiles used rather like Roman roof tiles. The flat tiles had flanges on their long sides and the gaps between these were covered with curved tiles to produce an effect rather like the later pantiles. This type of tiling may have been introduced into England by tilers working on Norman castles and abbeys since similar tiles have been found in early contexts at Reading Abbey.[26] Shouldered peg tiles would have overlapped by two-thirds of their surface

22  J.P. Allan, *Medieval and Post Medieval Finds from Exeter, 1971-80* (1984), 227.
23  Salzman, *Building in England*, 230.
24  C. Hohler, 'Medieval Paving Tiles in Buckinghamshire', *Records of Bucks.* xiv (1942), 1-49, 99-131.
25  Salzman, *English Industries*, 177, and Salzman, *Building in England*, 230.
26  K.H. Armitage, J.E. Pearce and A.G. Vince, 'Early Medieval Roof-tiles from London', *Antiq. Journ.* lxi (1981), 359-62. For Reading see A. Vince, forthcoming.

as opposed to half of the surface for ordinary peg tiles. A roof covered with shouldered peg tiles would have been much heavier than either ordinary peg tiles or flanged and curved tiles and this may be the reason for their disappearance in the 13th century.

There were variations in the sizes of plain roof tiles. Among the smallest are those from Eynsford Castle (Kent) which measured nine inches by five. At the other extreme the very high price charged for roof tiles in York suggests that these may have been of exceptional dimensions.[27] In an attempt to remedy the lack of uniformity in tile size, an ordinance was passed in 1477 which stated that the standard for flat tiles should be 10½ by 6¼ inches with a thickness of at least ⅝ inch; ridge tiles or crests should be 13½ by 6¼ inches and gutter tiles 10½ inches long. This indicates that it was usual for one ridge tile to cover two plain tiles, as is confirmed by the archaeological evidence from Joydens Wood (Kent) and Southampton.[28] However, 19-inch-long ridge tiles have also been found at sites such as Penhallam (Cornwall) and Southampton. These would have covered three plain tiles.[29]

The earliest archaeological and documentary evidence for medieval ridge tiles dates from the 13th century. The crest of the ridge was often decorated with shapes such as knife-cut or moulded triangles (sometimes called 'cocks comb'), or with loops of clay, or knife-cut steps. The typology of ridge crests has been studied principally for the Midlands and less so for other areas.[30]

Louvers are structures in the centre of the roof to enable smoke to escape without letting in the rain. On grander buildings they were made of wood, often with horizontal slats which sometimes could be regulated by louver strings.[31] Pottery louvers, which could not be regulated in the same way, are of two types. The first is made in one piece with a ridge. The simplest of this type is a ridge tile with side vents; others rise up above the ridge by as much as 12 to 15 inches. At Goosegate, Nottingham, a notable example of this type was found with three tiers of apertures and with flanges and canopies to keep out the rain and wind. The second type is a separate structure inserted into a circular hole in a platform in the centre of the roof; this is represented by the Great Easton louver. The archaeological evidence suggests a date range for ceramic louvers of *c.* 1250 to *c.* 1425. No specific trade of louver maker

27  S.E. Rigold, 'Excavations at Eynsford Castle', *Archaeologia Cantiana*, lxxxvi (1971), 109-71; Salzman, *Building in England*, 230.

28  P.J. Tester and J.E.L. Caiger, 'Medieval Buildings in Joydens Wood', *Archaeologia Cantiana*, lxxxii (1959), 27, Fig. 3; C. Platt and R. Coleman Smith, *Excavations in Medieval Southampton, 1953-1969* (1975), ii, 214, No. 1409.

29  G. Beresford, 'Penhallam, Cornwall', *Med. Arch.* xviii (1974), 135, Fig. 43; Platt and Coleman Smith, op. cit. note 28, 192, Nos. 1395, 1401.

30  Attention was first drawn to the development

of pottery ridge tiles by E.M. Jope, 'The Development of Pottery Ridge Tiles in the Oxford Region', *Oxoniensia*, xvi (1951), 86-8. Subsequent studies are J.M. Steane, 'Excavations at Lyveden, 1965-7', *Jnl. Northampton Museum*, ii (1967), 27-9; Clare E. Allin, 'The Ridge Tiles', in Mellor and Pearce, op. cit. note 19, 52-70. The regional and chronological variations in ridge crest typology need further study.

31  Margaret Wood, *The English Medieval House* (1966), 277-80.

*Fig. 88* Pottery roof-finial in the form
of a human face. Late 13th or early 14th
century. From Reading.
(*British Museum, 1966, 4-1, 1*)

has been identified and it seems that ceramic louvers were fired in pottery kilns like ridge tiles.[32]

Finials of stone, wood, or pottery were used from the 11th century onwards to decorate the gable ends of the ridges of medieval roofs. Some were in the form of spikes, others like human faces, and some represented standing animals such as horses, bears, dragons or lions (Fig.88).[33]

Chimney pots of baked clay were used in south-eastern and southern England from the 13th century. They do not occur elsewhere and their use is clearly a regional speciality. Up to 15 inches high, they are conical, being wider at the base and tapering to the top. They often have two holes, one in each side to increase the up-draught. It seems that they were often used on a ground-floor hall or manor house with an open timber roof. Chimney pot fragments have been found at medieval kiln sites, notably at Laverstock (Wilts.) where they occur alongside other roofing materials such as ridge tiles and finials. They were probably produced by potters rather than tilers.[34]

32  For louvers see G.C. Dunning, 'A Pottery Louver from Great Easton, Essex', *Med. Arch.* x (1966), 74-80.

33  For finials see Wood, op. cit. note 31, 296-9; G.C. Dunning, 'A Horse and Knight Roof Finial' in D. Baker, 'Excavations in Bedford', *Beds. Arch. Jnl.* ix (1974), 99-128; G.C. Dunning

in L. Ketteringham, *Alsted* (Surrey Arch. Soc. Research Reports 2, 1976), and J. Fairbrother, *Excavations at Netherton*, forthcoming.

34  G.C. Dunning, 'Medieval Chimney Pots', in E.M. Jope (ed.), *Studies in Building History* (1961), 78-93.

*Floor Tiles*

We know very little about the way in which the tile industry was organised. The only evidence is the tiles and kilns themselves and occasionally, at the end of the period, records of purchases of tiles. The discovery of decorated floor tiles at major Anglo-Saxon monastic sites such as Winchester, St. Albans, Bury St. Edmunds and Canterbury suggests that monastic patronage played a large part in the organisation of their production.[35]

Two-coloured tiles were produced in the second quarter of the 13th century, probably by foreign craftsmen and perhaps under royal or monastic patronage. It is therefore likely that the kilns were created for specific flooring programmes connected with major royal or monastic buildings and were used until that programme was completed. The kiln excavated at the royal palace of Clarendon illustrates this (Fig. 87), and provides one example of a type of kiln which may have been far more widespread. Monastic building programmes were often spread over long periods: it may be that tileries were established initially for paving the monastery but subsequently went on to serve other monastic houses, and even came to operate in a commercial manner. It is possible that the tile kiln excavated at Repton provides an example of this.[36]

Until recently it was the accepted view that commercial tile industries were not established until the 14th century. It now seems clear, however, that commercial tile production was already being undertaken in the last quarter of the 13th century in at least two areas: the South Midlands, where the 'stabbed Wessex' series of tiles were produced, and Essex, where the 'central Essex' group of tiles were made. Commercial tileries in the 14th century were sited sometimes in towns, such as Nottingham, sometimes outside towns as at Tyler Hill near Canterbury, and occasionally in the country, as at Penn in Buckinghamshire.[37]

The mosaic tiles for the northern Cistercian abbeys such as Fountains, Byland, Rievaulx or Meaux were probably made from local clay and fired in kilns at each site. A sequence for paving the different Cistercian sites in northern England –Fountains, Byland, Rievaulx, Newbattle, Meaux, Newminster, Thornton – has been worked out on the supposition that the number and complexity of the mosaic arrangements increased as time went on.[38]

During the 14th and 15th centuries there is evidence for the increasing use of tiles in royal buildings, manor houses, and town houses. However, it seems likely that

35   R. Gem and L. Keen, 'Late Anglo-Saxon Finds from the Site of St. Edmunds Abbey', *Proc. Suffolk Inst. of Arch.* xxxv (1981-4), 1-30.

36   The best account of the Clarendon tiles is in Eames, op. cit. note 7, 186-200.

37   For a lengthier study of the development of commercialised tile production see ibid., 278-283. The situation in the North Midlands is discussed by John Cherry, 'The Develop-ment of Tile Production in the North Midlands of England' in D. Deroeux (ed.), *Terres Cuites Architecturales au Moyen Age* (Arras, 1986), 227-33.

38   E.S. Eames and G.K. Beaulah, 'The 13th-Century Tile Mosaic Pavements in the York-shire Cistercian Houses', *Cîteaux in de Nederlanden*, vii (Antwerp, 1956), 264-77, Pls. i and ii.

*Fig. 89* Segment of a circular pattern from the first-floor chapel, Clarendon Palace, built for Henry III by Elias of Dereham, 1240-4; assembled in the British Museum from tiles removed during excavation and plaster casts. (*British Museum*)

ecclesiastical and monastic institutions provided a major stimulus to the craft. Indeed, from the mid 15th to the early 16th century the tile-making industry flourished under monastic patronage. The late medieval tiles from Malvern and Hailes are among some of the finest products of the industry.

Floor tiles were used for paving the principal rooms of palaces, churches and – in the later Middle Ages – of manor houses and large town houses. Surviving pavements are mainly in or from churches or monastic sites; smaller fragments of paving *in situ* occur in parish churches. The design of tile pavements is made up of two features: the division into panels, where the pattern is created by a number of tiles, and the decoration of the surface of each tile.

The only surviving pavements from an English royal palace are those from Clarendon (Wilts.) displayed in the British Museum. The pavement from the King's Chapel (laid in 1240-44) is circular, even though the chapel itself was rectangular in shape. It consists (Fig.89) of bands of narrow green-glazed tiles alternating with bands of wider brown and yellow tiles. The other pavement from Clarendon, from the ground floor of the chamber block built for Queen Philippa by Elias of Dereham in 1251-2, demonstrates how tiles could be used as single designs, or using one or two designs to make groups of four. The panels are divided by strips of plain tiles.[39]

39   The two pavements from Clarendon are illustrated in E.S. Eames, *English Medieval Tiles* (1985), Pls. 13, 61, and Eames, op. cit. note 7, Pl. VIa, V.
A full discussion is given by E.S. Eames, 'A Decorated Tile Pavement from the Queen's Chamber, Clarendon Palace, Wiltshire, dated 1250-2', *British Museum Quarterly*, xxii (1960), 34-7; and E.S. Eames, 'A 13th-Century Tiled Pavement from the King's Chapel, Clarendon Palace', *J.B.A.A.* 3rd ser. xxvi (1963), 40-50.

The most impressive surviving pavement is that in the chapter-house at Westminster Abbey, completed by 1258-9. This is laid in long rectangular strips although the building itself is octagonal. The octagonal chapter-house at Salisbury is the only medieval English building where it is clear that the 13th-century tile floor was deliberately designed in relation to the structure, although this medieval floor no longer exists.[40]

The tile mosaic pavements found principally at Cistercian abbeys such as Byland and Rievaulx are composed of rectangular and square panels, some having circles in them. The panels are divided by borders formed of mosaic tiles. This type of arrangement may have been developd in imitation of Italian stone mosaic floors. The late 13th-century pavement at Cleeve Abbey (Somerset) shows how diagonally set heraldic tiles divided by a thin border could be used to floor the refectory of a modest Cistercian house. The flooring of the east end of a major abbey church is illustrated by the pavement made in 1455 to the order of Abbot Sebrok at Gloucester. This is composed of panels each of which comprises sixteen inlaid tiles and four inlaid divided by strips of plain tiles.[41]

A similar arrangement of sixteen and four tile patterns divided by plain tiles is found in the pavement laid between 1481 and 1515 in the house that belonged to William Canynges of Bristol (now in the British Museum). Another pavement from a private house, Clifton House in King's Lynn, is composed of long thin panels divided by single tile borders; within the panels the tiles are arranged in a number of different ways. These include groups of alternating four-tile patterns with differently coloured plain tiles and plain and patterned tiles arranged in alternating chevrons.[42]

Within the decorative panels the tiles could be arranged in a number of ways, the most complex arrangement being that of pictorial tile mosaic. At Warden Abbey (Beds.) arabic numerals were used as an aid to laying. Some individual pieces have the names of the parts written on them, notably *tibia* (for shin or leg), *pes* (foot) and *sella* (saddle).[43] Plain mosaic pavements that appear complex are often found on examination to be composed of a limited number of shapes. Two-colour tiles were laid in a number of ways, either as single designs, or in groups of four, nine or sixteen tile patterns. These larger patterns can be built up in a number of ways, depending on the number of repeats in the pattern. The patterns themselves can then be used as small panels.

40   The chapter-house of Salisbury Cathedral was repaved in the 19th century. For the medieval pavement see H. Shaw, *Specimens of Tile Pavements* (1858), Pls. xxiii, xxiv.

41   For Westminster see P.B. Clayton, 'The Inlaid Tiles of Westminster', *Arch. Jnl.* lxix (1912), 36-73. For Cleeve, see J.B. Ward-Perkins, 'A Late 13th-century Tile Pavement from Cleeve Abbey', *Proc., Somerset Arch. and Natural History Soc.* lxxxvii (1941), 39-55. Part of Sebrok's pavement is illustrated in Eames, op. cit. note 39, Pl. 14, from Shaw, op. cit. note 40.

42   Plans and discussions of these two major tile pavements are in E.S. Eames, 'Decorated Tile Pavements in English Medieval Houses', in J.G.N. Renaud (ed.), *Rotterdam Papers*, ii (Rotterdam, 1975).

43   E. Baker, 'Craftsmanship and Design in Floors for the Wealthy – Some Implications of the Warden Abbey Tile Pavements', in J.G.N. Renaud (ed.), *Rotterdam Papers*, iv (Rotterdam, 1982), 5-21.

*Fig. 90* Panel of inlaid mosaic tiles from Chertsey Abbey (Surrey) showing the combat between Richard I and Saladin; *c.* 1250. (*British Museum*)

The surfaces could be decorated in a number of ways. Decoration was produced with wooden stamps, altough it is possible that for the very fine tiles produced at Chertsey metal stamps were used (Fig. 90).[44] Carved stamps were often used to produce relief tiles whose decoration is either above the surface or below it in counter-relief; alternatively, stamps were occasionally used to make line-impressed patterns. For inlaid tiles a stamp was used to impress a pattern which was then filled with white clay. Many two-colour tiles are inlaid in this way, though in the late 13th and 14th centuries techniques were developed which involved either covering the whole of the surface with white slip and stamping through it, or else filling in pre-stamped cavities with a thick white slip. An unusual technique for English tiles is the use of *sgraffito* that occurs on a series of tiles from Tring (Herts.), decorated with figural scenes illustrating the childhood of Christ from the Apocryphal Gospels.[45]

## Pottery

In the 7th century wheel-made pottery was produced in East Anglia and Northumbria. Over the rest of England at this period only hand-made pottery was produced. By 900 wheel-thrown pottery had spread over a large part of eastern

---

44   The use of metal stamps at Chertsey is suggested by Eames, op. cit. note 7, 153-4.
45   For the Tring tiles see ibid., 56-61, and M.R.

James, 'Rare Medieval Tiles and their Story',
*Burlington Magazine*, xiii (1923), 32-7.

England and by 950 was made in some thirty centres, although not in the north-west and only in some parts of southern England. In the 11th century there was apparently an increase in hand-made pottery. Wheel-made pottery was made at urban centres and the rural ones were slow to adopt the use of the wheel. In the 13th century some of the potters at Lyveden (Northants.) and Ham Green (Bristol) still produced pottery by hand.[46]

We have no direct evidence of the nature of the wheels used in the production of medieval pottery. Pottery could be made on a turntable. A French 13th-century illustration shows a potter using the right hand for turning the wheel with a stick and the left hand for raising the pot from the inside.[47] A recent study of pottery from Haarlem distinguishes between two different types of wheel. One is the kick wheel, where the bottom of the vertically set wheel is kicked around leaving the hands free for raising the pot. The other consists of a large cartwheel on a vertical pivot with a small turntable fastened in the centre; the 'cart wheel' has the characteristic of tending to revolve more slowly. The study of the Haarlem potters concluded that they used the 'cart wheel', but in England it is likely that both types of wheel were used.[48]

There is very little evidence as to the actual tools used by the potters. It can be assumed from the pots themselves that various decorative implements such as knives, combs and roulettes were used and that slip was applied with such implements as cowhorns. A few tools have been found in and around kilns and workshops, but the knives and combs that may have been used to decorate pots are difficult to distinguish from similar items used for domestic purposes. Some tools from Lyveden show how particular features on the pots were made. Bung holes, for instance, were probably pierced by worked and pointed antler tines. Sharpened bones at the Ashton (Cheshire) kiln site were used to produce incised decoration. Stamps and moulds, made of earthenware, stone or bone, were cut to produce grid patterns, human heads, or animals. Two examples found at a kiln site at St. Mary le Wigford (Lincoln) are of hard-baked clay. They are a lady with an elaborate nebuly headdress that may be dated to the 1360s or 1370s, and a bearded man's head.[49]

Glaze was used decoratively on the outside of jugs. It is rarely found on cooking pots, and only from the 14th century is it found on the inside of cooking vessels and bowls where it had a more functional use. Some vessels containing residues of glaze ingredients have been found on kiln sites. At the Hallgate (Doncaster) kilns a shelly ware vessel contained residues of lead compounds, and was interpreted as having

46   For mid and late Saxon pottery see J.G. Hurst, 'The Pottery', in D.M. Wilson (ed.), *The Archaeology of Anglo-Saxon England* (1976), 283-348.

47   Singer, *History of Technology*, ii (1956), 288.

48   S.E. van der Leeuw, 'Medieval Pottery from Haarlem: a Model', in Renaud, op. cit. note 42, 67-87.

49   A. Trollope, *Meeting of the Archaeological Institute at Lincoln, 1848* (1850), xliii; and S. Moorhouse, 'The Medieval Pottery Industry and its Markets', in D.W. Crossley (ed.), *Medieval Industry* (C..B.A. Research Rep. xl, 1981), 106.

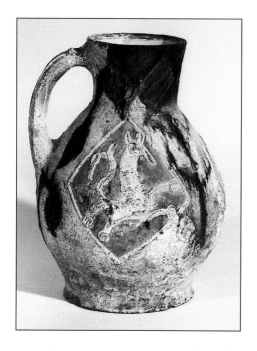

*Fig. 91* Pottery jug found in Cannon St.,
London showing use of slip and green, brown,
and clear-coloured glazes. Late 13th century.
(*British Museum 56, 7-1, 1566*)

been used to produce glaze.[50] Glaze was usually applied with a brush, though particularly in the 11th and 12th centuries it appears often to have been splashed or flicked onto the surface of the vessels.

Excavation has produced an increasing amount of evidence for pottery production sites. Recent discoveries have been well synthesised in two articles[51] and since these contain much information on the subject, only a few general remarks are made here. Excavations have usually been only of the kilns themselves and not of the surrounding structures. A potter would require a workshop, a kiln and a covered area to dry the pots and store them after firing. At Lyveden (Northants.) an excavated pottery working area revealed stone-lined wall footings and opposed entrances with a clay store in a lean-to at the rear. Areas of paving and pairs of stones were interpreted as a store shed.[52]

It is the structure of kilns that has received most attention. Medieval kilns were updraught and have been classified by the number of holes through which fires were drawn in from the outside. Single-flue kilns appear in the pre-Conquest period. Double-flue and multi-flue kilns were introduced in the 13th century and the latter became the commonest type in the late Middle Ages.[53]

The superstructure of kilns has not survived, so the nature of the roofing remains

50   P.C. Buckland, M.J. Dolby, C. Hayfield, and J.R. Magilton, *The Medieval Pottery Industry at Hallgate, Doncaster* (1979), 12, 51, Fig. 19, No. 528, 53.

51   The two articles are Moorhouse, op. cit. note

49, and J. Musty, 'Medieval Pottery Kilns', in V.I. Evison, H. Hodges and J.G. Hurst (ed.), *Medieval Pottery from Excavations* (1974).

52   Moorhouse, op. cit. note 49, 88-9, Figs. 83-4.

53   Musty, op. cit. note 51.

an open question. Some kilns (notably at Thetford) have provided evidence that the clay dome had collapsed into the oven pit, sealing the smashed remains of the stacked pots. One of the kilns at Laverstock (Wilts.) had the lower layers of jugs in position, with no sign of a clay dome above.[54] The multi-flue kilns with a walk-in entrance probably always had a permanent structure above.

Many kilns had internal structures to support the floor or to enable the pots to be raised above the entry of the fire. However, in the multi-flue kiln the pots were usually stacked on the floor. Saggars (vessels made specifically to protect the pottery) are not known in medieval kilns, though it is possible that cooking pots may have served to protect odd-shaped vessels such as aquamaniles or statuettes. Kiln props (long cylindrical or dumb-bell-shaped pots) are known mainly from multi-flue kilns. From the way that the glaze has run on many jugs, it is clear that they were stacked upside down.

The three fuels that were available to the medieval potter were coal, wood and peat. The use of coal was restricted to the coalmining areas in the Midlands and Yorkshire. Peat was particularly used in eastern England and evidence has been produced for the use of peat at both Cowick (Yorks.) and Toynton (Lincs.). The wood used was likely to have been in the form of bundles of loppings or brushwood. In 1355 at the manor of Wye in Kent a thousand bundles were required for the burning of ten tile kilns, at a total cost of 45*s*. This suggests that the cost of fuel in a small pottery kiln was quite low.[55]

The term potter by itself is ambiguous since it could mean a worker in either clay or metal (see Blair and Blair, above, p.93). Sometimes the meaning is made clear either by context or by the price of the goods supplied. In the town a potter must be considered to be a metal potter unless there is proof to the contrary, while in a village he can be assumed to be a clay worker unless there is other evidence. The words crocker, *figulus* and *figulator* were restricted to the clay potter.

Down to the end of the 12th century the surname may be assumed to have remained an occupational name, and to indicate a working potter. In the course of the 13th century the working potters are increasingly joined by other potters who do not bear the craft surname, whilst there are references to the surname in a context which makes it clear that the bearer followed a different trade. Towards the end of the 13th century, some villages added the term Potter as a prefix: thus Lyveden (Northants.) is recorded as Potters Lyveden in 1285 and Marston (Leics.) is recorded as Potters Marston from 1267[56]

The pottery industry appears to have been more prosperous in the 11th century than in the later Middle Ages. The archaeological evidence from the east of England suggests a sophisticated urban industry producing a wide range of products. St. Neots ware production, of a shelly unglazed ware, was principally of jugs and

54  J.W. Musty, D. Algar, and P.F. Ewence, 'The Medieval Pottery Kilns at Laverstock, near Salisbury, Wiltshire', *Archaeologia*, cii

(1969), 83-150.
55  Le Patourel, art. cit. note 2, 117.
56  Ibid. 124.

inturned bowls used more for culinary or dairy purposes, whilst the finer glazed pottery of Stamford, in a white clay, was used more for vessels for the table and drinking.[57]

The picture of the industry revealed by Domesday Book is geographically quite different. Only three potteries are mentioned – in Oxfordshire, Gloucestershire and Wiltshire. They all paid remarkably high sums. At Westbury in Wiltshire the payment was 20*s*. per year. It may be that pottery was more profitable at this time than it was later in the Middle Ages, though we know nothing of the precise way in which it was organised.[58]

In the 13th to the 15th centuries the potters were among the poorest groups of the craftsmen. In the country potting was often pursued as a part-time occupation in conjunction with small-scale agriculture. Even in towns potters were among the poorest members of the taxable population when they figure in the records at all. In many towns where kilns have been discovered, such as Exeter, Nottingham and Lincoln, there is a total absence of documentary evidence for the activities of potters. In Colchester, in the subsidy of 1301, the only person mentioned who appears to have been a potter was among the bottom 11% of the taxable population.[59]

There do not appear to be any references to potters in the late 14th-century poll tax returns where so many trades are indicated. The lack of profit in the craft must have been the principal reason why the urban clay potters (unlike the metal potters) never achieved any formal gild organisation. Some potters, particularly in smaller towns, were quite well established. Adam Beneyth at Woodstock (Oxon.) in 1279 had a tenement with a kiln and garden, with two stalls and a workshop all joined together with a small yard outside the workshop.[60]

In the countryside the majority of clay potters were cottagers with holdings of land in the three to five acre range. At Cowick (Yorks.), where from 1375 to 1400 five potters were paying 20*s*. each annually in clay rent – the highest payment yet found in England – the potters were only part-time workers giving their main attention to agricultural land. Pottery was often a subsidiary craft which formed part of a web of interwoven rural activity, of which little evidence found its way into the written record.

Potters did not have apprentices and only rarely had paid assistants. Additional help could be provided by the family or by hired labour. Most potters mentioned in the documents are men but in Woodstock (Oxon.) Agnes Siber rented a kiln for a penny a year. There is some evidence, notably at Toynton (Lincs.), that sons followed their fathers as potters. Family involvement in potting, as well as the part-time nature of the work, may have encouraged the tendency of the pottery industry to last for a very long time in the same place. The Black Death in the mid-14th century wiped out the potting community at Hanley (Worcs.) but at Ringmer (Sussex) the plague reduced the numbers of the potters without destroying the industry.[61]

57   Hurst, art. cit. note 46, 320-26.
58   Le Patourel, art. cit. note 2, 102-6.
59   Ibid. 113.
60   Ibid. 109.
61   Ibid. 108.

The quantity of evidence for the products of the medieval pottery industry is large and this is not the place for a general review of all the pottery types; a general introductory idea of the principal types may be obtained from the surveys by Rackham, Hurst and Jennings.[62] All that will be attempted here is an indication of the pattern of changes in both the form of vessels and the nature of the industry.

Pottery-making in the Middle Ages was conservative. Both fabrics and forms persisted for long periods. The late Saxon spouted pitcher lasted in eastern and southern England for some three hundred years, from the 9th to the 12th century. Yet despite this general conservatism change did occur, and occasionally, particularly in the second half of the 12th century, it appears to have taken place quite quickly. Two main periods will be considered – the change from the late Saxon tradition to the medieval, in the 12th century, and the change in the latter half of the 14th to the production of late medieval shapes and fabrics. In both periods it is difficult to analyse the real change in usage since little is known of how the usage of pottery related to other materials, such as metal vessels and vessels of wood and leather.

The Saxo-Norman wheel-made tradition is illustrated by the three main wares. Thetford, Stamford and St. Neots wares had as their principal products the large storage jar, the *olla* or jar-shaped cooking pot, the bowl with inturned rim and the spouted pitcher. The spouted pitcher (see Fig.92), derived ultimately from Merovingian and Carolingian traditions, is common to all the pottery fabrics.[63]

Two changes in form may be noted. The first is the replacement of the late Saxon type of cooking pot by the early medieval forms. The second is the change from the spouted pitcher to the medieval jug. Rough hand-made pottery continued in use in London and Kent until the Norman Conquest and beyond. The major change in cooking pots came through the development of the larger medieval type whose width was greater than its height.[64]

In the 12th century the late Saxon pottery industry appears to have collapsed and there was a definite decline in the quality of wheel-thrown pottery. It was only in the major towns such as London, Stamford and York that the wheel-made pottery continued. Characteristic of all three centres is the use of the wheel to make jugs (rather than the pitcher of Saxo-Norman pottery). The typical 'developed' Stamford-ware jug is tall and thin with a long strap handle, all covered with a lustrous green glaze.[65]

62  B. Rackham, *Medieval English Pottery*, ed. J.G. Hurst (1972); S. Jennings, *Eighteen Centuries of Pottery from Norwich* (1931).

63  The best general survey of Saxo-Norman pottery is J.G. Hurst, art cit. note 46, 314-346.

64  G.C. Dunning et al., 'Anglo-Saxon Pottery: a Symposium', *Med. Arch.* iii (1959), 44-8; J.G. Hurst, 'Excavations at Barn Road, Norwich, 1954-55', *Norfolk Arch.* xxxiii (1963), 131-179; J.G. Hurst, 'The Kitchen Area of Northolt Manor, Middlesex', *Med. Arch.* v

(1961), 211-99; B. Cunliffe, *Winchester Excavations 1949-60* (1964), 123.

65  For the change in Stamford ware see K. Kilmurry, *The Pottery Industry of Stamford, Lincs., c. 850-1250* (1980); for York see J. Holdsworth, *Selected Pottery Groups, A.D. 650-1780* (1978): for London see A.G. Vince et al., *Medieval Pottery, London Type Ware* (London and Middlesex Arch. Soc. Special Paper No. 6, 1985).

*Fig. 92* Late Saxon pottery pitcher found on the site of the Angel Inn, Oxford. (*British Museum OA 200*)

*Fig. 93* Pottery jug in the form of a man pulling his beard. Late 13th century. (*British Museum 55, 10-29, 11*)

*Fig. 94* Pottery baluster jug. Mid 14th century. Found near Cannon St., London. (*British Museum 54, 12-27, 102*)

*Fig. 95* Pottery jug in the form of a woman. Early 14th century. Found near Worcester Cathedral. (*British Museum 1974, 10-1, 1*)

In the 13th and 14th centuries the pottery industry was marked by regional variations. Some pottery was still wheel-made; hand-made jugs were fired at kilns such as Ham Green (Gloucs.) and Lyveden (Northants.). The range of products before the 13th century has been estimated as relatively small, being about one-third of the maximum range of about 30 pottery types produced up to the 15th century. This increase in the types of pottery produced went together with an increase in the number of potters and places where pottery was made. The decline in coarse wares, specially cooking pots, was possibly caused by an increase in the use of metal. In Colchester the chattels valued for the lay subsidy of 1301 show that 44% of the taxable population owned one or more metal cooking-pots.[66] Bronze vessels affected the pottery industry not only by reducing the quantity of certain sorts of pots but also by stimulating imitations of metal vessels. There are some pottery jugs whose decoration suggests that the potter was trying to copy metal vessels, and pottery versions of latten aquamaniles (vessels in the shape of mounted knights or animals such as rams or cows) were produced. The imitation of vessels in more expensive fabrics such as metal may be seen as evidence of a spread of ideas and fashion and is indicative of the methods by which decorative ideas such as heraldry or animals of the bestiary were adopted as ornament on decorative jugs. Highly decorated jugs, of which the most elaborate examples are the knight jugs, were particularly popular at the end of the 13th and the beginning of the 14th centuries and it may be that they were a response to a relatively prosperous market (Figs.93, 95).

The state of the industry at the end of the Middle Ages is not easy to summarise and is not susceptible of a single interpretation. The main features of what happened to the products of the industry are clear. Pottery was produced on a larger scale, and the types of vessels widened and became more specialised whereas the size of jugs became smaller and plainer. Jean le Patourel summarised the late medieval changes as follows:

In the last quarter of the 14th century, the industry passed into the hands of a different type of man whose main interest was in agriculture. The change seems to be associated with a decline in potting standards and the disappearance of elaborate decoration, which, in turn, must owe something to the general economic depression and the fall in demand for high-class pottery.[67]

Stephen Moorhouse saw a general change in pottery production as taking place during the first half of the 15th century. There were developments in the pottery traditions in the East Midlands, south-eastern Pennines, in the white wares of Surrey and Hampshire, in the supersession of West Sussex wares, and in the establishment of Midland purple. Each of these new traditions introduced a new range of forms, and often, as in the East Midlands, more technically competent methods of manufacture. He suggested that the reason for the wholesale change in the ceramic industry coupled with the introduction of fine ceramic table wares may be related to

66   Le Patourel, art. cit. note 2, 101.                    67   Ibid. 122.

the change in social structure which led to the formation of a wealthier middle class who could afford a greater freedom of choice.[68]

Christopher Dyer, following a similar line of thought, placed the emphasis slightly differently.[69] He noted that the demand for pottery was elastic and that its use must be related to that for metal, wood, and leather. The increasing spending-power of the more prosperous peasants in the 15th century did not create an extension of the use of metal as a substitute for pottery. However, the increased production of cups and drinking vessels by potters may suggest that the industry was making inroads into the wood-turners' traditional market. The growing wealth of the consumers and the partial substitution of pottery for treen prevented any major shrinkage of the industry.

Grenville Astill has painted the most expansive picture of the late medieval pottery industry.[70] He suggests that by the 15th century pottery production was becoming based in grouped workshops located in the vicinity of towns. The large scale of these workshops attracted middlemen to the potteries and ensured a wider distribution of the products, while an increased uniformity of production made the products of particular kilns acceptable over a wide area. Demand must have been sufficiently strong to offset increasing transportation costs. The expansion of potteries located close to towns may indicate their vitality in the 15th century. More work is clearly needed before the changes in the industry that undoubtedly took place at the end of the Middle Ages can be more clearly understood.

68   Stephen Moorhouse, 'Tudor Green: some Further Thoughts', *Medieval Ceramics*, iii (1979), 58.

69   Christopher Dyer, 'The Social and Economic Changes of the Late Middle Ages, and the Pottery of the Period', *Medieval Ceramics*, vi (1982), 38.

70   G.G. Astill, 'Economic Change in Late Medieval England: an Archaeological Review', in T.H. Aston et al. (ed.), *Social Relations and Ideas: Essays in Honour of R.H. Hilton* (1983), 219-30.

## Further Reading

The best introduction for medieval pottery is Michael R. McCarthy and Catherine M. Brooks, *Medieval Pottery in Britain AD 900-1600* (1988). This has an extensive bibliography. The article by S. Moorhouse, 'The Medieval Pottery Industry and its Markets', in D.W. Crossley (ed.), *Medieval Industry* (1981), 96-125 is a wide-ranging survey of the industry. For kilns the best general survey is J.W.G. Musty, 'Medieval Pottery Kilns', in V.I. Evison et al. (ed.), *Medieval Pottery from Excavations* (1974), 41-65. For medieval floor tiles the best introduction is Elizabeth Eames, *English Medieval Tiles* (1985), with short bibliography. A survey of the industry and extensive bibliography occurs in the same author's *Catalogue of Medieval Lead-glazed Earthenware Tiles in the Department of Medieval and Later Antiquities British Museum* (1980). For floor and roof tiles P.J. Drury, 'The Production of Brick and Tile in Medieval England', in D.W. Crossley (ed.), *Medieval Industry* (1981), 126-42 (with bibliography) is a most useful survey. There is also some valuable evidence for roofing materials from documentary sources published in L.F. Salzman, *Building in England to 1540* (1952), 223-36.

9

*Brick*

NICHOLAS J. MOORE

Very little is known from contemporary sources about brick making and building before the 14th century, and even for the later period documentary material is slight in relation to the known scale of work. It seldom offers more than a glimpse into some aspects of the industry's workings, but a wealth of surviving buildings adds much to our knowledge of the manufacture, distribution and uses of brick.

*The Use of Brick to 1550*

The development of the craft of brick building falls into three distinct but overlapping phases.

The earliest application of brick was as a coursable material, for which it was in demand for building quoins and vaults, and dressing windows and doorways; by the end of the 14th century it was widely obtainable in several of the stoneless counties of eastern and southern England, such as Norfolk, Suffolk and Kent, and in London and towns such as Norwich, Beverley and Hull. It was generally used sparingly and was concealed by render or used internally and plastered (although occasionally in the 14th century it appears openly as a facing material, especially in the North). Good examples of such work are Norwich city walls, built between 1294 and 1343, with arches, windows, arrowslits and copings of brick-dressed flint rubble, brick-vaulted towers and at least one vaulted staircase; Claxton Castle (Norfolk) begun by William de Kerdeston *c.* 1340, which includes lacing courses in the rubble, a fireplace, and the dressings to doorways and windows; and the mid-14th-century chancel ruins at Covehithe (Suffolk) with brick structural work such as lacing-courses and relieving-arches.

Brick was particularly in demand for vaulting, sometimes in combination with other materials. At Coggeshall Abbey (Essex) the vaulted corridor of the 1220s has stone webs on chamfered brick ribs, whereas at Exchequer Gate, Lincoln, and Butley Priory Gatehouse (Suffolk) in the 14th century, the webs are of brick and the ribs are stone. The latter form is common, especially in Norfolk and Suffolk in the 14th century, and was also used for several high vaults including the nave of Beverley Minster (begun 1308), and at Norwich Cathedral the Bauchun chapel (*c.* 1450), nave (*c.* 1463-72) and transepts (after 1509). The vaulted undercrofts which are a feature of Norwich's domestic architecture[1] generally have brick webs and chamfered brick ribs and are predominantly 15th-century.

Brick's fire-resistance was also understood and the building of chimneys and lining of hearths, both in timber-framed and stone or rubble buildings, preceded the more general adoption of brick across England in the 15th and 16th centuries. Among earlier examples are the royal manor of Gravesend where, in 1366, John Gardinere built three reredoses or firebacks in the kitchen by taskwork, utilising 7,000 bricks,[2] and Portchester Castle (Hants.), where a fireplace of white brick surviving in the west range (apartments) was probably built with the 1,000 'white tiles of Flanders' bought for 'reredoses' in 1397.[3]

Although there are 14th-century buildings in the south and east constructed chiefly of brick, such as the chapel of St. Nicholas, King's Lynn (begun after 1371) and Cow Tower, Norwich (1398-9), these were more common in the north, especially in Hull. Here, the transepts and chancel of Holy Trinity church (*c.* 1315-70), the town walls with their four main gates and about 30 towers built in 1321-1400 (using an estimated 4,700,000 bricks),[4] were all of brick, as were the palace and three houses built by Michael de la Pole (d. 1389). Recent excavation has partly supported Leland's statement that the ordinary houses were mostly of brick at this time.[5] Brick must have been common in Beverley by 1409-10, when 21 suppliers provided the 112,300 bricks for building the North Bar, which suggests a relatively large number of makers operating on a small scale. At Beverley Bar the decoration consists mainly of raised bands and the use of cusped and chamfered apertures, but the brickwork of Thornton Abbey Gatehouse (Lincs.) (*c.* 1382) and Cow Tower is very plain. There was some attempt at English bond in buildings such as Hull's town walls and Beverley Bar, but fine work is not possible with bricks of such varied size (Fig. 96).

In the early 15th century an altogether higher standard of brick building was introduced. Makers began to produce a brick of consistent shape and good red colour, doing so on a huge scale when necessary. This made possible the high-quality walling in English bond, fine structural techniques and wealth of decorative detail brought in at this period. These innovations extended from the nature of the decoration (with the introduction of diapering, elaborate corbel-tables and the ornamental chimney) and the design of mouldings, to the method of constructing vaulting or seating a chimneyshaft on its breast, and the way in which whole elevations were articulated. There can be no doubt that this impetus came from abroad. Within many of these new features there was much variation, suggesting more than one centre of influence; corbelling, for instance, may be trefoiled or

1  A recent survey alleges 88, of which 54 survive: R. Smith and A. Carter, 'Function and Site', *Vernacular Architecture*, xiv (Vernacular Architecture Group, 1983), 6.
2  *King's Works*, ii, 947.
3  Salzman, *Building in England*, 99; B. Cunliffe and J. Munby, *Excavations at Portchester Castle*,

iv (1985), 185.
4  J. Bartlett, 'The Medieval Walls of Hull', *Kingston upon Hull Museum Bulletin*, iii & iv (revised edn. 1971), 21.
5  E.g. P. Armstrong, 'Grimsby Lane Excavations 1972', ibid. x (1973), 2-44.

*Fig. 96* North Bar, Beverley, inward face, 1409-10; minor alterations 1867.

cinquefoiled, or constructed as a series of pointed or rounded archlets (Fig. 97).

Most of these features had appeared previously in Poland, the Low Countries or Germany. The documentary evidence mirrors that of the buildings, a considerable number of brick makers and layers being called 'Flemynges', 'of Holland', 'born in Teutonic parts', 'from Gelderland', and 'Docheman', or when not so identified, having foreign-sounding names such as 'Sondergyltes', 'Maligoo', and 'Turkyn Horwynd'. The introduction of high-quality work and foreign craftsmen appears to date from shortly after 1410, the earliest surviving building to combine them being the chapel tower at Stonor Park (Oxon.) with its diapering and moulded brick corbelling, under construction by Michael Warrewyk and his Flemings in 1416-17. Buildings of this phase show a diversity of design, and a contrast in appearance between those most obviously 'alien' (such as Faulkbourne Hall (Essex), begun *c.* 1439, and Prior Overton's Tower at Repton Priory (Derbs.) of 1437-8), and those of generally English character, such as Eton College, founded in 1440, and Herstmonceux Castle (Sussex), begun *c.* 1441. These contrasts provide the strongest evidence that Europeans were employed not only as brick makers and brick layers but also as architects (Figs. 102, 107-8). The highly-developed diapering at Eton, for example, suggests that foreign brickmakers constructed their work in accordance with their native training even when working under an English master mason, Robert Westerley; just as surely as the character of the stone chimneypieces and windows at Tattershall Castle (Lincs.) (begun *c.* 1432) is English in an otherwise largely 'foreign' building.

These buildings, which effectively introduced brick as a first-class building material, were spread throughout England. Henry V's work at Sheen, where he rebuilt the palace in 1414 with brick and stone and founded three monasteries, suggests that the Crown may have taken the lead. The Charterhouse certainly employed two bricklayers from Holland. Royal influence is also suggested by the Manor of the More (Herts.), built with 'brik' by Henry's uncle, Cardinal Beaufort *c.* 1427, and the brick and stone castle of Henry's brother John, duke of Bedford (d. 1435) at Fulbrook (Warwicks). These and several other early patrons of brick played a prominent part in the French wars, which may account for the rapid adoption here of the word 'brick' in the early 15th century; it was in current French use, but unusual here before 1400. The French war may also account for the introduction of brickmakers from the Low Countries, since the English at Calais were accustomed both to employing them directly and to buying their wares for the King's Works there.[6]

The extensive use of foreign detail on the finest buildings shows the domination of the industry by foreigners for a considerable period, tailing off only in the 1470s and 1480s. Among the last buildings with strongly alien detailing are Fox's Tower at Farnham Castle (*c.* 1470-75), where Dutch or Flemish 'brekemasons' were employed, and Wolsey's Tower at Esher Place (before 1484) (Fig. 103), both built for

6 *King's Works*, i, 427 n.4.

*Fig. 97a* Brick corbelling: Faulkbourne Hall (Essex), *c.* 1439

*Fig. 97b* Brick corbelling: Fox's Tower, Farnham Castle, 1473.

*Fig. 98* Tower, Buckden Place (Hunts.), built for Thomas Rotherham, Bishop of Lincoln 1472-80.

William Waynflete (bishop of Winchester, 1447-86), and the tower at Buckden Palace (Hunts.) built for Thomas Rotherham (bishop of Lincoln 1472-80) (Fig. 98). Foreign brickmasons were still much in evidence in the building-accounts of Kirby Muxloe Castle (Leics.), 1481-4.

In the third phase, brick emerged as a high-quality and decorative building material confidently handled by English designers and bricklayers and popular for buildings of all types; especially for bishops' palaces and country seats, such as those of John Alcock (bishop of Ely, 1486-1500) at Ely and Little Downham (Cambs.) and Cardinal Morton at Hatfield, Lambeth, Charing (Kent) and Croydon (Fig. 99). Imported details such as diapering and the spiral chimney were assimilated and developed, while the trefoiled corbel-table became a common design element in domestic and ecclesiastical architecture in the eastern counties until the mid 16th century. The development of more elaborate diaper patterns and chimney-shaft

*Fig. 99* Diapers on Cardinal Morton's palaces: (a) Croydon, chapel gable, late 15th century. (b) Hatfield Old Hall, porch, 1480s.

designs than those of the previous generation peaked in 1470-1500 with such buildings as the tower at Buckden Palace, Hatfield Old Hall (Herts.), and Tendring Hall (demolished) and Hadleigh Deanery, both in Suffolk. By about 1520 this impetus was largely exhausted, and the further development of brick decoration was mainly confined to East Anglia.

During the next two decades the architectural possibilities of terracotta were explored. Initially, if not continuously, it was made by foreign craftsmen clearly working to the directions of English designers, with typically English architectural members ornamented with detail current in North Italy before 1500, and/or heraldic and gothic designs. Again, it was introduced as a prestige material and has a national distribution. Terracotta was made by carefully refining good brickearth so that it adopts the finely-carved detail of special moulds; it is generally of pale buff colour. Usually it is cast in units much larger than the standard brick, and therefore requires greater manufacturing skill. Its most ambitious employment was at Sutton Place (Surrey), begun after 1521 and well advanced by 1527, in which a serious attempt was made to cast all the detailing of an elaborate building in terracotta: doorways, windows and chimney-pieces, plinths, friezes and stringcourses, even panel-cladding of external surfaces, quoins and the cupolas of turrets. Cardinal Wolsey also appears to have experimented with architectural terracotta at Hampton Court Palace.[7] Lesser although appreciable use was made of terracotta at such buildings as Layer Marney Hall (Essex), under construction in 1523,[8] Laughton Place (Sussex), which has plaques dated 1534, and Great Cressingham Manor House (Norfolk), perhaps *c.* 1540.[9] This work was mostly of high quality and used large units, with plinths measuring 11½ by 8½ by 8 inches (maximum) at Laughton Place and mullions 21 inches long at Layer Marney. But impurities and careless drying caused cracks in the work at Cressingham.

For Old Hall Farm, Kneesall (Notts.), a relatively small house (perhaps built in 1522-5 for Sir John Hussey, executed 1537), the terracottas may have been transported ready-made from London.[10] Small terracotta items may also have been made centrally, for example Wolsey's arms at Hampton Court, dated 1525, the arms of Charles Brandon, duke of Suffolk, on three 15-inch high panels at Westhorpe Hall (Suffolk) (Fig. 100), and five identical plaques, 7½ inches square, of Anne Boleyn and her badge *ex situ* at Poxwell House and West Lulworth (Dorset); and it has even been suggested that the group of seven terracotta tombs, centred on Norfolk and made *c.* 1530 from a common set of moulds, were manufactured abroad.[11]

7  A section of window mullion and two fragments of moulding with Italianate detail have been excavated, from a burial position of *c.* 1534, by D. Batchelor: 'Excavations at Hampton Court Palace', *Post-Med. Arch.* xi (1977), 44 and Fig. 8.

8  Terracotta window mouldings now at Shrubland Old Hall and Barham, Barking and Henley churches (Suffolk), with design elements and measurements similar to those at Layer Marney, were originally intended for a single

building, probably at Shrubland.

9  Where there was formerly more terracotta than now: excavations by R.B. Woodings in 1966-8 revealed many more, probably from the hall.

10  The suggestion of N. Summers, 'Old Hall Farm, Kneesall, Notts.', *Trans. Thoroton Soc.*, lxxvi (1972), 17-25.

11  A.P. Baggs, 'Sixteenth-century Terra-cotta Tombs in East Anglia', *Arch. Jnl.* cxxv (1969), 297-301.

*Fig. 100* Terracotta arms of Charles Brandon, Duke of Suffolk, at Westhorpe Hall (Suffolk); reset.

*Fig. 101* Finely finished crocket, Wallington Hall (Norfolk), *c.* 1525.

The finely-detailed work of the terracotta makers had a limited effect in East Anglia during the second quarter of the 16th century, stimulating the use of bricks of extra large size and carved and cast decoration generally. Among examples of the first are the gatehouse of Leiston Abbey (Suffolk), for the mouldings of the arch and for cinquefoiled panelling on its turrets,[12] and Wolterton Hall, East Barsham (Norfolk), where the gatehouse (after 1527) has rich architectural and ornamental detail carved on specially large bricks as if they were stones.

## Materials and Manufacture

It is generally agreed that brick manufacture changed only slowly before the 19th century, and that 17th-, 18th- and early 19th-century accounts of the process are broadly applicable to the 15th century.[13] This view is generally supported by such evidence as an examination of the bricks and documents provides.

The first step was to find suitable brickearth or clay. Medieval bricks were normally made from shallow deposits of clay, and the early type was nearly always made from the widely-available silts deposited in estuaries, lakes and fens. The 15th century preferred bricks which fired red, and it was the task of the brickmaker to find clay with the right iron compounds, such as sandy boulder clays of glacial origin. He expected to find these beneath a top-soil containing small flints.[14] White bricks were also sometimes wanted or at least used, as in the construction of Hengrave Hall (Suffolk) in 1525-38. The three-colour diapering at Old Warden Abbey (Beds.) of similar date required lime-rich clays.

Having found the right clay, the maker had to knead it, mould it into bricks and dry them. He then fired them carefully, to give not only a well-formed and durable product, but also one of consistent good colour. Diaper patterns of darker or glazed bricks became a desirable feature in the 15th century and these bricks were produced in the hottest part of the kiln or clamp, adjacent to the fire-channels.[15] Both kilns and clamps were used, but kilns are much the more frequently met with in documents. A kiln has the advantage over a clamp of firing about three times as fast (in five or six days at the Hull corporation kiln), and over a small clamp of firing the bricks more efficiently since those around the edges of a clamp never fired fully. Because of its permanent nature, with walls and a paved floor (but no fixed roof), a kiln was more appropriate to the longer-term supply but a clamp had the advantages of flexibility,

---

12  The cast bricks measure 9 × 8 × 2½, 13 × 7 × 2¼ and 13 × 7 × 3½ ins.

13  E.g. N. Lloyd, *A History of English Brickwork* (1925), 29-38, and T.P. Smith, *The Medieval Brickmaking Industry in England 1400-1450* (1985), 39-57. However, there must be serious doubt that bricks were ever made by the 'pastry' method (L.S. Harley, 'A Typology of Brick', *J.B.A.A.* 3rd ser. xxxvii (1974), 64), in which clay is supposed to have been spread thinly on straw and chopped up with a spade, a poor

and laborious process. The 'pastry' bricks were usually made with very wet clay, giving distortions, and probably in moulds of various sizes, a matter of little consequence in the buildings for which they were intended.

14  R.J. and P.E. Firman, 'Geological Approach to the Study of Medieval Bricks', *Mercian Geologist*, ii (1967), 312-4.

15  Brickmakers say that a dark-glazed effect can also be obtained by throwing salt into the kiln three-quarters of the way through firing.

its siting and capacity being determined as need arose.

So far very few of either have been found in England. An early 14th-century kiln excavated at Thornholme Priory (Lincs.) was very small, only about 10 feet across internally and circular, with a single flue aligned east-west.[16] Another 14th-century one at Boston (Lincs.) was essentially a tile-kiln in which bricks were also fired[17] (the dual role may have been common but there is little documentary evidence for it in England). This had three parallel flues slightly below ground-level, stoked from the north and with chimneys at the south end, the bricks and tiles stacked between and above the flues where the fuel burned. The site of a clamp, in which the bricks to build the kiln had been fired in the early 14th century, was found alongside; this was of three or possibly only two flues, and nicely demonstrates the use of a clamp.

Three clamps excavated at Wijk bij Duurstede in Holland, probably of late 15th-century date, were somewhat larger, one being of six flues aligned east-west and one of four aligned north-south, with estimated capacities of 30,000 and 20,000 bricks,[18] but nevertheless small by contemporary English standards: a 'clamp of brick' purchased at Bury St. Edmunds in 1530 yielded 124,000 bricks,[19] some at Hunsdon (Herts.) in 1525 about 166,000,[20] while one at Little Saxham Hall (Suffolk) in 1509-10 apparently held 300,000.[21] But the capacity of late medieval Dutch kilns at up to 100,000 bricks[22] was similar to English ones: John Ellis's 'kylne' supplying Kirby Muxloe Castle in March 1483 fired 100,000 bricks in the course of a week,[23] an earlier firing having yielded 81,900 and a cartload; at Caister Castle (Norfolk) in 1433-4, 550,000 were apparently produced from three firings of two kilns,[24] and Henry Sondergyltes made 345,000 bricks in three 'kylnes' at Deptford in 1418.[25] A kiln at Hull firing bricks for the royal fortifications in 1542 had ten 'holes' or flues.[26] The early 15th-century corporation kiln at Hull, therefore, was small, with a capacity of about 47-48,000 bricks,[27] and firings were usually of only 33,000 to 35,000, which may explain why it never made satisfactory profits and had gone out of production by 1436-7.

Two to four firings a year seem to have been usual, as at the Hull corporation brickyard; the kilns at Caister Castle were fired three times in 1433-4. If there was

16 *Arch. Excavations, 1974* (C.B.A. 1975), 12-13; *Arch. Excavations, 1975* (1976), 98.

17 P. Mayes, 'A Medieval Tile Kiln at Boston', *J.B.A.A.* 3rd ser. xxviii (1965), 86-105.

18 J. Hollestelle, 'Soil-marks of Late Medieval Brick Clamps at Wijk bij Duurstede', *Overdruk uit Berichten van de Rijksdienst voor het Oudheidkundig Bodemonderzoek*, xxiv (1974), 185-9.

19 J. Gage, *History and Antiquities of Hengrave, in Suffolk* (1822), 49.

20 14 clamps at 20*d*. and 21*d*. the thousand bricks cost £199 10*s*.: Salzman, *Building in England*, 144.

21 J. Gage, *History and Antiquities of Suffolk: Thingoe Hundred* (1838), 150.

22 J. Hollestelle, *De Steenbakkerij in de Nederlanden*

(1976), 271.

23 A.H. Thompson, 'The Building Accounts of Kirby Muxloe Castle, 1480-84', *Trans. Leics. Arch. Soc.* xi (1913-20), 307.

24 H.D. Barnes and W.D. Simpson, 'The Building Accounts of Caister Castle', *Norfolk Archaeology*, xxx (1952), 182-3.

25 Salzman, *Building in England*, 143.

26 *King's Works*, iv, 475.

27 93,000 were made in two firings in 1422-3, but 98,000 in three in 1427-8: F.W. Brooks, 'A Medieval Brick-yard at Hull', *J.B.A.A.* 3rd ser. iv (1939), 165-7, 169-70. All references to brick-making at Hull in 1395-1433 are from this source.

*Fig. 102* Faulkbourne Hall (Essex), begun by Sir John Montgomery *c.* 1439.

only one kiln at Eton in the 1440s it must have been a large one as it supplied an average of 430,000 bricks a year over the first five years, with a maximum of 1,036,500.[28] The relatively well-documented building programmes of Henry VIII show that firing normally took place in the summer months, but at Kirby Muxloe it must have happened as early as February for the first building season.[29] This seasonal practice was normal in Northern Europe, although in Italy kilns could work all year round.[30]

The normal fuel was wood (stakes, faggots, logs and greenwood) but turves ignited by wood were also used at the kilns of Hull corporation in 1395-1433, Caister Castle in the 1430s, Wisbech Castle in 1333[31] and Ely Priory in 1339 and 1345-6.[32] This use of turf in the eastern counties may reflect the local economy, or possibly the influence of the Netherlands where peat was commonly used.[33] Coal and firewood are listed among the requisites of William Vesey upon his appointment as royal brickmaker in 1437, but although coal was used to fire lime-kilns there is scant evidence for its use with brick.[34]

There is only one documentary source for the cost of establishing a kiln, that of William Vesey for Henry VI's work at Eton College. In April 1442, 'uppon making of a breke kylne', he was paid 28s. 4d., and his second instalment ten months later formed part of a further 25s.;[35] it seems improbable that these figures include the building materials. Eton's direct responsibility for the kiln was unusual, and was reflected in the price Vesey was paid for the bricks, only 10d. the thousand.

### The Organisation of the Brick Trade

By the early 16th century there were numerous independent brickmakers in the south of England and the same name is seldom heard twice, except in the royal works. Henry VIII either summoned makers to work at his building sites (as many as 30 at Nonsuch in 1541,[36] and 30 were envisaged at Hull in 1542)[37] or he contracted with them at their own kilns. John Lawrence sold large quantities of bricks for building the Savoy Hospital in 1510-15 from his kiln at Charing Cross,[38] and he supplied the bricks for Hampton Court Palace in 1529-30 until a kiln was set up in the park.[39] Sometimes the employer had to provide suitable brickearth at a distance from his building. For Hunsdon House the bricks were made three miles away at Great Parndon, where a croft was specially hired for two years,[40] kilns invariably

28  R. Willis and J.W. Clark, *The Architectural History of the University of Cambridge* (1886), i, 385.
29  Thompson, 'Kirby Muxloe', 228-9.
30  R.A. Goldthwaite, *The Building of Renaissance Florence* (1980), 187.
31  Cambridge University Library MS EDR D7/1/3, Wisbech Castle compotus 6-7 Edward III, kindly communicated by Dr. Dorothy Owen.
32  F.R. Chapman, *Sacrist Rolls of Ely*, ii (1908), 87, 137.
33  Hollestelle, *De Steenbakkerij*, 272.

34  The 14th-century kiln excavated at Boston was coal-fired, the brick clamp probably also, possibly with coal-dust mixed into the clay during manufacture: Mayes, op. cit. note 17, 93, 91.
35  Willis and Clark, *Architectural History*, i, 385.
36  J. Dent, *The Quest for Nonsuch* (1962), 49.
37  *King's Works*, iv, 474.
38  Ibid. iii, 203.
39  Ibid. iv, 132.
40  In or after 1525: ibid. iv, 155.

being situated by the source of clay. Four acres seem to have been sufficient for even the large-scale brick-making operations of Nonsuch Palace[41] and Caister Castle.[42]

Those who established kilns to serve their own works commonly parted with small quantities to outsiders. At Caister Castle 4,000 were sold for 20s. 'in the country' in 1433-4, and at Eton 18,000 were sold to one Robert Manfelde, also at 5s. the thousand, in 1449-50;[43] other small sales from Eton at this time were frequently made.[44] At Tattershall Castle, four lots of between 1,000 and 3,000 were sold to individuals in 1437-9 (perhaps for building hearths), and at least 35,400 were made available to Kirkstead Abbey and 20,000 to Bardney Abbey in 1434, while 8,000 or more were given to Edlington church over the years.

There were municipal kilns at Hull between 1303 and 1433, and at Beverley in 1391 and Sandwich in 1463.[45] Towns such as King's Lynn, Norwich and London were probably supplied from privately-owned kilns, but almost nothing is known of the self-employed brickmaker. There is relatively little evidence, either, for the entrepreneurial construction of a kiln as an investment before the 16th century, although it was common practice in Italy and the Netherlands in the late Middle Ages. Ralph, Lord Cromwell, owned a kiln in Boston between 1431 and 1452, leased to John Chamberleyn, from which he had bricks sent for the construction of Tattershall Castle, partly for cash and partly as arrears of rent in kind.[46] The vicars choral of York Minster manufactured bricks in the 15th century as a source of income.[47] Rent in kind was also accepted for the municipal brickworks at Beverley in 1391, Richard Hamondson and others paying 3,000 bricks a year.[48]

A number of brickmakers' contracts have survived. One of the most detailed is that of 1534, in which New College, Oxford, made an agreement with Richard Whitby and Clement Peake of London for 800,000 bricks, 500,000 to be made at Stanton St. John and the remainder at Tingewick (Bucks), in each case in three clamps or kilns. The men were to be paid £63 6s. 8d. in all: £6 when they started digging the brickearth, £4 at the start of moulding the bricks, and £3 6s. 8d. every fortnight thereafter (i.e. for 16 weeks). This allowed them 19d. a thousand, with the college providing all sand, straw and firewood on site.[49] Similarly, in April 1496, the Prior of Westminster agreed with James Powle of New Brentford and Robert Slyngisby of Hertfordshire for the manufacture of 400,000 bricks at Belsize (Middlesex) by Michaelmas; they were to be paid 18d. per thousand, with pasture for two horses, a lodging house and their cooking fuel provided, with the prior finding

41 Dent, *Quest for Nonsuch*, 265.
42 Barnes and Simpson, 'Caister Castle', 186. It is not certain that the 'Brick Pits' supplied both phases of the Castle's construction.
43 Knoop and Jones, *Med. Mason*, 217.
44 Willis and Clark, *Architectural History*, i, 384 n. 3.
45 It is not clear why Beverley Corporation owned a kiln. It leased it out, and when building the North Bar in 1409-10 had to acquire the bricks in 40 lots from 21 people.
46 E.g. W.D. Simpson (ed.), *The Building Accounts of Tattershall Castle 1434-1472* (Lincoln Record Soc. lv, 1960), 73. All references to the building accounts of Tattershall Castle are from this source.
47 *R.C.H.M. York*, v, p.xcvi.
48 Brooks, 'Medieval Brick-yard', op. cit. in n. 27, 161.
49 Harvey, *Mediaeval Craftsmen*, 197-8.

*Fig. 103* Wolsey's Tower, Esher Place, built by Bishop Waynflete before 1484; stonework 18th century.

*Fig. 104* The ultimate in carved chimneys: Thornbury Castle (Glos.), for Edward Stafford, Duke of Buckingham, dated 1514.

wood and straw and paying half the cost of the carriage of sand.[50] These terms, with the patron providing the site and the major proportion of the raw materials from his own resources, were normal. Sometimes he also paid for the collection of his bricks from within the kiln, as at Caister Castle in 1433-4. In such ways payments to brickmakers may appear comparatively low, the open market price of bricks from 1400 to 1550 being generally between four and five shillings the thousand.[51]

The specification of a size of brick was a natural consideration, not only in defining the product of the contract; it was a necessity in building work of any quality employing more than one maker. When the prior of Westminster ordered his bricks from two makers in 1496, their moulds were to be 9½ inches long 'or more'.[52] At Little Saxham Hall the contracts with two (or possibly four) makers in 1505 stipulated bricks 10 by 5 by 2½ inches when burned (bricks shrink in firing).[53] At

50  Ibid. 142-3.
51  But generally cheaper at Beverley; e.g. those bought by the thousand for Beverley Bar all cost less than 3*s*. 9½*d*. a thousand: A.F. Leach, 'The Building of Beverley Bar', *Trans. E. Riding*

*Antiq. Soc.* iv (1896), *passim.*
52  Harvey, *Mediaeval Craftsmen*, 142-3.
53  Gage, op. cit. note 21, 140, 141, 144. Four brickmakers were employed but only two contracts are known.

Tattershall Castle in the 1430s the bricks were made by Baldwin and Foys in two sizes according to the accounts, the 'larger' 10 by 5 by 2½ inches and the 'smaller' 9 by 4 by 2 and 'four parts of an inch'.[54] Henry VIII's bricks were to be 9½ by 4¾ by 2⅜ inches both at the Manor of the More (Herts.) in 1530[55] and Woking Manor in 1534.[56]

In practice the sizes of bricks in medieval buildings fall into three categories. Much the most common one was about 9-9½ by 4-4½ by 2-2¼ inches, found from the late 13th century onwards, as at Little Wenham Hall (Suffolk), c.1265, and perhaps developed from the small Dutch brick;[57] this size extends up to about 10 by 5 by 2½-3 inches, especially in 14th-century Norfolk. Secondly, there were the large or 'great' bricks, generally found in or near Essex, especially in the 12th and 13th centuries and probably not made after the 14th century. These were of very variable size, but with such dimensions as 13 by 6 by 2 inches (Coggeshall Abbey guesthouse, c.1190), 13 by 5½ by 1¾-2 inches (Copford church (Essex) c.1200) and 15 by 7 by 2¼ and 3 inches (Waltham Abbey gatehouse, late 14th-century).[58] They normally occur in ecclesiastical contexts, and have affinities with 13th-century Dutch bricks which commonly measure 11¾-12⅝ by 6-6¼ by 2¾-3½ inches (30-32 by 15-16 by 7 -9 cm.),[59] and the Florentine *mattone* of 1325, at 11⅜ by 5¾ by 2⅞ inches (29 by 14½ by 7¼ cm.).[60] The third size prevailed in the north where, appropriately, the names *teguli* and 'wall-tiles' lingered longest, and 14th-and 15th-century bricks measuring 10-11 by 5-5½ by 1½-2¼ inches were made in towns such as Boston, Beverley, Hull and York.

Doubts over the lasting qualities of brick were occasionally expressed. Corpus Christi College, Cambridge, wanted only 'best endureng breke' in their new bakehouse in 1460.[61] John Baret, providing for the rebuilding of Risby Gate, Bury St. Edmunds, in his will of 1463 specified freestone and brick unless his executors felt it 'not sufficient to endure', when they might substitute flint rubble;[62] Henry VI in his 'avyse' of 1449 for replanning the chapel at Eton expressly forbade the use of brick (also chalk and Reigate stone) in the walls or foundations.[63] Inferior bricks were occasionally supplied to the Crown, the parapets of Berwick-upon-Tweed fortifications built in about 1565 being reported as 'rotted and fretted away' by 1595;[64] in 1554-5 some surplus bricks at Hull were worth only 3s. 4d. a thousand because of their small size and poor firing.[65] Quality control was bound to break down occasionally: 10,000 bricks from the Hull yard, sold to St. Mary's chapel at

54  Simpson, *Tattershall Castle*, 56-7.
55  M. Biddle and others, 'Excavations of the Manor of the More', *Herts. Arch. Jnl.* cxvi (1959), 189.
56  *King's Works*, iv, 346.
57  Although Dr. Hollestelle believes that Dutch bricks of this size date from after 1300.
58  For other examples of 'great bricks' and their dimensions see P.J. Huggins, 'Monastic Excavations, Waltham Abbey, Essex, 1970-72', *Essex Archaeology and History*, iv (1972), 111-14. But

bricks of comparable dimensions occur apparently in 16th-century contexts in S. Bucks.: *R.C.H.M. Bucks. (South)*, 3, 207, 311.
59  Hollestelle, *De Steenbakkerij*, 273.
60  Goldthwaite, *Renaissance Florence*, 209.
61  Willis and Clark, *Architectural History*, i, 309.
62  J.H. Harvey, *English Mediaeval Architects*, 2nd edn. (1984), 57.
63  *King's Works*, i, 288.
64  Ibid. iv, 620.
65  Ibid. 475 and n. 1.

Hull, were rejected as weak and inadequately fired in 1423-4,[66] while others at Loseley (Surrey) in 1561 were re-fired.[67] £10 worth went unpaid for at Tattershall Castle in 1434-5 because they were insufficiently kneaded. Some losses were inevitable, and contracts generally guarded against under-fired and broken bricks: at Little Saxham Hall in 1505 'no semel [half-burnt] breke nor broken breke [were] to be told but only ij half brekes for oon breke'.[68] In the New College contract of 1534 the makers covenanted to provide free of charge 10,000 bricks 'in recompense of the waste of the same 800,000'[69] (1¼ per cent), and at Caister Castle in 1433-4 550,000 bricks were made but only 537,765 accepted for payment (2¼ per cent loss).

### Carved and Moulded Brickwork

An important part of a skilled bricklayer's work was the preparation of moulded bricks; 15th-and 16th-century buildings often use them generously. The brick as a unit cast in a mould might seem ideally suited to the continuous repetition of simple detail such as trefoil-corbelling and window mouldings. Much of this was however hand-carved, as is apparent both from building-accounts and from the bricks themselves, the worked parts often revealing a core quite different from the fired face. Some clays made bricks too hard to be worked and others had to be obtained, as at Wallington Hall (Norfolk) *c.*1525, where the ornamented bricks are orange-red. At Fox's Tower the false machicolations have multiple convex and concave mouldings topped by trefoil-corbelling, built in 1473 with 3,000 'hewen bryke' (Fig. 97b).[70] At Tattershall Castle 2,200 'worked bricks called hewentile' were provided for the chimneys and windows of the great stable (which have not survived) in 1438. At Kirby Muxloe Castle the hewing of bricks was a winter task apart from an early payment for laying and working some in June 1481; fireplaces and the ribs ('seynters') of the gatehouse vault were specified, although the work must have included certain doorways and windows, moulded with chamfers, ogees and hollow-chamfers (Fig. 106). Tools for this must have been among the dozens of axes, chisels and 'other' or 'small' tools frequently sharpened by the smith. In 1533-4 a brick-axe at 8*d.* and three stone hammers at 6*d.* each were bought for the bricklayers at Windsor Castle.[71] At Stonor Park there is corbelling with chamfers and simple mouldings on the chapel tower, cut with the aid of four hand-saws provided in 1416-17.[72] Chimneys in the early 16th century, even octagonal ones, were commonly hewn (Fig. 104);[73] those of Hengrave Hall (*c.*1530) were to be of 'roubed bryck',[74] and at

66 Brooks, 'Medieval Brick-yard', op. cit. note 27, 168.
67 J. Evans, 'Extracts from the Private Account Books of Sir William More of Loseley', *Archaeologia*, xxxvi (1956), 295.
68 Gage, op. cit note 21, 141.
69 Harvey, *Mediaeval Craftsmen*, 198.
70 M.W. Thompson, 'The Date of "Fox's Tower", Farnham Castle', *Surrey Arch. Collections*, lvii

(1960), 88.
71 W.H. St. John Hope, *Windsor Castle* (1913), i, 263, 264.
72 C.L. Kingsford (ed.), *The Stonor Letters and Papers, 1290-1483* (2 vols., Camden 3rd ser. xxix, xxx, 1919), i, 30.
73 Salzman, *Building in England*, 145.
74 Gage, op. cit. note 19, 42.

*Fig. 105* Moulded brick for forming an octagon, Baconsthorpe Castle (Norfolk), 15th century.

*Fig. 106* Hewn bricks of doorway, Kirby Muxloe Castle (Leics.), probably 1482.

least some of the moulded bricks of *c*.1525 at Wallington Hall were finely finished with an abrasive (Fig. 101). It is therefore not surprising that bricklayers were commonly called 'breekmasons' in the 15th and 16th centuries.

Nevertheless, some chamfers and mouldings were cast by the brickmaker (Fig. 105); Nathaniel Lloyd observed that shaped bricks at Coggeshall Abbey repeat a fault in the mould.[75] Several kinds of moulded bricks were made for the exceptionally early work at Coggeshall and occur in three building phases between *c*.1160 and 1220 (although there are also hewn bricks).[76] This raises the question why special bricks more than two centuries later were usually hewn. The answer probably lies in the nature of the clay used, its ability to keep a moulded shape and to fire with little shrinkage. The Coggeshall bricks are thought to be unique in having had sand added to the clay to improve its qualities; later brickmakers relied on trying to find naturally sandy clays.[77] In the Netherlands the difference was a regional matter, with the northern districts and Flanders forming their shaped bricks in moulds. In Holland they were cut subsequent to firing, the distinction being attributed to the monastic tradition of brickmaking in the north.[78]

75  Lloyd, *English Brickwork*, 71-2.
76  J.S. Gardner, 'Coggeshall Abbey and its Early Brickwork', *J.B.A.A.* 3rd ser. xviii (1955), 19-32.
77  Firman, op. cit. note 14, 305. It has been

suggested that moulded bricks would have required special kiln furniture to fire them: Smith, *Medieval Brickmaking Industries*, op. cit. note 13, 50.
78  Hollestelle, *De Steenbakkerij*, 273.

Another bricklayer's task was to finish his work with a treatment of ochre, and this is occasionally met with in accounts. 200 pounds of it were bought for 'colouring' Fox's Tower at Farnham Castle in 1475.[79] Seven pounds, together with 14 gallons of small ale and some glovers' offal, were bought for colouring a brick chimney at Collyweston Manor House (Northants.) in 1504.[80] It was presumably applied to brickwork as a wash. The patrons there were the bishop of Winchester and Lady Margaret Beaufort, mother of the king, which suggests that special trouble was taken to achieve a perfect finish on the best work, of which we now know little.[81]

## The Location of Kilns and Transportation of Bricks

The Boston tile kiln lay about 500 yards east of the medieval town boundary and the Hull corporation brickyard immediately south of the town,[82] situations similar to those usual in the Netherlands[83] and North Italy.[84] In 1461 the authorities at Beverley decreed that (tile) kilns should not be built nearer the town than they were 'on account of the stench, fouling the air and destruction of fruit trees'.[85]

Such restrictions did not apply to the kiln set up for a country building, which was established upon the nearest available suitable brickearth. This was generally within a mile or two, the 'Brick Pits' supplying Caister Castle being 1¼ miles to the south.[86] The clay pits for Coggeshall Abbey, discovered in 1887, were 'immediately N.E. of the Abbey',[87] and the Eton kiln of 1442 was a mile away at Slough, the cost of transporting the bricks from there being 6*d*. the thousand. The necessity of using the right clay led to the brickworks for Tattershall Castle being ten miles away by water on Edlington Moor, the carriage of 490,700 bricks made by Foys in 1438-9 costing £21 10*s*. 2*d*. or 10½*d*. the thousand.[88] Water was the cheapest form of transport, the Caister Castle bricks apparently making a journey of 2½ miles by water in preference to 1½ miles by road. For the Low Countries it has been calculated that a day's travel by horse and cart doubled the cost of bricks, the rural brickfields all being developed adjacent to good water transport.[89] Occasionally bricks travelled long distances. Sir John Fastolf sent some 25 miles across Norfolk, no doubt by water, from Caister to his manor house at Hellesdon, despite the availability of

79  Thompson, 'Date of "Fox's Tower"', 88.
80  Salzman, *Building in England*, 144.
81  Ruddling is not to be confused with the external 'pencilling' often performed by bricklayers from the mid 16th to the early 17th century (e.g. on the royal works); it was commonly in red, black or white, or some combination of them, apparently over a thin skim of plaster upon inferior brickwork or mixed materials. Early examples include Great Cressingham Manor House (Norfolk) and Beckingham Hall, Tolleshunt Major (Essex), both *c*.1540-50.
82  Brooks, 'Medieval Brick-yard', 157.
83  Hollestelle, *De Steenbakkerij*, 275.

84  Goldthwaite, *Renaissance Florence*, 178.
85  Salzman, *Industries*, 126.
86  Barnes and Simpson, 'Caister Castle', 186.
87  P.J. Drury, 'The Production of Brick and Tiles in Medieval England', in D.W. Crossley (ed.), *Medieval Industry* (C.B.A. Research Rep. xl, 1981), 139 n. 4.
88  St. John's College, Cambridge, was prepared to obtain its brick for Second Court in 1598 from Stow (Bardolph) 'where very good bricke is to be had', some 32 miles away: Willis and Clark, *Architectural History*, i, 251.
89  Hollestelle, *De Steenbakkerij*, 272, 275.

bricks two miles away at Norwich.[90]

In the 13th and 14th centuries such distances were less exceptional, and there is also evidence that bricks were imported. Internal distribution, then as later, was mainly by water. Among the earliest references to the brick trade are purchases of bricks for buildings at Ely from Wisbech in 1339 and King's Lynn in 1325, 1345 and 1354, and for King's Hall, Cambridge, from Lynn in 1400; these towns are linked by rivers but involved distances of over 20 and even over 40 miles. It is clear that many bricks purchased in ports were not imported but made there. The earliest documented manufactures of English bricks are at Hull in 1303 and at Ely and Wisbech in 1334. Part of the output in the 14th and 15th centuries of kilns at Hull and Boston, both situated at the mouths of rivers, must have contributed to English internal trade. Nevertheless, bricks bought in eastern ports were sometimes foreign; Dutch bricks from Antwerp and Gouda were imported as ballast in the course of the wool trade and sold as far north as Newcastle.[91] Such a consignment and its use are probably illustrated in the proposed purchase of a shipload of 'Flanderstiles' at London in 1370; their value at ten marks suggests a quantity of 12-15,000. They were to be sufficient for building the chimney flues above mantel level of ten fireplaces, of which eight were double ones, in a row of timber-framed shops.[92] A further use may be suggested in the decorative work of early to mid 14th-century date at Lawford and Purleigh churches near the Essex coast, where the pale yellow bricks are probably Dutch because of their exceptionally small size.[93] Bricks from Calais were imported to London for royal projects, as, for example, 114,000 in 1422 for Sheen Palace, which cost £19 to make and £28 10s. to transport.[94] At a time when stone was commonly brought over from France, however, the significance of such trade can easily be overstated.[95]

### Organisation of the Craft

In Italy and the Netherlands local legislation to control the industry developed much earlier than in England. There were one or more kilns at such towns as Venice, Padua and Pisa by the 13th century, where regulations were thought desirable to control the price and size of a vital public necessity. The kilnmen's gilds commonly took over enforcement from the community, their most frequent problem being fraudulent brick size.[96] In the Low Countries municipal policy often encouraged the

90 Barnes and Simpson, 'Caister Castle', 182, 185. However, Fastolf used a different supply to build Drayton Lodge, near Hellesdon, for its bricks are uniquely of a striking pink colour.
91 Hollestelle, *De Steenbakkerij*, 272, 275.
92 Salzman, *Building in England*, 443-4.
93 At Purleigh 7½-8½ by 3⅜-4 by 1¾-2ins., at Lawford 7¾ by ? by 1¾ ins. See Hollestelle, *De Steenbakkerij*, 273-4.
94 *King's Works*, ii, 999 n. 3.
95 Salzman considered the *Libelle of Englyshe*

*Polycye* of 1436 to be incomplete because it omits from its account of contemporary imports the 'Flanders tiles' known from building accounts (Salzman, *English Trade*, 360); but 'Flanders tiles' was an identifying name, obsolete in 1436, which does not necessarily denote a country of origin, and the omission from the *Libelle* seems to confirm the unimportance then of brick as an import.
96 Goldthwaite, *Renaissance Florence*, 178-211.

replacement of timber and thatch with brick and tiles; therefore the price and size of bricks had to be strictly controlled. Municipal kilns were often deliberately operated without profit. From the 14th century onwards Dutch towns strove for standardisation of size and against bricks becoming too small. This resulted in the development of two or even three permitted sizes.[97]

In London, by contrast, it was not until 1605 that timber frontages were forbidden, as a means of saving timber, impeding outbreaks of fire and imposing a degree of uniformity; the fixing of the size and price of bricks followed in 1622.[98] Some English towns had taken an initiative a little earlier; Worcester required all timber chimneys to be replaced in brick or stone within the year in 1467.[99] Size was occasionally regulated in the 16th century, though perhaps not very effectively. The New College contract of 1534 adopted 'the largest assize of the Chamber of the City of London',[100] possibly the 'lawfull scantlyng' referred to at Eton in a contract of 1543/4 with William Martyn, brickmaker, 9½ by 4½ by 2¼ inches.[101] Knight, the resident brickmaker at Southampton, was fined 50s. in 1551 for making his mould larger than that fixed by statute.[102] In 1571 the London Tilers' and Bricklayers' Company charter established a size of 9 by 4¼ by 2¼ inches for bricks when fired within a 15-mile radius of London.[103] At York in 1590-1 it is said to have been fixed at 10 by 5 by 2½ inches.[104]

Very little is known of brick gilds or their charters until after 1560, when the gilds were in decline and the value of charters much reduced. In these respects the stonemasons were scarcely more ordered, as is to be expected with crafts which were essentially itinerant whereas gilds were locally based.[105] Nevertheless the Beverley bricklayers claimed in 1596 that their craft had been organised since 1426; at a similar date the Newcastle wallers, bricklayers and daubers professed the grant of a charter by Henry VI.[106] This lack of a clearly-demarcated craft is reflected in the gilds which were eventually established, commonly incorporating a large number of crafts, not all of them even involved in building.

Neither does the organisation of formal apprenticeship seem to have been common among bricklayers; no apprentices have been identified among the dozens of layers at Eton in the 1440s.[107] Cornelius Brekemason, however, had his apprentice Jacob at Farnham Castle in 1475 and 1477.[108] At Kirby Muxloe, John Corbell had Antony Yzebronde alias Docheman as apprentice from 3 March until 16 June 1483 at 4d., although he spent eight of those weeks helping the brickmaker for 2d. a day, and helping Henry Corbell, no doubt a relation, for 3d. a day. All three men ceased employment together that month on the death of their employer. Subsequently

97 Hollestelle, *De Steenbakkerij*, 273-5.
98 *King's Works*, iii, 140, 142.
99 Knoop and Jones, *Med. Mason*, 6-7.
100 Harvey, *Mediaeval Craftsmen*, 198.
101 Willis and Clark, *Architectural History*, i, 419 n. 4.
102 *V.C.H. Hants and Isle of Wight*, v, 465.
103 Lloyd, op. cit. note 13, 12.
104 J. Bilson, 'The North Bar, Beverley', *Trans. E.*

*Riding Antiquarian Soc.* iv (1896), 47n.
105 Knoop and Jones, *Med. Mason*, 135-43, 207-9.
106 Ibid. 13, 207.
107 D. Knoop and G.P. Jones, 'The Building of Eton College 1442-60', *Ars Quatuor Coronatorum*, xlvi (1937), 90.
108 Thompson, 'Date of "Fox's Tower"', 88.

*Fig. 107* Eton College, Long Chamber, begun *c.* 1441.

Nicholas Bentson and Thomas Bentson his apprentice were employed for the same 13½ days (at 6*d.* and 3*d.*) in October, before work finally ceased. J. Horne, senior bricklayer for six months in 1481, was accompanied by John Prentes for 4 days and Thomas 'lernyng' for 1½ days, both at 6*d.* per day, and by William Prentes for 5 days at 3*d.*, while Horne was on day-work.[109]

The lack of demarcation is also evident in the men's employment, the bricklayers at Kirby Muxloe in 1482 digging foundations, at full rates of pay. The corporation brickmakers at Hull performed all kinds of work, J. Drinkale and Richard Southwell, for example, spending several days in 1422-3 carrying sand at 4*d.* as against the craftsman's daily rate of 6*d.* At the royal manor of Dartford in 1541, the bricklayers were not only employed to lay bricks and hew mouldings on them, but on demolition work, building a stone wall galleted with flint, and plastering and decorating their work.[110]

Building accounts including both brick and stone construction often show the interchangeability of brick and stone layers. At Eton, although there were 13 men in

109  For some of the general problems of apprentice-ships in the building crafts see L.R. Shelby, 'The Education of Medieval English Master

Masons', *Mediaeval Studies*, xxxii (1970), 19-23.
110  *King's Works*, iv, 70, 72.

1444-6 who were paid only as bricklayers, there were also 18 stonelayers of whom ten worked partly as bricklayers. In 1442 there were only two 'brikemen', who worked for four weeks each, but 38 stonelayers of whom 20 were also paid as 'brikemen'.[111] The clerks distinguished them as *positores de brike alias roughmasons* or *positores vocati rough leyers et brekemen*. Again at Kirby Muxloe some of the most skilled bricklayers were paid in May-July 1482 as 'roughmasons'. At Nonsuch Palace men employed as bricklayers in 1538 were 'roughlayers' subsequently, while working under the same warden.[112] Men found employment both as bricklayers and masons at Sandgate Castle in 1539-40.[113] In Calais in the 14th and 15th centuries bricklaying was always done by 'masons' and their materials were called 'brickestones' or *lapides vocati brykkes*.[114] Robert Newby was both master bricklayer and chief mason to Lincoln Cathedral in the 1520s. Christopher Dickinson, who was nominally master-mason to Windsor Castle and at Nonsuch Palace, appears in the Nonsuch general accounts as master-mason, but the detailed accounts consistently refer to him by his role there of master bricklayer.[115]

That some antagonism grew up between the crafts of stonemasonry and bricklaying, caused no doubt by the steady increase of bricklayers' work, is suggested at York where a dispute broke out in 1490 between masons and the 'tilers' working on a tower, with a tiler killed and tilers' tools broken. It has been suggested that the tower was the Red Tower and that the dispute arose because the masons were accustomed to working on the city walls and resented this incursion by the bricklayers.[116] This craft distinction was also displayed in appointments as Common Mason of York: two of the seven known holders of this office between 1464 and 1533 being made free of the city as 'tilers' rather than masons.[117]

No defined hierarchy developed among bricklayers as there had with masons, as at Eton in 1442-60 with a master-mason, freemasons, freemason setters, hardhewers and roughmasons. At Kirby Muxloe there was a chief bricklayer at 8*d*. a day; others earned 7*d*. or 6*d*. at summer rates, whether laying or hewing bricks, building vaults or creating the diaper patterns and pictures. At Tattershall Castle the accounts mention 'masons called brekmasons' and 'roughbrekmasons'; possibly only the first category laid the facing bricks and built the vaulting and corbelling.[118] Bricklayers were normally served by at least their own number of servants: 'trowel men' or labourers who received about half their masters' pay, or by one or more apprentices generally earning the same as, or more than, the labourers.

Some bricklayers also made bricks. Antony Yzebronde, apprentice bricklayer at Kirby Muxloe, spent more time at the kiln than with his master. The brickmaker in 1470 for Fox's Tower, Farnham Castle, was called Brian Brekemason. Robert Nevill worked as both maker and layer in the London area *c*.1500.[119] One of Henry VIII's

111 Knoop and Jones, 'Eton College', 106.
112 *King's Works*, iv, 181.
113 Ibid. 573 n. 3.
114 Ibid. i, 427 n. 4.
115 Harvey, *English Mediaeval Architects*, op. cit.

note 62, 213.
116 *R.C.H.M. York*, ii, 19-20.
117 Ibid. 174.
118 Simpson, *Tattershall Castle*, 60.
119 Harvey, *English Mediaeval Architects*, 246.

*Fig. 108* Prior Overton's Tower, Repton (Derbys.), 1437-8.

makers at Oatlands Palace and Woking Manor House was Edward Lydger, 'bricklayer'.[120] At Camber Castle in 1539 Gilbert Drynkherst was successively head bricklayer at 7*d.* a day, brickmaker at 8*d.*, and warden of the bricklayers.[121]

At Kirby Muxloe the building accounts of 1481-4 are sufficiently detailed to reveal the bricklayers' terms of employment. At any one time there was one senior bricklayer, who generally laid bricks 'in gross' at 18*d.* a thousand, any other contractor taking 14*d.* for the same work; occasionally he was paid instead at the daily rate of 8*d.* (the same as the visiting master-mason). When on wages he was given a maximum of five 'trowel men' and servants, costing in all 16*s.* per week; this was equivalent in cost to 10,700 bricks laid in gross. The contractors on taskwork

---

120 *King's Works*, iv, 346.                    121 Ibid. 423.

averaged 20,300 bricks per week throughout the period of laying, proving that they then provided their own auxiliaries. The way in which names occur in the accounts for a while and then disappear, possibly to surface again later, implies either a fluid labour force, or (as some evidence suggests) that at times these men were taken on as sub-contractors by the master bricklayer. Some brick-hewing was paid for during the winter months by weekly wage or by the week in gross. In addition John Corbell, senior bricklayer, received £4 12s. 6d. in October 1482 for hewing bricks at 5s. the thousand; there were further payments to him for 26,000 hewn bricks at 1s. 6d. the thousand in March and April 1483, which could easily account for the employment that winter of bricklayers Maligoo, Dale, Milner and Ruddicourt. The flexibility of the bricklayers' terms was also demonstrated in February and March 1483 when several of them were paid almost in alternate weeks for laying in gross or by the day, presumably reflecting the incidence of rapid bricklaying and fiddly jobs.

At least once Corbell undertook to mend and level a wall for a fee (1s.). Records of such taskwork are more common in the 16th century: Christopher Dickinson, master bricklayer at Hampton Court Palace, built the vault under the Great Watching Chamber in 1535 'by convention' for £37.[122] The garden and orchard walls at Hunsdon House were laid by task c.1530.[123] At Hengrave Hall (Suffolk), chimneys were made by bargain by Robert Davyson c.1536.[124] The brickmakers of Hull's corporation yard had flexible terms of employment, the accounts generally including some men paid by the task and some by the day, or even the same men paid by both methods in one account. J. Drynkale made three batches of *teguli* for lump sums in 1422-3, also filling, emptying, and watching the firing of the kiln on a daily basis, and Thomas Tokill in 1432-3 was paid separate sums for digging the clay, tempering it and making the bricks; he then loaded the kiln and ignited, watched and emptied three firings for two further payments. At Farnham Castle, the bricks for Fox's Tower were made and laid under contract in 1469-73 but in 1475 both jobs were performed by direct labour.[125]

The employment of brickmakers during the winter months was uncertain, although Tokill and his mate received £13 10s. 6d. in 1432-3, or sufficient for 324½ days' work (allowing them 6d. and 4d. a day); no doubt they spent the winter months digging and preparing their clay. At Camber Castle in 1539-40 the brickmakers are not however named in the accounts between about October and March-April.[126] The employment of bricklayers during the winter months was also uncertain. Although at Eton in the 1440s they continued for much of the winter at their summertime rates,[127] and at Kirby Muxloe at least some of the 'brekeleyers' continued to be paid as 'brekehewers' in 1482-3, the previous winter they had been excluded from the accounts between 5 November and 25 March; nothing implies their alternative employment.

122  Ibid. 132.
123  Ibid. 155.
124  Gage, op. cit. note 19, 53.

125  Thompson, 'Kirby Muxloe', 87-8.
126  *King's Works*, iv, 425, 426.
127  Knoop and Jones, 'Eton College', 85, 99-100.

## Further Reading

The only specific study of English medieval brickmaking or laying is T.P. Smith's *The Medieval Brickmaking Industry in England 1400-1450* (1985), the other principal compilations being Nathaniel Lloyd's *History of English Brickwork* (1925), Salzman's *Building in England down to 1540* (revised edn. 1967), J.A. Wight's *Brick Building in England, from the Middle Ages to 1550* (1972), and N.J. Moore's *Brick Building in Medieval England* (unpublished M.Phil. thesis, University of East Anglia, 1969). The most thorough account yet published, however, is of Dutch brickmaking in Dr. J. Hollestelle's *De Steenbakkerij in de Nederlanden* [Brickmaking in the Netherlands down to 1560] (Arnhem, 1976), which provides valuable analogies for our industries; it comes with an English summary but deserves full translation for its uniquely comprehensive and detailed knowledge.

The only substantial medieval account of bricks being made and fired in England is F.W. Brooks's 'Medieval Brick-yard at Hull', *J.B.A.A.* 3rd ser. vi (1939), and the only published set of building accounts for a medieval brick construction are those of Kirby Muxloe Castle, published by A. Hamilton Thompson in 1920; summary information on the industry is presented in A.F. Leach's 'The Building of Beverley Bar', *Trans. E. Riding Antiquarian Soc.* iv (1896), H.D. Barnes and W.D. Simpson's 'Building Accounts of Caister Castle', *Norfolk Archaeology*, xxx (1952), and W.D. Simpson's *Tattershall Castle* (Lincoln Rec. Soc. lv, 1960). Studies of specific topics include R.J. and P.E. Firman's 'Geological Approach to the Study of Medieval Bricks', *Mercian Geologist*, ii (1967), J.S. Gardner's 'Coggeshall Abbey and its Early Brickwork', *J.B.A.A.* 3rd ser. xviii (1955), and L.S. Harley's 'Typology of Brick', *J.B.A.A.* 3rd ser. xxxvii (1974), while the volumes of the *History of the King's Works*, the *Inventories* of the Royal Commission on Historical Monuments, the writings of John H. Harvey, and R. Willis and J.W. Clark's three-volume *Architectural History of the University of Cambridge* (1886) are invaluable sources of material.

10

*Vessel Glass*

R. J. CHARLESTON

The evidence on which to base an account of glass-making in medieval England is sketchy in the extreme. Although there is a plethora of excavated glasses (not always accurately dated by context), there is a great lack of documentation dating from before 1500. The industry, however, was a profoundly traditional one and there seems to be a smooth progression from the medieval period to the middle of the 16th century, when there is a sharp technical leap forward, thanks mainly to the immigration of workers from the Continent of Europe. This, however, represents an accelerated progression along existing lines, and so it has seemed legitimate in many aspects of the subject to argue from the later period to the earlier.

*Methods of Production*

Modern technology has established that glass is an extremely complex substance. Before 1500 and right back to Roman times and beyond, glass was a material made by fire from a mixture of sand (or crushed siliceous pebbles) and plant-ash. In the Mediterranean area and further East, the ash used was that of maritime plants of various kinds, notably those of the *salicornia* family. These are rich in soda, and this alkali tends to give a more lustrous and quick-working 'metal', the best properties of which may be seen in the perfected Venetian 'crystal' of the 15th-17th centuries. Up to the beginning of our period soda-ash seems to have been available in northern Europe, but after about 1000 these supplies appear to have been disrupted or to have dried up, and the northern glass-makers were forced back on the ashes of inland vegetation. These are rich in potash, and also normally have a reasonably large lime content, a necessary constituent which gives stability to glass. Different ashes give different results, but the favoured variety was beech. Theophilus at the very head of his Second Book, on 'The Art of the Worker in Glass', writes: 'If you have the intention of making glass, first cut many beechwood logs and dry them out. Then burn them all together in a clean place and carefully collect the ashes, taking care that you do not mix any earth or stones with them. . .'[1] This predilection was

1   Theophilus, *On Divers Arts*, ed. Hawthorne & Smith, 49.

probably not exclusive. Agricola,[2] writing half a century after the end of our period but probably throwing light backward on it, writes: 'But those who have none of the above-mentioned saps (i.e. the soda-ashes) take two parts of ashes of oak or ilex or of hard wood (*roborei*) or of turkey oak, or if these are not to hand, of beech or of fir, and mix them with one of gravel or sand, adding a little salt made from brackish or sea water . . . and a minute quantity of manganese; but the glass made with these latter is less white and translucent.' The French glass-makers certainly used bracken-ash (whence the name *verre de fougère*), and half a century after Agricola the priest-technologist Antonio Neri, compiler of the first printed book of glass technology (1612), although brought up in the Italian tradition, admits the efficacy of bracken, bean-cods and -stalks, coleworts, brambles, millet-stalks, rushes and reeds.[3] Beech, however, was certainly appreciated in the Middle Ages, for it has a high content of manganese, and this element made it possible to extract from the glass a wide range of different colours without recourse to added colorants, a great boon to the makers of window-glass.[4] Not many analyses have been published of English medieval glasses,[5] and it is in any case impossible to decide from an analysis alone just what form of alkali was used in a particular glass.

In the primitive and usually isolated conditions under which the medieval glass-maker worked, the sand which he used was normally of local origin, the woodland site being presumably chosen as far as possible to be within reach of such a source. One of the most critical qualities of sand is the proportion of iron oxide which it contains. A percentage as low as 0.5 or less can produce a distinct green colour, and this is almost universally present in English medieval glass. In the Weald of Surrey and Sussex, probably the most important English centre of the craft in medieval times, it is known that white sand from Lodsworth Common was used for glass-making, and a modern sample from this source was found capable of furnishing 'material for making glass of a pale colour'.[6] A second possible source was the white sand which outcrops at Hambledon Common, and a known glass-making site at Broomfield Hanger has a fine greyish sand in the vicinity: both are close to Chiddingfold (Surrey), the most important centre of the Wealden industry.[7] Glassmen were discriminating about their sand, although the medieval practitioner, with his simple green glass, probably did not need to be too selective. Merrett, however, writing in 1662, mentions that the London glasshouses used for crystal

2  Georg Agricola, *De Re Metallica* (Basle, 1556), Book XII, translated by S.E. Winbolt, *Wealden Glass* (1933), 79.

3  A. Neri, *L'Arte Vetraria* (Florence, 1612), translated by Christopher Merrett as *The Art of Glass* (1662). The passage is in Book I, chaps. 5 and 6. That bracken was used in England in the 16th century appears from W. Harrison, *Description of England* (1577); see R.J. Charleston, *English Glass*, 86: 'glass . . . made at home of ferne and burned stone'. Ferns were sold to glass-makers at Wolseley

(Staffs.) in 1479 – see Crossley, op. cit. in note 24, 47.

4  W.E.S. Turner, 'Studies in Ancient Glasses and Glassmaking Processes, Part V, Raw Materials and Melting Processes', *Trans. Soc. of Glass Technology*, xl (1956), 289.

5  Ibid. Part IV, 'The Chemical Compositions of Ancient Glasses', 173; J.C. Harrington, *Glass-making at Jamestown* (1952), 34.

6  G.H. Kenyon, *The Glass Industry of the Weald* (1967), 35.

7  Ibid.

*Fig. 109* Miniature from a MS of 'Sir John Mandeville's Travels'. Probably Bohemian; *c.* 1420 (B.L., MS Add. 24189 f.16).

glass 'the white Sand . . . from Maidstone in Kent, and for Green-glasses, a coarser from Woolwich. The former will not mix with ordinary green metall. Both these cost but little besides their bringing by water'.[8] At a later date glass-making sand was brought from Alum Bay, in the Isle of Wight, and from Lynn (Norfolk);[9] there is no evidence, however, that these sands were used in the Middle Ages. Suitable sands were also found in Cheshire and Staffordshire, both counties that are known to have sustained glasshouses in the medieval period.[10]

The third important raw material necessary for a glasshouse was a fire-clay suitable for the making of the glass-pots (crucibles) in which the mixture of ash and sand was melted. This clay might have to resist temperatures of more than 1200°C, and such clays are not readily available. There is plenty of evidence, mainly from the 16th and 17th centuries, that clay was regularly transported to glasshouses from a distance.[11] The best English fire-clay came from the Stourbridge area of Worcestershire, and analyses carried out on pots from the St. Weonard's glasshouse (Herefords.), probably late 16th century, suggested that the clay used there came mainly from this source;[12] and when in about 1617 Sir Robert Mansell built furnaces in Newcastle he complained that the Stourbridge clay brought for his pots had been 'corrupted' and rendered useless.[13] The Wealden clays are not suitable, and the medieval glass-makers there may well have used the same source of supply. Merrett, however, writes (1662): '. . . those for *Green Glass* are made of *Non-such* clay, mixed with another clay brought from *Worcestershire*, which bears the fire better than that of *Nonsuch*, but both together make the best pots'.[14]

The making of clay pots was a craft apart. Theophilus says (Book II, Ch. 5): ' . . . take some white pottery clay, dry it out, grind it carefully, pour water on it, knead it hard with a piece of wood, and make your pots. These should be wide at the top, narrowing at the bottom, and should have a small in-curving lip around their rims. When they are dry, pick them up with the tongs and set them in the red-hot furnace . . .'[15] Although an Italian writer of 1540 says that the pots were made on the wheel,[16] the normal tradition of northern Europe has been for them to be built up of rolls of clay, starting from a flat circular base formed on a board. It was important that all air-bubbles should be eliminated – Merrett writes: 'This clay being well washed from all impurities is calcin'd in a *furnace* for this purpose, and then ground in

8   Merrett, *Art of Glass*, 261.

9   *Encyclopaedia Britannica* (3rd edn., 1797), article 'Glass', 767; Susan Frank, *Glass and Archaeology* (1982), 73.

10  Ruth Hurst Vose, *Glass* (1980), 111-12; that calcined stones were occasionally used in England, as in Italy, is suggested by the passage from Harrison, op. cit. note 3.

11  E.g. from Scotland to England: Eleanor S. Godfrey, *The Development of English Glass-making, 1560-1640* (1975), 97, n. 5; within Ireland: M.S. Dudley Westropp, *Irish Glass* (n.d. [?1920]), 26.

12  N.P. Bridgewater, 'Glasshouse Farm, St. Weonards: a Small Glass-working Site', *Trans. Woolhope Naturalists' Field Club*, xxxvii (1963), 304-5.

13  Godfrey, op. cit. note 11, 88. Eventually suitable clay was found in Northumberland.

14  Merrett, *Art of Glass*, 246. The second constituent was presumably Stourbridge clay.

15  Theophilus, *On Divers Arts*, ed. Hawthorne & Smith, 53-4.

16  Vannoccio Biringuccio, *Pirotechnia* (Venice, 1540), translated by C.S. Smith and M.T. Gnudi (New York, 1942), 128.

their Mill into a fine powder, which being mixed with water is trod with their bare feet till it come to a good consistence, fit to mould, which they do with their hands, and when fashioned, dry them in a convenient place, and afterwards anneal them in or over the *furnace* . . .'[17]

Theophilus's description of the shape of a glass-pot is vague enough, the only distinct trait being the incurved lip, and this feature survives sporadically right through to the 18th century. No satisfactory chronological evolution of the glass-pot has been worked out, although an attempt has been made.[18] The great majority of the glass-pots found on English medieval and late-medieval sites have been bucket-shaped or roughly cylindrical.[19] The foot of a pot from the pre-conquest Glastonbury site[20] showed an everted side, and a rim fragment had an out-turned lip, the latter feature also to be observed on the Mandeville miniature (Fig. 109), and in Agricola's illustrations (the pots there being described as 'bellied' and having a maximum diameter of 1½ feet, the diameter of foot and lip being 1 foot and the height 2 feet).[21] Pots found in the Weald seem on average to measure about a foot at the base, expanding to some 14-15 in. at the rim of an everted shape, but about a foot for the barrel-shaped variety (Fig. 113). The average thickness was slightly less than an inch for the walls, but some 2-3 inches for the base.[22] Smaller round-based crucibles were made probably for more specialised glasses, one of them from Chaleshurst containing the residues of sealing-wax red glass. These, the 'piling pots' of Merrett, were probably placed on top of the main pots.[23] The Wealden pots correspond pretty well in size with those of Staffordshire.[24] The size of the pot probably tended to grow as time went on. Records of the Knole glasshouse (1585/6) show that '2 lode pot clay for makyng 12 pots' were brought to the site, and the pots were presumably made up there. Later this speciality seems to have run in families, but in the medieval period it may be presumed that one of the glasshouse team worked as pot-maker.[25] The suggestion that glass-pots were deliberately glazed or decorated can be scouted: the external glassy coating was acquired in the atmosphere of the furnace.[26]

Far less important than the materials already mentioned were certain oxides which may have been imported for the colouring of glass. These include cobalt for making blue glass, manganese both for colouring glass purple and for neutralising the green tone of glass to make it appear colourless,[27] and copper to produce a

17  Merrett, *Art of Glass*, 245-6.
18  R. Chambon, 'Esquisse de l'Evolution Morphologique des Creusets de Verrerie, de l'Antiquité à la Renaissance', *Annales du 1ᵉʳ Congrès des 'Journées Internationales du Verre'* (Liège, 1959), 115-7.
19  Kenyon, *Glass Industry of the Weald*, 49-50.
20  9-10th century – D.B. Harden, 'Domestic Window Glass: Roman, Saxon and Medieval', in E.M. Jope (ed.), *Studies in Building History . . .* (1961), 53; *Somerset and Dorset Notes and Queries*, xxvii, 68 ff., 165 ff., 251 ff.
21  Winbolt, *Wealden Glass*, 80.
22  Kenyon, *Glass Industry of the Weald*, 49-53, 55-8.
23  Ibid. 52-3; Merrett, *Art of Glass*, 246.

24  T. Pape, 'Medieval Glassworkers in North Staffordshire', *N. Staffs. Field Club Trans.* lxviii (1934), 36; at Bagot's Park the pots were slightly larger at the rim than suggested for the Weald: D.W. Crossley, 'Glassmaking in Bagot's Park, Staffordshire, in the Sixteenth Century', *Post-Med. Arch.* i (1967), 44-83, at 62, 73-4.
25  Kenyon, *Glass Industry of the Weald*, 53, suggests that a dense aggregation of glasshouses such as that in the Weald may have supported a specialist potmaker.
26  Vose, op. cit. note 10, 161.
27  R.W. Douglas and Susan Frank, *A History of Glassmaking* (Henley-on-Thames, 1972), 7.

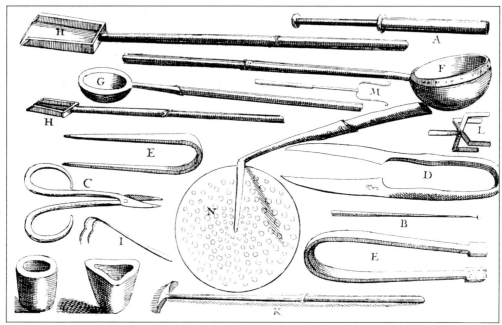

*Fig. 110* Glassmaker's tools, from Haudicquer de Blancourt, *De l'Art de la Verrerie* (Paris, 1697), 48. A. Blowing-iron with wooden handle (note swelling at end); B. Pontil, solid iron; C,D. Shears, D also used for opening up a glass; E. Two types of *procello* (*pucellas*); F. Large ladle for filling the working-pots; G. Small ladle for scumming the pots and removing glass for purification; I. Fork for stirring the pots: K. Rake for stirring the metal in the pots and also the frit; M. Fork for removing finished glasses to the lehr.

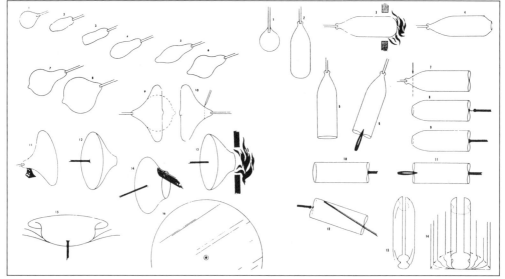

*Fig. 111* *Left:* Stages of making a 'crown'. (After Chambon, 'L'Evolution des Procédés . . . du Verre à Vitres'.) *Right:* Stages of making a 'muff'. (Same source)

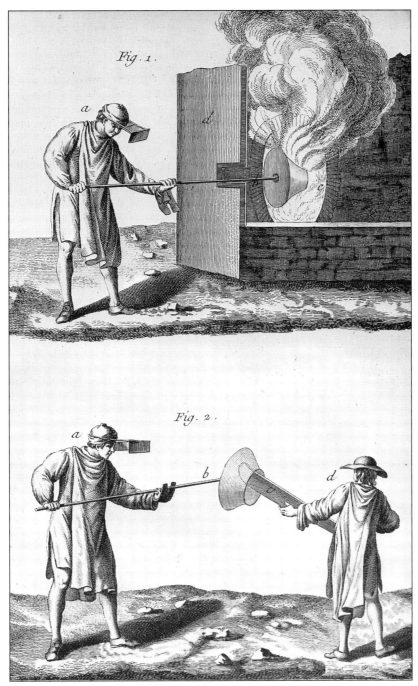

*Fig. 112* Penultimate operations of making a 'crown'. The paraison has been transferred to the pontil and is warmed up (1), then opened up by an assistant (2) prior to rewarming and spinning to finish the sheet. Diderot et al., *Encyclopédie . . . des Arts et des Métiers, Recueil de Planches . . .*, x (1772), Pl. 14.

translucent ruby or an opaque sealing-wax red. The English medieval glass-maker seems to have made little or no coloured glass for windows, this being imported from the Continent.[28] Blue glass vessels are known, although they too may have been Continental imports.[29] In the medieval period cobalt (in the form of 'zaffre', a diluted colorant) seems to have derived mainly from the Levant,[30] probably by way of Venice.[31] Manganese came from Piedmont, Tuscany and Liguria, but by Merrett's time was also derived from the lead-mines on Mendip.[32] Blue and purple glasses, however, found on glasshouse sites were more probably brought there as cullet (glass scrap helpful in promoting the founding of the batch). This, however, is not the case with the copper ruby. Copper is an extremely powerful colorant and for windows it was normally 'flashed', a thin layer of ruby diluted by superimposition on more or less colourless glass, and this technique was probably not practised in England before 1500. Reduced copper (melted in a smoky atmosphere) produces an opaque sealing-wax red, a type of glass which was popular in the Middle Ages, being used to make both complete vessels[33] and threads for decorating green glasses.[34] The Chaleshurst crucible has already been mentioned: while at Malham Ashfold, near Wisborough Green, dating probably before 1500, a considerable number of sealing-wax red lumps were found, apparently made on site.[35] Outside the Weald, a crucible containing red glass was found at the glasshouse site at Kingswood, Delamere (Cheshire), dated tentatively to the late 14th or 15th century.[36]

The most critical of all raw materials, however, was wood for firing. This could be consumed at a prodigious rate. At Knole (Kent) in 1585-6, a four-pot glasshouse consumed 543 cords of wood in 32 weeks.[37] It has been calculated that this would clear about 4 acres of 15-year-old coppice wood per month.[38] The furnaces were usually extinguished for eight to ten weeks a year, and it has been calculated that about 700 cords a year would be a normal consumption.[39] At Knole, 'Adams and George . . . do not sett upp the cords halfe so fast as they are caryed away, therefore . . . you must ether graunte that more woodcutters may be sett at worke or ells suffer to carry out of some other place in the parke. . .'[40] This is hardly surprising, for Agricola says of the founding process: 'Two boys taking turns night and day feed the

28  Kenyon, *Glass Industry of the Weald*, 88; J.A. Knowles, 'The Source of the Coloured Glass used in Medieval Stained Glass Windows', *Glass* (June, 1926), 157-9, 201-3, 295-6.

29  G. Beresford, 'The Medieval Manor of Penhallam, Jacobstow, Cornwall', *Med. Arch.* xviii (1974), 90-139.

30  Douglas and Frank, *History of Glassmaking*, 135.

31  Cipriano Piccolpasso, the maiolica potter of Castel Durante in Umbria, says in his book, finished in 1558, that 'the zaffre comes from Venice' – R.W. Lightbown and A. Caiger-Smith, *The Three Books of the Potter's Art* (1980).

32  Merrett, *Art of Glass*, 289-90. The Italian locations come from Neri, *L'Arte Vetraria*, 15, and Piccolpasso, op. cit. note 31.

33  R.J. Charleston, 'Glass of the High Medieval Period (12th to 15th Century)', *Bull. de l'Association Internationale pour l'Histoire du Verre*, viii (1977-80), 69.

34  Ibid.

35  Kenyon, *Glass Industry of the Weald*, 88, 161-2, 190-1.

36  Ibid. 220-1; R. Newstead, 'Glasshouse in Delamere Forest, Cheshire', *Chester and N. Wales Architectural, Archaeol. and Historic Soc. Jnl.*, n.s. xxxiii (1939), 35.

37  Kenyon, *Glass Industry of the Weald*, 47, 219. A cord is 128 cubic feet.

38  Crossley, 'Bagot's Park', art. cit. note 24, 63.

39  Kenyon, *Glass Industry of the Weald*, 47. Godfrey, op. cit. note 11, 191, suggests that consumption as high as 900 or 1,000 cords.

40  Kenyon, *Glass Industry of the Weald*, 47.

fire by putting dry logs on the hearth',[41] and this incessant stoking is attested from other sources.[42] Agricola mentions logs and the Knole papers record 'clefte cords' and '28 cords of log wood',[43] but the timber used was probably more often thinnings or pollardings. A Wealden glass-maker wrote in 1567: 'we do not mean to cut the actual trunks of good trees but only the branches . . .'[44] A contract of 1380 refers to 'underwood' but a deed relating to the same glasshouse five years later mentions 'the said underwood . . . to have, cut down, cleave and expend', so the lop and top may in fact have been of considerable size.[45] Underwood could not be cut in June and July, when the sap was flowing most strongly.[46] Whether small wood or grown timber, much foresight was required to ensure a steady supply to the furnaces, especially since allowance had to be made for drying the wood before use.[47] Some glassmen depended on buying from their landlords,[48] while others contrived to buy woodland for their own use. Thus in 1557 Henry Strudwick, of Kirdford (Sussex), left to his sons 'the profyt of my Glasse Howse, withall the beches that I have bought, and half the beches in and upon Idehurst and Crofts . . .';[49] and a later and larger operator, Isaac Bongar, in 1615 sold two manors near Alfold with extensive woodlands, and remained owner of further land in Sussex.[50] The tenure of a glass-maker who depended on other men's woodland was obviously uncertain, and this situation contributed to the wandering propensity of his life, a tradition within the woodland glass-making communities.

Theophilus, having described his furnace, says: 'take beechwood logs completely dried out in smoke, and light large fires in both sides of the bigger furnace . . .'[51] Beech indeed seems to have been the preferred fuel, and it was natural that beech ashes should be used as a source of potash (see p. 237 above). Both beech and oak grew well on the Weald. Other types of wood, however, could be used if available. Merrett mentions ash, juniper and (disparagingly) tamarisk.[52] Alder, ash and poplar were apparently used at Bagot's Park (Staffs.).[53]

The most important tool of the glass-maker was naturally his furnace, probably his largest single capital investment. It would probably be a mistake, however, to think of large and permanent structures such as characterised the mainly urban glass-making of, say, contemporary Italy. The building of them seems to have involved local stone, clay, and some brickwork.[54] Theophilus (see below) recommends stone and clay, and the probably near-contemporary Eraclius, in his *De Coloribus et Artibus Romanorum*, says: '. . . make a furnace of stones, faced with clay mixed with horse-dung'.[55] The only excavated English furnace of pre-1500 date conforms to this

41 Winbolt, *Wealden Glass*, 80.
42 R.J. Charleston, 'A Gold and Enamel Box in the form of a Glass Furnace', *Jnl. of Glass Studies*, xx (1978) 39-40.
43 Kenyon, *Glass Industry of the Weald*, 47, 220.
44 Ibid. 45.
45 Ibid. 31-2.
46 Ibid.
47 Godfrey, op. cit. note 11, 148, 192.
48 Crossley, op. cit. note 24, 45-8.

49 Kenyon, *Glass Industry of the Weald*, 45-6.
50 Godfrey, op. cit. note 11, 56.
51 Bk. II, chap. iv, ed. Hawthorne & Smith, 52.
52 Op. cit. note 3, 275.
53 Crossley, op. cit. note 24, 57, 78.
54 Kenyon, *Glass Industry of the Weald*, 220.
55 M.P. Merrifield, *Original Treatises . . . on the Arts of Painting*, 2 vols. (1849), i, 212. For the dating of the Eraclius MS see Theophilus, *De Div. Artibus*, ed. Dodwell, xiv.

general prescription,[56] and regularly shaped and solidly built furnaces probably become usual only in the 16th century.[57] The first description of this 'Northern' tupe of furnace[58] appears in Theophilus (Book II, Ch. I):–

> . . . After this build a furnace of stones and clay, fifteen feet long and ten feet wide, in this way.
>
> First, lay down foundations on each long side, one foot thick, and in between them make a firm, smooth, flat hearth with stones and clay. Mark off three equal parts and build a cross-wall separating one third from the other two. Then make a hole in each of the short sides through which fire and wood can be put in, and building the encircling wall up to a height of almost four feet, again make a firm, smooth, flat hearth over the whole area, and let the dividing wall rise a little above it. After this, in the larger section, make four holes through the hearth along one of the long sides, and four along the other. The work pots are to be placed in these. Then make two openings in the centre through which the flame can rise. Now, as you build the encircling wall, make two square windows on each side, a span long and wide, one opposite each of the flame openings, through which the work pots and whatever is placed in them can be put in and taken out. In the smaller section also make an opening (for the flame) through the hearth close to the cross-wall, and a window, a span in size, near the short wall, through which whatever is necessary for the work can be put in and taken out.
>
> When you have arranged everything like this, enclose the interior with an outer wall, so that the inside is in the shape of an arched vault, rising a little more than half a foot, and the top is made into a smooth, flat hearth, with a three-finger-high lip all round it, so that whatever work or implements are laid on top cannot fall off. This furnace is called the work furnace.[59] [Cf. Fig. 116]

The essence of this furnace was that it was in two parts, one larger and one smaller, with a firebox below (probably running throughout its length, although this is not stated) and a level 'hearth' above, having the glass-pots in the larger part and a working surface in the smaller part on which the sand and ashes could be given a preliminary heating and fusion, or 'fritting'. Above these chambers was simply a 'reverberatory' vault from which the heat was reflected down on to the glass in the pots. The pots were accessible through apertures in the sides of the structure, and the fritting-furnace had its own access-hole on one side. The description is in a number of ways unclear[60] and some of the details are in themselves inherently improbable

56   Eric S. Wood, 'A Medieval Glasshouse at Blunden's Wood, Hambledon, Surrey', *Surrey Arch. Coll.* lxii (1965), 54-79.

57   Cf. e.g. Blunden's Wood with Vann Copse, in the same area – Kenyon, *Glass Industry of the Weald*, 193-200.

58   For this distinction, see R.J. Charleston, 'Glass Furnaces through the Ages', *Jnl. of Glass Studies*, xx (1978), 9-33.

59   Theophilus, *On Divers Arts*, ed. Hawthorne &

Smith, 49-51.

60   As differing interpretations make evident – compare Hawthorne and Smith, 50-1 with Charles de L'Escalopier, *Théophile* . . . (Paris, 1843), 80, or the scheme published by J.A. Knowles, 'Medieval Processes of Glass Manufacture', *Glass* (July, 1927), 349: this formulation was followed in the Science Museum reconstruction illustrated by e.g. Charleston, op. cit. note 58, Fig. 15, and present Fig. 116.

(for instance, no furnace is known in which holes were made to hold the pots, a procedure which would make it difficult to insert them and virtually impossible to remove them; and which is totally unnecessary, since the heat plays more effectively on the open tops of the pots, not their bases). The presence of eight pots would be highly unusual and would imply an exceptionally large furnace (cf. pp. 248-9). With this puzzling structure should be compared the furnace described by Eraclius, with three chambers, the largest and central one (the founding furnace) with four pots and a single aperture on either side: of the subsidiary chambers, that on the right is smaller and its use is unexplained, while that on the left is larger and is used for fritting, pre-heating pots, and annealing.[61] Theophilus caters for a second separate furnace for annealing,[62] and the Eraclius text may be corrupt (left exchanged for right?) in giving all these functions to a single subordinate furnace. Eraclius does, however, seem to describe a feature which is common to most early Northern furnaces – the fire-trench running right through the long axis of the furnace, leaving a smooth 'base' (*fundamentum*) on either side (to take the pots).[63] The one aperture to service two pots seems to correspond with the ratio prescribed by Theophilus, awkward though this arrangement would have been in practice.

From these confused and difficult texts it is a relief to turn to a straightforward picture (Fig. 109). This well-known miniature illustrates a MS of Sir John Mandeville's *Travels*, in the British Library (Add. MS 24189), ascribed to Bohemia and dated to the early years of the 15th century. Two glass-blowers work at a furnace with two openings on the visible side; to the left is an ancillary smaller furnace with an arched opening from which a workman is extracting finished glasses. A workman to the right tends the hearth at the entry to the fire-trench, which probably extends the length of the combined furnaces; its further 'tease-hole' may in fact be just visible at the left-hand side. Behind the lehr (annealing oven) the owner or chief workman shows emotion over a finished jug, while in the background workmen dig and carry off sand, while others carry sacks (? of potash) and baskets (? of finished glasses) off-scene. Over the furnace is built a light open shed for protection from the weather,[64] while to the right is a timber structure on top of which are probably stacked billets of wood drying off preparatory to use.[65] The furnace, which seems to have a straight ground-line, is nevertheless obviously domed over the founding area and the annealing chamber. The pots in the furnace have the bellied shape with out-turned rim which recurs in the illustrations to Agricola, and the access-holes reveal the screens of fire-clay which are broken down for the removal of a broken or worn-out

---

61 Merrifield, *Original Treatises*, i, 212-6.
62 Op. cit. 52 (Bk. II, chap. II).
63 Merrifield, *Original Treatises*, i, 212.
64 A number of excavated sites show post-holes which presumably served to support such sheds, sometimes tiled – see Vose, op. cit. note 10, 138. At Ballynegery, Ireland, in 1621, £8 was paid 'To Tipton in gross for the glass-

house itself viz. – all the timber frame, board-ing, floors, ladders, stairs and shindling (?shingling) and other workings' (Westropp, *Irish Glass*, op. cit. note 11, 26).

65 The 'caramal' of Venetian practice – see Charleston as in n.58, 16, n.19; idem, 'A Gold and Enamel Box in the Form of a Glass Fur-nace', *Jnl. of Glass Studies*, xx (1978), 40, Fig. 11.

pot and rebuilt when the new pot has been inserted.[66]

The miniature well illustrates the essential character of the 'Northern' furnace, with its central founding chamber and annexed ancillary chamber receiving its lowered heat requirements mainly from the founding-chamber, and usable for a variety of purposes – fritting, 'pot-arching' or annealing, as local conditions might require.

With this illustration in mind, we may turn to the one early medieval furnace in England which has been excavated in the era of scientific archaeology – Blunden's Wood (Surrey) (Fig. 119).[67] Pottery and magnetic dating of the kiln gave a date about 1330. The furnace, about 11 feet long, was 8 feet wide at the eastern end and 10 at the western, the slightly bowed plan being 11 feet wide in the middle. Down the centre ran a fire-trench with packed clay floor, about 10 ft. 6 in. long and 1 ft. to 1 ft. 10 in. wide, passing between the two 'sieges', built as dry-stone banks, on each of which there were originally two pots, their positions marked by depressions in the clay covering the stones. At each end the fire-hearths were marked by blackened patches. The containing wall, 8 in. wide, left between it and the siege-bank a gap of some 11 in. filled with clay and stones.[68] The northern wall and siege had collapsed down the slope on which the furnace stood. The roof had fallen in and the site was strewn with stones and burned clay, presumably from this source. No furnace-site with roof even partially preserved has been found in this country, but a fallen section of a stone-built furnace-roof has been recorded in Denmark, this furnace dating probably from the 1580s.[69] At Bagot's Park (Staffs.), on a furnace-site dating from the early 16th century, there was evidence to suggest that the roof was shaped by stiffening clay with twigs which burned away when the fire was lit.[70]

No further comprehensible furnace remains of the period before 1500 seem to have survived. It may, however, be permissible to look forward in time to two furnaces dating from the first half and middle of the 16th century, one in Staffordshire, one in Surrey. A comparison with Blunden's Wood may suggest what development, or lack of it, there was in the intervening two centuries. In 1966 D.W. Crossley began excavation at a furnace-site in Bagot's Park, near Abbots Bromley, in an area where deep ploughing had revealed at least 15 furnace-sites.[71] He uncovered two furnaces on his selected site, dated 'by magnetic, ceramic and documentary evidence' to the early years of the 16th century.[72] The first, evidently the founding furnace, consisted of two stone-built sieges, each showing the marks where three pots (with base-diameter of 12-14 in.) had stood, with built-up projections following the lines of the

66   Art. cit. note 58, 15, n. 16. Changing the pots while the fire was still burning was the most arduous task of the glass-maker. It is graphically described by Haudicquer de Blancourt, *De l'Art de la Verrerie* (Paris, 1697), 34-5.

67   Wood, 'A Medieval Glasshouse at Blunden's Wood', as note 56, 54-79; Kenyon, *Glass Industry of the Weald*, 59-68.

68   The suggestion that this was an 'insulation cavity' should probably be scouted: there is no parallel phenomenon known from either excavated sites or the literature.

69   Thelma Jexlev et al., *Dansk Glas i Renaessan-cetid, 1550-1650* (Copenhagen, 1970), 43ff. and Pl. 3.1.

70   Crossley, 'Bagot's Park', as note 24, 57.

71   Ibid. 44, 49ff.

72   Ibid. 60.

sieges and marking the alignment of the two stoke-holes, one of which was floored with flat stones. The whole structure was some 12 feet long. The arches over the flues had collapsed, and the firing-trench was partly blocked by a glassy froth, as at Blunden's Wood. Both stone and brick had been used in the construction. The roof-material has already been described (p.248). Four large post-holes at the corners of the furnace-area probably indicate the roughly rectangular shape of the protective 'shed' superstructure, probably tiled.[73] The smaller furnace at Bagot's Park was less well preserved, being represented by a semi-circular line of bricks. It was presumably an ancillary furnace, perhaps used for annealing.[74]

The Surrey furnace site was at Knightons, Alfold, excavated by Eric S. Wood between 1965 and 1973.[75] The glasshouse was dated to the 1550s by the find of a coin of 1550 and by archaeomagnetic means, but the glass was mainly 'early' in type and possibly ante-dated 1550, suggesting an extended life for this house. Two probable, and one possible, founding furnaces were traced, the second overlying the first, both identified as six-pot furnaces, roughly rectangular in plan, the first measuring some 14½ ft. by 10½ ft. externally and 11 ft. by 7½ ft. internally, with a 2 ft. 6 in. fire-trench between the sieges, apparently stoked from one end only: the second had much the same dimensions, but was slightly narrower, with a 23¾ in. fire-trench. A third furnace of apparently the same type had been entirely robbed out, but annexed to it were two small subsidiary furnaces of roughly square plan, overlapping each other and sharing a common wall for about a yard, within which was a gap of some 23¾ in. 'representing a passage for hot gases to pass from one chamber to the other'. The natural clay round the conjoined furnace was unburnt, suggesting that no great heat was developed in it.[76] This furnace is interpreted as an annealing furnace for 'crown' window glass, of which many fragmented sheets were found on the site.[77] 'Crown' fragments were found in abundance at Bagot's Park too,[78] and these two six-pot furnaces may well represent a revival of this technique in the late medieval period (see pp.251-2).

The Knightons annealing furnace was well-built of roughly squared stones, and this solid type of construction seems characteristic of this later period. Thus at Bishop's Wood, in Staffordshire (*c.* 1584-1604), the four-pot furnace was solidly built of good masonry,[79] and in the Weald itself the 'late' furnaces at Vann, Hambledon,[80] and at Fernfold, Wisborough Green, were well made of regular brickwork. The Fernfold site has been plausibly connected with Jean Carré, who in 1567 stated that he had erected two furnaces there for making 'Normandy' ('crown') and 'Lorraine' ('muff') glass respectively.[81] The Vann furnace also appears to have had diagonal 'wings' running from it, providing small chambers heated from the main furnace, for

73 Ibid. 53, 59.
74 Ibid. 55, 59.
75 E.S. Wood, 'A 16th century Glasshouse at Knightons, Alfold, Surrey', *Surrey Arch. Coll.* lxxiii (1982), 1-47.
76 Ibid. 8-10, Figs. 3-6.
77 Ibid. 10, 19, 34.

78 Crossley, op. cit. note 24, 62-3.
79 T. Pape, 'An Elizabethan Glass Furnace', *Connoisseur*, xcii (Sept., 1933), 172-7.
80 Winbolt, *Wealden Glass*, 29-31; Kenyon, *Glass Industry of the Weald*, 193-200.
81 Kenyon, *Glass Industry of the Weald*, 120-4, 185-8.

the subsidiary processes. This feature is found again at Rosedale and Hutton Common, in N. Yorks., both dating from the years about 1600.[82] It is found earlier, however, at Buckholt (Hants.), where glass-making is recorded about 1575-80,[83] and even earlier occurrences are found on the Continent, from where these refinements undoubtedly came.[84] It is therefore not beyond the bounds of possibility that medieval furnaces of this pattern may yet be found in England.

The furnace and the pots being available, the glassman had first to prepare his 'batch' by taking ashes and sand and mixing them in proper proportions on the fritting hearth, whether in an annexe of the founding furnace or in a separate reverberatory structure. Theophilus says (Book II, Ch. IV):

> Then take two parts of the ashes . . . and a third part of sand, collected out of water, and carefully cleaned . . . Mix them in a clean place, and . . . lift them up with the long-handled iron ladle and put them in the upper hearth in the smaller section of the furnace . . . When they begin to get hot, stir at once . . . to prevent them from melting with the heat of the fire and agglomerating. Continue doing this for a night and a day. [85]

It was important that the frit should not become too compacted. The fritting furnace was called 'calcar' (*carcaise* in French). The frit was transferred into the pre-heated pots with the long-handled ladle (Fig. 110F), and the founding process began. The mixing of the batch and the supervision of the melting were the province of the 'founder' (the equivalent of the Venetian *conciatore*), [86] but medieval English glasshouses could probably not afford such specialisation, leaving the task to the master workman. After the necessary founding (to melt the glass) and 'fining' (to clear the bubbles), the temperature was dropped to working level. Theophilus says (Book II, Ch. VI):

> At the first hour next morning . . . take the iron blowpipe, put its end in the pot full of glass, and when the glass sticks to it turn the pipe in your hand until as much glass as you want agglomerates around it. Take it out at once, put it to your mouth, and blow gently . . . You should also have a smooth, flat stone in front of the window [i.e. the gathering-hole] on top of which you should gently strike the glowing glass, so that it hangs down equally on all sides . . . [87]

Eraclius says of the pipe: 'take iron tubes of the length of one cubit (18—22 in.) more or less . . . and at the end of each tube a little wooden tube, having a very small hole, through which you must blow . . . and form whatever you please upon the iron slab

82   D.W. Crossley and F.A. Aberg, '16th Century Glass-making in Yorkshire: Excavations at Furnaces at Hutton and Rosedale . . .', *Post-Med. Arch.* vi (1972), 107-59.

83   A. Hartshorne, *Old English Glasses* (1897), 170-4; Kenyon, *Glass Industry of the Weald*, 214-7.

84   Charleston, 'Furnaces', art. cit. note 58, 23-6,

esp. n. 42.

85   Theophilus, *On Divers Arts*, Hawthorne & Smith, 52-3.

86   The Ballynegery records speak of 'The consore or founder'—Westropp, *Irish Glass*, 25.

87   Theophilus, *On Divers Arts*, ed. Hawthorne & Smith, 54-5.

which is placed at the mouth of the furnace . . . which is called *marmor*. [88] By the 12th century, therefore, the marble (*marmor*) marver was already being replaced by its iron counterpart. Marble survived in use long after this, although no authenticated examples survive. However, at a furnace site at Idehurst, Kirdford, in the Weald, a slab of Purbeck marble about 10 by 4 in. was found which might have been a marver or part of one. [89] Both Theophilus and Eraclius say that the marver is placed by the gathering-hole, but the Mandeville miniature (Fig. 109) shows it on the ground and this detail is confirmed by the illustrations to Agricola. [90] On the whole, 'Northern' glassmen worked standing, perhaps because their code was dominated by window-production. Italians sat on stools. [91] The wooden handle of the pipe is also attested by the Mandeville illumination and by Agricola's engravings. The metal portion of the pipe was probably formed by wrapping a strip of iron round a mandrel and welding it, and no doubt this tool was an expensive one to make. [92] If it was extended by a wooden section, rather than merely being covered by it, this would be an economy. Pipes were also made of bronze. [93] At Knole '6 pypes' were purveyed to the glasshouse (1585/6) [94] and at Ballynegery '6 pipe handles' for 2 *s.* (1621). [95] A number of glass-maker's tools are shown in Fig. 110 A-E, taken from Haudicquer de Blancourt's *De l'Art de la Verrerie*, based for the most part on the Latin editions of Neri (from 1668). Although derived from Italian practice, there is no reason to suppose that they were very different from those used in the rest of Europe.

As has already been suggested, window-glass making was the most significant branch of the business throughout the Middle Ages. There were two main methods of manufacture – 'crown' and 'muff'. The 'crown' method had its home in Normandy and probably reached England with immigrant workmen, perhaps early in the 14th century. (It was apparently made at Blunden's Wood *c.* 1330.) [96] The method was practised in the Near East and in Byzantine territory from an early date, [97] and consisted of blowing a paraison (glass bubble), transferring it to a pontil (a solid iron rod), cutting it from the blowing-iron, then spinning it after reheating so that centrifugal force opened up the paraison into a flattish circular disc (Fig. 111A). [98] The method, once claimed for Normandy, was probably really only developed there in such a way that considerably larger 'crowns' could be made. From these in turn

88  Merrifield, *Original Treatises*, 212.
89  Kenyon, *Glass Industry of the Weald*, 54, 176-7.
90  See e.g. R.J. Charleston, 'Glass', in Singer, *Hist. of Technology*, iii (1957), Fig. 140.
91  R.J. Charleston, 'Some Tools of the Glass-maker in Medieval and Renaissance Times, with Special Reference to the Glass-maker's Chair', *Glass Technology*, iii, No. 3 (June, 1962), 107-11.
92  R.J. Charleston, 'Our Forefathers in Glass', *Glass Technology*, xxi, No. 1 (Feb., 1980), 31-3.
93  Agricola, quoted by Winbolt, *Wealden Glass*, 81.
94  Kenyon, *Glass Industry of the Weald*, 220.

95  Westropp, *Irish Glass*, 27.
96  Kenyon, *Glass Industry of the Weald*, 68.
97  D.B. Harden, 'Ancient Glass, III: Post-Roman', *Arch. Jnl.* cxxviii (1972), 84; id., 'Domestic Window Glass: Roman, Saxon and Medieval', in E.M. Jope (ed.), *Studies in Building History* (1961), 39-41, 55.
98  R. Chambon, 'L'Evolution des Procédés de Fabrication manuelle du Verre à Vitres . . .', *Advances in Glass Technology*, ed. F.R. Matson and G.E. Rindone, Part 2 (New York, 1963), 165-78.

smaller panels could be cut for the glazier's use.[99] The disadvantages were that only a limited number of regular panels could be cut from a large circular disc, the thickened centre of which is occupied by a rough protruding 'bull's eye' (French *boudine*), where the pontil had been affixed; the advantage was that the glass had a fine unblemished 'fire polish' from its reheating at the 'glory hole' – a quality which gave it popularity well into the 19th century.

The second main method ('muff') is first described by Theophilus in the continuation of the passage just quoted:

> . . . When you see it [the paraison] hanging down like a long bladder, put the end into the flame and as soon as it melts, a hole will appear. Then take a round piece of wood made for the purpose, and make the hole as wide as the middle [of the cylinder] . . .[100] [cf. Fig. 111B.]

This end is then pinched together to make a figure-of-eight, the pipe knocked off and attached to the centre of the eight; after reheating, the same is done at the other end, and the 'muff' is ready for annealing. In due course the fire is lit in a special furnace, and when it

> is red-hot, take a hot iron, split the glass along one side and put it on the hearth of the red-hot furnace. When it begins to soften, take iron tongs and a smooth, flat piece of wood, and opening it up on the side where it is split, spread it out and flatten it with the tongs as you want it. When the glass is completely flat . . . put it in the annealing furnace . . . in such a way that the sheet does not lie down but stands up against the wall . . .[101]

This method had been practised since Roman times, and 'muff' glass was found at the 9th to 10th-century Glastonbury site.[102] Although perhaps never lost, the technique seems not to have flourished in England in the medieval period. It came into its own after 1567, when French Huguenot families brought an improved method with them from Lorraine.[103] Its advantages were that it produced a large almost rectangular sheet which could be cut more economically than a 'crown'; the disadvantage was that its surface lacked brilliance, having been manipulated with tools in the spreading furnace.

The same glass-blowers who made window-glass also normally made vessel-glass, as is proved from documentary sources[104] and by the fact that evidence of both types of manufacture is found on some glass-making sites.[105] Complete specialisation in one or other branch probably did not come in until the latter part of the 16th century. Theophilus makes no distinction, saying simply (Book II, Ch.X):

---

99   For alternative schemes of dividing 'crowns', see Winbolt, *Wealden Glass*, 59, and W. Cooper, *The Crown Glass Cutter and Glazier's Manual* (1835), Pls. VI-VIII. Cutting was probably done mainly in glaziers' workshops.

100  Theophilus, *On Divers Arts*, ed. Hawthorne &

Smith, 55.

101  Ibid. 107.

102  Harden, 'Domestic Window Glass . . .', 53.

103  Kenyon, *Glass Industry of the Weald*, 125ff.

104  E.g. ibid. 31-2.

105  Ibid. 68.

When you want to make vessels, prepare the glass in the way described above [i.e. for making 'muff']. When you have blown the amount of glass you want, do not make a hole in the base as you did above, but separate it intact from the pipe using a flat piece of wood that has been dipped in water. Quickly heat the pipe and immediately stick it to the base. Now lift up the vessel, heat it in the flame, and with a round piece of wood enlarge the hole whence you separated the pipe. Shape its rim and enlarge it as much as you like . . .[106]

The base can then be pushed in with the iron and handles and threaded decoration added if desired by drawing threads from the pot on a slender iron rod. Again, it may be seen that Theophilus uses the blowing-iron as a pontil. His next chapter gives directions for making 'long-necked flasks' by swinging the paraison round on the iron to extend it, holding the thumb over the mouthpiece of the pipe. No mention is made of a tool such as a pair of shears (for finishing the lip) or pucellas (for shaping the glass by constricting it). In his chapter on spreading window-glass (ch. III), however, 'two pairs of tongs each hammered out of a single piece of iron, two long-handled iron ladles, and such other wooden and iron tools as you want'[107] are specified; and the spring-handled tongs made in a single piece are essentially the same tool as the *borsella* or *procello* (whence *pucellas*) of Italian practice (Fig. 110E). These tools, with various wetted wooden instruments, make up Theophilus's simple kit. He does not mention moulds, but simple rib-moulding is often found on medieval glass, and occasionally more complex designs,[108] and moulds were among the tools bequeathed by a Sussex glass-maker to his son in 1553.[109] Solid bronze 'dip-moulds' with mesh and other patterns are known from the medieval Near East,[110] but European moulds seem more often to have been of clay.[111] They seem to have been open at the base, as they are seen on the glasshouse floor in Agricola.[112] With these simple tools the English glass-maker could easily have made the range of objects discussed below, although it would have required exceptional skill to blow the alembic (see p.260), and occasional fragments are found which seem to demonstrate the inhalation technique used for making the conjoined tube neck of the German *Kuttrolf*.[113]

It was with this rudimentary equipment that the medieval glass-maker went to work, doing almost all of it himself, with occasional help from another member of the team. Thus at Ballynegery in 1621 there was only one glass-maker, Davy Francois

106 Theophilus, *On Divers Arts*, ed. Hawthorne & Smith, 57-8.
107 Ibid. 52.
108 As on the base of a 14th-century goblet found at Winchester – R.J. Charleston, 'Vessel Glass of the Late Medieval to Modern Periods', in M. Biddle and D. Keene, *The Crafts and Industries of Medieval Winchester*, Winchester Studies, vii, part ii (forthcoming).
109 Winbolt, *Wealden Glass*, 11.
110 See Sotheby's sales of 15 October 1985, lot 44, and 16 April 1986, lot 33.

111 See e.g. Hermann Günter Rau, 'Spätmittel-alterlicher Tonmodel aus dem Nordspessart', *Glastechnische Berichte*, 46. Jahrg., Heft 2 (1973), 36, ribbed mould from Schöllkrippen, 8 cm. high; O. Bloss, *Die älteren Glashütten in Südniedersachsen* (Hildesheim, 1977), Pl. 5, finely ribbed mould with four apertures.
112 See e.g. Charleston, as note 90.
113 H. Löber, 'Guttrolfe, Formgebung und Herstellungstechnik', *Glastechnische Berichte*, 39. Jahrg., Heft 12 (1966), 539-47.

(*sic*) as against one 'tezer' (i.e. 'teaser', or stoker), one 'consore' (founder) and 3 other men.[114] The glasshouse made 'broad' window-glass (i.e. probably 'muff'). It is difficult to see how one man could have made muff single-handed, so presumably an assistant was trained to open up the cylinder. On the 'crown' side, even in the 18th century, at the time of the *Encyclopédie*, the master seems to have had only one assistant (Fig. 112). The age of the team of three or four men to a 'chair' was still in the future.[115]

### Organisation of the Craft

A critical difficulty in working on the documentary side of the history of the English medieval glass-industry is the uncertainty of nomenclature. The Latin *vitrearius* becomes in French *verrier* (*verrer, verrir*, etc.), but this word can mean either 'glass-maker' or 'glazier' (who makes windows of glass brought from elsewhere); this reflects back on *vitrearius*, which becomes equally ambiguous. The English word 'glassman' is correspondingly unclear, and to add to the confusion a glass-*maker* could be referred to as a 'glasiere'. Only sometimes does the context make the position clear. When, therefore, we read of Henry Daniel, *vitrearius* in the reign of King Stephen (1135-54), or of William de Auckland *verrour* of York (*c.* 1351),[116] we should beware. But when we read of Lawrence Vitrearius obtaining a grant of twenty acres of land at Chiddingfold in the years before 1240,[117] we may conclude that he was a glass-maker, or at least a glazier buying glass from local glass-makers, for Chiddingfold was the recognised centre of a glass-industry which lasted until well after the medieval period. Further evidence comes from the royal Works accounts, dealing with the royal buildings. In April 1351 John Alemayne (presumably, by his name, a Continental or of recent Continental origin) purveyed 43*s.* 6*d.* worth of 'white glass' for glazing which was carried by a certain William Holmere from Chiddingfold to London; further substantial purchases (for St. Stephen's, Westminster) followed in October and November, and 53*s.* worth for St. George's, Windsor, in 1355. Alemayne was a Chiddingfold man, with holdings of land locally, and it is therefore likely that he was a glass-maker; even if only a dealer, his presence in Chiddingfold for 40 years would nevertheless testify to the continuity of the local industry.[118] That Alemayne in 1367 granted a twenty-year lease of his property in Hazelbridge to one John Schurterre 'glazier' makes it even more probable that he made glass, for the Schurterres became one of the leading glass-making families of the district. John Schurterre died before 1380, in which year his widow Joan 'granted to John Glasewryth (*sic*) of Staffordshire, half a [glass] house in Shuerewode . . . in the parish of Keuredeforde (Kirdford) . . . with the underwood growing . . . in the

114  Westropp, *Irish Glass*, 26-7, 29-30.
115  See Charleston, 'Our Forefathers in Glass', as in note 92, 28-30.
116  'The Earliest Recorded Glassmaker in England', *Glass Technology*, i, No. 4 (1960),

137; W.A. Thorpe, *History of English and Irish Glass* (1929), i, 52.
117  Kenyon, op. cit. note 6, 26-7.
118  Ibid. 27-9.

aforesaid place called Shuerewode and Strowykeswode' to be worked at his own cost, she to pay him for his production of 'brode' ('broad' = window, probably 'muff') and 'vessel' glass.[119] That both types of glass were made together in one glasshouse is also suggested by the finds on the site of Blunden's Wood, datable to *c*. 1330 (see p.248 above).

John Schurterre's son, another John, was associated in 1385 with a certain Robert Pikeboussh in a 'Glashous' in Kirdford, the first time this term is explicitly used in the Wealden records.[120] A furnace-site at Crouchland, Kirdford, has been suggested as the possible location of this glasshouse.[121] The last Schurterre mentioned as a glass-maker was Peter (*c*. 1400), although the family survived, and some members may have followed the calling. After Peter 'Shortere' the Chiddingold records fall silent until 1495, when Thomas Shorter (? Schurterre) conveyed a croft to Henry Ropley, 'glassecaryour'.[122] The Ropleys too were a local family, and a glass-carrier would hardly settle in an area where there was no glass. In the 16th century the records multiply, with the families of Peytowe and Strudwick replacing the Schurterres as the leading glass-makers.[123]

Although the Weald is the best-documented area of medieval glass-making, there is plenty of evidence to show that glass was made in a number of other areas, notably Staffordshire, Shropshire and Cheshire.

In Staffordshire,[124] a number of references are made to Bromley Hurst, near Abbots Bromley, beginning with a charter of 1289 mentioning 'le Glaslone' ('Glass Lane'); in 1416 a field near Bromley Hurst was called 'Glasshouse Field', while the proper names 'Glasemon' and 'Glasman' occur in 1333 and later. In 1616 Sir Walter Bagot claimed that glass had been made on his land for 200 years, and the family of Harvey occupied part of the Bagot's Park estate from 1493, although not referred to as glass-makers until 1501. Members of the family were also substantial yeoman farmers with lands in the Abbots Bromley and Bromley Hurst areas, but a number of them were referred to as glass-makers in the 1530s and 1540s. The finding of fifteen glasshouse-sites in Bagot's Park in the 1960s shows what an important centre this was, the one fully excavated furnace dating from the early part of the 16th century. The second main area of manufacture was Wolseley, near Rugeley. William and Ralph Glasemon were summoned for trespass in 1408, and John Glasman, of Rugeley, is known to have sold glass in York in 1418-19. References to a glasshouse occur in the mid15th century, and ferns were sold to glass-makers in 1479. A Thomas Wakelen was described as a glass-maker of Abbots Bromley in 1471, but of Rugeley in 1480. The Bagot's Park furnace-site shows that glass-making continued in the area into the 16th century, as does the Harvey connexion. In 1543 Thomas and John Harvey paid rent of cash plus *unam fen(estram)* for a holding in Abbots Bromley,

119  Ibid. 31-3.
120  Ibid. 32.
121  Ibid. 170-2; on the Schurterres generally, see
　　　ibid. 115-16.
122  Ibid. 29.
123  Ibid. 117-20.

124  The majority of the following references are
　　　taken from Crossley, 'Bagot's Park', art. cit.
　　　note 24, 44-7. See also J. Knowles, *The York
　　　School of Glass-Painting* (1936), 198-9; Godfrey,
　　　op. cit. note 11, 10.

indicating that they made window-glass, as the Bagot's Park furnace did.

In 1349 John de Brampton, a glazier who became the third Master of the Glaziers' Company and who also procured glass in the Weald, was ordered to buy glass in Staffordshire and Shropshire for the glazing of St. Stephen's, Westminster.[125] No medieval site in Shropshire has been identified, but it was certainly a glass-making area in the 16th century.

From 1284 to 1309, and probably later, the abbey of Vale Royal, in Cheshire, is known to have been concerned in the manufacture of glass, and an apparent glass-making site has been located in Delamere Forest, although it cannot confidently be associated with Vale Royal. As might have been expected, only window-glass was discovered, apparently mostly made by the 'muff' technique. Pottery suggested a 15th-century date, but a silver penny of Edward I (1272-1307) might be an indication that the site was used in the 14th century.[126]

Apart from the places named, Colchester records show a number of men with the surname 'le Verrer' (1295 and 1300). They might, of course, have been merely glaziers, but in 1300 Robert le Verrer had among his goods 'biletts pret. xviii *d*.', a store of wood which might suggest that he was a glass-maker.[127] It might also be borne in mind that when in 1352 John Geddyng, a well-known glazier (Upper Warden of the Glaziers' Gild 1373-81) was sent on the same errand as John de Brampton in Staffordshire, he was despatched to Kent and Essex,[128] although the suspicion must remain that he perhaps went to collect glass from the ports rather than from local glasshouses.

Mention should also be made of the 'glashous' belonging to Salisbury Cathedral in the 15th century: this might at first sight be deemed to have been merely a glazier's workshop, were it not for the fact that it required considerable quantities of sand.[129]

The men who worked in these glasshouses often belonged to the same families, and although some of them were prepared (like John Glaswryth) to migrate in search of work, many of them had landed property and pursued the calling of farmers in addition to that of glass-maker, a dual role perhaps helped by the seasonal nature of the craft itself, with its long break at the end of the working year.[130]

*Products*

The potash-lime glass of medieval England was particularly prone to decay, and excavated fragments nearly always suffer in varying degrees from brown weathering,

125  L.F. Salzman, 'The Glazing of St. Stephen's Chapel, Westminster, 1351-2', *J.B.S.M.G.P.* iv.4 (April, 1926), 14.

126  Salzman, *Building in England*, 182; R. Newstead, art. cit. note 36, 32-9; M.H. Ridgway and G.B. Leach, 'Further Notes on the Glasshouse Site at Kingswood, Delamere, Cheshire', *Chester Arch. Soc. Jnl.* n.s. xxxvii, pt. 1 (1948), 133-40.

127  A. Nesbitt, *Descriptive Catalogue of the Glass Vessels in the South Kensington Museum* (1878), p.cxxxi.

128  Salzman, *Building in England*, 182.

129  Ibid.

130  Kenyon, *Glass Industry of the Weald*, 14-15, 117-20; idem., 'A Sussex Yeoman Family as Glass-makers', *Jnl. Soc. of Glass Technology*, xxxv, No. 162 (Feb., 1951), 6-8; see also Crossley, art. cit. note 24, 45-6, for the Harveys.

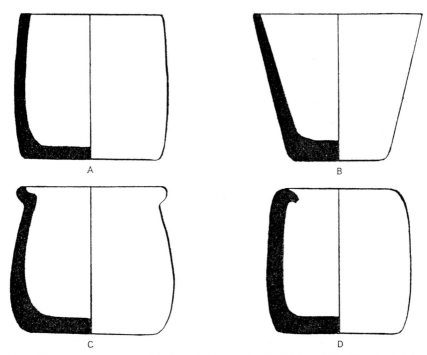

*Fig. 113* Wealden excavated pots. A-B from Malham Ashfold, 'Early': C. Blunden's Wood, *c.* 1330; D. Woodhouse, Wisborough Green, 'Late'. (After Kenyon, *Glass Industry of the Weald*, 50)

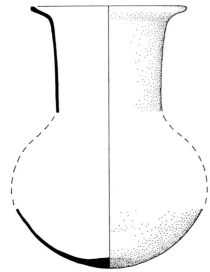

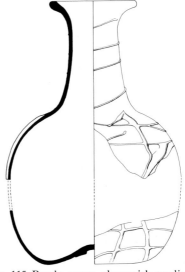

*Fig. 114* Urinal, clear green glass with patchy weathering. From Winchester. 14th century. Scale approx. 1:4.

*Fig. 115* Bottle, green glass with applied trailed decoration. From Tynemouth Priory. Height 11½ in. Probably 14th century. After D. Charlesworth, *Arch. Aeliana*, 4th ser. xlv (1967), 85.

either in patches or sometimes in an overall coating, inside which the sound glass is often no more than a paper-thin layer: sometimes the whole glass is denatured, and crumbles to black or brown powder. Somewhere about 1500 the metal seems to have been generally improved, giving a more robust glass with less weathering, often of a milky-green colour, and sometimes with a tendency to opalescence. This 'transitional' phase led to the perfected green glass of the late 16th century, thin, glossy, and far more resistant to weathering.

English green 'forest' glass of this period seems to have been virtually restricted to household, and to a lesser degree industrial, uses. Table-glass, if used at all, was more probably furnished from the Continent, mainly from Italy. Notable among 14th-century types of glass, however, found normally on sites of 'upper-class' character, is a wide-bowled green goblet, usually ribbed, with tall thin stem and conspicuously wide foot.[131] This follows the style of the colourless glasses, often with applied blue thread decoration, which were perhaps the most refined (and no doubt most expensive) glasses of the century.[132] The green goblets are widespread in France, Holland, Belgium and Germany.[133] No fragments have yet been found on an English glass-making site, and on present evidence it seems more likely that such glasses are Continental imports, northern Europe's reply to the colourless goblets of Italy.

Chief among the more mundane uses for which glass was employed in England (as elsewhere) was the hanging lamp (Figs. 117, 118). This is ubiquitous in manuscript illustrations of, say, the Nativity, and appears to change its shape little in the course of five hundred years. It survived into the 16th century, and seems by then to have become a little more straight-sided in the bowl, but otherwise little changed.[134] Its characteristic residue is the often solid base of the stem, where the pontil-wad adds extra thickness. The rim-fragments can often be mistaken for those of cups or bowls, for they can range in diameter from 3¾ to 6 in.[135] Examples of the base-stumps have been found on a number of English glass-making sites, notably the early 14th-century Blunden's Wood site, and other 'Early' furnace-sites in the Weald.[136] The complete Winchester lamp (Fig. 117) is datable to the 13th century, and a number of 13th- and 14th-century finds are known.

Almost as ubiquitous was the urinal, uroscopy being a vital ancillary of medieval medical diagnosis. For this purpose it was desirable to have as much of the body-glass as possible sufficiently thin to make colour-judgment possible. Inevitably most

131  E.g. D.B. Harden, 'Medieval Glass in the West', in *Eighth International Congress on Glass* (1969), 106, Figs. 16-7.

132  E.g. R.J. Charleston, 'The Glass', in C. Platt and R. Coleman-Smith (ed.), *Excavations in Medieval Southampton, 1953-69*, ii, *The Finds* (Leicester, 1975), No. 1513.

133  E. Baumgartner and Ingeborg Krueger, 'Zu Gläsern mit hohem Stiel oder Fuss des 13. und 14. Jahrhunderts', *Bonner Jahrbücher*, clxxxv

(1985), 363-413.

134  G.E. Oakley and J. Hunter, 'The Glass', in J.H. Williams, *St. Peter's Street, Northampton: Excavations, 1973-6* (1979), 298 (GL53).

135  R.J. Charleston, 'Vessel Glass', in Anthony Streeten, *Bayham Abbey* (Sussex Arch. Soc. Monograph 2, 1983), 113, 115 (Nos. 3-10).

136  Charleston, op. cit. note 33, 70-1.

*Fig. 116* Reconstruction of the founding furnace after Theophilus's description. (*Science Museum, London*)

*Fig. 117* Lamp, green glass. From a pit near Westgate, Winchester. Early 13th century. Height 6⅞ in. (*Winchester City Museum*)

*Fig. 118* Martyrdom of St. Thomas Becket (from a Latin psalter of *c.* 1200, B.L., MS Harl. 5102, f. 32).

of such thin glass has broken and dispersed, leaving behind only the spreading rim and the thick base-fragment with its pontil-mark on the convex outer surface. Two main types of the thin-walled urinal seem to predominate – one with spherical body, cylindrical neck and spreading flat rim, often with up-turned lip (Fig. 114), the other with piriform body leading straight into the tapering neck, with the same broad rim (Fig. 124). A third type of urinal, however, would have been impossible to use for uroscopy, being made of notably thick glass, and probably used as a *vase de nuit*.[137]

All these glasses, with their convex bases, were unstable. They were, therefore, normally kept in a cylindrical wickerwork case with cover and loop-handle: with this in hand, the patient waited for audience with the doctor.[138] Strangely, examples are rare on English manufacturing sites, but fragments were found at the mid 16th-century Wealden site at Knightons (Sussex).[139] It seems most unlikely that so common a domestic utensil was not normally made in the country. A neck-fragment found at Bramber Castle is almost certain to have been made in the neighbouring Weald.[140] Very many fragments have been found at occupation-sites up and down the country, dating from about 1300 until well into the 16th century, if not later.[141]

Even more common was the green glass flask, characteristically some 9 in. tall, but with infinite nuances of shape and size.[142] Normally it was roughly globular in body with a slightly rising 'kick' in the base (see p.253 above) to give stability and to accommodate the rough pontil-mark. Not infrequently the neck or body, or both, were blown with vertical ribbing, which can be 'wrythen' after delivery from the mould to give a spiral effect. The ribbing may be close or well-spaced, the neck tubular or tapering, and the spreading lip is frequently cut off at a slight slant. Many fragments are found on glasshouse sites, notably Blunden's Wood (early 14th century), and there can be little doubt that such products were indigenous (Fig. 120).[143] Other variant bottles, both larger (Fig. 115) and smaller (Fig. 125) were also made.[144]

A third area in which the English glass-maker played an important role was in the provision of utensils for distillation. Tubing has been found on a number of sites, but more important was the distilling complex (Fig. 121) of the alembic (Fig. 122) sitting on top of its cucurbit (Fig. 123) and discharging the distillate into the 'receiver' (a vessel of indeterminate type for which ordinary bottles would serve). Numerous fragments have been found on monastic and castle sites, no doubt from full-blown still-rooms.[145] An alembic fragment from Bramber Castle was almost certainly

137 Charleston, art. cit. note 135, 113, 115 (Nos. 12-16).
138 See e.g. the wood-cut attributed to Gentile Bellini from Ketham's *Fasciculus Medicinae* (Venice, 1522), illustrated by C. Zigrosser, *Ars Medica* (Philadelphia Museum of Art, 2nd edn., 1959), 26-7 (No. 61).
139 Wood, 'A 16th century Glasshouse at Knightons. . .', art. cit. note 75, 31 (Nos. 31-6).
140 Stephen Moorhouse, 'The Glass', in K.J. Barton and E.W. Holden, 'Excavations at Bramber Castle, Sussex, 1966-7', *Arch. Jnl.*

cxxxiv (1977), 70-72 (No. 3).
141 Charleston, as note 136, 71-2.
142 Ibid. 72.
143 Wood, 'A Medieval Glasshouse . . .', as in note 56, 65-6, Figs. 6a, c, d.
144 Charleston, *English Glass*, 35-6.
145 S. Moorhouse et al., 'Medieval Distilling-apparatus of Glass and Pottery', *Med. Arch.* xvi (1972), 79-121; id., 'Vessel Glass' in P. Mayes and L.A.S. Butler, *Sandal Castle Excavations, 1964-73* (1983), 225, 227 (Nos. 1-30).

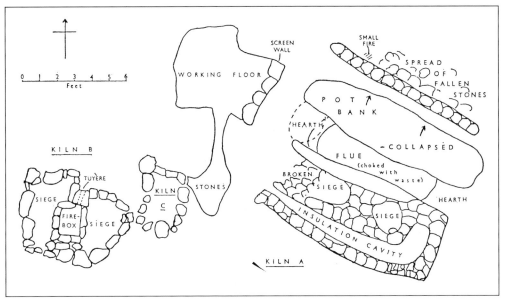

*Fig. 119* Furnaces at Blunden's Wood, Hambledon, *c.* 1330. Founding furnace to right, ancillary furnaces to left. (After Kenyon, *Glass Industry of the Weald*, 61)

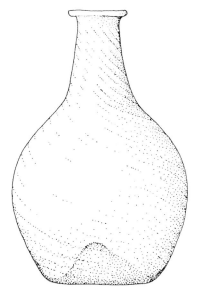

*Fig. 120* Bottle with 'wrythen' mould-blown ribbing. Late medieval or 16th century. (*Artist's impression based on fragments in the Museum of London*)

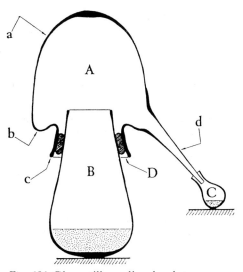

*Fig. 121* Glass still, medieval or later.
A. alembic; B. cucurbit; C. receive; D. lute;
(a. dome of alembic: b. collecting channel:
c. rim of alembic: d. spout).
(After S. Moorhouse)

made in the Weald,[146] and fragments were found at the mid 16th-century Knightons glasshouse.[147] It was to some such centre as this that the often-quoted lines from T. Charnock's *Breviary of Philosophy* relate.[148] No examples of such glass earlier in date than 1400 seem yet to have come to light.

Lastly, mention should be made of the solid green glass 'slick-stones' (Merrett's phrase) or linen-smoothers which recur on numerous archaeological sites. These are flattened balls of glass, convex on the underside (the working surface) and slightly concave on the back, their diameters varying from about 2½ in. to about 3½ in. Into the cavity on the back is often curled the 'tail' which connected the ball to the iron rod in its making: later, in the 16th century, the smoother was furnished with a vertical handle to afford greater purchase.[149] At Winchester no less than eleven examples were found in an industrial area of the city, dating between the 12th and 14th centuries,[150] and it must be supposed that these smoothers were used for such tasks as flattening stitching in saddlery, or smoothing vellum, as well as for the calendering of linen, a function for which they were used right up to modern times.

## Further Reading

Medieval glass has only relatively recently been established as a recognizable entity, although some of the documentary evidence was assembled as early as 1897 by A. Hartshorne in *Old English Glasses*. This was resumed and slightly expanded by W.A. Thorpe in his *History of English and Irish Glass* (1929) and *English Glass* (3rd edn. 1961). Only with the growth of archaeological excavation did a knowledge of the artefacts develop, together with an increasing understanding of the sites on which they might have been made, the first publication in this field being S.E. Winbolt's *Wealden Glass* (1933), which established the Weald as a major centre of the medieval glass industry. Winbolt's work was taken up, systematized and expanded by his co-worker G.H. Kenyon in *The Glass Industry of the Weald* (1967). The first truly scientific excavation of a medieval Wealden site, however, was undertaken and published in 1965 by Eric S. Wood, 'A Medieval Glasshouse at Blunden's Wood, Hambledon, Surrey', *Surrey Arch. Coll.* lxii (1965).

A broader view of medieval glass was taken by D.B. Harden in 1969 in his review lecture 'Medieval Glass in the West' (8th International Congress on Glass, Sheffield). Harden had already done important work on window glass ('Domestic Window Glass: Roman, Saxon and Medieval', in E.M. Jope (ed.), *Studies in Building History* (1961)), following up in some measure the beginning made by L.F. Salzman in *Building in England down to 1540* (1952; repr. with additions 1967). A review

146  Moorhouse, as note 140, 71-2 (Nos. 4-5).
147  Wood, art. cit. note 75, 33-5.
148  Thorpe, *English and Irish Glass*, op. cit. note 116, 55.
149  Charleston, op. cit. note 33, 72-3; id., '16th to 17th century English Glass', *Bull. de l'Association Internationale pour l'Histoire du Verre*, viii (1977-80), 87.
150  Charleston, art. cit. note 108.

*Fig. 122* Alembic, green glass. From
Eccleshall Castle. Perhaps made in
Staffordshire; probably 17th century. Height
5⅛ in. (*Stafford and Mid-Staffordshire Arch.
Soc., Stafford*)

*Fig. 123* Cucurbit, green glass. From
Chester. Perhaps made in Cheshire; probably
17th century. Height 11¼ in.
(*Grosvenor Museum, Chester*)

*Fig. 124* Urinal, green glass. From
Walbrook, London. Probably English;
*c.* 1500. Height 8⅞ in.
(*Museum of London*)

*Fig. 125* Phial, pale green glass. From
Walbrook, London. Probably English;
*c.* 1500. Height 2½ in.
(*Museum of London*)

restricted to England, but including foreign imports, was undertaken by R.J. Charleston in 'Glass of the High Medieval Period (12th-15th Centuries)', *Bull. de l'Association Internationale pour l'Histoire du Verre* (1977-80)) and this material was resumed and somewhat extended in his *English Glass* (1984), 17-49. A comparable review, but with different emphasis, was undertaken by J.R. Hunter in 1981 ('The Medieval Glass Industry', in D.W. Crossley (ed.) *Medieval Industry*, (C.B.A. Research Rep. xl, 1981)). A useful survey of the archaeology of glass-making in England is Ruth Hurst Vose's *Glass* (1980).

# 11

# Window Glass

## RICHARD MARKS

The practices of contemporary glass-painters working in a traditional manner have not changed substantially from those described in the various medieval technical treatises: those of Theophilus (early 12th century), Eraclius (late 12th – early 13th century), Anthony of Pisa and Cennino Cennini (late 14th century).[1]

The glazier obtained his raw material in sheets from the glass-makers. The techniques of glass-making as opposed to glass-painting are discussed in chapter 10 and are only considered here in so far as they appertain to windows. As was shown there, the major centres in England for the manufacture of glass were the Weald, and in particular the locality of Chiddingfold on the Surrey-Sussex border, and Staffordshire. In 1351 and 1355 John Alemayne of Chiddingfold supplied considerable quantities of white glass for the glazing of St. Stephen's Chapel, Westminster, and for the new chapel in Windsor Castle.[2] Other supplies of glass for St. Stephen's were obtained in 1349 from Shropshire and Staffordshire. Glass from the latter county was purchased for York Minster in 1418 and Tattershall (Lincs.) in 1480.[3]

There has been considerable debate as to whether coloured as well as white glass was made in English medieval glass-houses.[4] In 1449 a monopoly was granted to a Fleming, John Utynam, to make coloured glass for the windows of Eton and King's College, Cambridge, and to instruct others in the process 'because the said art has never been used in England'.[5] No coloured window glass has so far been found on any medieval kiln-sites and there is no documentary evidence that coloured glass

1 Theophilus, *On Divers Arts*, trs. J.G. Hawthorne and C.S. Smith (New York, 1979), 45-74; for Eraclius, *De Coloribus et Artibus Romanorum*, see Mrs. M.P. Merrifield, *Original Treatises ... on the Arts of Painting* (1849), i, 166-252: Anthony of Pisa's treatise is published by R. Bruck, 'Die Tractat des Meisters Antonio von Pisa über die Glasmalerei', *Repertorium für Kunstwissenschaft*, xxv (1902), 240-69. For Cennini's *Il Libro dell'Arte* see *The Craftsman's Handbook*, trans. D.V. Thompson (New York, 1960), 111-212.

The best modern account is E. Frodl-Kraft, *Die Glasmalerei: Entwicklung, Technik, Eigenart* (Vienna & Zurich, 1970).

2 G.H. Kenyon, *The Glass Industry of the Weald* (1967), 27-9.

3 R. Marks, *The Stained Glass of the Collegiate Church of the Holy Trinity, Tattershall (Lincs.)* (1984), 23, 31.

4 Ibid., 31-2 for bibliography on this controversy.

5 *Cal. Pat. R., 1446-1452*, 255.

was ever purchased in England, so it must be doubted whether Utynam's efforts met with success.

Even English white glass was considered inferior to that produced on the Continent. The contract of 1447 for the glazing of the Beauchamp Chapel at Warwick went so far as to stipulate that the glazier, John Prudde, was to use '... Glasse beyond the Seas, and with no Glasse of England'.[6] The principal sources of this 'glasse beyond the seas' were those parts of Burgundy and Lorraine which border the Rhine (known as 'Rhenish' glass), Flanders and Normandy. The earliest reference known to me for the purchase of foreign glass is in 1318, when 628 weys of white and 203 weys of coloured glass were obtained for Exeter Cathedral at Rouen.[7] Coloured glass for the windows of St. Stephen's Chapel, Westminster, and for Windsor was bought in 1351-2 from the London warehouses of the Hanse merchants in the Steelyard at the bottom of Thames Street.[8]

East coast ports such as Hull and King's Lynn tended to be the entry-points for glass from the Rhineland and Flanders, but in the 15th and early 16th centuries glaziers throughout the country used the products of glass-houses from all the areas mentioned above. The York glass-painters, who through the proximity of Hull availed themselves of glass from Flanders and the Rhineland, are also known to have purchased glass from Burgundy (in 1535-6) and Normandy (1537).[9] In 1508 the York glazier John Petty bequeathed to the Minster six tables of Normandy glass as well as ten sheaves of Rhenish glass.[10] For the windows of Coldharbour in London in 1485 glass was used from Normandy, England, *dusche* (i.e. the Rhineland) and Venice; the last appears to be the first reference to the use in the British Isles of glass from this famous centre.[11] Frequently in the early 16th century a combination of glass from the Rhineland and Normandy was used in glazing schemes.[12]

The sheets of glass supplied to the glass-painting workshops were usually priced by weight. In the 14th and 15th centuries this was expressed in terms of a *wey* or *ponder* which weighed 5 lbs; 24 weys comprised a *seam* or *hundred*, i.e. 120 lbs. In October 1351 John Alemayne of Chiddingfold received 37s. 6d. for '303 weys of white glass, each hundred of 24 weys, and each wey of 5 lbs'; these were destined for the windows of St. Stephen's Chapel.[13] During the 15th and early 16th centuries some new terms appeared, the *wawe, sheaf, wisp, case* and *cradle*. The wisp appears to have corresponded with the wey and weighed 5 lbs., and the case and cradle were the same as the seam. The sheaf seems to have weighed 6 lbs. and the wawe comprised 60 sheaves. At Collyweston (Northants.) a wawe of white glass cost 30s., exclusive of

6  W. Dugdale, *Antiquities of Warwickshire*, i (2nd edn., 1730), 446-7.

7  *The Accounts of the Fabric of Exeter Cathedral, 1279-1353*, ed. A.M. Erskine (Devon & Cornwall Record Society, n.s. xxiv, 1981), 98.

8  J.T. Smith, *Antiquities of Westminster* (1807).

9  *The Fabric Rolls of York Minster*, ed. J. Raine (Surtees Soc. xxxv, 1858), 108, 109.

10  *Test. Ebor.* iv, 334.

11  L.F. Salzman, 'Medieval Glazing Accounts', *J.B.S.M.G.P.* iii (1929-30), 29.

12  A. Oswald, 'Barnard Flower, the King's Glazier', *J.B.S.M.G.P.* xi (1951-5), 12.

13  L.F. Salzman, 'The Glazing of St. Stephen's Chapel, Westminster', *J.B.S.M.G.P.* i (1926-7), 38.

carriage, in the early 16th century. In 1537 the costs of glass bought for Sheriff Hutton Castle (N. Yorks.) were as follows:

> Payed to Robert Hall, merchant of Yorke, for iiij cradyll of Normandye glasse, at xviijs. a cradyll – lxxijs. Item payed to Robert May of Yorke, merchant, for a chest of wyspe glasse, xvijs. vjd. Item to the said Robert for x wyspses glasse, at ixd. a wyspe – vijs vjd[14]

Normandy glass was generally considered to be superior to both Rhenish and English glass and this is reflected in the price. For the glazing of Croydon Manor in 1505 the King's Glazier Barnard Flower supplied 16 square feet of Rhenish glass at 4d. per square foot; the same amount of glass from Normandy cost 5d. per square foot. This price included the glass-painters' labour.[15]

The costs quoted above all refer to white glass; coloured glass was always more expensive. In 1253 glass purchased for Westminster Abbey cost 3d. per wey for white and 6d. for coloured glass.[16] A century later the accounts for St. Stephen's Chapel and Windsor reveal the disparity in price between white and coloured glass. For both chapels white glass purchased from Chiddingfold was priced at 6d. per wey and foreign white glass cost between 8d. and 9d. per wey. Coloured glass was very much more expensive. At St. Stephen's red (ruby) glass cost 2s. 2d. per wey, azure (blue) and sapphire 3s.[17] These are the prices of the raw materials and do not include the cost of painting the glass and installing it in windows.

### *Methods of Working*

The first stage in the making of a window was the preparation of a full-size drawing, or cartoon, of the design. The cartoon itself would usually be based on a preliminary drawing, known in the 16th century as a *vidimus*, supplied by the patron of the window or made for his approval (see below pp.283-5 for a fuller discussion of the *vidimus*). The *vidimus* could be supplemented by stock design features such as canopies taken from the glass-painters' own working sketchbooks. The will of the York glazier William Thompson (d. 1539) makes reference to a 'book of portitour' which he left to his partner or apprentice; this is presumably such a sketchbook.[18] The well-known book of drawings in the Pepysian Library at Magdalene College, Cambridge (MS 1916) seems to have incorporated part of a glass-painter's sketchbook, at least towards the end of the Middle Ages.[19] Most of the drawings,

14 Idem, *Building in England* (1967), 184.
15 A. Oswald, 'The Glazing of the Savoy Hospital', *J.B.S.M.G.P.* xi (1951-5), 227 n. 1.
16 H.M. Colvin (ed.), *The Building Accounts of King Henry III* (1971), 286-7.
17 Salzman, op. cit. note 11, 35, 38, 41; for Windsor see idem, *J.B.S.M.G.P.*, ii (1927-8) 120.
18 J.A. Knowles, *Essays in the History of the York School of Glass-Painting* (1936), 36.
19 M.R. James, 'An English Medieval Sketchbook, No. 1916 in the Pepysian Library, Magdalene College, Cambridge', *Walpole Soc.* xiii (1924-5), 1-17. Some of my remarks are based on a paper given by Professor Robert Scheller at a symposium on the *Age of Chivalry* exhibition.

*Fig. 126 Virgin and Child*, canopy-work and sacred monograms in the *Pepysian Sketch-Book*, late 15th century (Cambridge, Magdalene College, Pepysian Library MS 1916, f. 22).

which are by various hands and were probably originally loose sheets, date from *c.* 1390-1400. They depict animals, birds, ornamental motifs and human figures, including angels, the Virgin and what appear to be apostles and prophets. Further drawings were added later (probably in the late 15th century), including a section of an architectural canopy of a design confined almost exclusively to stained glass; the sacred monograms IHC and the crowned M on the same folio also occur frequently in this medium (Fig. 126). Although it is unlikely that the book was originally formed for use by a glazier, the original drawings of birds are closely comparable with the exquisite bird drawings in the nave south windows at Salehurst (E. Sussex).

It was by means of such artisan sketchbooks that designs and motifs must have been disseminated between different crafts. They explain the similar, sometimes identical, ornamental repertoire common to tile-makers, wall-painters, glaziers and the limners of illuminated manuscripts. Presumably it must have been via a working model-book that the famous border scene of the monkey funeral at York Minster was adapted from the iconographical 'type' of the funeral procession of the Virgin as

*Fig. 127* Monkey's funeral, from the Pilgrimage window in the nave north aisle of York Minster, early 14th century.

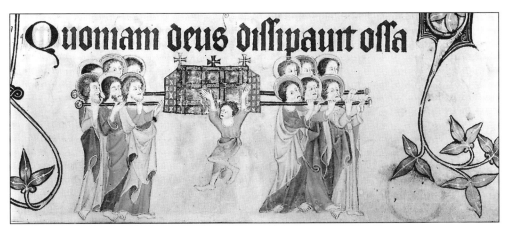

*Fig. 128 Funeral of the Virgin* (Luttrell Psalter, *c.* 1330-40, B.L. MS Add. 42130, f. 99).

depicted in contemporary illuminated manuscripts (Figs. 127, 128).[20]

The preliminary design, or *vidimus*, having been agreed by glazier and patron, the full-size cartoon was now prepared. This guided the work at all subsequent stages and so was precisely set out and included all subject-matter and the lead-lines, and had the required colours indicated by a letter or even by a sample of the colour itself. From the time of Theophilus (and probably before) down to at least the late 14th century, cartoons were drawn on boards or trestle tables prepared with chalk or whitewash and sized with water or ale. None of these boards has yet been discovered in England, although a pair of whitewashed tables bearing designs for stained glass panels and dating from the early 14th century exists at Gerona in Spain (Fig. 129).[21] Cartoons were still being prepared on such tables in 1351-2 at St. Stephen's Chapel, Westminster:

For ale bought to wash the drawing tables for the glaziers' work, 3*d*. ... Masters John de

20  D. O'Connor and J. Haselock, 'The Stained and Painted Glass', in G.E. Aylmer and R. Cant (eds.), *A History of York Minster* (1977), Plate 113.

21  J. Vila-Grau, 'El Vitrall Gotic a Catalunya descoberta de la Taula de Vitraller de Girona', *Reial Acadèmia Catalana de Belles Arts de Sant Jordi* (Barcelona, 1985), 5-27.

*Fig. 129  left:* Part of a glass-painter's table with design for a canopy, Gerona, Spain, early 14th century.

*Figs. 130 a and b  opposite: Angels* from the same cartoon, originally in the chancel of Tattershall church (Lincs.), St. Martin's church, Stamford (Lincs.).

Chestre, John Athelard, John Lincoln, Hugh Licheffeld, Simon de Lenne, and John de Lenton, 6 master glaziers, designing and painting on white tables various designs for the glass windows of the Chapel...[22]

Cartoons on tables were unwieldy and, as the Gerona boards show, had to be erased when new designs were required; notwithstanding this, such cartoons were sometimes used for commissions in separate locations, for example the early 14th-century panels depicting the Virgin and Child at Fladbury and Warndon (Herefs. and Worcs.).[23]

By the time Cennini compiled his treatise, Italian glaziers had replaced cartoons drawn on wooden tables by those on parchment. Probably their English counterparts had adopted the same practice in the same period, although there is no documentary evidence until the 15th century for the use of parchment cartoons here.[24] The introduction of cartoons traced on parchment greatly facilitated the glazier's work, for they could be rolled up, stored and reused, if necessary with slight

22  Salzman, op. cit. note 13, 35.

23  J. Alexander and P. Binski (eds.), *Age of Chivalry* (Exhibition Catalogue, Royal Academy of Arts, 1987), Nos. 472, 473.

24  *The Craftsman's Handbook*, op. cit. note 1, 111; for Exeter see C. Brooks and D. Evans, *The Great East Window of Exeter Cathedral: a Glazing History* (1988), 36.

alterations dictated by iconographical changes. Several instances of the adaptation and reuse of cartoons in York glass have been identified by Knowles, and many others are known (Fig. 130, a, b).[25]

The passing-down of cartoons from one generation of glass-painters to another in York is well documented. William Inglish (d. 1480) bequeathed to his son Thomas 'all the cartoons belonging to my work', and Robert Petty (d. 1528) obtained his 'scroes' from his elder brother John.[26] No doubt this practice was quite common.

The cartoon having been laid out on a flat work-top, pieces of glass of the required colours were laid over it and cut to the approximate shape by splitting with a hot iron and then trimmed with a grozing-iron. In 1351-2 *groisours* from St. Stephen's Chapel cost 1¼d. each.[27] The glass having been cut and shaped, it was painted by means of a pigment formed by a mixture of ground copper or iron oxide, powdered glass and wine, urine or vinegar, and gum arabic: the last makes the pigment adhere to the glass. Purchases of *arnement* (iron oxide) and *gumme arabik* are recorded in the St.

25  Knowles, op. cit. note 18, Plate xlv.

26  Ibid. 38.

27  Salzman, op. cit. note 13, 32, 40.

*Fig. 131* Shield of arms of the Somery family, *c.* 1330-50. (*Burrell Collection, Glasgow*)

*Fig. 132* St. Anne teaching the Virgin Mary to read, Thenford (Northants.).

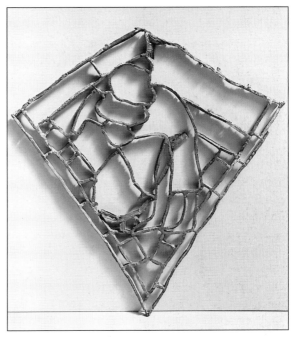

*Fig. 133* Early 14th century leading from a panel at Helmdon (Northants.).

Stephen's accounts.[28] The pigment was applied with brushes made of the hair of various animals, including hog, squirrel, badger and cat. Painting was usually done in several layers: a light overall wash, a second wash over selected areas with a heavily-charged brush, and then the outlines of facial features and draperies. Fully translucent highlights were created by picking out with the tip of the brush-handle letters of inscriptions, background ornamental patterns and other details. This process is usually termed stickwork (Fig. 131). From at least the 12th century the external surface of the glass was painted to reinforce shadows and give a three-dimensional effect to the medium. Back-painting at its most sensitive can be observed in early 15th-century glass, when the trace-lines of a veil or headdress might be painted on the outside and the principal facial shading applied to the inner surface (Fig. 132).

After the pieces of glass making up the panel or window had been painted, the pigment was fired on to them in an annealing furnace. Several references to such furnaces exist in documents. The accounts of 1469 for the glazing of the nave of Westminster Abbey include a payment 'for brike and other necessaries for making the anelyng herth'.[29] After the glass pieces with the pigment fired into them were removed from the furnace they were laid out again for leading. The individual pieces

28 Ibid. 14, 33, 35, 39, 41.  29 Idem, *Building in England*, 179.

were held together by closing or cloring nails. On 1 August 1351, 250 'clozngnaill' costing 18*d*. were purchased for St. Stephen's Chapel.[30] The lead was cast with an I-shape in cross-section and was supplied in strips known as *calmes* (from the Latin *calamus*, reed). The lead was soldered at all joins and the gaps between it and the glass were made waterproof by a filling (Fig. 133). At St. Stephen's Chapel tallow was used for this purpose, but nearly 200 years later some kind of cement was employed.[31] Soldering irons are mentioned occasionally, as in the 1474 inventory of the glazing stores at Shene (Surrey).[32]

The final stage was the insertion of the glass panels into the window openings. Whilst the glass was still being prepared and painted the openings were sometimes temporarily filled. In 1253 canvas was purchased for this purpose for Westminster Abbey.[33] A century later 350 yards of the same material were bought for the St. Stephen's Chapel windows.[34] The glass panels were set into the frames and held in place by armatures, stanchions and saddle-bars, to which they were secured either by strips soldered to the leading, or by clips. The armatures, stanchions and saddle-bars were usually of iron and were supplied by smiths, although evidence has been found in France of wooden armatures dating from as early as the 12th century.[35] During this and the following century the elaborate historiated windows of Canterbury, Chartres, Sens, Laon, Bourges and elsewhere in France had armatures echoing the quatrefoils, circles and other geometrical shapes found in the composition of the glazing itself. Stanchions and saddle-bars also exist from these centuries in association with single figure, non-figured and ornamental or heraldic panels, but as these geometrical shapes were discarded in window design during the late 13th century armatures fell into disuse and stanchions and saddle-bars were employed for all types of window. Stanchions are vertical members and sometimes are found on both the exterior and interior of the window. They were not always required, but the horizontal support, the saddle-bar, is invariably present. In the St. Stephen's accounts saddle-bars are termed *soudeletts*:

12 Dec. 1351 'To Master Andrew the Smith for 120 soudelett for the glass of the said windows, weighing 190 lbs. at 1½*d*. a pound, 23*s*. 9*d*.'[36]

This could mark the final stage in the installation of a window, but sometimes a thin iron protective grille or screen, such as are common in 19th-century windows, was placed on the exterior. In 1445 lattices were set in the King's Chapel at Clarendon (Wilts.), to protect three glazed windows.[37]

---

30  Idem, op. cit. note 13, 33.
31  Idem, *Building in England*, 181.
32  Salzman, op. cit. note 11, 29. For a recent study of medieval leading see B. Knight, 'Researches in Medieval Window Lead', *Jnl. Stained Glass*, xviii.1 (1983-4), 49-51.
33  Colvin, op. cit. note 16, 228-9.
34  Salzman, op. cit. note 13, 14.
35  J. Lafond, *Le Vitrail* (Paris, 1966), 49. For late 12th- and early 13th-century armatures see M. Caviness, *The Early Stained Glass of Canterbury Cathedral, c. 1175-1220* (Princeton, 1977), 42-3.
36  Salzman, op. cit. note 13, 39.
37  Salzman, op. cit. note 11, 28.

The above is a general account of the making and installation of a stained glass window in medieval times. Space does not allow for discussion of detailed points of technique such as silver staining, jewelling and the use of unfired pigments.[38]

## Organisation of the Craft

Throughout the late Middle Ages glass-painting seems to have been a highly organised craft. From the 13th century onwards, when the documentary evidence becomes plentiful, a large number of glaziers are recorded in association with many different centres. In the 13th century a large proportion came from the major towns and cities, such as Bath, Canterbury, Chester, Colchester, Coventry, Lincoln, London, Norwich and Oxford.[39] No names of York glass-painters have been discovered for this century, but the craft took swift root there in the following centuries, with the result that more is known about the York glaziers than about those associated with any other centre. Walter le Verrour is the first recorded, in 1313; thirteen others are named before 1363, 21 names occur between 1363 and 1413, 23 between 1413 and 1463 and 27 between 1463 and 1513.[40] The York glaziers were concentrated in Stonegate, particularly around St. Helen's church, where many of them were buried (Fig. 134). Recently more than 2,000 window glass fragments, apparently rejects from one of the workshops, were found in a medieval pit in Blake Street, a few yards from Stonegate.[41] From the early 14th century the York glass-painters seem to have obtained most of the important glazing commissions in the North (Fig. 135). In similar fashion, Norwich seems to have been the dominant centre in East Anglia in the second half of the 15th century (Fig. 136). At least 70 glaziers are known from this city between 1280 and 1570.[42] East Anglia in general was well-supplied with glass-painters: the names of nearly 100 craftsmen are recorded prior to the Reformation in the counties of Norfolk, Suffolk, Cambridgeshire and Essex.

There is surprisingly little evidence until the 16th century that the London area was a major centre for glass-painting. From the late 13th century the glaziers responsible for the making and repair of the windows for the royal residences were based at Westminster.[43] At about the same time glass-painters occur across the river in Southwark: Nicholas de Creping, who in 1292 made windows for Guildford Castle (Surrey), was a resident of Southwark.[44] It was also in Southwark that the foreign glaziers settled from the late 15th century in order to escape from the control of the

38  For these and other techniques see C. Winston, *Hints on Glass Painting* (2nd edn., 1867); idem, *Memoirs Illustrative of the Art of Glass Painting* (1865); J.D. Le Couteur, *English Mediaeval Painted Glass* (1926); Salzman, *Building in England.*

39  C. Woodforde, 'Glass-Painters in England before the Reformation', *J.B.S.M.G.P.* vi (1935-7), 62-9, 121-8.

40  Knowles, op. cit. note 18, 11-12.

41  D. O'Connor, 'Débris from a Medieval Glazier's Workshop', *Bull. of the York Archaeological Trust,* iii, No. 1 (August 1975), 11-17.

42  Information from Mr. David King. See also C. Woodforde, *The Norwich School of Glass-Painting in the Fifteenth Century* (1950), 9-15.

43  *King's Works,* i, 226.

44  L.F. Salzman, 'Medieval Glazing Accounts', *J.B.S.M.G.P.* ii (1927-8), 118.

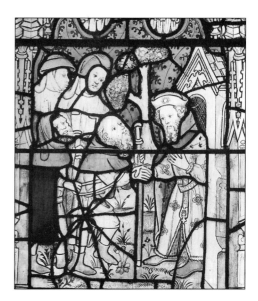

*Fig. 134 top left:* Shield of arms of the York Glaziers in St. Helen's church, Stonegate, York. Early 16th century with later repairs.

*Fig. 135 above: Entertaining the Stranger,* from a Works of Mercy window in All Saints' church, North Street, York. Early 15th century.

*Fig. 136 left: Sir Robert Wingfield* (d. 1480) at East Harling (Norfolk).

Glaziers Company of the City of London. Little can be said about the City glass-painters except that the Company existed by 1328, and that by 1364-5 it had a set of craft ordinances. In *c.*1523 there were seven glaziers practising within the boundaries of the City of London, although it was claimed that until recently there had been at least twenty-two.[45]

The documentary evidence suggests that even in the 14th century most major towns south of the Trent had a resident glazier. Exeter provides a series of names from the beginning of the 14th century to the Reformation, several Salisbury craftsmen are also recorded and Chester was a centre of some importance. The wide distribution of glaziers by the middle of the 14th century is demonstrated by the writ for the collection of craftsmen for the glazing of St. Stephen's Chapel, Westminster, and by the names of those who worked here and at the royal chapel in Windsor Castle. The writ covers 27 counties and the glaziers recruited from them bear the names of King's Lynn, Bury St. Edmunds, Norwich, Halstead, Dunmow, Waltham, Sibton and Haddiscoe (all in East Anglia), Lincoln, Lichfield, Coventry, Bramley, Chester, Thame and Hereford.[46]

By the 15th and early 16th centuries even minor towns and villages sometimes had a glazier. Probably many of these were capable of little more than cutting and leading clear glass, or at best painting simple figures or ornamental patterns for local churches. John Glasier of Coningsby (Lincs.) falls into this category. In 1457-8 he glazed the windows in a chamber in the nearby collegiate establishment at Tattershall, but the glazing of the collegiate church itself with rich coloured glass and complex iconography was beyond his capabilities. Glass-painters from much further afield were brought in for this task. In 1482 these included John Glasier of Stamford, John Wymondeswalde of Peterborough, Robert Power of Burton-on-Trent and Richard Twygge and Thomas Wodshawe from the Malvern area (Fig. 145).[47] More highly-regarded glaziers could travel considerable distances to undertake commissions. Richard Twygge also worked on the nave of Westminster Abbey, whilst Thomas Glazier of Oxford painted glass for Winchester College. John Thornton seems to have run workshops concurrently in Coventry and York in the early 15th century; not surprisingly, there are strong stylistic affinities between the glass of both centres in this period (Figs. 134, 137, 142).[48]

As was mentioned earlier, in some large cities the glaziers were sufficiently numerous to form a craft gild. In London and York they had a gild of their own (Fig. 134); the Chester glass-painters in 1534 were incorporated into a gild which included the painters, embroiderers and stationers (this charter ratified an existing practice as these trades had long before combined to perform one of the mystery plays). Similarly the Norwich glass-painters formed part of the gild of St. Luke with the bell-founders, brasiers, painters, pewterers and plumbers.[49] At Shrewsbury the glass-

45  D.R. Ransome, 'The Struggle of the Glaziers' Company with the Foreign Glaziers, 1500-1550', *Guildhall Miscellany*, ii No. 1 (Sept. 1960), 13.

46  *Cal. Pat. R., 1348-50*, 481; *Cal. Pat. R., 1350-4*, 308.

47  Marks, op. cit. note 3, 32-4.

48  O'Connor and Haselock, op. cit. note 20, 367.

49  Woodforde, op. cit. note 42, 14.

*Fig. 137 far left: Cherubim,* from St. Michael's church, Coventry. Early 15th century.

*Fig. 138 left: St. John of Bridlington* in the Beauchamp Chapel, St. Mary's church, Warwick, 1447-64.

painters combined with the saddlers.[50] In common with other craft gilds, the glaziers were concerned with the regulation of commercial practices in their field, and their rules were equally self-protective. When a city had a craft trade that could meet all demands on it (and take on outside commissions) it had an interest in protecting the indigenous masters. The York regulations of 1463-4 are particularly restrictive:

> Item, that no maister of the said craft supporte any maner of foreyner within this citee or without ayeinst any other maister in any poynt concerning the wele, worship and proffecte of the same craft, on payne of leisyng of xiij*s.* iiij*d.* to be payed as is aforewriten, and that noo foreyne sett up a shop as a master in the said crafte unto suche tyme he aggre with the serchours of the said craft for a certain some.[51]

50 Knowles, op. cit. note 18, 214 note 2.

51 *York Memorandum Book*, ed. M. Sellers, pt. ii (Surtees Soc. cxxv, 1915), 209.

It is significant that this 'some' is not specified, making it possible, if the assessors so decided, to demand a prohibitive payment. At this time the York glaziers consisted of a small number of inter-related family firms, the Chambers, Pettys, Shirleys and Inglishes, and this clause shows how concerned they were to preserve their oligarchy.[52]

The London rules of 1364-5 also laid down precise selection procedures for the admission of outsiders:

> ... if any stranger come to the City and desires to use the said mistery as a master, the good folk elected and sworn to the said mistery shall come to the Mayor and Aldermen and inform them of the name of such person, and the Mayor and Aldermen shall cause him to appear before them, and he shall be examined by good folk of the mistery to see if he be fit and sufficiently informed to use the mistery and of character to remain in the City.[53]

To avoid subjection to these rules was one of the principal reasons why the Flemish and German glaziers who came to England in steadily increasing numbers from the late 15th century took up residence in Southwark. So successful were the foreign glaziers that after 1500 they monopolised the major glazing contracts, a situation which led to a bitter dispute with the Glaziers Company.

The master glass-painter was also protected from unfair competition from his fellow-craftsmen. A York ordinance of 1463-4 stated that a glass-painter could not take a second apprentice until his first apprentice had completed four of his seven years' service.[54] This regulation was designed to prevent the formation of large workshops based on the cheap semi-skilled labour of apprentices.

During the late Middle Ages most urban glazing firms probably consisted of no more than the master glass-painter, one or two servants and perhaps an apprentice. In 1337 John de Walworth was employed at Westminster at the rate of 5*d*. per day and his 'garcio' had 3*d*. a day.[55] Master Walter *le verrator* had two boys assisting him in setting in place two clerestory windows in the choir of Exeter Cathedral in 1310-11, whereas his successor Robert Lyen at Exeter had only one servant towards the end of the same century.[56] The wills of York glaziers provide further information.[57] John Chamber the younger (d. 1450) had three 'servants', a term which may include apprentices, and a son in his practice. The will of Thomas Shirley (d. 1458) names two servants and mentions other men and women servants who may, however, be domestic. His son Robert was also in the firm, and his father left him 'all my drawings, appliances and necessaries, also the tables and trestles belonging in any way to my craft'.[58] No apprentices are mentioned in the will of John Petty (d. 1508), only two servants and his 'scribe' or book-keeper. Even John

52 Knowles, op. cit. note 18, 246-9.
53 C.H. Ashdown, *History of the Worshipful Company of Glaziers* (1948), 17.
54 *York Memorandum Book*, 209.
55 Salzman, op. cit. note 44, 119.

56 Erskine, op. cit. note 7, 56-7; Brooks and Evans, op. cit. note 24, 13, 37, 167.
57 For the following remarks see Knowles, op. cit. note 18, 38, 249-251.
58 Ibid. 38.

Prudde, the King's Glazier, seems to have employed no more than two servants: in 1443-4 his employees Richard and William were paid for work at Fromond's Chantry, Winchester College.[59]

When a large quantity of glazing was required, the work was sometimes entrusted to several glaziers or their firms. This occurred, as we have seen, at Tattershall in 1482, and again with King's College Chapel, Cambridge, in 1526. At St. Stephen's Chapel, Westminster, there were 20 to 30 glaziers at work in addition to the five or six master glass-painters. The entry in the accounts for 3 October 1351 is typical:

> ... Masters John de Chestre, John Athelard, John Lincoln, Hugh Licheffeld, Simon de Lenne, and John de Lenton, 6 master glaziers, designing and painting on white tables various designs for the glass windows of the chapel, for 6 days, at 12*d.* each, 36*s.* William Watton, John Waltham, John Carleton, John Lord, William Lichesfeld, John Alsted, Edward de Bury, William Dodyngton, Thomas Yong, Robert Norwic and John Geddyng, 11 glaziers painting glass for the said windows, each at 7*d.*, 28*s.* 6*d.* John Couentr', William Hamme, William Hereford, John Parson, William Nafreton, John Cosyn, Andrew Horkesle, W. Depyng, Geoffrey Starley, William Popelwic, John Brampton, Thomas Dunmowe, John atte Wode and William Bromley, 14 glaziers breaking and fitting glass upon the painted tables, for the same time, at 6*d.* a day, 42*s.* Thomas Dadyngton and Robert Yerdesle, 2 glaziers' mates (*garcionibus vitriariis*) working with the others at breaking glass, each of them at 4½*d.* a day, 4*s.* 6*d.*[60]

The role of the master-glaziers is worth noting. The restriction of their labour to the cartoons was almost certainly dictated by the desire to finish the glazing speedily and the availability of a large work-force to paint and lead the glass. A similar situation applied to John Thornton, when in 1405 he undertook to glaze the great east window of York Minster. It was laid down that Thornton should 'pourtray the said window with his own hand, and the histories, images and other things to be painted on the same'; but he was only to 'paint the same necessary'. As the contract refers to workmen provided by Thornton it is clear that it was not envisaged that he would personally execute all the glass (Fig. 142).[61] Given the size of the average workshop such a degree of specialisation was, one suspects, exceptional. The contract of 1447 for the Beauchamp Chapel, Warwick (Fig. 138) states that the cartoons for the windows were not to be done by the main glazier, John Prudde, but by another painter. Prudde himself was to paint and lead the glass, 'to fine, glaze, enelyn it, and finely and strongly set it in lead and souder as well as any Glasse in England'.[62]

Prudde worked at Westminster and Shene Palaces in 1442 and *c.* 1445, and an inventory of stores in both places compiled in 1443 provides useful information on the contents of the medieval glazier's workshop:

59  J.D. Le Couteur, *Ancient Glass in Winchester* (1920), 103, 120.
60  Salzman, op. cit. note 13, 35.
61  G. Benson, *The Ancient Painted Glass Windows in*

*the Minster and Churches of the City of York* (1915), 86-7.
62  Dugdale, op. cit. note 6, 446.

... 1 iron compace for the use of the glaziers ... 25 shields painted on paper with various arms of the King for patterns for the use of glaziers working there, 6 crestis with various arms for the same works ... 12 payntyng dyssches of lead ... 12 patterns made in the likeness of windows, 8 iron grosyeres [grozing irons] ... 42 glosyng nayle used up in glosyng work ... a leaden wasschbolle used to make leads for glazing windows ... 2 portreyying tables of waynescote, 2 tables of popeler [poplar], 11 trestles, used for glazing work.[63]

At the other end of the spectrum, some local glaziers were evidently incapable of making their own cartoons and had them supplied by others. In the early 16th century Sir Thomas Lucas paid one Wright 10*s.* 'for portraying of my chapel windowe and settyng out the coloures of the same unto my glazier'.[64]

It was in his capacity of King's Glazier that Prudde was employed at Westminster and Shene. The existence of such a post can be traced back at least to the late 13th century. In 1297 William of Kent, glazier:

> took office in place of Robert the glazier, to mend defects where necessary in many places and to receive the same wages that Robert received, namely 4*d.* a day. And he found as security for his faithful service to the King, Henry le Plomer.[65]

The daily wage or retainer varied in amount. John Brampton, when he was appointed in 1378, received 12*d.* per day only whilst he was engaged on the King's Works. His successor, Richard Savage, did not receive a set wage, but only 'whatever shall be agreed between the Clerk of the King's Works and the said Richard'. Savage was followed in 1412 by Roger Gloucester, for whom the 12*d.* fee was reinstated. It remained at this rate (except between 1461 and 1472 when it was reduced to 8*d.*) until the early 16th century.[66] The Fleming, Barnard Flower, who was King's Glazier from at least the end of March 1505 until 1517, received slightly more, for he had £24 per annum.[67] From at least the 15th century the King's Glazier had a shed or lodge in the western part of Westminster Palace; the dimensions of this are given as 60 feet by 20 feet.[68]

The office of King's Glazier was prestigious and worth more than the daily fee, for it did not preclude the holder from undertaking work outside the royal palaces and castles; indeed, it attracted important and lucrative commissions. This certainly happened to John Prudde with the Beauchamp Chapel glazing (Fig. 138). He also worked in 1441 at All Souls College, Oxford, and, as referred to above, at Fromonds Chantry, Winchester College, in 1443-4.[69]

Although almost all the named English medieval English glass-painters are known to us from contracts and accounts, a few 'signed' their works. The east window of York Minster bears John Thornton's initials together with the year of

63  Salzman, op. cit. note 11, 27.
64  Idem, *Building in England*, 178.
65  Idem, op. cit. note 44, 118.
66  For these figures and dates see *King's Works*, i, 226.
67  Oswald, 'Barnard Flower', op. cit. note 12, 13.
68  *King's Works*, i, 226.
69  H. C[hitty], 'John Prudde, "King's Glazier"', *Notes and Queries*, 12th ser. iii (1917), 419-21.

*Fig. 139* Signature of John Thornton in the
east window of York Minster, 1408.
(*After J. A. Knowles*)

completion (1408) (Fig. 139).[70] There are several examples of glaziers' signatures in
Continental glass, ranging in date from the mid 13th century 'Frater Lupuldus' at
Haina, Germany, down to the 16th-century windows signed by Arnoult de
Nijmuegen at Rouen and Tournai.[71] A few North European glaziers are also
depicted in their windows (Gerlachus in a German panel of *c.* 1150-60 and Clement
of Chartres in a window dating from *c.* 1220-30 at Rouen Cathedral).[72] None
survives in England, but a copy made in 1822 of the original figure of Thomas
Glazier of Oxford is in Winchester College Chapel; the original dates from the
1390s.[73] A south transept window in York Minster also once contained a figure of
John Petty (d. 1508).[74]

### The Commissioning of Windows

As in other fields of medieval artistic activity, the choice of subjects and type of
glazing were not matters left to the discretion of the glass-painters; nor was it their
normal practice to make windows for stock and sell them to chance customers.
Instead everything was executed to the specific commissions of those paying for the
work, be they monarch, prelate, noble, merchant or churchwarden.

The wishes expressed by a donor or testator had to be incorporated into a binding
agreement. The normal form that this took, as for other commercial transactions,
was a written contract. The earliest reference to such an agreement is in 1237, when
Peter the Painter received 5*s.* 6*d.* as agreed by contract for making a glass window for
Marlborough Castle (Wilts.).[75] Very few of these contracts survive; for the most part
they are only abstracts giving very little more than the name of the glazier, the patron
and the price. Some contracts are known from later copies which should be treated

70  Knowles, op. cit. note 18, 217.
71  For Haina see H. Wentzel, 'Die Glasmalerei
    der Zisterzienser in Deutschland', *Die Kloster-
    baukunst* (Arbeitsbericht der Deutsch-Fran-
    zösischen Kunsthistoriker-Tagung, Mainz,
    1951); the De Nijmuegen references are taken
    from J. Lafond, *La Résurrection d'un Maître
    d'autrefois* (Rouen, 1942), 5-6, 7, 9. For a general
    survey see M.P. Lillich, 'Gothic Glaziers:
    Monks, Jews, Taxpayers, Bretons, Women',
    *Jnl. Glass Studies*, xxvii (1985), 72-92.
72  For Gerlachus see R. Becksmann and H.
    Waetzoldt, 'Glasmalerei des Mittelalters'; in

*Vitrea Dedicata. Das Stifterbild in der deutschen
Glasmalerei des Mittelaters* (Berlin, 1975), 66,
text Fig. 1, and for Clement of Chartres see
G. Ritter, *Les Vitraux de la Cathédrale de Rouen*
(Cognac, 1926), Plate xiv.
73  J.H. Harvey and D. King, 'Winchester College
    Stained Glass', *Archaeologia*, ciii (1971), Plate
    lxvii b.
74  F. Harrison, *The Painted Glass of York* (1927),
    16, citing Oxford, Bodleian Library, MS Top.
    Yorks.c.14, f.74 (notes by Henry Johnston,
    1669-70).
75  Salzman, op. cit note 44, 116.

with caution. Nonetheless there are certain features common to most of these documents.

Glazing contracts do not differ in essence from other medieval European commercial agreements, such as those between patrons and the limewood retable sculptors of South Germany;[76] they combine the deposit or earnest by the patron to the craftsman which bound the latter to complete within an agreed period, a bond or surety by the glazier to fulfil the contract, and the obligation of the patron in turn to pay the balance as necessary. They also frequently include instructions to the glazier regarding subject-matter and (sometimes) they detail the type of glass to be used.

Several of the documents give detailed instructions to the glazier or mention that these will be supplied. The St. John's College, Cambridge, contract of 1513 mentions a figure of St. John the Evangelist to be placed in the hall windows, with detailed instructions to follow for the chapel.[77] We do not know what form these instructions were to take, but in several other instances it is made clear. The 1447 contract with John Prudde, the King's Glazier, for the windows of the Beauchamp Chapel, Warwick, states that 'the matters Images, and stories ... shall be delivered and appointed by the said Executors in patterns in paper'.[78] Another reference to a drawing, or *vidimus* (see above, p. 267), is in Henry VII's will: the iconographical scheme for the windows of his chapel at Westminster Abbey was to be delivered 'in picture' to the Master of the Works.[79]

There survive several 14th-century German examples of *vidimuses*,[80] but none is known from England prior to the end of the 15th century. The first is extremely interesting in that it seems to have been the work of the prospective donor himself. On f. 191 of London, British Library, Lansdowne MS 874 is a very rough drawing of a kneeling man and his wife (Fig. 140). The drawing can be dated to between *c.*1484 and 1498 and the heraldry on the man's tabard identifies him as Thomas Froxmere. The sketch is accompanied by detailed instructions relating to the heraldic charges to be depicted.[81]

In most instances these drawings were probably prepared for the patrons by professional *limnours* or draughtsmen. In 1505, 7*s.* were paid to John Delyon, the glazier of Lady Margaret Beaufort's manor at Collyweston (Northants.), 'for the changyng of the Antelope into an Ivell in the bay wyndowe in the grett chambre, wt xx*d* yevyn to William Hollmer for the draght of the said Ivell at London'.[82]

A number of *vidimuses* exist for glazing schemes in English churches of the early 16th century. The most elaborate, for a thirteen-light window containing the Crucifixion, Last Judgement, Passion scenes and four saints, is in the National Galleries of Scotland, Edinburgh. As the four saints include St. William of York (as

76 M. Baxandall, *The Limewood Sculptors of Renaissance Germany* (New Haven, 1980), 102-6.
77 R. Willis and J.W. Clark, *Architectural History of the University of Cambridge and of the Colleges of Cambridge and Eton* (1886), ii, 347-8.
78 Dugdale, op. cit. note 6, 446-7.
79 Le Couteur, op. cit. note 38, 11.
80 H. Wentzel, 'Un Projet du Vitrail au XIV<sup>e</sup> Siècle', *Revue de l'Art*, x (1970), 7-14.
81 J.A. Goodall, 'Two Medieval Drawings', *Antiq. Jnl.* lviii (1978), 160-2, Plate L(b).
82 Salzman, *Building in England*, 178.

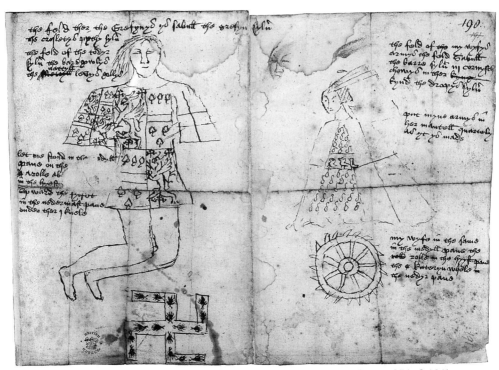

*Fig. 140* Drawing of a donor and his wife, *c.* 1484-98 (B.L., MS Lansdowne 874, f. 191).

well as St. Thomas of Canterbury), the *vidimus* can perhaps be connected with Cardinal Wolsey, who was Archbishop of York between 1515 and 1529. From the size of the composition it was almost certainly for the east or west windows of a large ecclesiastical edifice, perhaps one of the Cardinal's grandiose unfinished schemes at York Place (later Whitehall Palace) or Cardinal College (Christ Church), Oxford. The *vidimus* is also interesting in that the inscriptions do not tally with the subjects depicted; for instance 'Ecce homo' is written over the St. Thomas of Canterbury and the Entombment; presumably these were corrections or alterations to the subjects requested by the patron. From the occasional Dutch word in the inscriptions and the figure style it is likely that this *vidimus* was prepared by a Netherlandish artist, possibly James Nicholson, who was employed by Wolsey at Cardinal College. He may also have been the artist of a similar series of 24 *vidimuses* in the Musée des Beaux-Arts in Brussels, which are probably for another Wolsey project, the glazing of Hampton Court Chapel (Fig. 141).[83]

Three *vidimuses* for surviving windows in King's College Chapel, Cambridge, were discovered twenty years ago in the library of Bowdoin College, Maine, in the United States. The drawings can be associated in general terms with the four indentures

83  For the Edinburgh and Brussels *vidimuses* see H. Wayment, 'Twenty-four Vidimuses for Cardinal Wolsey', *Master Drawings*, xxiii-xxiv No. 4 (1988), 505-17.

*Fig. 141 Vidimus* probably for a window in the chapel of Hampton Court Palace, early 16th century. (*Musée des Beaux-Arts, Brussels*)

signed in 1526 with Galyon Hone, Richard Bond, Thomas Reve and James Nicholson (for eighteen windows) and with Francis Williamson and Simon Symondes (for four windows). One of these indentures stipulates that the representatives of the King and of the College must deliver to Williamson and Symondes 'patrons otherwyse called a vidimus ... for to form glass and make by the foresaid four windows of the said church'. The main indenture signed by Hone and his three fellow-glaziers states that they themselves had to hand over the *vidimuses* in question to Williamson and Symondes. As Wayment has pointed out, the presence of grid-lines representing the *ferramenta* suggests that these drawings are not the original *vidimuses* but copies made as guides for the maker of the cartoon.[84]

As an alternative to 'patrons', written instructions were supplied to glaziers. Two rolls concerning the glazing of the Observant Friars' church at Greenwich in *c.* 1493-4 show how detailed such instructions could be. A section is transcribed here:

Lowes kyng of Fraunce of whos body kyng Henry the vij[th] kyng of Englond is lynyally dyscended and sonne to hym in the ix[th] degree. Make hym armyd wyth a mantill over his harnes an opyn crowne and a berde a septure in his lefte hande and a ball wyth a crosse in his ryght hande. His armes the felde asure flourte golde.

Ethelbert kyng of Kent shryned at Seint Austynes at Caunterbury. Make hym in the abytte of a peasible kyng with a berde & a ball wyth a crosse theron in the ryght honde & a cepture in the lefte hande & an opyn crowne. His armes the feld golde iij roundells gowles in the fyrst roundell halff an ymage of a kynge crowned in the roobis of astate in the ii[de] a lyon sylver in the iij[de] a dragon golde.

84 Idem, 'The Great Windows of King's College Chapel and the Meaning of the Word "Vidi-mus"', *Proc. Cambridge Antiquarian Soc.* lxix (1979), 53-69.

In the left margin the arms so described are blazoned.[85]

Such detailed heraldic instructions were no doubt considered necessary as glaziers could not be expected to be expert in the blazoning of arms. In 1540 at St. Margaret's, Westminster, a herald was consulted: 'To Symon Symones glasier for making and setting up of divers armes in the Trinity chapell by the advice and commandement of Mr. Lancaster Herrold at armes xs.'[86]

Time limits are specified in some of the more complete contracts. In 1405 John Thornton of Coventry was allowed three years by the Dean and Chapter of York to complete the great east window of the Minster (Fig. 142).[87] The contracts of 1526 for the glazing of King's College Chapel stipulate that Hone, Bond, Reve and Nicholson had to finish six windows within one year and twelve in the following four years; the first indenture for Williamson and Symondes gave them two years for two windows and another three years for two more; this was amended to give them five years for all four windows.[88]

To ensure that glass-painters kept to the agreed dates 'bonds' or penalty clauses were included in contracts. John Thornton merely swore an oath, but later agreements specify a financial penalty payable by the glazier to the patron for failure to complete the contract on time. Richard Wright at St. John's College, Cambridge, was bound in £50 and the two teams of King's College Chapel glaziers in 500 marks and £200 respectively.

By the same token it was recognised that it was unreasonable for glaziers to have to wait for payment until the work was completed. In 1391, for the great east window of Exeter Cathedral, Robert Lyen received a weekly rate of 3s. 4d. for adapting the old glass, with a further 2s. for his assistant. For the new glass Lyen was paid 20d. per square foot, but it is not clear whether he received this on a weekly basis (Fig. 143).[89] John Thornton had 4s. per week during his work on the York Minster east window, in addition to a lump sum of £5 per year and £10 on completion of the contract. By the early 16th century at least it had become customary to pay a 'prest' or advance. In 1511 Barnard Flower received £20 as an advance for work at the Chapel of Our Lady, at Walsingham (Norfolk),[90] and four years later he had a down payment of £100 on his glazing at King's College Chapel. Hone, Bond, Reve and Nicholson were to receive £60 as an advance as well as further sums at half-yearly intervals.[91]

It was necessary for the patron to make such payments on account in order to enable glaziers undertaking major projects to fulfil the contract, particularly in those instances when the glass-painter, not the patron, had to supply the glass, lead and so forth, as well as meet transportation costs. These were taken into consideration in

85 London, British Library, Egerton MS 2341. See *Hasted's History of Kent*, ed, H.H. Drake, Pt. 1, *The Hundred of Blackheath* (1886), 86-7, No. 6.
86 J.C. Cox, *Churchwardens' Accounts* (1913), 87.
87 Benson, op. cit. note 61, 86-7.
88 H. Wayment, *The Windows of King's College*

*Chapel, Cambridge* (*Corpus Vitrearum Medii Aevi: Great Britain*, Supplementary Vol. 1, 1972), 124-5.
89 Brooks and Evans, op. cit. note 24, 37-8, 167.
90 Oswald, art. cit. note 12, 15.
91 Wayment, op. cit. note 88, 123-4.

*Fig. 142* Panel in the east window of York Minster by John Thornton, 1405-8.

*Fig. 143* Head of *St. Edward the Confessor* in the east window of Exeter Cathedral, *c.* 1391.

pricing the work, but nonetheless the glaziers had to expend considerable sums during the course of the contract.

Turning to prices and payments, evidence from contracts is greatly augmented by a number of sources, especially building accounts. The majority of new glazing schemes were priced per square foot. Costs fluctuated considerably between the early 13th and early 16th centuries and it is impossible to quantify what this meant in real terms as so many of the accounts are too imprecise regarding the glass, and only a small and unrepresentative proportion of the glass mentioned in documents survives. There is no means of knowing, for example, whether the white glass which, at a rate of 12*d*. per square foot, was purchased from Henry Staverne and John Brampton in 1364 for Hadleigh Castle (Essex), was the same in quality and decoration (or plainness) as that for which William Burgh in 1400 received only 10*d*. per square foot for a window in the Exchequer at Westminster.[92] On the other hand, the survival of some glass associated with accounts gives an indication of the types of glazing purchased by the various rates. In August 1253 the windows of Westminster Abbey cost 8*d*. per square foot for painting and working coloured glass and 4*d*. for white glass.[93] The few panels of coloured glass which survive from Henry III's glazing take the form of small but detailed narrative scenes, and it is known that the white glass depicted geometrical designs of stylised stems and leaves in conventional 13th-century fashion.[94] In the Exeter Cathedral accounts for the new presbytery windows in the period 1301-7, no distinction is made between white and coloured glass and the cost is merely given as 5½*d*. per square foot; in the years 1309-11 the rate rose to 6½*d*. per foot. These prices were for already painted glass.[95] Of the glass referred to in the 1301-7 accounts only parts of the east window and a north clerestory window survive; they contain figures under canopies in coloured glass which in the latter window are set on white (*grisaille*) grounds within a border. The prices quoted in the accounts do not include the expense of setting the glass in the windows, which is costed separately.[96] In 1338-9 the Dean and Chapter of York Minster agreed with a glass-painter named Robert a rate of 6*d*. per square foot for white and 12*d*. per foot for coloured glass for the great west window in the Minster (Fig. 144).[97] This window exists and contains figures and scenes under canopies. In 1363-4 glass with royal arms in the borders placed in the royal apartments at Windsor Castle cost 13*d*. per square foot.[98] This rate remained fairly constant for the next three decades. Thus at Windsor in 1383 John Brampton received 13*d*. per square foot for 160 feet of coloured glass decorated with falcons and the royal arms.[99] For the glazing which William Burgh carried out around 1400 in the royal palaces at Westminster and Eltham, prices rose very sharply. In 1399 he was paid 12*d*. a foot for

92  Salzman, op. cit. note 44, 189; op. cit. note 11, 25.
93  Colvin, op. cit. note 16, 286-7.
94  *Age of Chivalry*, op. cit. note 23, Nos. 735-6.
95  *Accounts of Exeter*, op. cit. note 7, 24, 28, 30, 32, 35, 42, 49, 50, 56, 57.
96  *Age of Chivalry*, No. 739; Brooks and Evans, op.

cit. note 24, 11-13, 15.
97  T. French and D. O'Connor, *York Minster: A Catalogue of Medieval Stained Glass* 1: *The West Windows of the Nave* (*Corpus Vitrearum Medii Aevi Great Britain*, iii.1, 1987), 85.
98  Salzman, op. cit. note 44, 189.
99  Ibid. 192.

*Fig. 144 St. John the Evangelist* in the great west window of York Minster, *c.* 1339.

glass decorated with birds and 1*s.* 8*d.* for glass with the royal arms and those of St. Edward in Westminster Palace. In the following year glass embellished with birds was priced at 16*d.* per square foot; plain white glass cost the King 10*d.* per square foot. In 1401 Burgh charged 2*s.* a square foot for a four-light window at Eltham which contained 'Escuchons, garters and colers of the Bagez of our Lord the King'. This was surpassed by the 3*s.* 4*d.* per foot which Burgh received for another window containing the figures of SS. John the Baptist, Thomas, George, the Annunciation, the Holy Trinity, and St. John the Evangelist.[100] In the following year Eltham was glazed with more very expensive glass:

> For 91 square feet of new glass, diapered and worked with broom-flowers, eagles and rolls inscribd Soueraigne, bought of William Burgh, glasier, for the said 3 Baywyndowes and costres, each of 2 lights, at 3*s.* 4*d.* a foot, 15*li.* 3*s.* 4*d.* And for 54 square feet of new glass worked with figures and canopies, the field made in the likeness of cloth of gold, bought of the same William for 3 windows each of 2 lights in the new oratory, at 3*s.* 4*d.* a foot, 9*li* - 24*li* 3*s.* 4*d.*[101]

The Eltham glazing was evidently very sumptuous, and the rate of 3*s.* 4*d.* per square foot is never repeated in any surviving accounts. The most expensive glazing

100  Ibid. iii (1929-30), 25-6.                    101  Ibid. 27.

*Fig. 145* Detail of *Sacrament of Confirmation* by Richard Twygge and Thomas Wodshawe, Tattershall (Lincs.), *c.* 1482.

scheme subsequently was the Beauchamp Chapel at Warwick, the 1447 contract for which stated that John Prudde was to receive 2*s.* per square foot (Fig. 138).[102]

During the 15th century, glazing ranged from plain white glass to complex iconographical schemes. From the accounts concerned with John Prudde quite an accurate picture can be obtained of what the various piecework rates purchased, inclusive of the cost of materials.[103] For Shene Palace in *c.* 1445 he made a window of white glass for 7*d.* per foot. The costs of his figural glass here and at Eton College (the latter in 1445-6) varied between 8*d.* and 12*d.*[104] The differences in price can be explained in terms of the respective amounts of coloured glass used and additional elements such as canopies and borders.

Prudde also glazed windows at Eton College with *vitri historiales*, that is, scenes rather than single figures. The rate was 1*s.* 2*d.*[105] Nearly forty years later, in 1482, *vitri historiales* made for Tattershall (Lincs.) still cost the same. Several panels from these windows survive (Fig. 145). Even as late as 1526 the rate for the historiated windows in King's College Chapel had only risen by 2*d.* to 1*s.* 4*d.* from Prudde's prices of 1445-6.[106] The price of unpainted white glass declined in the early 16th century. In 1513 Richard Wright received 4*d.* per square foot for installing white glass at St. John's College.[107] By *c.* 1517-20 the price of white glass had fallen still

102  Dugdale, op. cit. note 6, 446-7.
103  Knowles, *Essays*, p.48, Fig. 5.
104  Salzman, op. cit. note 11, 28; Willis and Clark, op. cit. note 77, i, 393-4.

105  Willis and Clark, op cit. note 77.
106  Wayment, op. cit. note 88, 123-5.
107  Willis and Clark, ii, 347-8.

further, for at the Savoy Hospital Chapel Richard Bond was only paid 2*d*.[108] The same rate occurs in 1533.[109]

The Savoy accounts are particularly informative with regard to precisely what the various prices purchased, as this entry reveals:

> Paid ffor the Glasyng off the South Wyndowe . . . with the Cruciffyxe Mary and John the Kyngis Armes And the Orate cont' in colored glasse xlvj ffote price le ffote xij*d* . . . £2 6*s*. 0*d*.
>
> Paid ffor the glasyng off the seid wyndowe with whyte glass cont' clxviij ffote price le ffote ij*d* . . . £1 8*s*. 0*d*.[110]

So far only payment by piecework has been discussed. Some glazing contracts named a fixed price for the work, as in the contract of 1338-9 for the two windows at the west end of York Minster nave aisles, which each cost 11 marks (£7 6*s*. 8*d*.).[111]

In certain circumstances glass-painters were paid on a day-work basis and not by fixed price/piecework. This seems to have been the case with certain very large royal contracts, such as the glazing of St. Stephen's Chapel, Westminster. As was mentioned above, a large team of glaziers was employed here and payment was by a daily wage. The extract from the accounts cited above (p. 280) reveals that master glaziers received 1*s*. per day, 'working' glaziers (for want of a better term) 6*d*. or 7*d*. and their assistants 4*d*. or 4½*d*. Similar rates applied at Windsor in *c*. 1351-2.[112] As there were so many compulsory feast and saints' days, it was arranged at St. Stephen's that the men would be paid for every alternate holiday. At both St. Stephen's and Windsor, although the glass was obtained by the glaziers direct from manufacturers at Chiddingfold (Surrey) and other centres, their wages did not include the purchase of the material.

The most frequent occurrence of payments by wage as opposed to piecework is in connection with glazing repairs. This system was already in operation in 1240 at Chichester Cathedral, where John the glazier undertook to keep the windows in repair in return for a daily allowance of bread and an annual fee of 13*s*. 4*d*.[113] At Eltham Palace in 1406 a team of four men were each paid 6*d*. a day for making a panel for a window in the King's Chamber and for mending various defective windows.[114] Included in this account is a payment of 4½*d*. for 3 lbs. of candles bought and used by the four glaziers for working at night. Evidently it was considered unreasonable that the workmen should have to meet such expenses out of their own pockets. There are occasional references to incidental expenses paid to glaziers, chiefly for travel, board and lodging when they were working away from home. In 1443-4, Richard and William, two assistants of John Prudde, King's Glazier, were given 3*s*. 4*d*. by the Warden of Winchester College for their expenses.[115]

108  Oswald, op. cit. note 15, 228.
109  Salzman, *Building in England*, 177.
110  Oswald, op. cit. note 15, 228-9.
111  French and O'Connor, op. cit. note 97, 85.
112  Salzman, op. cit. note 13; idem, op. cit. note

44, 120, 188.
113  Idem, *Building in England*, 175.
114  Idem, op. cit. note 11, 27.
115  Le Couteur, op. cit. note 59, 120.

*Fig. 146* Two apostles and a prophet from the side windows of
Winchester College Chapel, *c.* 1393.

Winchester is one example of glaziers undertaking commissions at considerable distances from their workshops. The expense involved in transporting the finished glass from the latter to the places for which they were destined could be considerable. The cost of the careful packing required was an important element, as the accounts for the carriage of the Windsor windows from Westminster in 1352 demonstrate:

> For 18 boards to make cases for carrying glass panels from Westminster to Windsor, 3*s*. For 38 elm-boards for the same, at 4*d*. a piece, 13*s*. 8*d*. For carriage of the same from London to Westminster, 5*d*. For hay and straw to put in the said cases for safe-keeping of the glass panels, 14*d*. For a 'palet' with 1 soldur [soldering-iron] bought for the glazing, 12*d*. For 300 nails for making the said cases, 12*d*. To John Wodewyk for freight of the said cases with the glass panels for the chapel windows from Westminster to Windsor, 4*s*.[116]

The cost of carriage was much higher for the windows made in 1393 by Thomas Glazier of Oxford for Winchester College Chapel. 19*s*. 3*d*. was paid for two waggons going from Esher (the residence of the patron, Bishop William of Wykeham) to pick up the glass at Oxford and take it via Highclere to Winchester (Fig. 146). The task took nine days and involved twelve horses and six waggoners.[117] Whenever it was convenient, water transport was used. In 1332 John de Walworth took some windows from Candlewick Street (now Cannon Street) to Westminster via the River Thames.[118]

From the foregoing it can be seen that there is a considerable body of contemporary information on the craft of glass-painting in the Middle Ages, largely because glazing is included in building accounts. As a result, far more is known concerning this branch of painting than about manuscript illumination. Furthermore, the large amount of medieval glass of high quality that survives in cathedrals and parish churches the length and breadth of the country reveals that the English glass-painter was well capable of matching the achievements of his continental counterparts.

## Further Reading

For a comprehensive bibliography on English medieval stained glass see M. Caviness and E.R. Staudinger, *Stained Glass before 1540: an Annotated Bibliography* (Boston, 1983), and D. Evans, *A Bibliography of Stained Glass* (1982). The following works contain useful information:

S. Crewe, *Stained Glass in England c. 1180-1540* (1987).

E. Frodl-Kraft, *Die Glasmalerei: Entwicklung, Technik, Eigenart* (Vienna & Zurich, 1970).

116  Salzman, op. cit. note 44, 188.

117  C. Woodforde, *The Stained Glass of New College,*

*Oxford* (1951), 5.

118  Salzman, op. cit. note 44, 119.

R. Marks, *Stained Glass in England during the Middle Ages* (forthcoming).

L.F. Salzman, *Building in England down to 1540* (reprinted with additions 1967).

N.H.J. Westlake, *A History of Design in Painted Glass* (i-iv, [1879]-94).

C. Winston, *An Inquiry into the Difference of Style Observable in Ancient Glass Paintings* (i-ii, 2nd edn., 1867).

C. Winston, *Memoirs Illustrative of the Art of Glass-Painting* (1865).

12

## Leather

### JOHN CHERRY

Leather was an important material in the Middle Ages. It provided for many needs in daily life: for clothing, particularly boots, shoes, gloves, and belts; for the harnessing of animals, saddles and harness; for the carriage of liquid in sacks and bottles; and for military purposes for scabbards, quivers, helmets and armour. Leather and leather goods were made throughout the country. The manufacture of leather and leather objects was an important urban activity since hides were often available as a by-product of meat consumption and towns were markets for leather goods.

Leather is the preserved hide of animals such as oxen, cows, calves, pigs, deer, horses, sheep and goats. Leather is produced by a series of operations which make it stable under warm moist conditions, and thus is capable of being repeatedly wetted and dried without losing this property. Skin or hide is composed of three layers: the outer layer containing the hair and hair root system, the corium or main skin structure, and the fleshy fat layer underneath. It is the treatment of the central layer of the skin by tanning or tawing that makes it most suitable for its ultimate use. The basic technology of tanning and tawing did not change from the Graeco-Roman world to the late 18th century.

In contrast to other manufacturing trades there was a division between those who prepared the raw material – the tanners, curriers, and tawyers – and the leather-workers who made the actual objects. This survey will therefore be divided into two main parts: the treatment of the skin to provide a workable material, and the use of that material by a variety of crafts to make objects.

### Techniques of Leather Preparation

The tanners acquired the hides from the butcher, who cut out all that was useful or profitable. The hides were delivered to the tanners with horns and hooves attached. This is confirmed by the discovery of a great quantity of cattle horn cores in pits at a tannery in Tanner Street, Northampton, and the preponderance of lower leg-bones at Tanner Street in Winchester.[1] The first job of the tanner was therefore to trim these from the hides and wash the hides free of blood, dung, and any salt that might have been applied by the butcher. This washing was often by immersion in the local stream. At Colchester in 1425-6 there was a complaint that the River Colne was polluted by the laying of many hides in the water to the detriment of those that brewed their ale.[2]

Next it was necessary to treat the hides to loosen the hair and enable it to be scraped off without damping the grain surface. This was achieved most simply by folding the hides hair-side in and piling them in a warm atmosphere until the hair roots began to rot and loosen. This action could be encouraged by sprinkling the hair-side of the skins with urine. An alternative method was to soak the skins in alkaline liquor prepared from wood ash or lime. Pairs of probable tanning pits, with one of each pair containing lime, have been excavated in a late 13th-century context at Exe Bridge and at High Street, Exeter.[3]

When the hair was loosened sufficiently, the hide was spread over a wooden beam and both sides were scraped with two-handled knives. The hair or grain side was scraped with a blunt single-edged unhairing knife and the flesh side with a sharper two-edged fleshing knife. After more soaking, the skin was scraped with a blunt scudding knife. Although these knives are known from post-medieval illustrations, and although two-handled scrapers are known from the Roman tannery in Pompeii, no example of a medieval two-handled knife has yet been found. Engravings of the 16th and 17th centuries show the technique of working with these implements over a beam.[4]

The next stage was to wash and open up the skins using either the alkaline bating, puering or mastering process or the acidic raising or drenching process. In the first the skins were immersed in a warm infusion of bird droppings or dog dung which removed the lime and gave the hide structure a softer, more flexible grain. The drenching process, which also removed lime, treated the hides in liquors prepared by fermenting barley or rye often with stale beer or urine added. It was the nature of the materials used in these processes that made tanneries unpleasant neighbours.

If one considers the archaeological evidence for the siting of tanneries, or at least those sites which have been identified as tanneries, it is apparent that they are not always near rivers. In York, tan pits of the Viking period were excavated in 1902 between High Ousegate and Coppergate some 500ft. from the river Ouse.[5] At Northampton, the medieval tanning quarter was located on the south-west edge of the town by the northern arm of the Nene. The tannery excavated north of Tanner Street is almost 400 feet from the river – a surprising distance, which possibly indicates that the tannery used well water[6] (Fig. 147). At Exeter the pits excavated at

1  M. Shaw, 'Northampton', *Current Arch.* xci (1984), 241-4; and D. Keene, *Survey of Medieval Winchester:* Winchester Studies 2 (1985), i, 287.
2  *V.C.H., Essex*, ii, 459.
3  J.P. Allan, *Medieval and Post Medieval Finds from Exeter, 1971-1980* (1984), 325.

4  For a modern illustration of the tanner's hand tools see H.G. Bennett, *The Manufacture of Leather* (1909), 67.
5  J. Radley, 'Economic Aspects of Anglo-Danish York', *Med. Arch.* xv (1971), 46.
6  Shaw, art. cit. in note 1, 241-4.

the Exe Bridge were near the river but those in the High Street were not.[7]

A further washing of the skins completed the preparatory work on the hides, and the 'rounding' or division of the hide into its different qualities was carried out, since if a complete hide was immersed the coarse-grained parts would absorb the best tanning solution. The tanning process had two stages. In the first the hides were immersed in weak tanning liquor and moved around almost continuously until they had a uniform surface colour. These pits were called the handlers since the hides were handled in and out of the pit at least daily. Once the colour was satisfactory, the hides were taken to pits called the layaways. In these, layers of vegetable tanning material and the hides alternated until the pit was full. It was then filled with cold water or a mixture of cold water and weak tanning material. The vegetable tanning material was usually oak bark, which yields 10 per cent liquor per unit of its volume. The time taken for tanning depended on the thickness of the hide, the tanning materials employed, and the properties of the leather. In Leicester the oath of the tanners specified that they should not sell any leather not well tanned, adding that the leather should be for a year and a day in the same face or liquor.[8] The leather act of 1563 laid down minimum times of 12 months for outer sole leather and nine months for uppers.[9] When it was judged that they were fully tanned, the hides were rinsed off and smoothed using a two-handled setting pin, which had a blunt triangular cross-section. The leather was then dried out slowly in a dark shed fitted with louvred panels.

If one applied this description of the technical process to the archaeological sites which have been identified as tanneries then one would expect two different types of pits: one probably shallow, in which the skins were easily handled, and the other probably deeper, in which the hides could be left for a long period of probably twelve months or more. At the Rhaedr tannery, erected in the second half of the 18th century and now preserved in the Welsh Folk Museum at St. Fagans near Cardiff, the pits are arranged in three groups: the 16 central leaching or suspender pits, the 22 handler or floater pits, and the 12 layer pits.[10] The tannery at High Ousegate, York, possessed three large tan pits, some seven or eight feet deep under a timber-framed building. This was only part of the tannery, probably the suspender pits.[11] At Northampton the tanning area can be divided into three main complexes (see Fig. 147). It is not clear, however, whether the northern and eastern complexes were two separate tanneries or different parts of the same tannery fulfilling different purposes. The western complex may have been either one complex with two different types of pits or one complex with pits serving different functions. The analysis of the need for different functions suggests that the latter explanation may be more acceptable for these pits lined with clay or staves with wood set inside them.[12]

7   Allan, *Exeter*, op. cit. in note 3, 235.
8   M.P. Dare, 'Medieval Shoemakers and Tanners in Leicester, Northampton and Nottingham', *Associated Architectural Societies' Reports*, xxxix (1928-9), 155.

9   Statute 5 Eliz.I, c. 8.
10  J.G. Jenkins, *The Rhaedr Tannery* (1973).
11  Radley, art. cit. note 5, p. 46, Fig. 10.
12  Shaw, 'Northampton', art. cit. note 1.

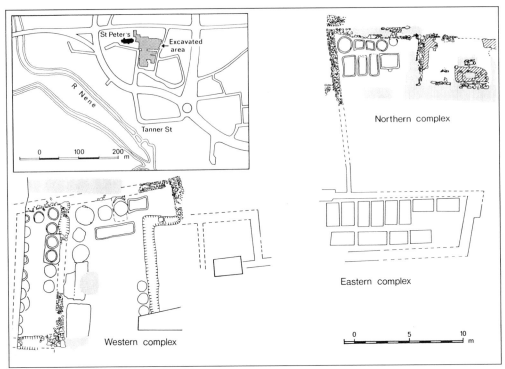

*Fig. 147* Plan of the tannery excavated in Northampton. Drawing by K. Hughes after M. Shaw and John Williams.

In order to minimise unfair competition and to control the quality of each stage of the production of a leather object, no one craftsman had control of the whole leather-making operation from the raw skin to the finished product. The tanner was not permitted to be a butcher, and was required to sell the rough dried leather to the curriers who converted it into a material having the necessary thickness, softness and flexibility suitable to its final use. The currier was not permitted to be tanner, nor the shoemaker a currier.

It is unlikely that a currier's workshop would leave any archaeological traces, since all the activities took place above ground. The currier dampened the leather in warm water and softened it by pummelling or trampling. The surfaces were then secured by stiff brushes or smoothed out using stone or metal-bladed slickers. In order to prove a leather of a standard thickness, the currier's shaving-knife was used. This had a rectangular double-edged blade ten inches long and six inches wide. It had two handles, one in line with the blade and the other at right-angles to it. The dampened leather was placed over a currier's beam, and shavings were pared off, the knife-blade being held at right-angles, until the leather was the right thickness. This type of knife was employed from Roman times to the 20th century and was undoubtedly used in the medieval period, although as far as I am aware no medieval examples have ever been found.[13]

The shaved hides were once again washed clean and worked on a flat wooden or stone bench with stones, slickers or brushes to flatten the leather and stretch it. It was then stuffed or impregnated with a warm dubbin of mixed tallow and fish oils. After the skins had been piled up to allow the fats to penetrate evenly, they were hung in a warm room and the surplus grease removed. If a firm leather product was required for shoe soles, harness, or other purposes, the hides were simply hung out to dry and season before selling. If a softer, finer product was required, further operations such as 'boarding' (rubbing on a flat table) were carried out. The leather was then coloured or the surface polished using a smooth stone.

There was a clear separation between the heavy leather trades of tanning and currying. It was much more difficult to separate the light leather trades, those of the whittawyers, the glovers and the leather dressers. The distinction between the tanner and the tawyer is that the tanner took cattle hides and used oak bark, whereas the tawyer took the skins of other animals and used only alum and oil. The 15th-century customal of Northampton confirms the basic difference: while the 'tanner shall tan no sheeps' leather, goats' leather, deers' leather, horse leather or hounds' leather', the whittawyer was only to process those types of skins.[14]

Skins were received by the tawyer from the butcher in a similar state to those delivered to the tanner, although it is likely that the tawyer used many more casualty skins from animals which had died naturally. Once the skins had been taken through the preparatory cleaning process they were placed in large tubs where they were trampled in a paste of alum, egg-yolks, oil and flour. They were then stretched, flattened and hung to dry. (Alum had to be imported. In the 13th and 14th centuries it was brought from the eastern Mediterranean, especially the Greek islands and from Phocaea near Izmir. After the fall of Byzantium to the Turks in 1453 an alum famine developed and new supplies were found in Italy.)[15] The leather was then softened by drawing it over a blunt blade used in the slaking or perching process. The most common tool for this, used from Egyptian times, was to set a blunt semi-circular blade about eight inches in diameter in a vertical wooden upright; the leather was then rubbed to and fro over it. Another method was to force a crutch stake, a smaller blade set in a T-shaped handle, across the skin between two wooden poles forming a frame known as the perch. Skins were also softened by using a lunette or circular blade against a skin held in the perch. The leather would then be dyed if necessary.

---

13  For the currier's tools see Bennett, op. cit. note 4, 287.

14  *Records of the Borough of Northampton*, ed. C.A. Markham and J.C. Cox (1898), i, 348.

15  F. Sherwood Taylor and C. Singer, 'Pre-Scientific Industrial Chemistry' in Singer and Holmyard, *History of Technology*, ii, 367-9. Alum was imported into Exeter from the Low Countries in the 15th century: see E.M. Carus-Wilson, *Expansion of Exeter at the Close of the Middle Ages* (1963), 15. See also W.R. Childs, *Anglo-Castilian Trade in the Later Middle Ages* (1978), 109.

*Mechanical Aids*

The gradual introduction of mechanical aids that occurred in many other industries by-passed the leather trades. It was only in grinding the oak bark into powder that mechanical aid was adopted. Bark was most easily peeled or stripped when the sap was rising in the trees in the period April to June. Although bark could be stripped from trees of all ages, oak coppice worked on a rotation of 25 to 30 years was ideal.[16] Grinding could be carried out in a large mortar or in a stone-lined pit, though none has been discovered on an archaeological site. The application of grinding by millstones driven by either animal or water-power certainly occurred in the Middle Ages. It is suggested that horse-driven bark mills were used in the medieval period. Although these were certainly used later, and there is no reason why they should not have been used in the Middle Ages, no evidence of this has so far been produced. In Europe, water-driven bark mills are referred to as early as 1138 in a document belonging to the chapter of Notre Dame in Paris, and a 13th-century writer suggested that leather working could only be carried out efficiently if water-power was available.[17] The dissemination of the techniques of water-power by various monastic orders throughout Europe may have had its effects on the tanning industry, but while monastic tanneries clearly existed, the only example known to me where a bark mill was employed was at Marley, the tannery of Battle Abbey.

At Clairvaux a 12th-century description indicates a tannery beside the stream that drove the corn-mill and the fulling-mill, though there is no specific reference to the use of the stream to drive a tanning-mill (the water is simply said to enter the tannery where, in preparing the leather for the shoes of the monks, it exercises as much exertion as diligence).[18] By the end of the 13th century tanning mills are recorded in English towns, notably at Newbury where a mill is recorded in 1297, and another (or possibly the same) is recorded as having been valued at 26s. 8d. before the Black Death and nothing afterwards, and also at Okehampton in Devon.[19] It is not recorded that these were powered, but it seems reasonable to suggest that since water was required for washing the leather, its power was probably used for the tan bark mills. In order to need such a mill it is clear that the tannery must have been operating on a considerable scale, since it would need a bark store as well as a mill. No tannery with a bark grinding mill has been excavated, and it would be of the greatest interest if one could be found and excavated.

16   For a good account of bark stripping see W. Linnard, 'Bark stripping in Wales', *Folk Life*, xvi (1978), 54-60.

17   The 1138 document is referred to without reference in J. Gimpel, *The Medieval Machine* (1977), 14.

18   For Clairvaux see Abbé Vacandard, *Vie de St.* *Bernard* (Paris, 1894), 416-18, translated by D. Luckhurst, *Monastic Watermills* (S.P.A.B., n.d.), 6.

19   *V.C.H., Berks*. i, 298. For Okehampton see *Calendar of Inquisitions Post Mortem*, xiv (1952), p. 310, No. 325.

## The Distribution of Tanning

For tanning to take place three essentials are necessary: animal skins, water and oak bark. Certain parts of the country were favoured since oaks do not grow much above 1,000 feet (excluding the Pennines, Lake District and Wales and Devon), and their growth is more difficult on wet, cold soils such as the Fens, Vale of York, Sedgemoor and Ouse Valley, or on chalk and limestone soils where beech and ash are favoured.[20] Certain areas were favoured for cattle grazing, notably the Midland clay plain. Norden in 1591 noted in Northamptonshire 'the greate heardes of cattle longinge to every small parish, village and hamlett, which when in my small travayle I did behold by such general multitudes'.[21] It was the combination of good grazing with oak trees that provided the geographical basis for tanning.

Tanning was certainly an urban occupation, but how far was it also a rural one? In 1184 the Assize of the Forest ordered tanners and tawyers to dwell within a borough, implying that tanning and tawing were proceeding in forest areas.[22] There is a constant repetition by modern authors that tanning was widespread. Thorold Rogers declared that tanning or tawing of leather was a by-product in most villages, and the *Victoria County History for Wiltshire* notes that Tanner was a common surname and that most towns and some villages had at least one tanner.[23] In the late 16th century a contemporary record states that 'in most villages in the realm there is some one dresser or worker of leather, and for the supplies of such as have not, there are in most market towns three, four, or five and in many great towns and cities ten or twenty and in London and its suburbs nearly two hundred'.[24] Even in the early 19th century a wide dispersal of tanning persisted: for example, at that time 131 towns and villages in Cornwall and Devon possessed tanners.[25] The subject of the village tanner deserves further attention and research to assess its real extent in the Middle Ages. The absence of any excavated tanneries in medieval villages, or any reference in a well-documented village such as Cuxham (Oxon.), is notable.[26]

With urban tanneries the evidence is clearer, or at least the pits more substantial. At York tan-pits of Danish date were discovered, and finds from 11th- and 12th-century contexts in Dublin suggest that there was a specialised industry there.[27] Tanning went on in all English towns in the Middle Ages and, as has been noted above, some large-scale establishments with bark-grinding mills were sited in towns,

20  For the discussion of the geographical factors affecting the location of the leather industry see C.P. Sargent, 'Physical Factors Affecting the Localisation of the Boot and Shoe Trade in England', *Geography*, xxiii (1938), 250-8. Sargent's arguments are summarised and critically analysed by P.R. Mountfield, 'The Footwear Industry of the East Midlands', *East Midland Geographer*, xxiii (1965), 394-413.

21  J. Norden, *A Delineation of Northamptonshire* (1720), 43.

22  For the Assize of the Forest see W. Stubbs,

*Select Charters* (9th edn. 1913), 185.

23  J.E. Thorold Rogers, *A History of Agriculture and Prices in England*, i (1866), 402: and *V.C.H. Wilts.* iv, 233.

24  B.L., Lansdowne MS 74, f.154.

25  J.W. Waterer, 'Leather', in Singer, *Hist. of Technology*, ii, 147-190.

26  P.D.A. Harvey, *A Medieval Oxfordshire Village: Cuxham 1240-1400* (1965).

27  B. O'Riordain, 'Excavations at High St. and Winetavern St., Dublin', *Med. Arch.* xv (1971), 75.

obtaining their supplies of hides from the cattle-market. By the end of the 17th century the most important centre of the leather-processing industry was London, based on the abundant supply of hides which were a by-product of the City's meat consumption. By *c.* 1700 there were about 80 tanneries, mainly sited in Bermondsey and Southwark, which served the leather workers of London. London was described in the Curriers' Company minute book as 'the place of greatest concourse of trades-men dealing in leather'.[28]

In considering the distribution of tanneries in the Middle Ages a third type must be considered: the monastic tannery. We have already noted the example at Clairvaux, and there is some evidence that the Cistercian order often had their own tanneries. The tannery at Rievaulx (Yorks.) still possesses brick tanning-pits.[29] Quarr Abbey had its own tannery from 1291 and Meaux Abbey had a tannery in 1396.[30] There were also tanneries in the Welsh Cistercian abbeys of Margam and Tintern. For the latter, situated close to the abbey, Gilbert Marshal, 6th Earl of Pembroke (1234-42), gave to the abbey *c.* 1240 all the bark of the lower forest of Went from the wood felled there, whether given or sold, for 2*d.* for each load.[31]

Very little has been written on the running of monastic establishments such as these. David Williams in his study of the Welsh Cistercians notes that the Tintern tannery failed to meet its needs in 1388, for the grange at Merthyrgeryn had to buy leather to mend flails.[32]

The best example of a monastic tannery that has been recently studied is the tannery of Battle Abbey situated in the manor of Marley near the town. The tannery had a bark-mill and clearly represented a major investment by the monastery in the early 14th century. It was managed sometimes in hand and sometimes at farm, bringing in between £2 and £10 during the 14th century. Repairs and running expenses could amount to over £6 in a single year (1384-5), but net profits as high as £20 in a year were recorded. The skins of many of the animals consumed in the refectory and guesthouse provided the tannery with much raw material. Most of the prepared leather was worked up by leather craftsmen in the town. In the 13th century leather workers are by far the most numerous among the burgesses: cordwainers lead, followed by glovers in abundance, saddlers, cobblers, curriers and tanners. At Battle even tailors worked in leather. Their jerkins, hoods and cloaks were purchased by the abbey and were no doubt sold to local buyers and possibly to more distant middlemen. Eleanor Searle suggests that the production of ready-to-wear leather clothing – the heavy inelegant waterproofs, shoe soles, leggings and heavy gloves – may have been demanded by the armies that poured through south-eastern England for France in the 14th century.[33]

28   L.A. Clarkson, 'The Leather Crafts in Tudor and Stuart England', *Agricultural History Review*, xiv (1966), 26-7.

29   Helen Clarke, *The Archaeology of Medieval England* (1984), 138.

30   For Quarr see S.F. Hockey, *Quarr Abbey and its Lands 1132-1631* (1970), 55, and for Meaux see

B.L., Cotton MS Vitellius C. vi, f. 139.

31   D.H. Williams, *The Welsh Cistercians* (1984), ii, 270.

32   Ibid. 301.

33   E. Searle, *Lordship and Community, Battle Abbey and its Banlieu, 1066-1538* (Toronto, 1974), 299-303.

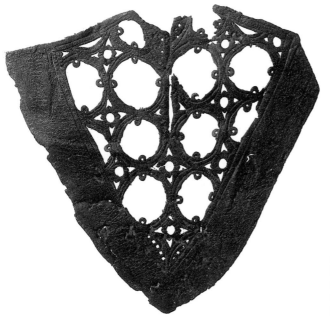

*Fig. 148* Front of leather shoe found in London, showing cut-out patterns. 14th century. Height 17 cms. (*British Museum 56, 7-1, 1708*)

## Techniques of Leather Working

Prepared leather was sold by the currier to the various trades who manufactured the final products. I will consider first the techniques and tools common to the construction and decoration of different objects, and then those objects in relation to the specific trades.

The correct cutting of the skin or hide provided adequately-sized pieces of material of the right thickness without blemish. Several kinds of knives were used for leather cutting, and some of these are indistinguishable from other knives. One of the most distinctive and also the most ancient is the half-moon knife. This must have existed in the Middle Ages, although no convincing example of a complete half-moon shaped knife has been found in medieval excavations. The closest examples are those from Badby (Northants.) and Wallingstones (Hereford and Worcester).[34] A different type of knife was used by the shoemaker to trim leather and cut soles. Cutting in patterns was also used for decorative purposes. In particular, some medieval shoes were elaborately cut to reveal the hose beneath (Fig. 148). Chaucer describes them as 'Paul's window carven on his shoes', presumably referring to the east window of St. Paul's Cathedral, London (*Canterbury Tales*, line 3318).[35]

Leather objects could be assembled by a number of techniques. Stitching is the

34  I.H. Goodall, 'The Medieval Blacksmith and his Products', in D.W. Crossley (ed.), *Medieval Industry* (C.B.A. Research Rep. xl, 1981), 54

and Fig. 53.

35  J.M. Swann, 'Shoe Fashions to 1600', *Trans. of the Museum Assistants Group*, xii (1973), 21.

most common, with holes made in leather by awls. Thread was made from flax or hemp yarn rolled with beeswax. The other principal assembly technique is sticking, which is particularly used for the attachment of leather to a wooden structure (see Fig. 149). The traditional adhesive for box covering is hot animal glue, which was often created as a by-product of the fleshings taken by the tanner from the skins or hides.

Leather objects can also be created by moulding, particularly such objects as armour, great tankards and drinking vessels, bottles and buckets. The traditional medieval term was *cuir bouilli*. The technique is quite simple, and consists of soaking the leather in cold water until thoroughly saturated. The leather is then very plastic and can be modelled over formers in moulds of plaster, wood or metal. If the surface is to be ornamented by tooling, stamping or punching, this must be done while the leather is damp. The leather is then dried gradually, supported by its mould or filling which can be removed later.

Ornamentation played a considerable part in medieval leatherwork. The most common processes of decorating smooth-surfaced leather were:

1. Incising with blunt or sharp tools (Fig. 150).
2. Punching, which was often used to give a texture to the background of incised designs and for which a variety of small iron or bronze punches were used. An example is the punch from Bury St. Edmunds in the form of a fleur-de-lis (see Figs. 151 and 152). Stamps were used widely in book-binding in the Middle Ages, Ages, and examples range from those with David playing the harp, or a griffin, in the 12th century, to stamps engraved with foliage or inscriptions dating from the 14th and 15th centuries (Figs. 153 and 154).[36]
3. Modelling, to leave the important features in low relief.
4. Embossing, which is performed with a ball tool from the flesh side of leather which has previously been dampened.

Finally, the object is decorated with coloured dyes, usually with some paint (tempera). Little work has been carried out on the analysis of medieval dyes on leather, but red is a common colour. Some leather was gilded using glaire (white of an egg) or gold size in order to attach the gold leaf, which adhered to the prepared surface under the heat and pressure of the book-binding tools.

*Nomenclature*

The names of the trades producing particular goods will be discussed as we consider the products. The names tanner and tawyer represent distinct trades based on

36  G.D. Hobson, *English Book Binding before 1500* (1929). For Romanesque bookbindings and stamps see G. Zarnecki (ed.), *English Roman-* *esque Art, 1066-1200* (Exhibition catalogue, British Museum, 1984), 342-9.

Fig. 149 Leather casket mounted on wooden structure. 14th century. Width 21 cms. (*British Museum 56, 7-1, 1664A*)

Fig. 150 Leather scabbard from the Blackfriars, Hull, showing incised decoration. 14th century. (*Hull Museum*)

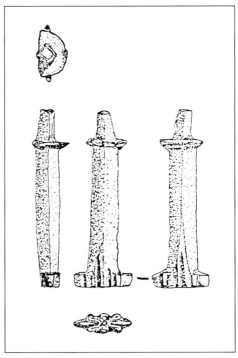

Fig. 151 Copper-alloy fleur-de-lis stamp from Bury St. Edmunds. Scale 1:1. (*Moyse's Hall Museum, Bury St. Edmunds*)

*Fig. 152* Detail of leather sheath showing fleur-de-lis stamps. (*British Museum 56, 7-1, 1945*)

*Fig. 153* Book-binding stamp and impression with griffin. Width 28 mm.
(*British Museum 72, 5-20, 28*)

*Fig. 154* Book-binding stamp and impression showing a knight fighting a lion. Height 24 mm.
(*British Museum, OA 7414*)

different methods of treating the leather, as seen above. Tanner was a common name in the later Middle Ages, and care must be taken in assuming a widespread distribution of tanning based on a wide distribution of tanner names in the 13th and 14th centuries. The presence of the surname Tanner in forests does not necessarily imply that tanning took place there.[37]

A curiosity of the naming of tanners was pointed out by Paul Dare in his study of Leicester shoemakers and tanners. Between 1335 and 1342 in the Leicester tallage rolls 16 tanners are mentioned and 14 men who are styled 'barkers'. In the rolls after 1348 and 1400 no-one styled tanner is mentioned, yet there are gild entry records of 12 barkers and mention of five or six others. It seems as if all the tanners were called barkers in the later 14th century.[38] The role of the barker needs further work. One would expect that there would be a similar number of curriers as tanners, but Dare notes that only one currier is mentioned in Leicester from 1200 and 1318, and in Oxford in 1381 there were 12 tanners employing 11 servants but only two curriers employing two servants.[39] It may be that some currying was carried out by the manufacturing trades. Tawyers tawed leather with alum, often producing a leather with a white colour; hence they are sometimes called whit-tawyers. The Latin word *alutarii* could include both tawyers and regular tanners. The distinction between tawyer and whit-tawyer is complex. Sometimes whit-tawyer meant nothing more than tawyer, sometimes it referred solely to those who made white or alum-dressed leather only, and there was a specialised regional use of the term in the North Midlands where it meant a saddler or mender of harness.[40]

In London there were separate ordinances for whit-tawyers (1346) and tawyers (1365), though the ordinances of the latter are basically concerned with fur rather than leather.[41]

## Organisation

We have seen that the location of tanning was determined by hide, water and bark supplies, but in contrast the location of a leather craft such as shoemaking was related to the distribution of population. This has been well brought out by a study of the location of industry in Worcestershire in the 17th century.[42]

The importance and the widespread nature of the leather crafts in Tudor and Stuart England has been analysed by L.A. Clarkson.[43] There has been no comparable survey of the whole of medieval England, but it is likely that a similar

37  J. Birrell, 'Peasant Craftsmen in the Medieval Forest', *Agricultural History Review*, xvi-xvii (1968-9), 103-4.

38  Dare, op. cit. note 8, 146.

39  *V.C.H.*, *Oxon.* iv, 45. The 1380-1 poll tax is printed in *Oxford City Documents, 1268-1665*, ed. J.E. Thorold Rogers (Oxford Historical Society, xviii, 1891), 1-75.

40  A. Betts, 'White Tawyers', *Arch. Journ.* lxviii

(1911), 149-56.

41  For the whit-tawyers see Riley, *Memorials*, 232-4, and for the tawyers see Ibid. 330-1.

42  K. Mc P. Buchanan, 'Studies in the Localisation of 17th-century Worcestershire Industries, 1600-1650', *Trans. Worcs. Arch. Soc.*, xvii (1940), 44-8.

43  Clarkson, op. cit. note 28, 25-46.

picture of widespread activity could be drawn for the medieval period.

The leather trades were clearly prominent in the Middle Ages. They were the most important trades in York in the late 13th century. The admissions to the freedom of the city in the reign of Edward I indicate that the leather trades were numerically the most important group in the city, representing 30 per cent of the freemen.[44] However, in York this proportion steadily declines until only 13 per cent were employed in the second half of the 15th century. This contrasts with the picture presented by the figures from Oxford, where in 1381, 99 householders and 45 servants were employed in the leather trade, and there was a rise in the status of leather workers in the 15th century chiefly associated with the growth of gloving, so that by the early 16th century leatherworking was, with tailoring and building, one of the chief trades of Oxford.[45] It may well be that a detailed analysis might show variations in the employment and relative strengths of the different leather trades in different parts of the country in the Middle Ages.

The division between the preparatory trades of the tanner and tawyer and the manufacturing trades of shoemakers, glovers or saddlers seems to have worked well, especially for the larger towns. The main difficulty seems to have occurred with smaller concerns and in tawing and fellmongering. There were occasional attempts to reverse the separation. At Chester in 1362 the tanners obtained a charter forbidding the cordwainers to meddle with their trade, but this was reversed in 1370 as contrary to the interests of the city, and a joint charter was granted to the skinners, shoemakers and tanners; nonetheless, the three crafts eventually separated.[46] It may be that in village tanneries there was little division between the tanners and leatherworkers.

The leatherworking trades may be divided into the heavy and light. The heavy trades consist of the manufacture from cattle-hide of footwear, saddles, harness, costrels, sheaths, belts or leather-covered coffers. The light trades manufactured gloves, purses and bags from sheep- and goat-skins.

### Shoes

In the 12th century there were three terms used for the makers of medieval shoes: cordwainers (*cordwanarii*), corvesers (*corvesarii*) and cobblers (*sutores*). Both the cordwainer and the corveser made new shoes, while the cobbler either repaired old shoes or remade old shoes for sale. In London and Leicester the cordwainers were divided into two: the *alutarii* and the *basanarii* (the latter using *bazen* or inferior leather made from sheepskin). The term cordwainer comes from the use of leather brought from Cordova in Spain. In London in the late 13th century cordwainers joined together to buy leather from Spanish merchants, but the term was clearly applied, possibly at

---

44   *V.C.H. City of York*, 86.                    46   Salzman, *Industries*, 246-7.
45   *V.C.H. Oxon.* iv, 35-45.

that time and certainly later, to makers of better shoes regardless of the source of the leather.[47] Although the three principal terms were used until the end of the Middle Ages, Derek Keene suggests that by the later 14th century the terms were synonymous, and by the early 15th century interchangeable.[48]

The vernacular term 'shoemaker' first appears in the Winchester records in the 15th century and becomes progressively more frequent. Figures from the 1381 poll tax in Oxford suggest that there was more profit in tanning than in shoemaking. Those who paid most tax tend to be the skinners or tanners, the cordwainers and cobblers paying smaller sums. Although cobblers were more frequent than cordwainers in Oxford (24 to 12) they only possessed one servant among them while the cordwainers had 11.[49]

A vivid impression of the belongings of a shoemaker in Winchester is recorded in 1408-9 when his goods were seized on account of debt. They included three pairs of boots and three pairs of boteaux worth 6*s*.; 25 pairs of shoes and 14 and a half dozen (presumably single) shoes, eight pairs of new galoches worth 8s, pieces of sole leather, leather for uppers, white sheepskins, carving knives, draw-knives, a paring knife, a shaver, chisel, a piece of lead, a *turnyngstaf*, stools, benches, tables, a chest, beef and bacon.[50]

The correlation of terms used in the Middle Ages for footwear, such as the boteaux, shoes, and galoches referred to above, with the examples of footwear found on excavations requires further work. Among studies of medieval shoes from excavations and in museum collections, one of the most thorough is the survey of medieval footwear from Coventry[51] (Fig. 155).

Medieval shoes were made by the turnshoe method of construction. In this method, the upper, which had been turned flesh side out, was lasted onto the sole and joined to the edge by an edge/flesh seam. The shoe was then turned inside out so that the grain side was outside (see Fig. 156). A rand was sometimes introduced to produce a stronger, more waterproof join. The turnshoe was replaced by the welted method of construction introduced about 1500. Flax was often used to stitch the parts together.

It is not possible to relate particular shoes to cordwainers as opposed to cobblers, though the incidence of repairs in some collections is high. Although Cordovan leather was known by 1100, it is not possible to point to any medieval shoe made of it. Methods of fastening boots and shoes varied. The instep strap fastening with a buckle first appears on the late 12th-century tombs of Henry II and Richard I at Fontevrault.[52] Shoes laced at the side and front and button-fastened were known by the early 14th century.

One of the most interesting developments in medieval footwear was the wooden patten. It first appears in the Luttrell Psalter (*c.* 1340) worn by a peasant. It is not

47 G. Unwin, *Gilds and Companies of London*, 4th edn. (London, 1963), 83.
48 Keene, op. cit. note 1, 289.
49 *V.C.H., Oxon.* iv, 45.

50 Keene, op. cit. note 1, 290.
51 S. Thomas, *Medieval Footwear from Coventry* (1980).
52 Swann, op. cit. note 35, 20.

*Fig. 155* Leather shoe from London. 14th century. Length 29 cms. (*British Museum 56, 7-1, 1726*)

possible to distinguish between the galoche and patten, though it may be that the patten always had an iron ring fitted under the wooden sole whereas the galoche did not. The wooden sole was common to both. Galoches are first mentioned in 1306 when John le Galocher and Christina his wife challenge a will. They were kept on by a leather band or, more commonly in the 15th century, with leather straps fastening with a buckle. It the was leather parts of the pattens that led to the association of the pattenmakers with the pouchmakers in 1379.[53]

### Saddles

Saddlers were widespread in English towns by the 14th century, reflecting the importance of the horse for carriage and transport. For instance, Oxford had seven saddlers each with one servant in 1381.[54] A saddle is primarily a wooden structure designed to take the weight off the horse's spine. While in the modern saddle the leather conceals the tree (the wooden structure of the saddle), this structure was more obvious in the medieval saddle. This lies behind the difficulties that occurred between the saddlers and the joiners, as revealed in the ordinances of the London Saddlers' Company in 1309. Complaints about collapsing saddles were blamed by the saddlers on the joiners. The joiners in turn blamed apprentices, who ran away and secretly patched up saddle bows of unseasoned wood which was often only glued together. These were sold to dishonest saddlers and painters who, after covering them with leather, velvet or cloth, would offer them for sale with the consequent collapse of saddle and rider.[55]

53   C. Fitch, *History of the Patten Makers Company*
     (1926). For a recent survey of shoes and pat-
     terns see F. Grew and M. de Neergard, *Shoes
     and Patterns* (Museum of London, 1988).

54   *V.C.H.,* *Oxon.* iv, 45.
55   J.W. Sherwell, *History of the Guild of Saddlers*
     (1937), 10.

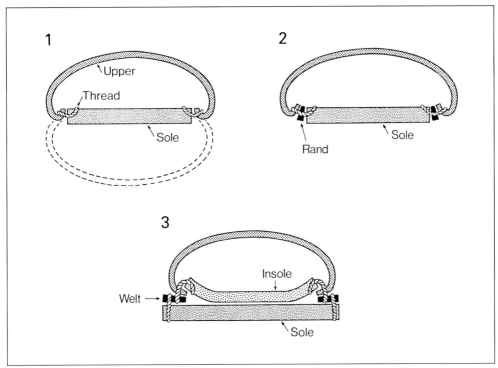

*Fig. 156* Method of producing a medieval turn-shoe.

Another area of dispute was between the saddlers and the lorimers, the makers of bits and other metalwork for horses. The saddlers clearly saw this as an infringement of their own rights, since they wished to control the sale of everything connected with horse trappings. Eventually the hostility between the trades led to bloody conflicts in Cheapside and Cripplegate in 1327 between the saddlers on one side and the lorimers, joiners and painters on the other.[56]

The only published history of the saddle gives a very short space to the medieval saddle.[57] Some leather fragments which are likely to have been part of a saddle were found at Trig Lane in London in 1974.[58] The only complete surviving saddle is that of Henry V, carried in his funeral procession in 1422 and still preserved at Westminster Abbey. It consists of two oblong side panels some 24 by 4 inches which rested on either side of the horse's spine, and has an upright pommel and rounded castle of wood. It was covered with purple velvet powdered with gilt fleurs-de-lis. Leather was not particularly important in this saddle.[59] However, a king's funeral

56    Ibid., 11 and 12.
57    John W. Waterer, *A Short History of Saddles in Europe* (Museum of Leathercraft, Northampton, *c.* 1960).
58    Unpublished. Trig Lane, Context 368.
59    Sir W.H.St.J. Hope, 'The Funeral, Monument, and Chantry Chapel of King Henry V', *Archaeologia*, lxv (1914), 129-86.

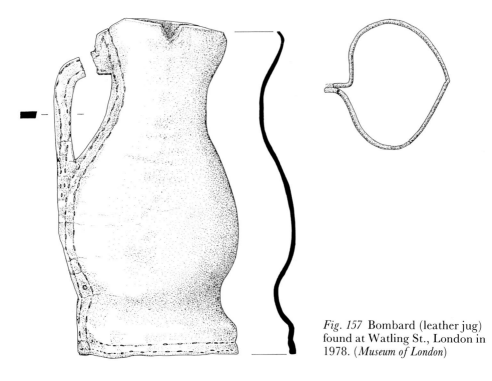

*Fig. 157* Bombard (leather jug) found at Watling St., London in 1978. (*Museum of London*)

saddle is not necessarily typical, and one can only wish that more were known of the simple types of saddles used in the medieval period.

### Leather Bottles

Costrels, leather vessels for carrying liquid, are known from the late Anglo-Saxon period, and much of our evidence for their forms at this period is due to ceramic skeuomorphs of the leather forms such as the Winchester-ware costrel.[60] Costrels were of two forms, either pear-shaped or barrel-shaped. An insight into the small size of the organisation of those who made leather bottles in London is given by a lawsuit in which the powerful Sir William Windsor, husband of Alice Perrers, was involved. He had lost 180 gallons of wine that he had taken with him to France owing to defective bottles. In the course of the case it appears that there were only eight botellers, including the culprit who was not a freeman.[61] The great leather jugs sometimes known as black jacks or bombards are first recorded in the 14th century (Fig. 157). They were frequently purchased for monastic houses, colleges, or great households. At New College in 1414 four leather jacks, two of a gallon size and two

60    M. Biddle and K. Barclay, 'Winchester Ware', in *Medieval Pottery from Excavations*, ed. V.I. Evison, H. Hodges and J.G. Hurst (1974), 146.
61    E.M. Veale, 'Craftsmen and the Economy of London in the Fourteenth Century', in A.E.J. Hollander and W. Kellaway (eds.), *Studies in London History* (1969), 142.

*Fig. 158* Lid of Talbot casket. Flemish, late 14th century. Width 26 cms. (*British Museum, 1977, 5-2, 1*)

*Fig. 159* Top of leather box, 14th century. (*Yorkshire Museum*)

half-gallon, were bought for a total of 4s. 8d.[62] The long-lasting quality of leather pots as opposed to pottery vessels is revealed by the decision in 1512 to replace earthen pots with leather vessels in the earl of Northumberland's castles of Wressle and Leconfield (Yorks.).[63]

### Chests, Coffers and Containers

The chest made of wood was used to keep clothes, linen or plates or other domestic gear, while the coffer was a travelling trunk covered with leather in order to transport these articles.[64] The chest was made by the carpenter or joiner whereas the coffer was made by a leatherworker – the cofferer. Large coffers were known as standards. Smaller coffers were used for the carriage of clothes. Trussing coffers were carried as pairs on sumpter horses. A small coffer for jewels or other valuables was known as a coffret, or casket. Such small boxes made of wood covered with leather were often decorated with elaborate decorated and embossed scenes. A notable example of this is the 'Talbot' casket in the British Museum (1977,5-2,1)[65] (Fig. 158). Although this was probably made in northern France or Flanders, at least twelve leather-covered boxes are known from England. The cylindrical box or chalice-case belonging to Cawston church (Norfolk) has a series of shields engraved around the sides which have been identified as English arms of the mid 14th century, suggesting an English origin. One of these is the shield of the family of Ufford, the family who held the principal manor in Cawston from 1330 to 1382.[66] A rectangular 14th-century box from a London collection (B.M. 56, 7-1 1664a) (Fig.149) is also likely to be of English origin, as is the circular box from York, the top of which is decorated with animals against a punched background (Fig.159).[67]

### Sheaths and Belts

It is surprising that there was a separate trade of sheathmaking, which owed much to the popularity of knives, daggers and swords in the medieval period. Sheathmakers are referred to at both York and Leicester, so they were not purely London-based. In 1381 there were three in Oxford, but they employed no servants.[68] Knives and scabbards from London have recently been surveyed by J. Cowgill, M.de Neergaard and N. Griffiths.[69] Sheaths were often decorated with shields, animals or foliate patterns. The use of heraldry to decorate scabbards is discussed by T. Wilmott in the

62  J.E. Thorold Rogers, *History of Prices* (7 vols, 1866-1902), iv, 612.
63  O. Baker, *Black Jacks and Leather Bottells* (c. 1920), 90.
64  R.W. Symonds, 'The Chest and the Coffer', *Connoisseur*, cvii (1941), 15-21.
65  J. Cherry, 'The Talbot Casket and Related Late Medieval Leather Caskets', *Archaeologia*, cvii (1982), 131-40.

66  A.W. Franks, 'Note on some Ornamental Cases of Leather', *Proc., Soc. Antiqs.* 2nd ser. xiv (1891-3), 246-54.
67  *Handbook to the Antiquities of the York Museum* (1891), 236.
68  *V.C.H., Oxon.* iv, 35.
69  J. Cowgill, M. de Neergaard, and N. Griffiths, *Medieval Finds from Excavations in London: Knives and Scabbards* (1987).

*Fig. 160* Fragment of leather armour for the right upper arm. 14th century. Height 28.5 cms. (*British Museum 56, 7-1, 1665*)

survey of London scabbards. London scabbards were usually made from calf since in 1350 the Gild of Furbishers forbade the use of any other for scabbards.[70] Sheath-makers may have been responsible for the manufacture of leather armour used for both men and horses. Such armour is known both from documents, such as the inventory of Sir Simon Burley (executed in 1388) where a helmet of *quier boyllé* is mentioned, or from actual examples such as the shoulderpiece of leather with embossed designs of birds in foliage from London.[71] (Fig. 160).

The girdlers of London obtained a charter in 1327 and their articles were established in 1344. It is noticeable that these were mostly concerned less with the quality of leather than with the nature and quantity of the metal fittings attached to the belts.[72]

## Gloves

Gloves were worn widely in the medieval period by all sections of society. They were made from the lighter alum-tawed leathers of sheepskin, goatskin, deerskin or horse.

70   Riley, *Memorials*, 259.
71   A.V.B. Norman, 'Notes on a Newly Discovered Piece of 14th-Century Armour', *Journal of the Arms and Armour Society*, viii.3 (June, 1975),

229-33.
72   W. Dumville Smythe, *Historical Accounts of the Worshipful Company of Girdlers* (1905), 61-4.

The giving of gloves was a general custom in medieval England. In Tudor England, gloving and leather-dressing tended to be concentrated in the west of England, possibly because this area had a plentiful supply of calfskin and sheepskin and possibly because in places there was a good quality water supply. In the Oxford area, for instance, the water was such that 'all skins of a more delicate kind . . . are so well seasoned with it for making of white leather that more whiter, softer or better is hardly found'.[73] It was certainly practised as a cottage craft in medieval England. The skin was alum tawed, worn grainside inwards and the outerside buffed and stained. The making of gloves requires a high degree of skill in cutting, so that the gloves can give with the movement of the hand yet continue to fit well. There was a London gild of glovers whose ordinances were proclaimed in 1349.[74] In Oxford in 1381 there were eight glovers with three servants, but the nature of the medieval craft may be more clearly perceived when the burgesses of Malmesbury (Wilts.) forbade non-resident makers of horseskin gloves to sell their wares within the town. The mention in the same document of Alice le Glovaire and Agnes le Glovaire indicates the role that women may have played in the manufacture of such gloves.[75] So far no certain glove fragments appear to have been found in archaeological contexts.

## Purses

Purses and pouches were both made from tawed and chamosed leather. In London there were different gilds of pouch-makers and pursers, both of whom merged with the leather sellers in the early 16th century. Both derived their leathers from the whit-tawyers, the suppliers of tawed and chamosed leather who merged with the leather sellers in 1479. When the glovers merged with them in 1502 the leather sellers continued the production and sale of a wide variety of small leather goods. Leicester and Oxford did not have pursers or pouch-makers although York did. An illustration of the connection of the selling of gloves and purses is provided by John le Stainton in London in 1396 who had 134 pairs of gloves and 118 purses of different types for sale, and, as well as leather laces, possessed 23 patterns for purses (Figs. 161 and 162).[76]

73    A. Wood, *Survey of the Antiquities of the City of Oxford 1661-6*, ed. A. Clark, i (Oxford Historical Society, xv, 1889), 395.
74    Riley, *Memorials*, 245.
75    *V.C.H. Wilts.* iv, 236.
76    P.R.O., Chancery Extents on Debts, 46/17, quoted by Veale, op. cit. note 61, 145.

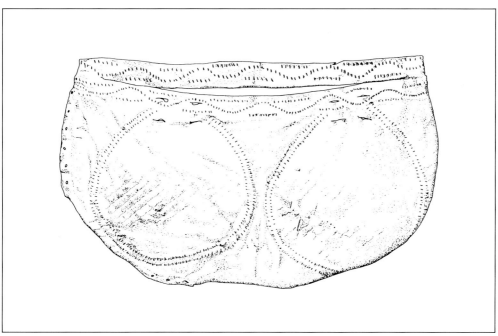

*Fig. 161* Drawing of bag from Trig Lane, London. (*Museum of London*)

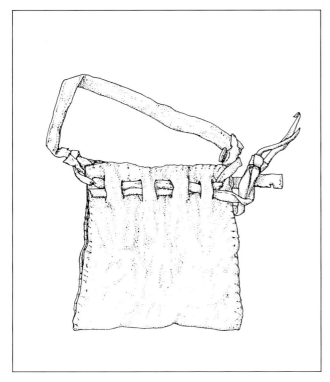

*Fig. 162* Drawing of purse from Baynards Castle. (*Museum of London*)

## Further Reading

The most comprehensive bibliography of works on leather is the *Shoe and Leather Bibliography* issued by Northampton Museum. The basic general work on the craftsmanship involved in leather from prehistoric times to the present day is J.W. Waterer, *Leather Craftsmanship* (New York, 1968). For tanning the most recent account of the technology and historical development of the process is R.S. Thomson, 'Tanning, Man's First Manufacturing Process?', *Trans. Newcomen Society*, lii-liii (1980-2), 139-56. A good account of the tanning and leather crafts with illustrations of tools is given by J.G. Jenkins, *Traditional Country Craftsmen* (1965), 189-220; he has also published a booklet on the *Rhaedr Tannery* (1973). Two general surveys which are of considerable use are John W. Waterer, 'Leather', in Singer and Holmyard, *History of Technology*, ii, 147-90, and John W. Waterer, 'Leathercraft', in the *Oxford Companion to Art*, ed. H. Osborne (1970). See also R.A. Salaman, *Dictionary of Leather – Working Tools, c. 700-1950* (1986).

The historical sources for tanning and leather working are best approached through L.A. Clarkson, 'The Leather Crafts in Tudor and Stuart England', *Agricultural History Review*, xiv (1966), 25-46. This has a good regional survey. The organisation of the leather industry is discussed by the same author in *Economic History Review*, 2nd ser. xiii (1960-61), 245-56.

Detailed studies of particular areas have concentrated on the Midlands, perhaps because of Northampton's considerable importance to the boot and shoe trade in the post-medieval period. For these areas see M.P. Dare, 'Medieval Shoemakers and Tanners in Leicester, Northampton and Nottingham', *Associated Architectural Societies' Reports*, xxxix (1928-9), 141-77; P.R. Mountfield, 'The Footwear Industry of the East Midlands', *East Midland Geographer*, xxiii (1965), 394-413; R. Thomson, 'Leather Manufacture in the Post-Medieval Period with Special Reference to Northamptonshire', *Post-Med. Archaeology*, xv (1981), 161-77; and Clare E. Allin, 'The Medieval Leather Industry in Leicester', *Leicester Museum Arch. Report No. 3* (1981). A good survey of medieval and post-medieval leather is contained in S. Thomas, L.A. Clarkson, and R. Thomson, *Leather Manufacture through the Ages* (East Midlands Industrial Archaeology Conference, 27) (1983). For shoes and pattens see F. Grew and M. de Neergard, *Shoes and Pattens* (1988).

Different types of object are referred to in Waterer's *Leather Craftsmanship*, but there are some particular studies of objects that may be recommended. For shoes, the *Transactions of the Museum Assistants Group*, xii (1973), and S. Thomas, *Medieval Footwear from Coventry* (1980). For saddles see John Waterer, *A Short History of Saddles in Europe* (Northampton Museum of Leathercraft, c. 1960). The Museum of Leathercraft, Northampton, is particularly worth visiting to see the uses to which leather has been put.

# 13

## Textiles

### PENELOPE WALTON

The story of medieval English clothmaking is a complex one. It begins in the 11th and 12th centuries with a women's domestic craft being taken up by professional male artisans. At this stage the volume of production was comparatively small and focussed in urban centres. Then followed a period of crisis in the late 13th and 14th centuries, during which rural weavers started to play a more important role. From this point production began to increase and exports to rise, so that by the mid 16th century England was a major European supplier of wool cloth.

There were many factors which effected these changes: social, economic and political pressures all played a part, as did advances in technology. However, one of England's major advantages over her competitors was a ready supply of a variety of raw materials.

### Wool

By the close of the Anglo-Saxon period, sheep were to be found in most parts of the country[1] and flocks of considerable size were recorded in Domesday Book and other inquisitions.[2] At first the value of the fleece was considered second in importance to the sheep's milk-yield,[3] but by the late 12th century the quality of wool was beginning to merit interest. In 1194 we find that 'the price . . . of a curly-fleeced sheep shall be 10d.; and of a sheep with coarser wool 6d.'.[4] In the same year the manor at Sulby (Northants.) was re-stocked with fine-woolled animals;[5] and by the early 13th century the Hungerford family in Wiltshire was importing rams from Lindsey (Lincs.),[6] an area soon to be famous for its fine wools.

The medieval sheep was a small animal[7] with a relatively short fleece: examples of

---

1  R. Trow-Smith, *British Livestock* (1957), 59.
2  Ibid. 61, 65-6.
3  Ibid. 74: P.H. Sawyer, 'The Wealth of England in the 11th Century', *T.R.H.S.* 5th ser. xv (1965) has suggested a more prominent role for England's wool in the late Anglo-Saxon period, but there is as yet no firm evidence for this –

see T.H. Lloyd, *The English Wool Trade* (1977), 2-4.
4  *Eng. Hist. Docs. (1189-1327)*, 305.
5  Trow-Smith, op. cit. note 1, 96, 110-11.
6  Ibid. 111, 161-2.
7  M.L. Ryder, *Sheep and Man* (1983), 465-7.

raw wool from archaeological sites have staple lengths ranging from 40mm. to 90mm.[8] Consequently the fleece weight was comparatively light, calculated from the records of 13th- to 14th-century flocks as 1 lb. to 2½ lbs. (less for a lamb or after murrain).[9] Most wool was white, but naturally coloured fleeces, *nigra* and *grisia*, were still included in the clip at Fountains Abbey in the mid 15th century.[10]

England was particularly fortunate in having a range of different wools on which to draw. Studies of excavated specimens of wool textiles[11] have shown that one particularly common type has a few coarse fibres combined with a soft crimpy underwool much like a Shetland fleece. Another type is not quite as fine as the modern Merino, but fine enough, both to the touch and to the naked eye: the best of this group may well be the famous 'Lemster ore', wool from the Leominster district of the Welsh marches.[12] Goat hair and hairy carpet wools are also to be found, particularly in textiles from northern sites.[13] Less frequently there is a long-stapled, smooth-fibred type resembling a primitive longwool and another crimpier type comparable with the modern shortwool.[14]

It is impossible to say in which locality the wools in these textiles originated, since most finds come from urban market centres. However, schedules of the 13th, 14th and 15th centuries[15] all show a similar geographical distribution of wool prices (Fig. 163). These can be correlated with the regional types of sheep which emerge in later history.[16] We can therefore assume that in outline there were coarse-woolled animals, ancestors of the modern mountain and hill breeds, in the uplands of northern England, Scotland, Wales and the South-West peninsula; sheep with shorter, crimpier fleeces in much of the rest of the country, the finest-woolled and most expensive being in the Welsh borders and Lincolnshire; and probably also primitive longwools in the salt marshes of East Anglia and Kent.[17] In tracing the sources of supply for the textile industry, it is also important to remember the fine Spanish wool imported at least as early as the 12th century[18] and the hairy fleeces of goats which were herded in open woodland.[19]

8  Ibid. 474; Ryder in P. Walton, 'Textiles, Cordage and Raw Fibre from 16-22 Coppergate', *Archaeology of York* 17.5 (1989).

9  D. Postles, 'Fleece Weights and the Wool Supply *c.* 1250-*c.* 1350', *Textile History*, xii (1981), 93-103.

10  *Memorials of Fountains Abbey*, ed. J.T. Fowler (Surtees Soc. cxxx, 1918), 39.

11  Ryder, op. cit. note 7, 472-7.

12  *V.C.H. Herefs.* i, 409.

13  H. Bennett, *Perth High Street* (forthcoming); Ryder, op. cit. note 7, 475-6.

14  This true shortwool becomes more common towards the 16th century: P. Walton, 'Textiles from Castle Ditch, Newcastle upon Tyne', *Archaeologia Aeliana*, 5th ser. ix (1981), 190-1.

15  J.H. Munro, 'Wool Price Schedules', *Textile History*, ix (1978), passim; J.H. Munro, 'The 1357 Wool-Price Schedule and the Decline of Yorkshire Wool Values', *Textile History*, x (1979), 211-19. Only the 1343 Parliamentary Ordinance shows inconsistencies. It is unfortunate that this is the list used by R.A. Pelham for his much-quoted map 'Wool Prices in England' in *An Historical Geography of England before 1800*, ed. H.C. Darby (1948).

16  M.L. Ryder, 'History of Sheep Breeds in Britain', *Agric. Hist. Rev.* xii (1964), 70-82.

17  Ibid.; P.J. Bowden, *The Wool Trade in Stuart England* (1962), 25-37.

18  Bowden, op. cit. note 17, 47; *Liber Custumarum*, ed. F.B. Bickley (2 vols., Bristol and London, 1900), ii, 125.

19  Trow-Smith, op. cit. note 1, 75.

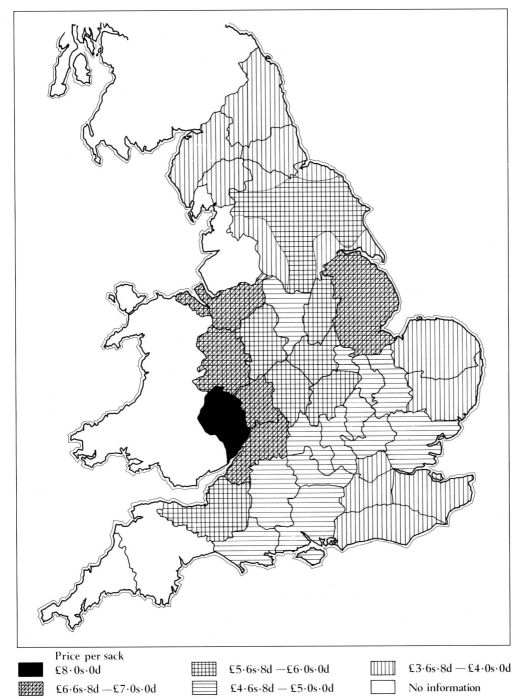

Price per sack

■ £8·0s·0d

▦ £6·6s·8d —£7·0s·0d

▦ £5·6s·8d —£6·0s·0d

▤ £4·6s·8d — £5·0s·0d

▥ £3·6s·8d — £4·0s·0d

☐ No information

*Fig. 163* Relative values of wools in 1336-7. This map is based on the parliamentary schedule known as the 'Nottingham Prices', which set a fixed price on the *best* wool of each district (see J.H. Munro in *Textile History*, ix (1978)).

## Flax and Hemp

Fibres from the stems of plants such as flax (*Linum usitatissimum* L.) and hemp (*Cannabis sativa* L.) were also used for making cloth. One of the duties of the Anglo-Saxon reeve was to cultivate flax for the weaving workshops[20] and a tithe was set on both crops in 1175.[21] Native supplies were evidently not enough, as flax from Hamburg was imported into Newcastle in 1390,[22] while Wilton was bringing in supplies via Southampton in the 15th century.[23] In the 16th century the Tudor countrywoman was advised to sow flax and hemp in March for pulling later in the year[24] and in 1532-3 Henry VIII ordered that for every 60 acres of land fit for tillage, one rood should be sown with hemp or flax seed.[25] Yet imports continued to come in from the Baltic and Russia.[26] The London Customs in 1550 rated 100 lbs. flax 'wrought' at 10s. and 'unwrought' at 6s. 8d.[27]

## Silk

Since England's climate is unsuitable for the cultivation of silk, full-size silk fabrics were imported at considerable expense. Some raw fibre was also brought in from the Mediterranean, especially Italy, to supply the silk braid-makers and embroiderers. The London silkwomen had transactions with merchants of Lombardy, Genoa and Venice[28] and in 1469, for example, one Alexandro Spynel, alien, landed a cargo at Southampton which included 220 lbs. of raw silk valued at £110.[29] There appear to have been different grades of fibre, as the London Customs charged separately for 'long silk' at 6s. 8d. per lb., 'short silk' at 4s. per lb., 'raw and dyed' at 8s., and 'thrown' (i.e. made into yarn) at 13s. 4d.[30]

## Cotton

The seed fibre of *Gossypium* spp. was imported in the 13th and 14th centuries for use in candle-wicks and as a padding for garments.[31] There is, however, no evidence for its use in English textiles before the late 16th century, although some cotton stuffs were probably being imported from Italy.[32] Confusingly, 'cottons' is a term commonly used in the later medieval period for certain coarse woollen cloths.[33]

---

20  *Gerefa*, translated in M. Swanton (ed.), *Anglo-Saxon Prose* (1975), 26.
21  J. Horner, *The Linen Trade of Europe during the Spinning Wheel Period* (1920), 216.
22  Salzman, *English Trade*, 363.
23  C. Platt, *The English Medieval Town* (1976), 78.
24  A. Fitzherbert, 'Boke of Husbandry' (1523): *Eng. Hist. Docs. (1485-1558)*, 922-4.
25  *Statutes of the Realm*, iii, 421-2: 24 Hen. VIII c.4.
26  Salzman, *English Trade*, 364.
27  Rate Book of 1550 in the London Custom House. Extracts published in T.F. Willan (ed.), *A Tudor Book of Rates* [*The Rates of the Custome House 1562*] (Manchester, 1962), 6-7.
28  *Cal. Plea & Mem. R., 1364-81*, 99-106.
29  'Port Book of Southampton, 1469', *Eng. Hist. Docs. (1327-1485)*, 1043-4.
30  Willan op. cit. note 27, 9.
31  Beck, *Draper's Dictionary*, 81.
32  Ibid. 82.
33  Ibid. 85-8.

*Fig. 164 above:* Carding wool and spinning with the spindle wheel (Luttrell Psalter, B.L., MS Add. 42130, f. 193).

*Fig. 165 left:* Wool-combing (Decretals of Gregory IX, B.L., MS Royal 10.E.iv).

### Fibre Preparation

Silk would have arrived partly prepared, and the long filaments would require little more than twisting together for a yarn.[34] However, wool, flax and hemp require more preparation. Sheep were washed and sheared in June[35] and the fleeces sorted for quality. At Beaulieu Abbey the clip for the year 1269-70[36] was divided into 'good', 'medium', 'coarse lockets' (loose pieces of wool), 'warpelok' and 'gardus' (wool with impurities in it). Each fleece has finer and coarser parts to it, but it was not until the 16th century, when the requirements of the industry changed, that the careful dividing-up of individual fleeces was practised.[37] There were also many prohibitions on the mixing of different qualities of wool.[38]

After sorting, wool went through a further preparation process. From the 14th century onwards, short-stapled wools were prepared with hand-carders, flat square boards with handles and many small iron teeth, prior to spinning into a soft light yarn. The earliest English illustration of carding, in the Luttrell Psalter, is datable to

34  M. K. Dale, 'London Silkwomen of the Fifteenth Century', *Econ. Hist. Rev.* 1st ser. iv (1932-4), 329-30.
35  Trow-Smith, op. cit. note 1, 245-6.
36  *Account-Book of Beaulieu Abbey*, ed. S.F. Hockey (Camden 4th ser. xvi, 1975), 33, 164.
37  Bowden, op. cit. note 17, 80; *V.C.H. Berks.* i, 389.
38  J. Strutt, *Dress and Habits of the People of England* (2 vols., 1842), ii, 86-7.

about the 1330s, not long after carders first appeared in north-west Europe (Fig. 164). An illustration of similar date in the 'Smithfield' Decretals of Gregory IX (Fig. 165)[39] shows the process used for long-fibred wools: the oiled wool[40] is mounted onto a long-toothed iron comb and then a second comb is drawn down through the first.[41] This makes the fibres lie straight and parallel, ready for a smooth firm yarn.

Before the arrival of hand-carders, only combs were in existence, and it is possible that short-staple wools were simply teased by hand before spinning.[42] However, it may also be that combs were used in a more general way on all fibres. In some northern countries the woolcomb fell out of use once carders arrived, as if one served the same purpose as the other;[43] and in countries where combs did survive, they seem to have become longer-toothed and heavier, suggesting that their role had changed.[44]

Flax and hemp, according to the *Boke of Husbandry*, were 'rippled, watered, washed, dried, beaten, braked, tawed, heckled, spun, wound, wrapped and woven'.[45] Rippling removes the seeds, and watering is the soaking of the stems ('retting') to soften the woody matter surrounding the fibre. When washed and dried the stems were beaten with heavy wooden tools with cylindrical heads[46] and then scraped with scutching knives[47] (wooden blades), used against a vertical board, to remove the outer fibre. The fibres were then drawn through successively finer heckles (sets of teeth mounted vertically in a stand).[48] The tow or 'hurdes' left over from heckling were used in a coarser kind of cloth called harden[49] while the finer fibres went into linen.

## Spinning

Processed flax and the longer-stapled wools were mounted on a distaff or 'rock' for spinning. This long wooden rod could be set in a stand[50] or slotted through the belt so that the spinner was free to move about (Fig. 166). Shorter-stapled wools were simply held in the hand as a roll of prepared fibre. The fibres were then drawn out

39  These Decretals were probably illustrated in England in the 1330s: L.F. Sandler, *Gothic Manuscripts, 1283-1385* (2 vols., 1986), ii, 111-12, No. 101.
40  *Eng. Hist. Docs. (1327-1485)*, 1053-5.
41  One woolcomb has been recovered from 11th century York: s.f. 10786 in P. Walton (ed.) 'Textile Implements from 16-22 Coppergate', *The Archaeology of York* (in preparation).
42  A bow was used to open out the fibres in Flanders (G. de Poerck, *Draperie Médiévale en Flandre et en Artois* (3 vols., Bruges 1951), i 52-5) but there is no evidence for it in England.
43  M. Hoffmann, *The Warp-Weighted Loom* (1964), 286.
44  Ibid. 286, 382; P. Baines, *Spinning Wheels*

(1977), 32-5.
45  See note 24.
46  Examples have been excavated from Perth High Street and several Irish sites: C. Morris, *Woodworking Crafts* (Cambridge PhD., 1984) T1, T9-17, pp. 31-2.
47  Examples from medieval Beverley, Macclesfield and Kings Lynn: ibid. T22, T24-7, p. 32.
48  Baines, op. cit. note 44, 21-4. Iron spikes either from flax heckles or woolcombs are a relatively common find on archaeological sites: P.J. Ottaway, 'Anglo-Scandinavian Ironwork from 16-22 Coppergate', *Archaeology of York*, 17.6 (forthcoming).
49  Beck, *Draper's Dictionary*, 160
50  B.L., MS Stowe 17 f. 34.

*Fig. 166* Distaff and suspended spindle, in a Book of Hours of Maastricht, *c.* 1300 (B.L., MS Stowe 17 f. 190.)

from the distaff, or the roll, and twisted by means of a free-hanging spindle, a short wooden stick[51] weighted at one end by a whorl, which also acted as a fly-wheel.

These whorls, made from stone, pottery, wood, bone etc., are common finds on archaeological sites. They vary considerably in weight, different weights being used for different types of yarn.[52] Medieval textiles were woven with a fine smooth warp (the threads under tension in the loom) and a softer, thicker weft (the yarn woven back and forth across the warp).[53] It is probable that to achieve this effect, the warp was spun with a heavy whorl and the weft with a light one.

The process was speeded up by the arrival of the spinning-wheel, which replaced the suspended spindle for the softer weft yarn. A simple form of spindle-wheel seems to have reached Flanders in the second half of the 13th century[54] although the earliest English illustrations belong to the 14th.[55] When spinning, the spinster would turn the wheel with one hand and draw the yarn off the head of the spindle. She would then reverse the action of the wheel in order to wind the yarn on to the spindle. The attachment called the U-flyer, which allows continuous spinning and wind-on, did not arrive in this country until the late 15th or 16th century,[56] and the treadle was even later.[57]

51 Examples from medieval York, Nantwich, Kings Lynn and London: Morris, op. cit. note 46, 40-2.
52 J. Kamińska and A. Nahlik, 'L'Industrie Textile en Pologne', *Archaeologia Polona*, iii (1960), 100.
53 Weft syn. woof, 'ab'.
54 De Poerck, op. cit. note 42, i, 62.
55 Baines, op. cit. note 44, 54-5.
56 Ibid. 85-91.
57 Ibid. 92.

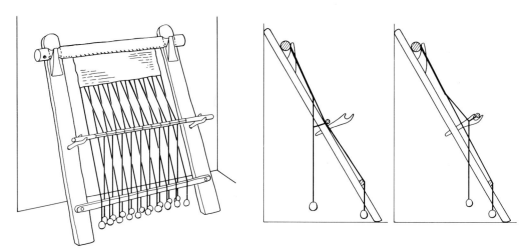

*Fig. 167* The warp-weighted loom.

For several centuries after the arrival of the wheel, spinning with distaff and suspended spindle still continued for flax, for combed wool and for yarn intended for the warp.[58] Included in the *Livre des Mestiers* of Bruges (*c.*1340) is a Picard French rhyme which says '. . . the spinner . . . much values her thread which was spun on the distaff; but the thread which is spun on the wheel has too many lumps and she says that she earns more to spin warp at the distaff than to spin weft with the wheel'.[59] Evidently the same could be said at the Middlesex manor of Laleham, where in 1295 the cost of spinning warp yarn was 2*d.* the lb., while weft was only 1½*d.*[60]

This difference in quality between warp and weft explains the Bristol and London weavers' regulations that the two should not be transposed.[61] Moreover, examination of medieval textiles shows that the fibres of warp and weft often lie in opposite directions, the spindle having been turned clockwise for the warp and anticlockwise for the weft:[62] thus the medieval merchant or weaver could tell at a glance whether yarn was intended for warp or for weft.

After spinning the yarn was wound on to hanks by means of a reel[63] at which stage it might be washed and dyed. The hank was then placed on a revolving swift and transferred on to spools[64] by means of a wheel resembling a spinning-wheel.[65] If the

58  J. de L. Mann, 'A Document Regarding Jersey Spinning in the P.R.O.', *Textile History*, iv (1973), 140-1.
59  Baines, op. cit. note 48, 94.
60  T.H. Lloyd, 'Sale Costs of Cloth Manufacturing', *Textile History*, i (1971), 332-6.
61  *Item quod nulla trama que dicitur ab sit in loco panni ubi stamen quod dicitur warp poni debet: Little Red Book of Bristol. Que stame ne soit en lu de trame: Lib. Cust.*op. cit. note 18, 125.
62  E. Crowfoot, 'Textiles from Durham', *Med. Arch.* xxiii (1979), 38.

63  De Poerck, op. cit. note 42, i, 65-6; remains of a late medieval drum-winder have been found at Blackfriars, Oxford: Morris, op. cit. note 46, T107, p. 46. (However, the excavator interprets this as an hourglass fragment: see G. Lambrick in *Oxoniensia*, l(1985), 167-9.)
64  Wooden spools from 12th-century York, 13th-century Kings Lynn, 14-15th century Hull: Morris, op. cit. note 46, 46-7.
65  The illustration in Salzman, *Industries*, 216, is of a spool-winder, and not a spinning-wheel as the caption suggests.

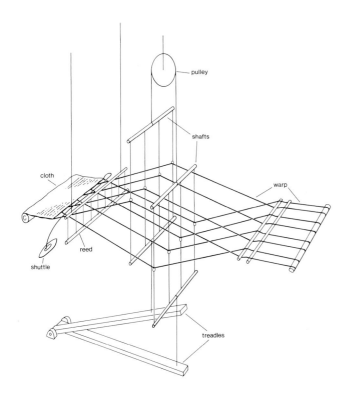

*Fig. 168* The horizontal loom.

cloth was to be woven on a horizontal loom, which has a particularly long web, then the warp threads would be pulled off from a rack of spools, several at a time, and wrapped on to a large wooden warping-frame (Fig. 171).[66] The warp would then be transferred to the loom and the weft spools inserted into shuttles.[67]

## Weaving

Prior to the 11th century, cloth was usually produced on the warp-weighted loom. This consisted of two uprights with an upper cross-beam which could be revolved and a lower, fixed, cross-bar (Fig. 167). The loom was leaned against the wall of the house or set upright in the ground.[68] The warp was suspended from the upper beam and weighted with heavy clay weights. Heddle rods across the front of the warp were attached by twine loops to the warp threads themselves so that when the heddle rods were lifted forward, one at a time, they made space for the passage of the weft. As weaving progressed, the weft was beaten upwards with a long sword-beater.

66 A warping-stick, warping-tree and spool-winder appear in the Nottingham records in the 15th century: *V.C.H. Notts.* ii, 345.

67 Shuttle-makers had a gild in their own right at Reading in the time of Queen Mary: *V.C.H. Berks.* i, 390-1.

68 The angle at which the loom was used is discussed in J.W. Hedges's contribution to A. MacGregor, 'Anglo-Scandinavian finds from Lloyds Bank, Pavement, and other sites', *Archaeology of York*, xvii, 3.

Some time around the year 1000 a new type of loom arrived in north-west Europe. In this, the forerunner of the modern handloom, the warp was stretched between two beams in the horizontal plane (Fig. 168). Each warp thread was slotted through a separate loop in the heddles, which were now mounted between shafts. These shafts were operated by a system of pulleys and treadles which separated the warp for the passing of the weft. The weft was now mounted in a boat-shaped shuttle which travelled smoothly across the warp. The horizontal loom operates considerably faster than the warp-weighted and has a smoother beating-in action because of its 'reed', a grill-like object which keeps the warp evenly spaced and the weft straight.[69] It is also able to deal with much longer pieces of cloth than is the warp-weighted loom.[70]

The treadle-operated loom was evidently in France[71] and Poland[72] by the 11th century. Evidence from England is sparse, but a wooden object, tentatively identified as the pivot from which the shafts of a horizontal loom would hang, has been found at York in levels dated to the 12th or 13th century.[73] Certainly it seems unlikely that the urban English weaving centres of the 12th century, such as York, Lincoln and Beverley, could have been using anything else. However, how soon or how completely the earlier loom was superseded by the later is open to question. Loomweights are rare in archaeological sites after the 10th century, but a line of weights between two postholes, obviously the remains of a loom, has been found with 12th-century pottery at St. Cross (Hants.).[74] Objects identified as weaving-swords have also been discovered at several medieval sites,[75] one (from Aberdeen) even as late as the 14th century.[76]

If this loom did survive, was it purely as a tool for the housewife's weaving, or did it have a more significant role to play? The answer depends on the date of the introduction of the two-man horizontal loom for broader fabrics. The one-man horizontal loom of early illustrations (Fig. 169) was capable of producing cloth only as wide as the weaver could comfortably reach out on either side to pass the shuttle. Yet in 1196 the standard size of cloth was set by royal proclamation at two ells wide.[77] If, as is suggested by one continental historian, the broader horizontal loom was not invented until the 13th century,[78] then the warp-weighted loom may have continued in use for these broader fabrics. However, the list of towns which paid fines to avoid conforming with the cloth assize suggests that the use of the narrow

---

69  A 'slay' (syn. reed) was made specially for the Laleham loom (Lloyd, 'Costs of Cloth Manufacture', 333) and another was bought for the weavers at Ramsey in 1338 (W. Dugdale, *Monasticon Anglicanum* (1846), ii, 585).
70  Hoffmann, op. cit. note 43, 130-1, 225, 258.
71  See note 248 below.
72  Kamińska and Nahlik, op. cit. note 52, 93-7.
73  Morris, op. cit. note 46, T130; revised date supplied by the archaeologist, R.A. Hall.
74  J. Collins, *Winchester Excavations 2: 1949-1960*

(1978), 29-39.
75  Late 13th-century Kings Lynn, medieval London and ? medieval Perth: Morris, op. cit. note 46, T155-162, pp. 51-2.
76  J. Murray (ed.), *Excavations in the Medieval Burgh of Aberdeen, 1973-81* (Soc. Antiq. Scot. Monog. Ser. 2), 179-80.
77  *Eng. Hist. Docs. (1189-1327)*, 320; the regulation was repeated in 1215 and 1216: ibid. 330.
78  Endrei, cited in Hoffmann, op. cit. note 43, 271.

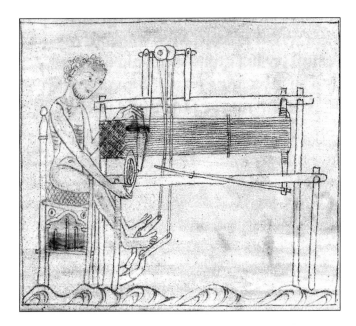

*Fig. 169* Horizontal loom,
*c.* 1250 (Trin. Coll., Camb.
MS. 0. 9. 34, f. 34ᵛ).

horizontal loom was widespread.[79]

The wide horizontal loom should not be confused with the loom of the challoners or tapiters, makers of hangings, rugs and coverlets. This was a two-beam vertical loom, a development of the one illustrated in the Utrecht Psalter (which in turn was copied into the Eadwine Psalter (Fig. 170)). Wide short-toothed iron combs found at York, Winchester and Newbury[80] – all chalon-making towns – were probably used for the heavy, downward, beating action which this loom requires. The 13th-century Winchester Customs describe the chalon looms as 'little looms', presumably from their lack of height, but some were producing wide cloth as much as 2 yards across.[81]

By the 14th century there were three main types of loom, the chalon loom, the narrow horizontal and the broad horizontal. A sophisticated version of this last is illustrated in the Ypres Kuerboek (Book of Ordinances) of 1363, along with a warping frame, reel, swift and spoolwinder (Fig. 171). The loom was called the broadcloth loom in England, where it existed side-by-side (even in the same workshop) with the narrow horizontal loom, sometimes called the kersey loom.[82] The Nottingham records[83] also draw a distinction between a linen loom and a woollen loom.

79  *Pipe Roll 4 John*, xx.
80  P.J. Ottaway in Walton (ed.) op. cit. note 41.
81  J.S. Furley, *The Ancient Uses of the City of Winchester* (Oxford, 1927), 28-31. The standard dimensions of the Winchester chal-

ons in 1275 were 4 ells/2 yds., 3½ ells/1¾ yds., 3¼ ells/1⅝ yds., 3 ells/1½ yds.
82  A.R. Bridbury, *Medieval English Clothmaking* (1982), 78.
83  *V.C.H. Notts.* ii, 345.

*Fig. 170* Early vertical two-beam loom, mid 12th century (Eadwine Psalter, Trin. Coll., Camb., MS R.17.1, f. 263).

## Finishing Processes

Once taken from the loom, linen cloth would be washed and laid out to bleach in the sunshine.[84] Woollen cloth, however, as Langland says:

> is not comely to wear,
> Till it be fulled under fote, or in fulling stocks;
> Washen well with water, and with teasels scratched,
> Towked and teynted, and under talour's hands.[85]

At first, cloth was fulled in a tub of water, by trampling or 'walking' it underfoot. Fullers earth, a naturally occurring clay, of which there are extensive beds in Surrey and Bedfordshire, was used in the tub to remove grease and speed the matting process.[86]

In Flanders a hollowed-out tree-trunk seems to have been used for fulling[87] and just such a tub, 70-80cm. across, with a rounded base, has been found in a clothworking area of 13th-century Beverley.[88] The Beverley tub seems to have been through two phases of use, but its first function may have been as a *truncum ad fullandum pannos*, such as one of the abbot's tenants kept illegally in his house at St. Albans in 1294.[89]

In 1295-6, cloth was still expected to be fulled by foot (*sub pedibus hominum*) in London.[90] However, the ordinances of the Lincoln gild of fullers in 1337 forbid gild members to work 'in the trough' (*in alveo*) and instead refer to fullers working 'at the perch' (*ad perticam*).[91] The word *pertica* is ambiguous, but could be a wooden bar for

84  Ibid. 348.
85  W. Langland, *The Vision of William concerning Piers Plowman*, B text, xv, 444.
86  *V.C.H. Surrey*, iii, 279.
87  De Poerck, op. cit. note 42, i, 101.
88  P. Armstrong, M. Brooks, M. Foreman, pers. comm.
89  *Gesta Abbatum Monasterii Sancti Albani*, ed. H.T. Riley (Rolls Ser. xxviii.4, 1867), i, 416.
90  *Lib. Cust.* op. cit. note 18, 128.
91  *English Gilds*, ed. J. and L. Toulmin Smith (E.E.T.S. orig. ser. xl, revised edn. 1892), 180.

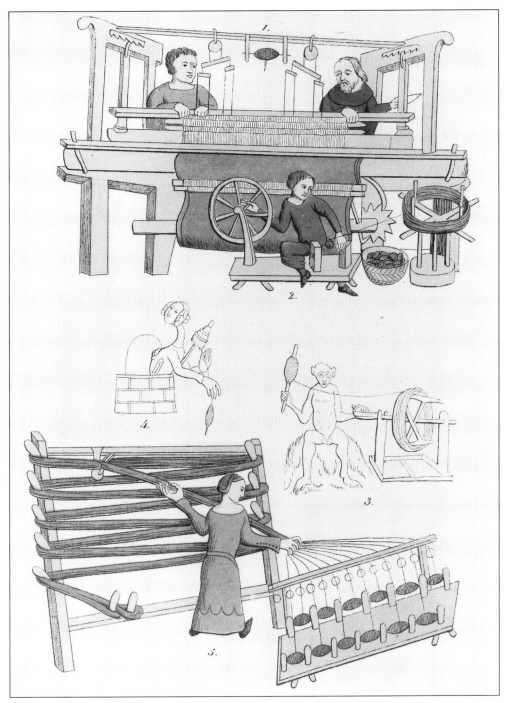

*Fig. 171* Weaving processes as illustrated in the Kuerboek of Ypres, 1363. After F. de Vigne, *Recherches Historiques sur les Costumes Civils et Militaire des Gildes et Corporations de Metiers* (Ghent, 1847).

beating the cloth.[92] This would bring it close to the mechanised process whereby a water-driven wheel was used to operate large wooden tilt-hammers. The earliest documentary references to such mills belong to the late 12th century, but although they soon became established in rural districts, particularly in the western half of the country,[93] they met with opposition in many towns.[94] Norwich, for example, did not acquire a fulling-mill until 1429.[95]

Fulling not only mats the fabric, but shrinks it considerably too. In 1505-6 weavers and walkers (or fullers) of York agreed that a cloth of 32 yards long would shrink to 25 yards after fulling.[96] The cloth would therefore have to be stretched on tenters, long wooden fences with iron hooks at top and bottom.[97] Even after tentering, a length of 28 yards of cloth was expected to be 4 yards shorter than when it began.[98] Over-tentering 'by wrenche rope and ringe' was a common problem,[99] which parliament attempted to control,[100] along with the use of flour, starch and chalk to make the cloth look thicker.[101]

For some cloth the treatment ended here, but for fabrics such as broadcloth, the matted effect of fulling was further developed by raising a 'nap' with teasels set in a frame. Teasels 'that longyn to the office of fullers'[102] were cultivated on a large scale from at least the early 13th century.[103] Iron-toothed cards were considered too rough for the purpose and were forbidden in 1465.[104] The process was evidently mechanised by 1436 when a gig-mill was in the possession of one wealthy clothier.[105]

After the nap had been raised, the cloth was clipped to a board with double-ended hooks called havettes[106] and the surface sheared back with large iron cropping-shears.[107] The processes of raising and shearing were repeated several times until the cloth had a smooth velvety finish, which would then be finished by pressing. When fine broadcloth was napped and sheared in this way, the result was an even, softly-draping fabric, such as can be seen in rich tones of red or blue alongside patterned silks in Renaissance paintings.

## *Dyes and Dyeing*

Dyeing could be carried out when the cloth was at any stage of manufacture: as 'wolles, clothe or garnes', as the York dyers' ordinances have it.[108] The raw materials

92  In France, clubs were used for fulling hats and caps: E. Carus-Wilson, *Medieval Merchant Venturers* (1967), 187.

93  Ibid. 194 ff; Bridbury, op. cit. note 82, 17-19.

94  *Lib. Cust.* op. cit. note 18, 128-9.

95  S. Kelly et al., *Men of Property* (1983), 25.

96  A. Raine (ed.), *York Civic Records*, iii, 21.

97  In 1494 the Nottingham Borough Records mention two tenters, one narrow and one broad, which must correspond to the two different loom-widths: *V.C.H. Notts.* ii, 346.

98  *Eng. Hist. Docs. (1327-1485)*, 1025.

99  *V.C.H. Sussex*, ii, 257.

100  As note 98.

101  Strutt, op. cit. note 38, ii, 87.

102  *The English Register of Godstow Nunnery*, ed. A. Clark (E.E.T.S., orig. ser. cxxix, cxxx, cxlii, 1905-11), ii, 648.

103  E. Carus-Wilson, 'The Significance of the Secular Sculptures in the Lane Chapel, Cullompton', *Med. Arch.* i (1957), 104-17.

104  As note 98.

105  *Eng. Hist. Docs. (1327-1485)*, No. 585.

106  G. Egan, 'A Shearman's Hook from London', *Trans. London & Middlesex Arch. Soc.* xxx (1979), 190-2.

107  As note 103.

108  *York Mem. Book*, ed. M. Sellers, ii (Surtees Soc. cxxv, 1915), 206.

*Fig. 172* The boy Jesus as an apprentice dyer, *c.* 1300 (Bodleian Library, MS Selden supra 38, f. 27).

available to the medieval dyer included cultivated plants, such as madder for red[109] and woad for blue;[110] the meadow plants weld [111] and woadwaxen[112] (also known as dyer's greenweed) for yellow; and the imported dyes kermes, orchil and brazilwood for richer reds and purples. Indigo,[113] although used as an artist's pigment at an early stage, does not seem to have been recognised as a dye in Europe until the mid 15th century, when it met with much opposition in woad-growing countries.[114]

The cultivation of madder and woad is recommended in an 11th-century estate memorandum[115] and both dyes were paying toll at Winchester in the 13th century.[116] Since foreign supplies of woad were readily available from the English possessions in Gascony,[117] imports of the dye were considerable. In the early 13th century it was entering England through many ports of the south and east coast[118] and Bristol[119] and Norwich[120] both had merchants specialising in the commodity. Dyers also drew on the woad of Picardy and Toulouse (Languedoc) [121] and at a later date imported from the Azores and from Genoa.[122] As the quality of the dye was important, woad assayers were set up at Exeter, Winchester[123] and York.[124] By the second half of the 16th century there was an even greater demand for woad and, as

109 Obtained from the roots of *Rubia tinctorum* L.
110 Leaves of *Isatis tinctoria* L.
111 *Reseda luteola* L. (whole plant, apart from roots).
112 *Genista tinctoria* L. (ends of branches while in blossom).
113 *Indigofera tinctoria* L.
114 F. Brunello, *Art of Dyeing* (1973), 144; C. Bolton, 'Contributions to the History of Dyeing', *The Dyer and Textile Printer*, lxxiii-lxxxiii (1935-40), lxxiv, 440, 483-4, 582.
115 As note 20.

116 Furley op. cit. note 81, 40-1.
117 Carus-Wilson, 'Trade and Industry', 377; Carus-Wilson, op. cit. note 92, 36.
118 J.B. Hurry, *The Woad Plant and its Dye* (1930), 55.
119 J.H. Bettey, 'Cultivation of Woad', *Textile History*, ix (1978), 112.
120 Kelly et al., op. cit. note 95, 24.
121 *Little Red Book*, op. cit. note 61, ii, 16.
122 Willan, op. cit. note 27, 10.
123 Furley op. cit. note 81, 40-1.
124 *York Mem. Book*, i, 43, 45.

farming practices changed, it was possible to give more land over to its production: Lincolnshire and the Salisbury-Somerset areas both became important producers.[125]

It is, however, remarkable that there is no record of the import of madder before the 14th century. This is by far the most common dye to be found in medieval textiles[126] and 'waranciers', traders or dyers in madder, were resident in Winchester as early as 1148.[127] In 1326 the export of madder, along with other native products such as teasels, was forbidden.[128] This suggests that madder, although it was not a native plant, was being cultivated in England, and that home supplies were sufficient for the dyers' needs. However, in 1347-8 'xi pokes de madder' were imported into Lynn[129] and by the 15th century the madder fields of Brabant and Zealand were more regularly supplying the English dyer.[130]

In 1582, Richard Hakluyt remarked that 'yellowes and greenes are colours of small prices in this realme by reason that Olde [weld] and Greenweed wherewith they be died be naturall here, and in great plenty'.[131] For this reason they rarely appear in trade documents, although their remains are to be found in archaeological sites.[132] The yellow dye saffron was also cultivated in East Anglia from the 14th century[133] although on the whole its use in textiles seems to have been limited.[134]

The most prestigious dye of the Middle Ages was kermes, obtained from an insect of the Mediterranean and Near East, *Kermes vermilio* Planch. These small round insects were known as 'vermilium' ('little worm') to the Italians (hence 'vermilion') and as 'grain' to the English.[135] The dye was expensive[136] and the tax on cloth dyed in grain could be double that of cloth without,[137] which explains why kermes is only to be found in the very best wool textiles and in silks.[138]

Reds and purples were always in demand for richer fabrics, but the fiery red of brazilwood could only be used with care because of its poor light-fastness. Although the dye (obtained from the heartwood of *Caesalpinia* spp. from the East Indies) seems to have been imported from at least the early 14th century,[139] its use was prohibited in some cloths[140] and it was denounced as 'disceytfull brasell' and 'a fauls colour' in 1553.[141] Similarly Hakluyt noted of logwood (*Haematoxylon Campechianum*, a dyewood

125  Bettey, art. cit. note 119, 112-17; Hurry, op. cit. note 118, 60-75.
126  P. Walton, 'Dyes on Medieval Textiles', *Dyes on Historical and Archaeological Textiles*, iii (1984), 30-4.
127  M. Biddle, *Winchester in the Early Middle Ages* (Winchester Studies, 1 1976), 430.
128  *Eng. Hist. Docs. (1189-1327)*, 546-7.
129  *Rot. Parl.* ii, 215, No.41.
130  *Libelle of Englysche Polycye*, ed. G.F. Warner (Oxford, 1926), 7.
131  Bolton, op. cit. note 114, lxxiv, 66.
132  P. Tomlinson and A.R. Hall, 'Progress in Palaeobotanical Studies of Dye Plants 1983/4', *Dyes on Historical and Archaeological Textiles*, iii

(1984), 28-9.
133  Brunello, op. cit. note 114, 147.
134  Saffron-dyed wimples and kerchiefs are mentioned by Chaucer, possibly as a prophylactic against jaundice: M. Harrison, *The History of the Hat* (1960), 48-9.
135  Brunello, op. cit. note 114, 137, 364.
136  Willan op. cit. note 27, 7.
137  *Eng. Hist. Docs. (1189-1327)*, 517.
138  As note 126.
139  N.S.B. Gras, *Early Eng. Customs System* (1918), 166.
140  Bolton, op. cit. note 114, lxxiv, 582.
141  Ibid. 552.

*Fig. 173* A 12th-century wooden vat fed by a boxed pipe at Eastgate, Beverley.

introduced from the Americas) that 'it is cheape and yeeldeth a glorious blew, but our workmen can not make it sure'.[142]

For the same reason orchil, which gives a reddish purple, was only to be used in combination with other dyes such as woad.[143] The name orchil first appears as a Florentine monopoly in about 1300, when it was prepared from Mediterranean lichens,[144] but the same dye, from British lichens, was traded under the name of 'cork' in the 13th century;[145] as 'lacmus', the Norwegian dye, it was imported into England in the 14th.[146]

Dark blues and blacks could be produced by repeated dyeing with woad and then 'saddening' the colour with madder or weld.[147] This was a costly process and cheaper blacks were made with tannin-bearing dyes such as oak galls and sumach.[148] Unfortunately, these did not give such a good result as the traditional woaded black and were treated with suspicion.

In order to fix most dyes on to the fibre, the cloth must first be dipped in a

142  Ibid. lxxiv, 66; see also lxxv, 59, 357.
143  *Rot. Parl.* v, 562 col. 1 (1464).
144  A. Kok, 'A Short History of the Orchil Dyes', *Lichenologist*, iii (1966), 252-3.
145  Furley op. cit. note 81, 40-1. Kok, art. cit. note

144, 254.
146  Kok, op. cit. note 144, 252.
147  Bolton, art. cit. note 114, lxx, 14, 19.
148  Ibid.

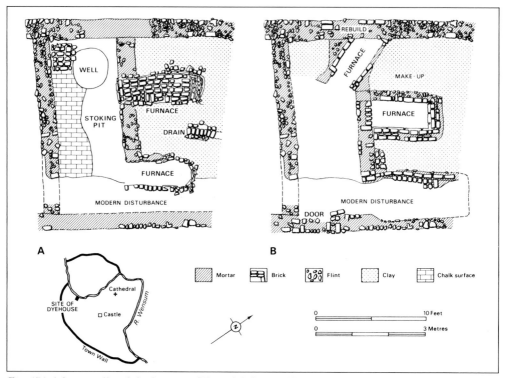

*Fig. 174* A late medieval dyehouse at Westwick Street, Norwich (from Platt 1976).

mordant. Vitriol or copperas (ferrous sulphate) could be used for darker shades[149] but for the rich warm tones which in general were preferred, alum was imported from Asia Minor, the Greek Islands and eventually Italy.[150] Woad requires no mordant, but an alkali such as potash is necessary to make the dye soluble. For this purpose wood ashes (both native and imported) and 'argol' scraped from the inside of wine-vats were used.[151]

The dye bath was usually prepared in a cauldron over a direct flame. The cloth might be dipped straight into this, or the liquor might be transferred to a separate vat.[152] The tub excavated at Beverley, in the second phase of its use in a dyehouse, was set into the ground with shuttering round its edge and with a wooden channel leading into it (Fig. 173). A small pit full of madder-root was found nearby, and a keyhole-shaped hearth which was probably used to heat the dye solution.[153] A whole

149  Green and white copperas are listed in the contents of a London grocer's shop in 1399: *Eng. Hist. Docs. (1327-1485)*, 1075-9. See also J.H. Bettey, 'Production of Alum and Copperas in Southern England', *Textile History*, xiii(1) (1982), 91-8.

150  C. Singer, *The Earliest Chemical Industry* (1948), 138 ff. Native alum mines were eventually

opened up in the late 16th century at Guisborough and Whitby: Singer op. cit. 182 ff.

151  Carus-Wilson, op. cit. note 92, 221-2.

152  De Poerck, op. cit. note 42, 162-3.

153  Humberside County Council Archaeology Unit, *The Archaeology of the Medieval Cloth Industry in Beverley* (1985), 16.

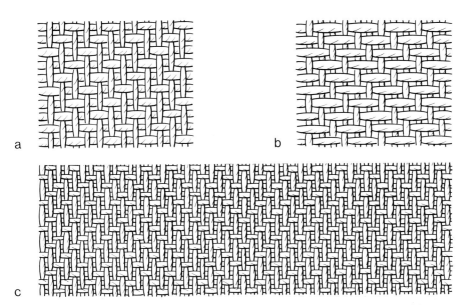

*Fig. 175 a, b, c:* 11th- to 13th-century weaves: (a) 3-shaft twill (front); (b) 3-shaft twill (back); (c) diamond twill.

series of similar keyhole-shaped hearths together with fullers earth have been found in London at Swan Lane,[154] not far from the medieval woadmarket at Candelwick Street.[155] Another medieval dyehouse, excavated at Westwick Street, Norwich, has a single hearth and a well (Fig. 174). A good supply of water was essential to the dyers' craft and was also a place to dump the waste from the dye-vat: wharfside dumping of madder and weld has been found at 14th-century Bristol.[156]

Finally, the cloth was checked for quality and size by gild searchers[157] and, from the late 13th century, by a Crown officer called the aulnager. From at least the 14th century the cloth was marked with a lead seal, to show that it had paid the aulnage tax.[158] These seals, many of which have been recovered from London excavations, may show the name of the cloth, its size, weight and place of origin; in the late 16th century dyers also began to affix their own seals.[159]

### *The Appearance and Names of Textiles: 11th to early 14th centuries*

During the 11th century the variety of weaves which had existed in the Anglo-Saxon period gave way to one particular type of twill.[160] This weave was worked on three

154 G. Egan, Museum of London, pers. comm.
155 Hurry, op. cit. note 118, 75-7.
156 As note 132.
157 *York Civic Records*, op. cit. note 96, iii, 21 ff.
158 W. Endrei and G. Egan, 'The Sealing of Cloth in Europe', *Textile History*, xiii (1982), 1, 54-6;

Carus-Wilson, op. cit. note 92, ch. VIII.
159 G. Egan, *Leaden Cloth Seals* (Finds Research Group 700-1700, Datasheet 3 (1985)).
160 F.A. Pritchard, 'Late Saxon Textiles from the City of London', *Med. Arch.* xxviii (1984), 68-9.

loom-shafts in such a way that the warp predominated on one face (Fig. 175a) while the softer weft tended to mat up on the opposite side (Fig. 175b). From the evidence of seams it would appear that the matted face was worn on the inside.[161] This kind of fabric remained the standard clothing material until well into the 14th century.[162]

Lighter and heavier weights of cloth were produced in this three-shaft weave. It is possible that some of the coarsest pieces are 'burel', a cheap cloth of poor wool given as alms by the king.[163] Some may also be russets, undyed cloth in natural greys and browns, which by sumptuary law were the proper clothing of country folk.[164] Blankets and says were medium-price and presumably medium-quality fabrics.[165]

One of the more expensive cloths of this period was 'scarlet' which was among the small number of English cloths to be exported at this date.[166] Scarlet was made from the finest wools[167] and bought for the royal houses of England[168] and Norway.[169] Its distinguishing feature was originally not its colour, but a densely teaselled and sheared surface.[170] However, because it was a cloth of high quality, it was often dyed with the expensive kermes so that the cloth-name, scarlet, eventually transferred to the vibrant red colour of this dye.[171] Regrettably there is nothing in the collections of excavated early textiles which compares with the documentary picture of this cloth – possibly because it was a valuable fabric, often exported and rarely discarded. It is not until the 14th century, when some tailor's offcuts from the royal residence at Baynard's Castle were laid down, that heavily teaselled cloth, sometimes kermes-dyed, is to be found.[172]

Although the name scarlet is misleading, many other cloths were in fact designated by their colours: burnets, plunkets, azures, blues, greens.[173] Most medieval fabrics seem to have been of one all-over colour, although simple stripes and checks were occasionally used. One group of fragments from Saxo-Norman Durham has alternating dark and light threads in warp and weft,[174] which is reminiscent of the London weavers' regulations that certain patterns should be woven 'thread and thread' (*un fil et un*).[175] The pattern names listed in these ordinances are quite bewildering: 'andley, porreye, or marbled ground with vetch-blossom, or green upon vair . . . menuet, virli, lumbard and such manner of cloths'. 'Ray' was a more commonly used term, to indicate a striped cloth.[176]

Alongside the rather soft wool twills, whether patterned or otherwise, was one other much finer and rarer type of fabric. This was woven in glossy yarns made from combed wool in a pattern of repeating diamonds (Fig. 175c, 176). The earliest

161 Crowfoot, art. cit. note 62, 38.
162 Ibid. 39.
163 Salzman, *Industries*, 197.
164 Strutt, op. cit. note 38, ii, 105 ff.
165 Salzman, *Industries*, 198.
166 H. Heaton, *The Yorkshire Woollen and Worsted Industries* (1920), 4.
167 J.H. Munro, 'Medieval Scarlet', in N.B. Harte and K.G. Ponting (eds.), *Cloth and Clothing in Medieval Europe* (1983), 30.

168 Salzman, *Industries* 198.
169 Hill, *Med. Lincoln*, 325.
170 Munro, op. cit. note 167, 29.
171 Ibid. 60.
172 E. Crowfoot et al., *Textiles and Clothing* (forthcoming); Walton, op. cit. note 126, 30-4.
173 Salzman, *Industries*, 199.
174 Crowfoot, op. cit. note 62, 36-9.
175 *Lib. Cust.* op. cit. note 18, ii, 125, 549.
176 Beck, *Draper's Dict.*, 272-3.

*Fig. 176* 11th-century diamond twill from York.

English examples of this textile are from 10th- to 11th-century York[177] and the latest from 13th-century Canterbury,[178] a date-range which coincides with documentary references to an expensive cloth called 'haberget'. Etymologically the origin of the name seems to be connected with hauberks, garments of mail.[179] Since the fine diamond twills have an overall appearanc of interlocking circles (and indeed in Scandinavian countries such fabrics are still called 'ring-woven'), the one may tentatively be identified with the other. At any rate, the diamond weaves were obviously valuable, since one example from York has been deeply dyed with kermes.[180]

### The Appearance and Names of Textiles: 14th to 16th centuries

Changes in technology were taking place in the late 13th and early 14th centuries. The spindle wheel arrived, allowing faster production of weft yarn, and the hand-carder took its place alongside the woolcomb. The wool textile industry now split into two specialist branches, the worsted weavers producing light, crisp textiles of

177  Hedges, 'Textiles from Lloyds Bank'.
178  Grave of Abbot Roger II (d. 1272) at St. Augustine's Abbey, Canterbury: E. Crowfoot in P.J. Ottaway, 'Burial from of Winchester Cathedral', *Arch. Jnl.* cxxix (1982), 128.
179  E. Carus-Wilson, 'Haberget', *Med. Arch.* xiii (1969), 148-66.
180  Petergate, York, *c.* 1200, unpublished.

*Fig. 177* 15th- and 16th-century worsted and woollens from Newcastle upon Tyne.

combed wool[181] and the woollen weavers working soft cloth of hand-carded wool (Fig. 177).

Woollens were by far the largest category, and within this group a change in cloth structure can be seen to have occurred in the course of the 14th century. The twill weave, which had previously been so popular, now steadily gave way to simpler plain weave (Fig. 178a).[182] At the same time, the difference between the yarns of warp and weft became less marked. Both these changes gave the cloth a more uniform appearance on front and back, and may well have been aimed at producing a cloth more suitable for fulling and teaselling. Certainly, later medieval textiles are more frequently heavily finished than earlier ones.[183]

It is hardly surprising to find that fabric names also changed at this time. Burel and haberget disappear from the records[184] and scarlet is less common; in their

181 Technically speaking, worsteds had been in existence for several centuries (e.g. haberget). However the term first appears in the early 14th century and seems to mark the beginning of a change in the classification of wool cloth.

182 Crowfoot et al. op. cit. note 172.

183 Walton, op. cit. note 14, 197-8.

184 Carus-Wilson, op. cit. note 179; A. Woodger, 'The Eclipse of the Burel Weaver: Some Technological Developments in the 13th Century', *Textile History*, xii (1981), 59-76.

places are broadcloth, northern cloths, dozens, straits, 'cottons', Kendal cloth, cocksals, Manchester rugs, friezes, cogware, kersies, sorting kersies, check kersies and many more.[185] To the merchant these cloths were identifiable by their dimensions and weight: according to regulations of 1553, the size of broadcloth was set at 28-30 yards × 7 quarters and its weight was 90 lbs. – although broadcloths called Tauntons and Bridgwaters were only 12-13 yards and 34 lbs; a dozen was 12-13 yards and 6½ quarters and 28 lbs. – or narrower and lighter if it was a Devonshire dozen; kersies were 17-18 yards long and 20 lbs; sorting kersies 23 lbs., and so on.[186] Stripes of colour in the selvedge were used as a guide to the fabric-type.[187] The appearance of these cloths also varied according to how much time they had spent at the fulling mill, or being teaselled and sheared. In 1477 the fullers and dyers of Newcastle upon Tyne set their prices as follows: to full a kersey cost 2*d.* the yard, as did 'wadded' blue; broadcloth cost 4*d.* per yard and friezes 1½*d.* The shearing of fustian (a coarse twill) cost 1½*d.* per yard, whereas broadcloth (which was evidently both fulled and teaselled) was 3*d.* and 'tilted cloth' was 3*d.* per dozen yards.[188]

There can be little doubt that the best wool cloth which England was producing at this time was the heavily-finished broadcloth, successor to the scarlet of the earlier period. By chance, three snippets have survived in Toulouse, pinned to a merchant's contract of 1458.[189] All three are of medium weight and in plain weave, the weave structure being completely obscured by a dense nap, making the cloth some 1.5-2.0mm. thick. In colour they are shades of red and reddish purple, the dyes various combinations of madder, woad (or indigo) and brazilwood. There are also some finer varieties of the same cloth in a collection of tailors' offcuts from 15th- and 16th-century Newcastle upon Tyne.[190]

Most cloth continued to be mono-colour. Names such as broad plunkets, azures, blues and russet straits[191] show that the same range of colours was in use as before, although russet was now more frequently dyed rather than being the natural brown of the wool.[192] One patterned fabric, the striped ray, still appears in the documents, although this too seems to have been through a change. A political poem concerning the reign of Edward II (1307-27) states that 'the raye is turned overthuert that sholde stonde adoun'.[193] It is probable that this refers to a new weave which appears in the late 13th century,[194] a finely-woven cloth with densely-packed weft-stripes which stand out as coloured ribs (Fig. 178b), unlike the simpler stripes of the earlier period.

Among worsteds, weaves were more variable, since their smooth yarns showed off their structure much better than did the felted woollens. The names of such worsteds

185 Strutt, op. cit. note 38, ii, 78-80.
186 Ibid.
187 *V.C.H. Essex*, ii (1981), 385.
188 J. Brand, *History of Newcastle upon Tyne* (1789), 320.
189 P. Wolff, 'Three Samples of English 15th Century Cloth', in N.B. Harte and K.G. Ponting (eds.), *Cloth and Clothing in Medieval Europe* (1983), 120-5.

190 As note 183.
191 Strutt, op. cit. note 38, ii, 79.
192 'russettes . . . woaded, boyled and maddered', 1549-50, Stat. 3 and 4 Edw. VI c.2 (*Statutes of the Realm*, iv, 101).
193 *The Political Songs of England*, ed. T. Wright (Camden Soc., vi, 1839), 326.
194 Walton, op. cit. note 8, Pritchard, op. cit. note 160, 200.

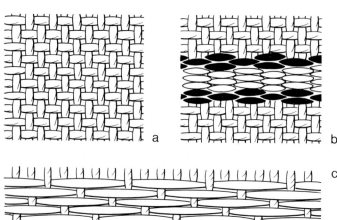

*Fig. 178 a, b, c:* 14th-16th-century weaves: (a) plain weave; (b) striped fabric; (c) true satin.

occur as 'streites, brodes . . . mantelles, sengles, doubles, et demy doubles, si bien les motles, paules, chekeres, raies, flores, pleynes, monkes-clothes et autres mantelles . . . chanonclothes, sengles, demy doubles et doubles'.[195] Surviving examples prove to have been woven in a variety of twills, some of them imitating the appearance of satin,[196] which the medieval weaver would have seen in imported silks. The more difficult technique of weaving true satin (Fig. 178c) does not appear to have reached England much before the mid 16th century.[197]

Worsteds in general seem to have become more common towards the end of the Elizabethan era, when there occurred an even greater proliferation of fabric names: bayes, sayes, serges, perpetuanas, rashes, frisadoes, minikins, bombasines, grograines, buffins, russels, sagathies, mockadoes, shalloons and tammies, to name a few.[198] However, most of these were dress-weight fabrics, and English wearers always preferred heavily napped woollens for outer garments.[199]

## *Linens*

The linen industry is on the whole poorly documented, largely because it lacked the economic importance of wool cloth. It is also ill-represented in the archaeological record, as the fibres rot quickly in damp conditions. There can, however, be little doubt that linen production was widespread (see below), its products being used for

195  Salzman, *Industries*, 230.
196  Pritchard, op. cit. note 160, 205; Walton, op. cit. note 14, 194-5.
197  Walton, loc. cit. note 196.
198  Bowden, op. cit. note 17, 41.

199  P. Walton, 'Textiles', in M. Ellison and B. Harbottle, 'Excavation of a 17th-century Bastion in the Castle of Newcastle upon Tyne', *Archaeologia Aeliana* 5th ser., xi (1983), 217-40, 262-3.

'sheets, broadcloths, towels, shirts, smocks and such other necessaries'.[200]

Linens mostly seem to have been in plain weave[201] and bleached white, although towels with blue stripes were included in an inventory of 1460.[202] Linens from Wilton were among the finest, supplying the royal household throughout the 13th century,[203] while 'diaper linen', probably some sort of white damask, was a speciality of Norfolk in the 16th century.[204] At the other end of the scale, coarse cheap types of cloth were made from linen tow and sold under the names of harden and sameron.[205] Many kinds of linen were also imported, including coarse 'Barras canvas' from Holland, dowlas and poldavy from Brittany, sieve-cloth from Rennes and finer linens such as bysse and cambric (originally from Cambrai).[206] A group of seals from London show that cloth of St. Gall on the Upper Rhine, one of the main European producers of linen, was being brought into England in the late 15th century.[207]

### Felt

Not all cloth was woven: wool fibres could be compacted together with the help of heat and moisture to make felt. Although felt production was probably negligible before Henry VIII's reign,[208] it is an occasional find on archaeological sites from the 12th century onwards,[209] and seems to have been used mainly for hats and hat brims. In the 16th century the finest felts were made from Spanish wool, while the coarsest, which were 'covered with veluytt Taffittaes and such like', were often made of Eastland and French wools.[210] A small wool felt hat dated to *c.* 1350 from the church at Little Sampford (Essex) has a silk lining and a satin covering to the brim.[211] At such a date this may be an import, similar to the fine felt hats which Flemish merchants were selling outside Westminster in the 15th century.[212]

### Knitted Goods

The art of knitting probably reached Europe with the Arabs, although it took some time to travel into the north.[213] The earliest example from England is a pair of silk knitted gloves kept at New College, Oxford, since its foundation in 1386.[214] These

200 A. Fitzherbert, 'The Boke of Husbandry' (1523): *Eng. Hist. Docs. (1485-1558)*, 922-4.
201 E.g. Pritchard, op. cit. note 160, 207.
202 *Eng. Hist. Docs. (1327-1485)*, 1146-1150.
203 Salzman, *Industries*, 239.
204 Beck, *Draper's Dict.* 96-8.
205 *York Civic Records*, op cit. note 96, iv, 139.
206 Willan op. cit. note 27, *passim*.
207 G. Egan, 'A Group of Seals found at Bankside from St. Gallen Linens or Fustians' *Trans. Lond. & Middlesex Arch. Soc.*, xxxi (1980), 116-8.
208 Bowden, op. cit. note 17, 47; Beck, *Draper's Dict.*, 125.
209 H.G. Bennett, *Perth High St. Textiles*

(forthcoming).
210 B.L., MS Lansdowne 29, f. 56.
211 K. Finch, 'A Medieval Hat Rediscovered', *Textile History*, xiv (1) (1983), 67-70.
212 B.L., MS Harl. 542; *Eng. Hist. Docs. (1327-1485)*, 1079-80.
213 S.M. Levey, 'Illustrations of the History of Knitting Selected from the Collection of the Victoria and Albert Museum', *Textile History*, i (2) (1969), 186; I. Turnau, 'Diffusion of Knitting in Medieval Europe', *Cloth and Clothing in Medieval Europe*, op. cit. note 189, 386.
214 M. Hartley and J. Ingilby, *The Old Hand-Knitters of the Dales* (1951), 4.

are likely to have been imports, as were the 'Spanish silke stockings from Spaine' worn by Henry VIII.[215] References to English knitters do not occur until the later 15th century, when 'cappe knytters' appear in Ripon (1465) and Nottingham (1478);[216] in 1488 it was stated that the price of knitted woollen hats was 2s. 8d.[217]

Once the craft was established it became widespread. In 1552 an Act of Parliament listed 'knitte hose, knitte petticotes, knitte gloves, knitte slieves',[218] and between 1563 and 1597 every person not possessed of 20 marks' worth of land was obliged to wear on Sundays and holidays one cap of wool, knit, finished and dressed in England.[219] Several styles of heavily felted, knitted hats have been found in London[220] and two other examples, of a 'flat cap' design, have been excavated at Newcastle upon Tyne.[221]

Elizabeth I actively encouraged handknitting, particularly among the poor, and when William Lee invented the first stocking frame (1589), she refused him a patent on the grounds that 'I have too much love for my poor people who obtain their bread by the employment of knitting, to give my money to forward an invention that will tend to their ruin'.[222] Elizabeth's enthusiasm for silk stockings may also have contributed to the establishment of a silk hose-making centre at Wokingham in the late 16th century.[223]

## Embroidery and Other Silkwork

Since England lacked its own silk industry, full-size silks were imported from Italy and Spain for use in churches and at the royal court.[224] Some comparable luxury goods were also produced at home, namely the rich embroideries called *opus anglicanum*. These were reaching the continent by the 8th century[225] and in the 13th and 14th centuries appear in several foreign inventories, including those of the Vatican.[226]

The Bayeux 'tapestry' (so-called) is in fact an embroidery, probably English in origin.[227] It is a hanging over 230 feet long, depicting the events surrounding the Norman invasion, and, unusually, it is worked in dyed wools on a linen ground. Most surviving embroideries are worked in couched gold (or silver-gilt) thread, with

215　Ibid.
216　K. Buckland, 'The Monmouth Cap', *Costume*, xiii (1979), 23.
217　Hartley and Ingilby, op. cit. note 214, 8.
218　Quoted in Beck, *Draper's Dict.* 184 [source not given].
219　'Statute of Servants', 1563, 5 Eliz. c. 4; 'An Act for the Continuance of the making of Caps', 13 Eliz. c. 19; see also Buckland, op. cit. note 216, 25.
220　K.G. Ponting, 'Knitted Caps', *Bulletin de Liaison du Centre International d'Etude des Textiles Anciens*, xlix (1979), 78-81.
221　Walton, art. cit. note 14, 200-3.
222　Quoted in Hartley and Ingilby, op. cit. note 214, 8 [source not given].
223　*V.C.H. Berks.* i, 395.
224　K. Staniland, 'Clothing and Textiles at the Court of Edward III, 1342-1352', in J. Bird, H. Chapman, J. Clark (eds.), *Collectanea Londiniensia* (London & Middlesex Arch. Soc. Special Paper 2, 1978), 231-2.
225　M. Budny and D. Tweddle, 'The Maaseik Embroideries', *Anglo-Saxon England* xiii (1984), 65-96.
226　A.F. Kendrick, *Eng. Embroidery* (1913), 4; J. Evans, *English Art 1307-1461* (1949), 17; A.G.I. Christie, *English Medieval Embroidery* (1938).
227　D.M. Wilson, *The Bayeux Tapestry* (1985).

coloured silks in split stitch, on a silk or linen ground. They are largely ecclesiastical – copes, amices, orphreys, altar frontals and palls – although there must have been a considerable amount of secular work which has not come down to us.

Many embroideries were designed by artists[228] and executed by needleworkers. Since the Anglo-Saxon period the craft had been practised in the convent and nuns were still embroidering in the 14th century.[229] However, by the 13th century female (and occasionally male)[230] needleworkers were employed in city workshops: the demands of the royal court alone were probably enough to keep quite a large number in full employment.[231]

Early designs include formal repeating patterns, such as those of the 12th-century fragments at Sens cathedral.[232] During the following century, figures within compartments began to appear, reaching their highest standard in the Syon[233] and Vatican[234] copes. By the late 13th and 14th centuries, English embroidery was at its peak, producing designs skilfully crafted to the shape of the garment. Fluid Tree of Life or Tree of Jesse motifs appear, as in the red silk 'Jesse' cope in the Victoria and Albert Museum[235] and lively biblical scenes set under arcades: many of these vestments can be seen in continental cathedral treasuries, such as those at Toledo, Pienza and Bologna.[236]

In the late 14th century embroiderers began to take short-cuts in their techniques. Motifs were worked separately and then applied to the ground fabric (now often of velvet or silk satin) and the quicker brick, satin and long and short stitches were introduced, along with surface couching and stem stitch.[237] Despite attempts to protect workshops, standards and design declined.[238] Only with the Tudor period did embroidery begin to recover, with a proliferation of designs and techniques, the products now being available to the affluent lay middle classes.[239]

In parallel with embroidery runs the craft of tablet-weaving, a technique for making narrow decorative braids. Silk examples, with designs ranging from geometric patterns to imaginative free-hand animals and birds, were used to attach seals to charters.[240] Others, brocaded with gold or silver-gilt thread, have been found

228 A designer's pattern-book, the 'Pepysian Sketchbook', used between *c.* 1280 and the end of the 14th century, contains sketches of birds and beasts similar to those in contemporary embroideries: Evans, op. cit. note 226, 19; J.J.G. Alexander and P. Binski (eds.), *Age of Chivalry: Art in Plantagenet England 1200-1400* (Royal Academy of Arts, 1987), No. 466.
229 Evans, op. cit. note 226, 18.
230 L. Parry in Bridgman and Drury, *Needlework*, 33.
231 K. Staniland, 'Medieval Courtly Splendour', *Costume*, xiv (1980), 13.
232 Christie, op. cit. note 226, Nos. 11-12; illustrated in Bridgman and Drury, op. cit. note 230, 32.
233 In the Victoria and Albert Museum; illus-

traded in Kendrick, op. cit. note 226, plates VI and VIa and in D. King, *Opus Anglicannum* (1963), pl. 7; see also Christie, op. cit. note 226, No. 75.
234 In the Museo Sacro, Vatican, Rome; illustrated in Bridgman and Drury, op. cit. note 230, 33; Christie op. cit. note 226, No. 51.
235 Illustrated in Kendrick, op. cit. note 226, pl XVII and XVIII.
236 Ibid. pls. X-XIII; King, op. cit. note 233, pls. 10 and 11.
237 Parry, op. cit. note 230, 34-5.
238 Kendrick, op. cit. note 226, 46-50.
239 Ibid., 50ff.; Parry, op. cit. note 230, 36-42.
240 A. Henshall, 'Five Tablet-Woven Seal-Tags', *Arch. Jnl.* cxxi (1964), 154-62.

in ecclesiastic's tombs, such as those of Archbishop de Gray at York[241] and Abbots Roger II and Dygon at Canterbury.[242] Some of these braids, particularly the later examples, were probably the work of the silkwomen, whose craft included the making of ribbons, laces, fringes and tassels.[243] Belt-braids in poorer materials such as linen and wool have also been found inside the plates of excavated buckles.[244]

### *Siting and Organisation of the Industry: 11th to early 14th centuries*

In the centuries before the Norman Conquest, spinning and weaving were domestic chores with which every woman in the household would have been familiar.[245] The tools – woolcomb, distaff, spindle and warp-weighted loom – were simple and comparatively slow and the products variable in both design and quality.[246]

However, in the course of the 11th century, the housewife's loom acquired a rival in the treadle-operated horizontal loom, capable of producing greater lengths of cloth at considerably increased speed.[247] Although the two looms probably existed side-by-side for some time, the new loom marked the beginning of cloth manufacture in the professional weaver's workshop. Rashi of Troyes (1040-1105) illustrates this when he distinguishes between 'the loom of [professional] weavers who weave by foot' (treadles) and 'the loom used by women' which has a 'rod that goes up and down' (sword-beater).[248]

It is in the towns, with their ready market for cloth, that we first hear of this new breed of textile workers, banded together in associations. By 1129-30 Lincoln had its weavers' gild[249] and by Henry II's reign there were others at London, York, Winchester, Oxford, Huntingdon and Nottingham, with a gild of fullers at Winchester.[250] These early gilds were paying the king for a monopoly in their craft over the surrounding district. However, regulations of later years show that gild members were also collecting together for feasts and pageants and were attempting to control the techniques of manufacture and the terms of apprenticeship.[251]

241  D. King, 'The Textiles', in H.G. Ramm, 'The Tombs of Archbishops Walter de Gray and Godfrey de Ludham in York Minster', *Archaeologia*, ciii (1971), 127-9.

242  E. Crowfoot, 'Textiles from the Tomb of Abbot Roger II and Abbot Dygon', A.M. Lab. Report No. 2793 (unpublished); E. Crowfoot, 'Textiles', in J.C. Thorn, 'Burial of John Dygon, Abbot of St. Augustine's', in A. Detsicas (ed.), *Collectanea Historica: Essays in Memory of Stuart Rigold* (1983), 81-3.

243  Dale, op. cit. note 34.

244  P. Walton, 'The Textiles', in P. Armstrong, 'Excavations in High Street and Blackfriargate, Hull', *East Riding Archaeologist*, viii (Hull Old Town Series) (forthcoming).

245  P. Walton, 'Textiles from 16-22 Coppergate', *Archaeology of York*, 17.5 (1989).

246  Ibid.; Pritchard, op. cit. note 160.

247  Experiments suggest that the horizontal loom was six times as fast the warp-weighted: A. Nahlik, *Tkaniny wsi Wschodnioeuropejskiej X-XIII w.* (Acta Arch. Lódziensia xiii, Lódz 1965), 100.

248  The Babylonian Talmud, Tractat Shabbat 105a, discussed by Carus-Wilson, op. cit. note 179, 165.

249  *Pipe Roll 31 Henry I*, 109.

250  *Pipe Roll II Henry II*, 46 and *12 Henry II*, 117; see also E. Miller, 'The Fortunes of the English Textile Industry during the 13th Century', *Econ. Hist. Rev.* 2nd ser. xviii (1965), 68-70.

251  *Lib. Cust.* op. cit. note 18, 122 ff; *English Gilds*, op. cit. note 91, passim; see also E. Lipson, *Woollen and Worsted Industries* (1921), 27-35.

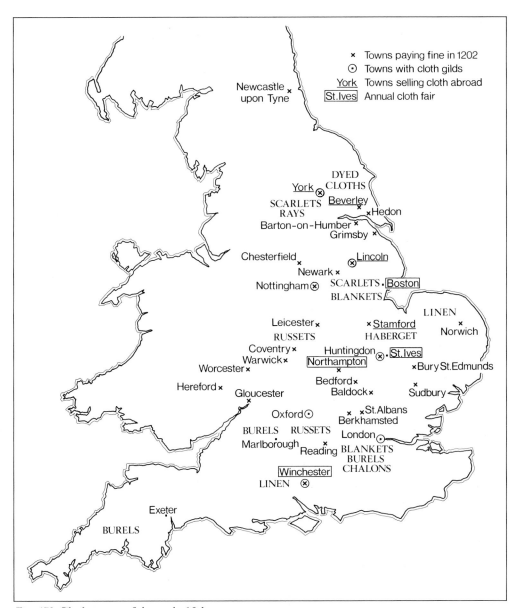

*Fig. 179* Cloth towns of the early 13th century.

Although documents tell us most about the royal boroughs, the cloth trade was evidently also important to many other towns, with or without gilds: for example, Newcastle, Leicester and several others were paying fines in 1202 to avoid complying with the regulations concerning the size of cloth (Fig. 179).[252] Nor was cloth

252 *Pipe Roll 4 John*, p. xx.

production confined to towns. By the 13th century many districts had a weaver, fuller or dyer who was either independent or attached to a manor.[253] Even in a largely rural county such as Northumberland, there were clothworkers of all sorts dotted about among the villages.[254] Although some of the products of this rural industry may have been reaching the towns,[255] they seem largely geared towards the needs of the local village communities.

The best-quality fabrics were produced in the York-Lincoln-Stamford region, close to the supply of fine Lindsey wool, in an area with well-established trade contacts with the Continent.[256] Their most famous product was scarlet, but York, Beverley and other East Riding towns were also making 'dyed and rayed' cloth;[257] Lincoln sold blanket and say,[258] while Stamford made blanket and haberget.[259] By the mid 13th century a significant number of these cloths were circulating in the markets of northern Italy, the Iberian peninsula and Germany,[260] although the volume of English export was not to be compared with that of the major producers in Flanders and northern France.

Cheaper cloths were also being produced for inland trade: for example, burels were made at Winchester and London, and russets at Colchester, Oxford and Leicester.[261] At the same time, Guildford and Winchester were weaving coverlets and hangings (chalons).[262]

Although wool cloth is the better-documented, the linen industry can also be glimpsed in town and country. In the 12th century Winchester had a linen market and a century later a church called St. Mary of the Linen Cloth.[263] Wilton seems to have been another important centre, importing foreign flax and selling fine linen to the royal household.[264] A metrical list of the 13th century also mentions 'Linen cloth of Aylsham' along with 'Coverchief of Shaftesbury', 'Wimple of Lewes' and 'Cambric of Bridport'.[265]

At Norwich in the early 14th century there were seven linen-drapers, whose by-names confirm that there was a linen-weaving area to the north of the town in the Aylsham district.[266] Linens called Aylshams were also being traded in North Yorkshire at this time.[267] Indeed in the 13th and 14th centuries flax, hemp and linen of all sorts were regularly exchanged in the markets of the North-East.[268]

253 Abbeys such as Laleham and Beaulieu built their own looms and employed their own weavers.

254 *Northumberland Assize Rolls* (Surtees Soc., lxxxvii, 1890), passim.

255 In the 12th century Newcastle burgesses were buying in cloth for dyeing: *Eng. Hist. Docs. (1042-1189)*, No. 298.

256 Lloyd, op. cit. note 3, 4.

257 *V.C.H. Yorks*, iv, 407.

258 Salzman, *Industries*, 198.

259 Ibid. 199.

260 P. Chorley, 'Thirteenth-Century Cloth Exports', *Historical Research*, lxi, No. 144

(1988), 1-10; see also Heaton, op. cit. note 166, 4: Carus-Wilson, op. cit. note 179, 151; F. Hill, *Med. Lincoln*, 325.

261 Salzman, *Industries*, 198-9; *Eng. Hist. Docs. (1189-1327)*, 881.

262 Furley op. cit. note 81, 28-9. *Eng. Hist. Docs. (1189-1327)*, 883.

263 Biddle, op. cit. note 127, 435.

264 Salzman, *Industries*, 239.

265 *Eng. Hist. Docs. (1189-1327)*, 882-3.

266 Kelly et al., op. cit. note 95, 24.

267 C.M. Fraser, 'Pattern of Trade in N.E. England', *Northern History*, iv (1969), 66.

268 Ibid. 46.

*Fig. 180* Cloth-making districts *c.* 1500 (from Bowden 1962).

## Siting and Organisation of the Industry: 14th to 16th centuries

As far as wool cloth is concerned, the 13th-century picture of widespread rural weaving for local needs, but urban production for long-distance trade, was to alter radically in the 14th and 15th centuries. The overall output was to increase, and it was in the countryside that the next phase of expansion was to be felt most.

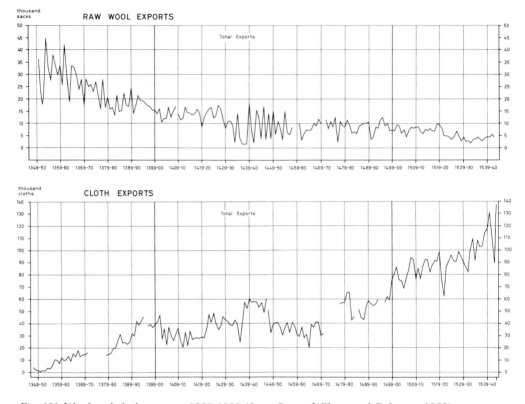

*Fig. 181* Wool and cloth exports, 1350-1550 (from Carus-Wilson and Coleman 1963).

In the 12th and 13th centuries the bulk of England's exports had been in raw wool, bought mainly by Flemings.[269] However, strained relations between England and France as well as the King's financial needs led to an export tax on wool in 1275.[270] This was increased in following years and followed in 1326 by a temporary prohibition on the import of foreign cloth and a ban on the export of raw materials such as madder and teasels.[271] Whatever the political intentions of these acts, they fostered the home cloth industry at the expense of the most important rival, Flanders.

At the same time Flanders was suffering political disturbances, causing interruption in her own cloth production.[272] The Flemish refugees who were actively encouraged to come to England at this time[273] may have brought with them new techniques such as the striped weave described above (Fig. 178b). At any rate, by

269  Lloyd, op. cit. note 3, 6-24.
270  *Eng. Hist. Docs. (1189-1327)*, 410.
271  Ibid. 469, 473-7, 488, 544-7.

272  Carus-Wilson, op. cit. note 117, 398-407.
273  Ibid. 414-15.

the mid 1360s English cloth had ousted foreign goods from the home market. English wool was now increasingly channelled into native-made cloth. As wool exports decreased, cloth exports recovered from a late 13th-century decline and started on an upward climb which was to continue into the 16th century (Fig. 181).[274]

Nonetheless, in the 14th century there were several complaints from towns such as Lincoln, Leicester and Northampton that their clothworkers had declined to a fraction of their number in the previous century.[275] Other towns such as York, Winchester and Oxford had not been making their gild payment to the crown for some time.[276] At first sight it would appear that urban cloth production was sadly in decline. Yet an Exchequer enquiry at Lincoln in 1348 showed that although there were few gildsmen in the town, there were plenty of weavers who either could not or would not pay the gild fee.[277] As A.R. Bridbury suggests, the crisis in town cloth production may not have been a lack of trade but rather a failure of the gilds to enforce their authority.[278]

Whatever the facts of this supposed urban decline, there can be little doubt that the countryside was now playing a far larger role than formerly in the production of cloth for trade. The place-names attached to cloths were now Tauntons, Bridgwaters, Coggeshalls, Kendals, northerns and westerns – quite different from the pre-14th-century names of cloths.

Professor Carus-Wilson has related this rise in rural clothmaking to the arrival of the fulling-mill, which seems to have found its place more readily in the north and west of the country.[279] In fact, there is no technological reason why such mills should not have been built on the slower-moving rivers of the eastern plain,[280] but the high cost of riverside space in towns may have been a factor. Moreover, the towns which resisted the coming of the fulling-mill may have been attempting to preserve the quality of their products made with the more laborious hand- or foot-fulling.

Surviving examples of textiles indicate that there was an increase in cloth-finishing, especially by teaselling, in the later medieval period. This meant that slight flaws and irregularities in the weaving were more readily obscured, and thus the skills of the carefully-trained gild weavers were no longer of such critical importance. As exports rose, the merchants' demand for large quantities of medium-quality cloth could now be met by rural weavers, whose living expenses, and consequently products, were comparatively cheap. The lord mayor of York put the matter clearly when he said that in West Yorkshire they had 'kine, fire and other relief good and cheap which is in this city very dear and wanting'.[281]

One of the major clothworking regions was now the Gloucestershire-Wiltshire-

274 E.M. Carus-Wilson and O. Coleman, *England's Export Trade, 1275-1547* (1963), 122-3, 138-9.
275 Salzman, *Industries*, 202.
276 Miller, op. cit. note 250, 69-70.
277 Hill, op. cit. note 260, 326-7.
278 Bridbury, op. cit. note 82, 31.

279 Carus-Wilson, op. cit. note 92, 194 ff.
280 Bridbury, op. cit. note 82, 19-21.
281 D.M. Palliser, 'York under the Tudors: The Trading Life of the Northern Capital', in A. Everitt (ed.), *Perspectives in English Urban History* (1973), 44.

Somerset area, with prominent centres at Castlecombe and Stroudwater.[282] This region could draw on the fine wools of the Welsh borders and the good carding wools of the Cotswolds and the Downs.[283] The trade was organised by clothiers who would buy the wool, give it out for spinning, take the yarn to the weavers, and then arrange for the cloth to be finished.[284] Some more affluent clothiers might have looms and fulling-mills of their own.[285] With the clothiers' capital to back them, the craftsmen were able to work large cloths and devote time to their careful finishing. The products of this region were therefore the finest-quality broadcloth. The main area for linen weaving at the same time seems to have moved further north, Shrewsbury acting as a centre for the whole of the Shropshire-Herefordshire linen trade.[286]

In West Yorkshire and Lancashire the picture was quite different.[287] Here there were small family units buying wool and then spinning and weaving it up for sale at the following week's market. Fulling might be carried out at the local landowner's mill. Cloth production was part-time work, alongside farming and other household tasks, and as capital was small only short cloths, kersies and dozens, were produced.[288] The raw material was poor and the Yorkshire products were therefore coarse and cheap. Knitting for trade was also practised in the cottages of the Yorkshire Dales in the 16th century.[289]

Another important area existed in Suffolk and Essex.[290] As in the West of England the craftsmen were backed by capital, and dynasties of wealthy clothiers, such as the Paycocks of Coggeshall, the Springs of Lavenham and the Webbs of Dedham, were founded in the 15th century. This region had a reputation for good workmanship, but mainly produced undyed cloth for finishing elsewhere. Indeed, by the 16th century, much of England's broadcloth production (one contemporary commentator put the figure at 150,000 cloths per year)[291] was being sent abroad to be dyed and finished.

In Norfolk the local longwools went into the worsted industry which had been established there since the early 14th century.[292] By 1547 it could be claimed that almost all the poor inhabitants of Norfolk and Norwich gained their living by spinning wool 'upon the rock into yarn',[293] although linen production was also important.[294] An influx of foreign weavers into this area probably introduced new techniques[295] and by the end of the 16th century Norwich was making complex patterned fabrics both in linen and in wool.[296]

282  K.G. Ponting, 'The West of England Cloth Industry', *Wool Text. Ind.*, 235-47; *V.C.H. Wilts*. iv, 121f, 128f.

283  Bowden, op. cit. note 17, 27-33, 45-50.

284  Carus-Wilson, op. cit. note 103, 114.

285  *Eng. Hist. Docs. (1327-1485)*, No. 588; *Eng. Hist. Docs. (1485-1558)*, No. 148.

286  *Eng. Hist. Docs. (1327-1485)*, 1094-5.

287  Heaton, op. cit. note 166; M.T. Wild, 'The Yorkshire Wool Textile Industry', *Wool Text. Ind.*, 185-234.

288  Bowden, op. cit. note 17, 54-6.

289  Hartley and Ingilby, op. cit. note 214.

290  J.E. Pilgrim, 'The Cloth Industry in East Anglia', *Wool Text. Ind.*, 252-68; *V.C.H. Essex*, ii, 381 ff.; *V.C.H. Suffolk*, ii, 254-5.

291  William Cholmeley: Bolton, op. cit. note 114, lxxiv, 18.

292  Pilgrim, op. cit. note 290, 265-7; Beck, *Draper's Dict.*, 373-6.

293  *Eng. Hist. Docs. (1485-1558)*, 998-9.

294  Kelly et al., op. cit. note 95, 24-5.

295  Pilgrim, art. cit. note 290, 265.

296  Beck, *Draper's Dict.*, 99-100, 373-6.

Other areas of manufacture included the South-West peninsula in an area focussed on Exeter, where medium-quality kersies and dozens were produced.[297] The coarse wools of Wales were woven into friezes and cottons, especially in the Pembrokeshire-Monmouthshire region.[298] In the North-West there were also Kendals and other woollens.[299] Linens continued to be made in the North-East, Newcastle giving its name to one particular type of canvas;[300] York for a while had its own gild of linen-weavers[301] and Nottingham also had linen looms and linen-weavers.[302]

As the making of standard fabrics moved out into the countryside, the towns with their tradition of craft skills began to concentrate on the more valuable textiles requiring greater skill in production. At Salisbury rays were a speciality[303] and at Winchester[304] and York[305] hangings and coverlets continued to be made long after woollen weaving had declined. The pattern-weaving of Norwich has already been mentioned and London of course had its embroiderers and silkworkers.

By the mid 16th century England was established as a major European producer of woollen cloth, exporting undyed undressed goods to Italy and the Low Countries, and kersies and other woollens to Poland, Holland, Germany and Hungary. English kersies were even being taken as far as Turkey by Italian merchants.[306] Yet the market on the continent was beginning to change, as, at the dictates of fashion, light worsteds were beginning to replace woollens: by the end of the century these 'new draperies' had established themselves in England. However, the way in which the English weavers, clothiers and merchants adapted to meet this change in demand belongs to another chapter in the cloth industry's history.

## Further Reading

M.L. Ryder, *Sheep and Man* (1983) includes an exhaustive survey of medieval sheep-farming and wools; P. Baines, *Spinning Wheels: Spinners and Spinning* (1977) has a detailed and scholarly account of fibre preparation and spinning techniques. Similarly thorough works on weaving, dyeing and cloth-finishing have yet to be written, although L.F. Salzman's *English Industries of the Middle Ages* (2nd edn. 1923) still contains the largest collection of documentary references on the subject.

Of archaeological finds of medieval textiles, little has as yet been published. However H. Bennett's study of the textiles from medieval Perth and E. Crowfoot's analysis of the textiles from Baynards Castle in London both promise to add conisderably more to the data already published in P. Walton, 'Textiles from Newcastle upon Tyne', *Archaeologia Aeliana* 5th ser. lx (1981), and F. Pritchard, 'Late

297 Ponting, op. cit. note 282, 242.
298 J.G. Jenkins, 'The Welsh Woollen Industry', *Wool Text. Ind.*, 281-4.
299 Bowden, op. cit. note 17, 56.
300 Canvas called newcastell: 'Rates of London Custom', 5.
301 *York Civic Records*, iii, 65, 112.
302 *V.C.H. Notts.* ii, 345.
303 Bridbury, op. cit. note 82, 68-9.
304 Woodger, 'Burel Weaver', passim.
305 *York Civic Records*, iv, 92.
306 Salzman, *English Trade*, 345-8.

Saxon Textiles from the City of London', *Med. Arch.* xxviii (1984). Surviving examples of embroidery are illustrated in several books such as A.G.I. Christie's *English Mediaeval Embroidery* (1938) and D. King's *Opus Anglicanum* (Exhibition Cat., Arts Council 1963).

The economic aspects of the medieval textile industry have of course received much greater attention. E. Carus-Wilson's contribution to the *Cambridge Economic History of Europe* is a standard work and her essays for *The Economic History Review*, etc, partly collected together in *Medieval Merchant Venturers* (2nd edn. 1967) are essential reading. More recent accounts include E. Miller, 'The English Textile Industry in the 13th Century', *Econ. Hist. Rev.* 2nd ser. xviii (1965), and a particularly stimulating work by A.R. Bridbury, *Medieval English Clothmaking* (1982). Regional studies include K.G. Ponting, *The Woollen Industry of South-West England* (1971), H. Heaton, *Yorkshire Woollen and Worsted Industries* (1920), and the individual essays in J.G. Jenkins (ed.), *The Wool Textile Industry of Great Britain* (1972) and in the *Victoria County Histories*.

# 14

# Antler, Bone and Horn

## ARTHUR MACGREGOR

Industries based on the skeletal elements of mammals – bone and antler – might reasonably be expected to share much in common with those relying on horn, supplied to medieval Europe from the carcasses of cattle, sheep and goats.[1] In practice, however, no such relationship can be established: the personnel involved, their sources of supply and their working methods were for the most part quite distinct. Evidence in support of this proposition, although patchy and diverse, is none the less compelling. In this chapter a consideration of the early character of each of these industries will be attempted, followed by an assessment of their output and relative importance in the medieval period.

### The Pre-Conquest Antler Industry

Although antlers are no more than bony outgrowths of deer skeletons, it is worth maintaining here the distinction between antlers and skeletal bone for two reasons: in the first instance, there is ample evidence to demonstrate widespread discrimination in favour of red deer antler by manufacturers up to the time of the Conquest,[2] and, secondly, the supply mechanisms necessary to support an industry based on antler were different from those required to maintain one using bone.

In the matter of supply, a certain amount of antler would have been available for manufacture from slaughtered carcasses. Hunting was, however, a jealously guarded privilege in England throughout much of our period; hence supplies of antler from the chase would have been restricted in availability, disposal being channelled through the noble households.[3] The presence of deer bones amongst

1 For a summary account of the biological differences between antler, bone and horn see A. MacGregor, *Bone, Antler, Ivory and Horn: the Technology of Skeletal Materials since the Roman Period* (1985).

2 Red deer was the only species whose antlers were utilised consistently in medieval England. Remarks made here concerning antler refer specifically to red deer.

3 Even by the late Saxon period there is evidence of extensive restriction on hunting; 31 deer

parks in nine separate counties are mentioned in Domesday Book. On the Continent some evidence has been found to suggest a relationship between the emergence of certain 'schools' of antler workers and the presence of identifiable noble seats; see Z. Kurnatowska, 'Hornworking in Mediaeval Poland', in *La Formation et le Développement des Métiers au Moyen Age (Vᵉ-XIVᵉ Siècles)*, ed. L. Gerevich (Budapest, 1977), 123-4.

urban food refuse indicates that some venison did filter through to the general populace, but the quantities involved were always small and any accompanying antler would still have been inadequate in volume to support a viable industry.

These considerations are in any case rendered less important by the fact that the bulk of the utilised material came not from dead animals but from antlers shed naturally in the wild. Wherever analyses have been carried out on large assemblages of antlers of *c.*10th- to 11th-century date, shed specimens have invariably predominated by a significant proportion.[4] Acquisition of naturally-shed antlers clearly involved means quite different from those entailed in the industrial consumption of food refuse. Antler gathering would have been to some extent a seasonal activity and the need to search over a wide terrain, much of it forested or overgrown, would have made it uneconomical for those involved in manufacture to collect their own raw materials. More probably, antlers would have been picked up by those whose everyday life took them into such areas – foresters, herders, and the like – and would later have been exchanged or sold.[5]

In considering the organisation of the pre-Conquest antler industry in England we have to rely on conclusions reached on the basis of more extensive continental evidence. Amongst even the most productive of continental sites it has long been recognised that the volume of industrial output (as represented by offcuts and other waste material from industrial activity) was insufficient at any time up to and including the Viking period to indicate full-time long-term manufacturing. Until recent years this situation was usually explained by the assumption that, until the advent of urban centres sufficiently populous to support full-time craftsmen, the needs of individual communities were met by workers who combined antler working with some other pursuit. Lately, however, an alternative and more convincing explanation has been gaining ground: in this hypothesis the antler workers (and more specifically those making antler combs) are seen as having been engaged in full-time manufacture for several centuries before the development of urbanised society, but as spending part of each year in an itinerant way of life owing to the dispersed nature of their markets.[6]

In England no site (or series of sites) yet excavated has proved rich enough to

4    See for example, A. MacGregor, 'Industry and Commerce in Anglo-Scandinavian York', in R.A. Hall (ed.), *Viking Age York and the North*, (Council for British Archaeology Research Report 27, 1978), 46. Similar evidence is widespread on the continent: the proportion was 3:1 in favour of shed antler at Wolin in Poland (D. Müller-Using, 'Über die früh-mittelalterlichen Geweihreste von Wollin', *Säugetierkundliche Mitteilungen*, i (1953), 64-7) and 4:1 at Ribe in Jutland (K. Ambrosiani, *Viking Age Combs, Comb Making and Comb Makers in the Light of Finds from Birka and Ribe* (Stockholm, 1981), 99).

5    Analyses of raw material and manufacturing

waste from Continental sites have shown that antlers were in some instances traded over considerable distances before being utilised. For further discussion of these factors see MacGregor, *Bone, Antler, Ivory and Horn*, 32-8.

6    Ambrosiani, *Viking Age Combs*, passim; A. Christophersen, 'Raw Material, Resources and Production Capacity in Early Medieval Comb Manufacture in Lund', *Meddelanden från Lunds Universitets Historiska Museum*, new ser. iii (1980), 150-65; idem, *Håndverket i Forandring. Studier i Horn- og Beinhåndverkets Utvikling i Lund, ca. 1000-1350* (Acta Archaeologica Lundensia, 4° ser. xiii, Lund, 1980), passim.

provide a basis for similar analyses. For the moment it may simply be said that such evidence as there is seems entirely alike in character to that from the more productive contemporary settlements on the Continent.

This similarity of character is important, for it justifies the application to English finds of conclusions based on seemingly remote evidence. Throughout northern Europe the same practices and routines in antler working can be detected again and again, with only small variations of style in the finished products – a consistency which may have been promoted by the diffusing influences of itinerant production. Nowhere have these systematic and exhaustive methods of utilisation been more convincingly demonstrated than at Hedeby in Schleswig-Holstein where, in a study of over a quarter of a million fragments and finished products of antler, Ulbricht was able to reduce the bulk of the evidence to schematic form (Fig. 182).[7]

The antler-worker's tool-kit, as revealed by traces of working on finished products and on waste materials generated by the industry, was a simple one. Saws, varying in size according to the task in hand, were used at every stage. Double-bladed saws were used for cutting decorative incisions on the side-plates of combs and very likely were also used in cutting the teeth, in order to achieve even spacing; a double-bladed saw or *stadda*[8] was a standard item in the tool kits of comb-makers up to the 19th century. Axes were used for less delicate cutting operations and evidence has been found for the use of wedges in splitting up antler beams. Knives were also used in shaping routines, and draw-knives played an important role in shaving antler blanks into the required shapes for tooth-plates and the like. Files appear from working traces to have been more widely used than the paucity of surviving examples might suggest. A range of mineral and organic substances no doubt served for the final stages of smoothing and polishing, although their use is more easily suggested than demonstrated. Scribers embodying a cutting tooth rotating at a fixed radius about a centre point would have been used to produce incised ring-and-dot motifs and the drills used by antler-workers no doubt operated on the same centre-bit principle. A few items show by their regular outlines that lathes were occasionally used.

The craftman's sensitivity to the nature of his material is clearly demonstrated in the manufacture of composite combs, which accounted for the bulk of the output of the antler industry. The fact that for comb-making antler was used at all, in preference to the more readily available animal bone, demonstrates an appreciation of the mechanical superority of antler – a superiority which has been confirmed only recently by objective scientific methods.[9] Likewise the rationale behind the design of

7    I. Ulbricht, *Die Geweihverarbeitung in Haithabu* (Die Ausgrabungen in Haithabu, 7, Neumünster, 1978), 25-32. I am grateful to Dr. Ulbricht for discussing the Hedeby material with me and for allowing me to reproduce her diagram here.

8    The *O.E.D.* cites a description of 1846 thus: 'The comb-cutter's double saw . . . is called a *stadda*, and has two blades so contrived as to

give, with great facility and exactness, the intervals between the teeth of combs.' For an illustration see MacGregor, *Bone, Antler, Ivory and Horn*, Fig. 33.

9    A. MacGregor and J. Currey, 'Mechanical Properties as Conditioning Factors in the Bone and Antler Industry of the 3rd to 13th century AD', *Jnl. of Arch. Science*, x (1983), 71-7.

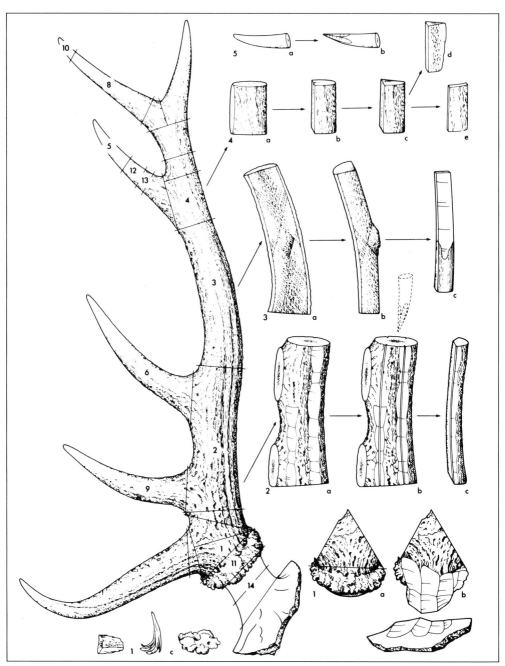

*Fig. 182* Schematic representation of methods of cutting and utilising antler (after Ulbricht). The left half of the figure illustrates the way in which antlers at Hedeby were most commonly dissected, while the right half shows some of the principal products (and offcuts) generated by the industry. Many parts of the antler were used in comb-making (1-6); composite combs were produced from them in a number of well-defined stages (7). Other parts were used in the manufacture of various smaller items (8-15).

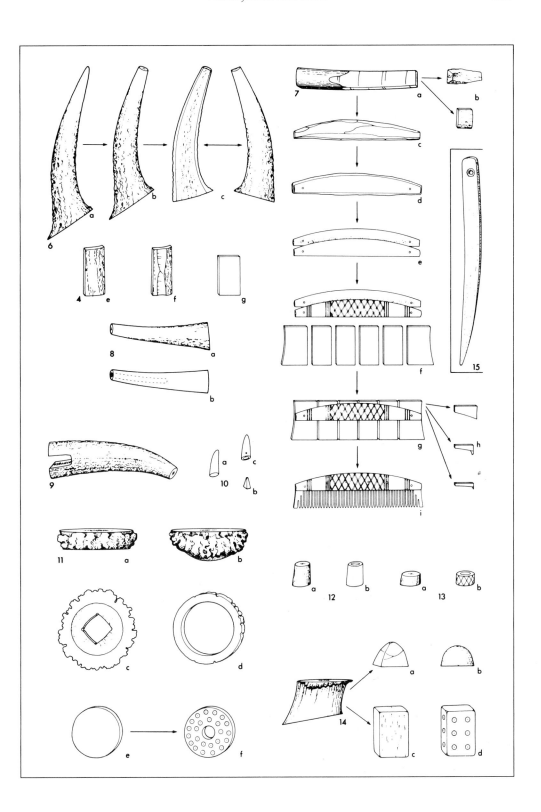

these combs (Fig. 183b) has been shown to reflect a highly evolved appreciation of the raw material. Matching cases produced for these combs provided protection for the teeth in an elegant and pleasing manner.

Amongst the other items produced by this industry were dice and playing pieces. The demand for these items was met by utilising solid tissue from the basal area of the antler, which played no part in comb making. Further items made from the same solid part of the antler (although these are rare) include sword pommels and guards (Fig. 183d), while the tines provided a natural source of implement handles (Fig. 183h).

All of these factors – the evidence for systematic collection and working of raw material with a standardised tool-kit and a range of specific skills – suggest that the pre-Norman antler industry gave employment to specialist craftsmen who concentrated on working this one material into a range of products, practising their trade initially on an itinerant basis but becoming progressively more sedentary as centres of population capable of supporting their activities gradually developed.

### The Pre-Conquest Bone Industry

To the late Saxon craftsman, bone was potentially a more accessible raw material than antler. That bones were not more commonly utilised at that time is a reflection of the mechanical superiority of antler. Some regularly utilised bones could have been supplied by slaughterers or butchers: prolonged cooking of bones has a deleterious effect on their mechanical properties (by leaching out collagen) as well as on their appearance, so that the butcher's shop would have represented to the manufacturer a more fruitful source of raw material than the kitchen.[10] For the lower limbs (particularly the metapodials of cattle and horses) which feature so strongly among the utilised bones, the same source is possible, but it has been suggested that skinners and tanners may also have formed important links in the supply chain.[11] The bones of large cetaceans (whales) provided raw material for certain items. These are most numerously represented around the 10th to 12th centuries, that is to say, at the time when Scandinavian intercourse brought England most directly into contact with more northerly latitudes.[12] Although size alone ensures that these are among the most impressive objects made in bone (Figs. 183a, 184), supplies in England

10   In early medieval Schleswig, however, Ingrid Ulbricht (*Die Verarbeitung von Knochen, Geweih und Horn im mittelalterlichen Schleswig* (Ausgrabungen in Schleswig, Berichte und Studien, 3, Neumünster, 1984), 18) has found evidence that certain utilised bones may have been boiled to rid them of their flesh and fat, supporting the assertion of L.E. Andés (*Bearbeitung des Horns, Elfenbeins, Schildplatts, der Knochen und Perlmutter* (Leipzig and Vienna, 1925), 157ff.) that defatting would have been necessary in order to produce articles of shining white bone.

11   See MacGregor, *Bone, Antler, Ivory and Horn*, 30. Barbara Noddle ('A Comparison of the Animal

Bones from 8 Medieval Sites in Southern Britain', in A.T. Clason (ed.), *Archaeozoological Studies* (Amsterdam, etc., 1975), 257) finds later evidence that tanners played a key role in the animal trade in 18th-century Norfolk. However, a cursory search of the records of the Butchers' Company and the Skinners' Company of London has failed to reveal any indication that either gild took special account of bones in the medieval period.

12   On the natural distribution of whales and the availability of their carcasses for utilisation, see MacGregor, *Bone, Antler, Ivory and Horn*, 31-2.

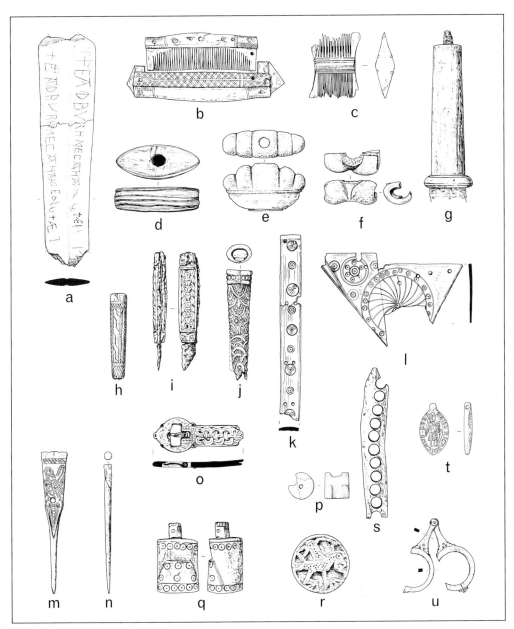

*Fig. 183* Products of the bone and antler industries. *a* cetacean bone weaving-sword (inscribed), Wallingford; *b* antler composite comb and case, York; *c* bone comb, Oxford; *d* antler sword-guard, Lakenheath; *e* cetacean bone sword-pommel, York; *f* bone dagger-guard, Sandal Castle; *g* antler sword-hilt, Oddington; *h* antler handle, Whitby; *i* bone-handled knife, Canterbury; *j* bone handle, London; *k* antler casket-mount, York Minster; *l* bone casket-mount, York Minster; *m* bone pin, London; *n* bone pin, York; *o* bone/antler buckle, Goodmanham; *p* antler crossbow-nut, Goltho; *q* antler chessman, London (?); *r* cetacean bone tableman, London (?); *s* bone waste from button/bead making, London; *t* bone seal-matrix, Old Sarum; *u* bone spectacle-frames, London.

*Fig. 184* Cetacean bone chessman from
Witchampton (Dorset). (*British Museum*)

were too restricted to promote large-scale utilisation on a systematic basis.

Evidence for an exclusively bone-based industry is hard to find in pre-Conquest
England. Saxon Southampton has produced a group of seven rubbish-pits filled with
detached articular ends from cattle metapodials, but without further clues it is
impossible to identify precisely what was being produced from the missing shafts.[13]
At Leadmill Lane in York a refuse pit of Saxo-Norman date was filled with offcuts of
bone, mostly ribs, together with some finished fragments which suggested that comb
cases were being manufactured (and possibly repaired) there.[14] Elsewhere, as at
Lincoln and Northampton,[15] such evidence as has been found for pre-Conquest bone

13  P. Holdsworth, 'Saxon Southampton; a New
    Review', *Med. Arch.* xx (1976), 45. Of the sug-
    gestions made by the excavators, only handle-
    making seems plausible, as has been postula-
    ted on the basis of similar evidence from
    Tudor levels at Baynards Castle, London
    (P. Armitage, 'Studies on the Remains of
    Domestic Livestock from Roman, Medieval
    and Early Modern London: Objectives and
    Methods', in A.R. Hall and H.K. Kenward
    (eds.), *Environmental Archaeology in the Urban
    Context* (C.B.A. Research Rep. 43, 1982), 104).
    Elsewhere, however, similar waste has been
    found to be generated by comb making
    (Ulbricht, *Die Verarbeitung von Knochen, Geweih*

*und Horn*, 18) and by glue making (E. Schmid,
    'Beindrechsler, Hornschnitzer und Leimsieder
    im römischen Augst', in E. Schmid et al. (eds.),
    *Provincialia, Festschrift für Rudolf Laur-Belart*
    (Basle, 1968), 185-98).

14  A MacGregor, 'Anglo-Scandinavian Finds
    from Lloyds Bank, Pavement and other Sites',
    in P.V. Addyman (ed.), *The Archaeology of
    York*, 17 (1982), 94-5, 151-2.

15  J.E. Mann, 'Early Medieval Finds from Flax-
    engate', in M.J. Jones (ed.), *The Archaeology of
    Lincoln*, 14 (1982), 42, 44-5; G.E. Oakley,
    'The Worked Bone', in J.H. Williams, *St.
    Peter's Street Northampton, Excavations 1973-1976*
    (1979), 308.

working has been scattered and small in scale.

Working traces from industrial waste and from finished items are almost equally unhelpful. It is worth mentioning, however, that cutting with a saw is in itself indicative of the use of a somewhat specialised tool-kit and, furthermore, that when saw-cuts are found on waste bone they may be taken as indicators of manufacturing rather than butchering: no evidence has been found for the use of saws by butchers before the 18th century.[16]

Bone was less well suited than antler to the manufacture of composite combs, and only a minority of such combs have elements that prove to be of bone rather than antler. Others have been noted which combine elements of both bone and antler, but their significance (perhaps indicative of no more than temporary shortages of antler) is difficult to assess.

Both bone and antler feature in the manufacture of casket mounts. Two forms are commonly found: flat plates, which may be combined in mosaic form to cover a large surface area and which are generally cut from scapulae (Fig. 183l); and elongated strips, which are sometimes of antler and sometimes of bone, cut either from long bones or from split ribs (Fig. 183k). The strips are arranged parallel to the sides of the casket walls, usually being mitred at the corners; the way in which decorative patterns (usually incised ring-and-dot motifs) are interrupted by the mitred ends shows that the ornament was executed beforehand and without reference to the final dimensions of the casket. Hence there is an implication that the mounts were not made by the casket makers but were supplied to them in bulk by bone and antler workers.

There is of course no scarcity of items of late Saxon and Viking date made of bone, but it may be doubted that the majority are the products of professional bone workers. One of the commonest categories of material, for example, is that associated with textile production – pin-beaters, spindle-whorls and the like – and since the majority of these require no more than shaping with a knife, it seems almost inconceivable that they were not produced by the weavers themselves according to need. The other major category of pre-Norman bonework comprises bone pins. Many of these again seem too rudimentary to indicate any need for professional involvement. Others display more skill, however, suggesting that some part of the market may have been supplied by skilled craftsmen: some Viking-age pins with decorative heads (Fig. 183m-n) may be counted among these. A small number of items such as buckles (Fig. 183o) and cetacean bone pommels (Fig. 183e) might be added to this list of 'professionally made' items, but its validity must be admitted to be extremely dubious owing to the impossibility of distinguishing the work of inspired amateurs from that of full-time workers.

On the evidence given, therefore, we may conclude that there probably were some

---

16   Dr. Philip Armitage, personal communication. See also J. Bourdillon and J. Coy, 'The Animal Bones', in P. Holdsworth, *Excavations at Melbourne Street, Southampton, 1971-76* (C.B.A. Research Rep. 33, 1980), 97.

individuals who specialised in bone working before the Conquest, but that their numbers were limited. Considering the small quantities of material involved, it seems not improbable that the same individuals may also have worked in antler, perhaps even producing most of their output in this medium.

### The Pre-Conquest Horn Industry

Our knowledge of early horn industries is severely limited by the poor survival potential of horn under normal conditions of burial. From the fact that horns had a price placed upon them under Anglo-Saxon law[17] it is clear that they had a quantifiable commercial value. The use of entire horns as drinking vessels or as containers provides the most obvious scope for utilisation, and for this the horn sheath required little more than removal from its bony core before it could be used. The bond between the sheath and its core decays naturally after death to the point where (given time) the sheath can simply be pulled off. In England a lengthy period of soaking has long been held to be a prerequisite of successful horn working (see p.371), a factor which could hardly be reconciled with an itinerant phase in the development of the craft. On the Continent, however, it seems that until recent times little was done to aid removal of the sheath beyond loosening it with a knife around the root, which would allow some degree of itinerant production as at least a theoretical possibility.[18]

As well as being used in their entire form, horns could be utilised in their raw state simply by cutting and shaping, much as one might do with wood. The solid tips of the sheaths provided ideal material for manufacturing into handles and hilts (an opportunity successfully exploited in the complete 7th-century sword-hilt from Cumberland, for example),[19] while the sheath itself could be sawn into narrow scales for handles. The paucity of surviving horn handles might be advanced as an argument against this latter suggestion, but recently a programme of microscopic examination of the corrosion products on Anglo-Saxon knives and swords which have lost their handles due to decay has revealed that considerable numbers of them were indeed originally hafted with horn.[20]

17  According to the Laws of Ine (*c*.688-94) an ox horn was valued at 10*d*. and a cow's horn at 2*d*. (see *English Historical Documents*, *c.500-1042*, ed. D. Whitelock (2nd edn., 1979), 405). Although the values quoted are for damages – the eye of an ox is valued at 5*d*. – the proposition relating to the commercial value of horn may stand.

18  See Andés, op. cit. note 10, 43. The picture drawn by G.B. Hughes (*Living Crafts* (1953), 151-2) is certainly difficult to reconcile with the view presented here and is unsupported by independent evidence: Hughes envisages a time (up to the 17th century) in which 'there were many itinerant horners to take their skill up and down the country', producing 'spoons,

ladles, scoops, and other simple domestic ware from ram horns which they boiled, split and flattened'.

19  MacGregor, op. cit. note 1, 166.

20  See, for example, J. Watson, 'Catalogue of Identified Organic Material', in C. Hills et. al., *The Anglo-Saxon Cemetery at Spong Hill, North Elmham*, Part III: *Catalogue of Inhumations* (East Anglian Arch. Rep. 21, 1984), 158-9. I am grateful to Jacqui Watson of the Ancient Monuments Laboratory of the Historic Buildings and Monuments Commission for discussion of her work in this field, an account of which will be published in *UKIC Occasional Papers*.

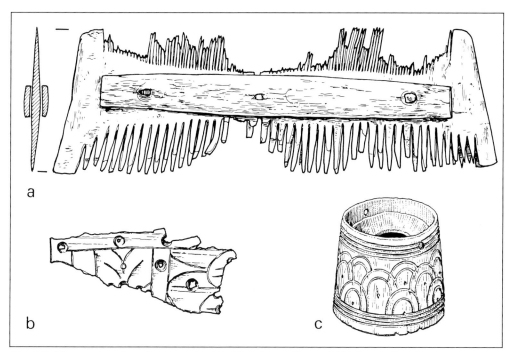

*Fig. 185* Horners' work: *a* horn comb with side-plates of bone, Milk Street, London; *b* casket-mount (?), York; *c* ink-well, London.

A major virtue of horn from the point of view of manufacturing is that it can be rendered plastic, allowing the hollow conical sheath to be opened up, flattened out and worked in sheets (see p.371). Evidence of this technologically more advanced use of horn is harder to find before the Conquest. The 7th-century Benty Grange helmet is judged to have been clad in sheets of horn bent into shape in this manner and gives us the earliest evidence from England for the use of this technique.[21] A horn comb from a 9th- or 10th-century pit at Milk Street in the City of London (Fig. 185a) must have been subjected to a flattening process; it is of an unusual type, having riveted bone side-plates on either side, a feature which may have been intended to prevent warping of the comb at a time when the technique of preparing horn was still imperfectly developed.[22] Thin strips of horn applied as decorative inlay to a 10th-century wooden saddle-bow from York provide a further instance of a technique which may have been widespread but for which little evidence has survived.[23]

In summary, therefore, it may be said that horn was utilised in some quantities before the Conquest and that there are clear signs that the techniques of flattening

21 R. Bruce-Mitford and R. Luscombe, 'The Benty Grange Helmet', in R. Bruce-Mitford (ed.), *Aspects of Anglo-Saxon Archaeology* (1974), 223-42.

22 Only two similar combs have so far been noted, one from York (said to have come from a Roman grave) and the other unstratified from Queen Victoria Street, London: see MacGregor, *Bone, Antler, Ivory and Horn*, 95.

23 R.A. Hall, *The Viking Dig* (1984), 82-3.

horn into sheets had already been developed. As suggested below, however, the horn industry as it developed in post-Conquest England depended upon a settled workplace with adequate space for the processing of large quantities of horn over periods of several weeks. Only with a degree of urbanisation could these preconditions be met.

### Antler and Bone in the Post-Conquest Period

In the centuries immediately following the Conquest far-reaching developments were wrought on the industries outlined above. For the antler workers they were centuries of decline, leading to the extinction of their most characteristic product – the composite comb – by around 1300. In the more amply provided Continental sites (notably at Schleswig)[24] the proportion of shed antler to that from slaughtered deer is markedly reduced at this time and, more significantly, there is a shift away from antler and a corresponding rise in the use of bone. In England large bodies of material capable of forming the basis of similar analyses are again lacking, but antler artefacts are certainly far fewer in number on post-Conquest settlement sites, with bone becoming more prevalent.

There seems to be no single factor that would offer a simple explanation for this change. No decline can be detected in the deer population at this time, although there was a great extension of the laws governing access to the English forests and their resources from the earliest years of Norman rule.[25] Access to the antlers of slaughtered deer would inevitably have become more restricted.

Two documentary references serve to illustrate the considerable value attributed to antler as a raw material for utilisation. The late 12th-century Miracles of St. Cuthbert recount an incident in Lothian in which the carcass of a stag (abandoned by its Norman slayers when it was revealed to have killed a boy after being forced from sanctuary in a churchyard) came to the attention of a skilled servant (*artificiosus minister*) from a nearby estate. This covetous fellow, who specialised in making combs, tablemen, chessmen, dice, pins and other such things from antlers and bones, is said to have rejoiced that with the remains of this one stag he had provided himself with means for plentiful profit. His plans were soon frustrated, however, when his attempts to remove the antlers were foiled by a miraculous flow of blood from the cuts he inflicted on them.[26]

24  Ulbricht, *Die Verarbeitung von Knochen, Geweih und Horn im mittelalterlichen Schleswig*, 73.

25  William I extended controls in England many-fold, as recorded in the *Anglo-Saxon Chronicle*, ed. D. Whitelock (1961) (*sub anno* 1087):
> He made great protection for the game
> And imposed laws for the same,
> That who so slew hart or hind
> Should be made blind.

26  *Reginaldi Monachi Dunelmensis Libellus de Admirandis Beati Cuthberti Virtutibus* . . . (Surtees Soc. i, 1835), cap. lxxxvi-lxxxviii. In the list of items made by the craftsman (*pectinibus, tabulatis, sacaccariis, talis, spiniferis*) only the last named presents problems of translation: the edition quoted above suggests 'spigots' – an unlikely product in antler; an allusion to pins or bodkins with thorn-like tips seems more probable.

A more prosaic reference from the Close Rolls of Henry III demonstrates that even shed antlers were at times regarded as a resource to be husbanded: hence in 1225 a certain Hasculf de Adhelakeston received orders that he should 'make over all the antler beams (*perchias*) which he has at his disposal from our forest which is in his care to Philip Convers the crossbow-maker for the manufacture of crossbow nuts'.[27] The extent to which this arrangement was more widely applied is, however, impossible to gauge.

Progressive urbanisation, with its consequent concentration of food resources and hence of animal bones, may in itself have acted as an incentive in the trend away from antler as a major raw material.

In the production of combs, which remained the major item of manufacture, two developments can be noted. In the first instance there was a move towards the utilisation of bone in the production of composite combs, later types being more commonly found in bone than in antler. More significantly, however, there was also a move away from composite combs altogether, with a new vogue developing for small one-piece combs (Fig. 183c). In conditions of appropriate dampness, similar combs in wood (mostly boxwood) and horn also survive, as well as others in ivory.

Whilst it is possible to argue that composite combs of the pre-Norman period were the products (indeed the principal products) of a well-developed antler industry, post-Conquest combs seem to represent the output of an industry that was essentially product-based. In other words, the characteristic feature of the manufacturers was no longer the raw material they consumed but the goods they produced. Hence comb-making had become a craft whose practitioners might be expected to produce combs in any number of materials but few (if any) other lines. Wood, ivory, bone, antler and horn – the latter supplied in ready-flattened sheets by the horners (see p.373) – might be worked by the same craftsman, the choice of material being determined by the taste and spending-power of the client.[28] A similar process took place in other areas where the antler workers had previously been strongly represented, as for example in the manufacture of knife handles, for which antler tines had been admirably suited. From the records of London's medieval Cutlers' Company, for instance, it appears that from their earliest days their numbers included not only bladesmiths but also a sub-group of hafters who made handles of every material, combining work in bone or ivory (or horn) with metalwork and even with precious materials, according to demand.[29] The successful operation of their monopoly depended not on their exploitation of a single material but on their

27  *Rotuli Litterarum Clausarum*, ed. T.D. Hardy (1844), ii, 50.

28  There appears to be no mention of materials in the Royal Charter granted to the London Combmakers in 1635 (Guildhall Library, London, MS 5415). While it is difficult to guess at the antiquity of this arrangement the archaeological evidence suggests that its origins lay as early as the Norman period.

29  C. Welch, *History of the Cutlers' Company of London* (1916), i, 19-21. The other branches of the Company encompassed the bladesmiths, the sheathers, and finally the cutlers who assembled and marketed the finished products.

very ability to work and combine a whole range of substances.[30] In any attempt to
evaluate the medieval bone industry in the capital, therefore, the numerous well-
made handles found there (Fig. 183j) must be seen not as testimonies to the well-being
of professional bone workers but as tokens of the success of the cutlers who had
cornered this part of the market.

Sword hilts of bone and antler (Fig. 183f-g) would almost certainly have been
manufactured and fitted to their blades under a comparable arrangement, allowing
little or no scope for a freelance bone or antler worker.

Another branch of the armourer's craft in which antler was commonly utilised was
the manufacture of crossbows, and more specifically in the making of the nut, the
cylindrical element designed to hold and release the string (Fig. 183p).[31] These too
would normally have been lathe-turned and fitted to their cradles in the crossbow-
maker's shop, providing no opportunity for outside enterprise.

The manufacture of playing pieces represented one area in which no particular
craft gild exercised exclusive rights. Discoid tablemen of standardised form make
their appearance around the time of the Conquest (Fig. 183r), the commonest kind
being made from transverse sections cut from antler beams or from discs excised
from bovine or horse jawbones. More elaborate examples feature combinations of
perforated ornament with sheet-metal backing, while a recent find at Gloucester of a
set of bone playing-men in association with a bone-mounted board (Fig. 186) displays
a much higher level of skill.[32] The earliest chessmen (from around the time of the
Conquest) are generally of bone or antler and of simple appearance (Fig. 183q, 184).
Later medieval examples correspond more closely in form with those of today: they
are more delicately and intricately carved than those mentioned above and they are
frequently of ivory. A different basis of production seems to be implied here: the
costly raw materials and finer workmanship speak of a more clearly-defined luxury
market which may well have been supplied largely from the well-developed French
ivory-working centres rather than by home producers (see Appendix).

A trade in buttons and beads of bone is attested by waste material and finished
products from a number of sites. Bone blanks (mostly metapodial fragments) from
which discs have been excised have been found on some of these (Fig. 183s), although
the relatively great thickness of the bone compared with the diameter of the holes
makes it difficult to decide whether the products were destined to be buttons or
beads.[33] Larger discs with central perforations, some of them cut from scapulae, are
more certainly buttons, although the further possibility that both types were

---

30   Evidence for the working of bone (and per-
     haps horn) in association with iron and bronze,
     as found in medieval Worcester, has been
     taken to suggest that knives were being made
     on the site: M.O.H. Carver (ed.), *Medieval
     Worcester: an Archaeological Framework* (*Trans.
     Worcestershire Arch. Soc.* 3rd ser. vii, 1980),
     174.
31   For reference to the collection of antler for the

manufacture of crossbow nuts see p.367. For
crossbows in general see R. Payne-Gallwey,
*The Crossbow* (1903).

32   I.J. Stewart and M.J. Watkins, 'An 11th-Cen-
     tury Bone *Tabula* Set from Gloucester', *Med.
     Arch.* xxviii (1984), 185-90.

33   See MacGregor, *Bone, Antler, Ivory and Horn*,
     99-102.

*Fig. 186* The Gloucester tablemen and board. (*Gloucester Museum and Art Gallery*)

combined in rosaries cannot be excluded.[34]

While these items could have been the products of specialist bone workers there are many others which clearly formed no part of a cohesive bone industry. For example, the seal matrices occasionally found in ivory and even more rarely in bone (Fig. 183t)[35] exhibit all the skills of the specialist die-cutter rather than those of the jobbing bone-worker. Other items requiring less artistic skill were married up with elements in other materials in such a way that a single craftsman must have had overall control. For instance, the 15th-century bone spectacle-frames (Fig. 183u) recovered at Trig Lane in the City of London[36] would almost certainly have been made and fitted to the lenses in the oculist's shop. Similarly, the 15th-century bone tuning-pegs found together with manufacturing evidence at St. Aldates, Oxford, have been interpreted convincingly as representing debris from the workshop of a musical instrument maker rather than that of a bone worker.[37]

34  For evidence for the manufacture of bone rosaries at Saint-Denis see O. Meyer (ed.), *Archéologie Urbaine à Saint-Denis* (Saint-Denis, 1971), section 2.2.1.

35  J. Cherry, 'The Seal Matrix of Richard Cano', *Wiltshire Arch. Magazine*, lxvii (1972), 162-3.

36  M. Rhodes, 'A Pair of Fifteenth-Century Spectacle Frames from the City of London', *Antiq. Jnl.* lxii (1982), 57-73.

37  M. Henig, in B. Durham, 'Archaeological Investigations in St. Aldates, Oxford', *Oxoniensia*, xlii (1977), 163-6.

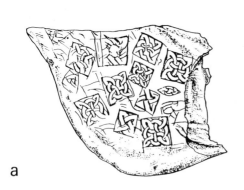

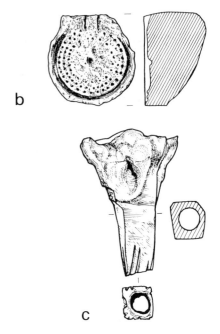

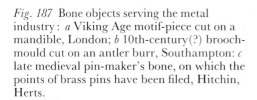

*Fig. 187* Bone objects serving the metal industry: *a* Viking Age motif-piece cut on a mandible, London; *b* 10th-century(?) brooch-mould cut on an antler burr, Southampton: *c* late medieval pin-maker's bone, on which the points of brass pins have been filed, Hitchin, Herts.

Yet other items in the corpus of medieval bone objects are to be seen not as products of a bone industry but as by-products of metalworking: in the early post-Conquest phase these include bone 'motif pieces' (Fig. 187a) and moulds (Fig. 187b)[38] and from the late medieval period pinners' bones on which the makers of brass pins filed the points on their products (Fig. 187c).

And finally there are those artefacts made neither by nor for professionals of any sort. Bone skates, for example, required only a minimum of skill in their preparation and in no instance is there any need to suggest that production was in the hands of any but the final user.[39]

### The Post-Conquest Horner

In contrast to the picture of fragmentation which has been painted above for the bone and antler industries, the horners present an image of successful development during the medieval period, the unity of their craft being recognised by the formation of professional gilds in London and York. Even in those areas where the horners lost control of the production of finished products, their grip on processing the raw material remained secure.

---

38  A. MacGregor, 'A Pre-Conquest Mould of Antler from Medieval Southampton', *Med. Arch.* xxiv (1980), 203-5.

39  A. MacGregor, 'Bone Skates: a Review of the Evidence', *Arch. Jnl.* cxxxiii (1976), 57-74.

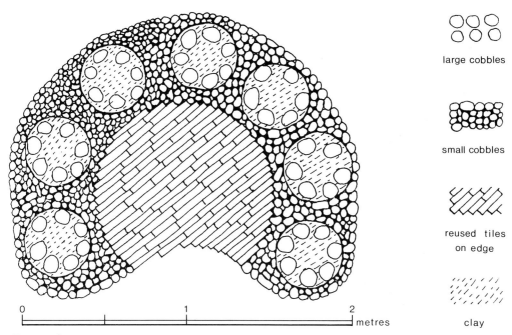

large cobbles

small cobbles

reused tiles
on edge

clay

*Fig. 188* Reconstructed plan of the multiple hearths of a horner's workshop, Hornpot Lane, York.

A considerable amount of information survives to illustrate working practices from this period. The most impressive English find is that made at Hornpot Lane, York: here a shallow clay- and timber-lined pit containing nearly 200 horn-cores (mostly of cattle and goat) was uncovered along with a series of hearths (Fig. 188), the whole complex being interpreted as a horner's workshop.[40] The pits correspond with the soaking pits used by English horners until recent times: horns were steeped in water for a matter of weeks (depending on the ambient temperature) to loosen the sheaths, the tips of which were sometimes removed in advance.[41] The sheaths, either cut into cylindrical sections while still on the core or removed in their entirety, were then slit lengthwise on the inside of the curve and set to boil in a cauldron; on being removed they were held over a fire for a few moments before being prised open with tongs and pressed flat. After some basic scouring and trimming the flattened plates of horn were ready for working into finished items.

On other excavated sites the presence of horn industries has been postulated on the basis of concentrations of waste material in the form of detached horn-cores,

40   Hornpot (Horn-pit) Lane is first recorded as a street name in 1295. For the site see L.P. Wenham, 'Hornpot Lane and the Horners of York', *Annual Rep. Yorkshire Philosophical Soc.* (1964), 23-54; for the bones see M.L. Ryder, 'The Animal Remains from Petergate, York, 1957-58', *Yorkshire Arch. Jnl.* xlii (1970), 418-

28.

41   Removal of the tips promoted the essential process of decay in the tissue connecting the sheath to the *os cornu*. Being made up of solid material, the horn tips could in any case be utilised (e.g. for handles) without further preparation.

usually chopped from the skull with an axe and sometimes showing knife-cuts around the base. At Angel Court in the City of London fifty horn-cores of cattle and fifteen of sheep – many of them sawn into sections – were recovered from a single medieval layer,[42] and at Baynards Castle, also in the City, cattle, sheep and goat horn-cores were well represented in Tudor levels.[43] Quantities of medieval cattle and goat horn-cores have also been recovered at Kingston-on-Thames, Bristol, Exeter, Hereford, Oxford, Coventry and King's Lynn.[44] The main urban centres with their concentrated demand for meat are likely to have attracted most of the horning activity, but the discovery of numerous sheep horn-cores at Ospringe (Kent)[45] suggests that it was not a purely urban pursuit.

Some caution is necessary, however, when postulating the presence of an industry on the evidence of a mere concentration of intact horn-cores. A butcher or, more particularly, a tanner with quantities of horns passing through his hands would have been foolish to discard them when they could have been sold in bulk to supply a horn industry operating even at some distance.[46] If any such long-distance transport were involved, it is not inconceivable that the sheaths might have been removed on the spot to save the unnecessary labour of carting the useless cores. In this context it may be noted that an Act of Parliament of 1465 forbade the export of rough horns from within a 24-mile radius of London until the needs of the London Horners' Company had been satisfied. The same Act extended the right of the Company to search for defective wares from the City as far afield as the fairs at Ely and Stourbridge.[47]

By this time the London Company had reached the zenith of its powers and had evidently come a long way since its earliest surviving ordinances were drawn up in 1391, in which the members described themselves modestly as 'the pour men of the littell crafte of the Horneris'. Amongst the disciplines to which they submitted themselves on that occasion were 'to eschewe anoyawnce and grevaunce . . . by cause of the gret noys that thei maken doyng ther craft', to seek out and destroy any 'fals werkis and deffectis' produced by their brethren and to exclude from their

42  J. Clutton-Brock and P. Armitage, in T.R. Blurton, 'Excavations at Angel Court, Walbrook, 1974', *Trans. London and Middlesex Arch. Soc.* xxviii (1977), 88-97.

43  P.L. Armitage, 'The Mammalian Remains from the Tudor Site of Baynards Castle, London: a Biometrical and Historical Analysis', Ph.D. thesis, University of London, 1977.

44  P.L. Armitage, 'A Preliminary Description of British Cattle from the Late Twelfth to the Early Sixteenth Century', *Ark*, vii (1980), 405-12; B.A. Noddle, art. cit. note 11, 248-60; eadem, 'Mammal Bone', in H. Clarke and A. Carter, *Excavations in King's Lynn, 1963-1970*, (Soc. for Medieval Arch. Monograph VII 1977), 378-99; M. Maltby, *Faunal Studies on Urban Sites: the Animal Bones from Exeter, 1971-1975* (1979), 39; R. Wilson in N. Palmer, 'A Beaker Burial and Medieval Tenements in

The Hamel, Oxford', *Oxoniensia*, xlv (1980), 198; R.E. Chaplin in E. Gooder et al., 'The Walls of Coventry', *Trans. and Proc. Birmingham Arch. Soc.* lxxxi (1964), 130-8.

45  S.M. Wall, 'The Animal Bones from the Excavation of the Hospital of St. Mary of Ospringe', *Archaeologia Cantiana*, xcvi (1980), 227-65.

46  In this context it is interesting to note a complaint of 1465 that 'People of strange Lands' were buying 'the great and chief stuff of English horns unwrought, of Tanners and Butchers', and were carrying it abroad to the detriment of the London horners: Statute 1 Edward IV, c.8.

47  Statute 1 Edward IV, c.8. Some element of ancient practice may be incorporated in the act.

number all 'forreynis'. By 1455 further ordinances were added to strengthen their defences against the 'people of other londes and places' who came yearly to buy horns in London, while at the same time agreeing to banish from within the City 'the grete and corrupt stenche and grevous noyance of neyghbours before tymes caused . . . by bying and cuttyng of greene hornes out of hides within this Citie'.[48]

Outside London, only York provides documentary evidence for the activities of medieval horners. The date of foundation of the York Horners' Gild is unknown, although one Adam de Wederhale is named as a horner in the Freemen's Rolls in 1309.[49] A late copy (*c*.1500) of their ordinances survives, similar in framework to those from London and specifying in addition that a seven-year apprenticeship must be served.[50]

Elsewhere in the provinces there is, as we have seen, a certain amount of archaeological evidence for horn working which suggests that Fisher, the historian of the London Company, may have been over-cautious in his view that the craft was little practised outside the capital.[51]

The London horners' claim in 1455 that their craft was 'not profitely hadd nor conned in any region or place of the world except in this land'[52] seems quite extravagant, and evidence for horning can be found on an number of medieval sites on the Continent.[53] North of the Scottish border, excavations in Perth have produced about 1,500 horn cores, taken to indicate 13th-century occupation of a tenement in the High Street by a horner.[54]

We may speculate for a moment on the nature and extent of the activities which the horners themselves undertook. By the 17th century over 2,000,000 leaves of horn were being exported yearly from London:[55] that is to say, what must have been a large proportion of the horn passing through the horners' hands was simply processed into flat sheets before being sold on to other craftsmen for working into finished products. The greater part of the Company's membership by that time must therefore have been made up of what were known (at least in the later parlance of the trade) as horn pressers or horn breakers.[56] Opening the horn and pressing it into

48   F.J. Fisher, *A Short History of the Worshipful Company of Horners* (1936), 19-22.
49   Wenham, op. cit. note 40, 29.
50   Ibid. 45-6.
51   Fisher, *Short History of the Horners*, 135
52   Ibid. 135.
53   See MacGregor, *Bone, Antler, Ivory and Horn*, 51-2. In addition it may be noted that the *peigniers* and *lanterniers* of Paris listed in Etienne Boileau's *Le Livre des Métiers* were certainly working horn as is shown by one of their ordinances: 'Nus Pigniers ne doit ne ne puet metre cor nuef ne viez en merrien de viez lenternes pour vendre . . .' (*Les Métiers et Corporations de la Ville de Paris, XIII^e Siecle. Le Livre des Métiers d'Etienne Boileau*, ed. R. de Lespinasse and F. Bonnardot, Paris, 1879, 139).

54   N.Q. Bogdan and J.W. Wordsworth, *The Medieval Excavations at the High Street, Perth, 1975-76* (1978), 27. For a further find of horn cores from Perth see *Med. Arch.* xxv (1981), 214-5.
55   Fisher, *Short History of the Horners*, 14.
56   Joseph Collyer, *The Parent's and Guardian's Directory* (1761), distinguishes three types of horn worker: the horner (producing a variety of wares), the button maker, and the horn presser, a trade regarded as requiring 'more strength than ingenuity'. In York the first 'hornebreker' is recorded in 1607; they continued to form a distinct division of the craft until the early years of the present century (Wenham, op. cit. note 40, 49, appendix IIc.).

sheets must always have been regarded as central to the horner's craft and even in the late 17th century the London horners were still seeking to prevent the comb-makers from encroaching on this aspect of their trade.[57]

By 1692 the London horners acknowledged that their trade 'chiefly depends in making lanthorn leaves'.[58] Throughout the medieval period these had formed a mainstay of the industry, although demand increased in the 17th century with the adoption of new patterns of lanterns with multiple panes. After opening and flattening a suitably light-coloured horn in the normal way, lantern leaves were produced by delaminating or splitting the horn into thin sheets, which were then further pressed between well-greased and heated iron plates. The translucency of the leaves could be further improved by smearing them with oil and warming them over a fire.[59] Surviving medieval lanterns are rare, but two examples of *c.* 14th-century date can be seen in the Museum of London, both with their tall horn windows now missing.[60] Excavations at Baynards Castle produced two fragments of pressed horn, tentatively identified as lantern panes, from a 14th-century layer.[61]

Similar leaves were in demand as window-panes throughout much of the medieval period. In the course of the 16th century, however, glass overtook the more traditional medium to the point where a writer in 1580 could record that 'horn in windows is now quite laid down'; the loss of this major market was judged to be one of the principal reasons for the temporary eclipse of the Horners' Company at this time.[62] Another outlet – albeit modest – for pressed horn is represented by a plate with incised decoration found at York, seemingly a fragmentary casket mount (Fig. 185b).

A new demand for leaves which may have helped to soften a little the loss of the window-pane trade came from the increasing use of horn books in schools. Small wooden tablets inscribed with alphabets and syllabaries were commonly used throughout medieval Europe, but from around the mid 15th century a seemingly peculiarly English variant emerged in which the text was printed on a slip of paper, fixed to the tablet and covered with a sheet of translucent horn to protect it.[63] Their vast popularity must have ensured a regular source of income to the horner. The earliest surviving example, in the Museum of London, is of 16th-century date.

The glass industry also made inroads into another of the horner's provinces – the production of drinking vessels. The more impressive medieval examples consisted of entire horns embellished with metal mounts. The surviving vessels have been reviewed by Oman, who found evidence that they had already taken on antiquarian overtones in the medieval period, their use being particularly associated with the

57   Fisher, op. cit. note 48, 6.
58   Ibid. 6.
59   Andés, op. cit. note 10, etc. Up to five leaves are said to have been produced from a single thickness (Hughes, op cit. note 18, 157).
60   London Museum, *Medieval Catalogue* (1954), 185, Fig. 58.

61   Armitage, op. cit. note 13, 102.
62   Fisher, op. cit. note 48, 13.
63   See A.W. Tuer, *History of the Horn Book* (1896). Small panels of translucent horn are also found riveted to the covers of conventional books to protect the gold blocked title lettering.

celebration of ancient custom.[64] More modest drinking vessels in the form of cups and tumblers formed until comparatively recently an important element in the horner's repertoire, although their popularity is again thought to have suffered from the rise of glass in the Tudor period.[65] The production of tumblers would have been true horner's work and is unlikely to have been devolved to a separate craft. The natural curvature of the horn had to be eliminated by heating the sheath and forcing it over a former.[66] Trimming and decorating with incised circumferential lines could be done on the lathe, as could the cutting of an internal groove for the base-plate. This plate, formed by a disc of prepared horn, was slipped into place while the bottom of the tumbler was rendered soft by heating; once cool, the two elements were firmly united. Some horn inkwells (inkhorns) were produced in much the same way: an example from London is illustrated in Fig. 185c;[67] others consisted of entire horns.

Spoon-making is likely to have formed part of the horner's own craft too, since he was well-placed to make the most economical use of his raw material and was well-furnished with the equipment and skills necessary for shaping, heating and moulding the bowls. Knife-handles of horn, on the other hand, are more likely to have been produced in the medieval period by the specialist hafters already mentioned.[68]

Armourers (or rather bowyers) were consumers of horn in the production of springs for composite bows, which in medieval England were limited to crossbows. In 1225, in the reign of Henry III, a certain 'Master Peter the Crossbowmaker' was awarded half a mark for the 'nuts, strings and horn which he bought at our command for the repair of our crossbows at Corfe',[69] and in 1419-20 'horning' was still listed among the processes used in the bowyer's craft.[70]

From these examples it will be clear that the medieval horn industry had two principal aspects. The horners themselves took care of processing the rough horns and probably retained control of those parts of the trade which involved the plastic

---

64   C.C. Oman, 'English Medieval Drinking Horns', *Connoisseur*, xiii (1944), 20-3, 60. Entire horns were still used for a variety of other purposes, including blast horns and money horns, while a tradition of holding property by 'cornage' also survived: for the latter see J.C. Bridge, 'Horns', *Jnl. Architectural, Arch. and Hist. Soc. of Chester and North Wales*, new ser. xi (1904), 85-166.

65   An assertion made by F.J. Fisher (*Short History of the Horners*, 28-36), who blames the same development for the ruin of the [leather] Bottlemakers Company, which was forced to amalgamate with the Horners in 1476. This association may reflect their common source of raw material as well as their common market interest. The Bottlemakers eventually died out, but the association of the two gilds is enshrined in the Horners' arms (argent, three leather bottles sable; on a chevron of the 2nd, 3 hunting horns of the 1st).

66   This process is illustrated by Diderot, *Encyclopédie, ou Dictionnaire Raisonné des Sciences, des Arts et des Métiers*, xxvi (Paris, 1771), *s.v. Tabletier-cornetier*, pl.1.

67   See also London Museum, *Medieval Catalogue*, 292, pl.xc. Amongst the York freemen, one Samuel Fountaine is listed in 1706 as an 'inkhorn maker and comb maker' (Wenham, op. cit. note 40, appendix IIc).

68   In this context it is of interest that in 1415 the York horners joined with the cutlers, blade-smiths, sheathers, scalers [i.e. hafters] and bucklemakers to perform a mystery play, some degree of common interest perhaps being implied by this association; see L.T. Smith, *York Plays. The Plays Performed by the Crafts or Mysteries of York* (1885), p.xxiii.

69   *Rot. Litt. Claus.* ii, 63.

70   J. Raine, *Fabric Rolls of York Minster* (Surtees Soc. xxxv, 1859), 45-6.

moulding of the raw material and the subsequent selling of these wares.[71] On the other hand, the important trade in leaves of flattened horn, although first documented in the 17th century, had its origins in the medieval period, when raw material would have been supplied in this form to other craftsmen such as comb-makers and (after further preparation) to lantern-makers and the purveyors of horn books.

### Antler, Bone and Horn at the End of the Medieval Period

Far-reaching changes had overtaken all of these industries since the late Saxon period. The bone and antler industries had indeed ceased to exist as entities: some utilisation of these materials continued but it was now in the hands of a range of specialist manufacturers tied to the production of specific items rather than to the utilisation of specific materials. The comb-makers, button-makers, knife-hafters and others were all indiscriminate users of these amongst other media. They were also consumers of horn, but the horners had managed to retain command of some elements of their craft and to consolidate their position (in London and York, at least) by the formation of gilds. Crucial to their success was the fact that horn had to pass through a lengthy process of preparation requiring special facilities before it could be used for manufacturing purposes.[72] No doubt they also benefited from the versatility of their medium, which could be cut, filed and polished like bone and antler and could be moulded as well. This feature was to prove their salvation from the 17th century onwards, when horn proved well adapted to rudimentary mass production, so that the surfaces of box-lids and the like could be die-stamped with elaborate designs.

### Appendix: Ivory Working in Medieval England

Although ivories feature prominently in every corpus of English medieval carvings, production was never on a scale approaching industrial proportions.

Two media were utilised: during the Romanesque period walrus ivory was used virtually exclusively, declining from the end of the 12th century in favour of elephant ivory as England's economic links with the Scandinavian north loosened and as increasingly strong ties were formed with France and the rest of the Continental mainland. Elephant ivory was among the exotic materials available there through the important seasonal fairs, and as early as the late 13th century a certain amount

---

71   An important outlet for the London horners' products was provided by the annual Horn Fair at Charlton near Greenwich, granted a charter under Henry III in 1268; a 'great plenty of all sorts of winding horns, cups and other vessels of horn' was bought and sold there up to the mid 17th century, but thereafter it declined and was discontinued in 1768

(see Fisher, op. cit. note 48, 12).

72   Even the 'noysome' nature of these preparative processes may have been to the horners' benefit in the end, for having removed themselves from within range of the offended nostrils of the citizenry, they had also isolated themselves from competition.

was being directly imported to France through the Channel ports.[73]

Throughout the 10th to 12th centuries the bulk of the items produced in England were religious in function and iconography and highly competent in execution. Their manufacture is attributed not to secular workshops but rather to the monastic schools whose individual characters were developed in other media, notably in manuscript illuminations. Hence in a recent review of this material Beckwith was able to identify a large number of ivories with the distinctive styles of Canterbury, Winchester, Dorchester, Hereford, Lincoln, St. Albans and Bury St. Edmunds.[74] Even amongst the ivory tablemen that account for the majority of the secular pieces the influence of the St. Albans school in particular was detectable. Hence in Norman England as in contemporary France[75] the artist-craftsmen who produced crosses, pyxes and plaques for public consumption show a large measure of identity with those who worked within (and largely for) the great monasteries. The few secular ivories of this period include, in addition to the tablemen already mentioned, dice, seal-matrices and combs. The 12th-century chessmen found in the Isle of Lewis, perhaps the best-known of secular pieces, may have been made in England.[76]

Compared to the vast output of later medieval France,[77] England still produced relatively little in the 13th century and later. Amongst the Parisian corporations listed in Étienne Boileau's *Livre des Métiers* (c. 1250)[78] there is none dedicated specifically to the production of carvings in ivory; several crafts, however, are recorded as being users of ivory amongst other materials, including the makers of combs, lanterns, gaming equipment and writing tablets, as well as the *imagiers* and the *patenostriers* whose products included (besides rosary beads) buttons and buckles. In England a similar situation must be envisaged, in which any of the craftsmen who worked in bone, antler and horn might equally make use of ivory in supplying their more affluent clients with combs, chessmen, knife-handles[79] and the like. Hence production was largely dispersed amongst a variety of specialist craftsmen each manufacturing particular products, and there was no concentration of activity in workshops dedicated exclusively to ivory carving. This state of affairs is therefore comparable to that suggested above for the contemporary working of other skeletal materials.

During the 15th and 16th centuries production of religious carvings was reduced even further,[80] a decline reinforced by Reformation distaste for images. Small-scale production of items such as combs and seal-matrices nonetheless survived in a minor

73   R. Koechlin, *Les Ivoires Gothiques Français* 3 vols. (Paris, 1924), i, 29-30.

74   J. Beckwith, *Ivory Carvings in Early Medieval England* (1972).

75   D. Gaborit-Chopin, *Ivoires du Moyen Age* (Fribourg, 1978); Koechlin, op. cit. note 73.

76   Beckwith, *Ivory Carvings*, No. 166.

77   Gaborit-Chopin, op. cit. note 75, and Koechlin, op. cit. note 73, passim.

78   Boileau, *Livre des Métiers*, passim.

79   In this context it is interesting to note that for a time in the mid 15th century the London Cutlers' Company bought ivory in bulk for re-sale to its freemen at a fixed and advantageous rate; the scheme had quickly to be abandoned due to fluctuations in the market price (Welch, *History of the Cutlers' Company*, i, 174).

80   See, for example, M.H. Longhurst, *English Ivories* (1926), 58; P. Williamson, *Medieval Ivory Carvings* (1982), 19.

way throughout this period, until the opening up of direct trade routes in the 17th and 18th centuries brought African and Indian ivory to England in quantities sufficient to support manufacture of a wide range of utilitarian items as well as collectors' pieces for the developing art market.[81]

## *Further Reading*

A general introduction to the raw materials, manufacturing techniques and products of the industries discussed here is given by A. MacGregor, *Bone, Antler, Ivory and Horn: the Technology of Skeletal Materials since the Roman Period* (1985). Apart from this book (with full bibliography), most of the works dealing with the archaeology of these materials are of Continental origin, but are of importance in interpreting the English evidence. The following are particularly recommended: K. Ambrosiani, *Viking Age Combs, Comb Making and Comb Makers in the Light of Finds from Birka and Ribe* (Stockholm, 1981); A. Christophersen, 'Raw Material, Resources and Production Capacity in Early Medieval Comb Manufacture in Lund', *Meddelanden från Lunds Universitets Historiska Museum*, new ser. iii (1980), 150-65; A. St. Clair and E.P. McLachlan (ed.), *The Carver's Art. Medieval Sculpture in Ivory, Bone and Horn* (New Brunswick, 1989); I. Ulbricht, *Die Geweihverarbeitung in Haithabu* (Neumünster, 1978); I. Ulbricht, *Die Verarbeitung von Knochen, Geweih und Horn im mittelalterlichen Schleswig (Ausgrabungen in Schleswig, Berichte und Studien 3)* (Neumünster, 1984); V.T. van Vilsteren, *Het Benen Tijdperk. Gebruiksvoorwerpen van been, gewei, hoorn en ivoor 10.000 jaar geleden tot heden* (Drents Museum 1987).

For the technology of both horn and bone working see L.E. Andés, *Bearbeitung des Horns, Elfenbeins, Schildplatts, der Knochen und Perlmutter* (Leipzig and Vienna, 1925). The history of horning in London is surveyed by F.J. Fisher, *A Short History of the Worshipful Company of Horners* (1936), and in York by L.P. Wenham, 'Hornpot Lane and the Horners of York', *Annual Rep. Yorks. Philosophical Soc.* (1964), 23-54, the latter also containing the reminiscences of a practising horner. A useful survey of the horner's products is given by P. Hardwick, *Discovering Horn* (1981), although most of the items discussed and illustrated are of post-medieval date. Paul Williamson, *Medieval Ivory Carvings* (1982), provides a useful introduction to his subject. John Beckwith, *Ivory Carvings in Early Medieval England* (1972) presents a lavishly illustrated survey of the Romanesque material, while M.H. Longhurst, *English Ivories* (1926), is still the most useful general work on the medieval period. Neil Stratford's summary of 'Gothic Ivory Carving in England', in J.J.G. Alexander and P. Binski (ed.), *Age of Chivalry. Art in Plantagenet England, 1200-1400* (Catalogue of Exhibition, Royal Academy of Arts, 1987), 107-13, appeared after the present chapter had gone to press.

81  I am grateful to Pat Jacobs, who prepared
    drawings specially for this publication.

15

## *Wood*

### JULIAN MUNBY

The use of timber and wood was so widespread in the medieval period that we might justifiably think of it as an age of timber, despite the obvious importance of masonry and the widespread use of iron. For timber, quite apart from its use in roofs and walls, bridges and wharfs, was the major component of vehicles and vessels, and in the machinery of agriculture, industry and war. If more woodwork had survived, its domestic usage might be more prominent than pottery, in utensils, furniture, fittings and gadgets. That this could be so must have been a factor of the low cost and ready availability of the material, the ease with which it could be worked, and the lack of any possible substitute.

With the timber and wood crafts covering so many facets of life, it is impossible to give fair weight to them all, but the principal characteristics of the more important can be outlined.

### *Sources of Wood and Timber*

Woodland was as carefully managed as any agrarian resource, and was usually able to meet the needs of its consumers, although it was supplemented where necessary by imports of specific types.[1] The first overall account of English woodland cover, that of Domesday Book in 1086, has been carefully analysed by Rackham, who shows that a total of 15 per cent of the land may have been wooded (compared with some 5.4 per cent in 1895), and who estimates that this may have been about half the acreage of woodland present in Roman times.[2] The general trend of landscape studies would now put the clearance of wildwood far back into prehistoric times, and would treat the progress made by clearing for agriculture (assarting) in the centuries before and after the Norman Conquest as a comparatively minor episode.[3]

1  See Oliver Rackham, *Trees and Woodland in the British Landscape* (1976); a more detailed treatment is his *Ancient Woodland* (1980), and a briefer summary is 'The Growing and Transport of Timber and Underwood', in Sean McGrail (ed.), *Woodworking Techniques before A.D. 1500*, B.A.R. internat. ser. cxxix (1982), 199-218.

2  Rackham, *Ancient Woodland*, op. cit. note 1, 111-27; H.C. Darby, *Domesday England* (1977), ch. vi.

3  C. Taylor, *Fields in the English Landscape* (1975); O. Rackham, *The History of the Countryside* (1986), ch. 8.

The woods recorded in Domesday Book were mostly the demesne woodlands listed among the manorial resources, which in the hands of their lay or ecclesiastical lords were to remain the chief source of supply throughout our period. Depending on the nature of the landscape, there must also have been trees on wooded commons and in hedgerows, to which tenants would have had some access by ancient rights of *haybote* and *housebote* (for making hedges and houses). In a somewhat different category were the trees growing on hunting reserves, in private parks and the royal forests. While these were liable to be used as a source (particularly of outsize trees), they were not primarily managed for the production of timber, and indeed many 'forests' (such as Dartmoor) had few or no trees at all.[4]

The classic form of woodland management was that of coppicing with standards, where the underwood coppice (say of hazel) was cut in a regular cycle of between four and 28 years, while the standard, or full-size timber trees (usually of oak) were allowed to mature over a longer period. Studies of existing buildings have suggested that timber was often cut relatively young (at between 20 and 70 years' growth), and was often used in the form of complete trees, only branches and bark being removed.[5] The frequent cropping of underwood provided for a wide variety of woodland crafts, from the making of faggots and charcoal to the construction of hurdles and scaffolds, and any number of wooden artefacts for which large timber was not necessary. This form of management allowed for the renewal of the wood and timber stock, and was in no way destructive of the woods themselves. It was especially suited to the production of large amounts of fuel for domestic and industrial processes such as iron-working, which in the past have been blamed for the 'disappearance of woodland'. In the case of the Weald of Kent and Sussex it may be noted that far from being a scarce resource there, wood was even exported in the medieval period.[6]

Timber from local woodlands sufficed for most purposes, but there were occasions when larger building enterprises called for special resources. The Octagon of Ely Cathedral or the roof of Westminster Hall required exceptionally large timbers which demanded much larger trees. The royal forests (especially Dean) were a source of timber gifts for scores of building projects from the 13th century, often involving long-distance carriage; at a later date the Crown might ask for gifts of oaks from parks near to royal works.[7]

A flourishing import trade, especially from the Baltic, was another source which met special demands. Timber from Norway was being brought in from the 13th century, and along the Hanseatic routes from Prussia in the 14th century: this included fir and oak, and a range of finished products, from bowstaves, boards and

---

4 Rackham, *Ancient Woodland*, op. cit. note 1, 175-88; C.R. Young, *The Royal Forests of Medieval England* (1979).

5 Rackham, *Ancient Woodland*, ch. 10.

6 H.C. Darby (ed.), *An Historical Geography of England before A.D. 1800* (1936), 322, Fig. 61; E. Searle, *Lordship and Community: Battle Abbey*

*and its Banlieu, 1066-1538* (Toronto, 1974), 300-1.

7 Rackham, *Ancient Woodland*, op. cit. note 1, 152-3; Young, op. cit. note 4, 123-7; B. Cunliffe and J.T. Munby, *Excavations at Portchester Castle* IV (Society of Antiquaries of London, 1975), 154.

*Fig.189* Woodland coppice with standards. Flemish, *c.* 1530 (B.L., MS Add. 18855, f. 108ᵛ).

wainscot to masts and spars for ships (and even whole vessels). Some timber was also imported through Bristol from Ireland. Although remarkably little of this imported material has been recognized in surviving buildings, there is little doubt that the trade was of considerable size and importance.[8]

While it is certain that particular species of timber were recognized for their properties, and woodland crafts used a wide range of species (for example, ash for wheels, poplar for barrows, alder for scaffolding), the principal building material was oak. Elm has been found in small quantities (and was used more from the 16th century onwards), and there are instances of pine and poplar, but virtually none of (sweet) chestnut or, despite frequent claims, of the reuse of 'ships' timbers'.[9]

### Methods of Working Timber

The woodworking craftsmen may be divided into those using timber trees (building carpenters, engineers, millwrights and shipwrights), and those using underwood products and smaller fractions of timber (turners, joiners and carvers). For the first group, most is known about those who worked on buildings, since their activities are best recorded in contemporary documents as well as in surviving structures. Most of what follows is also probably applicable to engineers, millwrights and shipwrights, though much less is known of their products.

Timber was first selected by a carpenter who went to view the trees and mark them for felling. Immediately on felling, bark and branches were removed, much of it to be sold for use in tanning, and for making firewood or charcoal. The trunks were then 'scappled', that is squared up into beams. If further conversion was necessary, sawing (with a two-man saw over a pit) could be done close by, but otherwise timber was carted to the building site, or to a framing yard.[10]

Timber was usually worked when still 'green', shortly after felling and without seasoning. This was much easier, and the effect of seasoning *in situ* may have helped to tighten up a complex framework later. Structures were prefabricated, often off-site in a framing yard (the carpenter's workplace), where the members were laid out, marked, measured and cut before being put together and then dismantled for transport to site for re-erection.[11] Contemporary illustrations show carpenters working timber raised on trestles at a convenient height above ground and often out of doors (Figs. 191-2).[12]

---

8 Salzman, *Building in England*, 245-9; P. Dollinger, *The German Hansa* (English translation, 1970), 221, 232; E. Power and M.M. Postan (eds.) *Studies in English Trade in the Fifteenth Century* (1933), 140-1 and 198; Rackham, *Ancient Woodland*, op. cit. note 1, 151; D.M. Owen, *The Making of King's Lynn*, British Academy, Records of Social and Economic History n.s. ix (1984), 100, 258, 335, 352-62, 366-76; T. O'Neill, *Merchants and Mariners in Medieval Ireland* (1987), 99-102.

9 Salzman, *Building in England*, 249-52; M. Taylor, *Wood in Archaeology*, Shire Archaeology, (1981), 45-55; H.L. Edlin, *Woodland Crafts in Britain* (1949), *passim*; Rackham, *Ancient Woodland*, op. cit. note 1, 145 and 329.

10 Salzman, *Building in England*, 237; Cunliffe and Munby, op. cit. note 7, 136-9, 154.

11 *King's Works*, i, 529-30, for Westminster Hall.

12 Singer, *History of Technology*, ii, Pl.30, Fig. 352; see note 45 below.

*Fig. 190* Design for a timber-framed house. Early 16th century. (From binding of register of Bishop Ghinucci of Worcester: see footnote 15.)

Mortice-and-tenon joints, fixed with wooden pegs, were the most usual way of joining pieces of timber. Lapped dovetail joints were more widely used in the 12th and 13th centuries, but were generally abandoned later, though dovetails remained in use in certain places (for instance in joining tie-beams to wall-plates). Nails were rarely used in structural carpentry, though iron straps were increasingly used from the 16th century onwards. Scarf joints of great ingenuity were employed to join together lengths of timber; the general development of such joints forms a sequence that can (with care) be used for dating the structures in which they occur.[13]

The marking-out of timbers was done with a chalked line, and they were measured with compasses, squares and gauges. Carpenters' marks often survive, as scribed setting-out lines for mortices, as identificatory marks for joining together the members of a prefabricated truss or frame, and as numbers for marking a particular truss or frame in sequence along the length of a building. Additional indicators were used to show how the sections were to be placed in the building, so that they faced the right way.[14]

13  C.A. Hewett, *English Historic Carpentry* (1980), 263-71.
14  R. Harris, *Discovering Timber-framed Buildings*, Shire Archaeology (1978), 15; H. Janse and L. Devliegher, 'Middeleeuwse Bekappingen in het Vroegere Graafschap Vlaanderen', *Bul-* letin de la Commission Royale des Monuments et des Sites (*K.C.M.L.*), xiii (1962), 308-11; J.T. Munby, 'Medieval Carpentry in Chichester', in A. Down, *Chichester Excavations*, v (1981), 234-5.

The stage of design and planning of buildings and their roofs has left little evidence. Cathedral carpenters may have shared the masons' tracing floors such as those surviving at Wells and York, or they may have made their own drawings on parchment. One early 16th-century drawing survives from Worcestershire, with some indication that it was intended for showing to a client as well as being a working drawing (Fig. 190).[15] Mouldings will have followed templates similar to those used by masons, but details of joints could have been remembered, and reproduced by measurement from one half of the joint to the other.

## Methods of Working Wood

Much less is known of woodworking crafts, though the methods of their last practitioners in the present century can be related to surviving artefacts of earlier periods. Many underwood products, such as hurdles, have no doubt always been made in much the same way, by cleaving poles to a suitable size and finishing them by shaving. The use of the lathe is evident from earliest times, and the pole lathe could be constructed quite simply, operating on the reciprocating power of a bent sapling with a foot pedal. For making turned vessels, rough blocks were prepared from a half- or quarter-section of the tree, with the base of the vessel towards the outside to reduce warping. Initial work was done with green wood, though some seasoning might be allowed before finishing. The outside of the vessel was first prepared, and the inside removed later, leaving a conical core which often survives as a recognizable artefact (Fig. 197). Spindle turning (used, for example, for chair-legs) was a simpler process, using small poles with their grain parallel to the lathe.[16]

It is likely that many craftsmen in wood worked near to their source of supply, if not actually in the woods, and then carried their products to market or to the building site. But crafts such as joinery, turning or coopering could equally well be based in towns, since they used ready prepared materials. Illustrations of the Holy Family provide many detailed depictions of Joseph as a joiner or carver, working at a bench indoors rather than in the open.[17]

## Woodworking Tools

Few medieval woodworking tools survive, or can certainly be recognized as such from excavated examples. Most evidence comes from contemporary illustrations and written sources which name tools, and from early modern examples which seem

15  L.S. Colchester and J.H. Harvey, 'Wells Cathedral', *Arch. Jnl.* cxxxi (1974), 214 and Fig. 2; F.W.B. Charles and K. Down, 'A Sixteenth Century Drawing of a Timber-framed Town House', *Trans. Worcs. Arch. Soc.* 3rd ser. iii (1970-2), 67-79, Pls. 8-9.

16  C. Morris, 'Aspects of Anglo-Saxon and Anglo-Scandinavian Lathe-Turning', in McGrail (ed.), op. cit. note 1, 245-61; Singer, *History of Technology*, ii, Figs. 220 and 585-6; Edlin, *Woodland Crafts*, Pls. 21, 39, 45 and 82.

17  Singer, *History of Technology*, ii, Pl. 12 and Fig. 356.

*Fig. 191* Joseph the carpenter, from wall-painting in Carpenters Hall, London. (F. W. Fairholt: British Museum, Dept. of Prints and Drawings, 1866-5-12-209.) cf. p. 389.

to be survivors of much earlier traditions. A certain amount can also be deduced from the marks left on buildings and artefacts.[18]

The axe was the predominant tool of the carpenter, occurring in a variety of forms and sizes, and was, in addition to felling, used for much of the finishing of timber. Adzes may have been used for scappling timber, and for some rough finishing. Sawing of planks and baulks involved the long two-handed pit-saw, but a smaller 'bread-saw' type was used for cutting scarf-joints. Mortices were marked out with a square and some kind of knife or scribe, and initially cut with an augur. Spoon-bit augurs often leave their mark in the base of mortices, and were probably lop-sided for ease of entry. For smaller holes there were breast augurs (as depicted on the Bayeux Tapestry), whilst the later application of the crank principle to this tool resulted in the cranked brace-and-bit, which is often illustrated from the early 15th century.[19] Mortices could be cut out with a chisel and mallet, or with the longer bladed 'twybill', often mentioned in documents and thought to be a long tool with chisel-like ends, examples of which survive from later periods. Its longer blade would allow the waste to be levered out of a deep mortice.[20] Smooth finishing could generally be achieved by fine axe-work, or in the case of joinery by the plane. The devices for measuring and cutting mouldings have already been described.

Some features, especially of plank-framed doors, suggest that routing planes were used, whilst the fine V-edged panels that were produced in large numbers and with

18  See C.A. Hewett, 'Toolmarks on Surviving Works from the Saxon, Norman and later Medieval Periods', and P. Walker, 'The Tools available to the Mediaeval Woodworker', in McGrail (ed.), op. cit. note 1, 339-48 and 349-56; and Salzman, *Building in England*, ch. xxi,

for much of what follows.
19  Singer, *History of Technology*, ii, 653; Lynn White, *Medieval Technology and Social Change* (1962), 112-13.
20  Walker, op. cit. note 18, 351, Fig. 20.1.

*Fig. 192* Noah building the ark. English *c.* 1420-30. (Bodleian Library, MS Barlow 53 (R).)

great accuracy imply some degree of mechanisation in production (though this need not have happened in England if the majority of such boards were imported).[21]

A jocular poem of the 15th century, *The Debate of the Carpenter's Tools*, takes the form of a discussion between some 27 different named tools as to their individual merits in assisting their master to make a good living, while berating him for spending the fruits of their labours in the ale-house.[22]

### Nomenclature and Organisation of Trades

The different woodworking crafts are not easy to distinguish, as their practitioners were generally called 'carpenters' or 'wrights' whatever they did. Whilst the

21  Hewett, op. cit. note 18, 343 and 348; Rackham, 'Growing and Transport', op. cit. note 1, 215-6.
22  Oxford, Bodleian Library, MS Ashmole 61, fos. 23-6; Salzman, *Building in England*, 340-5. Max Müller, *Der Streit der Zimmermannswerkzeuge* (Inaugural Dissertation, Erlangen, 1899) prints a full text with discusion, as more recently E. Wilson, 'The Debate of the Carpenter's Tools', *Review of English Studies*, n.s. xxxviii (1987), 445-70, where an origin in Leicestershire is suggested.

distinction between those paid at different rates, such as sawyers or carvers, is often apparent in building accounts,[23] the difference between millwrights, shipwrights and plain building carpenters is less frequently made, though these were to some extent distinct crafts. In the 1381 Poll Tax returns for York, the 108 people working in wood were named as wrights (36), fusters (woodworkers) (3), joiners (4), turners (2), sawyers (7), bowyers (9), fletchers (makers of arrows) (9), coopers (7), saddlers (who made the wooden bases for saddles) (23), cartwrights (3) and shipwrights (5).[24] Other trades not represented on this list include arkwrights, cofferers, millwrights, wheelwrights, makers of musical instruments, and military engineers.

An example of the variety of work performed by a carpenter is provided by Master Thomas of Houghton, employed in royal service as a 'carpenter' and 'engineer' between 1288 and 1318: he oversaw building work at Westminster, made a pile-driving engine, carved a screen for Queen Eleanor's tomb, went to Wales to select timber, and made engines of war for use in Gascony and Scotland.[25] It is hardly surprising, then, that records of furniture-making imply no clear distinction between the carpenter and joiner in terms of what they made.[26]

Much less is known of the organisation of carpenters than of masons, probably because of the diversity of their trade. Carpenters in London and the larger provincial towns were organized in craft gilds, which managed the economic and social relations within the craft and between the crafts, but whose records tell us little of the nature of the craft itself.[27] The London Carpenters Company was only incorporated in 1477, but behind it lay a long history of controlling wages and ensuring craft membership for would-be citizens.[28] The 'Boke of Ordinances' of the Brotherhood of Carpenters of London had been drawn up in 1333, and dealt largely with charitable assistance to the brothers and sisters,[29] but a continuous identity between this fraternity and the nascent Company whose first hall was built in 1429 cannot be established; the Company accounts survive from 1438, and ordinances were drawn up in 1455. Apart from charitable aims, the Company sought to control the work of 'foreigners' in the City and to demarcate work with other trades, and it had authority to search for timber and boards of inferior quality. The posts of Master Carpenter of the Guildhall and of the Bridge House were reserved for freemen of the Company. The Company was minor by London standards, but maintained its membership numbers, though it is clear that it can never have contained a majority of all the carpenters working in London and, given the demand for building works in a growing city, it was able neither to enforce its monopoly nor to monitor standards as it aspired to do. Indeed one contract of 1510 went so far as to guarantee the

23  Salzman, *Building in England*, ch. iv.
24  J. Harvey, *Mediaeval Craftsmen* (1975), 152-4.
25  *King's Works*, i. 216-17.
26  P. Eames, *Furniture in England, France and the Netherlands from the Twelfth to the Fifteenth Century*, published as *Furniture History*, xiii (1977), 232-4.

27  C. Phythian-Adams, *Desolation of a City: Coventry and the Urban Crisis of the Late Middle Ages* (1979), 108.
28  B.W.E. Alford and T.C. Barker, *A History of the Carpenters Company* (1968), ch. i.
29  R.W. Chambers and M. Daunt, *A Book of London English, 1384-1425* (1931), 41-4.

carpenter against interference by the Company.[30]

The York carpenters by their ordinances of 1482 claimed authority over other woodworking trades, though the York joiners already had ordinances of their own, and were later, together with the carvers, to insist on the separateness of their craft. Shipwrights are not mentioned in the York ordinances and rarely occur in York records, though they were responsible for the pageant of building the ark in the Corpus Christi play.[31] In Coventry the carvers were in the carpenters' fellowship until they joined the painters in 1528.[32] Outside the larger towns that had a number of trade gilds there were many places with fraternities that had no particular association with any craft, and perhaps the majority of urban workers in wood, like their rural counterparts, did not belong to a gild that looked after their trade. This need not have affected their practice of carpentry nor have prevented the furtherance of the craft through the standard form of apprenticeship.[33] In Oxford, where over 400 carpenters are recorded as working between 1370 and 1530, there is no evidence of any lasting organisation.[34] Many came from elsewhere, for Oxford colleges, like the King's Works, were likely to attract men of national repute, together with a proportion of temporary and itinerant craftsmen.

Most of our information about the organisation of work again relates to constructional carpenters, whose activities are well recorded in the large number of building accounts and in the more than 50 contracts for carpentry work which have survived.[35] From the latter we see carpenters agreeing to build entire houses or parts of houses on prepared foundations, shops and rows of shops, inns, watermills, windmills, fulling-mills, bridges and wharves, to construct roofs, and to fit out chambers in existing buildings. Often the specifications of timber sizes or internal arrangements are given, and some must have been accompanied by drawings, though only one such drawing survives, unfortunately without its contract.[36] It is clear from many of these agreements that the carpenter is often acting as architect-contractor, both arranging for materials and sub-contracting with other craftsmen. For more important enterprises there might be separate contracts for parts of the work, as with the division of responsibility for stone and timber work in the rebuilding of Westminster Hall for Richard II.[37]

A marked feature of the royal building accounts is the division between 'taskwork' – that is, separate contracts for individual pieces of work – and the wagework by which the remainder was done at a daily rate of pay. Taskwork seems to have been introduced as an accounting control on the King's Works in the mid 13th century, but was also in general use. It was particularly appropriate for repetitive tasks such

---

30  Alford and Barker, op. cit. note 28, 18-26, ch. ii; Salzman, *Building in England*, 560.
31  H. Swanson, *Building Craftsmen in Late Medieval York* (Borthwick Papers, no. 63, York, 1983), 16-18; H. Swanson, *Medieval Artisans* (1989), 86.
32  Phythian-Adams, op. cit. note 27, 101.
33  See Harvey, op. cit. note 24, App. II, for the indenture of a bowyer's apprentice.
34  E.A. Gee, 'Oxford Carpenters, 1370-1530', *Oxoniensia*, xvii/xviii (1952/3), 112-84.
35  Most known contracts are given in Salzman, *Building in England*, App. B-D.; see also Harvey, op. cit. note 24, App. I and VI, and Swanson, *Medieval Artisans*, op. cit. note 31, ch. 7.
36  See above, note 15.
37  *King's Works*, i, 527 et seq.

as sawing or carving, which could be paid for by either length or item.[38]

Another prominent feature of the royal works was the use of impressed labour, often brought from far afield, to work in castles and palaces and on military expeditions.[39] This may have been a major factor in the spread of ideas, as carpenters travelled round the country (or across the Channel) at the Crown's behest, whilst there was also the greater adventure of going on crusade, as the carpenter of Chichester Cathedral did in the 1220s.[40]

Apart from the great royal building campaigns, institutional and private accounts record a large amount of carpenters' building and repair work, done either by task or daywork. Most other craftsmen in wood, making individual items, no doubt worked independently and sold their own products, though it is hard to come by any information on the organisation of their work, beyond the records of the purchase of their products.

Carpenters were paid on a comparable or higher rate than masons, on a scale that rose with inflation in the cost of living at various times in the medieval period.[41] As with all building wages, the time of year (and length of day) brought seasonal changes to wage-rates. There is some suggestion that the profession was not a very profitable one, judging from the standing of the London Company and the wealth of individuals recorded in wills.[42] The jobbing carpenter may frequently have been out of work, though provision for this was made by the York fraternity, and in Coventry those seeking work met at 5 a.m. on the city crossroads to find employment.[43] For the more skilled and fortunate there was the prospect of permanent employment by a corporation or the Crown, the pinnacle of success being the post of king's Master Carpenter.[44] The murals in the London Carpenters Hall served as an ever-present reminder of the ancient nobility of the craft, in their scenes of Noah building the ark, and Joseph working timber while the Christ child gathered up the chips in a basket (Fig. 192).[45]

### Timber Products

By its use in so many aspects of building and technology, timber proved its great versatility, and though its application to building work saw few limits, it cannot be

38  Ibid. i, 107-8; H.M. Colvin, (ed.), *Building Accounts of Henry III* (1971), 8-9; Swanson, *Building Craftsmen*, op. cit. note 31, 14; Cunliffe and Munby, op. cit. note 7, 154 (sawing); *King's Works* i, 529-30 (carving).
39  *King's Works*, i, 180-5, Fig. 25.
40  Munby, op. cit. note 14, 243 (n. 38).
41  E.H. Phelps-Brown and S.V. Hopkins, 'Seven centuries of Building Wages', *Economica* n.s. xxii (1955), repr. in E.M. Carus-Wilson (ed.), *Essays in Economic History*, ii (1962), 168-78; Salzman, *Building in England*, ch. iv.
42  Swanson, *Building Craftsmen*, op. cit. note 31, 14-15, *Medieval Artisans*, 84; Alford and Barker, opp. cit. note 31, 23; for carpenters' wills, see

Harvey, op. cit. note 24, 152-3 and App. VII.
43  Swanson, *Building Craftsmen*, op. cit. note 31, 15; Phythian-Adams, op. cit. note 27, 74-5.
44  Swanson, *Building Craftsmen*, op. cit. note 31, 13-14; Harvey, op. cit. note 24, 148-9; idem, 'The King's Chief Carpenters', *J.B.A.A.* 3rd ser. xi (1948); 13-34, and his *English Mediaeval Architects*, 2nd edn. (1984); *King's Works*, i, 176-8, 216-22; ii, 1050.
45  J.L. Nevinson in Alford and Barker, op. cit. note 28, 225-8, and frontispiece; E.B. Jupp, *An Historical Account of the Worshipful Company of Carpenters* (1848; 2nd edn, 1887), Pl. 3; parts of the cycle are preserved at Carpenters Hall in Throgmorton Avenue, London.

known how much it was a limiting factor in the development of medieval machinery, before the more general use of iron and steel in later ages. The following account will deal first with buildings, and then with other types of construction.

The high antiquity of the great timber hall (often aisled) has been proved by excavations throughout Europe. What probably began as an aristocratic dwelling, and served also as a farmhouse for men and beasts, survived longest as the standard form for medieval barns.[46] The earliest post-Roman examples, at sites such as Yeavering (Northumberland) and Cowdery's Down (Hants.), display a fairly sophisticated carpentry with accurately cut posts and planks, always earth-fast (though their reconstruction above ground-level remains problematic).[47] The one occurrence of stave-construction surviving above ground, at Greensted church (Essex) is difficult to interpret (or date) in an insular context.[48] The series of halls at the royal palace of Cheddar (Somerset) dating between the 9th and 11th centuries have earth-fast posts, with the early 12th-century East Hall being the first there of aisled form.[49] The great stone hall of William Rufus at Westminster was also aisled (perhaps in timber), and may represent a reintroduction of the type to England. One of the earliest surviving examples is provided by the late 12th-century arcades of the Bishop's Palace at Hereford.[50] An increasing number of domestic aisled halls dating from the 13th century are being recognised, but the most impressive examples of aisled buildings wholly in timber are the earliest barns, all with posts now set on ground sills or pads, and no longer earth-fast.[51] They are characterized by the long 'passing braces' which tie together the aisle walls both to the arcade posts and to the tie-beams and rafters, calling for long straight timbers that perhaps hark back to a northern European tradition of softwood timber.[52] In the later development of roofs, where the trusses provided their own longitudinal support, the structure of roof and wall are separated,[53] except in the large category of cruck buildings. These have a single construction for wall and roof, though they also occur in stone buildings; their origin is much debated, but apart from some documentary references to their use in

46　J.T. Smith, 'The Early Development of Timber Buildings: the Passing-Brace and Reversed Assembly', *Arch. Jnl.* cxxxi (1974), 238-63; Roar Hauglid, *Norske Stavkirker* (Oslo, 1976), 9-77 and 405-8.

47　Brian Hope-Taylor, *Yeavering, An Anglo-British Centre of Early Northumbria* (1977); M. Millett and S. James, 'Excavations at Cowdery's Down, Basingstoke, Hampshire, 1978-81', *Arch. Jnl.* cxl (1983), 151-279, and S. James, A. Marshall and M. Millett, 'An Early Medieval Building Tradition', ibid. cxli (1984), 182-215.

48　Hewett, op. cit. note 13, 5-13; H. Christie, O. Olsen and H.M. Taylor, 'The Wooden Church of St. Andrew at Greensted, Essex', *Antiq. Jnl.* lix (1979), 92-112.

49　P. Rahtz, *The Saxon and Medieval Palaces at Cheddar* (B.A.R. lxv, 1979).

50　*King's Works*, i, 45-7; C.A. Ralegh Radford, E.M. Jope and J.W. Tonkin, 'The Great Hall of the Bishop's Palace at Hereford', *Med. Arch.* xvii (1973), 78-86; W.J. Blair, 'The 12th-century Bishop's Palace at Hereford', *Med. Arch.* xxxi (1987), 59-72; now dated to 1179, D. Haddon-Reece in *Vernacular Architecture*, xx (1989), 46.

51　Hewett, op. cit. note 13, 53-5, 64, 108-9 (houses); 47-9, 59-63, 70-72, 87-8 (barns); K. Sandall, 'Aisled Halls in England and Wales', *Vernacular Architecture*, xvii (1986), 21-35.

52　Smith, op. cit. note 46; J.M. Fletcher, 'The Bishop of Winchester's Medieval Manor House at Harwell, Berkshire, and its Relevance in the Evolution of Timber-Framed Aisled Halls', *Arch. Jnl.* cxxxvi (1979), 173-92.

53　E.g. Hewett, op. cit. note 13, 122-3; see note 56 below.

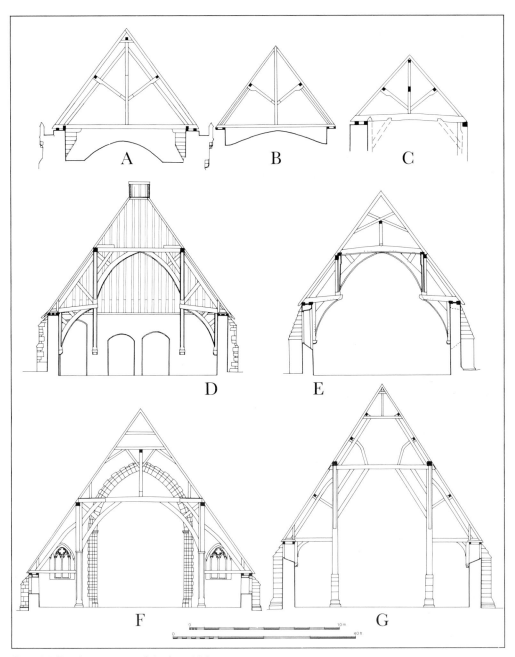

*Fig. 193* Roof carpentry of the late 13th century.
A-C King-post and purlin roofs (*c.* 1275-1300): A. Chichester Cathedral; B. Chichester
  Bishop's Palace; C. Bishop's Waltham (Hants.), 'Stable'.
D-E Hammer-beam roofs, *c.* 1290: D. Bishop's Kitchen, Chichester; E. Pilgrims' Hall,
  Winchester.
F-G Aisled buildings: F. St. Mary's Hospital, Chichester, *c.* 1290, with crown-post roof;
  G. Great Coxwell Barn, Oxon., *c.* 1310, with purlin roof.

vernacular buildings, they first occur as accurately finished pointed arches supporting roofs in the high gothic period.[54]

Churches and domestic buildings of stone have roofs showing a similar development to those of timber buildings (though it must be remembered that many church roofs were invisible above stone vaulting). Until the second half of the 13th century, longitudinal support is generally absent and rafter couples are braced internally (often with scissor-bracing), even in roofs so vast as those of Lincoln Minster.[55] Purlins, running along the roof and giving stability to the rafters, occur either at the sides of the roof, or centrally below the collar; support for the purlins was varied, but typically employed a crown-post, which seems to have been an insular development of the continental king-strut or king-post (Fig. 193, B-C), in the decades after 1250.[56] Later roof types are diversified so markedly in their regional distribution and status (in contrast with the more conservative continental practice) that it is hard to trace any single line of development.[57] Notable is the replacement of the tie-beam (and aisle-posts) by means of hammer-beams (Fig. 193, D-E) and then arch-braces, each in their way providing gothic arch-forms.[58] Later medieval roofs of stone buildings were often low-pitched to carry a lead roof covering; both these and roofs of steeper pitch had rows of purlins between the principal rafters, mounted on wind-braces.[59] The roof of Westminster Hall, rebuilt by Hugh Herland for Richard II in 1393-9, combines hammer-beams with a huge arch-brace, and marks the summit of medieval roof design.[60]

Timber-framed houses survive from the 13th century onwards, with plan-types showing regional variations, and distinguishing between urban and rural forms. The principal systems of framing were the box-frame, having a cubic shape with posts rising to the wall-plate that carries the roof, and the cruck-frame, where the curved principal supports for the roof also carry most of the framing for the walls. Regional and chronological differences in types of framing include differences in the type of bracing (arch and tension), the spacing of wall studs, the number of horizontal rails

54  E. Mercer, *English Vernacular Houses* (1975), ch. vii; N.W. Alcock and W.J. Blair, 'Crucks: New Documentary Evidence', *Vernacular Architecture*, xvii (1986), 36-8.

55  Smith, op. cit. note 46; Munby, op. cit. note 14, 247; C.A. Hewett, *English Cathedral and Monastic Carpentry* (1985).

56  J.T. Munby, M. Sparks and T. Tatton-Brown, 'Crown-post and King-strut Roofs in South-East England', *Med. Arch.* xxvii (1983), 123-35; Mercer, op, cit. note 54, ch. vi.

57  For the Continent see Janse and Devliegher, op. cit. note 14; H. Deneux, 'L'Evolution des Charpentes du XI^c au XVIII^c Siècle', *L'Architecte*, n.s. iv (1927), 49-53 etc.; F. Ostendorf, *Die Geschichte des Dachwerks* (Leipzig and Berlin, 1908; reprinted Hanover, 1982); for English developments, see J.T. Smith, 'The

Reliability of Typological Dating of Medieval English Roofs' in R. Berger (ed.), *Scientific Methods in Medieval Archaeology* (Berkeley, Calif., 1970), 239-69; and J.T. Smith, 'Medieval Roofs: a Classification', *Arch. Jnl.* cxv (1958), 111-49.

58  For a building with both, see J. Crook, 'The Pilgrims' Hall, Winchester', *Proc. Hants Field Club*, xxxviii (1982), 85-101.

59  F.E. Howard and F.H. Crossley, *English Church Woodwork* (2nd edn. 1927), 87-129.

60  L.T. Courtenay, 'The Westminster Hall Roof and its 14th-century Sources', *Jnl. Soc. of Architectural Historians*, xliii (1984), 295-309; L.T. Courtenay and R. Mark, 'The Westminster Hall Roof: An Historiographic and Structural Study', ibid. xlvi (1987), 374-93.

on each storey, and the amount of decoration introduced into the external facing of the walls.[61]

The origins of the jettied house, having a cantilevered support for the upper floor, are not known, and the phenomenon was not restricted to England.[62] Whatever its practical benefits, it became the essential feature of the storeyed timber town-house, occurring with regional variants across much of northern Europe from the 14th century onwards.[63] In rural houses it formed a display feature in timber-framed cross-wings, especially in the 'wealden house' so common in the wealthy south-east of England, where hall and cross-wings were integral beneath one roof.[64]

Apart from regular types of main-span roofing on rectangular walls, some of the most inventive of carpenters' designs were to be found on square and polygonal buildings with a function that demanded special treatment. Belfries, lineal descendants of the *berfroi*, mobile machines of war, had to support swinging bells at some height above ground and called for well-braced timber towers.[65] Kitchens required roofs that were kept well above the huge fires over which aristocratic meals were prepared, and both the 13th-century example at Chichester (Sussex) (Fig. 193, D) and the 15th-century one at Stanton Harcourt (Oxon.) are remarkable constructions that compare well with the most elaborate of stone-vaulted kitchens.[66] Cathedral chapter-houses, so often polygonal, provided scope for imaginative creations, whilst on a larger scale the internal framing of spires (whether with an outside covering of lead or of stone) had to meet the special need of anchoring the shell against wind-resistance, as can best be seen at Salisbury (Wilts.).[67] In a class of its own is the Octagon at Ely, where the daring cantilevered work (perhaps of William Hurley) has in part survived, despite much restoration.[68]

Most major bridges were built of timber until the 14th century, and although none survives intact, remnants of many minor bridges have been found in castle moats and similar places, indicating a fairly standard method of construction. Some large bridges used piles driven into the river bed, but smaller bridges employed braced trestles rising from a transverse sole-plate, carrying the roadway or serving as an abutment for a lifting or withdrawable bridge section. The simpler types have single trestles, with more elaborate forms having bracing in two directions, or fully braced square box-frames, closely resembling the frames for hanging bells. Excavated

61 J.T. Smith, 'Timber-Framed Building in England, its Development and Regional Differences', *Arch. Jnl.* cxxii (1965), 133-58; N.W. Alcock, *Cruck Construction, An Introduction and Catalogue* (C.B.A. Research Rep. 42, 1981).

62 Hewett, op. cit. note 13, 171-2 and 293-5.

63 E.g. R. Quenedey, *L'Habitation Rouennaise* (1926; repr. St.-Pierre de Salerne, 1977); G. Binding, U. Mainzer and A. Wiedenau, *Kleine Kunstgeschichte des Deutschen Fachwerkbaus* (Darmstadt, 1975).

64 S.E. Rigold, 'The Distribution of Wealden Houses', in I. Ll. Foster and L. Alcock (eds.),

*Culture and Environment* (1963), 351-4; Mercer, op. cit. note 54, 11-14.

65 C.A. Hewett, *Church Carpentry* (1982), ch. 4.

66 M. Wood, *The English Mediaeval House* (1965), ch. 17 and Pl. 20A; 'Proceedings of Summer Meeting . . . at Chichester in 1985', *Arch. Jnl.* cxlii (1985), Figs. 6 and 7.

67 Hewett, op. cit. note 55, 106-11, 139-45; J. Heyman, *Equilibrium of Shell Structures* (1977), 84-90.

68 Hewett, op. cit. note 55, 114-22; Courtenay, art. cit. note 60, 299-301.

examples date from the late 11th to the 16th centuries, and show few signs of development beyond the establishment of the basic type, apart from changes in bracing and jointing comparable with those taking place in timber framing above ground.[69]

At the time of the Domesday survey watermills were abundant in England (windmills had yet to be invented), and some 6,000 are listed within the area covered by the survey.[70] Remains of mills have been excavated at Old Windsor (Berks.) and Tamworth (Staffs). The latter, of 8th-century date, was of the horizontal type (with a horizontal wheel) similar to the many mills that have been found in Ireland, dating between the 7th and 10th centuries and thought to be of Norse origin, and of which examples were in use in Scotland in the present century.[71] Later mills had vertical wheels, either under- or overshot. In addition to the construction of the wheel, complex gearing and transmission elements must have been necessary, most of which were wooden. The teeth of the gears were made from individual blocks of wood.[72] The floating mill, familiar on many European rivers, does not seem to have made an appearance in England, though there were tide-mills at suitable coastal sites, and horsemills are recorded in towns from the 13th century.[73] At the same time fulling-mills became widespread, representing a significant mechanisation of one of the processes of cloth-making, though their physical components are not known beyond the fact that they were water-driven, and operated by rising and falling wooden mallets, presumably aided by camshafts. Similar techniques must have been used for the hammer-mills so important in the iron industry, and for other industrial mills.[74]

The development of the windmill in the late 12th century was an important advance, possibly invented in England if not originating in the Near East.[75] Much of the milling machinery was doubtless adapted from water mills, but new components included the sail arms, and the massive braced post on which the mill stood. Many illustrations of early windmills exist, giving a clear indication of their external appearance, and the earliest surviving mills from the post-medieval period provide some idea of their internal construction (Fig. 194).[76]

69  S.E. Rigold, 'Structural Aspects of Medieval Timber Bridges', *Med. Arch.* xix (1975), 48-91.

70  H.C. Darby, *Domesday England* (1977), 272 and App. 14.

71  P. Rahtz and K. Sheridan in *Trans. S. Staffs. Archaeol. and Hist. Soc.* xiii (1971), 9-16; R. Holt, *The Mills of Medieval England* (1988), 4-5, Figs. 1-2; McGrail (ed.), op. cit. note 1, 264-5; Singer, *History of Technology*, ii, 594-5. See E. Gauldie, *The Scottish Country Miller* (1981), ch. 7.

72  Singer, *History of Technology*, ii, 648; Edlin, op. cit. note 9, 140; Walter Rose, *The Village Carpenter* (1946), 104-11.

73  Singer, *History of Technology*, ii, 608 and 610-11; Holt, op. cit. note 71, 17-20 and 133-7.

74  E.M. Carus-Wilson, 'An Industrial Revolution of the Thirteenth Century', *Econ. Hist. Rev.* 1st ser. xi (1941), 39-60, repr. with additions in her *Medieval Merchant Venturers* (1954), 183-210; Singer, *History of Technology*, ii, 643 and 650; A.R. Bridbury, *Medieval English Cloth-making* (1982), ch. 2.

75  White, op. cit. note 19, 85-9; Singer, *History of Technology*, ii, 617-25; E.J. Kealey, *Harvesting the Air, Windmill Pioneers in Twelfth-Century England* (1987) proposes an earlier origin, but see Holt, op. cit. note 71, ch. 2 and app. 1.

76  C.A. Hewett, 'Some Developments in Carpentry Illustrated by Essex Millwrighting', *Art Bulletin*, 1 (1968), 70-4, Pls. 1-6; S. Freese, *Windmills and Millwrighting* (1957).

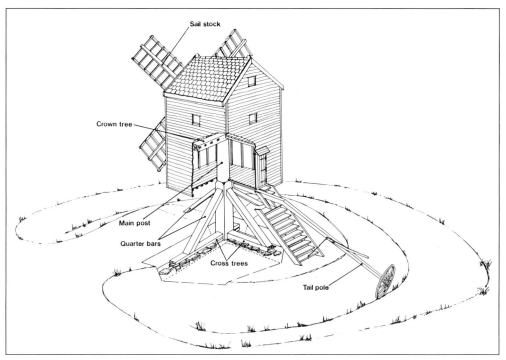

*Fig. 194* Reconstruction of the Great Linford post-mill. (*R. J. Zeepvat, Buckinghamshire Archaeological Unit*)

Other types of medieval wooden machinery made little advance on Roman practice, and are now represented solely by the hoisting mechanisms surviving in the towers of great churches – large treadwheels using manpower to raise stones and bells, sometimes with a moving arm known as a hawk or falcon.[77] Although principally of timber, these machines had parts of iron or copper alloy as building accounts testify.[78] Simpler hand-turned windlasses are also shown in illustrations, being used at ground level or on scaffolding, and are likely to have been used for rearing frames of timber buildings, perhaps in association with pairs of sheer-legs.[79] The great cranes in the ports of northern Europe were adaptations of the treadwheel type, though their structure was usually obscured by weatherboarding; the bird-like appearance of the angled jib and beaked head gave rise to the name.[80] Public cranes were to be found in the larger ports, as at York and Southampton, and are to be seen

---

77 Hewett, op. cit. note 55, 188-99; Singer, *History of Technology*, ii, Fig. 600.

78 Salzman, *Building in England*, 324-5.

79 F.W.B. Charles and W. Horn, 'The Cruck-Built Barn of Leigh Court, Worcestershire, England', *Jnl. Soc. of Architectural Historians*,

xxxii (1973), Figs. 30-31; Salzman, *Building in England*, 326-7 and 329; Singer, *History of Technology*, ii, 656 and Pl. 31.

80 For the Bruges crane see Singer, *History of Technology*, ii, Pl. 38.

*Fig. 195* Trebuchet and springald
from Carlisle charter of 1315.
(*Cumberland and Westmorland
A. & A.S.*)

by the side of the Thames in early views of London.[81]

The 'engines' of warfare mentioned in accounts and appearing in illustrations seem mainly to have been made of timber, with small parts of metal or other materials. Little is known of their form or function, but they seem either to have propelled large stones (the mangonel and trebuchet), or to have fired quarrels (the springald and arblast). A springald mounted on a tower at Carlisle castle, mentioned in building accounts, is shown in action against a trebuchet in a drawing of the 1315 siege by the Scots.[82] Siege towers were of similar construction to belfries, as mentioned above.

No great change in types of wheeled transport or in the technology of wheel construction seem to have taken place in the medieval period. Carts of two and four wheels were common, with superstructures of simple staves or hurdles, or a full carriage body.[83] The discovery of supension may have occurred within our period, but there is little evidence for its use.[84]

81  A. Raine, *Mediaeval York* (1955), 240-1; C. Platt, *Medieval Southampton* (1973), 143; M. Holmes, 'An Unrecorded Map of London', *Archaeologia*, c (1966), 105-28, pl. xlvib.

82  H.J. Hewitt, *The Organisation of War under Edward III* (1966), 71-2; for the illustration of a springald see *King's Works*, ii, 598, referring to *Trans. Cumb. & Westm. Antiq. Soc.*, vi (1881-2), 319, as Fig. 195.

83  Singer, *History of Technology*, ii, 546-55; J. Langdon, *Horses, Oxen and Technological Innovation* (1986), 14, 76-9, 142-56 and 246-50.

84  Lynn White, 'The Origins of the Coach', *Medieval Religion and Technology* (Berkeley, Calif., 1978), 205-16.

Despite the very great importance of shipping throughout the medieval period, and the considerable changes that occurred in shipbuilding, the few remains of ships available for study make it difficult at present to describe a chronological development, or even to observe the sort of technical advances such as are known in building carpentry.[85] There were changes in size and shape of the hull, in techniques of construction, and in the arrangement of mast and sails, but it is hard to localise these changes between the Baltic and the Mediterreanean, or to date them. Compared with building construction, records of English ship-building are few and the remains not yet sufficient to make a complete picture, but there are many illustrations of greater or less technical skill from which conclusions may be drawn about the general tendency of development.[86]

At the beginning of the period the Viking tradition produced the long ships that mastered the North Sea and crossed the Atlantic. These are well represented by surviving examples, and were clinker-built (with overlapping planking), with the outer shell being made first and the frames fitted afterwards; they could be rowed or fitted with a mast, and had a side-rudder.[87] The ships depicted under construction and sail on the Bayeux Tapestry are in this tradition, and the type probably survived as the royal 'snakes' used in later centuries for channel crossings.[88]

Ships after the Viking era are less well known from surviving vessels, but are often illustrated (especially on seals), and mentioned with great frequency in documents with a variety of names whose significance is not always understood. The round-hulled, clinker-built ship with decks and castles fitted fore and aft, stern-rudders and increasingly complex rigging, seems to represent the survival and adaptation of Viking techniques down to the 12th or 13th century.[89] The principal merchant ship of northern Europe by the 13th century was the 'cog', now identified with the type of ship recovered from the Weser at Bremen, having a flat, smooth-planked bottom and high clinker-built sides, with straight, steeply inclined stems.[90] The cog was pre-eminently the ship of the Hanseatic merchants, and provided a generous cargo space, whilst being easier and cheaper to build (using sawn rather than cleft planking). The 'hulc' is another type which is often referred to, and was very

85  B. Greenhill, *Archaeology of the Boat* (1976); G.F. Bass (ed.), *A History of Seafaring based on Underwater Archaeology* (1972); S. McGrail (ed.), *Medieval Ships and Harbours in Northern Europe*, (B.A.R. internat. ser. lxvi, 1979); R.W. Unger, *The Ship in the Medieval Economy* (1980).

86  D. Burwash, *English Merchant Shipping 1460-1540* (Toronto, 1947; repr. 1969); I. Friel, 'Documentary Sources and the Medieval Ship: some Aspects of the Evidence', *Internat. Jnl. of Nautical Archaeology*, xii (1983), 41-62; A.W. Farrell, 'The Use of Iconographic Material in Medieval Ship Archaeology', in McGrail (ed.), op. cit. note 85, 227-46.

87  O. Crumlin-Pedersen, 'The Vikings and the Hanseatic Merchants', in Bass (ed.), op. cit. note 85, 182-92; S. McGrail, *The Ship: Rafts, Boats and Ships* (1981), 26-36.

88  K.M.E. Murray, 'Shipping', in A.L. Poole (ed.), *Medieval England*, 2 vols. (1958), i, 176-7.

89  See illustrations on pp. 196-7 in Bass (ed.), op. cit. note 85; for seals see G. Pedrick, *Borough Seals of the Gothic Period* (1904) and H.H. Brindley, 'Medieval Ships in Painted Glass and on Seals', *Mariner's Mirror*, i (1911), 43-7, 71-5, 129-34 and 193-200.

90  D. Ellmers, 'The Cog of Bremen and related Boats', and O. Crumlin-Pedersen, 'Danish Cog-Finds', in McGrail (ed.), op. cit. note 85, 1-15 and 17-34; see illustrations on pp. 202-4 in Bass (ed.), op. cit. note 85.

*Fig. 196* Ships on stall ends from St. Nicholas's chapel, Kings Lynn. 15th century. (*Victoria and Albert Museum, W. 16-1921 and W. 16-1916*)

common in the 14th century, perhaps replacing the cog, but is better known from illustrations than from survivals (one is actually named on the late 13th-century seal of New Shoreham).[91] It seems to be characterised by a markedly round profile, with all the planks ending above the waterline, and lacking both stem and stern-post.

The major development in late medieval shipping is the least well understood of all – the appearance of the three-masted ship of smooth planking built on a skeleton framework, now known as the carrack. These ships could be built to a much larger size, and in addition to their increased cargo capacity were eventually able to carry guns. Their reliability, quite apart from their size, made them ideal for voyages of exploration and the discovery of the New World. They perhaps originated in the Mediterranean early in the 15th century, and underwent a steady development during that century, in their size, rigging, and the appearance of large fore- and aftercastles. These changes are known almost entirely from illustrations rather than from any surviving examples, and much remains to be discovered about this very important phase, which laid the basis of all later large wooden sailing ships.[92]

## *Wood Products*

The most significant use of wood (in terms of quantity) was for fuel; the production of bundles of faggots and sticks of all sizes must have been a major and widespread industry, though the details of its organisation, transport and marketing are barely known. The quantity of fuel required for London and the major provincial towns was enormous, quite apart from the needs of smaller towns, castles, manors and monasteries, and the gross demand must have kept many woodmen in work.[93] On a lesser scale, but equally widespread, was the production of charcoal for industrial and domestic use, and mention has been made of the use of oak bark for the tanning industry.[94]

A wide range of products for agricultural and domestic use was probably made by woodland craftsmen working in the woods or in village workshops, using underwood poles rather than larger fractions of timber trees. Prominent in building accounts are scaffold poles and hurdles, the latter being used (as planks are now) for staging. Hurdles were made in large numbers, being accounted for by the dozen, and were also used in agriculture for fencing and folding (appearing often in pictures of the Nativity), and in warfare.[95]

Wooden machinery for agriculture included the plough and harrow, which were

91 Ibid., p. 199 (Shoreham); McGrail, op. cit. note 87, 38-40.

92 A. McGowan, *The Ship: Tiller and Whipstaff* (1981), 8-17; F. Howard, *Sailing Ships of War* (1979), 13-41; I. Friel, 'England and the Advent of the Three-Masted Ship', *Internat. Congress of Maritime Museums, 4th Conference Proceedings* (Paris, 1983), 130-8.

93 Rackham, *Ancient Woodland*, op. cit. note 1,

142-3; M.K. McIntosh, *Autonomy and Community, The Royal Manor of Havering, 1200-1500* (1986), 143-4 (London supplies); O'Neill, op. cit. note 8, 99 (Ireland).

94 Rackham, *Ancient Woodland*, op. cit. note 1, 143; Edlin, op. cit. note 9, ch. xxv; Searle, op. cit. note 6, 300-1.

95 Hewitt, op. cit. note 82, 79 and 86-7; Rackham, *Ancient Woodland*, op. cit. note 1, 144.

mostly wooden, with a few iron fittings; the important development of the heavy plough, and its means of traction, need not concern us here, though another medieval invention, the wheelbarrow, deserves mention as a great labour-saving device.[96] Hand implements like the (iron-shod) shovel, rake, threshing flail and scythe handle must also have been regular products of the woodland or village craftsman.

Industrial machinery of the larger sort has already been described, but there were useful advances in the smaller machines used in the cloth industry that had an equally wide impact.[97] The spinning wheel and the horizontal loom were largely constructed of wood. The former appeared in the 13th century, and was the first application of continuous rotary motion to a mechanism; the latter, of similar date, was easier to work at and allowed the use of rising and falling sheds.[98]

Like tools, many weapons required wooden shafts, whilst the making of wooden shields was a craft of its own.[99] The most important weapon was the bow and arrow, made by bowyers and fletchers. During the Hundred Years' War, these were required by the Crown in such quantities (7,800 bows and 13,000 arrows were ordered in 1341 alone) that they were obtained from most of the counties of England. The Tower of London, where the ordnance supplies were kept, had its own bowyers and fletchers along with the armourers, carpenters and artillers on the establishment of the Privy Wardrobe.[100] Whether on account of scarcity, or quality of material, bow staves were being imported from the Baltic (probably Carpathian yew) and from Spain, though English elm might be used as well as yew.[101]

Minor domestic objects of wood are represented by finds from excavation of waterlogged sites. Most utensils from spoons to mousetraps could be made of wood, though this is not the place to enumerate the products of a large-scale but minor craft.[102] The majority of such items were carved, but a significant proportion were turned on a lathe. Typical products of turning were bowls and cups, the finer 'mazers' being trimmed and mounted with precious metals.[103] Turned wares were complementary to the larger range of pottery vessels and must have existed in great quantity, though their survival rate has necessarily been poorer. A smaller number of items was produced by spindle turning, and objects made by this method range from small handles and boxes to larger members for furniture.[104]

96 White, op. cit. note 19, ch. ii; Singer, *History of Technology*, ii, 642.

97 Cf. above, pp. 324-32.

98 Singer, *History of Technology*, ii, 202-5 and 644-5.

99 For a nearly complete buckler from London, see T. Tatton-Brown, 'Excavations at the Custom House Site . . . 1973', *Trans. London & Middlesex Archaeol. Soc.*, xxv (1974), 201-4.

100 Hewitt, op. cit. note 82, 63-71; T.F. Tout, *Chapters in the Administrative History of Mediaeval England*, iv (1926), 469-70, 476-7; L.R. Hardy, *Longbow: A Social and Military History* (1976).

101 Dollinger, op. cit. note 8, 221 and 232; Power

and Postan op. cit. note 8, 140, 152 and 207; W.R. Childs, *Anglo-Castilian Trade in the Later Middle Ages* (1978), 31, 120 and 185; Owen, op. cit. note 8, 370; Rackham, op. cit. note 3, 229-30 and 237.

102 E.H. Pinto, *Treen and Other Wooden Bygones* (1969).

103 Ibid., 43-7. Cf. above, pp. 151-2.

104 Morris, op. cit. note 16; and M. Hurley, 'Wooden Artefacts from the Excavation of the Medieval City of Cork', in McGrail (ed.), *Woodworking Techniques*, 245-61 and 301-11; Singer, *History of Technology*, ii, 249.

*Fig. 197* Lathe-turned bowls, cups and covers from York. Viking period.
(*York Archaeological Trust*)

## Other Products

There remain several types of wooden object, made by joiners, carvers, and other specialists, which do not easily fit the division between timber and wood crafts, and which might belong to either category. Some craftsmen, like saddlers, coopers and wheelwrights, might combine skill in working wood with the other parts of leather or metal required for their products. Saddles, for example, were built on a wooden base (which might be all that was necessary for a pack-horse), and upholstered in leather (see also John Cherry above, pp.311-12); a decorated wooden saddle-bow has been found in York.[105]

A recent survey of medieval furniture has described a fair number of surviving cupboards, chests, tables and chairs, and has considered the documentation for their production and use.[106] Most are made from oak boards, and are solid and relatively straightforward in their construction, often deriving their status from decoration (by

105 R.A. Hall, '10th Century Woodworking in Coppergate, York', in McGrail (ed.), op. cit. note 1, 234-5, Fig. 13.2.
106 Eames, op. cit. note 26.

painting or ironwork) or from the objects placed upon them. More elaborate are the chests and chairs whose flat surface could be carved with architectural motifs or figured scenes. The Coronation Chair in Westminster Abbey was painted and gilded, but the Guild Chair of Coventry was carved with traceried panels, in the manner of ecclesiastical bench-ends.[107] Chests, or coffers, were used for storing all manner of goods, from treasure and books to muniments and bread. Chests of the 14th century at York Minster and New College, Oxford, have fine carved scenes thought to be Flemish in origin, and there are numerous references to Flemish chests in inventories.[108] Armoires with drawers for storing records survive in the muniment rooms at Wells Cathedral and Winchester College, and in the treasury of St. George's Chapel, Windsor.[109]

More elaborate are the surviving ecclesiastical fittings, such as carved screens, pulpits, font covers and seating, which provide some of the most spectacular examples of the medieval joiner's work. The most frequently used decorative motifs are architectural, whether as blank traceried panels, or the fantastically elaborate tabernacle work with buttresses, pinnacles, crockets and spires. All these elements can be seen at their best on the Bishop's Throne at Exeter Cathedral, or on the East Anglian group of font covers.[110] Turned wooden seats also formed an important class, well represented in contemporary illustrations and many post-medieval examples, though the fine romanesque chair in Hereford cathedral is the sole representative of the type.[111] More basic forms of rustic furniture produced by woodland craftsmen have not survived, though their traditions no doubt formed the basis of the later industry.[112]

Medieval wood carving was a craft of its own, with specialist sculptors being hired to carve stalls or the angels on hammer-beam roofs.[113] Much has now been lost, but the survival of minor works, such as bench ends and the many lifting misericord seats, gives some idea of the range of the carver's skill, especially in the amount and depth of undercutting, and in the wide scope of subject matter illustrated.[114] The

107  W. Palmer, *The Coronation Chair* (H.M.S.O., 1953); F. Bond, *Wood Carvings in English Churches* II – *Stalls and Tabernacle Work* (1910), 117, also N. Pevsner and A. Wedgwood, *The Buildings of England: Warwickshire* (1966), Pl. 16.

108  Eames, op. cit. note 26, 145-8 and Pls. 36-7 (York); ibid., 137 (Flemish Chests); C. ffoulkes, 'A Carved Flemish Chest at New College, Oxford', *Archaeologia*, lxv (1913-14), 113-28; J.M. Fletcher and M.C. Tapper, 'Medieval Artefacts and Structures Dated by Dendrochronology', *Med. Arch.* xxviii (1984), 122-4; E.T. Hall, 'The Courtrai Chest from New College, Oxford, Re-examined', *Antiquity*, lxi (1987), 104-7. See also C.A. Hewett, 'English Medieval Cope Chests', *J.B.A.A.* xcli (1988), 105-23.

109  Eames, op. cit. note 26, 40-44.

110  F. Bond, *Screens and Galleries in English Chur-*

ches (1908); idem, op. cit. note 107; F.E. Howard and F.H. Crossley, *English Church Woodwork* (2nd edn. 1927), 191-5 and 321-37; C. Tracy, *English Gothic Choir Stalls 1200-1400* (1987).

111  Singer, *History of Technology*, ii, 248-9; Royal Commission on Historical Monuments (England), *Herefordshire* (1931), 106-7; Bond, op. cit. note 107, 115 regarded the Hereford chair as Jacobean.

112  Singer, *History of Technology*, ii, 252-3; Edlin, op. cit. note 9, ch. vi etc.

113  Harvey, op. cit. note 24, 157-8; E.S. Prior and A. Gardner, *An Account of Medieval Figure-Sculpture in England* (1912), 515-9.

114  F. Bond, *Wood Carvings in English Churches* I – *Misericords* (1910); M.D. Anderson, *Misericords* (1954); G.L. Remnant, *A Catalogue of Misericords in Great Britain* (1969).

*Fig. 198* Romanesque chair in Hereford Cathedral. (*R.C.H.M.E., National Monument Record*)

large number of rood screens is an indication of the very great loss of the carved roods themselves, but figure carving is also to be seen in the angels on late medieval roofs in East Anglia, in the bench-ends of East Anglia and the West Country, and in a number of monumental effigies.[115]

Medieval musical instruments are frequently illustrated in paintings and sculpture, from which much can be determined of their appearance; there are also a considerable number of parts of instruments from excavations (such as tuning pegs), though complete examples are rare.[116] Medieval instruments underwent many changes, with introductions from the arab world being rapidly assimilated, and their modifications leading to the forms that became the basis of the present families of instruments (albeit with regional variations). Instruments were not wholly the province of the woodworker, and there were always metal and bone pipes for wind

115 Prior and Gardner, op. cit. note 113, 524-42 and 661-71; Howard and Crossley, op. cit. note 110, 127-8 and 352-9; A. Gardner, *Minor English Wood Sculpture 1400-1550* (1958); A.C. Fryer, *Wooden Monumental Effigies in England and Wales* (2nd edn. 1924).

116 F. Crane, *Extant Medieval Musical Instruments* (Iowa City, 1972).

instruments,[117] whilst the construction of wooden instruments was affected by the limitations of using metal parts, especially the increased tension of wire strings. From earliest times skilled craftsmen must have specialised in the production of more elaborate instruments, while simpler instruments could even have been made by their players. Wind instruments required accurate boring of pipes, and positioning of holes. Stringed instruments came in many types, and ranged from the fiddle (which was basically a hollowed-out wooden box with a separate resonator board) to more complex instruments, such as the lute, the sound box of which was elaborately constructed from many bent staves. One rare survival is the 14th-century gittern from Warwick castle, now in the British Museum.[118] Lyres are represented by the Sutton Hoo instrument (as reconstructed), and the changing form of the harp is recorded in many illustrations, with a new type, developed in the 13th century, having a large sound-box: the 'Irish' harp, of which a 14th-century example is kept at Trinity College, Dublin.[119] Bone tuning pegs for the psaltery and another instrument have been excavated in Oxford on a site apparently occupied by a harp-maker in the mid 15th century.[120] Organs, either the small portative or the larger positive, were fitted with metal or wooden pipes, though many of their internal works were wooden, and they were often housed in decorative wooden cases with architectural motifs.[121] The increasingly sophisticated keyboard of the organ (and the re-invention of the stop) developed as other keyboard instruments now appeared, such as the clavichord and harpsichord, which are both illustrated in the windows of *c.* 1440 in the Beauchamp Chapel of St. Mary's Church, Warwick.[122] Unlike many of the crafts described here, there is some contemporary writing about musical instruments, and there are technical treatises on their construction that are most informative about late medieval instruments.[123]

This brief survey of a large field has examined the uses of a highly adapatable material in many different contexts, where it was employed to the extreme limits of its potential. The enormous versatility of wood is exemplified in many areas where it has continued to hold its own until the recent discovery of new materials better suited for particular tasks, and for many purposes it has not yet been superseded. The widespread use of wood and timber in medieval crafts and technology is a remarkable aspect of the age, which demonstrates both the properties of the material, and its adaptability for use in the many technological developments throughout the period.

117 Cf. above, p. 369.
118 Jeremy Montagu, *The World of Medieval and Renaissance Musical Instruments* (1976), Pl. 19; J.G. Alexander and P. Binski (eds.) *Age of Chivalry*, (Exhibition Catalogue, Royal Academy of Arts, 1987), No. 521.
119 Montagu, op. cit. note 118, Pls. 3 and 52.
120 B. Durham, 'Archaeological Investigations in St. Aldates, Oxford', *Oxoniensia*, xlii (1977),

163-6; for examples in wood, see Hurley, op. cit. note 104.
121 Montagu, op. cit. note 118, 36-7 and 63-5.
122 Ibid., Pl. 45; C.F. Hardy, 'On the Music in the Painted Glass of the Windows in the Beauchamp Chapel at Warwick', *Archaeologia*, lxi (1909), 583-614.
123 Montagu, op. cit. note 118, 56-8, Pls. 43-4, 46, 48 and 50-1.

## Further Reading

For many of the subjects dealt with here the fundamental text is L.F. Salzman's *Building in England down to 1540* (2nd edn., 1967) which provides a mass of detail derived from a wide reading of medieval accounts. Trees and forestry in the middle ages are considered by Oliver Rackham in his *Ancient Woodland* (1980), and more generally in his *The History of the Countryside* (1986). The careers of individual carpenters of note are listed in J.H. Harvey, *English Mediaeval Architects* (2nd edn., 1984), and techniques in several branches of the craft are discussed in his *Mediaeval Craftsmen* (1982), as also in S. McGrail (ed.), *Woodworking Techniques before A.D. 1500* (1982).

The History of the King's Works, ed. H.M. Colvin et al. (1963, etc.) deals with the royal building operations and much else besides. For some actual building accounts a parallel Latin and English text is printed in Colvin's *Building Accounts of King Henry III* (1971). Timber framing has a large bibliography: a general introduction is now provided by R.W. Brunskill, *Timber Building in Britain* (1985), which has an excellent glossary and select bibliography listing useful papers. Cecil Hewett's *English Historic Carpentry* (1980) summarises his work and is fully illustrated.

Shipping also has an extensive literature: a useful introduction is Basil Greenhill's *Archaeology of the Boat* (1976), and recent research is represented by the papers in S. McGrail (ed.), *Medieval Ships and Harbours in Northern Europe* (1979).

Other constructions in wood and timber are treated somewhat unevenly in C. Singer et al. (ed.), *A History of Technology*, ii (1956). Archaeological finds are considered by Maisie Taylor, *Wood in Archaeology* (1981), and more recent aspects by H.L. Edlin, *Woodland Crafts in Britain* (1949).

A catalogue and general discussion of furniture is provided by Penelope Eames, *Furniture in England, France and the Netherlands from the Twelfth to the Fifteenth Century* (published as *Furniture History*, xiii, 1977), whilst the furniture and fittings of churches are fully illustrated and discussed by F.E. Howard and F.H. Crossley, *English Church Woodwork* (2nd edn. 1927). This includes sculpture, for which see also E.S. Prior and A. Gardner, *An Account of Medieval Figure-Sculpture in England* (1912) and A. Gardner, *Minor English Wood Sculpture 1400-1550* (1958).

A general introduction to musical instruments, with bibliography, is Jeremy Montagu, *The World of Medieval and Renaissance Musical Instruments* (1976).

# Bibliography

The primary place of publication of all monographs is London, unless otherwise stated.

Addyman, P., 'Archaeology and Anglo-Saxon Society', in G. de G. Sieveking, I.H. Longworth and K.E. Wilson (eds.), *Problems in Economic and Social Archaeology* (1976), 309-22.

Agricola, Georg, *De Re Metallica* (Basle, 1556); ed. and transl. Herbert C. Hoover and L.H. Hoover (1912).

Alexander, Jonathan J.G., and Paul Binski (eds.), *Age of Chivalry: Art in Plantagenet England, 1200-1400* (Exhibition catalogue, Royal Academy of Arts, 1987).

Alexander, S.M., 'Towards a History of Art Materials – A Survey of Published Technical Literature in the Arts. Part I. From Antiquity to 1599', *Art and Archaeology Technical Abstracts*, vii (1969), 123-61.

Alford, Bernard W.E., and Theodore C. Barker, *A History of the Carpenters' Company* (1968).

Anthony of Pisa, *see* Bruck, R.

Arwidsson, Greta, and Gösta Berg, *The Mästermyr Find: A Viking Age Tool Chest from Gotland*, Kungl. Vitterhets Historie och Antikvitets Akademien (Stockholm, 1983).

Ashdown, C.H., *History of the Worshipful Company of Glaziers* [c.1918].

Astill, G.G., 'Economic Change in Late Medieval England: an Archaeological Review', in T.H. Aston, P.R. Coss, C. Dyer and J. Thirsk (eds.), *Social Relations and Ideas: Essays in Honour of R.H. Hilton* (Cambridge, 1983), 219-30.


Backhouse, J., D.H. Turner and L. Webster (eds.), *The Golden Age of Anglo-Saxon Art* (Exhibition catalogue, British Museum, 1984).

Badham, S., 'An Interim Study of the Stones used for the Slabs of English Monumental Brasses', *Trans. Monumental Brass Soc.* xiii (1985), 475-83.

Baines, Patricia, *Spinning Wheels. Spinners and Spinning* (1977).

Barnes, H.D., and W. Douglas Simpson, 'The Building Accounts of Caister Castle, A.D. 1432-1435', *Norfolk Archaeology*, xxx (1947-52), 178-88.

Barral I Altet, Xavier (ed.), *Artistes, Artisans et Production Artistique au Moyen Age.*

*Colloque International, Rennes, 2-6 mai 1983*, 3 vols. (Paris, 1986-90).

Bartholomew the Englishman, *see* Trevisa.

Bass, George F. (ed.), *A History of Seafaring based on Underwater Archaeology* (1972).

Baumgartner, Erwin, and Ingeborg Krueger, 'Zu Gläsern mit hohem Stiel oder Fuss des 13. und 14. Jahrhunderts', *Bonner Jahrbücher*, clxxxv (1985), 363-413.

Baxandall, Michael, *The Limewood Sculptors of Renaissance Germany* (New Haven and London, 1980).

Bayley, J., 'Roman Brass-Making in Britain', *Historical Metallurgy*, xviii.1 (1984), 42-3.

—, 'Non-Ferrous Metal Working: Continuity and Change', in E.A. Slater and J.O. Tate (eds.), *Science and Archaeology, Glasgow 1987. Proceedings of a Conference* (B.A.R. British Ser. 196, Oxford, 1988), 193-208.

Bazeley, Margaret L., 'The Forest of Dean in its Relations with the Crown during the Twelfth and Thirteenth Centuries', *Trans. Bristol and Glos. Archaeol. Soc.* xxxiii (1910),153-286.

Becksmann, R., and H. Waetzoldt, 'Glasmalerei des Mittelalters', in *Vitrea Dedicata. Das Stifterbild in der deutschen Glasmalerei des Mittelalters* (Berlin, 1975).

Beckwith, John, *Ivory Carvings in Early Medieval England* (1972).

Beeson, Cyril F.C., *English Church Clocks, 1280-1850* . . . (Antiquarian Horological Soc., Monograph 5, 1971).

Bell, Malcolm, *Old Pewter* (1905).

Bennett, H., *Excavations in Perth High Street: The Textiles* (forthcoming).

Bennett, Hugh G., *The Manufacture of Leather* (1909).

Benoit, Paul, and Denis Cailleaux (eds.), *Hommes et Travail du Métal dans les Villes Médiévales* (Paris, 1988).

Benson, George, *The Ancient Painted Glass Windows in the Minster and Churches of the City of York* (Annual Rep. of the Yorkshire Philosophical Society, 1915).

Beresford, Guy, 'The Medieval Manor of Penhallam, Jacobstow, Cornwall', *Med. Arch.* xviii (1974), 90-139.

Bessac, Jean-Claude, *L'Outillage Traditionnel du Tailleur de Pierre, de l'Antiquité à nos Jours. Revue Archéologique de Narbonnaise*, Supplément 14 (Paris, 1986).

Bettey, J.H., 'The Cultivation of Woad in the Salisbury Area during the late 16th and 17th Centuries', *Textile History*, ix (1978), 112-17.

Bickley, Francis B. (ed.), *The Little Red Book of Bristol* (2 vols., Bristol, 1900).

Biddle, Martin (ed.), *Winchester in the Early Middle Ages: an Edition and Discussion of the Winton Domesday*, Winchester Studies, 1 (Oxford, 1976).

—, (ed.), *Object and Economy in Medieval Winchester*, Winchester Studies, 7ii (2 vols., Oxford, 1990).

Biringuccio, Vannoccio, *Pirotechnia* (Venice, 1540), trans. C.S. Smith and M.T. Gnudi (New York, 1942).

Blair, C. (ed.), *Pollard's History of Firearms* (1983).

—, 'An Early Fifteenth-Century London Latoner', *Monumental Brass Soc. Bull.* 38 (Feb. 1985), 129.

—, J. Blair and R. Brownsword, 'An Oxford Brasiers' Dispute of the 1390s: Evidence for Brass-Making in Medieval England', *Antiq. Jnl.* lxvi (1986), 82-90.

Blair, John, 'Orsett, Essex: a New Clue to the Early London Brass Workshops?', *Monumental Brass Soc. Bull.* 23 (Feb. 1980), 15.

—, 'Henry Lakenham, Marbler of London, and a Tomb Contract of 1376', *Antiq. Jnl.* lx (1980), 66-74.

—, 'English Monumental Brasses before 1350: Types, Patterns and Workshops', in J. Coales (ed.), *The Earliest English Brasses: Patronage, Style and Workshops 1270-1350* (Monumental Brass Soc. 1987), 133-74.

—, 'An Early 12th-Century Purbeck Marble Graveslab from St. Frideswide's Priory', *Oxoniensia*, liii (1988), 266-8.

—, 'A Bishop Orders his Brass: Buying a Slab from the Purbeck Quarries, *c.* 1400', *Trans. Monumental Brass Soc.*, forthcoming.

Blanchard, I.S.W., 'Derbyshire Lead Production, 1195-1505', *Derbyshire Arch. Jnl.* xci, for 1971 (1973), 119-40.

—, 'Labour Productivity and Work Psychology in the English Mining Industry, 1400-1600', *Econ. Hist. Rev.* 2nd ser. xxxi (1978), 1-24.

—, 'Lead Mining and Smelting in Medieval England and Wales', in D.W. Crossley (ed.), *Medieval Industry* (C.B.A. Research Rep. xl, 1981), 72-84.

Blancourt, Haudicquer de, *De l'Art de la Verrerie* (Paris, 1697).

Boileau, Etienne, *see* Lespinasse, René de.

Bolton, C., 'Contributions on the History of Dyeing', *The Dyer and Textile Printer*, lxxiii-lxxxiii (1935-1940), passim.

Bony, Jean, 'French Influences on the Origins of English Gothic Architecture', *Jnl. of Warburg and Courtauld Insts.* xii (1949), 1-15.

—, *French Gothic Architecture of the Twelfth and Thirteenth Centuries* (1983).

Botfield, B., *Manners and Household Expenses of England in the Thirteenth and Fourteenth Centuries* [ed. T.H. Turner] (Roxburghe Club, No. 57, 1841).

Bowden, Peter J., *The Wool Trade in Tudor and Stuart England* (1962).

Braunstein, P., 'Innovations in Mining and Metal Production in Europe in the Late Middle Ages', *Jnl. of European Economic History*, xii (1983), 573-91.

Brepohl, Erhard, *Theophilus Presbyter und die Mittelalterliche Goldschmiedekunst* (Vienna etc., 1987).

Bridbury, Anthony R., *Medieval English Clothmaking: An Economic Survey* (1982).

Bridgewater, N.P., 'Glasshouse Farm, St. Weonards: a Small Glassworking Site', *Trans. Woolhope Naturalists' Field Club*, xxxvii (1961-3), pp. 300-15.

Briggs, M.S., 'Building-Construction', in *A History of Technology*, ed. Charles Singer et al., II (Oxford, 1956), 397-448.

Britnell, Richard H., *Growth and Decline in Colchester, 1300-1525* (Cambridge, 1986).

Brooks, Christopher, and D. Evans, *The Great East Window of Exeter Cathedral: a Glazing History* (Exeter, 1988).

Brooks, F.W., 'A Medieval Brick-yard at Hull', *J.B.A.A.* 3rd ser. iv (1939), 151-74.

Brownsword, Roger, *English Latten Domestic Candlesticks, 1440-1700*, Finds Research

Group 700-1700, Datasheet 1 ([Oxford, 1985]).

Bruck, R., 'Der Tractat des Meisters Antonio von Pisa über die Glasmalerei', *Repertorium für Kunstwissenschaft*, xxv (1902), 240-69.

Brunello, Franco, *The Art of Dyeing in the History of Mankind*, transl. B. Hickey (Vicenza, 1973).

Butler, L.A.S., 'Minor Medieval Monumental Sculpture in the East Midlands', *Arch. Jnl.* cxxi (1964), 111-53.


Calkin, J.B., 'Some Archaeological Discoveries in the Island of Purbeck: Part II', *Proc. Dorset Nat. Hist. and Arch. Soc.* lxxxi (1960), 121-2.

Cameron, H.K., 'Technical Aspects of Monumental Brasses', *Arch. Jnl.* cxxxi (1974), 215-37.

Campbell, Marian L., *An Introduction to Medieval Enamels* (1983).

Carter, A.C., and J.P. Roberts, 'Excavations in Norwich – 1972. The Norwich Survey – Second Interim Report', *Norfolk Archaeology*, xxxv (1970-3), 443-68.

Carus-Wilson, E.M., 'The Significance of the Secular Sculptures in the Lane Chapel, Cullompton', *Med. Arch.* i (1957), 104-117.

—, *Medieval Merchant Venturers: Collected Studies* (2nd edn., 1967).

—, 'Haberget: A Medieval Textile Conundrum', *Med. Arch.* xiii (1969), 148-66.

—, 'The Woollen Industry', in M.M. Postan and E. Miller (eds.), *Trade and Industry in the Middle Ages* (2nd edn., Cambridge, 1987), 613-90.

Caviness, Madeline, *The Early Stained Glass of Canterbury Cathedral, c.1175-1220* (Princeton, 1977).

—, and Staudinger, E.R., *Stained Glass before 1540: an Annotated Bibliography* (Boston, Mass. [1983]).

Cennini, Cennino d'Andrea, *The Craftsman's Handbook*, transl. D.V. Thompson (New Haven and London, 1933).

Chambon, R., 'Esquisse de l'Evolution Morphologique des Creusets de Verrerie, de l'Antiquité à la Renaissance', *Annales du 1er Congrès des 'Journées Internationales du Verre'* (Liège, 1959), 115-17.

—, 'L'Evolution des Procédés de Fabrication Manuelle du Verre à Vitres . . .', in F.R. Matson and G.E. Rindone (eds.), *Advances in Glass Technology*, part 2 (New York, 1963), 165-78.

Chamot, Mary, *English Mediaeval Enamels* (1930).

Charleston, R.J., 'Glass', in *A History of Technology*, ed. C. Singer et al., III, *From the Renaissance to the Industrial Revolution, c.1500-c.1750* (Oxford, 1957), 206-29.

—, 'Some Tools of the Glass-Maker in Medieval and Renaissance Times, with Special Reference to the Glass-Maker's Chair', *Glass Technology*, iii, No. 3 (June 1962), 107-11.

—, 'Glass of the High Medieval Period (12th to 15th Century)', *Bull. de l'Assoc. Internat. pour l'Hist. du Verre*, viii (1977-80), 65-76.

—, 'Glass Furnaces through the Ages', *Jnl. of Glass Studies*, xx (1978), 9-33.

—, 'A Gold and Enamel Box in the Form of a Glass Furnace', *Jnl. of Glass Studies*, xx

(1978), 35-44.

—, '16th to 17th Century English Glass', *Bull. de l'Association Internationale pour l'Histoire du Verre*, viii (1977-80).

—, 'Our Forefathers in Glass', *Glass Technology*, xxi, No. 1 (Feb. 1980), 27-36.

—, 'Vessel Glass', in A. Streeten, *Bayham Abbey* (Sussex Arch. Soc. Monograph 2, 1983).

—, *English Glass . . .* (1984).

Cheetham, Francis, *English Medieval Alabasters. With a Catalogue of the Collection in the Victoria and Albert Museum* (1984).

Cherry, J., 'A New Type of Dinanderie found in England', *British Museum Occasional Paper*, x (1980), 55-6.

C[hitty], H., 'John Prudde, "King's Glazier"', *Notes and Queries*, 12th ser. iii (1917), 419-21.

Chorley, P., 'English Cloth Exports during the Thirteenth and Early Fourteenth Centuries: the Continental Evidence', *Historical Research*, lxi (1988), 1-10.

Christie, A.G.I., *English Mediaeval Embroidery* (Oxford, 1938).

Clarkson, L.A., 'The Leather Crafts in Tudor and Stuart England', *Agricultural History Review*, xiv (1966), 25-39.

Cleere, Henry F., and D.W. Crossley, *The Iron Industry of the Weald* (Leicester, 1985).

Clifton-Taylor, A., *The Pattern of English Building* (4th edn., ed. J. Simmons, 1987).

—, and A.S. Ireson, *English Stone Building* (1983).

Coales, J. (ed.), *The Earliest English Brasses: Patronage, Style and Workshops 1270-1350* (Monumental Brass Soc., 1987).

Cohen, I., 'History of Ironworking in and near the Forest of Dean', *Trans. Woolhope Naturalists' Field Club*, xxxiv (1952-4), 161-77.

Coldstream, N., 'English Decorated Shrine-bases', *J.B.A.A.* cxxxix (1976), 15-34.

Collins, Francis (ed.), *Register of the Freemen of the City of York*, I, *1272-1558* (Surtees Soc. xcvi, 1897).

Colvin, H.M. (general ed.), *The History of the King's Works*, I-II, *The Middle Ages* (1963), III, *1485-1660 (Part I)* (1975); IV, *1485-1660 (Part II)* (1982).

—, (ed.), *Building Accounts of King Henry III* (Oxford, 1971).

Cooper, William, *The Crown Glass Cutter and Glazier's Manual* (Edinburgh and London, 1835).

Cowgill, Jane, M. de Neergard and N. Griffiths, *Knives and Scabbards*, Medieval Finds from Excavations in London, 1 (Museum of London, 1987).

Craddock, P.T., 'Medieval Copper Alloy Production and West African Brass Analysis: Part I', *Archaeometry*, xxvii (1985), 17-41.

Crewe, S., *Stained Glass in England c.1180-1540* (1987).

Crossley, David W., 'Glassmaking in Bagot's Park, Staffordshire, in the Sixteenth Century', *Post-Medieval Arch.* i (1967), 44-83.

—, (ed.), *Medieval Industry* (C.B.A. Research Rep. xl, 1981).

—, 'Medieval Iron Smelting', in D.W. Crossley (ed.), *Medieval Industry* (C.B.A. Research Rep. xl, 1981), 29-41.

—, and F.A. Aberg, '16th Century Glass-Making in Yorkshire: Excavations at Furnaces at Hutton and Rosedale', *Post-Med. Arch.* vi (1972), 107-59.

Crowfoot, Elisabeth, 'Textiles', in M.O.H. Carver, 'Three Saxo-Norman Tenements in Durham City', *Med. Arch.* xxiii (1979), 36-9.

—, F. Pritchard and K. Staniland, *Textiles and Clothing*, Medieval Finds from Excavations in London (Museum of London, forthcoming).

Dale, M.K., 'The London Silkwomen of the Fifteenth Century', *Econ. Hist. Rev.* 1st ser. iv (1932-4), 324-35.

Dare, M.P., 'Medieval Shoemakers and Tanners of Leicester, Northampton and Nottingham . . .', *Associated Architectural Societies' Reports & Papers*, xxxix (1928-9), 141-77.

Dexel, Thomas, *Gebrauchsgerät Typen* (Munich, 1981).

Dilks, T.D. (ed.), *Bridgwater Borough Archives*, i, 1200-1377 (Somerset Record Soc. xlviii, 1933).

Dodwell, C.R. (ed. and transl.), *Theophilus, De Diversis Artibus* (1961).

—, *Anglo-Saxon Art: a New Perspective* (Manchester, 1982).

Douglas, David C., and G.W. Greenaway (eds.), *English Historical Documents*, II, *1042-1189* (2nd edn., 1981).

Douglas, Ronald W., and Susan Frank, *A History of Glassmaking* (Henley-on-Thames, 1972).

Drescher, H., 'Mittelalterliche Dreibeintöpfe aus Bronze', in J.G.N. Renaud (ed.), *Rotterdam Papers* (Rotterdam, 1968), 23-33.

Drury, G. Dru, 'The Use of Purbeck Marble in Medieval Times', *Proc. Dorset Nat. Hist. and Arch. Soc.* lxx (1948), 74-98.

Drury, P.J., 'The Production of Brick and Tile in Medieval England', in D.W. Crossley (ed.), *Medieval Industry* (C.B.A. Research Rep. xl, 1981), 126-42.

Dugdale, William, *The Antiquities of Warwickshire* (2 parts, 2nd edn., 1730).

—, *Monasticon Anglicanum*, ed. J. Caley and others (6 vols., 1846).

Dunning, G.C., 'The Purbeck Marble Industry in the Roman Period', *Archaeological News Letter*, i.11 (March 1949), 15.

—, and others, 'Anglo Saxon Pottery: a Symposium', *Med. Arch.* iii (1959), 1-78.

—, 'Stone Mortars', *Med. Arch.* v (1961), 279-84.

—, 'Medieval Bronze Tap-Handles from Lewes and Kirkstall Abbey', *Antiq. Jnl.* xlviii (1968), 310-11.

Dyer, C., 'The Social and Economic Changes of the Later Middle Ages, and the Pottery of the Period', *Medieval Ceramics*, vi (1982), 33-42.

—, 'The Consumer and the Market in the Later Middle Ages', *Econ. Hist. Rev.* 2nd ser xli (1989), 305-27.

Eames, Elizabeth S., *Catalogue of Medieval Lead-glazed Earthenware Tiles in the Department of Medieval and Later Antiquities, British Museum* (2 vols., 1980).

—, *English Medieval Tiles* (1985).

Eames, Penelope, *Furniture in England, France and the Netherlands from the Twelfth to the Fifteenth Century, Furniture History*, xiii (1977).

Edlin, Herbert L., *Woodland Crafts in Britain* (1949).

Edwards, Joan, and J.L. Nevinson (eds.), 'The Rates of the London Custom House in 1550', *Costume*, iv (1970), 3-12.

Ekwall, E., *Two Early London Subsidy Rolls* (Lund, 1951).

Elphick, G.P., *Sussex Bells and Belfries* (1970).

—, *The Craft of the Bellfounder* (Chichester, 1988).

Emmerson, R., 'Monumental Brasses: London Design *c.*1420-85', *J.B.A.A.* cxxxi (1978), 50-78.

Eraclius, *De Coloribus et Artibus Romanorum*, see Merrifield, M.P.

Erskine, A.M. (ed.), *The Accounts of the Fabric of Exeter Cathedral, 1279-1353* (Devon and Cornwall Record Soc. n.s. xxiv, xxvi, 1981, 1983).

Evans, David, *A Bibliography of Stained Glass* (Cambridge, 1982).

Evans, Joan, *Magical Jewels of the Middle Ages and the Renaissance* (Oxford, 1922).

—, *A History of Jewellery, 1100-1870* (2nd edn., 1970).

Falke, Otto von, and E. Meyer, *Romanische Leuchter und Gefässe, Giessgefässe der Gotik*, Bronzegeräte des Mittelalters, I (repr. with additions, Berlin, 1983).

Feldhaus, F.M., *Die Technik* (2nd edn., Munich, 1965).

Fell, Alfred, *The Early Iron Industry of Furness and District* (Ulverston, 1908).

Fernie, E.C., and A.B. Whittingham (eds.), *The Early Communar and Pittancer Rolls of Norwich Cathedral Priory* (Norfolk Record Soc. xli, 1972).

Finberg, Herbert P.R., *Tavistock Abbey. A Study in the Social and Economic History of Devon* (2nd edn., Newton Abbot, 1969).

Firman, R.J., and P.E. Firman, 'A Geological Approach to the Study of Medieval Bricks', *Mercian Geologist*, ii.3 (1967), 229-318.

—, 'A Geological Approach to the History of English Alabaster', *Mercian Geologist*, ix.3 (1984), 161-78.

Fisher, Frederick Jack, *A Short History of the Worshipful Company of Horners* (1936).

Forbes, Robert J., 'Metallurgy', in *A History of Technology*, ed. Charles Singer et al., II (Oxford, 1956), 41-80.

—, *Studies in Ancient Technology*, VII and VIII (2nd edn., Leiden, 1966, 1971).

Frank, Susan, *Glass and Archaeology* (1982).

Fransson, Gustav, *Middle English Surnames of Occupation, 1100-1350*, Lund Studies in English, iii (1938).

Fraser, C.M., 'The Pattern of Trade in the North-East of England, 1265-1350', *Northern History*, iv (1969), 44-66.

French, T., and D. O'Connor, *York Minster: A Catalogue of Medieval Stained Glass*. I: *The West Windows of the Nave* (*Corpus Vitrearum Medii Aevi: Great Britain*, iii.1, 1987).

Fritz, Johann Michael, *Goldschmiedekunst der Gotik in Mitteleuropa* (Munich, 1982).

Frodl-Kraft, E., *Die Glasmalerei: Entwicklung, Technik, Eigenart* (Vienna & Zurich, 1970).

Gardner, Arthur, *Alabaster Tombs of the Pre-Reformation Period in England* (Cambridge, 1940).

—, *English Medieval Sculpture* (rev. edn., Cambridge, 1951).

—, *Minor English Wood Sculpture 1400-1550. An Essay on Carved Figures and Animals on Bench-Ends in English Parish Churches* (1958).

Gardner, J. Starkie, *Ironwork*, pt. I, 4th edn. by W.W. Watts (1927) and pt. III (1922); reprinted with supplementary bibliography (1978).

Gardner, J.S. 'Coggeshall Abbey and its Early Brickwork', *J.B.A.A.* 3rd ser. xviii (1955), 19-32.

Geddes, J., 'The Sanctuary Ring of Durham Cathedral', *Archaeologia*, cvii (1982), 125-30.

—, 'The Blacksmith's Life, Wife and Work, 1250-1450', *Tools and Trades*, i (1983), 15-37.

Gill, Margaret, *A Directory of Newcastle Goldsmiths* (Newcastle, 1980).

Giuseppi, M.S., 'Some Fourteenth-Century Accounts of Ironworks at Tudeley, Kent', *Archaeologia*, lxiv, for 1912-13 (1913), 145-64.

Godfrey, Eleanor, S., *The Development of English Glassmaking 1560-1640* (Oxford, 1975).

Goldberg, P.J.P., 'Women's Work, Women's Role, in the Late Medieval North', in Michael A. Hicks (ed.), *Profit, Piety and the Professions in Later Medieval England* (Gloucester etc., 1990), 34-50.

Goldthwaite, Richard A., *The Building of Renaissance Florence* (Baltimore, 1980).

Goodall, Alison R., 'The Medieval Bronzesmith and his Products', in D.W. Crossley (ed.), *Medieval Industry* (C.B.A. Research Rep. xl, 1981), 63-71.

Goodall, I.H., 'The Medieval Blacksmith and his Products', in D.W. Crossley (ed.), *Medieval Industry* (C.B.A. Research Rep. xl, 1981), 51-62.

Goodall, J.A., 'Two Medieval Drawings', *Antiq. Jnl.* lviii (1978), 160-2.

Graham-Campbell, James, *Viking Artefacts: A Select Catalogue* (Exhibition Catalogue, British Museum, 1980).

Gras, N.S.B., *The Early English Customs System*, Harvard Economic Studies, xviii (Cambridge, Mass., 1918).

Graves, Edgar B. (ed.), *A Bibliography of English History to 1485* (Oxford, 1975).

Greenhill, Basil, *Archaeology of the Boat* (1976).

Greenwood, John, *The Industrial Archaeology and Industrial History of London: A Bibliography* (1988).

Greeves, T.A.P., 'The Archaeological Potential of the Devon Tin Industry', in D.W. Crossley (ed.), *Medieval Industry* (C.B.A. Research Rep. xl, 1981), 85-95.

Grew, Francis, and M. de Neergard, *Shoes and Pattens*, Medieval Finds from Excavations in London, 2 (Museum of London, 1988).

Hall, D.W., 'Some Early London Pewterers', *Jnl. of the Pewter Soc.* iii.3 (1982), 78-9.

Halsey, R., 'The Galilee Chapel', in *Medieval Art and Architecture at Durham Cathedral*: British Arch. Association Conference Trans. for 1977 (1980), 59-73.

Hamilton, Henry, *The English Brass and Copper Industries to 1800* (2nd edn., 1967).

Harden, D.B., 'Domestic Window Glass: Roman, Saxon and Medieval', in E.M. Jope (ed.), *Studies in Building History* . . . (1961), 39-63.

—, 'Medieval Glass in the West', in *Eighth International Congress on Glass* (1969), 97-111.

—, 'Ancient Glass, III: Post-Roman', *Arch. Jnl.* cxxviii, for 1971 (1972), 78-117.

Harley, L.S., 'A Typology of Brick', *J.B.A.A.* 3rd ser. xxxvii (1974), 63-87.

Harrington, J.C., *Glassmaking at Jamestown* (1952).

Harris, Richard, *Discovering Timber-Framed Buildings*, Shire Archaeology (Princes Risborough, 1978).

Harrison, Frederick, *The Painted Glass of York* (1927).

Hartley, Marie, and Joan Ingilby, *The Old Hand-Knitters of the Dales* (Clapham, Lancaster, 1951).

Hartshorne, Albert, *Old English Glasses* (1897).

Harvey, B.F., 'Work and *Festa Ferianda* in Medieval England', *Jnl. of Ecclesiastical History*, xxiii (1972), 287-308.

Harvey, John H., *Mediaeval Craftsmen* (1975).

—, *English Mediaeval Architects. A Biographical Dictionary down to 1550* (2nd edn., Gloucester, 1984); *Supplement* (Isle of Wight, 1987).

—, and D. King, 'Winchester College Stained Glass', *Archaeologia*, ciii (1971), 149-77.

Hatcher, John, *English Tin Production and Trade before 1550* (Oxford, 1973).

—, and Theodore C. Barker, *A History of British Pewter* (1974).

Hawthorne, John G., and Cyril Smith, intro. and transl., *Theophilus, On Divers Arts* (Chicago, 1963; reprinted with additions, New York, 1979).

Heaton, Herbert, *The Yorkshire Woollen and Worsted Industries* (Oxford, 1920).

Hedges, Ernest S., *Tin in Social and Economic History* (1964).

Hemming, A.G., 'Mortars by English Church Bell Founders', *Connoisseur*, xciii (Jan.-June 1934), 392-5.

Hewett, Cecil, *English Historic Carpentry* (Chichester, 1980).

—, *Church Carpentry* (Chichester, 1982).

—, *Cathedral and Monastic Carpentry* (Chichester, 1985).

Hibbert, W.N., *History of the Worshipful Company of Founders* (1925).

Hildburgh, W.L., 'English Alabaster Tables of about the Third Quarter of the Fourteenth Century', *Art Bulletin*, xxxii (1950), 1-23.

Hill, James W. Francis, *Medieval Lincoln* (Cambridge, 1948).

Hilton, R.H., *A Medieval Society. The West Midlands at the End of the Thirteenth Century* (1966; reptd. with corrections, 1983).

Hoffmann, Marta, *The Warp-Weighted Loom* (Oslo, 1964).

Hollestelle, J., *De Steenbakkerij in de Nederlanden tot omstreeks 1560* (Arnhem, 1976).

Homer, Ronald F., *Five Centuries of Base Metal Spoons* (Worshipful Co. of Pewterers, 1975).

—, 'Medieval London Pewterers', *Jnl. of the Pewter Soc.* iv.2 (1983), 47-53.

—, 'The Origin of the Craft in London', *Jnl. of the Pewter Soc.* v.2 (1985), 54-7.

—, 'Chalices and Patens at Lincoln Cathedral', *Jnl. of the Pewter Soc.* v.3 (1986), 73-6.

—, 'The Medieval Pewterers of London, *c*.1190-1457', *Trans. London and Middlesex Arch. Soc.* xxxvi (1985), 137-63.

Hope, W.H.St.J., 'On the Sculptured Alabaster Tablets called Saint John's Heads', *Archaeologia* lii, pt. ii (1890), 669-708.

—, 'On the Early Working of Alabaster in England', *Arch. Jnl.* lxi (1904), 221-40.

Horner, John, *The Linen Trade of Europe during the Spinning-Wheel Period* (Belfast, 1920).

Hornsby, P.R.J., R.F. Homer and R. Weinstein, *Pewter, A Celebration of the Craft 1200-1700* (Museum of London, 1989).

How, G.E.P. and J.P., *English and Scottish Silver Spoons, Mediaeval to Late Stuart, and Pre-Elizabethan Hall-marks on English Plate* (3 vols., privately printed, 1952-7).

Howard, F.E., and F.H. Crossley, *English Church Woodwork* (2nd edn., 1927).

Hugo, Thomas, 'Notes on a Collection of Pilgrims' Signs', *Archaeologia*, xxxviii (1860), 128-34.

Hunter, J.R., 'The Medieval Glass Industry', in D.W. Crossley (ed.), *Medieval Industry* (C.B.A. Research Rep. xl, 1981), 143-50.

Hurry, Jamieson B., *The Woad Plant and its Dye*, ed. A.R. Horwood (1930).

Hurst, J.G., 'The Pottery', in David M. Wilson (ed.), *The Archaeology of Anglo-Saxon England* (1976), 283-348.

*Illustrated Catalogue of the Exhibition of English Medieval Alabaster Work, held in the Rooms of the Society of Antiquaries . . . 1910* (1913).

Jack, Sybil M., *Trade and Industry in Tudor and Stuart England* (1977).

Jackson, Charles J., *An Illustrated History of English Plate* (2 vols., 1911).

—, *English Goldsmiths and their Marks* (2nd edn., 1921).

Jackson, E., 'On a Bronze Tripod Vessel', *Trans. Cumberland and Westmorland Arch. Soc.* n.s. viii (1908), 72-4.

James, M.R., 'An English Medieval Sketch-Book, No. 1916 in the Pepysian Library, Magdalene College, Cambridge', *Walpole Soc.* xiii (1924-5), 1-17.

Jenkins, John G. (ed.), *The Wool Textile Industry in Great Britain* (1972).

Jennings, Sarah, *Eighteen Centuries of Pottery from Norwich* (East Anglian Archaeology, Rep. No. 13, 1981).

Jexlev, Thelma, P. Rissmøller and M. Schlüter, *Dansk Glas i Renaessancetid, 1550-1650* (Copenhagen, 1970).

Kahl, W.F., *The Development of London Livery Companies: an Historical Essay and a Select Bibliography* (Boston, Mass., 1960).

Kamińska, J., and A. Nahlik, 'Études sur l'Industrie Textile du Haut Moyen Âge en Pologne', *Archaeologia Polona*, iii (1960), 89-119.

Keene, Derek, *Survey of Medieval Winchester*, Winchester Studies, 2 (2 vols., Oxford, 1985).

Kelly, Serena, E. Rutledge and M. Tillyard, *Men of Property. An Analysis of the Norwich Enrolled Deeds, 1285-1311* (Norwich, 1983).

Kent, J.P.C., 'Monumental Brasses: a New Classification of Military Effigies, *c*.1360-*c*.1485', *J.B.A.A.* 3rd ser. xii (1949), 70-97.

Kenyon, G.H., 'A Sussex Yeoman Family as Glass-makers', *Jnl. Soc. Glass Technology*, xxxv, No. 162 (Feb. 1951), 6-8.

—, *The Glass Industry of the Weald* (Leicester, 1967).

Kerridge, Eric, *Textile Manufactures in Early Modern England* (Manchester, 1985).

Kilmurry, K., *The Pottery Industry of Stamford, Lincolnshire, c. A.D.850-1250 . . .*, British Archaeological Reports, British Ser. 84 (1980).

[King, Donald], *Opus Anglicanum: English Medieval Embroidery* (Catalogue of Arts Council exhibition at Victoria and Albert Museum, 1963).

Knight, B., 'Researches on Medieval Window Lead', *Jnl. of Stained Glass*, xviii.1 (1983-4), 49-51.

Knoop, D., and G.P. Jones, 'The Building of Eton College, 1442-1460', *Ars Quatuor Coronatorum*, xlvi (1937), 70-114.

—, and G.P. Jones, *The Mediaeval Mason* (3rd edn., Manchester, 1967).

Knowles, J.A., 'The Source of the Coloured Glass used in Medieval Stained Glass Windows', *Glass* (June 1926), 157-9, 201-3, 295-6.

—, 'Medieval Processes of Glass Manufacture', *Glass* (July 1927), 303, 305, 307, 309, 343, 345, 349, 359, 391, 395, 397, 399.

—, *Essays in the History of the York School of Glass-Painting* (London and New York, 1936).

Kren, Claudia (ed.), *Medieval Science and Technology: A Select Annotated Bibliography* (New York, 1985).

Kuile, Onno ter, *Rijksmuseum, Amsterdam, Koper & Brons* (s'Gravenhage, 1988).


Lacey, K.E., 'Women and Work in Fourteenth and Fifteenth Century London', in L. Charles and L. Duffin (eds.), *Women and Work in Pre-Industrial England* (1985), 24-82.

Lafond, J., *La Résurrection d'un Maître d'Autrefois* (Rouen, 1942).

—, *Le Vitrail* (Paris, 1966).

Lankester, P.J., 'A Military Effigy in Dorchester Abbey, Oxon', *Oxoniensia*, lii (1987), 145-72.

Lapsley, G.T., 'The Account Roll of a Fifteenth-century Ironmaster', *Eng. Hist. Rev.* xiv (1899), 509-29.

Leach, A.F., 'The Building of Beverley Bar', *Trans. East Riding Antiquarian Soc.* iv (1896), 26-37.

Leach, R., *An Investigation into the Use of Purbeck Marble in Medieval England* (2nd edn., privately printed, Crediton, 1978).

Le Couteur, J.D., *Ancient Glass in Winchester* (Winchester, 1920).

—, *English Mediaeval Painted Glass* (1926).

Le Goff, Jacques, *Time, Work and Culture in the Middle Ages*, transl. A. Goldhammer (Chicago, 1980).

Le Patourel, H.E. Jean, 'Documentary Evidence and the Medieval Pottery Industry',

*Med. Arch.* xii (1968), 101-26.

Lehmann-Brockhaus, O., *Lateinische Schriftquellen zur Kunst in England, Wales und Schottland, vom Jahre 901 bis zum Jahre 1307* (5 vols., Veröffentlichungen des Zentralinstituts für Kunstgeschichte in München, Munich, 1955-60).

Lespinasse, René de, and François Bonnardot (eds.), *Les Métiers et Corporations de la Ville de Paris. Le Livre des Métiers d'Etienne Boileau*, Histoire Générale de Paris, Collection de Documents (Paris, 1879).

Lewis, G.R., *The Stannaries. A Study of the Medieval Tin Miners of Cornwall and Devon* (Camb., Mass., 1908).

Lewis, J.M., R. Brownsword and E.E.H. Pitt, 'Medieval Bronze "Tripod" Ewers from Wales', *Med. Arch.* xxi (1987), 80-93.

Lightbown, R.W., *Secular Goldsmiths' Work in Medieval France* (1978).

Lillich, M.P., 'Gothic Glaziers: Monks, Jews, Taxpayers, Bretons, Women', *Jnl. of Glass Studies*, xxvii (1985), 72-92.

Lindsay, J. Seymour, *Iron and Brass Implements of the English House* (revised edn., 1970).

Lipson, Ephraim, *The History of the Woollen and Worsted Industries* (1921).

Lloyd, Nathaniel, *A History of English Brickwork* (1925).

Lloyd, Terence H., 'Some Costs of Cloth Manufacturing in 13th Century England', *Textile History*, i (1971), 332-6.

—, *The English Wool Trade in the Middle Ages* (Cambridge, 1977).

Lockner, Hermann P., *Messing. Ein Handbuch über Messinggerät des 15.-17.Jahrhunderts* (Munich, 1982).


McCarthy, Michael R., and Catherine M. Brooks, *Medieval Pottery in Britain, A.D. 900-1600* (Leicester, 1988).

McGrail, Sean (ed.), *Medieval Ships and Harbours in Northern Europe* (National Maritime Museum, Greenwich, Archaeological Series, No. 5; British Archaeological Reps. Internat. Ser. 66, 1979).

—, (ed.), *Woodworking Techniques before A.D. 1500* (National Maritime Museum, Greenwich Archaeological Series, No. 7; British Archaeological Reps. Internat. Ser. 129, 1982).

MacGregor, Arthur, 'Industry and Commerce in Anglo-Scandinavian York', in R.A. Hall (ed.), *Viking Age York and the North* (C.B.A. Research Rep. xxvii, 1978), 34-57.

—, *Bone, Antler, Ivory and Horn: the Technology of Skeletal Materials since the Roman Period* (1985).

Magnusson, G., 'Lapphyttan – an Example of Medieval Iron Production', in N. Bjorkenstam et al. (eds.), *Medieval Iron in Society*, Jernkontorets Publication 434 (Stockholm, 1985), 21-33.

Marks, R., *The Stained Glass of the Collegiate Church of the Holy Trinity, Tattershall (Lincs.)* (1984).

—, *Stained Glass in England during the Middle Ages* (forthcoming).

Marshall, K., 'Cast-Bronze Cauldrons of Medieval Type in the Belfast City Museum',

*Ulster Jnl. of Archaeology*, 3rd ser. xii (1950), 66-75.

Mende, U., *Die Türzieher des Mittelalters* (Munich, 1981).

Mercer, Eric, *English Vernacular Houses* (1975).

Merrett, Christopher, *see* Neri, Antonio.

Merrifield, Mary P., *Original Treatises . . . on the Arts of Painting in Oil, Miniature, Mosaic and on Glass* (2 vols., 1849).

Michaelis, Ronald F., *Antique Pewter of the British Isles* (1955).

—, *Old Domestic Base-Metal Candlesticks* (Woodbridge, 1978).

Mickenberg, David (ed.), *Songs of Glory: Medieval Art from 900-1500* (Exhibition catalogue, Oklahoma Museum of Art, 1985).

Miller, E., 'The Fortunes of the English Textile Industry during the Thirteenth Century', *Econ. Hist. Rev.* 2nd ser. xviii (1965), 64-82.

Mitchiner, Michael B., and Anne Skinner, 'English Tokens, c.1200-1425', *British Numismatic Jnl.* liii, for 1983 (1984), 29-77.

—, and Anne Skinner, 'Contemporary Forgeries of English Silver Coins: Henry III to William III', *Numismatic Chronicle*, cxlv (1985), 209-36.

Montague, Jeremy, *The World of Medieval and Renaissance Musical Instruments* (Newton Abbot, 1976).

Moore, Ellen Wedemeyer, *The Fairs of Medieval England* (Toronto, 1985).

Moore, N.J., *Brick Building in Medieval England* (unpublished MPhil thesis, University of East Anglia, 1969).

Moorhouse, S.A., et al., 'Medieval Distilling-Apparatus of Glass and Pottery', *Med. Arch.* xvi (1972), 79-121.

—, 'The Glass', in K.J. Barton and E.W. Holden, 'Excavations at Bramber Castle, Sussex, 1966-67', *Arch. Jnl.* cxxxiv (1977), 70-2.

—, 'The Medieval Pottery Industry and its Markets', in D.W. Crossley (ed.), *Medieval Industry* (C.B.A. Research Rep. xl, 1981), 95-125.

—, 'Vessel Glass', in P. Mayes and L.A.S. Butler, *Sandal Castle Excavations, 1964-1973*, ed. S. Johnson (Woolley, 1983), 225-30.

Morris, Carole A., 'Anglo-Saxon and Medieval Woodworking Crafts – the Manufacture and Use of Domestic and Utilitarian Wooden Artifacts in the British Isles, 400-1500 AD' (unpublished PhD thesis, University of Cambridge, 1984).

Muldoon, Sara, and Roger Brownsword, *Pewter Spoons and other Related Material of the 14th-17th Centuries in the Collection of the Herbert Art Gallery and Museum, Coventry* (Coventry, [1985]).

Munro, J.H., 'Wool Price Schedules and the Qualities of English Wools in the later Middle Ages c.1270-1499', *Textile History*, ix (1978), 119-69.

—, 'The Medieval Scarlet and the Economics of Sartorial Splendour', in N.B. Harte and K.G. Ponting (eds.), *Cloth and Clothing in Medieval Europe, Essays in Memory of Professor E.M. Carus-Wilson* (1983), 13-70.

Musty, John, 'Medieval Pottery Kilns', in Vera I. Evison, H. Hodges and J.G. Hurst (eds.), *Medieval Pottery from Excavations* (1974), 41-67.

Myers, Alec R. (ed.), *English Historical Documents*, IV, *1337-1485* (1969).

Neri, Antonio, *L'Arte Vetraria* (Florence, 1612); transl. Christopher Merrett, *The Art of Glass* (1662).

Nesbitt, Alexander, *A Descriptive Catalogue of the Glass Vessels in the South Kensington Museum, London* (1878).

Newstead, R., 'Glasshouse in Delamere Forest, Cheshire', *Jnl. of the Chester and N. Wales Architectural, Arch. and Historic Soc.* n.s. xxxiii (1939), 32-9.

Nichols, John, *A Collection of all the Wills . . . of the Kings & Queens of England . . . and the Blood Royal* (1780).

Norris, M., *Monumental Brasses: the Craft* (1978) and *Monumental Brasses: the Memorials* (2 vols., 1977).

North, John D., *Richard of Wallingford: an Edition of his Writings* (Oxford, 1976).


O'Connor, D.E., 'Débris from a Medieval Glazier's Workshop', *Interim (Bull. of the York Archaeological Trust)*, iii, No. 1 (August 1975), 11-17.

—, and J. Haselock, 'The Stained and Painted Glass', in G.E. Aylmer and R. Cant (eds.), *A History of York Minster* (Oxford, 1977), 313-93.

Oman, C.C., *English Church Plate, 597-1830* (1957).

—, 'English Medieval Base Metal Church Plate', *Arch. Jnl.* cxix (1962), 195-207.

Oswald, A., 'Barnard Flower, The King's Glazier', *J.B.S.M.G.P.* xi (1951-5).

—, 'The Glazing of the Savoy Hospital', *J.B.S.M.G.P.* xi (1951-5).

Owen, D.M. (ed.), *The Making of King's Lynn* (1984).


Palgrave, Francis, *Antient Kalendars and Inventories of the Treasury of His Majesty's Exchequer* (3 vols., 1836).

Pape, T., 'An Elizabethan Glass Furnace', *Connoisseur*, xcii (July-Dec. 1933), 172-7.

—, 'Medieval Glassworkers in North Staffordshire', *North Staffs. Field Club Trans.* for 1933-4, lxviii (1934), 74-121.

Papworth, W., 'Latten or Brass', *Notes and Queries*, 3rd ser. xii (July-Dec. 1867), 301-3.

Partingdon, J.R., *A History of Greek Fire and Gunpowder* (Cambridge, 1960).

Pinto, Edward H., *Treen and other Wooden Bygones* (1969).

Pirenne, H., 'Les Marchands-Batteurs de Dinant au XIV$^e$ et au XV$^e$ Siècle', *Vierteljahrschrift für Social- und Wirtschaftsgeschichte*, ii (1904), 442-9.

Platt, Colin P.S., *Medieval Southampton. The Port and Trading Community, A.D. 1000-1600* (1973).

—, *The English Medieval Town* (1976).

—, and R. Coleman-Smith (eds.), *Excavations in Medieval Southampton, 1953-69* (2 vols., Leicester, 1975).

Poerck, G. de, *La Draperie Médiévale en Flandre et en Artois. Technique et Terminologie* (3 vols., Bruges, 1951).

Ponting, Kenneth G., *The Woollen Industry of South-West England* (Bath, 1971).

Postan, Michael M., E.E. Rich and Edward Miller (eds.), *The Cambridge Economic History of Europe*. III, *Economic Organization and Policies in the Middle Ages* (Cambridge, 1963).

—, *The Medieval Economy and Society. An Economic History of Britain in the Middle Ages* (1972).

—, and Edward Miller (eds.), *The Cambridge Economic History of Europe*. II, *Trade and Industry in the Middle Ages* (2nd edn., Cambridge, 1987).

Power, Eileen, and M.M. Postan (eds.), *Studies in English Trade in the Fifteenth Century* (1933).

Prior, E.S., and A. Gardner, *An Account of Medieval Figure-Sculpture in England* (Cambridge, 1912).

Pritchard, Frances A., 'Textiles from Recent Excavations in the City of London', *Textilsymposium Neumünster* (Neumünster, 1982), 193-208.

—, 'Late Saxon Textiles from the City of London', *Med. Arch.* xxviii (1984), 46-76.


Rackham, Bernard, *Medieval English Pottery*, ed. J.G. Hurst (1972).

Rackham, Oliver, *Ancient Woodland* (1980).

—, *The History of the Countryside* (1986).

Raine, Angelo (ed.), *York Civic Records*, i-iv, *1475-1548* (Yorks. Archaeol. Soc., Record Ser. xcviii, 1938; ciii, 1940; cvi, 1942; cviii, 1943).

Raine, James (ed.), *Testamenta Eboracensia*, I-IV (Surtees Soc. iv, 1836, xxx, 1855, xlv, 1864, liii, 1868).

—, (ed.), *Fabric Rolls of the Minster of York* (Surtees Soc. xxxv, 1858).

Ramsay, N.L., 'Makers of Sixteenth-Century Church Monuments', *Monumental Brass Soc. Bull.* 27 (June 1981), 9-10.

—, 'Artists, Craftsmen and Design in England, 1200-1400', in J.J.G. Alexander and P. Binski (eds.), *Age of Chivalry: Art in Plantagenet England, 1200-1400* (Exhibition Catalogue, Royal Academy of Arts, 1987), 49-54.

Ransome, D.R., 'The Struggle of the Glaziers' Company with the Foreign Glaziers, 1500-1550', *Guildhall Miscellany*, ii, No. 1 (Sept. 1960).

Reddaway, T.F., and L.E.M. Walker, *The Early History of the Goldsmiths' Company, 1327-1509* (1975).

Ridgway, M.H., and G.B. Leach, 'Further Notes on the Glasshouse Sites at Kingswood, Delamere, Cheshire', *Jnl. of the Chester and N. Wales Architectural, Arch. and Historic Soc.* n.s. xxxvii (1948-9), 133-40.

Riley, Henry T. (transl. and ed.), *Memorials of London and London Life, in the XIIIth, XIVth and XVth Centuries* (1868).

Ritter, G., *Les Vitraux de la Cathédrale de Rouen* (Cognac, 1926).

Rothwell, Harry (ed.), *English Historical Documents*, III, *1189-1327* (1975).

Ruddock, Alwyn A., *Italian Merchants and Shipping in Southampton, 1270-1600* (Southampton Record Ser. i, 1951).

Ruette, M. de, 'Les Résultats d'Analyse de Teneurs des Laitons Coutes dans les Anciens Pays-Bas Méridionaux et la Principauté de Liège (Moyen Age et Temps Modernes)', *Revue des Archéologues et Historiens d'Art de Louvain*, xvi (1983), 252-79.

Ryde, C., 'An Alabaster Standing Angel with Shield at Lowick – a Chellaston Shop Pattern', *Derbys. Arch. Jnl.* xcvii (1977), 36-49.

Ryder, Michael L., *Sheep and Man* (1983).

Salter, E., 'A Complaint against the Blacksmiths', *Literature and History*, v (1979), 194-215.

Salzman, Louis F., *English Industries in the Middle Ages* (2nd edn., Oxford, 1923).

—, 'The Glazing of St. Stephen's Chapel, Westminster', *J.B.S.M.G.P.* i (1924-6), No. 4, 14-16; No. 5, 31-5; ii (1927-8), 38-41.

—, 'Medieval Glazing Accounts', *J.B.S.M.G.P.* ii (1927-8), 116-20, 188-92; iii (1929-30), 25-30.

—, *English Trade in the Middle Ages* (Oxford, 1931).

—, 'Mines and Stannaries', in J.F. Willard, W.A. Morris and W.H. Dunham jr. (eds.), *The English Government at Work, 1327-36*, III (Cambridge, Mass., 1950), 67-104.

—, *Building in England, down to 1540: a Documentary History* (rev. edn., Oxford, 1967).

Schubert, Hans R., *History of the British Iron and Steel Industry, from c.450 B.C. to A.D. 1775* (1957).

Sellers, Maud (ed.), *York Memorandum Book*, 2 parts (Surtees Soc. cxx, 1911, and cxxv, 1915).

Sharpe, Reginald R. (ed.), *Calendar of Letter-Books . . . of the Corporation of the City of London . . . Letter-Book A* (etc.) 11 vols. (1899-1912).

Shortt, H. de S., 'The Three Bishops' Tombs Moved to Salisbury Cathedral and Old Sarum', *Wilts. Arch. Mag.* lvii (1958-60), 217-19.

Simpson, W. Douglas (ed.), *The Building Accounts of Tattershall Castle 1434-1472* (Lincoln Record Soc. lv, 1960).

Singer, Charles, et al. (eds.), *A History of Technology*, II, *The Mediterranean Civilizations and the Middle Ages, c.700 B.C. to c. A.D. 1500* (Oxford, 1956); III, *From the Renaissance to the Industrial Revolution, c.1500-c.1750* (Oxford, 1957).

Smith, C.S., and J.G. Hawthorne, 'Mappae Clavicula. A Little Key to the World of Medieval Techniques', *Trans. American Philosophical Soc.* n.s. lxiv, pt. 4 (1974).

Smith, J.T., *Antiquities of Westminster* (1807).

Smith, Joshua Toulmin, and Lucy Toulmin Smith (eds.), L. Brentano (intro.), *English Gilds. The Original Ordinances of More than one Hundred early English Gilds . . .* (Early English Text Society, orig. ser. xl, 1870; reprinted with additions 1892).

Smith, Terence P., *The Medieval Brickmaking Industry in England, 1400-1450* (British Archaeological Reps. British Ser. 138, 1985).

Spencer, Brian, 'Medieval Pilgrim Badges', in J.G.N. Renaud (ed.), *Rotterdam Papers. A Contribution to Medieval Archaeology* (Rotterdam, 1968), 137-53.

—, 'Pilgrim Souvenirs from the Medieval Waterfront Excavations at Trig Lane, London, 1974-6', *Trans. London & Middlesex Arch. Soc.* xxxiii (1982), 304-23.

Stahlschmidt, J.C.L., *Surrey Bells and London Bell-Founders* (1884).

Stone, Lawrence, *Sculpture in Britain: The Middle Ages* (2nd edn., 1972).

Straker, Ernest, *Wealden Iron* (1931).

Strutt, Joseph, *A Complete View of the Dress and Habits of the People of England*, ed.

J.R. Planché (2 vols., 1842).

Swanson, Heather C., 'Craftsmen and Industry in Late Medieval York' (unpublished DPhil thesis, University of York, 1980-1).

—, *Building Craftsmen in Late Medieval York* (Borthwick Papers, No. 63, 1983).

—, *Medieval Artisans. An Urban Class in Late Medieval England* (Oxford, 1989).

Taylor, Maisie, *Wood in Archaeology*, Shire Archaeology (Princes Risborough, 1981).

Theophilus, *see* Brepohl, Erhard; Dodwell, C.R., J.G. Hawthorne and C.S. Smith.

Thomas, Arthur H. (ed.), *Calendar of Early Mayor's Court Rolls . . . of the City of London . . . 1298-1307* (Cambridge, 1924).

—, and Philip E. Jones (eds.), *Calendar of Plea and Memoranda Rolls . . . of the City of London, 1323-1482* (6 vols., Cambridge, 1926-61).

Thompson, A.H., 'The Building Accounts of Kirby Muxloe Castle, 1480-84', *Trans. Leics. Arch. Soc.* xi (1913-20), 193-345.

Thompson, D.V., 'Trial Index to some Unpublished Sources for the History of Mediaeval Craftsmanship', *Speculum*, x (1935), 410-31.

—, *The Materials and Techniques of Medieval Painting* (1936).

Thompson, M.W., 'The Date of "Fox's Tower", Farnham Castle, Surrey', *Surrey Arch. Collns.* lvii (1960), 85-92.

Thorpe, William A., *A History of English and Irish Glass* (1929).

—, *English Glass* (3rd edn., 1961).

Thrupp, Sylvia L., *The Merchant Class of Medieval London, 1300-1500* (Chicago, etc., 1948).

Thuresson, Bertil, *Middle English Occupational Terms* (Lund Studies in English, xix, 1950).

Tout, T.F., 'Firearms in England in the Fourteenth Century', *Collected Papers of T.F. Tout*, II (Manchester, 1934), 233-75; reprinted with an introduction by C. Blair (London, 1968).

Trevisa, John, *On the Properties of Things: Translation of Bartholomaeus Anglicus, De Proprietatibus Rerum. A Critical Text*, ed. [M.C. Seymour] (3 vols., Oxford, 1975-88).

Trow-Smith, Robert, *A History of British Livestock Husbandry to 1700* (1957).

Tudor-Craig, P., 'Archbishop Hubert Walter's Tomb and its Furnishings: The Tomb', in *Medieval Art and Architecture at Canterbury*, British Arch. Association Conference Trans. for 1979 (1982), 72-80.

Tummers, H.A., *Early Secular Effigies in England: the Thirteenth Century* (Leiden, 1980).

Turnau, Irena, 'The Organization of the European Textile Industry from the Thirteenth to the Eighteenth Century', *Jnl. of European Economic History*, xvii (1988), 583-602.

Turner, W.E.S., 'Studies in Ancient Glasses and Glassmaking Processes, Part IV, The Chemical Composition of Ancient Glasses', and 'Part V, Raw Materials and Melting Processes', *Jnl., Soc. Glass Technology*, xl (1956), 162-86, 277-300.

Tylecote, Ronald F., 'The Medieval Smith and his Methods', in D.W. Crossley (ed.), *Medieval Industry* (C.B.A. Research Rep. xl, 1981), 42-50.

—, *The Prehistory of Metallurgy in the British Isles* (1986).
—, *A History of Metallurgy* (revised edn., 1986).

Unwin, George (ed.), *Finance and Trade under Edward III* (1918).
—, *The Gilds and Companies of London* (3rd edn., rev. F.J. Fisher, 1938, and 4th edn., 1963).

Veale, Elspeth M., 'Craftsmen and the Economy of London in the Fourteenth Century', in A.E.J. Hollaender and W. Kellaway (eds.), *Studies in London History* (1969), 131-51.
Vellacott, C.H., 'Quarrying', in *V.C.H. Dorset*, ii (1908), 331-44.
Vince, Alan, 'The Medieval and Post-Medieval Ceramic Industry of the Malvern Region: The Study of a Ware and its Distribution', in David P.S. Peacock (ed.), *Pottery and Early Commerce* (1977), 257-305.
Viollet-le-Duc, Eugène Emmanuel, *Dictionnaire Raisonné de l'Architecture Française du XIᵉ au XVIᵉ Siècle* (10 vols., Paris, 1858-68).
Vose, Ruth Hurst, *Glass* (1980).

Wallingford, Richard of, *see* North, J.D.
Walters, H.B., 'The Gloucestershire Bell-Foundries', *Trans. Bristol & Glos. Arch. Soc.* xxxiv (1911), 110-19.
—, *Church Bells of England* (1912).
Walton, P., 'The Textiles', in B. Harbottle and M. Ellison, 'An Excavation in the Castle Ditch, Newcastle upon Tyne, 1974-6', *Archaeologia Aeliana*, 5th ser. ix (1981), 190-228.
—, 'Dyes on Medieval Textiles', *Dyes on Historical and Archaeological Textiles*, iii (1984), 30-4.
—, (ed.), 'Textile Implements from 16-22 Coppergate', *The Archaeology of York* (in preparation).
Ward Perkins, J.B., *London Museum: Medieval Catalogue* (1940).
Warner, George F. (ed.), *The Libelle of Englyshe Polycye* (Oxford, 1926).
Wayment, H., *The Windows of King's College Chapel, Cambridge (Corpus Vitrearum Medii Aevi: Great Britain*, Supplementary Vol. 1, 1972).
—, 'The Great Windows of King's College Chapel and the Meaning of the Word "Vidimus"', *Proc. Cambridge Antiquarian Soc.* lxix (1979), 53-69.
—, Twenty-Four Vidimuses for Cardinal Wolsey', *Master Drawings*, xxiii-xxiv (1988), 503-17.
Welch, Charles, *History of the Worshipful Company of Pewterers of the City of London* (2 vols., 1902).
—, *History of the Cutlers' Company of London* (2 vols., 1916).
Wenham, L.P., 'Hornpot Lane and the Horners of York', *Annual Rep. of Yorkshire Philosophical Soc.* (1964), 23-54.
Wentzel, H., 'Un Projet du Vitrail au XIVᵉ Siècle', *Revue de l'Art*, x (1970), 7-14.

Werner, O., 'Analysen Mittelalterlicher Bronzen und Messinge. I', *Archäologie und Naturwissenschaften*, i (1977), 144-20.

Westlake, N.H.J., *A History of Design in Painted Glass* (4 vols., [1879]-94).

Westropp, M.S. Dudley, *Irish Glass* . . . ([1920]).

White, Lynn, jnr., *Medieval Technology and Social Change* (1962).

Whitelock, Dorothy (ed.), *English Historical Documents*, I, *c.500-1042* (2nd edn., 1979).

Whittingham, Selby, *A Thirteenth-Century Portrait Gallery at Salisbury Cathedral* (2nd edn., Salisbury, 1979).

Wight, Jane A., *Brick Building in England, from the Middle Ages to 1550* (1972).

Williams, Charles H. (ed.), *English Historical Documents*, V, *1485-1558* (1967).

Williams, J.H., *St. Peter's Street, Northampton* (Northampton, 1979).

Willis, Robert, and J.W. Clark, *The Architectural History of the Colleges of Cambridge and Eton* (4 vols., Cambridge, 1886).

Wilson, David M. (ed.), *The Archaeology of Anglo-Saxon England* (1976).

—, 'Craft and Industry', in David M. Wilson (ed.), *The Archaeology of Anglo-Saxon England* (1976), 253-81.

Winbolt, S.E., *Wealden Glass* (1933).

Winston, C., *Memoirs Illustrative of the Art of Glass-Painting* (1865).

—, *An Inquiry into the Difference of Style Observable in Ancient Glass Paintings* . . . (2 pts., 2nd edn., Oxford and London, 1867).

Wood, Eric S., 'A Medieval Glasshouse at Blunden's Wood, Hambledon, Surrey', *Surrey Arch. Coll.* lxii (1965), 54-79.

—, 'A 16th Century Glasshouse at Knightons, Alfold, Surrey', *Surrey Arch. Coll.* lxxiii (1982), 1-47.

Wood, Margaret E., *The English Mediaeval House* (1965).

Woodforde, C., 'Glass-Painters in England before the Reformation', *J.B.S.M.G.P.* vi (1935-7), 62-9, 121-8.

—, *The Norwich School of Glass-Painting in the Fifteenth Century* (1950).

—, *The Stained Glass of New College, Oxford* (Oxford, 1951).

Woodger, A., 'The Eclipse of the Burel Weaver: Some Technological Developments in the 13th Century', *Textile History*, xii (1981), 59-76.

Zarnecki, George, *English Romanesque Lead Sculpture. Lead Fonts of the Twelfth Century* (1957).

—, (ed.), *English Romanesque Art, 1066-1200* (Exhibition catalogue, Arts Council of Great Britain, 1984).

—, 'Henry of Blois as a Patron of Sculpture', in S. Macready and F.H. Thompson (eds.), *Art and Patronage in the English Romanesque* (1986), 159-72.

Zupko, R.E., *Dictionary of Weights and Measures for the British Isles* (Philadelphia, 1985).

(Various compilers), 'List of Books and Articles on the Economic (and Social) History of Great Britain (and Ireland)', *Econ. Hist. Rev.* 1st ser. i (1927-8) and subsequently, annually.

# Index